Fundamentals of
Data Structures in Pascal

Fundamentals of
Data Structures in Pascal

FOURTH EDITION

Ellis Horowitz
University of Southern California

Sartaj Sahni
University of Florida

COMPUTER SCIENCE PRESS

An imprint of W. H. Freeman and Company

New York

Cover illustration by Richard Elmer

Fundamentals of Data Structures in Pascal is the result of the combined efforts of the authors. Their names have been listed in alphabetical order with no implication that one is senior and the other junior.

Printed in the United States of America

Computer Science Press

An imprint of W. H. Freeman and Company
The book publishing arm of Scientific American
41 Madison Avenue, New York, NY 10010
20 Beaumont Street, Oxford OX1 2NQ, England

1 2 3 4 5 6 7 8 9 0   R R D   9 9 8 7 6 5 4

CONTENTS

PREFACE

This edition retains the in-depth discussion of the algorithms and computing time analyses found in earlier editions of this book. In addition we have attempted to preserve the chapter organization and the presentation style of the earlier editions whenever it was desirable. But this has not kept us from making improvements. For example, the discussion of strings is now found in the chapter on arrays; internal and external sorting methods have now been combined into a single chapter, Chapter 7; the previous chapter on advanced data structures has been split into two chapters, Chapter 9 which deals with heap structures and Chapter 10 which deals exclusively with search structures; exercises are now placed immediately after the relevant section. We have rearranged the sections in each chapter so that the basic material appears early in the chapter and the difficult or optional material appears at the end of the chapter.

One of the major new features in this book, compared to its earlier version, is the inclusion of abstract data types. The major idea is to separate out the issue of data type specification from implementation. Languages such as Ada provide direct support for such a split, but in Pascal there is no equivalent construct. Therefore, we have devised a straightforward notation in which we express an abstract data type. Basically, we provide a description of the objects of the type followed by the names and arguments of the functions of the type. Instructors can discuss with the students the specification of the data type before moving on to implementation issues and concerns for efficiency of the algorithms.

In several sections, we have enhanced the presentation by including additional material. For example, the discussion on the representation of sets by trees has been enhanced by the inclusion of two additional strategies for tree compaction and an additional strategy for combining two trees during a union operation; the discussion on single-source/all-destinations shortest paths has been extended to include an algorithm for the case when edge weights may be negative; the discussion on binary search trees and red-black trees has been extended to include the operations of split, join, and combine.

USING THIS TEXT FOR A COURSE

For the instructor who intends to use this book and is teaching on a semester basis we present the following two possibilities, a medium pace and a rigorous pace. The medium pace is recommended when the course is for begining computer science majors, possibly their second or third course of the curriculum. Most people, including the authors, have taught according to the medium pace. The outline below corresponds to the curriculum recommended by the ACM, in particular course C2, (Curriculum '78, CACM 3/79, and CACM 8/85).

SEMESTER SCHEDULE - MEDIUM PACE

Week	Subject	Reading Assignment
1	Intro. to Algorithms and Data Organization	Chapter 1
2	Arrays	Chapter 2
3	Arrays (strings)	First program due
4	Stacks and Queues	Chapter 3
5	Linked Lists (singly and doubly linked)	Chapter 4
6	Linked Lists	Second program due
7	Trees (basic facts, binary trees)	Chapter 5
8	Trees (search, heap)	
9	Mid Term	
10	Graphs (basic facts, representations)	Chapter 6
11	Graphs (shortest paths, spanning trees, topological sorting)	Third program due
12	Internal Sorting (insertion, quick, and merge)	Chapter 7
13	Internal Sorting (heap, radix)	Fourth program due
14	Hashing	Chapter 8
15	Heap Structures (Selected Topics)	Chapter 9
16	Search Structures (Selected Topics)	Chapter 10

We recommend that several programming assignments be given, spaced somewhat evenly thoughout the semester. The aim of the first program is primarily to get the students familiar with the computing environment. The second program should emphasize list structures, as discussed in Chapter 4. There are several suggestions for projects at the end of the exercises of Chapter 4. One topic we have chosen to skip is external sorting.

This leaves time to cover one of the most important of techniques, hashing. This topic is used in several courses later on in the curriculum, so it is important to cover it this semester. The instructor will likely not have time to cover the material in the Search Structures chapter. Perhaps one or two topics can be selectively chosen.

The more rigorous pace would be appropriate when the book is used for a first year graduate course, or for an advanced undergraduate course. Our suggested outline follows.

SEMESTER SCHEDULE - RIGOROUS PACE

Week	Subject	Reading Assignment
1	Intro. to Algorithms and Data Organization	Chapter 1
2	Arrays	Chapter 2
3	Stacks and Queues	Chapter 3
		First program due
4	Linked Lists	Chapter 4
5	Trees	Chapter 5
6	Trees continued	Second program due
7	Mid Term	
8	Graphs	Chapter 6
9	Graphs continued	Third program due
10	Internal Sorting	Chapter 7
11	External Sorting	Chapter 7
12	Hashing	Chapter 8
13	Heap Structures	Chapter 9
		Fourth program due
14	Heap Structures	Chapter 9
15	Search Structures	Chapter 10
16	Search Structures	Chapter 10

The programming assignments and midterm exam are paced exactly as in the medium case. However, the lectures proceed at a faster rate. For the rigorous pace, two weeks are allotted for   Chapters 9 and 10. This allows the coverage of only a few topics selected from each chapter.

Finally we present a curriculum for an advanced Data Structures course. This presupposes that the student has already encountered the basic material, in particular the material on lists, trees, and graphs. Four weeks on advanced data structures gives the instructor enough time to cover all of the relevant topics in depth.

SEMESTER SCHEDULE - ADVANCED DATA STRUCTURES COURSE

Week	Subject	Reading Assignment
1	Review of Basic Material on Algorithms	Chapters 1-2
2	Review of Basic List structures	Chapters 3-4
3	Review of Trees	Chapter 5
4	Review of Graphs	Chapter 6
5	Review of Internal Sorting	Chapter 7
		First program due
6	External Sorting	Chapter 7
7	External Sorting (continued)	
8	Hashing	Chapter 8
		Second program due
9	Heap Structures (min-max heaps, deaps, leftist trees)	Chapter 9
10	Mid Term	
11	Heaps Structures (Fibonacci heaps)	Chapter 9
12	Search Structures (Optimal binary search trees)	Chapter 10
13	Search Structures (AVL trees, 2-3 trees, 2-3-4 trees)	Third program due
14	Search Structures (Red-black trees, splay trees, digital trees)	
15	Search Structures (B-trees, tries)	Fourth program due
16	Search Structures	

For schools on the quarter system, the following two quarter sequence is possible. It assumes prior exposure to algorithm analysis and elementary data structures at the level obtained from an advanced programming course.

QUARTER 1

Week	Subject	Reading Assignment
1	Review of algorithms and arrays	Chapters 1-2
2	Stacks and Queues	Chapter 3
3	Linked Lists (stacks, queues, polynomials)	Chapter 4
4	Linked Lists	
5	Trees (traversal, set representation)	Chapter 5
		First program due

6	Trees (heaps, search)	
	Mid Term	
7	Graphs (traversal, components)	Chapter 6
8	Graphs (minimum spanning trees)	
9	Graphs (shortest paths)	Second program due
10	Graphs	(activity networks)

QUARTER 2

Week	Subject	Reading Assignment
1	Internal Sorting (insertion, quick, bound, O(1) space merging, merge sort)	Chapter 7
2	Sorting (heap, radix, list, table)	
3	External Sorting	Chapter 7
4	Hashing	Chapter 8
5	Mid Term	First program due
6	Heap Structures (deaps, Min-Max heaps, Leftist trees)	Chapter 9
7	Heap Structures (Fibonacci Heaps)	
8	Search Structures (AVL trees, 2-3 trees, 2-3-4 trees)	Chapter 10
9	Search Structures (Red-black trees, splay trees, digital trees)	Second program due
10	Search Structures (B-Trees, tries)	

Once again we would like to thank the people who have assisted us in debugging this edition. Thanks go to Professor Dinesh Mehta, University of Tennessee Space Institute, and to Mr. Seonghun Cho, Mr. Venkatramanan Narayanan, and Mr. Vishal Walia, University of Florida and to Ms. Penny Hull, Associate Managing Editor, W. H. Freeman.

Ellis Horowitz
Sartaj Sahni
September 1993

CHAPTER 1

BASIC CONCEPTS

1.1 OVERVIEW: SYSTEM LIFE CYCLE

We assume that our readers have a strong background in structured programming, typically attained through the completion of an elementary programming course. Such an initial course usually emphasizes mastering the syntax of a programming language (its grammar rules) and applying this language to the solution of several relatively small problems. These problems are frequently chosen so that they use a particular language construct. For example, the programming problem might require the use of arrays or **while** loops.

In this text we want to move you beyond these rudiments by providing you with the tools and techniques necessary to design and implement large-scale computer systems. We believe that a solid foundation in data abstraction, algorithm specification, and performance analysis and measurement provides the necessary methodology. In this chapter, we will discuss each of these areas in detail. We will also briefly discuss recursive programming because many of you probably have only a fleeting acquaintance with this important technique. However, before we begin, we want to place these tools in a context that views programming as more than writing code. Good programmers regard large-scale computer programs as systems that contain many complex interacting parts. As systems, these programs undergo a development process called the system life cycle. This cycle consists of requirements, analysis, design, coding, and verification phases. Although we will consider them separately, these phases are highly interrelated and follow only a very crude sequential time frame. The References and Selected Readings section lists several sources on the system life cycle and its various phases that will provide you with additional information.

(1) Requirements. All large programming projects begin with a set of specifications that define the purpose of the project. These requirements describe the information that we, the programmers, are given (input) and the results that we must produce (output). Frequently the initial specifications are defined vaguely, and we must develop rigorous input and output descriptions that include all cases.

(2) Analysis. After we have delineated carefully the system's requirements, the analysis phase begins in earnest. In this phase, we begin to break the problem down into manageable pieces. There are two approaches to analysis: bottom-up and top-down. The bottom-up approach is an older, unstructured strategy that places an early emphasis on the coding fine points. Since the programmer does not have a master plan for the project, the resulting program frequently has many loosely connected, error-ridden segments. Bottom-up analysis is akin to constructing a building from a generic blueprint. That is, we view all buildings identically; they must have walls, a roof, plumbing, and heating. The specific purpose to which the building will be put is irrelevant from this perspective. Although few of us would want to live in a home constructed using this technique, many programmers, particularly beginning ones, believe that they can create good, error-free programs without prior planning.

In contrast, the top-down approach begins with the purpose that the program will serve and uses this end product to divide the program into manageable segments. This technique generates diagrams that are used to design the system. Frequently, several alternate solutions to the programming problem are developed and compared during this phase.

(3) Design. This phase continues the work done in the analysis phase. The designer approaches the system from the perspectives of the data objects that the program needs and the operations performed on them. The first perspective leads to the creation of abstract data types, whereas the second requires the specification of algorithms and a consideration of algorithm design strategies. For example, suppose that we are designing a scheduling system for a university. Typical data objects might include students, courses, and professors. Typical operations might include inserting, removing, and searching within each object or between them. That is, we might want to add a course to the list of university courses or search for the courses taught by a specific professor.

Since the abstract data types and the algorithm specifications are language-independent, we postpone implementation decisions. Although we must specify the information required for each data object, we ignore coding details. For example, we might decide that the student data object should include name, social security number, major, and phone number. However, we would not yet pick a specific implementation for the list of students. As we will see in later chapters, there are several possibilities, including arrays, linked lists, or trees. By deferring implementation issues as long as possible, we not only create a system that could be written in several programming languages, but we also have time to pick the most efficient implementations within our chosen language.

(4) Refinement and coding. In this phase, we choose representations for our data objects and write algorithms for each operation on them. The order in which we do this is crucial because a data object's representation can determine the efficiency of the algorithms related to it. Typically this means that we should write the algorithms that are independent of the data objects first.

Frequently at this point we realize that we could have created a much better system. Perhaps we have spoken with a friend who has worked on a similar project, or we realize that one of our alternate designs is superior. If our original design is good, it can absorb changes easily. In fact, this is a reason for avoiding an early commitment to coding details. If we must scrap our work entirely, we can take comfort in the fact that we will be able to write the new system more quickly and with fewer errors. A delightful book that discusses this "second system" phenomenon is Frederick Brooks's *The Mythical Man-Month*, cited in the References and Selected Readings section.

(5) Verification. This phase consists of developing correctness proofs for the program, testing the program with a variety of input data, and removing errors. Each of these areas has been researched extensively, and a complete discussion is beyond the scope of this text. However, we want to summarize briefly the important aspects of each area.

Correctness proofs: Programs can be proven correct using the same techniques that abound in mathematics. Unfortunately, these proofs are very time-consuming and difficult to develop for large projects. Frequently scheduling constraints prevent the development of a complete set of proofs for a large system. However, selecting algorithms that have been proven correct can reduce the number of errors. In this text, we will provide you with an arsenal of algorithms, some of which have been proven correct using formal techniques, that you may apply to many programming problems.

Testing: We can construct our correctness proofs before and during the coding phase, since our algorithms need not be written in a specific programming language. Testing, however, requires the working code and sets of test data. This data should be developed carefully so that it includes all possible scenarios. Frequently beginning programmers assume that if their program ran without producing a syntax error, it must be correct. Little thought is given to the input data, and usually only one set of data is used. Good test data should verify that every piece of code runs correctly. For example, if our program contains a **switch** statement, our test data should be chosen so that we can check each **case** within the **switch** statement.

Initial system tests focus on verifying that a program runs correctly. Although this is a crucial concern, a program's running time is also important. An error-free program that runs slowly is of little value. Theoretical estimates of running time exist for many algorithms, and we will derive these estimates as we introduce new algorithms. In addition, we may want to gather performance estimates for portions of our code. Constructing these timing tests is also a topic that we pursue later in this chapter.

Error removal. If done properly, the correctness proofs and system tests will indicate erroneous code. The ease with which we can remove these errors depends on the design and coding decisions made earlier. A large undocumented program written in "spaghetti" code is a programmer's nightmare. When debugging such programs, each corrected error possibly generates several new errors. On the other hand, debugging a well-documented program that is divided into autonomous units that interact through parameters is far easier, especially if each unit is tested separately and then integrated into the system.

1.2 ALGORITHM SPECIFICATION

1.2.1 Introduction

The concept of an algorithm is fundamental to computer science. Algorithms exist for many common problems, and designing efficient algorithms plays a crucial role in developing large-scale computer systems. Therefore, before we proceed further, we need to discuss this concept more fully. We begin with a definition.

Definition: An *algorithm* is a finite set of instructions that, if followed, accomplishes a particular task. In addition, all algorithms must satisfy the following criteria:

(1) **Input.** Zero or more quantities are externally supplied.

(2) **Output.** At least one quantity is produced.

(3) **Definiteness.** Each instruction is clear and unambiguous.

(4) **Finiteness.** If we trace out the instructions of an algorithm, then for all cases, the algorithm terminates after a finite number of steps.

(5) **Effectiveness.** Every instruction must be basic enough to be carried out, in principle, by a person using only pencil and paper. It is not enough that each operation be definite as in (3); it also must be feasible. □

In computational theory, one distinguishes between an algorithm and a program, the latter of which does not have to satisfy the fourth condition. For example, we can think of an operating system that continues in a "wait" loop until more jobs are entered. Such a program does not terminate unless the system crashes. Since our programs will always terminate, we will use algorithm and program interchangeably in this text.

We can describe an algorithm in many ways. We can use a natural language like English, although if we select this option, we must make sure that the resulting instructions are definite. Graphic representations called flowcharts are another possibility, but they work well only if the algorithm is small and simple. In this text we will present most of our algorithms in Pascal, occasionally resorting to a combination of English and Pascal for our specifications. Two examples should help to illustrate the process of translating a problem into an algorithm.

Example 1.1 [*Selection sort*]: Suppose we must devise a program that sorts a collection of $n \geq 1$ integers. A simple solution is given by the following:

From those integers that are currently unsorted, find the smallest and place it next in the sorted list.

Although this statement adequately describes the sorting problem, it is not an algorithm because it leaves several unanswered questions. For example, it does not tell us where and how the integers are initially stored or where we should place the result. We assume that the integers are stored in an array, a, such that the ith integer is stored in the ith position, $a[i]$, $1 \leq i \leq n$. Program 1.1 is our first attempt at deriving a solution. Notice that it is written partially in Pascal and partially in English.

```
for i := 1 to n do
begin
   examine a[i] to a[n] and suppose the smallest integer is at a[j];
   interchange a[i] and a[j];
end;
```

Program 1.1: Selection sort algorithm

To turn Program 1.1 into a real Pascal program, two clearly defined subtasks remain: finding the smallest integer and interchanging it with $a[i]$. We can solve the latter problem using the code:

$$t := a[i]; a[i] := a[j]; a[j] := t;$$

The first subtask can be solved by assuming the minimum is $a[i]$, checking $a[i]$ with $a[i+1]$, $a[i+2]$, $\cdots$ and whenever a smaller element is found, regarding it as the new minimum. Eventually $a[n]$ is compared to the current minimum, and we are done. Putting all these observations together, we get the procedure *sort* (Program 1.2). *ElementList* is an array of integers.

The obvious question to ask at this point is, Does this procedure work correctly?

```
 1  procedure sort (var a : ElementList; n : integer);
 2  {Sort the n integers a[1..n] into nondecreasing order.}
 3  var i, j, k, t : integer;
 4  begin
 5     for i := 1 to n do
 6     begin
 7        j := i;
 8        {Find smallest integer in a [i..n].}
 9        for k := i +1 to n do
10           if a [k ] < a [j] then j := k;
11           {interchange}
12           t := a [i]; a [i] := a [j]; a [j] := t;
13     end; {of for i}
14  end; {of sort}
```

Program 1.2: Selection sort

Theorem 1.1: Procedure $sort(a,n)$ correctly sorts a set of $n \geq 1$ integers; the result remains in $a[1..n]$ such that $a[1] \leq a[2] \leq \cdots \leq a[n]$.

Proof: We first note that for any i, say $i = q$, following the execution of lines 7-12, it is the case that $a[q] \leq a[r]$, $q < r \leq n$. Also observe that when i becomes greater than q, $a[1..q]$ is unchanged. Hence, following the last execution of these lines (i.e., $i = n$), we have $a[1] \leq a[2] \leq \cdots \leq a[n]$. $\square$

We observe at this point that the upper limit of the **for** loop in line 5 can be changed to $n - 1$ without damaging the correctness of the algorithm. $\square$

Example 1.2 [*Binary search*]: Assume that we have $n \geq 1$ distinct integers that are already sorted and stored in the array $a[1..n]$. Our task is to determine if the integer x is present and if so to return j such that $x = a[j]$; otherwise return $j = 0$. By making use of the fact that the set is sorted, we conceive of the following efficient method:

Let *left* and *right*, respectively, denote the left and right ends of the list to be searched. Initially, *left* = 1 and *right* = n. Let *middle* = (*left* +*right*) **div** 2 be the middle position in the list. If we compare $a[middle]$ with x, we obtain one of three results:

(1)   **x < a[middle].** In this case, if x is present, it must be in the positions between 1 and *middle* − 1. Therefore, we set *right* to *middle* − 1.

(2)   **x = a[middle].** In this case, we return *middle*.

(3)   **x > a[middle].** In this case, if x is present, it must be in the positions between *middle* + 1 and n. So, we set *left* to *middle* + 1.

If x has not been found and there are still integers to check, we recalculate *middle* and continue the search. The algorithm contains two subtasks: (1) determining if there are any integers left to check and (2) comparing x to $a[middle]$.

At this point you might try the method out on some sample numbers. This method is referred to as *binary search*. Note how at each stage the number of elements in the remaining set is decreased by about one-half. Note also that at each stage, x is compared with $a[middle]$ and depending on whether $x > a[middle]$, $x < a[middle]$, or $x = a[middle]$, we do a different thing. To implement this in Pascal we could use the **if-then-else** construct:

$$\textbf{if } x > a[middle] \textbf{ then } \dots$$
$$\textbf{else if } x < a[middle] \textbf{ then } \dots$$
$$\textbf{else } \dots$$

From this construct it is not readily apparent that we are considering the three cases that can result from the comparison between x and $a[i]$. To make the program more transparent, we introduce a compare function that has value >, <, or =, depending on the outcome of the comparison. This function is given in Program 1.3.

```
function compare(x, y : element) : char;
begin
  if x > y then compare := '>'
        else if x < y then compare := '<'
              else compare := '='
end; {of compare}
```

Program 1.3: Comparing two elements

We can now refine the description of binary search to get a pseudo-Pascal procedure. The result is given in Program 1.4.

Another refinement yields the Pascal procedure of Program 1.5. To prove this program correct we make assertions about the relationship between variables before and after the **while** loop of lines 6-14. As we enter this loop and as long as x is not found, the following holds:

$$left \leq right \textbf{ and } a[left] \leq x \leq a[right] \textbf{ and } SORTED(a, n)$$

Now, if control passes out of the **while** loop past line 14, then we know the condition of line 6 is false, so $left > right$. This, combined with the above assertion, implies that x is not present.

Unfortunately, a complete proof takes us beyond our scope but those who wish to pursue program-proving should consult our references at the end of this chapter. □

---

procedure *BinarySearch*(**var** *a* : *ElementList*; *x* : *element*; **var** *n,j* : **integer**);
{Search the sorted array *a* [1 .. *n*] for *x*.}
initialize *left* and *right*
while there are more elements **do**
begin
   let *a* [*middle*] be the middle element;
   case *compare*(*x*, *a* [*middle*]) **of**
     '>': set *left* to *middle*+1;
     '<': set *right* to *middle*−1;
     '=': found *x*;
   end; {of **case**}
end; {of **while**}
not found;
end; {of *BinarySearch*}

Program 1.4: Algorithm for binary search

```
1   procedure BinarySearch(var a : ElementList; x : element; var n,j : integer);
2   {Search the sorted array a [1 .. n ] for x.}
3   var left, right, middle : integer; found : boolean;
4   begin
5      left := 1; right := n; found := false; j := 0;
6      while (left <= right) and (not found) do  {while more elements}
7      begin
8        middle := (left+right) div 2;
9        case compare (x, a [middle]) of
10          '>': left := middle+1;   {x > a [middle]}
11          '<': right := middle−1;   {x < a [middle]}
12          '=': begin j := middle; found := true; end;  {x = a [middle]}
13        end; {of case}
14     end; {of while}
15  end; {of BinarySearch}
```

Program 1.5: Pascal procedure for binary search

1.2.2   Recursive Algorithms

We have tried to emphasize the need to structure a program to make it easier to achieve the goals of readability and correctness. One of the most useful syntactical features for accomplishing this is the procedure. A set of instructions that perform a logical operation, perhaps a very complex and long operation, can be grouped together as a procedure. The procedure name and its parameters are viewed as a new instruction that can be used in other programs. Given the input-output specifications of a procedure, we do not even have to know how the task is accomplished, only that it is available. This view of the procedure implies that it is invoked, executed and returns control to the appropriate place in the calling procedure. What this fails to stress is that procedures may call themselves (*direct recursion*) before they are done or they may call other procedures that again invoke the calling procedure (*indirect recursion*). These recursive mechanisms are extremely powerful, but even more importantly, many times they can express an otherwise complex process very clearly. For these reasons we introduce recursion here.

   Typically, beginning programmers view recursion as a somewhat mystical technique that is useful only for some very special class of problems (such as computing factorials or Ackermann's function). This is unfortunate because any program that can be written using assignment, the **if-then-else** statement, and the **while** statement can also be written using assignment, **if-then-else**, and recursion. Of course, this does not say that the resulting program will necessarily be easier to understand. However, there are many instances when this will be the case. When is recursion an appropriate mechanism for algorithm exposition? One instance is when the problem itself is recursively defined. Factorial fits this category, as well as binomial coefficients where

$$\binom{n}{m} = \frac{n!}{m!(n-m)!}$$

can be recursively computed by the formula

$$\binom{n}{m} = \binom{n-1}{m} + \binom{n-1}{m-1}$$

   We would like to use three examples to show you how to develop a recursive algorithm. In the first example, we take the binary search procedure that we created in Example 1.2 and transform it into a recursive procedure. In the second example, we recursively reverse a character string, and in the third, we generate all possible permutations of a list of characters.

Example 1.3 [*Recursive binary search*]: Program 1.5 gave the iterative version of a binary search. In the recursive version we pass *left* and *right* as parameters (Program 1.6). The **while** loop of Program 1.5 has been replaced by recursive calls in Program 1.6. To invoke the recursive procedure, we use the statement

BinarySearch (*a*, 1, *n*, *i*);

Notice that both the iterative (Program 1.5) and recursive (Program 1.6) procedures perform the same computation. □

```
1   procedure BinarySearch(var a : ElementList; x : element; var left,right,j : integer);
2   {Search the sorted array a [left..right] for x.}
3   var middle : integer;
4   begin
5       middle := (left+right) div 2;
6       case compare (x, a [middle]) of
7           '>': BinarySearch (a, x, middle +1, right,j);  {x > a [middle]}
8           '>': BinarySearch (a, x, left, middle−1, j);  {x < a [middle]}
9           '=': j := middle; {x = a [middle]}
10      end; {of case}
11  end; {of BinarySearch}
```

Program 1.6: Recursive implementation of binary search

Example 1.4 [*Recursive string reversal*]: Assume that the **type** string has been declared as

$$type\ string = \textbf{record}$$
$$length : \textbf{integer};\ \{length\ of\ string\}$$
$$c : \textbf{array}[1..100]\ \textbf{of char};$$
$$\textbf{end};$$

and that the following functions have already been defined:

(1)   *substring* (*s, i, j*) This yields the string made up of the ith through jth characters in s for appropriately defined i and j. Thus if $0 < i \le j \le s.length$, then the string $s.c [i] \cdots s.c[j]$ is the desired substring.

(2)   *concat*(*s1,s2*) This function yields a string of length $s1.length + s2.length$ obtained by concatenating $s1$ and $s2$ with $s1$ preceding $s2$.

Using these functions, a recursive function (Program 1.7) to reverse the string s is easily obtained. □

Example 1.5 [*Permutation generator*]: Given a set of $n \ge 1$ elements, the problem is to print all possible permutations of this set. For example if the set is $\{a, b, c\}$, then the set of permutations is $\{(a, b, c), (a, c, b), (b, a, c), (b, c, a), (c, a, b), (c, b, a)\}$. It is easy to see that given n elements, there are n ! different permutations. A simple algorithm can be obtained by looking at the the case of four elements (a,b,c,d). The answer can be

```
function reverse (s : string) : string;
{reverse the string s}
var n : integer;
begin
    n := s.length;
    if n <= 1
    then reverse := s
    else reverse := concat (reverse (substring (s,2,n)), s.c[1]);
end; {of reverse}
```

Program 1.7: String reversal

constructed by writing

(1) a followed by all permutations of (b,c,d)

(2) b followed by all permutations of (a,c,d)

(3) c followed by all permutations of (a,b,d)

(4) d followed by all permutations of (a,b,c)

The expression "followed by all permutations" is the clue to recursion. It implies that we can solve the problem for a set with n elements if we have an algorithm that works on $n-1$ elements. These considerations lead to Program 1.8, which is invoked by $perm(a, 1, n)$.

Try this algorithm out on sets of length one, two, and three to ensure that you understand how it works. □

Another time when recursion is useful is when the data structure that the algorithm is to operate on is recursively defined. We shall see several important examples of such structures in this book.

EXERCISES

1.   Horner's   rule   is   a   means   for   evaluating   a   polynomial $A(x)$ = $a_n x^n + a_{n-1} x^{n-1} + \cdots + a_1 x + a_0$ at a point x_0 using a minimum number of multiplications. This rule is:

$$A(x) = (\cdots (a_n x_0 + a_{n-1}) x_0 + \cdots + a_1) x_0 + a_0$$

Write a Pascal program to evaluate a polynomial using Horner's rule. Determine how many times each statement is executed.

```
procedure perm (a : ElementList; k,n : integer);
{Generate all the permutations of a [k..n].}
var t : element;  {type of entries in a}
    i : integer;
begin
  if k = n
  then begin {output permutation}
               for i := 1 to n do
                     write(a [i]);
               writeln;
       end
  else begin
          {a [k..n] has more than one permutation.
          Generate these recursively.}
          for i := k to n do
          begin
            {interchange a [k] and a [i]}
            t := a [k]; a [k] := a [i]; a [i] := t;
            perm (a, k+1, n); {all permutations of a [k +1 .. n]}
          end;
       end; {of else}
end; {of perm}
```

Program 1.8: Recursive permutation generator

2. Given n boolean variables $x_1, \cdots, x_n$ we wish to print all possible combinations of truth values they can assume. For instance, if $n = 2$, there are four possibilities: true, true; true, false; false, true; false, false. Write a Pascal program to accomplish this and do a frequency count.

3. Write a Pascal program that prints out the integer values of x, y, and z in nondecreasing order. What is the computing time of your method?

4. Write a Pascal procedure that searches an array $a [1 .. n]$ for the element x. If x occurs, then set j to its position in the array, else set j to zero. Try writing this without using the **goto** statement.

5. Use the *string* data type defined in this section for the following:

    (a) Write the functions *concat* and *substring* described in this section.

    (b) Write a function *index* (x,y) that searches string x for the first occurrence of string y. If y does not appear in x, then *index* equals zero. Otherwise, *index* is the starting position in x of the first occurrence of y.

(c) Write a function *compact* (*s*) that replaces each sequence of blanks in *s* by a single blank.

(d) Write a program that accepts as input a string *s* and determines the frequency of occurrence of each of the distinct characters in *s*.

Test each of your programs using suitable test data.

6. Trace the action of the code

$$
\begin{aligned}
&i := 1; j := n; \\
&\textbf{repeat} \\
&\quad k := (i + j)/2; \\
&\quad \textbf{if } a\,[k] < = x \textbf{ then } i := k + 1 \\
&\quad\quad\quad\quad\quad\quad\quad \textbf{else } j := k - 1; \\
&\textbf{until } i > j;
\end{aligned}
$$

on the elements 2, 4, 6, 8, 10, 12, 14, 16, 18, and 20 searching for $x = 1, 3, 13$, or 21.

7. Write a binary search procedure that initializes *left* to zero and *right* to $n + 1$.

8. Take any version of binary search, express it using assignment, **if-then-else**, and **goto**, and then give an equivalent recursive program.

9. The factorial function $n!$ has value 1 when $n \leq 1$ and value $n*(n-1)!$ when $n > 1$. Write both a recursive and an iterative C function to compute $n!$.

10. The Fibonacci numbers are defined as: $f_0 = 0$, $f_1 = 1$, and $f_i = f_{i-1}+f_{i-2}$ for $i > 1$. Write both a recursive and an iterative C function to compute f_i.

11. Write a recursive procedure for computing the binomial coefficient $\begin{bmatrix} n \\ m \end{bmatrix}$ as defined in Section 1.2.2, where $\begin{bmatrix} n \\ 0 \end{bmatrix} = \begin{bmatrix} n \\ n \end{bmatrix} = 1$. Analyze the time and space requirements of your algorithm.

12. Write an iterative function to compute a binomial coefficient; then transform it into an equivalent recursive function.

13. Ackermann's function $A\,(m,n)$ is defined as follows:

$$
A\,(m,n) = \begin{cases} n + 1 & \text{, if } m = 0 \\ A\,(m - 1, 1) & \text{, if } n = 0 \\ A\,(m - 1, A\,(m,n - 1)) & \text{, otherwise} \end{cases}
$$

This function is studied because it grows very fast for small values of *m* and *n*. Write a recursive procedure for computing this function. Then write a nonrecursive algorithm for computing Ackermann's function.

14. The *pigeonhole principle* states that if a function *f* has *n* distinct inputs but less than *n* distinct outputs, then there exist two inputs *a* and *b* such that $a \neq b$ and $f(a) = f(b)$. Write a program to find the values *a* and *b* for which the range values are equal. Assume that the inputs are $1, 2, \cdots, n$.

15. Given n, a positive integer, determine if n is the sum of all of its divisors — i.e., if n is the sum of all t such that $1 \le t < n$, and t divides n.

16. Consider the function $F(x)$ defined by

$$\textbf{if } x \text{ is even } \textbf{then } F := x \textbf{ div } 2$$
$$\textbf{else } F := F(F(3x + 1))$$

Prove that $F(x)$ terminates for all integers x. (Hint: Consider integers of the form $(2i + 1)2^k - 1$ and use induction.)

17. If S is a set of n elements, the *powerset* of S is the set of all possible subsets of S. For example, if $S = (a,b,c)$, then *powerset* $(S) = \{(\ ), (a), (b), (c), (a,b), (a,c), (b,c), (a,b,c)\}$. Write a recursive procedure to compute *powerset* (S).

18. [*Towers of Hanoi*] There are three towers and sixty-four disks of different diameters placed on the first tower. The disks are in order of decreasing diameter as one scans up the tower. Monks were supposed to move the disks from tower 1 to tower 3 obeying the following rules: (a) only one disk can be moved at any time and (b) no disk can be placed on top of a disk with smaller diameter. Write a recursive procedure that prints the sequence of moves that accomplish this task.

1.3 DATA ABSTRACTION

The reader is no doubt familiar with the basic data types of Pascal. These include **char**, **integer**, **real**, **string**, and **boolean**. Ultimately, the real world abstractions we wish to deal with must be represented in terms of these data types. In addition to these basic types, Pascal helps us by providing two mechanisms for grouping data together. These are the array and the record. *Arrays* are collections of elements of the same basic data type; *records* are collections of elements whose data types need not be the same.

All programming languages provide at least a minimal set of predefined data types, plus the ability to construct new, or *user-defined* types. It is appropriate to ask the question, What is a data type?

Definition: A *data type* is a collection of *objects* and a set of *operations* that act on those objects. □

Whether your program is dealing with predefined data types or user-defined data types, these two aspects must be considered: objects and operations. For example, the data type **integer** consists of the objects $\{0, +1, -1, +2, -2, \cdots, \textbf{maxint}, \textbf{minint}\}$, where **maxint** and **minint** are the largest and smallest integers that can be represented on your machine. The operations on integers are many and would certainly include the arithmetic operators $+$, $-$, $*$, and **div**. There is also testing for equality/inequality and the operation that assigns an integer to a variable.

In addition to knowing all of the facts about the operations on a data type, we might also want to know about how the objects of the data type are represented. For example, on most computers a **char** is represented as a bit string occupying 1 byte of memory, whereas an **integer** might occupy 2 or possibly 4 bytes of memory. If 2 eight-bit bytes are used, then **maxint** is $2^{15} - 1 = 32,767$.

Knowing the representation of the objects of a data type can be useful and dangerous. By knowing the representation we can often write algorithms that make use of it. However, if we ever want to change the representation of these objects, we also must change the routines that make use of it. It has been observed by many software designers that hiding the representation of objects of a data type from its users is a good design strategy. In that case, the user is constrained to manipulate the objects solely through the functions that are provided. The designer may still alter the representation as long as the new implementations of the operations do not change the user interface. This means that users will not have to recode their algorithms.

Definition: An *abstract data type* *(ADT)* is a data type that is organized in such a way that the specification of the objects and the specification of the operations on the objects is separated from the representation of the objects and the implementation of the operations. ◻

Some programming languages provide explicit mechanisms to support the distinction between specification and implementation. For example, Ada has a concept called a *package*, and C++ has a concept called a *class*. Both of these assist the programmer in implementing abstract data types. Although Pascal does not have an explicit mechanism for implementing ADTs, it is still possible and desirable to design your data types using the same notion.

How does the specification of the operations of an ADT differ from the implementation of the operations? The specification consists of the names of every function, the type of its arguments, and the type of its result. There should also be a description of what the function does, but without appealing to internal representation or implementation details. This requirement is quite important, and it implies that an abstract data type is *implementation-independent*. Furthermore, it is possible to classify the functions of a data type into several categories:

(1) **Creator/constructor**. These functions create a new instance of the designated type.

(2) **Transformer**. These functions also create an instance of the designated type, generally by using one or more other instances. The difference between constructors and transformers will become more clear with some examples.

(3) **Observer/reporter**. These functions provide information about an instance of the type, but they do not change the instance.

Typically, an ADT definition will include at least one function from each of these three categories.

Throughout this text, we will emphasize the distinction between specification and implementation. To help us do this, we will typically begin with an ADT definition of the object that we intend to study. This will permit the reader to grasp the essential elements of the object, without having the discussion complicated by the representation of the objects or by the actual implementation of the operations. Once the ADT definition is fully explained, we will move on to discussions of representation and implementation. These are quite important in the study of data structures. To help us accomplish this goal, we introduce a notation for expressing an ADT.

Example 1.6 [*Abstract data type NaturalNumber*]: As this is the first example of an ADT, we will spend some time explaining the notation. Structure 1.1 contains the ADT definition of *NaturalNumber*. The structure definition begins with the name of the structure and its abbreviation. There are two main sections in the definition: the objects and the functions. The objects are defined in terms of the integers, but we make no explicit reference to their representation. The function definitions are a bit more complicated. First, the definitions use the symbols x and y to denote two elements of the set *Natural-Number*, whereas **true** and **false** are elements of the set of *Boolean* values. In addition, the definition makes use of functions that are defined on the set of integers, namely, plus, minus, equal, and less than. This is an indication that in order to define one data type, we may need to use operations from another data type. For each function, we place the result type to the left of the function name and a definition of the function to the right. The symbols "::=" should be read as "is defined as."

The first function, *Zero*, has no arguments and returns the natural number zero. This is a constructor function. The function *Successor(x)* returns the next natural number in sequence. This is an example of a transformer function. Notice that if there is no next number in sequence, that is, if the value of x is already **maxint**, then we define the action of *Successor* to return **maxint**. Some programmers might prefer that in such a case *Successor* return an error flag. This is also perfectly permissible. Other transformer functions are *Add* and *Subtract*. They might also return an error condition, although here we decided to return an element of the set *NaturalNumber*. □

Structure 1.1 shows you the general form that all ADT definitions will follow. However, we will not often be able to provide a definition of the functions that is so close to Pascal code. In fact, the nature of an ADT argues that we avoid implementation details. Therefore, we will usually use a form of structured English to explain the meaning of the functions.

EXERCISES

For each of these exercises, provide a definition of the abstract data type using the form illustrated in Structure 1.1.

---

structure *NaturalNumber* is

objects: An ordered subrange of the integers starting at zero and ending at the maximum integer (**maxint**) on the computer.

functions:

for all *x*, *y* ∈ *NaturalNumber*; **true**, **false** ∈ *Boolean*
and where +, −, <, and = are the usual integer operations

Zero( ) : *NaturalNumber*	::=	0
IsZero(*x*) : *Boolean*	::=	**if** $x = 0$ **then** *IsZero* := **true**
		else *IsZero* = **false**
Add(*x*, *y*) : *NaturalNumber*	::=	**if** $x + y <=$ **maxint then** *Add* := $x + y$
		else *Add* := **maxint**
Equal(*x*, *y*) : *Boolean*	::=	**if** $x = y$ **then** *Equal* := **true**
		else *Equal* := **false**
Successor(*x*) : *NaturalNumber*	::=	**if** $x =$ **maxint then** *Successor* := *x*
		else *Successor* := $x + 1$
Subtract(*x*, *y*) : *NaturalNumber*	::=	**if** $x < y$ **then** *Subtract* := 0
		else *Subtract* := $x - y$

end *NaturalNumber*

Structure 1.1: Abstract data type *NaturalNumber*

1. Add the following operations to the *NaturalNumber* ADT: *Predecessor*, *IsGreater*, *Multiply*, *Divide*.

2. Create an ADT, *Set*. Use the standard mathematical definition and include the following operations: *Create*, *Insert*, *Remove*, *IsIn*, *Union*, *Intersection*, *Difference*.

3. Create an ADT, *Bag*. In mathematics a *bag* is similar to a *set* except that a bag may contain duplicate elements. The minimal operations should include *Create*, *Insert*, *Remove*, and *IsIn*.

4. Create an ADT, *Boolean*. The minimal operations are *And*, *Or*, *Not*, *Xor* (exclusive or), *Equivalent*, and *Implies*.

1.4 PERFORMANCE ANALYSIS AND MEASUREMENT

One goal of this book is to develop skills for making evaluative judgments about programs. There are many criteria upon which we can judge a program, for instance:

(1) Does it do what we want it to do?

(2) Does it work correctly according to the original specifications of the task?

(3)   Is there documentation that describes how to use it and how it works?

(4)   Are procedures created in such a way that they perform logical subfunctions?

(5)   Is the code readable?

The above criteria are all vitally important when it comes to writing software, most especially for large systems. Though we will not be discussing how to reach these goals, we will try to achieve them throughout this book with the programs we write. Hopefully this more subtle approach will gradually infect your own program-writing habits so that you will automatically strive to achieve these goals.

There are other criteria for judging programs that have a more direct relationship to performance. These have to do with their computing time and storage requirements.

Definition: The *space complexity* of a program is the amount of memory it needs to run to completion. The *time complexity* of a program is the amount of computer time it needs to run to completion. □

Performance evaluation can be loosely divided into two major phases: (1) a priori estimates and (2) a posteriori testing. We refer to these as *performance analysis* and *performance measurement* respectively.

1.4.1   Performance Analysis

1.4.1.1   Space Complexity

Function *abc* (Program 1.9) computes the expression $a+b+b*c+(a+b-c)/(a+b)+4.0$; function *sum* (Program 1.10) computes the sum $\sum_{i=1}^{n} a[i]$ iteratively, where the $a[i]$'s are real numbers; and function *rsum* (Program 1.11) is a recursive program that computes $\sum_{i=1}^{n} a[i]$.

```
function abc (a, b, c : real) : real;
begin
   abc := a +b +b *c +(a +b −c)/(a +b)+4.0;
end; {of abc}
```

Program 1.9: Function to compute $a+b+b*c+(a+b-c)/(a+b)+4.0$

The space needed by each of these programs is seen to be the sum of the following components:

line	function *sum(a : ElementList ; n :* **integer**) : **real**;
1	**var** *s* : **real**; *i* : **integer**;
2	**begin**
3	*s* := 0;
4	**for** *i* := 1 **to** *n* **do**
5	*s* := *s* + *a* [*i*];
6	*sum* := *s*;
7	**end**; {of *sum*}

Program 1.10: Iterative function for sum

line	function *rsum(a : ElementList ; n :* **integer**) : **real**;
1	**begin**
2	**if** *n*<=0 **then** *rsum* := **0**
3	**else** *rsum* := *rsum* (*a, n*−1) + *a* [*n*];
4	**end**; {of *rsum*}

Program 1.11: Recursive function for sum

(1) A fixed part that is independent of the characteristics (e.g., number, size) of the inputs and outputs. This part typically includes the instruction space (i.e., space for the code), space for simple variables and fixed-size component variables (also called *aggregate*), space for constants, etc.

(2) A variable part that consists of the space needed by component variables whose size is dependent on the particular problem instance being solved, the space needed by referenced variables (to the extent that this depends on instance characteristics), and the recursion stack space (insofar as this space depends on the instance characteristics).

The space requirement $S(P)$ of any program P may therefore be written as $S(P) = c + S_P$(instancecharacteristics) where c is a constant. When analyzing the space complexity of a program, we shall concentrate solely on estimating S_P (instance characteristics). For any given problem, we shall need to first determine which instance characteristics to use to measure the space requirements. This is very problem-specific, and we shall resort to examples to illustrate the various possibilities. Generally speaking, our choices are limited to quantities related to the number and magnitude of the inputs to and outputs from the program. At times, more complex measures of the interrelationships among the data items are used.

Example 1.7: For Program 1.9, the problem instance is characterized by the specific values of a, b, and c. Making the assumption that one word is adequate to store the values of each of a, b, c, and abc, we see that the space needed by function abc is independent of the instance characteristics. Consequently, S_P(instance~ characteristics) = 0. □

Example 1.8: The problem instances for Program 1.10 are characterized by n, the number of elements to be summed. Since a and n are value formal parameters, space for these must be allocated. The space needed by the variable n is one word, since it is of type **integer**. The space needed by a is the space needed by variables of type *ElementList*. This is at least n words, since a must be large enough to hold the n elements to be summed. So, we obtain $S_{sum}(n) \geq n$.

Notice that if we change the formal parameter a from value to reference (or *var*), only the address of the actual parameter gets transferred to the function, and the space needed by the function is independent of n. In this case, $S_{sum}(n) = 0$.

So, even though the values of the individual components of a do not get changed by *sum*, it is desirable to make a a variable parameter in order to conserve space. As a variable parameter, only enough space to store a memory address is needed. This is typically just one or two words. □

Example 1.9: Let us consider the function *rsum*. As in the case of *sum*, the instances are characterized by n. The recursion stack space includes space for the formal parameters, the local variables, and the return address. Since a is a value formal parameter, the values of all its components get saved on the stack. Assume that the return address requires only one word of memory. Each call to *rsum* requires at least $(n + 3)$ words (including space for the values of n, a, and *rsum* and the return address). More space is required if *ElementList* has been declared as an array [1..*MaxSize*] where *MaxSize* $> n$. In this case, each call to *rsum* takes up $(MaxSize + 3)$ space.

Since the depth of recursion is $n+1$, the recursion stack space needed is $(n+1)(MaxSize+3)$ or $(n+1)(n+3)$ depending on whether or not the size of *ElementList* is changed whenever n changes.

Now that we realize the space cost of having a a value formal parameter, we see that *rsum* will fail when n is suitably large. For example, when $n = 1000$, at least $1001*1003 = 1,004,003$ words of memory are needed for the recursion stack space alone.

If we make a a variable parameter, then each call to *rsum* requires only four words of space. The recursion stack space becomes $4(n+1)$ or 4004 words when $n = 1000$. We can solve much larger instances now with a given amount of memory. Of course, we can do much better by not using recursion at all and sticking with the modified version of Program 1.10 in which a is a variable formal parameter. □

1.4.1.2   Time Complexity

The time, $T(P)$, taken by a program P is the sum of the compile time and the run (or execution) time. The compile time does not depend on the instance characteristics. Also, we may assume that a compiled program will be run several times without recompilation. Consequently, we shall concern ourselves with just the run time of a program. This run time is denoted by t_P(instance characteristics).

Because many of the factors t_P depends on are not known at the time a program is conceived, it is reasonable to attempt only to estimate t_P. If we knew the characteristics of the compiler to be used, we could proceed to determine the number of additions, subtractions, multiplications, divisions, compares, loads, stores, and so on that would be made by the code for P. So, we could obtain an expression for $t_P(n)$ of the form

$$t_P(n) = c_a ADD(n) + c_s SUB(n) + c_m MUL(n) + c_d DIV(n) + \cdots$$

where n denotes the instance characteristics, and c_a, c_s, c_m, c_d, etc., respectively, denote the time needed for an addition, subtraction, multiplication, division, etc., and ADD, SUB, MUL, DIV, etc., are functions whose value is the number of additions, subtractions, multiplications, divisions, etc., that will be performed when the code for P is used on an instance with characteristic n.

Obtaining such an exact formula is in itself an impossible task, since the time needed for an addition, subtraction, multiplication, etc., often depends on the actual numbers being added, subtracted, multiplied, etc. In reality then, the true value of $t_P(n)$ for any given n can be obtained only experimentally. The program is typed, compiled, and run on a particular machine. The execution time is physically clocked and $t_P(n)$ obtained. Even with this experimental approach, one could face difficulties. In a multiuser system, the execution time will depend on such factors as system load, the number of other programs running on the computer at the time program P is run, the characteristics of these other programs, and so on.

Given the minimal utility of determining the exact number of additions, subtractions, etc., that are needed to solve a problem instance with characteristics given by n, we might as well lump all the operations together (provided that the time required by each is relatively independent of the instance characteristics) and obtain a count for the total number of operations. We can go one step further and count only the number of program steps.

A *program step* is loosely defined as a syntactically or semantically meaningful segment of a program that has an execution time that is independent of the instance characteristics. For example, the entire statement

$$abc := a + b + b * c + (a + b - c) / (a + b) + 4.0;$$

of Program 1.9 could be regarded as a step since its execution time is independent of the instance characteristics (this statement is not strictly true, since the time for a multiply and divide will generally depend on the actual numbers involved in the operation).

The number of steps any program statement is to be assigned depends on the nature of that statement. The following discussion considers the various statement types that can appear in a Pascal program and states the complexity of each in terms of the number of steps:

(1) *Comments*. Comments are nonexecutable statements and have a step count of zero.

(2) *Declarative statements*. This category includes all statements of type **const**, **label**, **type**, and **var**. These count as zero steps, since these are either nonexecutable or their cost may be lumped into the cost of invoking the procedure/function they are associated with.

(3) *Expressions and assignment statements*. Most expressions have a step count of one. The exceptions are expressions that contain function calls. In this case, we need to determine the cost of invoking the functions. This cost can be large if the functions employ many-element value parameters because the values of all actual parameters need to be assigned to the formal parameters. This is discussed further under procedure and function invocation. When the expression contains functions, the step count is the sum of the step counts assignable to each function invocation.

The assignment statement <variable> := <expr> has a step count equal to that of <expr> unless the size of <variable> is a function of the instance characteristics. In this latter case, the step count is the size of <variable> plus the step count of <expr>. For example, the assignment $a := b$, where a and b are of type *ElementList*, has a step count equal to the size of *ElementList*.

(4) *Iteration statements*. This class of statements includes the **for**, **while**, and **until** statements. We shall consider the step counts only for the control part of these statements. These have the following form:

> **for** i := <expr> **to** <expr1> **do**
> **for** i := <expr> **downto** <expr1> **do**
> **while** <expr> **do**
> **until** <expr>;

Each execution of the control part of a **while** and **until** statement will be given a step count equal to the number of step counts assignable to <expr>. The step count for each execution of the control part of a **for** statement is one, unless the counts attributable to <expr> and <expr1> are a function of the instance characteristics. In this latter case, the first execution of the control part of the **for** has a step count equal to the sum of the counts for <expr> and <expr1> (note that these expressions are computed only when the loop is started). Remaining executions of the **for** statement have a step count of one.

(5) *Case statement*. This statement consists of a header followed by one or more sets of condition-statement pairs.

```
case <expr> of
    cond1: <statement1>
    cond2: <statement2>
           .

           .

           .
    else: <statement>
end;
```

The header **case** <expr> **of** is given a cost equal to that assignable to <expr>. The cost of each following condition-statement pair is the cost of this condition plus that of all preceding conditions plus that of this statement.

(6) *If-then-else statement*. The **if-then-else** statement consists of three parts:

```
if <expr>
then <statements1>
else <statements2>;
```

Each part is assigned the number of steps corresponding to <expr>, <statements1>, and <statements2> respectively. Note that if the **else** clause is absent, then no cost is assigned to it.

(7) *Procedure and function invocation*. All invocations of procedures and functions count as one step unless the invocation involves value parameters whose size depends on the instance characteristics. In this latter case, the count is the sum of the sizes of these value parameters. If the procedure/function being invoked is recursive, then we must also consider the local variables in the procedure or function being invoked. The sizes of local variables that are characteristic-dependent need to be added to the step count.

(8) *Begin, end, with, and repeat statements*. Each **with** statement counts as one step. Each **begin**, **end**, and **repeat** statement counts as zero steps.

(9) *Procedure and function statements*. These count as zero steps because their cost has already been assigned to the invoking statements.

(10) *Goto statement*. This has a step count of one.

With the above assignment of step counts to statements, we can proceed to determine the number of steps needed by a program to solve a particular problem instance. We can go about this in one of two ways. In the first method, we introduce a new variable, *count*, into the program. This is a global variable with initial value 0. Statements to increment *count* by the appropriate amount are introduced into the program. This is done so that each time a statement in the original program is executed, *count* is incremented by the step count of that statement.

Example 1.10: When the statements to increment *count* are introduced into Program 1.10, the result is Program 1.12. The change in the value of *count* by the time this program terminates is the number of steps executed by Program 1.10.

Since we are interested in determining only the change in the value of *count*, Program 1.12 may be simplified to Program 1.13. It should be easy to see that for every initial value of *count*, Program 1.12 and Program 1.13 compute the same final value for *count*. It is easy to see that in the **for** loop, the value of *count* will increase by a total of $2n$. If *count* is zero to start with, then it will be $2n+3$ on termination. So, each invocation of *sum* (Program 1.10) executes a total of $2n+3$ steps. □

```
function sum(a : ElementList ; n : integer) : real;
var s : real; i : integer;
begin
  s := 0;
  count := count+1; {count is global}
  for i := 1 to n do
  begin
    count := count+1; {for for}
    s := s +a [i ];
    count := count+1; {for assignment}
  end;
  count := count+1; {for last time of for}
  sum := s;
  count := count+1; {for assignment}
end; {of sum}
```

Program 1.12: Program 1.10 with count statements added

```
function sum(a : ElementList ; n : integer) : real;
var s : real; i : integer;
begin
  for i := 1 to n do
    count := count+2; {end of for}
  count := count+3;
end; {of sum}
```

Program 1.13: Simplified version of Program 1.12

Example 1.11: When the statements to increment *count* are introduced into Program 1.11, Program 1.14 is obtained. In this program, we have assumed that the declared size of *ElementList* is m. Note that $m \geq n$. Let $t_{rsum}(n)$ be the increase in the value of *count* when Program 1.14 terminates. We see that $t_{rsum}(0) = 2$. When $n > 0$, *count* increases by $m+1$ plus whatever increase results from the invocation of *rsum* from within the **else** clause. From the definition of t_{rsum}, it follows that this additional increase is $t_{rsum}(n-1)$. So, if the value of *count* is zero initially, its value at the time of termination is $m+1+t_{rsum}(n-1)$, $n > 0$.

---

function *rsum*(*a* : *ElementList* ; *n* : **integer**) : **real**;
begin
   count := *count*+1; {for **if** conditional}
   if *n<=0* **then begin**
             rsum := 0;
             count := *count*+1; {for assignment}
        end
   else begin
        rsum := *rsum* (*a*, *n*−1) + *a* [*n*];
        count := *count*+*m*; {for assignment, *m* is the size of *ElementList*}
      end;
end; {of *rsum*}

Program 1.14: Program 1.11 with count statements added

When analyzing a recursive program for its step count, we often obtain a recursive formula for the step count (i.e., say $t_{rsum}(n) = m+1+t_{rsum}(n-1)$, $n>0$ and $t_{rsum}(0) = 2$). These recursive formulas are referred to as *recurrence relations*. This recurrence may be solved by repeatedly substituting for t_{rsum} as below:

$$t_{rsum}(n) = m +1+t_{rsum}(n-1)$$
$$= m +1 + m +1 + t_{rsum}(n-2)$$
$$= 2(m +1) + t_{rsum}(n-2)$$
$$\cdot$$
$$\cdot$$
$$\cdot$$
$$= n (m +1) + t_{rsum}(0)$$
$$= n (m +1)+2, n \geq 0.$$

So, the step count for procedure *rsum* (Program 1.11) is $n (m +1)+2$. This is significantly larger than that for the iterative version (Program 1.10). If *a* is made a variable parameter, then the step count becomes $2n +2$. □

Comparing the step count of Program 1.10 to that of Program 1.11 with *a* changed to a variable parameter, we see that the count for Program 1.11 is less than that for Program 1.10. From this, we cannot conclude that Program 1.10 is slower than Program 1.11. This is so because a step does not correspond to a definite time unit. Each step of *rsum* may take more time than every step of *sum*. So, it might well be (and we expect it) that *rsum* is slower than *sum*.

The step count is useful in that it tells us how the run time for a program changes with changes in the instance characteristics. From the step count for *sum*, we see that if *n* is doubled, the run time will also double (approximately); if *n* increases by a factor of 10, we expect the run time to increase by a factor of 10; and so on. So, we expect the run time to grow *linearly* in *n*. We say that *sum* is a linear program (the time complexity is linear in the instance characteristic *n*).

Example 1.12 [*Matrix addition*]: Program 1.15 is a program to add two $m \times n$ matrices *a* and *b* together. Introducing the *count*-incrementing statements leads to Program 1.16. Program 1.17 is a simplified version of Program 1.16 that computes the same value for *count*. Examining Program 1.17, we see that line 6 is executed *n* times for each value of *i* or a total of *mn* times; line 7 is executed *m* times; and line 9 is executed once. If *count* is zero to begin with, it will be $2mn + 2m + 1$ when Program 1.17 terminates.

From this analysis we see that if $m > n$, then it is better to interchange the two **for** statements in Program 1.15. If this is done, the step count becomes $2mn + 2n + 1$. Note that in this example the instance characteristics are given by *m* and *n*. □

```
line  procedure add (var a, b, c : matrix; m,n : integer);
 1     var i, j : integer;
 2     begin
 3       for i := 1 to m do
 4         for j := 1 to n do
 5           c [i,j] := a [i,j]+b [i,j];
 6     end; {of add}
```

Program 1.15: Matrix addition

The second method to determine the step count of a program is to build a table in which we list the total number of steps contributed by each statement. This figure is often arrived at by first determining the number of steps per execution of the statement and the total number of times (i.e., frequency) each statement is executed. By combining these two quantities, the total contribution of each statement is obtained. By adding up the contributions of all statements, the step count for the entire program is obtained.

There is an important difference between the step count of a statement and its steps per execution (s/e). The step count does not necessarily reflect the complexity of the statement. For example, the statement

$$x := sum(a,m);$$

```
procedure add (var a, b, c : matrix; m, n : integer);
var i, j : integer;
begin
  for i := 1 to m do
  begin
    count := count+1; {for for i}
    for j := 1 to n do
    begin
      count := count+1; {for for j}
      c [i,j] := a [i,j]+b [i,j];
      count := count+1; {for assignment}
    end;
    count := count+1; {for last time of for j}
  end;
  count := count+1; {for last time of for i}
end; {of add}
```

Program 1.16: Matrix addition with counting statements

```
line  procedure add (var a, b, c : matrix; m, n : integer);
1       var i, j : integer;
2       begin
3         for i := 1 to m do
4         begin
5           for j := 1 to n do
6             count := count+2;
7           count := count+2;
8         end;
9         count := count+1;
10      end; {of add}
```

Program 1.17: Simplified program with counting only

has a step count of m (assuming that a is defined to be an array of size m), while the total change in *count* resulting from the execution of this statement is actually m plus the change resulting from the invocation of *sum* (i.e., $2m+3$). The steps per execution of the above statement is $m+2m+3 = 3m+3$. *The s/e of a statement is the amount by which count changes as a result of the execution of that statement.*

In Table 1.1, the number of steps per execution and the frequency of each of the statements in procedure *sum* (Program 1.10) have been listed. The total number of steps required by the program is determined to be $2n+3$. It is important to note that the frequency of line 4 is $n+1$ and not n. This is so because i has to be incremented to $n+1$ before the **for** loop can terminate.

line	s/e	frequency	total steps
1	0	0	0
2	0	0	0
3	1	1	1
4	1	$n+1$	$n+1$
5	1	n	n
6	1	1	1
7	0	1	0
Total number of steps			$2n+3$

Table 1.1: Step table for Program 1.10

Table 1.2 gives the step count for procedure *rsum* (Program 1.11). Line 2(a) refers to the **if** conditional of line 2, and line 2(b) refers to the statement in the **then** clause of the **if**. Notice that under the s/e (steps per execution) column, line 3 has been given a count of $m+t_{rsum}(n-1)$. This is the total cost of line 3 each time it is executed. It includes all the steps that get executed as a result of the invocation of *rsum* from line 3. The frequency and total steps columns have been split into two parts: one for the case $n = 0$ and the other for the case $n > 0$. This is necessary because the frequency (and hence total steps) for some statements is different for each of these cases.

line	s/e	frequency $n = 0$	frequency $n > 0$	total steps $n = 0$	total steps $n > 0$
1	0	0	0	0	0
2(a)	1	1	1	1	1
2(b)	1	1	0	1	0
3	$m+t_{rsum}(n-1)$	0	1	0	$m+t_{rsum}(n-1)$
4	0	1	1	0	0
Total number of steps				2	$m+1+t_{rsum}(n-1)$

Table 1.2: Step table for Program 1.11

Table 1.3 corresponds to procedure *add* (Program 1.15). Once again, note that the frequency of line 3 is $m+1$ and not m. This is so as i needs to be incremented up to $m+1$ before the loop can terminate. Similarly, the frequency for line 4 is $m(n+1)$. When you have obtained sufficient experience in computing step counts, you may avoid constructing the frequency table and obtain the step count as in the following example.

line	s/e	frequency	total steps
1	0	0	0
2	0	0	0
3	1	$m+1$	$m+1$
4	1	$m(n+1)$	$mn+m$
5	1	mn	mn
6	0	1	0
Total number of steps			$2mn+2m+1$

Table 1.3: Step table for Program 1.15

Example 1.13 [*Fibonnaci numbers*]: The Fibonacci sequence of numbers starts as

$$0, 1, 1, 2, 3, 5, 8, 13, 21, 34, 55, \cdots$$

Each new term is obtained by taking the sum of the two previous terms. If we call the first term of the sequence F_0 then $F_0 = 0$, $F_1 = 1$, and in general

$$F_n = F_{n-1} + F_{n-2}, n \geq 2.$$

The program *fibonacci* (Program 1.18) inputs any nonnegative integer n and prints the value F_n.

To analyze the time complexity of this program, we need to consider the two cases: (1) $n = 0$ or 1 and (2) $n > 1$. Line 7 will be regarded as two lines: 7(a), the conditional part, and 7(b), the **then** clause. When $n = 0$ or 1, lines 6, 7(a), 7(b), and 19 get executed once each. Since each line has an s/e of 1, the total step count for this case is 4. When $n > 1$, lines 6, 7(a), 10, and 17 are each executed once. Line 11 gets executed n times, and lines 12-16 get executed $n-1$ times each (note that the last time line 11 is executed, i is incremented to $n + 1$ and the loop exited). Line 10 has an s/e of 2; the remaining lines that get executed have an s/e of 1. The total steps for the case $n > 1$ is therefore $4n + 2$. □

```
1  program fibonacci(input, output);
2  {compute the Fibonacci number F_n}
3  type natural = 0 .. maxint;
4  var fnm1, fnm2, fn, n, i : natural;
5  begin
6     readln(n);
7     if n <= 1 then writeln(n) {F_0 = 0 and F_1 = 1}
8              else
9              begin {compute F_n}
10                 fnm2 := 0; fnm1 := 1;
11                 for i := 2 to n do
12                 begin
13                     fn := fnm1+fnm2;
14                     fnm2 := fnm1;
15                     fnm1 := fn;
16                 end; {of for}
17                 writeln(fn);
18              end; {of else}
19 end. {of fibonacci}
```

Program 1.18: Fibonacci numbers

Summary

The time complexity of a program is given by the number of steps taken by the program to compute the function it was written for. The number of steps is itself a function of the instance characteristics. Although any specific instance may have several characteristics (e.g., the number of inputs, the number of outputs, the magnitudes of the inputs and outputs), the number of steps is computed as a function of some subset of these. Usually, we choose those characteristics that are of importance to us. For example, we might wish to know how the computing (or run) time (i.e., time complexity) increases as the number of inputs increase. In this case the number of steps will be computed as a function of the number of inputs alone. For a different program, we might be interested in determining how the computing time increases as the magnitude of one of the inputs increases. In this case the number of steps will be computed as a function of the magnitude of this input alone. Thus, before the step count of a program can be determined, we need to know exactly which characteristics of the problem instance are to be used. These define the variables in the expression for the step count. In the case of *sum*, we chose to measure the time complexity as a function of the number, n, of elements being added. For procedure *add* the choice of characteristics was the number, m, of rows and the number, n, of columns in the matrices being added.

Once the relevant characteristics (n, m, p, q, r, $\cdots$) have been selected, we can define what a step is. A step is any computation unit that is independent of the characteristics (n, m, p, q, r, $\cdots$). Thus, 10 additions can be one step; 100 multiplications can also be one step; but n additions cannot. Nor can $m/2$ additions, $p+q$ subtractions, and so on be counted as one step.

A systematic way to assign step counts was also discussed. Once this has been done, the time complexity (i.e., the total step count) of a program can be obtained using either of the two methods discussed.

The examples we have looked at so far were sufficiently simple that the time complexities were nice functions of fairly simple characteristics like the number of elements, and the number of rows and columns. For many programs, the time complexity is not dependent solely on the number of inputs or outputs or some other easily specified characteristic. Consider the procedure *BinarySearch* (Program 1.5). This procedure searches $a[1..n]$ for x. A natural parameter with respect to which you might wish to determine the step count is the number, n, of elements to be searched. That is, we would like to know how the computing time changes as we change the number of elements n. The parameter n is inadequate. For the same n, the step count varies with the position of x in a. We can extricate ourselves from the difficulties resulting from situations when the chosen parameters are not adequate to determine the step count uniquely by defining three kinds of step counts: best-case, worst-case, and average.

The *best-case step count* is the minimum number of steps that can be executed for the given parameters. The *worst-case step count* is the maximum number of steps that can be executed for the given parameters. The *average step count* is the average number of steps executed on instances with the given parameters.

1.4.1.3 Asymptotic Notation (O, Ω, Θ)

Our motivation to determine step counts is to be able to compare the time complexities of two programs that compute the same function and also to predict the growth in run time as the instance characteristics change.

Determining the exact step count (either worst-case or average) of a program can prove to be an exceedingly difficult task. Expending immense effort to determine the step count exactly is not a very worthwhile endeavor, since the notion of a step is itself inexact. (Both the instructions $x := y$ and $x := y + z + (x/y) + (x*y*z-x/z)$ count as one step.) Because of the inexactness of what a step stands for, the exact step count is not very useful for comparative purposes. An exception to this is when the difference in the step counts of two programs is very large, as in $3n + 3$ versus $100n + 10$. We might feel quite safe in predicting that the program with step count $3n+3$ will run in less time than the one with step count $100n+10$. But even in this case, it is not necessary to know that the exact step count is $100n+10$. Something like, "it's about $80n$, or $85n$, or $75n$," is adequate to arrive at the same conclusion.

For most situations, it is adequate to be able to make a statement like $c_1 n^2 \leq t_P(n) \leq c_2 n^2$ or $t_Q(n,m) = c_1 n + c_2 m$ where c_1 and c_2 are nonnegative constants. This is so because if we have two programs with a complexity of $c_1n^2 + c_2n$ and c_3n respectively, then we know that the one with complexity c_3n will be faster than the one with complexity $c_1n^2 + c_2n$ for sufficiently large values of n. For small values of n, either program could be faster (depending on c_1, c_2, and c_3). If $c_1 = 1, c_2 = 2$, and $c_3 = 100$ then $c_1n^2 + c_2n \leq c_3n$ for $n \leq 98$, and $c_1n^2 + c_2n > c_3n$ for $n > 98$. If $c_1 = 1, c_2 = 2$, and $c_3 = 1000$, then $c_1n^2 + c_2n \leq c_3n$ for $n \leq 998$.

No matter what the values of c_1, c_2, and c_3, there will be an n beyond which the program with complexity c_3n will be faster than the one with complexity $c_1n^2 + c_2n$. This value of n will be called the *break-even point*. If the break-even point is zero, then the program with complexity c_3n is always faster (or at least as fast). The exact break-even point cannot be determined analytically. The programs have to be run on a computer in order to determine the break-even point. To know that there is a break-even point, it is adequate to know that one program has complexity $c_1n^2 + c_2n$ and the other c_3n for some constants c_1, c_2, and c_3. There is little advantage in determining the exact values of c_1, c_2, and c_3.

With the previous discussion as motivation, we introduce some terminology that will enable us to make meaningful (but inexact) statements about the time and space complexities of a program. In the remainder of this chapter, the functions f and g are nonnegative functions.

Definition [*Big "oh"*]: $f(n) = O(g(n))$ (read as "f of n is big oh of g of n") iff (if and only if) there exist positive constants c and n_0 such that $f(n) \leq cg(n)$ for all $n, n \geq n_0$. □

Example 1.14: $3n + 2 = O(n)$ as $3n + 2 \leq 4n$ for all $n \geq 2$. $3n + 3 = O(n)$ as $3n + 3 \leq 4n$ for all $n \geq 3$. $100n + 6 = O(n)$ as $100n + 6 \leq 101n$ for $n \geq 10$. $10n^2 + 4n + 2 = O(n^2)$ as $10n^2 + 4n + 2 \leq 11n^2$ for $n \geq 5$. $1000n^2 + 100n - 6 = O(n^2)$ as $1000n^2 + 100n - 6 \leq 1001n^2$ for $n \geq 100$. $6*2^n + n^2 = O(2^n)$ as $6*2^n + n^2 \leq 7*2^n$ for $n \geq 4$. $3n + 3 = O(n^2)$ as $3n + 3 \leq 3n^2$ for $n \geq 2$. $10n^2 + 4n + 2 = O(n^4)$ as $10n^2 + 4n + 2 \leq 10n^4$ for $n \geq 2$. $3n + 2 \neq O(1)$ as $3n + 2$ is not less than or equal to c for any constant c and all $n, n \geq n_0$. $10n^2 + 4n + 2 \neq O(n)$. □

We write $O(1)$ to mean a computing time that is a constant. $O(n)$ is called linear, $O(n^2)$ is called quadratic, $O(n^3)$ is called cubic, and $O(2^n)$ is called exponential. If an algorithm takes time $O(\log n)$, it is faster, for sufficiently large n, than if it had taken $O(n)$. Similarly, $O(n \log n)$ is better than $O(n^2)$ but not as good as $O(n)$. These seven computing times, $O(1), O(\log n), O(n), O(n \log n), O(n^2), O(n^3)$, and $O(2^n)$ are the ones we will see most often in this book.

As illustrated by the previous example, the statement $f(n) = O(g(n))$ states only that $g(n)$ is an upper bound on the value of $f(n)$ for all $n, n \geq n_0$. It does not say anything about how good this bound is. Notice that $n = O(n^2), n = O(n^{2.5}), n = O(n^3), n = O(2^n)$, and so on. For the statement $f(n) = O(g(n))$ to be informative, $g(n)$ should be as small a function of n as one can come up with for which $f(n) = O(g(n))$. So, while we shall often say $3n + 3 = O(n)$, we shall almost never say $3n + 3 = O(n^2)$, even though this latter statement is correct.

From the definition of O, it should be clear that $f(n) = O(g(n))$ is not the same as $O(g(n)) = f(n)$. In fact, it is meaningless to say that $O(g(n)) = f(n)$. The use of the symbol "=" is unfortunate because this symbol commonly denotes the "equals" relation. Some of the confusion that results from the use of this symbol (which is standard terminology) can be avoided by reading the symbol "=" as "is" and not as "equals."

Theorem 1.2 obtains a very useful result concerning the order of $f(n)$ (i.e., the $g(n)$ in $f(n) = O(g(n))$) when $f(n)$ is a polynomial in n.

Theorem 1.2: If $f(n) = a_m n^m + \cdots + a_1 n + a_0$, then $f(n) = O(n^m)$.

Proof: $f(n) \leq \sum_{i=0}^{m} |a_i| n^i$

$$\leq n^m \sum_{0}^{m} |a_i| n^{i-m}$$

$$\leq n^m \sum_{0}^{m} |a_i|, \text{ for } n \geq 1$$

So, $f(n) = O(n^m)$. $\square$

Definition: [Omega] $f(n) = \Omega(g(n))$ (read as "f of n is omega of g of n") iff there exist positive constants c and n_0 such that $f(n) \geq cg(n)$ for all n, $n \geq n_0$. $\square$

Example 1.15: $3n + 2 = \Omega(n)$ as $3n + 2 \geq 3n$ for $n \geq 1$ (actually the inequality holds for $n \geq 0$, but the definition of Ω requires an $n_0 > 0$). $3n + 3 = \Omega(n)$ as $3n + 3 \geq 3n$ for $n \geq 1$. $100n + 6 = \Omega(n)$ as $100n + 6 \geq 100n$ for $n \geq 1$. $10n^2 + 4n + 2 = \Omega(n^2)$ as $10n^2 + 4n + 2 \geq n^2$ for $n \geq 1$. $6*2^n + n^2 = \Omega(2^n)$ as $6*2^n + n^2 \geq 2^n$ for $n \geq 1$. Observe also that $3n + 3 = \Omega(1)$; $10n^2 + 4n + 2 = \Omega(n)$; $10n^2 + 4n + 2 = \Omega(1)$; $6*2^n + n^2 = \Omega(n^{100})$; $6*2^n + n^2 = \Omega(n^{50.2})$; $6*2^n + n^2 = \Omega(n^2)$; $6*2^n + n^2 = \Omega(n)$; and $6*2^n + n^2 = \Omega(1)$. $\square$

As in the case of the "big oh" notation, there are several functions $g(n)$ for which $f(n) = \Omega(g(n))$. The function $g(n)$ is only a lower bound on $f(n)$. For the statement $f(n) = \Omega(g(n))$ to be informative, $g(n)$ should be as large a function of n as possible for which the statement $f(n) = \Omega(g(n))$ is true. So, while we shall say that $3n + 3 = \Omega(n)$ and $6*2^n + n^2 = \Omega(2^n)$, we shall almost never say that $3n + 3 = \Omega(1)$ or $6*2^n + n^2 = \Omega(1)$, even though both of these statements are correct.

Theorem 1.3 is the analogue of Theorem 1.2 for the omega notation.

Theorem 1.3: If $f(n) = a_m n^m + \cdots + a_1 n + a_0$ and $a_m > 0$, then $f(n) = \Omega(n^m)$.

Proof: Left as an exercise. $\square$

Definition: [Theta] $f(n) = \Theta(g(n))$ (read as "f of n is theta of g of n") iff there exist positive constants c_1, c_2, and n_0 such that $c_1 g(n) \leq f(n) \leq c_2 g(n)$ for all $n, n \geq n_0$. $\square$

Example 1.16: $3n + 2 = \Theta(n)$ as $3n + 2 \geq 3n$ for all $n \geq 2$, and $3n + 2 \leq 4n$ for all $n \geq 2$, so $c_1 = 3$, $c_2 = 4$, and $n_0 = 2$. $3n + 3 = \Theta(n)$; $10n^2 + 4n + 2 = \Theta(n^2)$; $6*2^n + n^2 = \Theta(2^n)$; and $10*\log n + 4 = \Theta(\log n)$. $3n + 2 \neq \Theta(1)$; $3n + 3 \neq \Theta(n^2)$; $10n^2 + 4n + 2 \neq \Theta(1)$; $10n^2 + 4n + 2 \neq \Theta(1)$; $6*2^n + n^2 \neq \Theta(n^2)$; $6*2^n + n^2 \neq \Theta(n^{100})$; and $6*2^n + n^2 \neq \Theta(1)$. $\square$

The theta notation is more precise than both the "big oh" and omega notations. $f(n) = \Theta(g(n))$ iff $g(n)$ is both an upper and lower bound on $f(n)$.

Notice that the coefficients in all of the $g(n)$'s used in the preceding three examples have been 1. This is in accordance with practice. We shall almost never find ourselves saying that $3n + 3 = O(3n)$, or that $10 = O(100)$, or that $10n^2 + 4n + 2 = \Omega(4n^2)$, or that $6*2^n + n^2 = \Omega(6*2^n)$, or that $6*2^n + n^2 = \Theta(4*2^n)$, even though each of these statements is true.

Theorem 1.4: If $f(n) = a_m n^m + \cdots + a_1 n + a_0$ and $a_m > 0$, then $f(n) = \Theta(n^m)$.

Proof: Left as an exercise. $\square$

Let us reexamine the time complexity analyses of the previous section. For procedure *sum* (Program 1.10) we had determined that $t_{sum}(n) = 2n + 3$. So, $t_{sum}(n) = \Theta(n)$. $t_{rsum}(n) = n(m+1) + 2 = \Theta(nm)$ and $t_{add}(m,n) = 2mn + 2n + 1 = \Theta(mn)$.

Although we might all see that the O, Ω, and Θ notations have been used correctly in the preceding paragraphs, we are still left with the question, Of what use are these notations if one has to first determine the step count exactly? The answer to this question is that the asymptotic complexity (i.e., the complexity in terms of O, Ω, and Θ) can be determined quite easily without determining the exact step count. This is usually done by first determining the asymptotic complexity of each statement (or group of statements) in the program and then adding up these complexities. Tables 1.4 through 1.6 do just this for *sum*, *rsum*, and *add* (Programs 1.10, 1.11, and 1.15).

Note that in the table for *add* (Table 1.6), lines 4 and 5 have been lumped together even though they have different frequencies. This lumping together of these two lines is possible because their frequencies are of the same order.

Although the analyses of Tables 1.4 through 1.6 are actually carried out in terms of step counts, it is correct to interpret $t_P(n) = \Theta(g(n))$, or $t_P(n) = O(g(n))$, or $t_P(n) = \Omega(g(n))$ as a statement about the computing time of program P. This is so because each step takes only $\Theta(1)$ time to execute.

After you have had some experience using the table method, you will be in a position to arrive at the asymptotic complexity of a program by taking a more global approach. We elaborate on this method in the following examples.

Example 1.17 [*Permutation generator*]: Consider procedure *perm* (Program 1.8). Assume that a is of size n. When $k = n$, we see that the time taken is $\Theta(n)$. When $k < n$, the

line(s)	s/e	frequency	total steps
1,2	0	–	$\Theta(0)$
3	1	1	$\Theta(1)$
4	1	$n+1$	$\Theta(n)$
5	1	n	$\Theta(n)$
6	1	1	$\Theta(1)$
7	0	–	$\Theta(0)$

$$t_{sum}(n) = \Theta(\max_{1 \le i \le 7}\{g_i(n)\}) = \Theta(n)$$

Table 1.4: Asymptotic complexity of *sum* (Program 1.10)

line	s/e	frequency $n = 0$	frequency $n > 0$	total steps $n = 0$	total steps $n > 0$
1	0	–	–	0	$\Theta(0)$
2(a)	1	1	1	1	$\Theta(1)$
2(b)	1	1	0	1	$\Theta(0)$
3	$m + t_{rsum}(n-1)$	0	1	0	$\Theta(m + t_{rsum}(n-1))$
4	0	–	–	0	$\Theta(0)$
	$t_{rsum}(n) =$			2	$\Theta(m + t_{rsum}(n-1))$

Table 1.5: Asymptotic complexity of *rsum* (Program 1.11)

else clause is entered. At this time, the second **for** loop is entered $n - k + 1$ times. Each iteration of this loop takes $\Theta(n + t_{perm}(k + 1, n))$ time. So, $t_{perm}(k, n) = \Theta((n - k + 1)(n + t_{perm}(k + 1, n)))$ when $k < n$. Since $t_{perm}(k + 1, n)$ is at least n when $k + 1 \le n$, we get $t_{perm}(k, n) = \Theta((n - k + 1)t_{perm}(k + 1, n))$ for $k < n$. Using the substitution method, we obtain $t(1, n) = \Theta(n(n!)), n \ge 1$. $\square$

Example 1.18 [*Binary search*]: Let us obtain the time complexity of procedure *BinarySearch* (Program 1.4). The instance characteristic that we shall use is the number n of elements in a. Each iteration of the **while** loop takes $\Theta(1)$ time. We can show that the **while** loop is iterated at most $\lceil \log_2(n+1) \rceil$ times (see the book by S. Sahni cited in the references). Since an asymptotic analysis is being performed, we do not need such an accurate count of the worst-case number of iterations. Each iteration except for the last results in a decrease in the size of the segment of a that has to be searched by a factor of

line(s)	s/e	frequency	total steps
1,2	0	0	$\Theta(0)$
3	1	$\Theta(m)$	$\Theta(m)$
4,5	1	$\Theta(mn)$	$\Theta(mn)$
6	0	–	$\Theta(0)$
		$t_{add}(m,n) =$	$\Theta(mn)$

Table 1.6: Asymptotic complexity of *add* (Program 1.15)

about 2. So, this loop is iterated $\Theta(\log n)$ times in the worst-case. As each iteration takes $\Theta(1)$ time, the overall worst-case complexity of *BinarySearch* is $\Theta(\log n)$. Note that, if *a* was not a **var** parameter, the complexity of using *BinarySearch* would be more than this because it would take $\Omega(n)$ time just to invoke the procedure. □

Example 1.19 [*Magic square*]: Our final example is a problem from recreational mathematics. A magic square is an $n \times n$ matrix of the integers 1 to n^2 such that the sum of every row, column, and diagonal is the same. Figure 1.1 gives an example magic square for the case $n = 5$. In this example, the common sum is 65.

15	8	1	24	17
16	14	7	5	23
22	20	13	6	4
3	21	19	12	10
9	2	25	18	11

Figure 1.1: Example magic square

H. Coxeter has given the following simple rule for generating a magic square when *n* is odd:

Start with 1 in the middle of the top row; then go up and left, assigning numbers in increasing order to empty squares; if you fall off the square imagine the same square as tiling the plane and continue; if a square is occupied, move down instead and continue.

The magic square of Figure 1.1 was formed using this rule. Program 1.19 is the Pascal program for creating an $n \times n$ magic square for the case when n is odd. This results from Coxeter's rule.

```
program magic (input, output);
{create a magic square of size n, n is odd}
const MaxSize = 50; {maximum square size − 1}
var square : array [0..MaxSize, 0..MaxSize] of integer;
    i, j, k, l : integer; {indices}
    key : integer; {counter}
    n : integer; {square size}
begin
  readln(n);  {input square size}

{check correctness of n}
  if (n > MaxSize+1) or (n < 1)
  then writeln('error..n out of range')
  else
  if n mod 2 = 0 then writeln('error..n is even')

{n is odd; Coxeter's rule can be used}
  else begin
  for i := 0 to n−1 do {initialize square to zero}
   for j := 0 to n−1 do square [i,j] := 0;
  square [0,(n−1) div 2] := 1; {middle of first row}
  {i and j are current position}
  key := 2; i := 0; j := (n−1) div 2;
  while key <= n*n do
  begin
    {move up and left. The next two if statements may
    be replaced by the mod operator if −1 mod n is implemented to have value n−1}
    if i−1 < 0 then k := n−1 else k := i−1;
    if j−1 < 0 then l := n−1 else l := j−1;
    if square [k,l] <> 0
    then i := (i+1) mod n {square occupied, move down}
    else begin {square [k,l] is unoccupied}
          i := k;
          {the mod operator may be used here if −1 mod n = n−1}
```

```
        if j−1 < 0 then j := n−1
                  else j := j−1;
      end;
   square [i,j] := key;
   key := key+1;
 end; {of while}

{output the magic square}
writeln('magic square of size', n);
for i := 0 to n−1 do
begin
  for j := 0 to n−1 do
    write(square [i,j]);
  writeln;
  end; {of for}
      end; {of n is odd}
end. {of magic}
```

Program 1.19: Magic square

The magic square is represented using a two-dimensional array having n rows and n columns. For this application it is convenient to number the rows (and columns) from zero to $n - 1$ rather than from one to n. Thus, when the program ''falls off the square,'' the **mod** operator sets i and/or j back to zero or $n - 1$.

The **while** loop is governed by the variable *key*, which is an integer variable initialized to 2 and increased by one each time through the loop. Thus, each statement within the **while** loop will be executed no more than $n^2 - 1$ times, and the computing time for *magic* is $O(n^2)$. Since there are n^2 positions in which the algorithm must place a number, we see that $O(n^2)$ is the best bound an algorithm for the magic square problem can have. □

1.4.1.4   Practical Complexities

We have seen that the time complexity of a program is generally some function of the instance characteristics. This function is very useful in determining how the time requirements vary as the instance characteristics change. The complexity function may also be used to compare two programs P and Q that perform the same task. Assume that program P has complexity $\Theta(n)$ and program Q is of complexity $\Theta(n^2)$. We can assert that program P is faster than program Q for sufficiently large n. To see the validity of this assertion, observe that the actual computing time of P is bounded from above by cn for some constant c and for all n, $n \geq n_1$, whereas that of Q is bounded from below by dn^2 for some constant d and all n, $n \geq n_2$. Since $cn \leq dn^2$ for $n \geq c/d$, program P is faster than program Q whenever $n \geq \max\{n_1, n_2, c/d\}$.

You should always be cautiously aware of the presence of the phrase "sufficiently large" in the assertion of the preceding discussion. When deciding which of the two programs to use, we must know whether the n we are dealing with is, in fact, sufficiently large. If program P actually runs in $10^6 n$ milliseconds, whereas program Q runs in n^2 milliseconds, and if we always have $n \le 10^6$, then, other factors being equal, program Q is the one to use.

To get a feel for how the various functions grow with n, you are advised to study Table 1.7 and Figure 1.2 very closely. It is evident from the table and the figure that the function 2^n grows very rapidly with n. In fact, if a program needs 2^n steps for execution, then when $n = 40$, the number of steps needed is approximately $1.1*10^{12}$. On a computer performing 1 billion steps per second, this would require about 18.3 minutes. If $n = 50$, the same program would run for about 13 days on this computer. When $n = 60$, about 310.56 years will be required to execute the program and when $n = 100$, about $4*10^{13}$ years will be needed. So, we may conclude that the utility of programs with exponential complexity is limited to small n (typically $n \le 40$).

$\log n$	n	$n \log n$	n^2	n^3	2^n
0	1	0	1	1	2
1	2	2	4	8	4
2	4	8	16	64	16
3	8	24	64	512	256
4	16	64	256	4096	65,536
5	32	160	1024	32,768	4,294,967,296

Table 1.7: Function values

Programs that have a complexity that is a polynomial of high degree are also of limited utility. For example, if a program needs n^{10} steps, then using our 1-billion-steps-per-second computer, we will need 10 seconds when $n = 10$; 3,171 years when $n = 100$; and $3.17*10^{13}$ years when $n = 1000$. If the program's complexity had been n^3 steps instead, then we would need 1 second when $n = 1000$; 110.67 minutes when $n = 10,000$; and 11.57 days when $n = 100,000$.

Table 1.8 gives the time needed by a 1-billion-steps-per-second computer to execute a program of complexity $f(n)$ instructions. You should note that currently only the fastest computers can execute about 1 billion instructions per second. From a practical standpoint, it is evident that for reasonably large n (say $n > 100$), only programs of small complexity (such as n, $n \log n$, n^2, n^3) are feasible. Further, this is the case even if one could build a computer capable of executing 10^{12} instructions per second. In this case, the computing times of Table 1.8 would decrease by a factor of 1000. Now, when $n = 100$ it would take 3.17 years to execute n^{10} instructions and $4*10^{10}$ years to execute 2^n instructions.

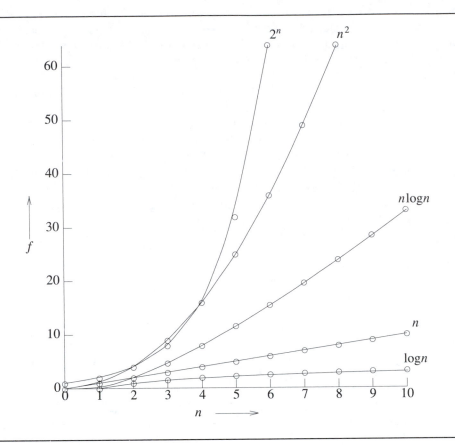

Figure 1.2: Plot of function values

1.4.2 Performance Measurement

Performance measurement is concerned with obtaining the actual space and time requirements of a program. These quantities are dependent on the particular compiler and options used as well as on the specific computer on which the program is run. Unless otherwise stated, all performance values provided in this book are obtained using the Turbo Pascal compiler, the default compiler options are used, and the computer used is an early model IBM-PC.

In keeping with the discussion of the preceding section, we shall not concern ourselves with the space and time needed for compilation. We justify this by the assumption that each program (after it has been fully debugged) will be compiled once and then executed several times. Certainly, the space and time needed for compilation are important during program testing, when more time is spent on this task than in actually running the compiled code.

Time for $f(n)$ instructions on a 10^9 instr/sec computer

n	$f(n)=n$	$f(n)=\log_2 n$	$f(n)=n^2$	$f(n)=n^3$	$f(n)=n^4$	$f(n)=n^{10}$	$f(n)=2^n$
10	.01µs	.03µs	.1µs	1µs	10µs	10sec	1µs
20	.02µs	.09µs	.4µs	8µs	160µs	2.84hr	1ms
30	.03µs	.15µs	.9µs	27µs	810µs	6.83d	1sec
40	.04µs	.21µs	1.6µs	64µs	2.56ms	121.36d	18.3min
50	.05µs	.28µs	2.5µs	125µs	6.25ms	3.1yr	13d
100	.10µs	.66µs	10µs	1ms	100ms	3171yr	$4*10^{13}$ yr
1,000	1.00µs	9.96µs	1ms	1sec	16.67min	$3.17*10^{13}$ yr	$32*10^{283}$ yr
10,000	10.00µs	130.03µs	100ms	16.67min	115.7d	$3.17*10^{23}$ yr	
100,000	100.00µs	1.66ms	10sec	11.57d	3171yr	$3.17*10^{33}$ yr	
1,000,000	1.00ms	19.92ms	16.67min	31.71yr	$3.17*10^7$ yr	$3.17*10^{43}$ yr	

Table 1.8: Times on a 1-billion-steps-per-second computer

We shall not explicitly consider measuring the run-time space requirements of a program. Rather, we shall focus on measuring the computing time of a program. To obtain the computing (or run) time of a program, we need a clocking procedure. We assume the existence of a procedure *time* (*hsec*) that returns in the variable *hsec* the current time in hundredths of a second.

Suppose we wish to measure the worst-case performance of the sequential search procedure (Program 1.20). Before we can do this, we need to: (1) decide on the values of *n* for which the times are to be obtained and (2) determine, for each of the above values of *n*, the data that exhibits the worst-case behavior.

```
line function seqsearch (a : ElementList ; n,x : integer): integer;
 1    var i : integer;
 2    begin
 3       i := n; a [0] := x;
 4       while a [i] <> x do
 5          i := i−1;
 6       seqsearch := i;
 7    end; {of seqsearch}
```

Program 1.20: Sequential search

The decision on which values of *n* to use is to be based on the amount of timing we wish to perform and also on what we expect to do with the times once they are obtained. Assume that for Program 1.20, our intent is simply to predict how long it will take, in the worst-case, to search for *x* given the size *n* of *a*. An asymptotic analysis reveals that this time is $\Theta(n)$. So, we expect a plot of the times to be a straight line. Theoretically, if we know the times for any two values of *n*, the straight line is determined, and we can obtain the time for all other values of *n* from this line. In practice, we need the times for more than two values of *n*. This is so for the following reasons:

(1)   Asymptotic analysis tells us the behavior only for "sufficiently large" values of *n*. For smaller values of *n* the run time may not follow the asymptotic curve. To determine the point beyond which the asymptotic curve is followed, we need to examine the times for several values of *n*.

(2)   Even in the region where the asymptotic behavior is exhibited, the times may not lie exactly on the predicted curve (straight line in the case of Program 1.20) because of the effects of low-order terms that are discarded in the asymptotic analysis. For instance, a program with asymptotic complexity $\Theta(n)$ can have an actual complexity that is $c_1 n + c_2 \log n + c_3$, or for that matter any other function of *n* in which the highest-order term is $c_1 n$ for some constant, $c_1, c_1 > 0$.

It is reasonable to expect that the asymptotic behavior of Program 1.20 will begin for some n that is smaller than 100. So, for $n > 100$ we shall obtain the run time for just a few values. A reasonable choice is $n = 200, 300, 400, \cdots, 1000$. There is nothing magical about this choice of values. We can just as well use $n = 500, 1000, 1500, \cdots, 10,000$ or $n = 512, 1024, 2048, \cdots, 2^{15}$. It will cost us more in terms of computer time to use the latter choices, and we will probably not get any better information about the run time of Program 1.20 using these choices.

For n in the range [0, 100] we shall carry out a more refined measurement, since we are not quite sure where the asymptotic behavior begins. Of course, if our measurements show that the straight-line behavior does not begin in this range, we shall have to perform a more detailed measurement in the range [100, 200] and so on, until the onset of this behavior is detected. Times in the range [0, 100] will be obtained in steps of 10 beginning at $n = 0$.

It is easy to see that Program 1.20 exhibits its worst-case behavior when x is chosen such that it is not one of the $a[i]$'s. For definiteness, we shall set $a[i] = i$, $1 \leq i \leq n$ and $x = 0$.

At this time, we envision using a program such as Program 1.21 to obtain the worst-case times.

The output obtained from this program is summarized in Figure 1.3. The times obtained are too small to be of any use to us. Most of the times are zero, indicating that the precision of our clock is inadequate. The nonzero times are just noise and are not representative of the actual time taken.

To time a short event, it is necessary to repeat it several times and divide the total time for the event by the number of repetitions.

Since our clock has an accuracy of about one-hundredth of a second, we should not attempt to time any single event that takes less than about 1 second. With an event time of at least 1 second, we can expect our observed times to be accurate to 1 percent.

The body of Program 1.21 needs to be changed to that of Program 1.22. In this program, $r[i]$ is the number of times the search is to be repeated when the number of elements in the array is $n[i]$. Notice that rearranging the timing statements as in Programs 1.14 or 1.15 does not produce the desired results. For instance, from the data of Figure 1.3, we expect that with the structure of Program 1.23, the value output for $n = 0$ will still be 0. With the structure of Program 1.24, we expect the program never to exit the **while** loop when $n = 0$ (in reality, the loop will be exited because occasionally the measured time will turn out to be five- or six-hundredths of a second). Yet another alternative is to move the first call to *time* out of the **while** loop of Program 1.24 and change the assignment to t within the **while** loop to

$$t := h1 - h;$$

This approach can be expected to yield satisfactory times. This approach cannot be used when the timing procedure available gives us only the time since the last invocation of *time*. Another difficulty is that the measured time includes the time needed to read the clock. For small n, this time may be larger than the time to run *search*. This difficulty

```
program TimeSearch(input,output);
{Program to time Program 1.20}
type ElementList = array [0..1000] of integer;
var z : ElementList;
    i, j, k, h, m, s, f, h1, m1, s1, f1, t1 : integer;
    n : array [1..20] of integer;


      .

      .

      .


begin {body of TimeSearch}
   for j := 1 to 1000 do {initialize z}
      z[j] := j;
   for j := 1 to 10 do   {values of n}
   begin
      n[j] := 10*(j−1); n[j+10] := 100*j;
   end;
   writeln('n':5, ' ', 'time');
   for j := 1 to 20 do {obtain computing times}
   begin
      time(h); {get time}
      k := seqsearch(z, n[j], 0); {unsuccessful search}
      time(h1); {get time}
      {time spent in hundredths of a second}
      t1 := h1−h;
      writeln(n[j]:5,' ',t1:5);
   end;
   writeln('Times are in hundredths of a second'};
end. {of TimeSearch}
```

Program 1.21: Program to time Program 1.20

can be overcome by determining the time taken by the timing procedure and subtracting this time later. In further discussion, we shall use the explicit repetition factor technique.

The output from the timing program, Program 1.22, is given in Figure 1.4. The times for n in the range $[0, 100]$ are plotted in Figure 1.5. The remaining values have not been plotted because this would lead to severe compression of the range $[0, 100]$. The linear dependence of the worst-case time on n is apparent from this graph.

The graph of Figure 1.5 can be used to predict the run time for other values of n. For example, we expect that when $n = 24$, the worst-case search time will be 0.87 hun-

n	time	n	time
0	0	100	0
10	6	200	5
20	0	300	6
30	0	400	0
40	0	500	0
50	0	600	0
60	5	700	0
70	0	800	0
80	0	900	6
90	5	1000	5

Times in hundredths of a second

Figure 1.3: Output from Program 1.21

dredths of a second. We can go one step further and get the equation of the straight line. The equation of this line is $t = c + mn$, where m is the slope and c the value for $n = 0$. From the graph, we see that $c = 0.78$. Using the point $n = 60$ and $t = 1.01$, we obtain $m = (t-c)/n = 0.23/60 = 0.00383$. So, the line of Figure 1.5 has the equation $t = 0.78 + 0.00383n$, where t is the time in hundredths of a second. From this, we expect that when $n = 1000$, the worst-case search time will be 4.61 hsec, and when $n = 500$, it will be 2.675 hsec. Compared with the actual observed times of Figure 1.4, we see that these figures are very accurate!

An alternate approach to obtain a good straight line for the data of Figure 1.4 is to obtain the straight line that is the least-squares approximation to the data. The result is $t = 0.77747 + 0.003806n$. When $n = 1000$ and 500, this equation yields $t = 4.583$ and 2.680.

Now, we are probably ready to pat ourselves on the back for a job well done. However, this action is somewhat premature, since our experiment is flawed. First, the measured time includes the time taken by the repetition **for** loop. So, the times of Figure 1.4 are excessive. This can be corrected by determining the time for each iteration of this statement. A quick test run indicates that 30,000 executions take only 65 hundredths of a second. So, subtracting the time for the **for** $b := 1$ **to** $r[j]$ **do** statement reduces the reported times by only 0.002. We can ignore this difference, since the use of a higher repetition factor could well result in measured times that are lower by about 0.002 hsec per search. Our times are not accurate to a hundredth of a second, and it is not very meaningful to worry about the two-hundredths of a second spent on each repetition.

The second and more serious problem is caused by the fact that *ElementList* has been defined to be an array of size 1000. Consequently, each invocation of *seqsearch* begins by copying the 1000 values of the actual parameter z into the value formal param-

---

```
{repetition factors}
const r: array[1..20] of integer =
        (700, 700, 600, 600, 600, 600, 500, 500, 500, 500, 500,
        400, 400, 300, 300, 200, 200, 200, 100, 100);
begin {body of TimeSearch}
    for j := 1 to 1000 do {initialize z}
      z[j] := j;
    for j := 1 to 10 do {values of n}
    begin
        n[j] := 10*(j−1); n[j+10] := 100*j;
    end;

    writeln('n':5, ' ', 't 1', ' ', 't');
    for j := 1 to 20 do {obtain computing times}
    begin
      time(h); {get time}
      for b := 1 to r[j] do
          k := seqsearch(z, n[j], 0); {unsuccessful search}
      time(h); {get time}
      {time spent in hundredths of a second}
      t 1 := h 1−h;
      t := t 1; t := t/r[j]; {time per search}
      writeln(n[j]:5, ' ', t 1:5, t:8:3);
    end;
    writeln('Times are in hundredths of a second'};
end. {of TimeSearch}
```

Program 1.22: Timing program

eter a. The measured times are therefore representative of the actual time to use *seqsearch* only when *ElementList* is of this size! If the size of *ElementList* is changed to 2000 or 10,000, the measured times will change. A substantial part of the time reported in this figure is the time spent copying the 1000 elements of the actual parameter into the formal parameter.

So, what constitutes a meaningful test for Program 1.20? The size of *ElementList* is not known to us, and yet it is perhaps the most important factor. The realization that the worst-case run time of Program 1.20 is a function of both n and s (the size of *ElementList*, i.e., 1001 in the case of Program 1.21) motivates us to obtain the time for the body of Program 1.20 and that for its invocation separately. The former is independent of s, and the latter is independent of n. The total time to use Program 1.20 is the sum of these two times.

```
t := 0;
for b := 1 to r [ j ] do
begin
    time (h);
    k := seqsearch (a,n [ j ],0);
    time (h);
    t := t + h 1 − h;
end;
t := t/r [ j ];
```

Program 1.23: Improper timing construct

```
t := 0; i := 0;
while t < DesiredTime do
begin
    time (h);
    k := seqsearch (a,n [ j ],0);
    time (h 1);
    t := t + h 1 − h;
    i := i +1;
end;
t := t/i;
```

Program 1.24: Another improper timing construct

To obtain the time for the body of Program 1.20, we place the timing loop directly into function *seqsearch* as in Program 1.25. This is preferable to placing the code of *seqsearch* directly into the body of *TimeSearch*. This is because the strategy of Program 1.25 yields times that include the overhead of using parameters.

When Program 1.25 is used in place of Program 1.20, and the timing and repetition statements removed from Program 1.21, the times shown in Figure 1.6 are obtained. The repetition factors used are $r[1..20] = [32,000, 12,000, 6000, 5000, 4000, 3000, 2500, 2000, 2000, 1500, 1500, 800, 600, 500, 400, 300, 200, 200, 150, 150]$.

The time of 0.002 for each execution of the repetition **for** statement needs to be subtracted from the times of Figure 1.6. This subtraction has a material effect (i.e., at least 10 percent) only on the time for $n = 0$.

To time the invocation of Program 1.20 for different sizes s of *ElementList*, we delete all statements between the **begin** and **end** statements of Program 1.20 and run Program 1.21 for different values of s. The repetition factor needed varies with s. The ob-

n	t1	t	n	t1	t
0	549	0.784	100	582	1.164
10	571	0.816	200	615	1.537
20	516	0.860	300	763	1.907
30	539	0.898	400	686	2.287
40	555	0.925	500	801	2.670
50	583	0.972	600	610	3.050
60	505	1.010	700	687	3.435
70	522	1.044	800	758	3.790
80	538	1.076	900	826	4.230
90	566	1.132	1000	922	4.610

Times in hundredths of a second

Figure 1.4: Worst-case run times for Program 1.20

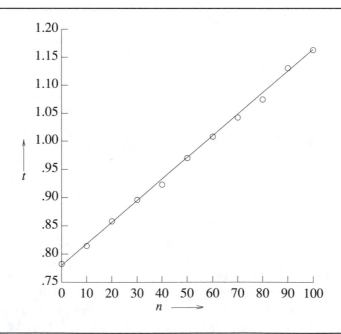

Figure 1.5: Plot of the data in Figure 1.4

```
function seqsearch (a : ElementList ; n,x : integer) : integer;
var i, k : integer;
begin
    time (h); {get time}
    for k := 1 to r [j] do {r [j] is global}
    begin
        i := n; a [0] := x;
        while a [i] <> x do
            i := i−1;
        seqsearch := i;
    end; {of repetition for}
    time (h 1); {get time}
    {time spent in hundredths of a second}
    t 1 := h 1−h;
    t := t 1; t := t/r [j]; {time per search}
    writeln(n [j]:5, ' ', t 1:5, t:8:3);
end; {of seqsearch}
```

Program 1.25: Timing the body of *seqsearch* (Program 1.20)

served times for various values of *s* are shown in Figure 1.7. Again, the time for the re-petition **for** loop has not been subtracted. This does not materially affect the times shown.

The least-squares straight line for the data of Figure 1.6 is $t = 0.008531 + 0.003785n$, and that for Figure 1.7 is $t = 0.018009 + 0.000756s$. Adding these two con-tributions, we get $t = 0.02654 + 0.000756s + 0.003785n$. We can see how good this equation is in predicting actual run times by using it with $s = 1000$. The equation be-comes $t = 0.78254 + 0.003785n$. This is quite close to the least-squares line for the data of Program 1.21.

Note that we can make the run time of *seqsearch* independent of *s* by making *a* a variable formal parameter.

Summary

To obtain the run time of a program, we need to plan the experiment. The follow-ing issues need to be addressed during the planning stage:

(1)   What is the accuracy of the clock? How accurate do our results have to be? Once the desired accuracy is known, we can determine the length of the shortest event that should be timed.

n	$t1$	t	n	$t1$	t
0	275	0.009	100	583	0.389
10	560	0.047	200	610	0.762
20	511	0.085	300	687	1.145
30	610	0.122	400	764	1.528
40	643	0.161	500	758	1.895
50	594	0.198	600	686	2.287
60	593	0.237	700	527	2.635
70	544	0.272	800	609	3.045
80	626	0.313	900	511	3.407
90	522	0.348	1000	571	3.807

Times in hundredths of a second

Figure 1.6: Times for body of Program 1.20 using Program 1.25

s	r	$time$	$time/r$
10	30,000	769	0.026
20	30,000	999	0.033
30	30,000	1225	0.041
40	20,000	967	0.048
50	12,000	670	0.056
60	12,000	767	0.064
70	10,000	714	0.071
80	10,000	791	0.079
90	10,000	862	0.086
100	10,000	939	0.094
200	5000	846	0.169
500	2000	795	0.398
1000	1000	774	0.774
5000	200	758	3.790
10,000	100	758	7.58

Times in hundredths of a second

Figure 1.7: Time needed to invoke Program 1.20

(2)   For each instance size, a repetition factor needs to be determined. This is to be chosen such that the event time is at least the minimum time that can be clocked with the desired accuracy.

(3)   Are we measuring worst-case or average performance? Suitable test data need to be generated.

(4)   What is the purpose of the experiment? Are the times being obtained for comparative purposes, or are they to be used to predict actual run times? If the latter is the case, then contributions to the run time from such sources as the repetition loop and data generation need to be subtracted (in case they are included in the measured time). If the former is the case, then these times need not be subtracted (provided they are the same for all programs being compared).

(5)   In case the times are to be used to predict actual run times, then we need to fit a curve through the points. For this, the asymptotic complexity should be known. If the asymptotic complexity is linear, then a least-squares straight line can be fit; if it is quadratic, then a parabola is to be used (i.e., $t = a_0 + a_1 n + a_2 n^2$). If the complexity is $\Theta(n\log n)$, then a least-squares curve of the form $t = a_0 + a_1 n + a_2 n\log_2 n$ can be fit. When obtaining the least-squares approximation, one should discard data corresponding to ''small'' values of n, since the program does not exhibit its asymptotic behavior for these n.

1.4.3   Generating Test Data

Generating a data set that results in the worst-case performance of a program is not always easy. In some cases, it is necessary to use a computer program to generate the worst-case data. In other cases, even this is very difficult. In these cases, another approach to estimating worst-case performance is taken. For each set of values of the instance characteristics of interest, we generate a suitably large number of random test data. The run times for each of these test data are obtained. The maximum of these times is used as an estimate of the worst-case time for this set of values of the instance characteristics.

To measure average-case times, it is usually not possible to average over all possible instances of a given characteristic. Although it is possible to do this for sequential and binary search, it is not possible for a sort program. If we assume that all keys are distinct, then for any given n, $n!$ different permutations need to be used to obtain the average time. Obtaining average-case data is usually much harder than obtaining worst-case data. So, we often adopt the strategy outlined above and simply obtain an estimate of the average time.

Whether we are estimating worst-case or average time using random data, the number of instances that we can try is generally much smaller than the total number of such instances. Hence, it is desirable to analyze the algorithm being tested to determine classes of data that should be generated for the experiment. This is a very algorithm-specific task, and we shall not go into it here.

EXERCISES

1. Compare the two functions n^2 and $2^n/4$ for various values of n. Determine when the second becomes larger than the first.

2. Prove by induction:

   (a) $\sum\limits_{1 \leq i \leq n} i = n(n+1)/2,\ n \geq 1$

   (b) $\sum\limits_{1 \leq i \leq n} i^2 = n(n+1)(2n+1)/6,\ n \geq 1$

   (c) $\sum\limits_{0 \leq i \leq n} x^i = (x^{n+1} - 1)/(x - 1),\ x \neq 1,\ n \geq 0$

3. Determine the frequency counts for all statements in the following two program segments:

   ```
   1  for i := 1 to n do              1  i := 1;
   2     for j := 1 to i do           2  while i ≤ n do
   3        for k := 1 to j do        3  begin
   4           x := x + 1 ;           4     x := x + 1 ;
                                       5     i := i + 1 ;
                                       6  end;
   ```
   (a)   (b)

4. (a) Introduce statements to increment *count* at all appropriate points in Program 1.26.

   (b) Simplify the resulting program by eliminating statements. The simplified program should compute the same value for *count* as computed by the program of (a).

   (c) What is the exact value of *count* when the program terminates? You may assume that the initial value of *count* is 0.

   (d) Obtain the step count for Program 1.26 using the frequency method. Clearly show the step count table.

5. Do Exercise 4 for procedure *transpose* (Program 1.27).

6. Do Exercise 4 for Program 1.28. This program multiplies two $n \times n$ matrices a and b.

7. (a) Do Exercise 4 for Program 1.29. This program multiplies two matrices a and b where a is an $m \times n$ matrix and b is an $n \times p$ matrix.

   (b) Under what conditions will it be profitable to interchange the two outermost **for** loops?

8. Show that the following equalities are correct:

   (a) $5n^2 - 6n = \Theta(n^2)$

```
procedure d (var x : list ; n : integer);
var i : integer;
begin
  i := 1;
  repeat
    x [i ] := x [i ] + 2;
    i := i + 2;
  until (i > n);
  i := 1;
  while i <= (n div 2) do
  begin
    x [i ] := x [i ] + x [i +1];
    i := i + 1;
  end;
end; {of d}
```

Program 1.26: Example program

```
line   procedure transpose(var a : matrix; n : integer);
1        var i, j : integer; t : element;
2        begin
3          for i := 1 to n−1 do
4            for j := i+1 to n do
5              begin
6                t := a [i,j ]; a [i,j ] := a [j,i ]; a [j,i ] := t;
7              end;
8        end; {of transpose}
```

Program 1.27: Matrix transpose

(b) $n! = O(n^n)$

(c) $2n^2 2^n + n\log n = \Theta(n^2 2^n)$

(d) $\sum_{i=0}^{n} i^2 = \Theta(n^3)$

(e) $\sum_{i=0}^{n} i^3 = \Theta(n^4)$

(f) $n^{2^n} + 6*2^n = \Theta(2^{2^n})$

```
procedure mult (var a, b, c : matrix; n : integer);
var i, j, k : integer;
begin
  for i := 1 to n do
    for j := 1 to n do
    begin
      c [i,j] := 0;
      for k := 1 to n do
        c [i,j] := c [i,j] + a [i,k] * b [k,j];
    end;
end; {of mult}
```

Program 1.28: Matrix multiplication

```
procedure prod (var a, b, c : matrix; m, n, p : integer);
var i, j, k : integer;
begin
  for i := 1 to m do
    for j := 1 to p do
    begin
      c [i,j] := 0;
      for k := 1 to n do
        c [i,j] := c [i,j] + a [i,k] * b [k,j];
    end;
end; {of prod}
```

Program 1.29: Matrix multiplication

(g) $n^3 + 10^6 n^2 = \Theta(n^3)$

(h) $6n^3/(\log n + 1) = O(n^3)$

(i) $n^{1.001} + n\log n = \Theta(n^{1.001})$

(j) $n^k + \varepsilon + n^k \log n = \Theta(n^k + \varepsilon)$ for all k and ε, $k \geq 0$, and $\varepsilon > 0$

(k) $10n^3 + 15n^4 + 100n^2 2^n = O(100n^2 2^n)$

(l) $33n^3 + 4n^2 = \Omega(n^2)$

(m) $33n^3 + 4n^2 = \Omega(n^3)$

9. Show that the following equalities are incorrect:

    (a) $10n^2 + 9 = O(n)$

    (b) $n^2 \log n = \Theta(n^2)$

    (c) $n^2 / \log n = \Theta(n^2)$

    (d) $n^3 2^n + 6n^2 3^n = O(n^3 2^n)$

10. Obtain the average run time of procedure *BinarySearch* (Program 1.4). Do this for suitable values of n in the range $[0, 100]$. Your report must include a plan for the experiment as well as the measured times. These times are to be provided both in a table and as a graph.

11. Analyze the computing time of procedure *sort* (Program 1.2).

12. Obtain worst-case run times for procedure *sort* (Program 1.2). Do this for suitable values of n in the range $[0, 100]$. Your report must include a plan for the experiment as well as the measured times. These times are to be provided both in a table and as a graph.

13. Consider procedure *add* (Program 1.15).

    (a) Obtain run times for $n = 1, 10, 20, \cdots, 100$.

    (b) Plot the times obtained in part (a).

14. Do the previous exercise for matrix multiplication (Program 1.29).

15. A complex-valued matrix X is represented by a pair of matrices (A,B) where A and B contain real values. Write a program that computes the product of two complex-valued matrices (A,B) and (C,D), where $(A,B) * (C,D) = (A + iB) * (C + iD) = (AC - BD) + i(AD + BC)$. Determine the number of additions and multiplications if the matrices are all $n \times n$.

1.5   REFERENCES AND SELECTED READINGS

For a discussion of programming techniques and how to develop programs, see *The Science of Programming*, by D. Gries, Springer Verlag, New York, NY, 1981; *A Discipline of Programming*, by E. W. Dijkstra, Prentice-Hall, Englewood Cliffs, NJ, 1976; and *The Elements of Programming Style*, Second Edition, by B. W. Kernighan and P. J. Plauger, McGraw Hill, New York, NY, 1978.

A good discussion of tools and procedures for developing very large software systems appears in the texts *Practical Strategies for Developing Very Large Software Systems*, by E. Horowitz, Addison-Wesley, Reading, MA, 1975, *The Mythical Man-Month*, by F. Brooks, Addison-Wesley, Reading, MA, 1979, and *Software engineering*, Third Edition, by I. Sommerville, Addison-Wesley, Workingham, England, 1989.

For a further discussion of abstract data types see *Abstraction and Specification in Program Development*, by B. Liskov and J. Guttag, MIT Press, Cambridge, MA, 1988;

Algorithms and Data Structures, by J. Kingston, Addison-Wesley, Reading, MA, 1990, and *Data Structures with Abstract Data Types and Pascal*, by D. Stubbs and N. Webre, Brooks/Cole Publishing Co., Monterey, CA, 1985.

Writing a correct version of binary search is discussed in the papers "Programming pearls: Writing correct programs," by J. Bentley, *CACM*, 26, 1983, pp. 1040-1045; and "Some lessons drawn from the history of the binary search algorithm," by R. Levisse, *The Computer Journal*, 26, 1983, pp. 154-163.

For a general discussion of permutation generation, see the paper "Permutation generation methods," by R. Sedgewick, *Computer Surveys*, 9, 1977, pp. 137-164.

For a more detailed discussion of performance analysis and measurement, see *Software Development in Pascal*, Third Edition, by S. Sahni, NSPAN Printing and Publishing, Gainesville, FL, 1993.

CHAPTER 2

ARRAYS

2.1 THE ARRAY AS AN ABSTRACT DATA TYPE

We begin our discussion by considering an array as an ADT. This is not the usual perspective, since many programmers view an array only as a consecutive set of memory locations. This is unfortunate because it clearly shows an emphasis on implementation issues. Although an array is usually implemented as a consecutive set of memory locations, this is not always the case. Intuitively an array is a set of pairs, *<index, value>*, such that each index that is defined has a value associated with it. In mathematical terms, we call this a *correspondence* or a *mapping*. However, when considering an ADT, we are more concerned with the operations that can be performed on an array. Aside from creating a new array, most languages provide only two standard operations for arrays, one that retrieves a value and a second that stores a value. Structure 2.1 shows a definition of the array ADT.

The *Create(j, list, item)* function produces a new, empty array of the appropriate size and type. All of the items are initially undefined. *Retrieve* accepts an *array* and an *index*. It returns the value associated with the index if the index is valid or an error if the index is invalid. *Store* accepts an *array*, an *index*, and an *item*, and returns the original array augmented with the new *<index, value>* pair. The advantage of this ADT definition is that it clearly points out the fact that the array is a more general structure than ''a consecutive set of memory locations.''

---

structure *Array* **is**

    objects: A set of pairs *<index, value>* where for each value of *index* there is a value from the set *item*. *Index* is a finite ordered set of one or more dimensions, for example, $\{1, \cdots, n\}$ for one dimension, $\{(1, 1), (1, 2), (1, 3), (2, 1), (2, 2), (2, 3), (3, 1), (3, 2), (3, 3)\}$ for two dimensions, etc.

    functions:

        for all $A \in Array, i \in index, x \in item, j, size \in$ integer

Create(j, list, item) : *Array*	::=	declare a *j* dimensional array; the range of the *i*th dimension is given by the *i*th element of *list*; the array elements are of type *item*;
Retrieve(A, i) : *Item*	::=	**if** *i* in *index* set of *A* **then** the item associated with index value *i* in array *A* is returned **else** error
Store(A,i,x) : *Array*	::=	**if** *i* in index set of *A* **then** an array that is identical to array *A* except the new pair *<i, x>* has been inserted is returned **else** error

end *Array*

Structure 2.1: Abstract data type *Array*

2.2   THE POLYNOMIAL ABSTRACT DATA TYPE

Arrays are not only data structures in their own right; we can also use them to implement other abstract data types. For instance, let us consider one of the simplest and most commonly found data structures: the *ordered*, or *linear, list.* We can find many examples of this data structure, including:

- Days of the week: (Sunday, Monday, Tuesday, Wednesday, Thursday, Friday, Saturday)
- Values in a deck of cards: (Ace, 2, 3, 4, 5, 6, 7, 8, 9, 10, Jack, Queen, King)
- Floors of a building: (basement, lobby, mezzanine, first, second)
- Years the United States fought in World War II: (1941, 1942, 1943, 1944, 1945)
- Years Switzerland fought in World War II: ( )

    Notice that "Years Switzerland fought in World War II" is different because it contains no items. It is an example of an empty list, which we denote as ( ). The other lists all contain items that are written in the form $(a_1, a_2, \cdots, a_n)$.

    We can perform many operations on lists, including:

(1)   Find the length, n, of the list.

(2)   Read the list from left to right (or right to left).

(3)   Retrieve the ith element, $1 \leq i \leq n$.

(4)   Store a new value into the ith position, $1 \leq i \leq n$.

(5)   Insert a new element at the position i, $1 \leq i \leq n + 1$, causing elements numbered $i, i + 1, \cdots, n$ to become numbered $i + 1, i + 2, \cdots, n + 1$.

(6)   Delete the element at position i, $1 \leq i \leq n$, causing elements numbered $i + 1, \cdots, n$ to become numbered $i, i + 1, \cdots, n - 1$.

It is not always necessary to be able to perform all of these operations; many times a subset will suffice. In the study of data structures we are interested in ways of representing ordered lists so that these operations can be carried out efficiently.

Rather than state the formal specification of the ADT *ordered list*, we want to explore briefly its implementation. Perhaps the most common way to represent an ordered list is by an array where we associate the list element a_i with the array index i. This we will refer to as *sequential mapping* because, using the conventional array representation, we are storing a_i and a_{i+1} into consecutive locations i and $i + 1$ of the array. This gives us the ability to retrieve or modify the values of random elements in the list in a constant amount of time, essentially because a computer memory has random access to any word. We can access the list element values in either direction by changing the subscript values in a controlled way. Only operations (5) and (6) require real effort. Insertion and deletion using sequential allocation force us to move some of the remaining elements so that the sequential mapping is preserved in its proper form. It is precisely this overhead that leads us to consider nonsequential mappings of ordered lists in Chapter 4.

Let us jump right into a problem requiring ordered lists, which we will solve by using one-dimensional arrays. This problem has become the classical example for motivating the use of list-processing techniques, which we will see in later chapters. Therefore, it makes sense to look at the problem and see why arrays offer only a partially adequate solution. The problem calls for building a set of subprograms (procedures and functions) that allow for the manipulation of symbolic polynomials. By ''symbolic,'' we mean the list of coefficients and exponents that accompany a polynomial; e.g., two such polynomials are

$$A(x) = 3x^2 + 2x + 4 \ \text{ and } \ B(x) = x^4 + 10x^3 + 3x^2 + 1$$

The largest (or leading) exponent of a polynomial is called its *degree.* Coefficients that are zero are not displayed. The term with exponent equal to zero does not show the variable, since x raised to a power of zero is 1. There are standard mathematical definitions for the sum and product of polynomials. Assume that we have two polynomials, $A(x) = \sum a_i x^i$ and $B(x) = \sum b_i x^i$; then

$$A(x) + B(x) = \sum (a_i + b_i)x^i$$

$$A(x) \cdot B(x) = \sum (a_i \, x^i \cdot \sum (b_j \, x^j))$$

Similarly, we can define subtraction and division on polynomials, as well as many other operations.

We begin with an ADT definition of a polynomial. The particular operations in part are a reflection of what will be needed in our subsequent programs to manipulate polynomials. The definition is contained in Structure 2.2.

We are now ready to make some representation decisions. A very reasonable first decision requires unique exponents arranged in decreasing order. This requirement considerably simplifies many of the operations. Using our specification and this stipulation, we can write a version of *Add* that is closer to a Pascal procedure (Program 2.1) but is still representation-independent.

The basic loop of this algorithm consists of merging the terms of the two polynomials, depending upon the result of comparing the exponents. The **case** statement determines how the exponents are related and performs the proper action. Since the tests within the **case** statement require two terms, if one polynomial gets exhausted we must exit, and the remaining terms of the other can be copied directly into the result. With these insights, suppose we now consider the representation question more carefully.

One way to represent polynomials in Pascal is to define the data type *poly*:

> **type** *poly* = **record**
>> *degree* : 0..*MaxDegree*;
>> *coef* : **array**[0..*MaxDegree*] **of real**;
> **end**;

where *MaxDegree* is a constant representing the largest-degree polynomial that is to be represented. Now, if *a* is of type *poly* and $n \leq MaxDegree$, then the polynomial $A(x)$ above would be represented as:

> *a.degree* = *n*
> *a.coef*[*i*] = a_{n-i}, $0 \leq i \leq n$

Note that *a.coef*[*i*] is the coefficient of x^{n-i} and the coefficients are stored in order of decreasing exponents. This representation leads to very simple algorithms for many of the operations you wish to perform on polynomials (addition, subtraction, evaluation, multiplication, etc.). It is, however, quite wasteful in its use of computer memory. For instance, if *a.degree* $\ll$ *MaxDegree* (the double "less than" should be read as "is much less than"), then most of the positions in *a.coef* [0..*MaxDegree*] are unused. To avoid this waste, we would like to be able to define the data type *poly* using records of variable size as below:

---

structure *Polynomial* **is**

   objects: $p(x) = a_1 x^{e_1} + \cdots + a_n x^{e_n}$; a set of ordered pairs of $<e_i, a_i>$, where $a_i \in$ *Coefficients* and $e_i \in$ *Exponents*, e_i are integers $>= 0$

   functions:

     for all *poly*, *poly*1, *poly*2 $\in$ *Polynomial*, *coef* $\in$ *Coefficients*, *expon* $\in$ *Exponents*

Zero() : *Polynomial*	::=	return the polynomial $p(x) = 0$
IsZero(*poly*) : *Boolean*	::=	**if** *poly* = 0 **then** *IsZero* := **true** **else** *IsZero* := **false**
Coef (*poly*,*expon*) : *Coefficient*	::=	**if** *expon* $\in$ *poly* **then** *Coef* := its coefficient **else** *Coef* := 0
LeadExp (*poly*) : *Exponent*	::=	*LeadExp* := the largest exponent in *poly*
Attach (*poly*, *coef*, *expon*) : *Polynomial*	::=	**if** *expon* $\in$ *poly* **then** error **else** *Attach* := the polynomial *poly* with the term $<coef, expon>$ inserted
Remove (*poly*, *expon*) : *Polynomial*	::=	**if** *expon* $\in$ *poly* **then** *Remove* := the polynomial *poly* with the term whose exponent is *expon* deleted **else** error
SingleMult (*poly*, *coef*, *expon*) : *Polynomial*	::=	*SingleMult* := the polynomial $poly \cdot coef \cdot x^{expon}$
Add (*poly*1, *poly*2) : *Polynomial*	::=	*Add* := the polynomial $poly1 + poly2$
Mult (*poly*1, *poly*2) : *Polynomial*	::=	*Mult* := the polynomial $poly1 \cdot poly2$

end *Polynomial*

Structure 2.2: Abstract data type *Polynomial*

```
type poly = record
              degree : 0..maxint;
              coef : array[0..degree] of real;
            end;
```

{$c := a + b$ where a and b are the input polynomials}
$c := Zero$;
while not $IsZero(a)$ **and not** $IsZero(b)$ **do**
begin
  case $compare(LeadExp(a), LeadExp(b))$ **of**
    '<': **begin**
        $c := Attach(c, Coef(b, LeadExp(b)), LeadExp(b))$;
        $b := Remove(b, LeadExp(b))$;
     end;
    '=': **begin**
        $c := Attach(c, Coef(a, LeadExp(a)) + Coef(b, LeadExp(b)), LeadExp(a))$;
        $a := Remove(a, LeadExp(a)); b := Remove(b, LeadExp(b))$;
     end;
    '>': **begin**
        $c := Attach(c, Coef(a, LeadExp(a)), LeadExp(a))$;
        $a := Remove(a, LeadExp(a))$;
     end
  end; {of **case**}
end; {of **while**}

insert any remaining terms of a or b into c

Program 2.1: Initial version of procedure to add polynomials

Such a declaration is, of course, not permitted in standard or Turbo Pascal. Although such a type definition solves the problem mentioned earlier, it does not yield a desirable representation. To see this, let us consider polynomials that have many zero terms. Such polynomials are called *sparse*. For instance, the polynomial $x^{1000} + 1$ has two nonzero terms and 999 zero terms. Using records of variable size as above, 999 of the entries in *coef* will be zero.

Suppose we take the polynomial $A(x)$ defined above and keep only its nonzero coefficients. Then we will really have the polynomial

$$b_{m-1}x^{e_{m-1}} + b_{m-2}x^{e_{m-2}} + \cdots + b_0 x^{e_0}$$

where each b_i is a nonzero coefficient of A and the exponents e_i are decreasing $e_{m-1} > e_{m-2} > \cdots > e_0 \geq 0$. If all of A's coefficients are nonzero, then $m = n + 1$, $e_i = i$, and $b_i = a_i$ for $0 \leq i \leq n$. Alternatively, only a_n may be nonzero, in which case $m = 1$, $b_0 = a_n$, and $e_0 = n$.

All our polynomials will be represented in a global array called *terms* that is defined as below:

> **type** *term* = **record**
> > *coef* : **real**; {coefficient}
> > *exp* : 0 .. **maxint**; {exponent}
>
> **end**;
> **var** *terms* : **array**[1 .. *MaxTerms*] **of** *term*;

where *MaxTerms* is a constant.

Consider the two polynomials $A(x) = 2x^{1000} + 1$ and $B(x) = x^4 + 10x^3 + 3x^2 + 1$. These could be stored in the array *terms* as shown in Figure 2.1. Note that *StartA* and *StartB* give the location of the first term of A and B respectively, whereas *FinishA* and *FinishB* give the location of the last term of A and B; *free* gives the location of the next free location in the array *terms*. For our example, *StartA* = 1, *FinishA* = 2, *StartB* = 3, *FinishB* = 6, and *free* = 7.

	StartA↓	FinishA↓	StartB↓			FinishB↓	free↓
coef	2	1	1	10	3	1	
exp	1000	0	4	3	2	0	
	1	2	3	4	5	6	7

Figure 2.1: Array representation of two polynomials

This representation scheme does not impose any limit on the number of polynomials that can be stored in *terms*. Rather, the total number of nonzero terms in all the polynomials together cannot exceed *MaxTerms*. It is worth pointing out the difference between our specification and our representation. Our specification used *poly* to refer to a polynomial, and our representation translated *poly* into a <*start*, *finish* > pair. Therefore, to use $A(x)$ we must pass in *StartA* and *FinishA*. Any polynomial A that has n nonzero terms has *StartA* and *FinishA* such that *FinishA* = *StartA* + n − 1. If A has no nonzero terms (i.e., A is the zero polynomial), then *FinishA* = *StartA* − 1.

Before proceeding, we should evaluate our current representation. Is this representation any better than the one that used records with large array size? Well, it certainly solves our problem when many zero terms are present. $A(x) = 2x^{1000} + 1$ uses only 6 units of space (one for *StartA*, one for *FinishA*, two for the coefficients, and two for the exponents). However, when all terms are nonzero, as in $B(x)$ above, the new scheme uses about twice as much space as the previous one that used variable-size records. Unless we know beforehand that each of our polynomials has very few zero terms in it, the representation using the array *terms* will be preferred.

Let us now write a Pascal procedure to add two polynomials A and B represented as above to obtain the sum $C = A + B$. Procedure *padd* (Program 2.2) adds $A(x)$ and $B(x)$ term by term to produce $C(x)$. The terms of C are entered into the array *terms* starting at the position *free* (procedure *NewTerm*, Program 2.3). In case there is not enough space in *terms* to accommodate C, an error message is printed and the program terminates.

Analysis of *padd*: It is natural to carry out this analysis in terms of the number of nonzero terms in A and B. Let m and n be the number of nonzero terms in A and B respectively. The assignments of line 5 are made only once and hence contribute O(1) to the overall computing time. If either $n = 0$ or $m = 0$, the **while** loop of line 6 is not executed.

In case neither m nor n equals zero, the **while** loop of line 6 is entered. Each iteration of the **while** loop requires O(1) time. At each iteration, the value of a or b or both increases by 1. Since the iteration terminates when either a or b exceeds *FinishA* or *FinishB* respectively, the number of iterations is bounded by $m + n - 1$. This worst-case is achieved, for instance, when $A(x) = \sum_{i=0}^{n} x^{2i}$ and $B(x) = \sum_{i=0}^{n} x^{2i+1}$. Since none of the exponents are the same in A and B, $terms[a].exp \neq terms[b].exp$. Consequently, on each iteration the value of only one of a or b increases by 1. So, the worst-case for the **while** loops of lines 23 and 29 is bounded by O($n + m$), since the first cannot be iterated more than m times and the second more than n. Taking the sum of all of these steps, we obtain O($n + m$) as the asymptotic computing time of this algorithm. $\square$

As we create polynomials, *free* is continually incremented until it tries to exceed *MaxTerms*. When this happens must we quit? We must unless there are some polynomials that are no longer needed. There may be several such polynomials whose space can be reused. We could write a procedure that would compact the remaining polynomials, leaving a large, contiguous free space at one end. But this may require much data movement. Even worse, if we move a polynomial, we must change its start and end pointers. This demands a sophisticated compacting routine coupled with a disciplined use of names for polynomials. In Chapter 4, we will see an elegant solution to these problems.

EXERCISES

1. Use the six operations defined in this section for an ordered list to arrive at an ADT specification for such a list.

2. If $A = (a_1, \cdots, a_n)$ and $B = (b_1, \cdots, b_m)$ are ordered lists, then $A < B$ if $a_i = b_i$ for $1 \leq i < j$ and $a_j < b_j$, or, if $a_i = b_i$ for $1 \leq i \leq n$ and $n < m$. Write a procedure that returns -1, 0, or $+1$, depending upon whether $A < B$, $A = B$, or $A > B$. Assume you can compare atoms a_i and b_j.

3. Assume that n lists, $n > 1$, are being represented sequentially in the one-dimensional array $space[1..m]$. Let $front[i]$ be one less than the position of the first element in the ith list, and let $rear[i]$ point to the last element in the ith list,

```
 1 procedure padd (StartA, FinishA, StartB, FinishB : integer;
                                    var StartC, FinishC : integer);
 2 {Add A (x) and B (x) to get C (x).}
 3 var a, b : integer; c : real;
 4 begin
 5    a := StartA; b := StartB; StartC := free;
 6    while (a <= FinishA) and (b <= FinishB) do
 7      case compare (terms [a ].exp, terms [b ].exp) of
 8        '=': begin
 9              c := terms [a ].coef + terms [b ].coef;
10              if c < > 0 then NewTerm (c, terms [a ].exp);
11              a := a + 1; b := b + 1;
12            end;
13        '<': begin
14              NewTerm (terms [b ].coef, terms [b ].exp);
15              b := b + 1;
16            end;
17        '>': begin
18              NewTerm (terms [a ].coef, terms [a ].exp);
19              a := a + 1;
20            end;
21      end; {of case and while}
22    {add in remaining terms of A (x)}
23    while a <= FinishA do
24    begin
25      NewTerm (terms [a ].coef, terms [a ].exp);
26      a := a + 1;
27    end;
28    {add in remaining terms of B (x)}
29    while b <= FinishB do
30    begin
31      NewTerm (terms [b ].coef, terms [b ].exp);
32      b := b + 1;
33    end;
34    FinishC := free − 1;
35 end; {of padd}
```

Program 2.2: Adding two polynomials

```
procedure NewTerm (c : real; e : integer);
{Add a new term to C (x).}
begin
  if free > MaxTerms
  then begin
         writeln('too many terms in polynomials');
         halt; {terminate program}
       end;
  terms [free].coef := c;
  terms [free].exp := e;
  free := free + 1;
end; {of NewTerm}
```

Program 2.3: Adding a new term

$1 \le i \le n$. Assume that $rear[i] \le front[i + 1]$, $1 \le i \le n$ and $front[n + 1] = m$. The functions to be performed on these lists are insertion and deletion.

(a) Obtain suitable initial and boundary conditions for $front[i]$ and $rear[i]$.

(b) Write a procedure $insert (i, j, item : \textbf{integer})$ to insert $item$ after the $(j - 1)$'st element in list i. This procedure should fail to make an insertion only if there are already m elements in $space$.

4. Using the assumptions of the preceding exercise, write a procedure $delete (i, j : \textbf{integer}; \textbf{var } item : \textbf{integer})$ that sets $item$ to the jth element of the ith list and removes it. The ith list should be maintained as sequentially stored.

5. Write Pascal procedures to input and output polynomials represented as in this section.

6. Write a Pascal procedure that multiplies two polynomials represented using the array $terms$. What is the computing time of your procedure?

7. Write a Pascal procedure that evaluates a polynomial at a value x_0 using the representation of the preceding exercise. Try to minimize the number of operations.

8. The polynomials $A(x) = x^{2n} + x^{2n-2} + \cdots + x^2 + x^0$ and $B(x) = x^{2n+1} + x^{2n-1} + \cdots + x^3 + x$ cause $padd$ to work very hard. For these polynomials, determine the exact number of times each statement will be executed.

9. The declarations that follow give us an alternate representation of the polynomial ADT. The number of nonzero terms in the ith polynomial is given in $terms [i, 0].expon$. These terms are stored, in descending order of exponents, in positions $terms [i, 1]$, $terms [i, 2]$, $\cdots$. Write and test Pascal procedures to input, output, add, multiply, and evaluate polynomials represented in this way. Is this

representation better or worse than the representation used in the text?

```
const MaxTerms = 100; {max number of terms in a poly}
      MaxPolys = 20; {max number of polynomials}
type poly = record
               degree : 0 .. maxint;
               coef : real;
            end;
var terms = array [MaxPolys, 0 .. MaxTerms ] of poly;
```

2.3   SPARSE MATRICES

A matrix is a mathematical object that arises in many physical problems. As computer scientists, we are interested in studying ways to represent matrices so that the operations to be performed on them can be carried out efficiently. A general matrix consists of m rows and n columns of numbers, as in Figure 2.2.

	col 1	col 2	col 3
row 1	−27	3	4
row 2	6	82	−2
row 3	109	−64	11
row 4	12	8	9
row 5	48	27	47

(a)

	col 1	col 2	col 3	col 4	col 5	col 6
row 1	15	0	0	22	0	−15
row 2	0	11	3	0	0	0
row 3	0	0	0	−6	0	0
row 4	0	0	0	0	0	0
row 5	91	0	0	0	0	0
row 6	0	0	28	0	0	0

(b)

Figure 2.2: Two matrices

The first matrix has five rows and three columns, the second six rows and six columns. In general, we write $m \times n$ (read "m by n") to designate a matrix with m rows and n columns. Such a matrix has mn elements. When m is equal to n, we call the matrix *square*.

It is very natural to store a matrix in a two-dimensional array, say $A[1 .. m, 1 .. n]$. Then we can work with any element by writing $A[i,j]$, and this element can be found very quickly, as we will see in the next section. Now if we look at the second matrix of Figure 2.2, we see that it has many zero entries. Such a matrix is called *sparse*. There is no precise definition of when a matrix is sparse and when it is not, but it is a concept that we can all recognize intuitively. Above, only eight out of 36 possible elements are nonzero, and that is sparse! A sparse matrix requires us to consider an alternate form of representation. This comes about because in practice many of the matrices we want to deal with are large, e.g., 1000×1000, but at the same time they are sparse: say only 1000 out of 1 million possible elements are nonzero. On many computers today it would be impossible to store a full 1000×1000 matrix in the memory at once. Therefore, we seek an alternative representation for sparse matrices. The alternative representation should explicitly store only the nonzero elements.

Before developing a particular representation, we first must consider the operations that we want to perform on these matrices. A minimal set of operations includes matrix creation, transpose, addition, and multiplication. Structure 2.3 contains our specification of the matrix ADT.

Before implementing any of these operations, we must establish the representation of the sparse matrix. By examining Figure 2.2, we know that we can characterize uniquely any element within a matrix by using the triple <*row, col, value* >. This means that we can use an array of triples to represent a sparse matrix. We require that these triples be stored by rows with the triples for the first row first, followed by those of the second row, and so on. We also require that all the triples for any row be stored so that the column indices are in ascending order. In addition, to ensure that the operations terminate, we must know the number of rows and columns and the number of nonzero elements in the matrix. Putting all this information together suggests that we use the following data types:

> **type** *MatrixTerm* = **record**
> > *row* : 1 .. *maxint*;
> > *col* : 0 .. *maxint*;
> > *value* : **integer**;
> > **end**;
> *SparseMatrix* = **array**[0 .. *MaxTerms*] **of** *MatrixTerm*;

where *MaxTerms* is a constant. Figure 2.3(a) shows the representation of the matrix of Figure 2.2(b) using an array *a* of type *SparseMatrix*. *a*[0].*row* contains the number of rows; *a*[0].*col* contains the number of columns; and *a*[0].*value* contains the total number of nonzero entries. Positions 1 through 8 store the triples representing the nonzero entries. The row index is in the field *row*; the column index is in the field *col*; and the value is in the field *value*. The triples are ordered by row and within rows by columns.

2.3.1 Transposing a Matrix

Figure 2.3(b) shows the transpose of the matrix of Figure 2.3(a). To transpose a matrix, we must interchange the rows and columns. This means that if an element is at position $[i,j]$ in the original matrix, then it is at position $[j,i]$ in the transposed matrix. The elements on the diagonal will remain unchanged, since $i = j$. Since the original matrix is

---

structure *SparseMatrix* is

    objects: A set of triples, *<row, column, value>*, where *row* and *column* are integers and form a unique combination, and *value* comes from the set *item*.

    functions:

        for all $a, b \in$ *SparseMatrix*, $x \in$ *item*, $i, j, MaxCol, MaxRow \in$ **integer**

        Create(MaxRow, MaxCol) : SparseMatrix ::=

                this function creates a *SparseMatrix* that can hold up to *MaxItems* = *MaxRow* × *MaxCol* and whose maximum row size is *MaxRow* and whose maximum column size is *MaxCol*

        Transpose (a) : SparseMatrix ::=

                the *SparseMatrix* produced by interchanging the row and column value of every triple is constructed

        Add (a, b) : SparseMatrix ::=

                if the dimensions of *a* and *b* are the same
                then the matrix produced by adding corresponding items, namely those with identical *row* and *column* values is created
                else error

        Multiply (a, b) : SparseMatrix ::=

                if number of columns in *a* equals number of rows in *b*
                then the matrix *d* produced by multiplying *a* by *b* according to the formula $d[i, j] = \sum(a[i, k] \cdot b[k, j])$, where $d[i, j]$ is the (i, j)th element, is constructed. *k* ranges from 1 to the number of columns in *a*
                else error

Structure 2.3: Abstract data type *SparseMatrix*

organized by rows, our first idea for a transpose algorithm might be the following:

        for each row *i* **do**
          take element (i, j, val) and
          store it in (j, i, val) of the transpose;

The difficulty is in not knowing where to put the element (j, i, val) until all other elements that precede it have been processed. In Figure 2.3(a), for instance, we encounter

	row	col	value		row	col	value
a[0]	6	6	8	b[0]	6	6	8
[1]	1	1	15	[1]	1	1	15
[2]	1	4	22	[2]	1	5	91
[3]	1	6	−15	[3]	2	2	11
[4]	2	2	11	[4]	3	2	3
[5]	2	3	3	[5]	3	6	28
[6]	3	4	−6	[6]	4	1	22
[7]	5	1	91	[7]	4	3	−6
[8]	6	3	28	[8]	6	1	−15
	(a)				(b)		

Figure 2.3: Sparse matrix and its transpose stored as triples

(1,1,15)	which becomes	(1,1,15)
(1,4,22)	which becomes	(4,1,22)
(1,6,−15)	which becomes	(6,1,−15)
(2,2,11)	which becomes	(2,2,11)

If we just place them consecutively, then we will need to insert many new triples, forcing us to move elements down very often. We can avoid this data movement by finding the elements in the order we want them, which would be

> **for** all elements in column j **do**
>   place element (i,j,val) in position (j,i,val);

This says "find all elements in column 1 and store them in row 1, find all elements in column 2 and store them in row 2, etc." Since the rows are originally in order, this means that we will locate elements in the correct column order as well. The procedure *transpose* (Program 2.4) computes the transpose of A. A is initially stored as a sparse matrix in the array a, and its transpose is obtained in the array b.

It is not too difficult to see that the procedure is correct. The variable *CurrentB* always gives us the position in b where the next term in the transpose is to be inserted. The terms in b are generated by rows. Since the rows of B are the columns of A, row c of B is obtained by collecting all the nonzero terms in column c of A. This is precisely what is being done in lines 12 to 20. On the first iteration of the **for** loop of lines 12 to 20, all terms from column 1 of A are collected, then all terms from column 2, and so on, until eventually all terms from the last column of A are collected.

```
 1  procedure transpose (a : SparseMatrix; var b : SparseMatrix);
 2  {b is set to be the transpose of a.}
 3  var terms,c,i,CurrentB : integer;
 4  begin
 5    terms := a [0].value; {number of terms in a}
 6    b [0].row := a [0].col; {rows in b = columns in a}
 7    b [0].col := a [0].row; {columns in b = rows in a}
 8    b [0].value := terms; {terms in b = terms in a}
 9    if terms > 0 then {nonzero matrix}
10    begin
11      CurrentB := 1;
12      for c := 1 to a [0].col do {transpose by columns}
13        for i := 1 to terms do
14          {find elements in column c}
15          if a [i ].col = c then
16          with b [CurrentB ] do
17            begin
18              row := c; col := a [i ].row;
19              value := a [i ].value;
20            end;
21    end; {of if terms > 0}
22  end; {of transpose}
```

Program 2.4: Transposing a matrix

Analysis of _transpose:_ Let _columns_ denote the number of columns in _A_. For each iteration of the loop of lines 12 to 20, the **if** clause of line 15 is tested _terms_ times. Since the number of iterations of the loop of lines 12 to 20 is _columns_, the total time for line 15 is _terms · columns_. The assignments of lines 18 and 19 take place exactly _terms_ times, since there are only this many nonzero terms in the sparse matrix being generated. Lines 5-11 take a constant amount of time. The total time for the algorithm is therefore $O(terms \cdot columns)$. In addition to the space needed for _a_ and _b_, the algorithm requires only a fixed amount of additional space, i.e., space for the variables _terms_, _c_, _i_, and _CurrentB_. □

We now have a matrix transpose algorithm that we believe is correct and that has a computing time of $O(terms \cdot columns)$. This computing time is a little disturbing, since we know that in case the matrices had been represented as two-dimensional arrays, we could have obtained the transpose of a _rows × columns_ matrix in time $O(rows \cdot columns)$. The algorithm for this has the simple form

$$\textbf{for } j := 1 \textbf{ to } columns \textbf{ do}$$
$$\textbf{for } i := 1 \textbf{ to } rows \textbf{ do}$$
$$B[j,i] := A[i,j];$$

The O($terms \cdot columns$) time for procedure $transpose$ becomes O($rows \cdot columns^2$) when $terms$ is of the order of $rows \cdot columns$. This is worse than the O($rows \cdot columns$) time using arrays. Perhaps, in an effort to conserve space, we have traded away too much time. Actually, we can do much better by using a little more storage. We can, in fact, transpose a matrix represented as a sequence of triples in time O($terms + columns$). This algorithm, *FastTranspose* (Program 2.5), proceeds by first determining the number of elements in each column of A. This gives us the number of elements in each row of B. From this information, the starting point in b of each of its rows is easily obtained. We can now move the elements of a one by one into their correct position in b. *MaxCol* is a constant such that the number of columns in A never exceeds *MaxCol*.

The correctness of procedure *FastTranspose* follows from the preceding discussion and the observation that the starting point, $RowStart[i]$, of row i, $i > 1$, of B is $RowStart[i-1] + RowSize[i-1]$, where $RowSize[i-1]$ is the number of elements in row $i-1$ of B. The computation of $RowSize$ and $RowStart$ is carried out in lines 11 to 15. In lines 16 to 23 the elements of a are examined one by one starting from the first and successively moving to the correct place in b. $RowStart[j]$ is maintained so that it is always the position in b where the next element in row j of B is to be inserted.

There are four loops in *FastTranspose*, which are executed *columns*, *terms*, $columns - 1$, and *terms* times respectively. Each iteration of the loops takes only a constant amount of time, so the asymptotic complexity is O($columns + terms$). The computing time of O($columns + terms$) becomes O($rows \cdot columns$) when *terms* is of the order of $rows \cdot columns$. This is the same as when two-dimensional arrays were in use. However, the constant factor associated with *FastTranspose* is bigger than that for the array algorithm. When *terms* is sufficiently small compared to its maximum of $rows \cdot columns$, *FastTranspose* will be faster. Hence in this representation, we save both space and time! This was not true of *transpose*, since *terms* will almost always be greater than max{$rows$, $columns$} and *columns.terms* will therefore always be at least $rows.columns$. The constant factor associated with *transpose* is also bigger than the one in the array algorithm. Finally, you should note that *FastTranspose* requires more space than does *transpose*. The space required by *FastTranspose* can be reduced by utilizing the same space to represent the two arrays *RowSize* and *RowStart*.

If we try the algorithm on the sparse matrix of Figure 2.3, then after execution of the third **for** loop, the values of *RowSize* and *RowStart* are:

	[1]	[2]	[3]	[4]	[5]	[6]
RowSize =	3	2	1	0	1	1
RowStart =	1	4	6	7	7	8

```
 1  procedure FastTranspose (a : SparseMatrix; var b : SparseMatrix);
 2  {The transpose of a is placed in b and is found in O(terms +columns) time.}
 3  var RowSize,RowStart : array[1 .. MaxCol] of integer;
 4        i,j,columns,terms : integer;
 5  begin
 6    columns := a [0].col; terms := a [0].value;
 7    b [0].row := columns; b [0].col := a [0].row; b [0].value := terms;
 8    if terms > 0 then {nonzero matrix}
 9    begin
10      {compute RowSize [i] = number of terms in row i of b}
11      for i := 1 to columns do RowSize [i] := 0; {initialize}
12      for i := 1 to terms do RowSize [a [i ].col] := RowSize [a [i ].col] + 1;

13      {RowStart [i] = starting position of row i in b}
14      RowStart [1] := 1;
15      for i := 2 to columns do RowStart [i] := RowStart [i −1] + RowSize [i −1];

16      for i := 1 to terms do {move from a to b}
17      begin
18        with  b [RowStart [a [i ].col]] do
19        begin
20          row := a [i ].col; col := a [i ].row; value := a [i ].value;
21        end;
22        RowStart [a [i ].col] := RowStart [a [i ].col] + 1;
23      end; {of for}
24    end; {of if}
25  end; {of FastTranspose}
```

Program 2.5: Transposing a matrix faster

2.3.2   Matrix Multiplication

Definition: Given A and B, where A is $m \times n$ and B is $n \times p$, the product matrix D has dimension $m \times p$. Its $[i, j]$ element is

$$d_{ij} = \sum_{k=1}^{n} a_{ik}\, b_{kj}$$

for $1 \le i \le m$ and $1 \le j \le p$. $\square$

The product of two sparse matrices may no longer be sparse, as Figure 2.4 shows.

$$\begin{bmatrix} 1 & 0 & 0 \\ 1 & 0 & 0 \\ 1 & 0 & 0 \end{bmatrix} \begin{bmatrix} 1 & 1 & 1 \\ 0 & 0 & 0 \\ 0 & 0 & 0 \end{bmatrix} = \begin{bmatrix} 1 & 1 & 1 \\ 1 & 1 & 1 \\ 1 & 1 & 1 \end{bmatrix}$$

Figure 2.4: Multiplication of two sparse matrices

We would like to multiply two sparse matrices A and B represented as ordered lists as in Figure 2.3. We need to compute the elements of D by rows so that we can store them in their proper place without moving previously computed elements. To do this we pick a row of A and find all elements in column j of B for $j = 1, 2, \cdots, ColB$, where $ColB$ is the number of columns in B. Normally, we would have to scan all of B to find all the elements in column j. However, we can avoid this by first computing the transpose of B. This puts all column elements in consecutive order. Once we have located the elements of row i of A and column j of B, we just do a merge operation similar to that used for polynomial addition in Section 2.2. An alternate approach is explored in the exercises.

Before we write a matrix multiplication procedure, it will be useful to define a subprocedure as in Program 2.6, which stores a matrix term.

```
procedure StoreSum(var d : SparseMatrix; var LastD : integer;
                    r, c : integer; var sum : integer);
{If sum ≠ 0, then it along with its row and column position are stored
as the LastD+1'st entry in d. sum is reset to zero and LastD incremented.}
begin
  if sum < > 0 then
    if LastD < MaxTerms then begin
                        LastD := LastD + 1;
                        d [LastD ].row := r;
                        d [LastD ].col := c;
                        d [LastD ].value := sum;
                        sum := 0;
                    end
    else begin
          writeln('Number of terms in product exceeds MaxTerms');
          halt; {terminate program}
        end;
end; {of StoreSum}
```

Program 2.6: Storing a matrix term

The procedure *mmult* (Program 2.7) multiplies the matrices A and B to obtain the product matrix D using the strategy outlined above. A, B, and D are stored as sparse matrices in the arrays a, b, and d respectively. Procedure *mmult* makes use of variables i, j, q, r, c, and *RowBegin*. The variable r is the row of A that is currently being multiplied with the columns of B. *RowBegin* is the position in a of the first element of row r. c is the column of B that is currently being multiplied with row r of A. *LastD* is the position occupied by the last element of d. i and j are used to examine successively elements of row r and column c of A and B respectively. In addition to all this, line 20 of the algorithm introduces a dummy term into each of a and d. This enables us to handle end conditions (i.e., computations involving the last row of A or last column of B) in an elegant way. This, however, requires that the number of terms in A and B be fewer than *Max-Terms* (lines 12 to 16), as otherwise we will not have the space for the dummy term.

```
 1  procedure mmult (var a, b, d : SparseMatrix);
 2  {Multiply two sparse matrices A and B producing D.}
 3  var RowsA,ColsA,ColsB,LastD,TermsA,TermsB,i,j,r,c,sum,RowBegin : integer;
 4    e : SparseMatrix;
 5  begin
 6    RowsA := a [0].row; ColsA := a [0].col; TermsA := a [0].value;
 7    if ColsA < > b [0].row then begin
 8                          writeln('Incompatible matrices');
 9                          halt; {terminate program}
10                        end;
11    ColsB := b [0].col; TermsB := b [0].value;
12    if (TermsA = MaxTerms) or (TermsB = MaxTerms) then
13              begin
14                writeln('One additional space in a or b needed');
15                halt; {terminate program}
16              end;
17    FastTranspose (b,e);
18    i := 1; LastD := 0; RowBegin := 1; r := a [1].row;
19    {set boundary conditions}
20    a [TermsA +1].row := RowsA + 1; e [TermsB +1].row := ColsB + 1;
21    e [TermsB +1].col := 0; sum := 0;
22    while i <= TermsA do {generate row r of d}
23    begin
24      c := e [1].row; j := 1;
25      while j <= TermsB + 1 do {multiply row r of a by column c of b}
26      begin
27        if a [i ].row < > r
28        then begin  {end of row r}
29              StoreSum (d,LastD,r,c,sum);
30              i := RowBegin;
```

```
31                    {go to next column}
32                       while e [j ].row = c do j := j + 1;
33                       c := e [j ].row;
34                   end
35            else if e [j ].row < > c
36                   then begin {end of column c of b}
37                          StoreSum (d,LastD,r,c,sum);
38                          {set to multiply row r with next column}
39                          i := RowBegin; c := e [j ].row;
40                      end
41            else if a [i ].col < e [j ].col
42                   then i := i + 1 {advance to next term in row}
43                   else if a [i ].col = e [j ].col
44                       then begin {add to sum}
45                              sum := sum + a [i ].value * e [j ].value;
46                              i := i + 1;  j := j + 1;
47                          end
48                       else {advance to next term in column c}
49                              j := j + 1;
50       end; {of while j <= TermsB + 1}
51       while a [i ].row = r do {advance to next row}
52          i := i + 1;
53       RowBegin := i; r := a [i ].row;
54    end; {end of while i <= TermsA}
55    d [0].row := RowsA; d [0].col := ColsB; d [0].value := q;
56 end; {of mmult}
```

Program 2.7: Multiplying sparse matrices

Analysis of mmult: We leave the correctness proof of this algorithm as an exercise. Let us examine its complexity. In addition to the space needed for a, b, d, and some simple variables, space is also needed for the transpose matrix e. Algorithm *FastTranspose* also needs some additional space. The exercises explore a strategy for *mmult* that does not explicitly compute e, and the only additional space needed is the same as that required by *FastTranspose*. Turning our attention to the computing time of *mmult*, we see that lines 6 to 21 require only $O(ColsB + TermsB)$ time. The **while** loop of lines 22 to 54 is executed at most $RowsA$ times (once for each row of A). In each iteration of the **while** loop of lines 25 to 50 the value of i or j or both increases by 1, or i and c are reset. The maximum total increment in j over the whole loop is $TermsB$. If t_r is the number of terms in row r of A, then the value of i can increase at most t_r times before i moves to the next row of A. When this happens, i is reset to $RowBegin$ in line 30. At the same time c is advanced to the next column. Hence, this resetting can take place at most $ColsB$ times. The total maximum increment in i is therefore $ColsB \cdot t_r$. The maximum number of iterations of the **while** loop of lines 25 to 50 is therefore $ColsB + ColsB \cdot t_r + TermsB$.

The time for this loop while multiplying with row r of A is $O(ColsB \cdot t_r + TermsB)$. Lines 51 to 53 take only $O(t_r)$ time. Hence, the time for the outer **while** loop, lines 22 to 54, for the iteration with row r of A, is $O(ColsB \cdot t_r + TermsB)$. The overall time for this loop is then $O(\Sigma_r(ColsB \cdot t_r + TermsB)) = O(ColsB \cdot TermsA + RowsA \cdot TermsB)$.

Once again, we may compare the computing time with the time to multiply matrices when arrays are used. The classical multiplication algorithm is:

```
for i := 1 to RowsA do
  for j := 1 to ColsB do
  begin
    sum := 0;
    for k := 1 to ColsA do
      sum := sum + a [i,k] * b [k,j];
    c [i,j] := sum;
  end;
```

The time for this is $O(RowsA \cdot ColsA \cdot ColsB)$. Since $TermsA \leq RowsA \cdot ColsA$ and $TermsB \leq ColsA \cdot RowsB$, the time for *mmult* is at most $O(RowsA \cdot ColsA \cdot ColsB)$. However, its constant factor is greater than that for matrix multiplication using arrays. In the worst case, when $TermsA = RowsA \cdot ColsA$ or $TermsB = ColsA \cdot RowsB$, *mmult* will be slower by a constant factor. However, when $TermsA$ and $TermsB$ are sufficiently smaller than their maximum values, i.e., A and B are sparse, *mmult* will outperform the above multiplication algorithm for arrays.

The above analysis for *mmult* is nontrivial. It introduces some new concepts in algorithm analysis and you should make sure you understand the analysis. □

This representation for sparse matrices permits one to perform operations such as addition, transpose, and multiplication efficiently. There are, however, other considerations that make this representation undesirable in certain applications. Since the number of terms in a sparse matrix is variable, we would like to represent all our sparse matrices in one array (as we did for polynomials in Section 2.2), rather than use a separate array for each matrix. This would enable us to make efficient utilization of space. However, when this is done, we run into difficulties in allocating space from this array to any individual matrix. These difficulties also arise with the polynomial representation of the previous section and will become apparent when we study a similar representation for multiple stacks and queues in Section 3.5.

EXERCISES

1. How much time does it take to locate an arbitrary element $A[i,j]$ in the representation of this section and to change its value?

2. Analyze carefully the computing time and storage requirements of procedure *FastTranspose* (Program 2.5). What can you say about the existence of an even faster algorithm?

3. Write Pascal procedures to input and output a sparse matrix. You should design the input and output formats. However, the internal representation should be a one dimensional array of nonzero terms as used in this section. Analyze the computing time of your procedures.

4. Rewrite procedure *FastTranspose* (Program 2.5) so that it uses only one array rather than the two arrays required to hold *RowSize* and *RowStart*.

5. Develop a correctness proof for procedure *mmult* (Program 2.7).

6. Using the idea in *FastTranspose* of *ColsA* row pointers, rewrite *mmult* (Program 2.7) to multiply two sparse matrices *A* and *B* represented as in Section 2.3 without transposing *B*. What is the computing time of your algorithm?

7. A variation of the scheme discussed in this section for sparse matrix representation involves representing only the nonzero terms in a one-dimensional array v in the order described. In addition, a strip of $n \times m$ bits, $bits[1 .. n, 1 .. m]$ is also kept. $bits[i,j] = 0$ if $A[i,j] = 0$, and $bits[i,j] = 1$ if $A[i,j] \neq 0$. The figure below illustrates the representation for the sparse matrix of Figure 2.2(b).

$$\begin{bmatrix} 1 & 0 & 0 & 1 & 0 & 1 \\ 0 & 1 & 1 & 0 & 0 & 0 \\ 0 & 0 & 0 & 1 & 0 & 0 \\ 0 & 0 & 0 & 0 & 0 & 0 \\ 1 & 0 & 0 & 0 & 0 & 0 \\ 0 & 0 & 1 & 0 & 0 & 0 \end{bmatrix} \quad \begin{bmatrix} 15 \\ 22 \\ -15 \\ 11 \\ 3 \\ -6 \\ 91 \\ 28 \end{bmatrix}$$

(a) On a computer with w bits per word, how much storage is needed to represent a sparse matrix $A_{n \times m}$ with t nonzero terms?

(b) Write an algorithm to add two sparse matrices A and C, represented as above, to obtain $D = A + C$. How much time does your algorithm take?

(c) Discuss the merits of this representation versus the representation of Section 2.3. Consider space and time requirements for such operations as random access, add, multiply, and transpose. Note that the random access time can be improved somewhat by keeping another array ra such that $ra[i] =$ number of nonzero terms in rows 1 through $i - 1$.

2.4 REPRESENTATION OF ARRAYS

Even though the multidimensional array is provided as a standard data object in most high level languages, it is interesting to see how this object is represented in memory. Memory may be regarded as one-dimensional with words numbered from 1 to m. So, we are concerned with representing n dimensional arrays in a one-dimensional memory. We must develop a representation in which the location, in memory, of an arbitrary array element, say $A[i_1, i_2, \cdots, i_n]$, can be determined efficiently. This is necessary since programs using arrays may, in general, use array elements in a random order. In addition to being able to retrieve array elements easily, it is also necessary to be able to determine the amount of memory space to be reserved for a particular array. Assuming that each array element requires only one word of memory, the number of words needed is the number of elements in the array. If an array is declared $A[l_1 .. u_1, l_2 .. u_2, \cdots, l_n .. u_n]$, then it is easy to see that the number of elements is

$$\prod_{i=1}^{n} (u_i - l_i + 1)$$

One of the common ways to represent an array is in *row major order* (see Exercise 3 for column major order). If we have the declaration

$$A[4..5, 2..4, 1..2, 3..4]$$

then we have a total of $2*3*2*2 = 24$ elements. Using row major order, these elements will be stored as

$$A[4,2,1,3], A[4,2,1,4], A[4,2,2,3], A[4,2,2,4]$$

and continuing

$$A[4,3,1,3], A[4,3,1,4], A[4,3,2,3], A[4,3,2,4]$$

for three more sets of four until we get

$$A[5,4,1,3], A[5,4,1,4], A[5,4,2,3], A[5,4,2,4]$$

We see that the index at the right moves the fastest. In fact, if we view the indices as numbers, we see that they are, in some sense, increasing:

$$4213, 4214, \cdots, 5423, 5424$$

A synonym for row major order is *lexicographic order.*

From the compiler's point of view, the problem is how to translate from the name $A[i_1, i_2, ..., i_n]$ to the correct location in memory. Suppose $A[4,2,1,3]$ is stored at location 100. Then $A[4,2,1,4]$ will be at 101 and $A[5,4,2,4]$ at location 123. These two addresses are easy to guess. In general, we can derive a formula for the address of any element. This formula makes use of only the starting address of the array plus the declared dimensions.

To simplify the discussion we shall assume that the lower bounds on each dimension l_i are 1. The general case when l_i can be any integer is discussed in the exercises. Before obtaining a formula for the case of an n-dimensional array, let us look at the row major representation of one-, two-, and three-dimensional arrays. To begin with, if A is declared $A[1..u_1]$, then assuming one word per element, it may be represented in sequential memory as in Figure 2.5. If α is the address of $A[1]$, then the address of an arbitrary element $A[i]$ is just $\alpha + i - 1$.

array element:	$A[1]$	$A[2]$	$A[3]$	$\cdots$	$A[i]$	$\cdots$	$A[u_1]$
address:	α	$\alpha+1$	$\alpha+2$	$\cdots$	$\alpha+i-1$	$\cdots$	$\alpha+u_1-1$

Figure 2.5: Sequential representation of $A[1..u_1]$

The two-dimensional array $A[1..u_1,1..u_2]$ may be interpreted as u_1 rows, $row_1, row_2, \cdots, row_{u_1}$, each row consisting of u_2 elements. In a row major representation, these rows would be represented in memory as in Figure 2.6.

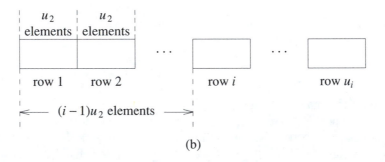

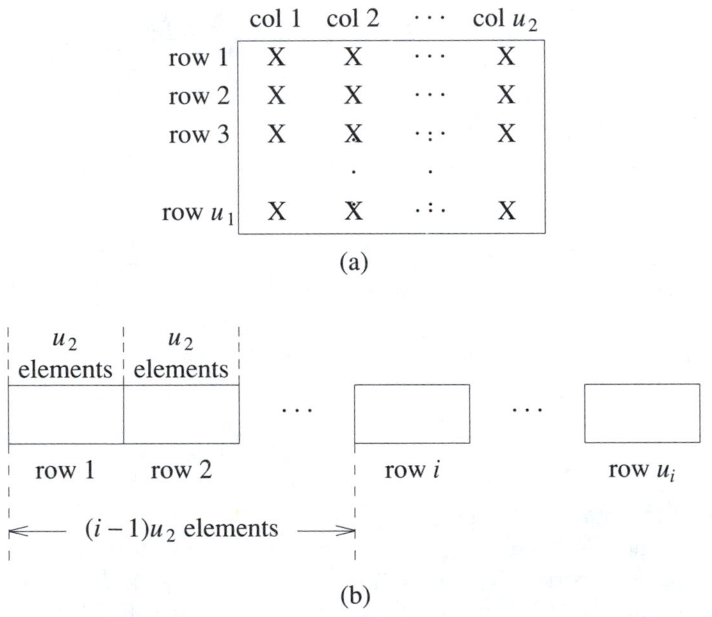

	col 1	col 2	$\cdots$	col u_2
row 1	X	X	$\cdots$	X
row 2	X	X	$\cdots$	X
row 3	X	X	$\cdot : \cdot$	X
row u_1	X	X	$\cdot : \cdot$	X

(a)

(b)

Figure 2.6: Sequential representation of $A[1..u_1,1..u_2]$

Again, if α is the address of $A[1,1]$, then the address of $A[i,1]$ is $\alpha + (i-1)u_2$, as there are $i-1$ rows, each of size u_2, preceding the first element in the ith row. Knowing the address of $A[i, 1]$, we can say that the address of $A[i, j]$ is then simply $\alpha + (i - 1)u_2 + (j - 1)$.

Figure 2.7 shows the representation of the three-dimensional array $A[1 .. u_1, 1 .. u_2, 1 .. u_3]$. This array is interpreted as u_1 two-dimensional arrays of dimension $u_2 \times u_3$. To locate $A[i, j, k]$, we first obtain $\alpha + (i - 1)u_2 u_3$ as the address for $A[i, 1, 1]$ since there are $i - 1$ two-dimensional arrays of size $u_2 \times u_3$ preceding this element. From this and the formula for addressing a two-dimensional array, we obtain $\alpha + (i - 1)u_2 u_3 + (j - 1)u_3 + (k - 1)$ as the address of $A[i, j, k]$.

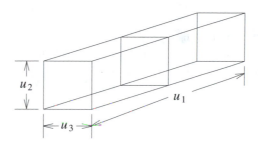

(a) 3-dimensional array $A[1 .. u_1, 1 .. u_2, 1 .. u_3]$ regarded as u_1 2-dimensional arrays

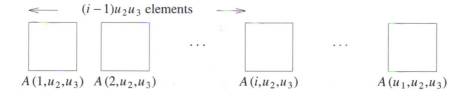

$A(1, u_2, u_3)$ $A(2, u_2, u_3)$ $A(i, u_2, u_3)$ $A(u_1, u_2, u_3)$

(b)   Sequential row major representation of a 3-dimensional array. Each 2-dimensional array is represented as in Figure 2.6

Figure 2.7: Sequential representation of $A[1 .. u_1, 1 .. u_2, 1 .. u_3]$

Generalizing on the preceding discussion, the addressing formula for any element $A[i_1, i_2, \cdots, i_n]$ in an n-dimensional array declared as $A[1 .. u_1, 1 .. u_2, \cdots, 1 .. u_n]$ may be easily obtained. If α is the address for $A[1, 1, \cdots, 1]$ then $\alpha + (i_1 - 1)u_2 u_3 \cdots u_n$ is the address for $A[i_1, 1, \cdots, 1]$. The address for $A[i_1, i_2, 1, \cdots, 1]$ is then $\alpha + (i_1 - 1)u_2 u_3 \cdots u_n + (i_2 - 1)u_3 u_4 \cdots u_n$. Repeating in this way, the address for $A[i_1, i_2, \cdots, i_n]$ is

$$\alpha + (i_1 - 1)u_2 u_3 \cdots u_n$$
$$+ (i_2 - 1)u_3 u_4 \cdots u_n$$

$$+ (i_3 - 1)u_4 u_5 \cdots u_n$$

.

.

.

$$+ (i_{n-1} - 1)u_n$$
$$+ (i_n - 1)$$

$$= \alpha + \sum_{j=1}^{n} (i_j - 1)a_j \text{ where } \begin{cases} a_j = \prod_{k=j+1}^{n} u_k & 1 \le j < n \\ a_n = 1 \end{cases}$$

Note that a_j may be computed from a_{j+1}, $1 \le j < n$, using only one multiplication as $a_j = u_{j+1}a_{j+1}$. Thus, a compiler will initially take the declared bounds $u_1, \cdots, u_n$ and use them to compute the constants $a_1, \cdots, a_{n-1}$ using $n - 2$ multiplications. The address of $A[i_1, \cdots, i_n]$ can then be found using the formula, requiring $n - 1$ more multiplications and n additions and n subtractions.

In this chapter we have used arrays to represent ordered lists of polynomials and sparse matrices. In all cases we have been able to move values around, accessing arbitrary elements in a fixed amount of time, and this has given us efficient algorithms. However, several problems have been raised. First, by using a sequential mapping that associates a_i of $(a_1, \cdots, a_n)$ with the ith element of the array, we are forced to move data around whenever an insert or delete operation is used. Second, once we adopt one ordering of the data, we sacrifice the ability to have a second ordering simultaneously.

EXERCISES

1. How many values can be held by an array with dimensions $a[0..n]$, $b[-1..n, 1..m]$, $c[-n..0, 1..2]$?

2. Obtain an addressing formula for the element $A[i_1, i_2, \cdots, i_n]$ in an array declared as $A[l_1..u_1, l_2..u_2, \cdots, l_n..u_n]$. Assume a row major representation of the array with one word per element and α the address of $A[l_1, l_2, ..., l_n]$.

3. Do the preceding exercise assuming a column major representation. In this, a two-dimensional array is stored sequentially by columns rather than by rows.

2.5 THE STRING ABSTRACT DATA TYPE

In this section, we turn our attention to a data type, the string, whose component elements are characters. As an ADT, we define a string to have the form $S = s_1, \cdots, s_n$, where s_i are characters taken from the character set of the programming language, and n is the length of the string. If $n = 0$, then S is an empty or null string.

There are several useful operations we could specify for strings. Some of these operations are similar to those required for other ADTs: creating a new empty string, reading a string or printing it out, appending two strings together (called *concatenation*), or copying a string. However, there are other operations that are unique to our new ADT, including comparing strings, inserting a substring into a string, removing a substring from a string, or finding a pattern in a string. We have listed the essential operations in Structure 2.4, which contains our specification of the string ADT.

---

structure *String* is
   objects: A finite ordered set of zero or more characters.
   functions:
      for all $s, t \in String$, $i, j, m \in$ nonnegative integers

Create (m) : *String*	::=	return a string whose maximum length is m characters but is initially empty
IsEqual (s,t) : *Boolean*	::=	**if** s equals t **then** *IsEqual* := **true** **else** *IsEqual* := **false**
IsNull (s) : *Boolean*	::=	**if** s is empty **then** *IsNull* := **true** **else** *IsNull* := **false**
Length (s) : *integer*	::=	*Length* := number of characters in s
Concat (s,t) : *String*	::=	**if** *IsNull* (s) **then** *Concat* := t **else** *Concat* := a string whose elements are those of s followed by those of t
Substr (s,i,j) : *String*	::=	**if** $((i >= 0)$ **and** $(j > 0)$ **and** $(i+j-1) < Length(s))$ **then** *Substr* := the string containing the characters of s at positions $i, i+1, \cdots, i+j-1$ **else** *Substr* := empty string

---

Structure 2.4: Abstract data type *String*

Turbo Pascal provides a data type **string** together with procedures to delete and insert substrings and to convert numbers into strings and vice versa. In addition, functions to concatenate strings, return a substring, return the length of a string, and to search for a substring are provided. The string data type of Pascal works much like an array. So, the declaration

$$\textbf{var } s : \textbf{string}[10];$$

declares variable s to be a string whose length is at most 10. $s[i]$ references the ith character of s. Using this referencing scheme and the function *length*, it is possible to write Pascal code for the string operations described above. In the remainder of this section, we shall examine the problem of string pattern matching only.

Assume that we have two strings, *s* and *pat*, where *pat* is a pattern to be searched for in *s*. We can determine if *pat* is in *s* by using the built-in function *pos*. *pos* (*pat*, *s*) returns an index *i* such that *pat* matches the substring of *s* that begins at position *i*. It returns zero iff *pat* is either empty or is not a substring of *s*. Let us examine how a function such as *pos* may be implemented.

The easiest but least efficient method is to sequentially consider each position of *s* and determine if it is the starting point of a match. Let *LengthP* and *LengthS* respectively, denote the lengths of the pattern *pat* and the string *s*. Positions of *s* to the right of position *LengthS* − *LengthP* + 1 need not be considered, as there are not enough characters to their right to complete a match with *pat*. Procedure *find* (Program 2.8) implements this strategy. The complexity of this procedure is O(*LengthP* · *LengthS*).

```
procedure find (s,pat : string; var i : integer);
{i is set to 0 if pat does not occur in s; otherwise i
 is set to point to the first position in s, where pat begins.}
var PosS, PosP, LengthP, LengthS : integer; found: boolean;
begin
 found :=false;
 LengthP := length (pat); LengthS := length (s);
 if (LengthS > 0) and (LengthP > 0)
 then begin
        i := 1; PosS := 1; PosP := 1; {i is starting point}
        while (i <= LengthS − LengthP + 1) and not found do
         if pat [PosP ] = s [PosS ]
         then {characters match}
               if PosP = LengthP then found := true {match found}
               else begin
                     PosP := PosP + 1; {next char in pat}
                     PosS := PosS + 1; {next char in s}
                   end
         else begin {no match}
               i := i + 1; PosS := i; PosP := 1;
              end;
 if not found then i := 0; {pat is empty or does not occur in s}
end; {of find}
```

Program 2.8: Exhaustive pattern matching

We can introduce heuristics into procedure *find* that improve its performance on certain pairs of *s* and *pat*. For example, for each position *i* of *s* considered in procedure *find*, we may check for a match of the last character of *pat* with the character at position *i* + *LengthP* − 1 of *s* before examining characters 1 through *LengthP* − 1 of *pat* for a

match. The asymptotic complexity of the resulting pattern matching procedure is still
O(*LengthP* · *LengthS*).

Ideally, we would like an algorithm that works in O(*LengthP* + *LengthS*) time.
This is optimal for this problem, as in the worst case it is necessary to look at all characters in the pattern and string at least once. We want to search the string for the pattern
without moving backwards in the string. That is, if a mismatch occurs we want to use
our knowledge of the characters in the pattern and the position in the pattern, where the
mismatch occurred to determine where we should continue the search. Knuth, Morris,
and Pratt have developed a pattern-matching algorithm that works in this way and has
linear complexity. Using their example, suppose

$$pat = \text{'} a\, b\, c\, a\, b\, c\, a\, c\, a\, b \text{'}$$

Let $s = s_1\, s_2\, \cdots\, s_{m-1}$ be the string and assume that we are currently determining
whether or not there is a match beginning at s_i. If $s_i \neq a$, then clearly we may proceed by
comparing s_{i+1} and a. Similarly, if $s_i = a$ and $s_{i+1} \neq b$, then we may proceed by comparing s_{i+1} and a. If $s_i s_{i+1} = ab$ and $s_{i+2} \neq c$ then we have the situation

$s =$	'-	a	b	?	?	?	.	.	.	.	?'
$pat =$		'a	b	c	a	b	c	a	c	a	b'

The ? implies that we do not know what the character in s is. The first ? in s represents
s_{i+2} and $s_{i+2} \neq c$. At this point we know that we may continue the search for a match by
comparing the first character in *pat* with s_{i+2}. There is no need to compare this character
of *pat* with s_{i+1}, since we already know that s_{i+1} is the same as the second character of
pat, b, and so $s_{i+1} \neq a$. Let us try this again assuming a match of the first four characters
in *pat* followed by a nonmatch, i.e., $s_{i+4} \neq b$. We now have the situation

$s =$	'-	a	b	c	a	?	?	.	.	.	?'
$pat =$		'a	b	c	a	b	c	a	c	a	b'

We observe that the search for a match can proceed by comparing s_{i+4} and the second
character in *pat*, b. This is the first place a partial match can occur by sliding the pattern
pat towards the right. Thus, by knowing the characters in the pattern and the position in
the pattern where a mismatch occurs with a character in s, we can determine where in the
pattern to continue the search for a match without moving backwards in s. To formalize
this, we define a failure function for a pattern.

Definition: If $p = p_1 p_2 \cdots p_n$ is a pattern, then its *failure function, f,* is defined as

$$f(j) = \begin{cases} \text{largest } i < j \text{ such that } p_1 p_2 \cdots p_i = p_{j-i+1} p_{j-i+2} \cdots p_j \text{ if such an } i \geq 1 \text{ exists} \\ 0 \qquad\qquad\qquad\qquad\qquad\qquad\qquad\qquad\qquad\qquad \text{otherwise.} \end{cases}$$

□

For the example pattern above, $pat = abcabcacab$, we have

j	1	2	3	4	5	6	7	8	9	10
pat	a	b	c	a	b	c	a	c	a	b
f	0	0	0	1	2	3	4	0	1	2

From the definition of the failure function, we arrive at the following rule for pattern matching: *If a partial match is found such that $s_{i-j+1} \cdots s_{i-1} = p_1 p_2 \cdots p_{j-1}$ and $s_i \neq p_j$ then matching may be resumed by comparing s_i and $p_{f(j-1)+1}$ if $j \neq 1$. If $j = 1$, then we may continue by comparing s_{i+1} and p_1.* This pattern-matching rule translates to procedure *pmatch* (Program 2.9).

```
1  procedure pmatch (s, pat : string; f : FailFun; var i : integer);
2  {Determine if pat is a substring of s.}
3  var PosP, PosS : integer;
4  begin
5      PosP := 1; PosS := 1;
6      while (PosP <= LengthP) and (PosS <= LengthS) do
7          if pat [PosP ] = s [PosS ]
8          then begin {character match}
9                  PosP := PosP + 1; PosS := PosS + 1;
10             end
11         else if PosP := 1
12             then PosS := PosS + 1
13             else PosP := f [j − 1] + 1;
14     if PosP <= LengthP then i := 0
15                         else i := PosS − LengthP;
16  end; {of pmatch}
```

Program 2.9: Pattern-matching with a failure function

Analysis of *pmatch*: The correctness of *pmatch* follows from the definition of the failure function. To determine the computing time, we observe that lines 9 and 12 can be executed for a total of at most *LengthS* times, since in each iteration *PosS* is incremented by 1 but *PosS* is never decremented in the algorithm. As a result, *PosP* can move right on *pat* at most *LengthS* times (line 9). Since each execution of the **else** clause in line 13 moves *PosP* left on *pat*, it follows that this clause can be executed at most *LengthS* times, since otherwise *PosP* becomes less than 1. Consequently, the maximum number of iterations of the **while** loop is *LengthS*, and the computing time of *pmatch* is O(*LengthS*). □

From the analysis of *pmatch*, it follows that if we can compute the failure function in O(*LengthP*) time, then the entire pattern-matching process will have a computing time proportional to the sum of the lengths of the string and pattern. Fortunately, there is a fast way to compute the failure function. This is based upon the following restatement of the failure function:

$$
f(j) = \begin{cases} 0 & \text{if } j = 1 \\ f^m(j-1) + 1 & \text{where } m \text{ is the least integer } k \text{ for which } p_{f^k(j-1)+1} = p_j \\ 0 & \text{if there is no } k \text{ satisfying the above} \end{cases}
$$

(Note that $f^1(j) = f(j)$ and $f^m(j) = f(f^{m-1}(j))$). This directly yields the procedure of Program 2.10 to compute f.

```
1  procedure fail (var p : string; var f : failure);
2  {Compute the failure function for the pattern p.}
3  var i, j, LengthP : integer;
4  begin
5    f [1] := 0; LengthP := length (p);
6    for j := 2 to LengthP do {compute f [j]}
7    begin
8      i := f [j−1];
9      while (p [j] <> p [i +1]) and (i > 0) do i := f [i ];
10     if p [j] = p [i +1] then f [j] := i +1
11                          else f [j] := 0;
12   end;
13 end; {of fail}
```

Program 2.10: Computing the failure function

Analysis of *fail*: In each iteration of the **while** loop the value of i decreases (by the definition of f). The variable i is reset at the beginning of each iteration of the **for** loop. However, it is either reset to 0 (when $j = 2$ or when the previous iteration went through line 11), or it is reset to a value 1 greater than its terminal value on the previous iteration (i.e., when the previous iteration went through line 10). Since only $LengthP - 1$ executions of line 8 are made, the value of i therefore has a total increment of at most $LengthP - 1$. Hence it cannot be decremented more than $LengthP - 1$ times. Consequently, the **while** loop is iterated at most $LengthP - 1$ times over the whole algorithm, and the computing time of *fail* is O(*LengthP*). $\square$

Note that when the failure function is not known in advance, pattern matching can be carried out in time O(*LengthP* + *LengthS*) by first computing the failure function using procedure *fail* and then performing a pattern match using procedure *pmatch*.

EXERCISES

Note: When doing the following exercises, you may use the Pascal string functions *length* and *concat* but no other built-in string function or procedure.

1. Write a procedure that accepts as input a string *s* and determines the frequency of occurrence of each of the distinct characters in *s*. Test your procedure using suitable data.

2. Write a procedure, *sdelete*, that accepts a string *s* and two integers, *start* and *length*. The procedure computes a new string that is equivalent to the original string, except that *length* characters beginning at *start* have been removed.

3. Write a function, *cdelete*, that accepts a string *s* and a character *c*. The function returns *s* with the all occurrences of *c* removed.

4. Write a procedure to make an in-place replacement of a substring of *x* by the string *y*. Note that the substring being replaced may not be of the same size as *y*. What is the complexity of your procedure?

5. If $x = (x_1, ..., x_m)$ and $y = (y_1, ..., y_n)$ are strings, where x_i and y_i are letters of the alphabet, then *x* is less than *y* if $x_i = y_i$ for $1 \le i \le j$ and $x_j < y_j$ or if $x_i = y_i$ for $1 \le i \le m$ and $m < n$. Write an algorithm that takes two strings *x,y* and returns either $-1, 0$, or $+1$ if $x < y$, $x = y$, or $x > y$ respectively.

6. (a) Find a string and a pattern for which procedure *find* (Program 2.8) takes times proportional to *LengthP* · *LengthS*.

   (b) Do part (a) under the assumption that the procedure *find* has been modified to check for a match with the last character of the pattern first (see text for an explanation of this heuristic).

7. Compute the failure function for each of the following patterns:

   (a) *a a a a b*;

   (b) *a b a b a a*; and

   (c) *a b a a b a a b b*.

8. Let $p_1 p_2 \dots p_n$ be a pattern of length *n*. Let *f* be its failure function. Define $f^1(j) = f(j)$ and $f^m(j) = f(f^{m-1}(j))$, $1 \le j \le n$ and $m > 1$. Show, using the definition of *f*, that

$$f(j) = \begin{cases} 0 & \text{if } j = 1 \\ f^m(j-1)+1 & \text{where } m \text{ is the least integer } k \text{ for which } p_{f^k(j-1)+1} = p_j \\ 0 & \text{if there is no } k \text{ satisfying the above} \end{cases}$$

9. The definition of the failure function may be strengthened to

$$f(j) = \begin{cases} \text{largest } i < j \text{ such that } p_1 p_2 \cdots p_i = p_{j-i+1} p_{j-i+2} \cdots p_j \text{ and } p_{i+1} \neq p_{j+1} \\ 0 \qquad \qquad \text{if there is no } i \geq 1 \text{ satisfying above} \end{cases}$$

(a) Obtain the new failure function for the pattern *pat* of the text.

(b) Show that if this definition for f is used, then algorithm *pmatch* (Program 2.9) still works correctly.

(c) Modify algorithm *fail* (Program 2.10) to compute f under this definition. Show that the computing time is still O(m).

(d) Are there any patterns for which the observed computing time of *pmatch* is more with the new definition of f than with the old one? Are there any for which it is less? Give examples.

2.6 REFERENCES AND SELECTED READINGS

The Knuth, Morris, Pratt pattern-matching algorithm can be found in "Fast pattern matching in strings," *SIAM Journal on Computing*, 6:2, 1977, pp. 323-350.

2.7 ADDITIONAL EXERCISES

1. Given an array $a[1 .. n]$ produce the array $z[1 .. n]$ such that $z[1] = a[n]$, $z[2] = a[n-1]$, ..., $z[n-1] = a[2]$, $z[n] = a[1]$. Use a minimal amount of storage.

2. Let $L = (a_1, a_2, \cdots, a_n)$ be a linear list represented in the array $M[1 .. n]$ using the following mapping: The ith element of L is stored in $M[i]$. Write an algorithm to make an in-place reversal of the order of elements in M. That is, the algorithm should transform M such that $M[i]$ contains the $(n - i + 1)$th element of L. The only additional space available to your algorithm is that for simple variables. The input to the algorithm is M and n. How much time does your algorithm take to accomplish the reversal?

3. An $m \times n$ matrix is said to have a saddle point if some entry $a[i][j]$ is the smallest value in row i and the largest value in column j. Write a C function that determines the location of a saddle point if one exists. What is the computing time of your method?

4. When all the elements either above or below the main diagonal of a square matrix are zero, then the matrix is said to be triangular. Figure 2.8 shows a lower and an upper triangular matrix. In a lower triangular matrix, A, with n rows, the maximum number of nonzero terms in row i is i. Hence, the total number of nonzero terms is $\sum_{i=1}^{n} i = n(n + 1)/2$. For large n it would be worthwhile to save the space

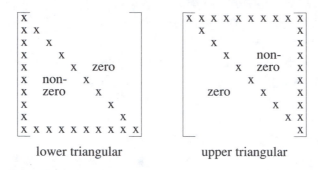

lower triangular   upper triangular

Figure 2.8: Lower and upper triangular matrices

taken by the zero entries in the upper triangle. Obtain an addressing formula for elements a_{ij} in the lower triangle if this lower triangle is stored by rows in an array $B[1 .. n(n + 1)/2]$ with $A[1,1]$ being stored in $B[1]$. What is the relationship between i and j for elements in the zero part of A?

5. Let A and B be two lower triangular matrices, each with n rows. The total number of elements in the lower triangles is $n(n + 1)$. Devise a scheme to represent both the triangles in an array $c[1 .. n, 1 .. n + 1]$. [Hint: Represent the triangle of A as the lower triangle of c and the transpose of B as the upper triangle of c.] Write algorithms to determine the values of $A[i,j]$, $B[i,j]$, $1 \le i$, $j \le n$, from the array c.

6. Another kind of sparse matrix that arises often in practice is the tridiagonal matrix. In this square matrix, all elements other than those on the major diagonal and on the diagonals immediately above and below this one are zero (Figure 2.9).

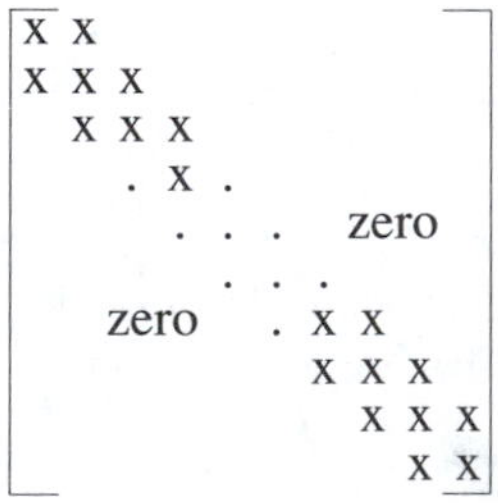

Figure 2.9: Tridiagonal matrix

If the elements in the band formed by these three diagonals are represented by rows in an array, b, with $A[1,1]$ being stored in $b[1]$, obtain an algorithm to determine the value of $A[i,j]$, $1 \le i, j \le n$ from the array b.

7. A square band matrix $A_{n,a}$ is an $n \times n$ matrix in which all the nonzero terms lie in a band centered around the main diagonal. The band includes $a-1$ diagonals below and above the main diagonal and also the main diagonal (Figure 2.10).

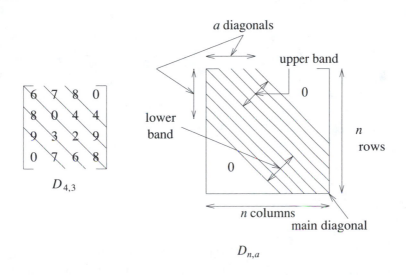

$$D_{4,3}$$

$$D_{n,a}$$

Figure 2.10: Square band matrix

(a) How many elements are there in the band of $A_{n,a}$?

(b) What is the relationship between i and j for elements a_{ij} in the band of $A_{n,a}$?

(c) Assume that the band of $A_{n,a}$ is stored sequentially in an array b by diagonals starting with the lowermost diagonal. Thus, $A_{4,3}$ above would have the following representation:

b[1]	b[2]	b[3]	b[4]	b[5]	b[6]	b[7]	b[8]	b[9]	b[10]	b[11]	b[12]	b[13]	b[14]
9	7	8	3	6	6	0	2	8	7	4	9	8	4
a_{31}	a_{42}	a_{21}	a_{32}	a_{43}	a_{11}	a_{22}	a_{33}	a_{44}	a_{12}	a_{23}	a_{34}	a_{13}	a_{24}

Obtain an addressing formula for the location of an element a_{ij} in the lower band of $A_{n,a}$, e.g., $LOC(a_{31}) = 1$, $LOC(a_{42}) = 2$ in the example above.

8. A generalized band matrix $A_{n,a,b}$ is an $n \times n$ matrix A in which all the nonzero terms lie in a band made up of $a - 1$ diagonals below the main diagonal, the main diagonal, and $b - 1$ diagonals above the main diagonal (Figure 2.11).

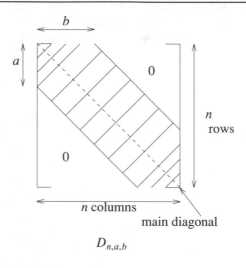

Figure 2.11: Generalized band matrix

(a) How many elements are there in the band of $A_{n,a,b}$?

(b) What is the relationship between i and j for elements a_{ij} in the band of $A_{n,a,b}$?

(c) Obtain a sequential representation of the band of $A_{n,a,b}$ in the one-dimensional array c. For this representation, write a Pascal procedure *value* (n,a,b,i,j,c) that determines the value of element a_{ij} in the matrix $A_{n,a,b}$. The band of $A_{n,a,b}$ is represented in the array c.

9. [*Programming Project*] There are a number of problems, known collectively as "random walk" problems, that have been of longstanding interest to the mathematical community. All but the most simple of these are extremely difficult to solve and for the most part they remain largely unsolved. One such problem may be stated as

A (drunken) cockroach is placed on a given square in the middle of a tile floor in a rectangular room of size $n \times m$ tiles. The bug wanders (possibly in search of an aspirin) randomly from tile to tile throughout the room. Assuming that he may move from his present tile to any of the eight tiles surrounding him (unless he is against a wall) *with equal probability*, how long will it take him to touch every tile on the floor at least once?

Hard as this problem may be to solve by probability theory techniques, it is easy to solve using the computer. The technique for doing so is called "simulation." This technique is widely used in industry to predict traffic flow, inventory control, and so forth. The problem may be simulated using the following method:

An $n \times m$ array *count* is used to represent the number of times our cockroach has reached each tile on the floor. All the cells of this array are initialized to zero. The position of the bug on the floor is represented by the coordinates (*ibug, jbug*). The eight possible moves of the bug are represented by the tiles located at (*ibug* + *imove* [*k*], *jbug* + *jmove* [*k*]), where $1 \leq k \leq 8$ and

$$
\begin{array}{ll}
imove[1] = -1 & jmove[1] = 1 \\
imove[2] = 0 & jmove[2] = 1 \\
imove[3] = 1 & jmove[3] = 1 \\
imove[4] = 1 & jmove[4] = 0 \\
imove[5] = 1 & jmove[5] = -1 \\
imove[6] = 0 & jmove[6] = -1 \\
imove[7] = -1 & jmove[7] = -1 \\
imove[8] = -1 & jmove[8] = 0
\end{array}
$$

A *random walk* to one of the eight given squares is simulated by generating a random value for *k* lying between 1 and 8. Of course, the bug cannot move outside the room, so coordinates that lead up a wall must be ignored and a new random combination formed. Each time a square is entered, the count for that square is incremented so that a nonzero entry shows the number of times the bug has landed on that square so far. When every square has been entered at least once, the experiment is complete.

Write a program to perform the specified simulation experiment. Your program *MUST*:

(a) handle all values of n and m, $2 < n \leq 40, 2 \leq m \leq 20$

(b) perform the experiment for (1) $n = 15$, $m = 15$, starting point: (20,10) and (2) $n = 39$, $m = 19$, starting point: (1,1)

(c) have an iteration limit, that is, a maximum number of squares the bug may enter during the experiment (this avoids getting hung in an infinite loop); a maximum of 50,000 is appropriate for this exercise

(d) for each experiment, print (1) the total number of legal moves that the cockroach makes and (2) the final *count* array (this will show the density of the walk, that is, the number of times each tile on the floor was touched during the experiment).

(Have an aspirin.) This exercise was contributed by Steve Olson.

10. [*Programming Project*] Chess provides the setting for many fascinating diversions
that are quite independent of the game itself. Many of these are based on the
strange L-shaped move of the knight. A classical example is the problem of the
knight's tour, which has captured the attention of mathematicians and puzzle
enthusiasts since the beginning of the eighteenth century. Briefly stated, the problem is to move the knight, beginning from any given square on the chessboard, in
such a manner that it travels successively to all 64 squares, touching each square
once and only once. It is convenient to represent a solution by placing the
numbers 1, 2, $\cdots$, 64 in the squares of the chessboard indicating the order in
which the squares are reached. Note that it is not required that the knight be able
to reach the initial position by one more move; if this is possible, the knight's tour
is called re-entrant. One of the more ingenious methods for solving the problem of
the knight's tour was that given by J. C. Warnsdorff in 1823. His rule was that the
knight must always be moved to one of the squares from which there are the
fewest exits to squares not already traversed. Use Warnsdorff's rule to construct a
particular solution to the problem by hand before reading any further.

The most important decisions to be made in solving a problem of this type are
those concerning how the data is to be represented in the computer. Perhaps the
most natural way to represent the chessboard is by an 8×8 array *board*, as shown
in Figure 2.12. The eight possible moves of a knight on square (5,3) are also
shown in this figure. In general a knight at (i,j) may move to one of the squares
$(i-2,j+1)$, $(i-1,j+2)$, $(i+1,j+2)$, $(i+2,j+1)$, $(i+2,j-1)$, $(i+1,j-2)$,
$(i-1,j-2)$, $(i-2,j-1)$. Notice, however, that if (i,j) is located near one of the
edges of the board, some of these possibilities could move the knight off the board,
and, of course, this is not permitted. The eight possible knight moves may con-
veniently be represented by two arrays *ktmov1* and *ktmov2*:

ktmov1	*ktmov2*
-2	1
-1	2
1	2
2	1
2	-1
1	-2
-1	-2
-2	-1

Then a knight at (i,j) may move to $(i + ktmov1[k], j + ktmov2[k])$, where k is
some value between 1 and 8, provided that the new square lies on the chessboard.

	1	2	3	4	5	6	7	8
1								
2								
3		8		1				
4	7				2			
5			K					
6	6				3			
7		5		4				
8								

Figure 2.12: Legal moves for a knight

An algorithm to solve the knight's tour problem using Warnsdoff's rule is described below.

(a) [***Initialize chessboard***] For $1 \leq i, j \leq 8$, set *board* $[i, j]$ to 0.

(b) [***Set starting position***] Read and print i, j and then set *board*$[i, j]$ to 1.

(c) [***Loop***] For $2 \leq m \leq 64$, do steps (d) through (g).

(d) [***Form set of possible next squares***] Test each of the eight squares one knight's move away from (i, j) and form a list of the possibilities for the next square (*nexti* $[l]$, *nextj* $[l]$). Let *npos* be the number of possibilities. (That is, after performing this step we will have *nexti* $[l] = i + ktmov1[k]$ and *nextj* $[l]$ $= j + ktmov2[k]$, for certain values of k between 1 and 8. Some of the squares $(i + ktmov1[k], j + ktmov2[k])$ may be impossible for the next move either because they lie off the chessboard or because they have been previously occupied by the knight (i.e., they contain a nonzero number). In every case we will have $0 \leq npos \leq 8$.)

(e) [***Test special cases***] If *npos* = 0, the knight's tour has come to a premature end; report failure and then go to step (h). If *npos* = 1, there is only one possibility for the next move; set *min* = 1 and go right to step (g).

(f)   [*Find next square with minimum number of exits*] For $1 \le l \le npos$ set
      exits[l] to the number of exits from square (*nexti* [l],*nextj* [l]). That is, for
      each of the values of l, examine each of the next squares
      (*nexti* [l]+*ktmov1*[k], *nextj* [l] + *ktmov2*[k]) to see if it is an exit from
      (*nexti* [l],*nextj* [l]), and count the number of such exits in *exits* [l]. (Recall
      that a square is an exit if it lies on the chessboard and has not been previous-
      ly occupied by the knight.) Finally, set *min* to the location of the minimum
      value of *exits*. (There may be more than one occurrence of the minimum
      value of *exits*. If this happens, it is convenient to let *min* denote the first
      such occurrence, although it is important to realize that by so doing we are
      not actually guaranteed finding a solution. Nevertheless, the chances of
      finding a complete knight's tour in this way are remarkably good, and that is
      sufficient for the purposes of this exercise.)

(g)   [*Move knight*] Set $i = nexti$ [*min*], $j = nextj$ [*min*], and *board*[i,j] $= m$.
      Thus, (i,j) denotes the new position of the knight, and board[i,j] records the
      move in proper sequence.

(h)   [*Print*] Print out *board* showing the solution to the knight's tour and then
      terminate the algorithm.

The problem is to write a Pascal program that corresponds to this algorithm. This
exercise was contributed by Legenhausen and Rebman.

CHAPTER 3

STACKS AND QUEUES

3.1 THE STACK ABSTRACT DATA TYPE

In this chapter, we shall study two data types that are frequently found in computer science. These data types, the stack and the queue, are special cases of the more general data type *ordered list* that we discussed in Chapter 2. Recall that $A = a_1, a_2, \cdots, a_n$ is an ordered list of $n \geq 0$ elements. We refer to the a_i's as *atoms* or *elements* that are taken from some set. The null or empty list, denoted by ( ), has $n = 0$ elements. In this section we begin by defining the ADT *stack* and follow with its implementation. In Section 3.2 we look at the queue.

A *stack* is an ordered list in which insertions and deletions are made at one end called the *top*. Given a stack $S = (a_1, \cdots, a_n)$, we say that a_1 is the bottom element, a_n is the top element, and a_i is on top of element a_{i-1}, $1 < i \leq n$. The restrictions on the stack imply that if we add the elements A, B, C, D, E to the stack, in that order, then E is the first element we delete from the stack. Figure 3.1 illustrates this sequence of operations. Since the last element inserted into a stack is the first element removed, a stack is also known as a *Last-In-First-Out (LIFO)* list.

Example 3.1 [*System stack*]: Before we discuss the stack ADT, we look at a special stack, called the system stack, that is used by a program at run time to process function calls. Whenever a function or procedure is invoked, the program creates a structure, referred to as an *activation record* or a *stack frame*, and places it on top of the system

97

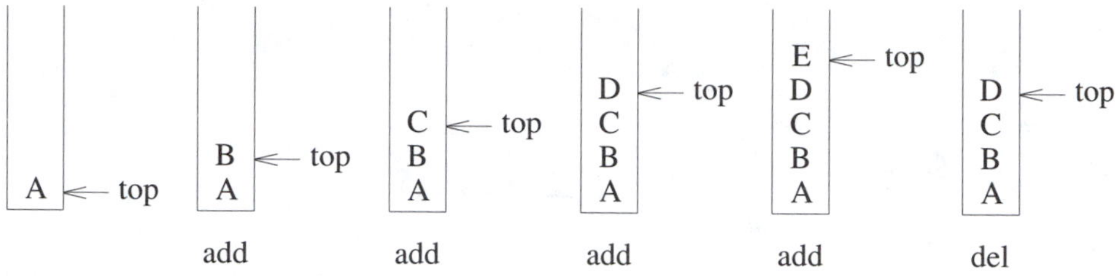

Figure 3.1: Inserting and deleting elements in a stack

stack. Initially, the activation record for the invoked subprogram (procedure or function) contains only a pointer to the previous stack frame and a return address. The previous stack frame pointer points to the stack frame of the invoking subprogram; the return address contains the location of the statement to be executed after the subprogram terminates. Since only one subprogram executes at any given time, the subprogram whose stack frame is on top of the system stack is chosen. If this subprogram invokes another subprogram, the local variables and the parameters of the invoking subprogram are added to its stack frame. A new stack frame is then created for the invoked subprogram and placed on top of the system stack. When this subprogram terminates, its stack frame is removed and the processing of the invoking subprogram, which is again on top of the stack, continues. A simple example illustrates this process. (We refer the reader who wants a more detailed discussion of stack frames to Holub's book on compiler design cited in the References and Selected Readings section.)

Assume that we have a main procedure that invokes function $a1$. Figure 3.2(a) shows the system stack before $a1$ is invoked; Figure 3.2(b) shows the system stack after $a1$ has been invoked. Frame pointer fp is a pointer to the current stack frame. The system also maintains separately a stack pointer, sp, which we have not illustrated.

Since all functions and procedures are stored similarly in the system stack, it makes no difference if the invoking subprogram calls itself. That is, a recursive call requires no special strategy; the run-time program simply creates a new stack frame for each recursive call. However, recursion can consume a significant portion of the memory allocated to the system stack; it could consume the entire available memory. □

Our discussion of the system stack suggests a basic set of operations, including insert an item, delete an item, and check for stack full or empty. These are given in the ADT specification (Structure 3.1).

The easiest way to implement this ADT is by using a one-dimensional array, say *stack* [1 .. *MaxStackSize*], where *MaxStackSize* is the maximum number of entries. The first, or bottom, element of the stack is stored in *stack* [1], the second in *stack* [2], and the *i*th in *stack* [*i*]. Associated with the array is a variable, *top*, which points to the top ele-

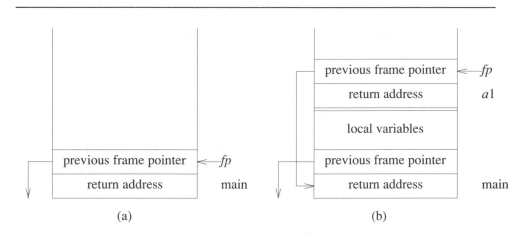

Figure 3.2: System stack after function call

ment in the stack. Initially, *top* is set to 0 to denote an empty stack. With these decisions made, the following implementations result:

$$CreateS\,(stack, MaxStackSize\,) ::= \textbf{var}\ stack : \textbf{array}[1 .. MaxStackSize\,] \ \textbf{of}\ items\,;$$
$$top : 0 .. MaxStackSize\,;$$
$$top := 0;$$
$$IsFull\,(stack, MaxStackSize\,)\quad ::= \textbf{if}\ top = MaxStackSize\ \textbf{then}\ IsFull := \ \textbf{true}$$
$$\textbf{else}\ IsFull := \ \textbf{false;}$$
$$IsEmpty\,(stack\,)\qquad\qquad ::= \textbf{if}\ top = 0\ \textbf{then}\ IsEmpty := \ \textbf{true}$$
$$\textbf{else}\ IsEmpty := \ \textbf{false;}$$

The implementations of these three operations using an array are so short that we need not make them separate procedures but can just use them directly whenever we need to. The *add* and *delete* operations are only a bit more complex. The corresponding procedures (Programs 3.1 and 3.2) have been written assuming that *stack, top*, and *Max-StackSize* are global.

Programs 3.1 and 3.2 are so simple that they need little explanation. *StackFull* and *StackEmpty* are procedures that we leave unspecified, since they will depend upon the particular application. Often when a stack becomes full, the *StackFull* procedure will signal that more storage needs to be allocated and the program rerun. *StackEmpty* is often a meaningful condition. In Sections 3.3 and 3.4, we will see important applications of stacks where *StackEmpty* signals the end of processing.

---

structure *Stack* **is**
    objects: A finite ordered list with zero or more elements.
    functions:
        for all *stack* ∈ *Stack*, *item* ∈ *Items*, *MaxStackSize* ∈ positive integer
        CreateS (*stack*, *MaxStackSize*) : *Stack* ::=
                      create an empty stack, *stack*, whose maximum size is
                      MaxStackSize
        IsFull (*stack*, *MaxStackSize*) : *Boolean* ::=
                      if number of elements in *stack* = *MaxStackSize*
                      then *IsFull* := **true**
                      else *IsFull* := **false**
        Add (*stack*, *item*) : *Stack* ::=
                      if *IsFull* (*stack*) **then** *StackFull*
                      else insert *item* into top of *stack*
        IsEmpty (*stack*) : *Boolean* ::=
                      if number of elements in *stack* = 0
                      then *IsEmpty* := **true**
                      else *IsEmpty* := **false**
        Delete (*stack*) : *Items* ::=
                      if *IsEmpty* (*stack*) **then** *StackEmpty*
                      else remove and return the *item* on the top of the stack

---

Structure 3.1: Abstract data type *Stack*

---

procedure *add* (*item* : *items*);
{Add *item* to the global stack *stack*; *top* is the current top of *stack*,
 and *MaxStackSize* is its maximum size.}
begin
 if *top* = *MaxStackSize* **then** *StackFull*
                        else begin
                            top := *top* + 1;
                            stack [*top*] := *item*;
                      end;
end; {of *add*}

Program 3.1: Adding to a stack

---

procedure *delete*(**var** *item* : *items*);
{Remove top element from the stack *stack* and put it in *item*.}
begin
  if *top* = 0 **then** *StackEmpty*
         else begin
               item := *stack* [*top*];
               top := *top* − 1;
          end;
end; {of *delete*}

Program 3.2: Deleting from a stack

EXERCISES

1. Write Pascal code for the *StackFull* and *StackEmpty* procedures.

2. Consider the railroad switching network given in Figure 3.3. Railroad cars num-
    bered 1, 2, 3, . . ., n are initially in the top right track segment (in this order, left to
    right). Railroad cars can be moved into the vertical track segment one at a time
    from either of the horizontal segments and then moved from the vertical segment
    to any one of the horizontal segments. The vertical segment operates as a stack as
    new cars enter at the top and cars depart the vertical segment from the top. For in-
    stance, if $n = 3$, we could move car 1 into the vertical segment, move 2 in, move 3
    in, and then take the cars out producing the new order 3, 2, 1. For $n = 3$ and 4
    what are the possible permutations of the cars that can be obtained? Are any per-
    mutations not possible?

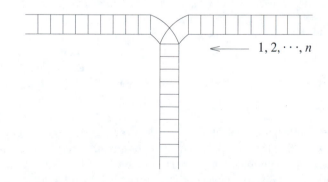

$$\longleftarrow \quad 1, 2, \cdots, n$$

Figure 3.3: Railroad switching network

3.2   THE QUEUE ABSTRACT DATA TYPE

A *queue* is an ordered list in which all insertions take place at one end and all deletions take place at the opposite end. Given a queue $Q = (a_1, a_2, \cdots, a_n)$, a_1 is the front element, a_n is the rear element, and a_i is behind a_{i-1}, $2 \le i \le n$. The restrictions on a queue imply that if we insert A, B, C, D, and E in that order, then A is the first element deleted from the queue. Figure 3.4 illustrates this sequence of events. Since the first element inserted into a queue is the first element removed, queues are also known as *First-In-First-Out (FIFO)* lists. The ADT specification of the queue appears in Structure 3.2.

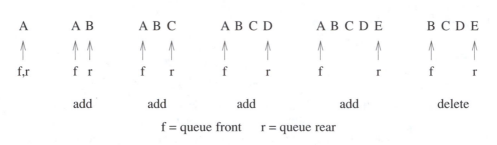

Figure 3.4: Inserting and deleting elements in a queue

The representation of a queue in sequential locations is more difficult than that of the stack. The simplest scheme employs a one-dimensional array and two variables, *front* and *rear*. *front* is one less than the position of the first element in the queue, and *rear* gives the position of the last element in the queue. With this scheme, the following implementation of *CreateQ*, *IsFullQ*, and *IsEmptyQ* results:

$CreateQ\,(q, MaxQueueSize\,) ::= \mathbf{var}\ q : \mathbf{array}\ [1 .. MaxQueueSize\,]\ \mathbf{of}\ items;$
$\qquad\qquad\qquad\qquad\qquad front, rear : 0 .. MaxQueueSize\,;$
$\qquad\qquad\qquad\qquad\qquad front := 0;\ rear := 0;$
$IsFullQ\,(q) \qquad\qquad := \mathbf{if}\ rear = MaxQueueSize\ \mathbf{then}\ IsFullQ = \mathbf{true}$
$\qquad\qquad\qquad\qquad\qquad\qquad\qquad \mathbf{else}\ IsFullQ = \mathbf{false};$
$IsEmptyQ\,(q) \qquad\quad := \mathbf{if}\ front = rear\ \mathbf{then}\ IsEmptyQ = \mathbf{true}$
$\qquad\qquad\qquad\qquad\qquad\qquad\qquad \mathbf{else}\ IsEmptyQ = \mathbf{false};$

The above implementation of *IsFullQ* does not correspond accurately to the specification provided in Structure 3.2, since it is possible that *rear* = *MaxQueueSize* and *front* > 0. In this case, the number of elements in the queue is less than *MaxQueueSize*. We shall account for this discrepancy later. Since the *IsEmptyQ* and *IsFullQ* operations are quite simple, we again implement them directly in the *addq* (Program 3.3) and *deleteq* (Program 3.4) procedures.

structure *Queue* is

   objects: A finite ordered list with zero or more elements.

   functions:

   for all *queue* ∈ *Queue*, *item* ∈ *Items*, *MaxQueueSize* ∈ positive integer

   CreateQ (*queue*,*MaxQueueSize*) : *Queue* ::=

   create an empty queue, *queue*, whose maximum size is *MaxQueueSize*

   IsFullQ (*queue*, *MaxQueueSize*) : *Boolean* ::=

   if number of elements in *queue* = *MaxQueueSize*
   then *IsFullQ* = **true**
   else *IsFullQ* = **false**;

   AddQ (*queue*, *item*) : *Queue* ::=

   if *IsFullQ* (*queue*) **then** *QueueFull*
   else insert *item* at rear of *queue* and return *queue*

   IsEmptyQ (*queue*) : *Boolean* ::=

   if number of elements in *queue* = 0
   then *IsEmptyQ* = **true**
   else *IsEmptyQ* = **false**;

   DeleteQ (*queue*) : *Items* ::=

   if *IsEmptyQ* (*queue*) **then** *QueueEmpty*
   else remove and return the *item* at front of *queue*

Structure 3.2: Abstract data type *Queue*

procedure *addq* (*item* : *items*);
{Add *item* to the queue *q*; *q*, *rear*, and *n* are global variables.}
begin
   if *rear* = *n* **then** *QueueFull*
            else begin
                     rear := *rear* + 1;
                     q [*rear*] := *item*;
                  end;
end; {of *addq*}

Program 3.3: Adding to a queue

---

procedure *deleteq*(**var** *item* : *items*);
{Delete from the front of *q* and put into *item*.}
begin
   if *front* = *rear* **then** *QueueEmpty*
             else begin
                   front := *front* + 1;
                   item := *q* [*front*];
              end;
end; {of *deleteq*}

Program 3.4: Deleting from a queue

This sequential representation of a queue has pitfalls that are best illustrated by an example.

Example 3.2 [*Job scheduling*]: Queues are frequently used in computer programming, and a typical example is the creation of a job queue by an operating system. If the operating system does not use priorities, then the jobs are processed in the order they enter the system. Figure 3.5 illustrates how an operating system might process jobs if it used a sequential representation for its queue.

---

front	rear	Q[1]	[2]	[3]	[4]	[5]	[6]	[7]	...	Comments
0	0		queue		empty					initial
0	1	J1								Job 1 joins *Q*
0	2	J1	J2							Job 2 joins *Q*
0	3	J1	J2	J3						Job 3 joins *Q*
1	3		J2	J3						Job 1 leaves *Q*
1	4		J2	J3	J4					Job 4 joins *Q*
2	4			J3	J4					Job 2 leaves *Q*

Figure 3.5: Insertion and deletion from a queue

It should be obvious that as jobs enter and leave the system, the queue gradually shifts to the right. This means that eventually the rear index equals *MaxQueueSize*, suggesting that the queue is full. In this case, *QueueFull* should move the entire queue to the left so that the first element is again at *queue* [1] and *front* is 0. It should also recalculate *rear* so that it is correctly positioned. Shifting an array is very time-consuming, particularly when there are many elements in it. In fact, *QueueFull* has a worst-case complexity of O(*MaxQueueSize*). □

As observed earlier, the *QueueFull* signal does not necessarily imply that there are *MaxQueueSize* elements in the queue. One obvious thing to do when *QueueFull* is signaled is to move the entire queue to the left so that the first element is again at $q[1]$ and *front* = 0. This is time-consuming, especially when there are many elements in the queue at the time of the *QueueFull* signal.

Let us look at an example (Figure 3.6) that shows what could happen, in the worst case, if each time a queue of size *MaxQueueSize* = n becomes full we choose to move the entire queue left so that it starts at $q[1]$. To begin, assume there are n elements J1, $\cdots$, Jn in the queue, and we next receive alternate requests to delete and add elements. Each time a new element is added, the entire queue of $n - 1$ elements is moved left.

front	*rear*	$q[1]$	[2]	[3]	$\cdots$	[n]	Next Operation
0	n	J1	J2	J3	$\cdots$	Jn	initial state
1	n		J2	J3	$\cdots$	Jn	delete J1
0	n	J2	J3	J4	$\cdots$	Jn+1	add Jn+1
							(jobs J2 through
							Jn are moved)
1	n		J3	J4	$\cdots$	Jn+1	delete J2
0	n	J3	J4	J5	$\cdots$	Jn+2	add Jn+2

Figure 3.6: Queue example

A more efficient queue representation is obtained by regarding the array $q[1..MaxQueueSize]$ as circular. It now becomes more convenient to declare the array as $q[0..MaxQueueSize-1]$. When *rear* = *MaxQueueSize*−1, the next element is entered at $q[0]$ in case that spot is free. Using the same conventions as before, *front* will always point one position counterclockwise from the first element in the queue. Again, *front* = *rear* if and only if the queue is empty. Initially we have *front* = *rear* = 1. Figure 3.7 illustrates some of the possible configurations for a circular queue containing the four elements J1-J4. The assumption of circularity changes the *addq* and *deleteq* procedures slightly. To add an element, it will be necessary to move *rear* one position clockwise, i.e.,

$$\textbf{if } rear = MaxQueueSize - 1 \textbf{ then } rear := 0$$
$$\textbf{else } rear := rear + 1.$$

Using the modulus operator, which computes remainders, this is equivalent to *rear* := (*rear* + 1) **mod** *MaxQueueSize*. Similarly, it will be necessary to move *front* one position clockwise each time a deletion is made. Again, using the modulus operator, this can be accomplished by *front* := (*front* + 1) **mod** *MaxQueueSize*. An examination of the al-

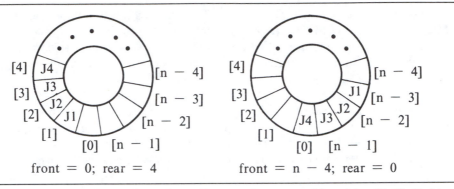

Figure 3.7: Circular queue of *MaxQueueSize* = *n* elements and four jobs: J1, J2, J3, J4

procedure *addq* (*item* : *items*);
{Insert *item* into the circular queue stored in *q*[0 .. *MaxQueueSize* −1].}
begin
 rear := (*rear* + 1) **mod** *MaxQueueSize*; {advance *rear* clockwise}
 if *front* = *rear* **then** *QueueFull*
              else *q* [*rear*] := *item*; {insert}
end; {of *addq*}

Program 3.5: Adding to a circular queue

gorithms (Programs 3.5 and 3.6) indicates that addition and deletion can now be carried out in a fixed amount of time or O(1).

One surprising point in the two algorithms is that the test for queue full in *addq* and the test for queue empty in *deleteq* are the same. In the case of *addq*, however, when *front* = *rear* is evaluated and found to be true, there is actually one space free, i.e., *q* [*rear*], since the first element in the queue is not at *q* [*front*] but is one position clockwise from this point. However, if we insert an item here, then we will not be able to distinguish between the cases full and empty, since this insertion would leave *front* = *rear*. To avoid this, we signal *QueueFull*, thus permitting a maximum of *n*−1 rather than *n* elements to be in the queue at any time.

One way to use all *MaxQueueSize* positions would be to use an additional variable, *LastOp*, to record the last operation performed on the queue. This variable is initialized to "delete." Following each addition, it is set to "add" and following each deletion, it is set to "delete." Now when *front* = *rear*, we can determine whether the queue is empty or full by examining the value of *LastOp*. If *LastOp* is "add," then the

---

procedure *deleteq*(**var** *item* : *items*);
{Remove front element from *q* and put into *item*.}
begin
  if *front* = *rear* **then** *QueueEmpty*
              else begin
                    front := (*front* + 1) **mod** *MaxQueueSize*; {advance *front* clockwise}
                    item := *q* [*front*];
              end;
end; {of *deleteq*}

Program 3.6: Deleting from a circular queue

---

queue is full. Otherwise, it is empty. The use of the variable *LastOp* as described above does, however, slow down the queue add and delete procedures. Since the *addq* and *deleteq* procedures will be used many times in any problem involving queues, the loss of one queue position will be more than made up for by the reduction in computing time. Hence, we favor the implementations of Programs 3.5 and 3.6 over those that result from the use of the variable *LastOp*.

    The procedures *QueueFull* and *QueueEmpty* have been used without explanation, but they are similar to *StackFull* and *StackEmpty*. Their function will depend on the particular application. Note, however, that when *QueueFull* is invoked, the rear pointer has already been moved. This should be taken into account by this procedure.

EXERCISES

1. Write procedures *addq* and *deleteq* (Programs 3.5 and 3.6) using the variable *LastOp* as discussed in this section. The queue should now be able to hold up to *MaxQueueSize* elements. The complexity of each of your procedures should be $\Theta(1)$.

2. A double-ended queue (deque) is a linear list in which additions and deletions may be made at either end. Obtain a data representation mapping a deque into a one-dimensional array. Write algorithms to add and delete elements from either end of the deque.

3. A linear list is being maintained circularly in an array $c[0..n-1]$ with *front* and *rear* set up as for circular queues.

    (a) Obtain a formula in terms of *front*, *rear*, and *n* for the number of elements in the list.

    (b) Write an algorithm to delete the *k*th element in the list.

    (c) Write an algorithm to insert an element *y* immediately after the *k*th element.

    What is the time complexity of your algorithms for (b) and (c)?

3.3   A MAZING PROBLEM

The rat in a maze experiment is a classical one from experimental psychology. A rat (or mouse) is placed through the door of a large box without a top. Walls are set up so that movements in most directions are obstructed. The rat is carefully observed by several scientists as it makes its way through the maze until it eventually reaches the exit. There is only one way out, but at the end is a nice hunk of cheese. The idea is to run the experiment repeatedly until the rat will zip through the maze without taking a single false path. The trials yield its learning curve.

We can write a computer program for getting through a maze, and it will probably not be any smarter than the rat on its first try through. It may take many false paths before finding the right one. But the computer can remember the correct path far better than the rat. On its second try it should be able to go right to the end with no false paths taken, so there is no sense rerunning the program. Why don't you sit down and try to write this program yourself before you read on and look at our solution. Keep track of how many times you have to go back and correct something. This may give you an idea of your own learning curve as we rerun the experiment throughout the book.

Let us represent the maze by a two-dimensional array, $maze[1..m, 1..p]$, where a value of 1 implies a blocked path, and a 0 means one can walk right on through. We assume that the rat starts at $maze[1,1]$, and the exit is at $maze[m,p]$. An example is given in Figure 3.8.

entrance

0	1	0	0	0	1	1	0	0	0	1	1	1	1	1
1	0	0	0	1	1	0	1	1	1	0	0	1	1	1
0	1	1	0	0	0	0	1	1	1	1	0	0	1	1
1	1	0	1	1	1	1	0	1	1	0	1	1	0	0
1	1	0	1	0	0	1	0	1	1	1	1	1	1	1
0	0	1	1	0	1	1	1	0	1	0	0	1	0	1
0	0	1	1	0	1	1	1	0	1	0	0	1	0	1
0	1	1	1	1	0	0	1	1	1	1	1	1	1	1
0	0	1	1	0	1	1	0	1	1	1	1	1	0	1
1	1	0	0	0	1	1	0	1	1	0	0	0	0	0
0	0	1	1	1	1	1	0	0	0	1	1	1	1	0
0	1	0	0	1	1	1	1	1	0	1	1	1	1	0

exit

Figure 3.8: An example maze (can you find a path?)

With the maze represented as a two-dimensional array, the location of the rat in the maze can at any time be described by the row, i, and the column, j, of its position. Now let us consider the possible moves the rat can make from a point $[i,j]$ in the maze. Figure 3.9 shows the possible moves from any point $[i,j]$. The position $[i,j]$ is marked by an X. If all the surrounding squares have a 0, then the rat can choose any of these eight squares as its next position. We call these eight directions by the names of the points on a compass: north, northeast, east, southeast, south, southwest, west, and northwest, or N, NE, E, SE, S, SW, W, and NW.

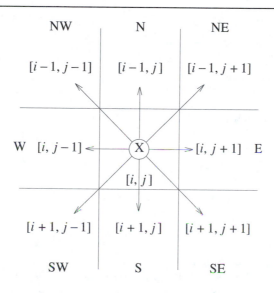

Figure 3.9: Allowable moves

We must be careful here because not every position has eight neighbors. If $[i,j]$ is on a border where either $i = 1$ or m, or $j = 1$ or p, then less than eight, and possibly only three, neighbors exist. To avoid checking for border conditions, we surround the maze by a border of ones. The array will therefore be declared as $maze[0..m+1, 0..p+1]$. Another device that will simplify the problem is to predefine the possible directions to move in a table, *move*, as in Figure 3.10. The data types needed are

type *offsets* = **record**
        $a : -1..1$;
        $b : -1..1$;
    end;
    directions = (N, NE, E, SE, S, SW, W, NW);
var *move* : **array**[*directions*] **of** *offsets*;

q	$move\,[q\,].a$	$move\,[q\,].b$
N	−1	0
NE	−1	1
E	0	1
SE	1	1
S	1	0
SW	1	−1
W	0	−1
NW	−1	−1

Figure 3.10: Table of moves

If we are at position $[i,j]$ in the maze and we wish to find the position $[g,h]$ that is southwest of us, then we set

$$g := i + move[SW].a; \quad h := j + move[SW].b;$$

For example, if we are at position $[3,4]$, then position $[3 + 1 = 4,\ 4 + (-1) = 3]$ is southwest.

As we move through the maze, we may have the chance to go in several directions. Not knowing which one to choose, we pick one but save our current position and the direction of the last move in a list. This way, if we have taken a false path, we can return and try another direction. With each new location we will examine the possibilities, starting from the north and looking clockwise. Finally, in order to prevent us from going down the same path twice, we use another array, $mark[0..m+1, 0..p+1]$, which is initially zero. $mark[i,j]$ is set to 1 once we arrive at that position. We assume $maze[m,p] = 0$, since otherwise there is no path to the exit. Program 3.7 is a first pass at an algorithm.

This is not a Pascal program, and yet it describes the essential processing without too much detail. The use of indentation for delineating important blocks of code plus the use of Pascal reserved words make the looping and conditional tests transparent.

What remains to be pinned down? Using the three arrays $maze$, $mark$, and $move$, we need only specify how to represent the list of new triples. Since the algorithm calls for removing first the most recently entered triple, this list should be a stack. We can use the sequential representation we saw before. All we need to know now is a reasonable bound on the size of this stack. Since each position in the maze is visited at most once, at most mp elements can be placed into the stack. Thus, mp locations is a safe but somewhat conservative bound. The maze of Figure 3.11 has only one path from entrance to exit. It has $\lceil m/2 \rceil (p-2) + 2$ positions.

initialize *stack* to the maze entrance coordinates and direction east;
while *stack* is not empty **do**
begin
 (*i*, *j*, *mov*) := coordinates and direction from top of *stack*;
 while there are more moves **do**
 begin
  (*g*, *h*) := coordinates of next move;
  if (*g* = *m*) **and** (*h* = *p*) **then** success;
  if *maze* [*g*, *h*] = 0 {legal move}
    and (*mark* [*g*, *h*] = 0) {haven't been here before}
  then begin
        mark [*g*, *h*] := 1;
        mov := next direction to try;
        add (*i*, *j*, *mov*) to top of *stack*;
        i := *g*; *j* := *h*; *mov* := *north*;
      end;
 end;
end;
writeln('no path found');

Program 3.7: First pass at finding a path through a maze

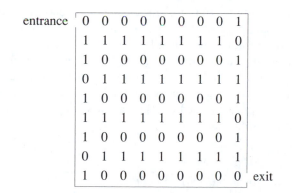

Figure 3.11: A maze with a long path

Thus, *mp* is not too crude a bound. We are now ready to give a precise maze algorithm (Program 3.8).

Although using nonnumeric indices for *move* keeps the correspondence with direction transparent, it makes the resulting Pascal program somewhat cumbersome. This is so because the predecessor of N and the successor of NW are not defined. So, in procedure *path* (Program 3.8), we assume that *move* is actually declared as

var *move*: **array**[1 .. 8] **of** *offsets;*

The correspondence is *move*[1] = *move*[N], . . ., *move*[8] = *move*[NW].

The arrays *maze, mark, move,* and *stack*, along with the variables or constants *top,* *m, p,* and *n*, are assumed global to *path*. Further, it is assumed that *stack* [1 .. *n*] is an array of *items* where the type *items* is defined as

type *items* = **record**
　　　　x : 1 .. *m*;
　　　　y : 1 .. *p*;
　　　　dir : 1 .. 9;
　　end;

If *n* is at least *mp*, then the *StackFull* condition will never occur.

Now, what can we say about the computing time of this procedure? It is interesting that even though the problem is easy to grasp, it is difficult to make any but the most trivial statement about the computing time. The reason for this is that the number of iterations of the main **while** loop is entirely dependent upon the given maze. What we can say is that each new position [*i, j*] that is visited gets marked, so paths are never taken twice. There are at most eight iterations of the inner **while** loop for each marked position. Each iteration of the inner **while** loop takes a fixed amount of time, O(1), and if the number of zeros in *maze* is *z*, then at most *z* positions can get marked. Since *z* is bounded above by *mp*, the computing time is O(*mp*). (In actual experiments, however, the rat may be inspired by the watching psychologists and the invigorating odor from the cheese at the exit. It might reach its goal by examining far fewer paths than those examined by algorithm *path*. This may happen despite the fact that the rat has no pencil and only a very limited mental stack. It is difficult to incorporate the effect of the cheese odor and the cheering of the psychologists into a computer algorithm.) The array *mark* can be eliminated altogether and *maze*[*g,h*] changed to 1 instead of setting *mark*[*g,h*] to 1, but this will destroy the original maze.

EXERCISES

1.　(a)　Find a path through the maze of Figure 3.8.

　　(b)　Trace out the action of procedure *path* (Program 3.8) on the maze of Figure 3.8. Compare this to your own attempt in (a).

2.　What is the maximum path length from start to finish for any maze of dimensions $m \times p$?

procedure *path*;
{Output a path (if any) in the maze; *maze*[0,*i*] = *maze* [*m* +1,*i*] =
maze [*j*,0] = *maze* [*j*,*p* +1] = 1, 0 ≤ *i* ≤ *p* +1, 0 ≤ *j* ≤ *m*+1.}
var *position* : *items*; *d*,*g*,*h*,*i*,*j*,*q* : **integer**; *found* : **boolean**;
begin
  {start at (1,1)}
  mark[1,1] := 1; *top* := 1; *found* := **false**;
  with *stack*[1] **do begin** *x* := 1; *y* := 1; *dir* := 3; **end**;

  while (*top* > 0) **and not** *found* **do** {stack not empty}
  begin
    delete (*position*); {unstack}
    with *position* **do begin** *i* := *x*; *j* := *y*; *d* := *dir*; **end**;
    while (*d* <= 8) **and not** *found* **do** {move forward}
    begin
      g := *i* + *move* [*d*].*a*; *h* := *j* + *move* [*d*].*b*;
      if (*g* = *m*) **and** (*h* = *p*) **then** {reached exit}
                              begin {output *path*}
                                for *q* := 1 **to** *top* **do writeln**(*stack* [*q*] .*x*, *stack* [*q*] .*y*);
                                writeln(*i*, *j*); **writeln**(*m*,*p*);
                                found := **true**;
                              end {of **then**}
                    else
                              begin
                                if (*maze* [*g*,*h*] = 0) **and** *mark* [*g*,*h*] = 0)
                                then begin {new position}
                                        mark [*g*,*h*] := 1;
                                        with *position* **do** *x* := *i*; *y* := *j*; *dir* := *d*+1; **end**;
                                        add (*position*); {stack it}
                                        i := *g*; *j* := *h*; *d* := 1; {move to (*g*,*h*)}
                                    end
                                    else *d* := *d*+1; {try next direction}
                              end; {of **else**}
    end; {of **while** *d* <= 8}
  end; {of *top* > 0}

  if not *found* **then writeln**('no path in maze');
end; {of *path*}

Program 3.8: Finding a path through a maze

3.4   EVALUATION OF EXPRESSIONS

3.4.1   Expressions

When pioneering computer scientists conceived the idea of higher-level programming languages, they were faced with many hurdles. One of these was how to generate machine-language instructions to evaluate an arithmetic expression. An assignment statement such as

$$X := A/B - C + D * E - A * C$$

might have several meanings, and even if it were uniquely defined, say by a full use of parentheses, it still seemed a formidable task to generate a correct instruction sequence. Fortunately the solution we have today is both elegant and simple. Moreover, it is so simple that this aspect of compiler writing is really one of the more minor issues.

An expression is made up of operands, operators, and delimiters. The expression above has five operands: A, B, C, D, and E. Though these are all one-letter variables, operands can be any legal variable name or constant in our programming language. In any expression the values that variables take must be consistent with the operations performed on them. These operations are described by the operators. In most programming languages there are several kinds of operators that correspond to the different kinds of data a variable can hold. First, there are the basic arithmetic operators: plus, minus, times, and divide ($+$, $-$, $*$, $/$). Other arithmetic operators include unary minus, **mod**, and **div**. The latter two may sometimes be library subroutines rather than predefined operators. A second class is the relational operators: $<$, $<=$, $=$, $<>$, $>=$, and $>$. These are usually defined to work for arithmetic operands, but they can just as easily work for character string data. ('CAT' is less than 'DOG' since it precedes 'DOG' in alphabetical order.) The result of an expression that contains relational operators is one of two constants: **true** or **false**. Such an expression is called boolean, named after the mathematician George Boole, the father of symbolic logic. There also may be logical operators such as **and**, **or**, and **not**.

The first problem with understanding the meaning of an expression is to decide in what order the operations are carried out. This means that every language must uniquely define such an order. For instance, if $A = 4$, $B = C = 2$, $D = E = 3$, then in the above equation we might want X to be assigned the value

$$((4/2) - 2) + (3 * 3) - (4 * 2)$$
$$= 0 + 9 - 8$$
$$= 1$$

However, the true intention of the programmer might have been to assign X the value

$$(4/(2 - 2 + 3)) * (3 - 4) * 2$$
$$= (4/3) * (-1) * 2$$
$$= -2.6666666$$

Of course, the programmer could specify the latter order of evaluation by using parentheses:

$$X := ((A/(B - C + D)) * (E - A) * C$$

To fix the order of evaluation, we assign to each operator a priority. Then within any pair of parentheses we understand that operators with the highest priority will be evaluated first. A set of sample priorities from Pascal is given in Figure 3.12. The highest priority is 1.

priority	operator
1	unary minus
2	**not**
3	$*, /,$ **div, mod, and**
4	$+, -,$ **or, xor**
5	$<, <=, =, <>, >=, >,$ **in**

Figure 3.12: Priority of operators in Pascal

Notice that all of the relational operators have the same priority. Unary minus has top priority, followed by boolean negation. When we have an expression where two adjacent operators have the same priority, we need a rule to tell us which one to perform first. For example, do we want the value of $A/B*C$ to be understood as $(A/B) * C$ or $A/(B*C)$? Convince yourself that there will be a difference by trying $A = B = C = 2$. The Pascal rule is that for all priorities, evaluation of operators of the same priority will proceed left to right. So, $A/B*C$ will be evaluated as $(A/B) * C$. Remember that by using parentheses we can override these rules, as expressions are always evaluated with the innermost parenthesized expression first.

Now that we have specified priorities and rules for breaking ties we know how $X : A/B - C + D*E - A*C$ will be evaluated, namely, as

$$X := (((A/B) - C) + (D * E)) - (A * C)$$

3.4.2   Postfix Notation

How can a compiler accept an expression and produce correct code? The answer is given by reworking the expression into a form we call *postfix notation.* If *e* is an expression with operators and operands, the conventional way of writing *e* is called *infix*, because the operators come *in-between* the operands. (Unary operators precede their operand.) The *postfix* form of an expression calls for each operator to appear *after* its operands. For example,

$$\text{infix } A*B/C \text{ has postfix } AB*C/$$

If we study the postfix form of $A*B/C$, we see that the multiplication comes immediately after its two operands A and B. Now imagine that $A*B$ is computed and stored in T. Then we have the division operator, $/$, coming immediately after its two operands T and C.

Let us look at our previous example

$$\text{infix:} \quad A/B - C + D * E - A * C$$

$$\text{postfix:} \quad AB/C - DE * + AC * -$$

and trace out the meaning of the postfix.

Suppose that every time we compute a value, we store it in the temporary location T_i, $i \geq 1$. If we read the postfix expression left to right, the first operation is division. The two operands that precede this are A and B. So, the result of A/B is stored in T_1, and the postfix expression is modified as in Figure 3.13. This figure also gives the remaining sequence of operations. The result is stored in T_6. Notice that if we had parenthesized the expression, this would change the postfix only if the order of normal evaluation were altered. Thus, $(A/B) - C + (D * E) - A * C$ will have the same postfix form as the previous expression without parentheses. But $(A/B) - (C + D) * (E - A) * C$ will have the postfix form $AB/CD + EA - * C * -$.

operation	postfix
$T_1 := A/B$	$T_1 C - DE * + AC * -$
$T_2 := T_1 - C$	$T_2 DE * + AC * -$
$T_3 := D * E$	$T_2 T_3 + AC * -$
$T_4 := T_2 + T_3$	$T_4 AC * -$
$T_5 := A * C$	$T_4 T_5 -$
$T_6 := T_4 - T_5$	T_6

Figure 3.13: Postfix evaluation

What the virtues of postfix notation that enable easy evaluation of expressions? To begin with, the need for parentheses is eliminated. Second, the priority of the operators is no longer relevant. The expression may be evaluated by making a left to right scan, stacking operands, and evaluating operators using as operands the correct number from the stack and finally placing the result onto the stack (see Program 3.9). This evaluation process is much simpler than attempting direct evaluation from infix notation.

procedure *eval* (*e* : *expression*);
{Evaluate the postfix expression *e*. It is assumed that the last token (a token is either an operator, operand, or '#') in *e* is '#.' A procedure *NextToken* is used to extract from *e* the next token. A one-dimensional array *stack*[1 .. *n*] is used as a stack.}
var *x* : *token*;
begin
 top := 0; {initialize *stack*}
 x := *NextToken* (*e*);
 while *x* <> '#' **do**
 begin
  if *x* is an operand
  then *add* (*x*) {add to *stack*}
  else begin {operator}
     remove the correct number of operands for operator *x* from *stack*; perform the operation *x* and store the result (if any) onto the stack;
    end;
  x := *NextToken* (*e*);
 end; {of **while**}
end; {of *eval*}

Program 3.9: Evaluating postfix expressions

3.4.3   Infix to Postfix

To see how to devise an algorithm for translating from infix to postfix, note that the order of the operands in both forms is the same. In fact, it is simple to describe an algorithm for producing postfix from infix:

(1)   Fully parenthesize the expression.

(2)   Move all operators so that they replace their corresponding right parentheses.

(3)   Delete all parentheses.

For example, $A/B - C + D * E - A * C$, when fully parenthesized, yields

$$((((A / B) - C) + (D * E)) - (A * C))$$

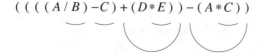

The arcs join an operator and its corresponding right parenthesis. Steps 2 and 3 yield

$$AB/C - DE * + AC * -$$

This algorithm requires two passes. The first one reads the expression and parenthesizes it, and the second actually moves the operators. Since the order of the operands is the same in infix and postfix, when we scan an expression for the first time, we can form the postfix by immediately passing any operands to the output. To handle the operators, we store them in a stack until it is time to pass them to the output.

For example, since we want $A + B * C$ to yield $ABC * +$, our algorithm should perform the following sequence of stacking (these stacks will grow to the right):

next token	stack	output
none	empty	none
A	empty	A
+	+	A
B	+	AB

At this point the algorithm must determine if $*$ gets placed on top of the stack or if the $+$ gets taken off. Since $*$ has higher priority, we should stack $*$, producing

$*$	$+*$	AB
C	$+*$	ABC

Now the input expression is exhausted, so we output all remaining operators in the stack to get

$$ABC * +$$

For another example, $A * (B + C) * D$ has the postfix form $ABC + *D *$, and so the algorithm should behave as

next token	stack	output
none	empty	none
A	empty	A
$*$	$*$	A
(	$*($	A
B	$*($	AB
+	$*(+$	AB
C	$*(+$	ABC

At this point we want to unstack down to the corresponding left parenthesis and then delete the left and right parentheses. This gives us

)	*	$ABC+$
*	*	$ABC+*$
D	*	$ABC+*D$
done	empty	$ABC+*D*$

These examples motivate a priority-based scheme for stacking and unstacking operators. The left parenthesis complicates things, since when it is not in the stack, it behaves as an operator with high priority, whereas once it gets in, it behaves as one with low priority (no operator other than the matching right parenthesis should cause it to get unstacked). We establish two priorities for operators: *isp* (in-stack priority) and *icp* (in-coming priority). The *isp* and *icp* of all operators in Figure 3.12 is the priority given in Figure 3.12. In addition, we define *isp* $['('] = 5$, *icp*$['('] = 0$, and *isp*$['#'] = 5$. These priorities result in the following rule: *Operators are taken out of the stack as long as their in-stack priority is numerically less than or equal to the in-coming priority of the new operator.* Our algorithm to transform from infix to postfix is given in Program 3.10.

Analysis of *postfix*: The algorithm makes only a left-to-right pass across the input. The time spent on each operand is $O(1)$. Each operator is stacked and unstacked once. Hence, the time spent on each operator is also $O(1)$. So, the complexity of procedure *postfix* is $\Theta(n)$, where n is the number of tokens in the expression. □

EXERCISES

1. Write the postfix form of the following expressions:

    (a) $A * B * C$

    (b) $-A + B - C + D$

    (c) $A * -B + C$

    (d) $(A + B) * D + E/(F + A * D) + C$

    (e) A **and** B **or** C **or** **not** $(E > F)$ (assuming Pascal precedence)

    (f) **not** $(A$ **and** **not** $((B < C)$ **or** $(C > D))) $ **or** $(C < E)$

2. Use the priorities of Figure 3.12 together with those for '(' and '#' to answer the following:

    (a) In procedure *postfix* (Program 3.10), what is the maximum number of elements that can be on the stack at any time if the input expression e has n operators and delimiters?

    (b) What is the answer to (a) if e has n operators and the depth of nesting of parentheses is at most 6?

3. Another expression form that is easy to evaluate and is parenthesis-free is known as *prefix*. In this way of writing expressions, the operators precede their operands. For example:

procedure *postfix(e : expression)*;
{Output the postfix form of the infix expression *e*. *NextToken* and *stack* are as in
  procedure *eval* (Program 3.9). It is assumed that the last token in *e* is '#.' Also, '#' is
  used at the bottom of the stack.}
var *x,y* : *token*;
begin
 stack[1] := '#'; *top* := 1; {initialize *stack*}
 x := *NextToken* (*e*);
 while *x* <> '#' **do**
 begin
  if *x* is an operand **then write**(*x*)
  else if *x* = ')' **then begin** {unstack until '('}
          while *stack* [*top*] <> '(' **do**
          begin *delete* (*y*); **write**(*y*); **end**;
          delete (*y*); {delete '('}
        end
      else begin
          while *isp* [*stack* [*top*]] <= *icp* [*x*] **do**
          begin *delete* (*y*); **write**(*y*); **end**;
          add (*x*);
        end;
  x := *NextToken* (*e*);
 end; {of **while**}

 {end of expression; empty stack}
 while *top* > 1 **do begin** *delete* (*y*); **write**(*y*); **end**;
 writeln('#'); {end of expression marker}
end; {of *postfix*}

[handwritten annotation:] — ERROR in while loop — (won't terminate) (on empty stack)

Program 3.10: Converting from infix to postfix form

infix	prefix
$A * B / C$	$/*ABC$
$A/B - C + D * E - A * C$	$- + - /ABC * DE * AC$
$A * (B + C)/D - G$	$-/* A + BCDG$

Notice that the order of operands is not changed in going from infix to prefix.

(a)   What is the prefix form of the expressions in Exercise 1?

(b)   Write an algorithm to evaluate a prefix expression *e*. (Hint: Scan *e* right to
       left and assume that the leftmost token of *e* is '#.')

(c)   Write an algorithm to transform an infix expression e into its prefix equivalent. Assume that the input expression e begins with a '#' and that the prefix expression should begin with a '#.'

What is the time complexity of your algorithms for (b) and (c)? How much space is needed by each of these algorithms?

4.   Write an algorithm to transform from prefix to postfix. Carefully state any assumptions you make regarding the input. How much time and space does your algorithm take?

5.   Do the preceding exercise, but this time for a transformation from postfix to prefix.

6.   Write an algorithm to generate fully parenthesized infix expressions from their postfix form. What is the complexity (time and space) of your algorithm?

7.   Do the preceding exercise starting from prefix form.

3.5   MULTIPLE STACKS AND QUEUES

Until now we have been concerned only with the representations of a single stack or a single queue in the memory of a computer. For these two cases we have seen efficient sequential data representations. What happens when a data representation is needed for several stacks and queues? We limit ourselves to sequential mappings of these data objects into an array $M[1..m]$. If we have only two stacks to represent, then the solution is simple. We can use $M[1]$ for the bottommost element in stack 1 and $M[m]$ for the corresponding element in stack 2. Stack 1 can grow toward $M[m]$ and stack 2 toward $M[1]$. It is therefore possible to utilize efficiently all the available space. Can we do the same when more than two stacks are to be represented? The answer is no because a one-dimensional array has only two fixed points, $M[1]$ and $M[m]$, and each stack requires a fixed point for its bottommost element. When more than two stacks, say n, are to be represented sequentially, we can initially divide out the available memory $M[1..m]$ into n segments and allocate one of these segments to each of the n stacks. This initial division of $M[1..m]$ into segments may be done in proportion to expected sizes of the various stacks if these are known. In the absence of such information, $M[1..m]$ may be divided into equal segments. For each stack i we shall use $b[i]$ to represent a position one less than the position in M for the bottommost element of that stack. $t[i]$, $1 \leq i \leq n$ will point to the topmost element of stack i. We shall use the boundary condition $b[i] = t[i]$ iff the ith stack is empty. If we grow the ith stack in memory indices lower than the $(i+1)$th, then with roughly equal initial segments we have

$$b[i] = t[i] = \lfloor m/n \rfloor (i-1), \ 1 \leq i \leq n$$

as the initial values of $b[i]$ and $t[i]$ (see Figure 3.14). Stack i, $1 \leq i \leq n$, can grow from $b[i]+1$ up to $b[i+1]$ before it catches up with the $(i+1)$th stack. It is convenient both for the discussion and the algorithms to define $b[n+1] = m$. Using this scheme, the *add* and *delete* algorithms of Programs 3.11 and 3.12 result.

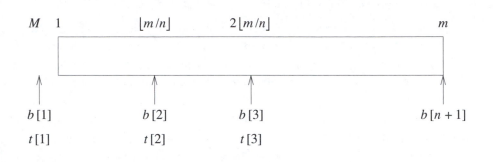

Figure 3.14: Initial configuration for n stacks in $M[1..m]$. All stacks are empty and memory is divided into roughly equal segments

procedure *add* (i : **integer**; x : *items*);
{Add x to the ith *stack*.}
begin
 if $t[i] = b[i+1]$ **then** *StackFull* (i)
                else begin
                       $t[i] := t[i] + 1$;
                       $M[t[i]] := x$; {add to ith stack}
                    end;
end; {of *add*}

Program 3.11: Adding to the ith stack

    The algorithms to add and delete appear to be as simple as in the case of only one or two stacks. This really is not the case, since the *StackFull* condition in algorithm *add* does not imply that all m locations of M are in use. In fact, there may be a lot of unused space between stacks j and $j + 1$ for $1 \le j \le n$ and $j \ne i$ (Figure 3.15). The procedure *StackFull*(i) should therefore determine whether there is any free space in M and shift stacks around so as to make some of this free space available to the ith stack.

    Several strategies are possible for the design of algorithm *StackFull*. We shall discuss one strategy in the text and look at some others in the exercises. The primary objective of algorithm *StackFull* is to permit the adding of elements to stacks so long as there is some free space in M. One way to guarantee this is to design *StackFull* along the following lines:

```
procedure delete (i : integer; var x : items);
{delete topmost item of stack i.}
begin
 if t [i] = b [i] then StackEmpty (i)
              else begin
                      x := M [t [i]];
                      t [i] := t [i] − 1;
                   end;
end; {of delete}
```

Program 3.12: Deleting from the *i*th stack

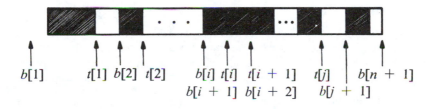

Figure 3.15: Configuration when stack *i* meets with stack *i* + 1 but there is still free space elsewhere in *M*

(1)   Determine the least, *j*, *i* < *j* ≤ *n*, such that there is free space between stacks *j* and *j* + 1, i.e., $t[j] < b[j+1]$. If there is such a *j*, then move stacks *i* + 1, *i* + 2, ..., *j* one position to the right (treating *M* [1] as leftmost and *M* [*m*] as rightmost), thereby creating a space between stacks *i* and *i* + 1.

(2)   If there is no *j* as in (1), then look to the left of stack *i*. Find the largest *j* such that 1 ≤ *j* < *i* and there is space between stacks *j* and *j* + 1, i.e., $t[j] < b[j + 1]$. If there is such a *j*, then move stacks *j* + 1, *j* + 2, ..., *i* one space left, creating a free space between stacks *i* and *i* + 1.

(3)   If there is no *j* satisfying either the conditions of (1) or (2), then all *m* spaces of *M* are utilized, and there is no free space.

The writing of algorithm *StackFull* using the above strategy is left as an exercise. It should be clear that the worst-case performance of this representation for the *n* stacks together with the above strategy for *StackFull* would be rather poor. In fact, in the worst case O(m) time may be needed for each insertion (see Exercises). In the next chapter we shall see that if we do not limit ourselves to sequential mappings of data objects into arrays, then we can obtain a data representation for m stacks that has a much better worst-case performance than the representation described here. Sequential representations for n queues and other generalizations are discussed in the exercises.

EXERCISES

1. Two stacks are to be represented in an array $M[1..m]$ as described in this section. Write algorithms *add* (i,x) and *delete* (i) to add x and delete an element from stack i, $1 \leq i \leq 2$. Your algorithms should be able to add elements to the stacks so long as there are fewer than m elements in both stacks together and should run in O(1) time.

2. Obtain a data representation mapping a stack s and a queue q into a single array $M[1..n]$. Write algorithms to add and delete elements from these two data objects. What can you say about the suitability of your data representation?

3. Write a Pascal procedure implementing the strategy for *StackFull*(i) outlined in this section.

4. For the *add* and *delete* algorithms (Programs 3.11 and 3.12) and the *StackFull*(i) algorithm of the preceding exercise, produce a sequence of adds and deletes that will require O(m) time for each add. Use $n = 2$ and start from a configuration representing a full utilization of $M[1..m]$.

5. It has been empirically observed that most programs that get close to using all available space eventually run out of space. In light of this observation, it seems futile to move stacks around providing space for other stacks to grow in if there is only a limited amount of space that is free. Rewrite the algorithm of the preceding exercise so that the algorithm terminates if there are fewer than c free spaces. c is an empirically determined constant that is provided to the algorithm.

6. Another strategy for the *StackFull*(i) condition is to redistribute all the free space in proportion to the rate of growth of individual stacks since the last call to *Stack-Full*. This would require the use of another array, $lt[1..n]$, where $lt[j]$ is the value of $t[j]$ at the last call to *StackFull*. Then the amount by which each stack has grown since the last call is $t[j] - lt[j]$. The amount for stack i is actually $t[i] - lt[i] + 1$, since we are not attempting to add another element to i.

   Write algorithm *StackFull*(i) to redistribute all the stacks so that the free space between stacks j and $j + 1$ is in proportion to the growth of stack j since the last call to *StackFull*. *Stackfull*(i) should assign at least one free location to stack i.

7. Design a data representation sequentially mapping n queues into an array $M[1..m]$. Represent each queue as a circular queue within M. Write procedures *addq*, *deleteq*, and *QueueFull* for this representation.

8. Design a data representation, sequentially mapping n data objects into an array $M[1..m]$. n_1 of these data objects are stacks, and the remaining $n_2 = n - n_1$ are queues. Write algorithms to add and delete elements from these objects. Use the same *SpaceFull* algorithm for both types of data objects. This algorithm should provide space for the ith data object if there is some space not currently being used. Note that a circular queue with space for r elements can hold only $r - 1$.

3.6   REFERENCES AND SELECTED READINGS

You will find an excellent discussion of the system stack and activation records in *Compiler Design in C*, by A. Holub, Prentice-Hall, Englewood Cliffs, NJ, 1990. The structure of our activation record (Figure 3.2) is based on Holub's discussion.

3.7   ADDITIONAL EXERCISES

1. [*Programming Project*] [Landweber] People have spent so much time playing card games of solitaire that the gambling casinos are now capitalizing on this human weakness. A form of solitaire is described below. Your assignment is to write a computer program to play the game, thus freeing hours of time for people to return to more useful endeavors.

    To begin the game, 28 cards are dealt into seven piles. The leftmost pile has one card, the next two cards, and so forth, up to seven cards in the rightmost pile. Only the uppermost card of each of the seven piles is turned face up. The cards are dealt left to right, one card to each pile, dealing to one less pile each time, and turning the first card in each round face up. On the topmost face-up card of each pile you may build in descending sequences red on black or black on red. For example, on the 9 of spades you may place either the 8 of diamonds or the 8 of hearts. All face-up cards on a pile are moved as a unit and may be placed on another pile according to the bottommost face-up card. For example, the 7 of clubs on the 8 of hearts may be moved as a unit onto the 9 of clubs or the 9 of spades.

    Whenever a face-down card is uncovered, it is turned face up. If one pile is removed completely, a face-up king may be moved from a pile (together with all cards above it) or the top of the waste pile (see below) into the vacated space. There are four output piles, one for each suit, and the object of the game is to get as many cards as possible into the output piles. Each time an ace appears at the top of a pile or the top of the stack, it is moved into the appropriate output pile. Cards are added to the output piles in sequence, the suit for each pile being determined by the ace on the bottom.

From the rest of the deck, called the stock, cards are turned up one by one and placed face up on a waste pile. You may always play cards off the top of the waste pile, but only one at a time. Begin by moving a card from the stock to the top of the waste pile. If there is ever more than one possible play to be made, the following order must be observed:

(a)   Move a card from the top of a playing pile or from the top of the waste pile to an output pile. If the waste pile becomes empty, move a card from the stock to the waste pile.

(b)   Move a card from the top of the waste pile to the leftmost playing pile to which it can be moved. If the waste pile becomes empty, move a card from the stock to the waste pile.

(c)   Find the leftmost playing pile that can be moved and place it on top of the leftmost playing pile to which it can be moved.

(d)   Try (a), (b), and (c) in sequence, restarting with (a) whenever a move is made.

(e)   If no move is made via (a) through (d), move a card from the stock to the waste pile and retry (a).

Only the topmost card of the playing piles or the waste pile may be played to an output pile. Once played on an output pile, a card may not be withdrawn to help elsewhere. The game is over when either all the cards have been played to the output, or the stock pile has been exhausted and no more cards can be moved.

When played for money, the player pays the house $52 at the beginning and wins $5 for every card played to the output piles. Write your program so that it will play several games and determine your net winnings. Use a random number generator to shuffle the deck. Output a complete record of two games in easily understood form. Include as output the number of games played and the net winnings (+ or −).

2.   [*Programming Project*] [Landweber] We want to simulate an airport landing and takeoff pattern. The airport has three runways, runway 1, runway 2, and runway 3. There are four landing holding patterns, two for each of the first two runways. Arriving planes will enter one of the holding pattern queues, where the queues are to be as close in size as possible. When a plane enters a holding queue, it is assigned an integer *id* number and an integer giving the number of time units the plane can remain in the queue before it must land (because of low fuel level). There is also a queue for takeoffs for each of the three runways. Planes arriving in a takeoff queue are also assigned an integer *id*. The takeoff queues should be kept approximately the same size.

At each time, up to three planes may arrive at the landing queues and up to three planes may arrive at the takeoff queues. Each runway can handle one takeoff or landing at each time slot. Runway 3 is to be used for takeoffs except when a plane is low on fuel. At each time unit, planes in either landing queue whose air time has reached zero must be given priority over other landings and takeoffs. If only one plane is in this category, runway 3 is to be used. If more than one, then the other runways are also used (at each time, at most three planes can be serviced in this way).

Use successive even (odd) integers for *id*'s of planes arriving at takeoff (landing) queues. At each time unit assume that arriving planes are entered into queues before takeoffs or landings occur. Try to design your algorithm so that neither landing nor takeoff queues grow excessively. However, arriving planes must be placed at the ends of queues. Queues cannot be reordered.

The output should clearly indicate what occurs at each time unit. Periodically output (a) the contents of each queue; (b) the average takeoff waiting time; (c) the average landing waiting time; (d) the average flying time remaining on landing; and (e) the number of planes landing with no fuel reserve. (b) and (c) are for planes that have taken off or landed, respectively. The output should be self-explanatory and easy to understand (and uncluttered).

The input can be from cards, a terminal, a file, or it can be generated by a random number generator. For each time unit the input is of the form

col1	0-3	indicating the number of planes arriving at takeoff queues
col2	0-3	indicating the number of planes arriving at landing queues
col4-5	1-20	
col6-7	1-20	units of flying time for planes arriving in landing queues
col8-9	1-20	(from col2)

CHAPTER 4

LINKED LISTS

4.1 SINGLY LINKED LISTS

In the previous chapters, we studied the representation of simple data structures using an array and a sequential mapping. These representations had the property that successive nodes of the data object were stored a fixed distance apart. Thus, (1) if the element a_{ij} of a table was stored at location L_{ij}, then $a_{i,j+1}$ was at the location $L_{ij} + c$ for some constant c; (2) if the ith node in a queue was at location L_i, then the $(i + 1)$th node was at location $L_i + c$ mod n for the circular representation; (3) if the topmost node of a stack was at location L_T, then the node beneath it was at location $L_T - c$, and so on. These sequential storage schemes proved adequate for the functions we wished to perform (accessing an arbitrary node in a table, insertion or deletion of nodes within a stack or queue). However, when a sequential mapping is used for ordered lists, operations such as insertion and deletion of arbitrary elements become expensive. For example, consider the following list of three-letter English words ending in AT:

(BAT, CAT, EAT, FAT, HAT, JAT, LAT, MAT, OAT, PAT, RAT, SAT, TAT, VAT, WAT)

To make this list complete we naturally want to add the word GAT, which means gun or revolver. If we are using an array to keep this list, then the insertion of GAT will require us to move elements already in the list either one location higher or lower. We must move either HAT, JAT, LAT, $\cdots$, WAT or BAT, CAT, EAT, and FAT. If we have to do many such insertions into the middle, neither alternative is attractive because of the amount of data movement. On the other hand, suppose we decide to remove the word LAT, which refers to the Latvian monetary unit. Then again, we have to move many elements so as to maintain the sequential representation of the list.

When our problem called for several ordered lists of varying sizes, sequential representation again proved to be inadequate. By storing each list in a different array of maximum size, storage may be wasted. By maintaining the lists in a single array a potentially large amount of data movement is needed. This was explicitly observed when we represented several stacks, queues, polynomials, and matrices. All these data objects are examples of ordered lists. Polynomials are ordered by exponent, whereas matrices are ordered by rows and columns. In this chapter we shall present an alternate representation for ordered lists that will reduce the time needed for arbitrary insertion and deletion.

An elegant solution to this problem of data movement in *sequential* representations is achieved by using *linked* representations. Unlike a sequential representation, in which successive items of a list are located a fixed distance apart, in a linked representation these items may be placed anywhere in memory. In other words, in a sequential representation the order of elements is the same as in the ordered list, whereas in a linked representation these two sequences need not be the same. To access elements in the list in the correct order, with each element we store the address or location of the next element in that list. Thus, associated with each data item in a linked representation is a pointer to the next item. This pointer is often referred to as a link. In general, a *node* is a collection of data, *data* 1, $\cdots$, *data n* and links *link* 1, $\cdots$, *link m*. Each item in a node is called a *field*. A field contains either a data item or a link.

Figure 4.1 shows how some of the nodes of the list we considered before may be represented in memory by using pointers. The elements of the list are stored in a one-dimensional array called *data*, but the elements no longer occur in sequential order, BAT before CAT before EAT, and so on. Instead we relax this restriction and allow them to appear anywhere in the array and in any order. To remind us of the real order, a second array, *link*, is added. The values in this array are pointers to elements in the *data* array. Since the list starts at *data*[8] = BAT, let us set a variable $f = 8$. *link*[8] has the value 3, which means it points to *data*[3], which contains CAT. The third element of the list is pointed at by *link*[3], which is EAT. By continuing in this way we can list all the words in the proper order. We recognize that we have come to the end when *link* has a value of zero. Some of the values of *data* and *link* (e.g., *data*[2], *link*[2], *data*[5], *link*[5]) are undefined. We shall ignore this for the moment.

It is customary to draw linked lists as an ordered sequence of nodes with links being represented by arrows, as in Figure 4.2. We shall use the name of the pointer variable that points to the list as the name of the entire list. Thus, the list of Figure 4.2 is the list *f*. Notice that we do not explicitly put in the values of the pointers but simply draw arrows to indicate they are there. The arrows reinforce in our own mind the facts that (1) the nodes do not actually reside in sequential locations and (2) the locations of nodes may change on different runs. Therefore, when we write a program that works with lists, we do not look for a specific address except when we test for zero.

	data	link
1	HAT	15
2		
3	CAT	4
4	EAT	9
5		
6		
7	WAT	0
8	BAT	3
9	FAT	1
10		
11	VAT	7
	.	.
	.	.
	.	.

Figure 4.1: Nonsequential list representation

Figure 4.2: Usual way to draw a linked list

Let us now see why it is easier to make arbitrary insertions and deletions using a linked list rather than a sequential list. To insert the data item GAT between FAT and HAT, the following steps are adequate:

(1)   Get a node that is currently unused; let its address be x.

(2)   Set the *data* field of this node to GAT.

(3)   Set the *link* field to x to point to the node after FAT, which contains HAT.

(4)   Set the *link* field of the node containing FAT to x.

Figure 4.3(a) shows how the arrays *data* and *link* will be changed after we insert GAT. Figure 4.3(b) shows how we can draw the insertion using our arrow notation. The new arrows are dashed. The important thing to notice is that when we insert GAT, we do not have to move any elements that are already in the list. We have overcome the need to move data at the expense of the storage needed for the second field, *link*, but we will see that this penalty is not too severe.

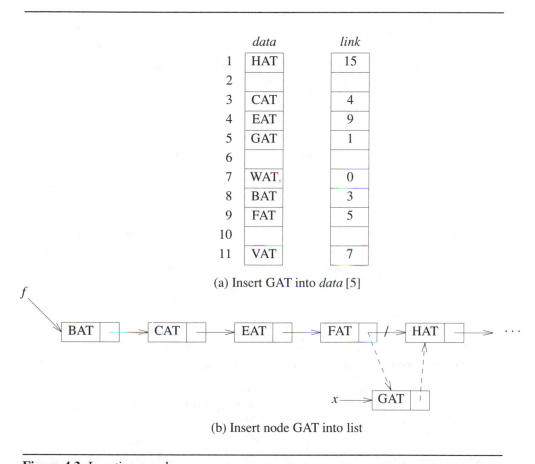

(a) Insert GAT into *data* [5]

(b) Insert node GAT into list

Figure 4.3: Inserting a node

Now suppose we want to delete GAT from the list. All we need to do is find the element that immediately precedes GAT, which is FAT, and set *link*[9] to the position of HAT which is 1. Again, there is no need to move the data around. Even though the *link* field of GAT still contains a pointer to HAT, GAT is no longer in the list (see Figure 4.4).

From our brief discussion of linked lists, we see that the following capabilities are needed to make linked representations possible:

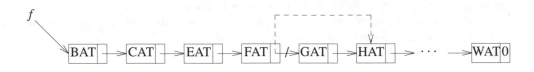

Figure 4.4: Delete GAT from list

(1)   a mechanism to define the structure of a node (i.e., its fields)

(2)   a means to create nodes as needed

(3)   a way to free nodes that are no longer in use

These capabilities are provided in the programming language Pascal. To define a node structure, we need to know the **type** of each of its fields. The *data* field in the preceding example is simply an array of characters, and the *link* field is a pointer to another node. In Pascal, pointer types are defined as

type *PointerType* = ↑*NodeType*;

where *NodeType* refers to the type of node that the pointer may point to. The symbol ↑ denotes the indirection operator ˆ. When keying in a Pascal program, you must use the ˆ key wherever the symbol ↑ appears in this text. In texts, it is customary to use ↑ rather than ˆ to denote a pointer.

If the type of the node in our earlier example is denoted by *ThreeLetterNode*, then *ptr* gives the type of the *link* field of the nodes:

type *ptr* = ↑*ThreeLetterNode*;

The data type *ThreeLetterNode* may itself be defined as a record, as

type *ThreeLetterNode* = **record**
data : **array**[1..3] **of char**;
link : *ptr*;
end;

Note that the variable *f* in the *ThreeLetterNode* example is also a pointer, and its type is to be declared as

var *f* : *ptr*;

The fields of the node pointed to by *f* may be referenced in the following way:

f↑. *data*, *f*↑. *link*

and the components of the *data* field are referenced as

$$f{\uparrow}.data\,[1],\ f{\uparrow}.data\,[2],\ f{\uparrow}.data\,[3]$$

This is shown diagrammatically in Figure 4.5.

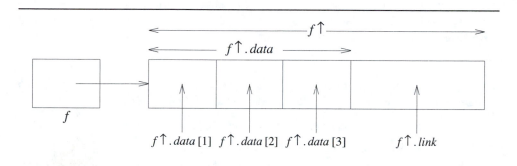

Figure 4.5: Referencing the fields of a node

Example 4.1: If a linked list is to consist of nodes that have a *data* field of type integer and a *link* field, the following type definition can be used:

> **type** *pointer* = ↑*ListNode*;
>   *ListNode* = **record**
>   *data* : **integer**;
>   *link* : *pointer*;
>   **end**;

The type definition

> **type** *ptra* = ↑*nodea*;
>   *ptrb* = ↑*nodeb*;
>   *nodea* = **record**
>   *data* 1 : **integer**;
>   *data* 2 : **char**;
>   *data* 3 : **real**;
>   *linka* : *ptra*;
>   *linkb* : *ptrb*;
>   **end**;
>   *nodeb* = **record**
>   *data* : **integer**;
>   *link* : *ptrb*;
>   **end**;

defines the type *nodea* to consist of three data fields and two link fields, whereas nodes of type *nodeb* will consist of one data field and one link field. Note that the *linkb* field of nodes of type *nodea* must point to nodes of type *nodeb*. □

Nodes of a predefined type may be created using the procedure *new*. If f is of type *ptr* then following the call *new* (f),$f\uparrow$ denotes the node (or variable) of type *ThreeLetter-Node* that is created. Similarly, if x, y, and z are, respectively, of type *pointer, ptra,* and *ptrb* (Example 4.1), then following the sequence of calls

$$new(x); \ new(y); \ new(z);$$

$x\uparrow$, $y\uparrow$, and $z\uparrow$ will, respectively, denote the nodes of type *ListNode, nodea,* and *nodeb* that are created. These nodes may be disposed in the following way:

$$dispose(f); \ dispose(x); \ dispose(y); \ dispose(z);$$

Note that some implementations of Pascal do not provide a *dispose* function.

Pascal also provides a special constant **nil**, which may be assigned to any pointer variable, regardless of type. This constant is generally used to denote a pointer field that points to no node (e.g., the *link* field in the last node of Figure 4.3(b)) or an empty list (as in $f =$ **nil**).

Arithmetic on pointer variables is not permitted. However, two pointer variables of the same type may be compared to see if both point to the same node. Thus, if x and y are pointer variables of the same type, then the expressions $x = y$, $x <> y$, $x =$ **nil**, and $x <>$ **nil** are valid, whereas the expressions $x + 1$ and $y * 2$ are invalid.

The effect of the assignments $x := y$ and $x\uparrow := y\uparrow$ on the initial configuration of Figure 4.6(a) is given in Figure 4.6(b) and (c). Note also that pointer values may neither be input nor output. In many applications, these restrictions on the use of pointers create no difficulties. In fact, in most applications, it does not even make sense to perform arithmetic on pointers. However, there are applications where we will want to perform arithmetic and/or input/output on pointers. In Sections 4.8 and 4.10, we shall see applications where arithmetic on pointers is required. Applications requiring input/output of pointer values will be seen in later chapters. When arithmetic and/or input/output on pointers is to be performed, we can implement our own pointer type by using integers (see Section 4.8).

Example 4.2: Procedure *create2* (Program 4.1) creates a linked list with two nodes of type *ListNode* (Example 4.1). The *data* field of the first node is set to 10 and that of the second to 20. *first* is a pointer to the first node. The resulting list structure is shown in Figure 4.7. □

Example 4.3: Let *first* be a pointer to a linked list, as in Example 4.2. *first* = **nil** if the list is empty (i.e., there are no nodes on the list). Let x be a pointer to some arbitrary node in the list. Program 4.2 inserts a node with *data* field 50 following the node pointed to by x. The resulting list structures for the two cases *first* = **nil** and *first* ≠ **nil** are shown in Figure 4.8. □

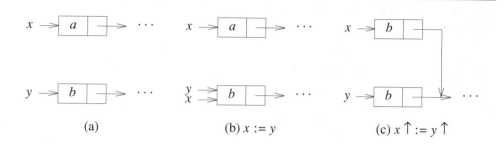

(a)   (b) $x := y$ (c) $x \uparrow := y \uparrow$

Figure 4.6: Effect of pointer assignments

```
procedure create 2(var first : pointer);
var second : pointer;
begin
  new (first);
  new (second);
  first ↑. link := second;  {link first node to second}
  second ↑. link := nil;  {last node}
  first ↑. data := 10;  {set data of first node}
  second ↑. data := 20;  {set data of second node}
end;  {of create2}
```

Program 4.1: Creating a two-node list

Figure 4.7: A two-node list

Example 4.4: Let *first* and *x* be as in Example 4.3. Let *y* point to the node (if any) that precedes *x*, and let *y* = **nil** if *x* = *first*. Procedure *delete* (Program 4.3) deletes node *x* from the list. □

```
procedure insert (var first : pointer ; x : pointer );
var t : pointer ;
begin
  new (t); {get a new node}
  t↑.data := 50; {set its data field}
  if first = nil then begin {insert into empty list}
                  first := t;
                  t↑.link := nil;
              end
  else begin {insert after x}
          t↑.link := x↑.link;
          x↑.link := t;
      end;
end; {of insert}
```

Program 4.2: Inserting a node

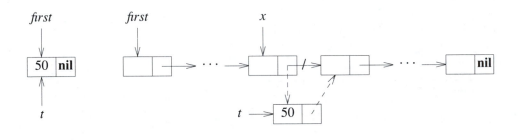

Figure 4.8: Inserting into an empty and nonempty list

EXERCISES

The following exercises assume that each node has two fields: *data* and *link*.

1. Write an algorithm *length* to count the number of nodes in a singly linked list p, where p points to the first node in the list. The last node has *link* field **nil**. What is the time complexity of your algorithm?

2. Let p be a pointer to the first node in a singly linked list and x a pointer to an arbitrary node in this list. Write an algorithm to delete this node from the list. If $x=p$, then p should be reset to point to the new first node in the list. What is the time complexity of your algorithm?

---

procedure *delete* (*x*,*y* : *pointer* ; **var** *first* : *pointer*);
begin
  if *y* = **nil then** *first* := *first*↑. *link*
         else *y* ↑. *link* := *x* ↑. *link*;
  dispose (*x*); {return the node}
end; {of *delete*}

Program 4.3: Deleting a node

---

3. Let p be a pointer to the first node in a singly linked list. Write a procedure to delete every other node beginning with node p (i.e., the first, third, fifth, and so on nodes of the list are deleted). What is the time complexity of your algorithm?

4. Let p be as in the preceding exercise. Write a procedure to reverse the order of nodes in the list. Do not use any additional nodes. Following the reversal, the original list should not exist. What is the time complexity of your algorithm?

5. Let $x = (x_1, x_2, \cdots, x_n)$ and $y = (y_1, y_2, \cdots, y_m)$ be two linked lists. Write an algorithm to merge the two lists together to obtain the linked list $z = (x_1, y_1, x_2, y_2, \cdots, x_m, y_m, x_{m+1}, \cdots, x_n)$ if $m \leq n$ and $z = (x_1, y_1, x_2, y_2, \cdots, x_n, y_n, y_{n+1}, \cdots, y_m)$ if $m > n$. Following the merge, x and y should not exist as individual lists because each node initially in x or y is now in z. No additional nodes may be used. What is the time complexity of your algorithm?

6. Let $x = (x_1, x_2, \cdots, x_n)$ and $y = (y_1, y_2, \cdots, y_m)$ be two chains. Assume that in each chain, the nodes are in nondecreasing order of their data-field values. Write an algorithm to merge the two lists to obtain a new chain z in which the nodes are also in this order. Following the merge, x and y should not exist as individual lists because each node initially in x or y is now in z. No additional nodes may be used. What is the time complexity of your algorithm?

7. It is possible to traverse a singly linked list in both directions (i.e., left to right and a restricted right-to-left traversal) by reversing the links during the left-to-right traversal. A possible configuration for a list p under this scheme is given in Figure 4.9. The pointer p points to the node currently being examined and l to the node on its left. Note that all nodes to the left of p have their links reversed.

  (a) Write an algorithm to move pointer p, n nodes to the right from any given position (l, p).

  (b) Write an algorithm to move p, n nodes to the left from any given position (l, p).

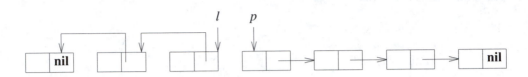

Figure 4.9: Possible configuration for a singly linked list traversed in both directions

4.2   LINKED STACKS AND QUEUES

We have already seen how to represent stacks and queues sequentially. Such a representation proves efficient if we have only one stack or one queue. However, when several stacks and queues coexist, there is no efficient way to represent them sequentially. In this section we present a good solution to this problem using linked lists. Figure 4.10 shows a linked stack and a linked queue.

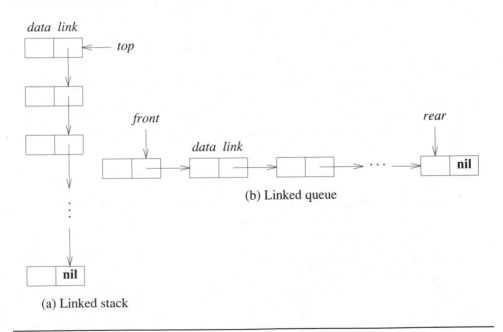

(a) Linked stack

(b) Linked queue

Figure 4.10: Linked stack and queue

Notice that the direction of links for both the stack and the queue is such that it facilitates insertion and deletion of nodes. In the case of Figure 4.10(a), you can easily add a node at the top or delete one from the top. In Figure 4.10(b), you can easily add a node at the rear, and both addition and deletion can be performed at the front, although for a queue we normally do not want to add nodes at the front. If we wish to represent n stacks and m queues simultaneously, the set of algorithms in Programs 4.4 - 4.7 will serve our purpose. The data type *pointer* is defined as:

$$\textbf{type } pointer = \uparrow node ;$$
$$node = \textbf{record}$$
$$data : \textbf{integer};$$
$$link : pointer;$$
$$\textbf{end};$$

```
procedure AddStack (i,y : integer);
{Add y to the ith stack, 1 ≤ i ≤ n.}
var x : pointer;
begin
 new (x); {get a node}
 x↑.data := y; {set its data field}
 x↑.link := top [i ]; {attach to top of ith stack}
 top [i ] := x; {update stack pointer}
end; {of AddStack}
```

Program 4.4: Adding to a linked stack

```
procedure DeleteStack (i : integer; var y : integer);
{Delete top node from stack i and set y to be its data field, 1 ≤ i ≤ n.}
var x : pointer;
begin
 if top [i ] = nil then StackEmpty
             else begin
                   x := top [i ];
                   y := x↑.data; {set data field of top node}
                   top [i ] := x↑.link; {remove top node}
                   dispose (x); {free the node}
                 end;
end; {of DeleteStack}
```

Program 4.5: Deleting from a linked stack

```
procedure AddQueue (i,y : integer);
{Add y to queue i, 1≤i≤m.}
var x : pointer;
begin
  new (x);
  x↑.data := y; x↑.link := nil;
  if front[i ] = nil then front[i ] := x {empty queue}
                  else rear [i ]↑.link := x;
  rear [i ] := x;
end; {of AddQueue}
```

Program 4.6: Adding to a linked queue

```
procedure DeleteQueue (i : integer; var y : integer);
{Delete the first node in queue i and set y to its data field, 1≤i≤m.}
var x : pointer;
begin
  if front[i ] = nil then QueueEmpty
              else begin
                    x := front[i ];
                    front[i ] := x↑.link; {delete first node}
                    y := x↑.data;
                    dispose (x); {free the node}
                  end;
end; {of DeleteQueue}
```

Program 4.7: Deleting from a linked queue

The following global arrays of type *pointer* are used:

$$top[i] = \text{node at top of } i\text{th stack, } 1 \leq i \leq n$$
$$front[i] = \text{node at front of } i\text{th queue, } 1 \leq i \leq m$$
$$rear[i] = \text{last node in } i\text{th queue, } 1 \leq i \leq m$$

The initial conditions are

$$top[i] = \textbf{nil}, 1 \leq i \leq n$$
$$front[i] = \textbf{nil}, 1 \leq i \leq m$$

and the boundary conditions are

$$top[i] = \textbf{nil} \text{ iff the } i\text{th stack is empty}$$
$$front[i] = \textbf{nil} \text{ iff the } i\text{th queue is empty}$$

This solution to the n-stack, m-queue problem is seen to be both computationally and conceptually simple. There is no need to shift stacks or queues around to make space. Computation can proceed as long as there are free nodes. Although additional space is needed for the *link* field, the cost is no more than a factor of 2. Sometimes the *data* field does not use the whole word, making it possible to pack the *link* and *data* fields into the same word. In such a case the storage requirements for sequential and linked representations would be the same. For the use of linked lists to make sense, the overhead incurred by the storage for links must be overridden by (1) the ability to represent complex lists in a simple way and (2) the fact that the computing time for manipulating the lists is less than that for a sequential representation.

EXERCISES

1. Do Exercise 1 of Section 4.1 for the case of circularly linked lists.
2. Do Exercise 2 of Section 4.1 for the case of circularly linked lists.
3. Do Exercise 3 of Section 4.1 for the case of circularly linked lists.
4. Do Exercise 4 of Section 4.1 for the case of circularly linked lists.
5. Do Exercise 5 of Section 4.1 for the case of circularly linked lists.
6. Do Exercise 6 of Section 4.1 for the case of circularly linked lists.
7. Consider the hypothetical data object $X2$. $X2$ is a linear list with the restriction that although additions to the list may be made at either end, deletions can be made from one end only. Design a linked-list representation for $X2$. Write addition and deletion algorithms for $X2$. Specify initial and boundary conditions for your representation.
8. Let p be a pointer to a circularly linked list. Show how this list may be used as a queue (i.e., write algorithms to add and delete elements). Specify the value for p when the queue is empty.

4.3 POLYNOMIALS

4.3.1 Polynomial Representation

Let us tackle a reasonable-size problem using linked lists. This problem, the manipulation of symbolic polynomials, has become a classic example of the use of list process. As in Chapter 2, we wish to be able to represent any number of different polynomials as long as their combined size does not exceed our block of memory. In general, we want to represent the polynomial $A(x) = a_m x^{e_m} + \cdots + a_1 x^{e_1}$, where the a_i are nonzero coefficients and the exponents e_i are nonnegative integers such that $e_m > e_{m-1} > \cdots > e_2 > e_1 \geq 0$. Each term will be represented by a node. A node will be of fixed size and have fields to represent the coefficient and exponent of a term plus a pointer to the next term.

Assuming that the coefficients are integers, the required type declarations are

$$\textbf{type } PolyPointer = \uparrow PolyNode;$$
$$PolyNode = \textbf{record}$$
$$coef : \textbf{integer}; \{\text{coefficient}\}$$
$$exp : \textbf{integer}; \{\text{exponent}\}$$
$$link : PolyPointer;$$
$$\textbf{end};$$

Polynodes will be drawn as

coef	exp	link

For instance, the polynomials $a = 3x^{14} + 2x^8 + 1$ and $b = 8x^{14} - 3x^{10} + 10x^6$ would be stored as in Figure 4.11.

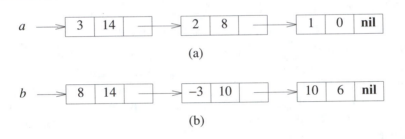

(a)

(b)

Figure 4.11: Polynomial representation

4.3.2   Adding Polynomials

To add two polynomials, we examine their terms starting at the nodes pointed to by a and b. Two pointers p and q are used to move along the terms of a and b. If the exponents of two terms are equal, then the coefficients are added and a new term created for the result. If the exponent of the current term in a is less than the exponent of the current term in b, then a copy of the term in b is created and attached to c. The pointer q is advanced to the next term. Similar action is taken on a if $p\uparrow.exp > q\uparrow.exp$. Figure 4.12 illustrates this addition process on the polynomials a and b of the preceding example.

Each time a new node is generated, its $coef$ and exp fields are set and it is appended to the end of the list c. To avoid having to search for the last node in c each time a new node is added, we keep a pointer d, which points to the current last node in c. The complete addition algorithm is specified by the procedure $padd$ (Program 4.8), which

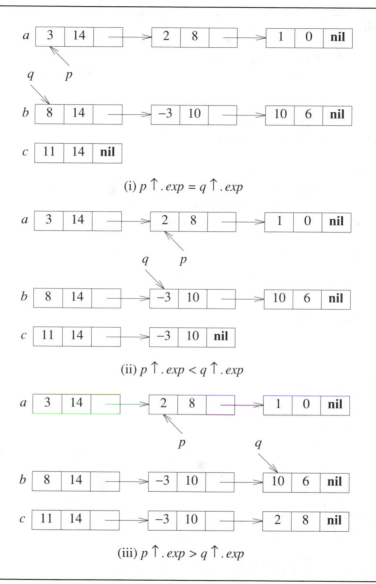

Figure 4.12: Generating the first three terms of $c = a + b$

makes use of a procedure *attach* (Program 4.9) to create a new node and append it to the end of c. To make things work out neatly, c is initially given a single node with no values, which is deleted at the end of the algorithm. Although this is somewhat inelegant, it avoids more computation. As long as its purpose is clearly documented, such a tactic is permissible.

```
 1 procedure padd (a,b : PolyPointer; var c : PolyPointer);
 2 {Polynomials a and b represented as singly linked lists
 3  are summed to form the new list named c.}
 4 var p,q,d : PolyPointer ; x : integer;
 5 begin
 6   p := a ; q := b; {p,q point to next term of a and b}
 7   new (c); d := c; {initial node for c, returned later}
 8   while (p <> nil) and (q <> nil) do
 9     case compare (p ↑ .^exp, q↑. exp) of
10       '=':begin
11             x := p↑. coef + q↑. coef;
12             if x <> 0 then attach (x,p↑. exp,d);
13             p := p↑. link ; q :=q↑. link; {advance to next term}
14           end;
15       '<': begin
16             attach (q ↑. coef, q↑. exp, d);
17             q := q↑. link; {next term of b}
18           end;
19       '>': begin
20             attach (p ↑. coef, p↑. exp, d);
21             p := p↑. link; {next term of a}
22           end;
23     end; {of case and while}
24   while p <> nil do {copy rest of a}
25   begin
26     attach (p ↑. coef, p↑. exp, d);
27     p := p↑. link;
28   end;
29   while q <> nil do {copy rest of b}
30   begin
31     attach (q ↑. coef, q↑. exp, d);
32     q := q↑. link;
33   end;
34   d↑. link := nil; {last node}
35   {delete extra initial node}
36   p := c ; c := c↑. link ; dispose (p);
37 end; {of padd}
```

Program 4.8: Adding two polynomials

---

procedure *attach*(*c*, *e* : **integer**; **var** *d* : *PolyPointer*);
{Create a new node with *coef=c* and *exp=e* and attach it to the
node pointed at by *d*. *d* is updated to point to this new node.}
var *x* : *PolyPointer*;
begin
  new (*x*);
  with *x*↑ **do begin** *coef* := *c*; *exp* := *e*; **end**;
  d↑. *link* := *x*;
  d := *x*; {*d* points to new last node}
end; {of *attach*}

Program 4.9: Attaching a node to the end of a list

This is our first complete example of the use of list processing, so it should be carefully studied. The basic algorithm is straightforward, using a merging process that streams along the two polynomials, either copying terms or adding them to the result. Thus, the main **while** loop of lines 8-23 has three cases depending upon whether the exponents of the terms are =, <, or >. Notice that there are five places where a new term is created, justifying our use of the procedure *attach*.

Analysis of *padd*: The following operations contribute to the computing time:

(1)   coefficient additions

(2)   exponent comparisons

(3)   additions/deletions to available space

(4)   creation of new nodes for *c*

Let us assume that each of these four operations, if done once, takes a single unit of time. The total time taken by algorithm *padd* is then determined by the number of times these operations are performed. This number clearly depends on how many terms are present in the polynomials *a* and *b*. Assume that *a* and *b* have *m* and *n* terms, respectively:

$$a(x) = a_m x^{e_m} + \cdots + a_1 x^{e_1}, \; b(x) = b_n x^{f_n} + \cdots + b_1 x^{f_1}$$

where

$$a_i, b_i \neq 0 \; \text{and} \; e_m > \cdots > e_1 \geq 0, f_n > \ldots > f_1 \geq 0$$

Then clearly the number of coefficient additions can vary as

$$0 \leq \text{coefficient additions} \leq \min\{m, n\}$$

The lower bound is achieved when none of the exponents are equal; the upper bound is achieved when the exponents of one polynomial are a subset of the exponents of the other polynomial.

As for exponent comparisons, one comparison is made on each iteration of the first **while** loop. On each iteration either p or q or both move to the next term in their respective polynomials. Since the total number of terms is $m + n$, the number of iterations and hence the number of exponent comparisons is bounded by $m + n$. You can easily construct a case when $m + n - 1$ comparisons will be necessary — e.g., $m = n$ and

$$e_n > f_n > e_{n-1} > f_{n-1} > \cdots > e_2 > f_2 > e_1 > f_1$$

The maximum number of terms in c is $m + n$, so no more than $m + n$ new nodes are created (this excludes the additional node that is attached to the front of c and later returned). In summary, the maximum number of executions of any of the statements in $padd$ is bounded above by $m + n$. Therefore, the computing time is $O(m + n)$. If the algorithm is implemented and run on a computer, the time taken will be $c_1 m + c_2 n + c_3$, where c_1, c_2, and c_3 are constants. Since any algorithm that adds two polynomials must look at each nonzero term at least once, algorithm $padd$ is optimal to within a constant factor. $\square$

4.3.3 Erasing Polynomials

The use of linked lists is well suited to polynomial operations. We can easily imagine writing a collection of procedures for input, output, addition, subtraction, and multiplication of polynomials using linked lists as the means of representation. A hypothetical user wishing to read in polynomials $a(x)$, $b(x)$, and $c(x)$ and then compute $d(x) = a(x) * b(x) + c(x)$ would write in the main program

$read(a);$
$read(b);$
$read(c);$
$t := pmul(a,b);$
$d: = padd(t,c);$
$print(d);$

Now our user may wish to continue computing more polynomials. At this point it would be useful to reclaim the nodes that are being used to represent $t(x)$. This polynomial was created only as a partial result toward the answer $d(x)$. The returned nodes of $t(x)$ may be used to hold other polynomials. Procedure $erase$ (Program 4.10) frees up the nodes in t one by one.

```
procedure erase(var t : pointer);
{Free all the nodes in the chain t.}
var x : PolyPointer;
begin
   while t <> nil do
   begin
      x := t↑.link;
      dispose (t);
      t := x;
   end;
end; {of erase}
```

Program 4.10: Erasing a polynomial

4.3.4 Circular List Representation of Polynomials

It is possible to free all the nodes in t more efficiently by modifying the list structure in such a way that the *link* field of the last node points to the first node in t (see Figure 4.13). A list in which the last node points back to the first is called a *circular list*. A singly linked list in which the last node has a **nil** link is called a *chain*.

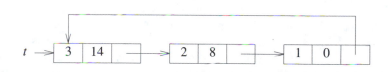

Figure 4.13: Circular list representation of $t = 3x^{14} + 2x^8 + 1$

The reason we dispose of nodes that are no longer in use is so that these nodes may be reused later. This objective, together with an efficient erase algorithm for circular lists, may be met by maintaining our own list (as a chain) of nodes that have been "disposed." When a new node is needed, we may examine this list. If this list is not empty, then one of the nodes on it may be made available for use. Only when this list is empty do we need to use procedure *new* to create a new node.

Let *av* be a variable of type *PolyPointer* that points to the first node in our list of nodes that have been "disposed." This list henceforth will be called the *available-space list* or *av list*. Initially, $av = $ **nil**. Instead of using the procedures *new* and *dispose*, we shall now use the procedures *GetNode* (Program 4.11) and *retnode* (Program 4.12).

---

procedure *GetNode*(**var** x : *PolyPointer*);
{Provide a node for use.}
begin
  if av = **nil**
  then *new* (x)
  else begin $x := av$; $av := av \uparrow. link$; **end**;
end; {of *GetNode*}

Program 4.11: Getting a node

---

procedure *retnode* $(x$: *PolyPointer*);
{Free the node pointed to by x.}
begin
  $x \uparrow. link := av$;
  $av := x$;
end; {of *retnode*}

Program 4.12: Returning a node

As illustrated by procedure *cerase* (Program 4.13), a circular list may now be erased in a fixed amount of time independent of the number of nodes on the list. Figure 4.14 is a schematic showing the link changes involved in erasing a circular list.

A direct changeover to the structure of Figure 4.13, however, causes some problems during addition and other operations, as the zero polynomial has to be handled as a special case. To avoid such special cases you may introduce a head node into each polynomial (i.e., each polynomial, zero or nonzero, will contain one additional node). The *exp* and *coef* fields of this node will not be relevant. Thus, the zero polynomial will have the representation of Figure 4.15(a), and $a = 3x^{14} + 2x^8 + 1$ will have the representation of Figure 4.15(b).

For this circular list with head node representation, the test for $t =$ **nil** may be removed from *cerase*. The only changes to be made to algorithm *padd* (Program 4.8) are

(1)	Change line 6 to	$p := a \uparrow. link$; $q := b \uparrow. link$;
(2)	Change line 8 to	**while** $(p <> a)$ **and** $(q <> b)$ **do**
(3)	Change line 24 to	**while** $p <> a$ **do**

```
procedure cerase (var t : PolyPointer);
{Erase the circular list t.}
var second : PolyPointer;
begin
  if t <> nil
  then begin
          second := t↑.link; {second node}
          t↑.link := av; {first node linked to av}
          av := second; {second node of t becomes front of av list}
          t := nil;
       end;
end; {of cerase}
```

Program 4.13: Erasing a circular list

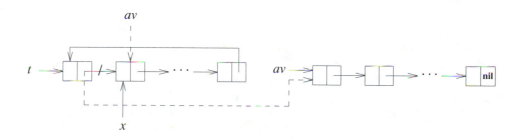

Figure 4.14: Dashes indicate changes involved in erasing a circular list

(4) Change line 29 to   **while** $q <> b$ **do**
(5) Delete lines 34 and 35
(6) Change line 36 to $d↑.link := c$:

Thus, the algorithm stays essentially the same. Zero polynomials are now handled in the same way as nonzero polynomials.

A further simplification in the addition algorithm is possible if the *exp* field of the head node is set to -1. Now when all nodes of *a* have been examined, $p = a$ and $exp(p) = -1$. Since $-1 \leq exp(q)$, the remaining terms of *b* can be copied by further executions of the case statement. The same is true if all nodes of *b* are examined before those of *a*. This implies that there is no need for additional code to copy the remaining

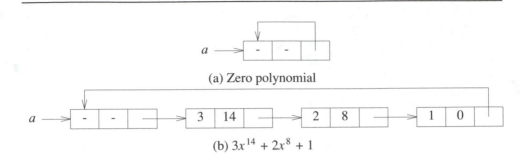

Figure 4.15: Example polynomials

terms as in *padd*. The final algorithm (*cpadd*) takes the simple form given in Program 4.14.

4.3.5 Summary

Let us review what we have done so far. We have introduced the notions of a singly linked list, a chain, and a singly linked circular list. Each node on one of these lists consists of exactly one link field and some number of other fields. In all of our examples, all nodes on any given list had the same fields. The concept of a singly linked list does not require this property and in subsequent sections we shall see lists that violate it.

In dealing with polynomials, we found it convenient to use circular lists. This required us to introduce the notion of an available space list. Such a list consists of all nodes that have been used at least once and are currently not in use. By using the available-space list and the procedures *GetNode*, *retnode*, and *cerase*, it became possible to erase circular lists in constant time and to reuse all nodes currently not in use. As we continue, we shall see more problems that call for variations in node structure and list representation because of the operations we wish to perform.

EXERCISES

1. Write an algorithm *pread*(x) to read in n pairs of coefficients and exponents, (c_i, e_i), $1 \leq i \leq n$, of a univariate polynomial, x, and to convert the polynomial into the circularly linked list representation described in this section. Assume that $e_i > e_{i+1}$, $1 \leq i < n$, and that $c_i \neq 0$, $1 \leq i \leq n$. Your algorithm should leave x pointing to the head node. Show that this operation can be performed in time O(n).

```
procedure cpadd (a,b : PolyPointer; var c : PolyPointer);
{Polynomials a and b are represented as circular lists with head
nodes so that a↑.exp = b↑.exp = -1. Their sum, c, is returned
as a circular list.}
var p,q,d : PolyPointer ; x : integer; done : boolean;
begin
    p := a↑.link ; q := b↑.link;
    GetNode (c); c↑.exp := -1; {head node for c}
    d := c; {last node in c}; done := false
    repeat
        case compare (p↑.exp, q↑.exp) of
        '=': if p = a then done := true
            else begin
                    x := p↑.coef + q↑.coef;
                    if x <> 0 then attach (x, p↑.exp, d);
                    p := p↑.link ; q := q↑.link;
                end;
        '<': begin
                attach (q↑.coef, q↑.exp, d);
                q := q↑.link;
            end;
        '>': begin
                attach (p↑.coef, p↑.exp, d);
                p := p↑.link;
            end;
        end; {of case}
    until done;
    d↑.link := c; {link last node to first}
end; {of cpadd}
```

Program 4.14: Adding circularly represented polynomials

2. Let a and b be pointers to the head nodes of two polynomials represented as circular lists. Write an algorithm to compute the product polynomial $c = a*b$. Your algorithm should leave a and b unaltered and create c as a new list. Show that if n and m are the number of terms in a and b, respectively, then this multiplication can be carried out in time $O(nm^2)$ or $O(mn^2)$. If a and b are dense, show that the multiplication takes $O(mn)$.

3. Let a be a pointer to the head node of a univariate polynomial represented as a circular list. Write an algorithm, $peval(a,x)$, to evaluate the polynomial a at the point x, where x is some real number.

4. [***Programming Project***] Design a linked allocation system to represent and manipulate univariate polynomials with integer coefficients (use circular linked lists with head nodes). Each term of the polynomial will be represented as a node. Thus, a node in this system will have three fields as below:

Exponent	Link
Coefficient	

To erase polynomials efficiently, we need to use an available-space list and associated procedures as described in Section 4.3. The external (i.e., for input or output) representation of a univariate polynomial will be assumed to be a sequence of integers of the form: n, e_1, c_1, e_2, c_2, e_3, c_3 ..., e_n, c_n, where e_i represents an exponent and c_i a coefficient; n gives the number of terms in the polynomial. The exponents are in decreasing order — i.e., $e_1 > e_2 > \cdots > e_n$.

Write and test the following procedures:

(a) *pread(x)* Read in an input polynomial and convert it to its circular list representation using a head node. Set x to point to the head node of this polynomial.

(b) *pwrite(x)* Convert the polynomial x from its linked list representation to its external representation and output it.

(c) *padd(x,y,z)* Compute $z = x + y$.

(d) *psub(x,y,z)* Compute $z = x - y$.

(e) *pmul(x,y,z)* Compute $z = x * y$.

(f) *peval(x,a,v)* a is a real constant and the polynomial x is evaluated at the point a. Set v to this value.

Note: Procedures (c)-(f) should leave the input polynomials unaltered after completion of their respective tasks.

(g) *perase(x)* Return the circular list x to the available space list.

4.4   ADDITIONAL OPERATIONS

4.4.1   Operations for Chains

It is often necessary and desirable to build a variety of routines for manipulating singly linked lists. Some that we have already seen are *GetNode* (Program 4.11) and *retnode* (Program 4.12) which get and return nodes to *av*. Another useful operation is one that inverts a chain (Program 4.15). This routine is especially interesting because it can be done ''in place'' if we make use of three pointers.

---

procedure *invert*(**var** *x* : *pointer*);
{A chain pointed at by *x* is inverted so that if $x = (a_1, \cdots, a_n)$, then after execution $x = (a_n, \cdots, a_1)$.}
var *p,q,r* : *pointer*;
begin
   p := *x*; *q* := **nil**; {*q* trails *p*}
   while *p* <> **nil do**
   begin
      r := *q*; *q* := *p*; {*r* trails *q*}
      p := *p*↑. *link*; {*p* moves to next node}
      q↑. *link* := *r*; {link *q* to preceding node}
   end;
   x := *q*;
end; {of *invert*}

Program 4.15: Inverting a list

     You should try out this algorithm on at least three examples, the empty list and lists of length 1 and 2, to convince yourself that you understand the mechanism. For a list of $m \geq 1$ nodes, the **while** loop is executed *m* times, so the computing time is linear or $O(m)$.
     Another useful procedure is one that concatenates two chains, *x* and *y* (Program 4.16). The complexity of this algorithm is also linear in the length of the list *x*.

4.4.2 Operations for Circular Lists

Now let us take another look at circular lists like the one in Figure 4.16. Suppose we want to insert a new node at the front of this list. We have to change the *link* field of the node containing x_3, which requires that we move down the entire length of *a* until we find the last node. It is more convenient if the name of a circular list points to the last node rather than to the first (Figure 4.17).
     Now we can write procedures that insert a node at the front (Program 4.17) or at the rear of a circular list in a fixed amount of time. To insert *x* at the rear, one needs to add only the statement *a* := *x* to the **else** clause of *InsertFront*.
     As a last example of a simple procedure for circular lists, we write a function (Program 4.18) that determines the length of a such a list.

---

procedure *concatenate* $(x, y : pointer;$ **var** $z : pointer)$;
$\{x = (a_1, \cdots, a_m)$ and $y = (b_1, \cdots, b_m)$, m, $n \geq 0$, produces the new chain $z = (a_1, \cdots, a_m, b_1, \cdots, b_n).\}$
var $p : pointer$;
begin
  if $x = $ **nil then** $z := y$
  else begin
      $z := x$;
      if $y <> $ **nil then begin** {find last node in x}
            $p := x$;
            while $p\uparrow.link <> $ **nil do** $p := p\uparrow.link$;
            $p\uparrow.link := y$; {link last of x to first of y}
        end;
    end;
end; {of *concatenate*}

Program 4.16: Concatenating two chains

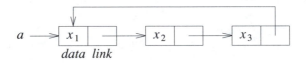

data link

Figure 4.16: Example of a circular list

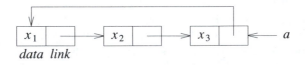

data link

Figure 4.17: Pointing to the last node of a circular list

---

procedure *InsertFront*(**var** *a* : *pointer* ; *x* : *pointer*);
{Insert the node pointed at by *x* at the "front" of the circular list *a*, where *a* points to the last node in the list.}
begin
  if *a* = **nil then begin** {empty list}
          a := *x*; *x*↑. *link* := *x*;
      end
  else begin
      x↑. *link* := *a*↑. *link*; *a*↑. *link* := *x*;
    end;
end; {of *InsertFront*}

Program 4.17: Inserting at the front

---

function *length* (*a* : *pointer*): **integer**;
{Find the length of the circular list *a*.}
var *x* : *pointer*;
begin
  length := 0;
  if *a* <> **nil then begin**
          x := *a*;
        repeat
          length := *length* + 1;
         x := *x*↑. *link*;
        until *x* = *a*;
      end;
end; {of *length*}

Program 4.18: Determining the length of a circular list

4.5 EQUIVALENCE RELATIONS

Let us put together some of these ideas on linked and sequential representations to solve a problem that arises in the design and manufacture of very large-scale integrated (VLSI) circuits. One of the steps in the manufacture of a VLSI circuit involves exposing a silicon wafer using a series of masks. Each mask consists of several polygons. Polygons that overlap are electrically equivalent. Electrical equivalence specifies a relationship among mask polygons. This relation has several properties that it shares with other relations, such as the conventional mathematical equivalence. Suppose we denote an arbitrary relation by the symbol ≡, and suppose that

(1)   For any polygon x, $x \equiv x$ (e.g., x is electrically equivalent to itself). Thus, $\equiv$ is *reflexive*.

(2)   For any two polygons x and y, if $x \equiv y$, then $y \equiv x$. Thus, the relation $\equiv$ is *symmetric*.

(3)   For any three polygons x, y, and z, if $x \equiv y$ and $y \equiv z$, then $x \equiv z$ (e.g., if x and y are electrically equivalent and y and z are also, then so also are x and z). The relation $\equiv$ is *transitive*.

Definition: A relation $\equiv$ over a set S, is said to be an *equivalence relation* over S iff it is symmetric, reflexive, and transitive over S. $\square$

Equivalence relations are numerous. For example, the "equal to" ($=$) relationship is an equivalence relation, since (1) $x = x$, (2) $x = y$ implies $y = x$, and (3) $x = y$ and $y = z$ implies $x = z$. One effect of an equivalence relation is to partition the set S into equivalence classes such that two members x and y of S are in the same equivalence class iff $x \equiv y$. For example, if we have 12 polygons numbered 1 through 12 and the following overlap pairs are defined:

$$1 \equiv 5, \ 4 \equiv 2, \ 7 \equiv 11, \ 9 \equiv 10, \ 8 \equiv 5, \ 7 \equiv 9, \ 4 \equiv 6, \ 3 \equiv 12, \ \text{and } 12 \equiv 1$$

then, as a result of the reflexivity, symmetry, and transitivity of the relation $\equiv$, we get the following partitioning of the 12 polygons into three equivalence classes:

$$\{1, 3, 5, 8, 12\}; \ \{2, 4, 6\}; \ \{7, 9, 10, 11\}$$

These equivalence classes are important, as each such class defines a *signal net*. The signal nets can be used to verify the correctness of the masks.

The algorithm to determine equivalence classes works in essentially two phases. In the first phase the equivalence pairs (i, j) are read in and stored. In phase two we begin at 1 and find all pairs of the form $(1, j)$. The values 1 and j are in the same class. By transitivity, all pairs of the form (j, k) imply k is in the same class as 1. We continue in this way until the entire equivalence class containing 1 has been found, marked, and printed. Then we continue.

The first design for this algorithm might be as in Program 4.19. Let m and n represent the number of related pairs and the number of objects, respectively. Now we need to determine which data structure should be used to hold these pairs. To do so, we examine the operations that are required. The pair (i, j) is two random integers in the range 1 to n. Easy random access would dictate an array, say *pairs*$[1..n, 1..m]$. The ith row would contain the elements j, which are paired directly to i in the input. However, this would potentially be very wasteful of space since very few of the array elements would be used. It might also require considerable time to insert a new pair, (i, k), into row i, since we would have to scan the row for the next free location or use more storage.

These considerations lead us to consider a linked list to represent each row. Each node on the list requires only a *data* and a *link* field. However, we still need random access to the ith row, so a one-dimensional array, *seq*$[1..n]$, can be used as the head nodes

```
procedure equivalence;
begin
    initialize;
    while more pairs do
    begin
        read the next pair (i, j);
        process this pair;
    end;
    initialize for output;
    repeat
        output a new equivalence class;
    until done;
end; {of equivalence}
```

Program 4.19: First pass at equivalence algorithm

of the n lists. Looking at the second phase of the algorithm we need a mechanism that tells us whether or not object i has yet to be printed. A boolean array, $out\,[1\,..\,n\,]$, can be used for this. The next refinement of the algorithm (Program 4.20) assumes that n is a global constant.

```
procedure equivalence;
declare seq, out, and other local variables;
begin
    initialize seq to nil and out to true;
    while more pairs do {input pairs}
    begin
        read the next pair (i, j);
        put j on the seq [i] list;
        put i on the seq [j] list;
    end;
    for i := 1 to n do {output equivalence classes}
        if out [i] then begin
                     out [i] := false;
                     output this equivalence class;
                 end;
end; {of equivalence}
```

Program 4.20: A more detailed version of equivalence algorithm

Let us simulate the algorithm, as we have it so far, on the previous data set. After the **while** loop is completed the lists will look as they do in Figure 4.18. For each relation $i \equiv j$, two nodes are used. $seq[i]$ points to a list of nodes that contains every number directly equivalenced to i by an input relation.

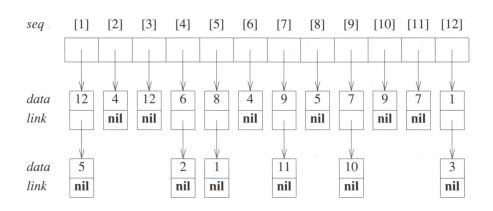

Figure 4.18: Lists after pairs have been input

In phase two we can scan the seq array and start with the first, i, $1 \le i \le n$ such that $out[i] = $ **true**. Each element in the list $seq[i]$ is printed. To process the remaining lists which, by transitivity, belong in the same class as i, a stack of their nodes is created. This is accomplished by changing the $link$ fields so they point in the reverse direction. The complete procedure is given in Program 4.21.

```
procedure equivalence;
{Input the equivalence pairs and output the equivalence classes.}
type pointer = ↑node;
     node = record
                data : 1..n;
                link : pointer;
            end;
var  seq : array [1..n] of pointer;
     out : array [1..n] of boolean;
     i,j : integer;
     x,y,top : pointer;
     done : boolean;
begin
   {initialize seq and out}
   for i := 1 to n do begin seq[i] := nil; out[i] := true; end;
   {Phase 1: input equivalence pairs}
   while not eof (input) do
```

```
begin
    readln(i, j);
    new (x); {add j to list seq [i ]}
    x↑.data := j; x↑.link := seq [i ]; seq [i ] :=x;
    new (x); {add i to list seq [j ]}
    x↑.data :=i; x↑.link := seq [j ]; seq [j ]:=x;
end;
{Phase 2: output equivalence classes}
for i := 1 to n do
if out [i ] {needs to be output}
then begin
        writeln('A new class:', i);
        out [i ] := false;
        x := seq [i ]; top := nil; {init stack} done := false;
        repeat {find rest of class}
            while x <> nil do {process the list}
            begin
                j := x↑.data;
                if out [j ]
                then begin
                        writeln(j); out [j ] := false;
                        y := x↑.link ; x↑.link := top;
                        top := x ; x := y;
                    end
                else x := x↑.link;
            end; {of while x <> nil}
            if top = nil then done := true
            else begin
                    x := seq [top↑.data ];
                    top := top↑.link; {unstack}
                end;
        until done;
    end; {of if}
end; {of equivalence}
```

Program 4.21: Algorithm to find equivalence classes

Analysis of *equivalence*: The initialization of *seq* and *out* takes $O(n)$ time. The processing of each input pair in phase 1 takes a constant amount of time. Hence, the total time for this phase is $O(n + m)$, where m is the number of input pairs. In phase 2 each node is put onto the linked stack at most once. Since there are only $2m$ nodes and the **for** loop is executed n times, the time for this phase is $O(m + n)$. Hence, the overall computing time is $O(m + n)$. Any algorithm that processes equivalence relations must look at all m equivalence pairs and at all n polygons at least once. Thus, no algorithm can have a computing time less than $O(m + n)$. This means that procedure *equivalence* is optimal to within a constant factor. Unfortunately, the space required by the algorithm is also $O(m + n)$. In Chapter 5 we shall see an $O(n)$-space solution to this problem.

4.6   SPARSE MATRICES

4.6.1   Sparse Matrix Representation

In Chapter 2, we saw that when matrices were sparse (i.e., many of the entries were zero), then much space and computing time could be saved if only the nonzero terms were retained explicitly. In the case where these nonzero terms did not form any "nice" pattern such as a triangle or a band, we devised a sequential scheme in which each nonzero term was represented by a node with three fields: row, column, and value. These nodes were organized sequentially. However, as matrix operations such as addition, subtraction, and multiplication are performed, the number of nonzero terms in matrices will vary. Matrices representing partial computations (as in the case of polynomials) will be created and will have to be destroyed later to make space for additional matrices. Thus, sequential schemes for representing sparse matrices suffer from the same inadequacies as similar schemes for polynomials. In this section we study a very general linked-list scheme for sparse-matrix representation. As we have already seen, linked schemes facilitate efficient representation of varying-size structures, and here, too, our scheme overcomes the aforementioned shortcomings of the sequential representation studied in Chapter 2.

In the data representation we use, each column of a sparse matrix is represented by a circularly linked list with a head node. In addition, each row is also a circularly linked list with a head node.

Each node has a field called *head*. This field is used to distinguish between head nodes and nodes representing nonzero matrix elements. Each head node has three additional fields: *down, right*, and *next*. The total number of head nodes is max {number of rows, number of columns}. The head node for row i is also the head node for column i. The *down* field of a head node is used to link into a column list; the *right* field is used to link into a row list. The *next* field links the head nodes together.

Every other node has six fields: *head, row, col, down, right*, and *value* (Figure 4.19). The *down* field is used to link to the next nonzero term in the same column and the *right* field links to the next nonzero term in the same row. Thus, if $a_{ij} \neq 0$, then there is a node with *head* = **false**, *value* = a_{ij}, *row* = i, and *col* = j. This node is linked into the circular linked lists for row i and column j. Hence, the node is simultaneously in two different lists.

As noted earlier, each head node is in three lists: a row list, a column list, and a list of head nodes. The list of head nodes itself has a head node that is identical to the six field nodes used to represent nonzero elements. The *row* and *col* fields of this node are used to store the matrix dimensions.

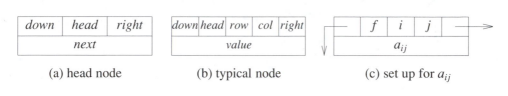

down	head	right
	next	

(a) head node

down	head	row	col	right
	value			

(b) typical node

	f	i	j	
	a_{ij}			

(c) set up for a_{ij}

Figure 4.19: Node structure for sparse matrices

$$\begin{bmatrix} 0 & 0 & 11 & 0 & 0 & 13 & 0 \\ 12 & 0 & 0 & 0 & 0 & 0 & 14 \\ 0 & -4 & 0 & 0 & 0 & -8 & 0 \\ 0 & 0 & 0 & 0 & 0 & 0 & 0 \\ 0 & 0 & 0 & 0 & 0 & 0 & 0 \\ 0 & -9 & 0 & 0 & 0 & 0 & 0 \end{bmatrix}$$

Figure 4.20: 6×7 sparse matrix A

The linked structure obtained for the 6×7 matrix, A, of Figure 4.20 is shown in Figure 4.21. Although Figure 4.21 does not show the values of the *head* fields, these values are readily determined from the node structure shown. For each nonzero term of A, we have one six-field node that is in exactly one column list and one row list. The head nodes are marked H1 to H7. As seen in the figure, the *right* field of the head node list header is used to link into the list of head nodes. Notice that the whole matrix may be referenced through the head node, a, of the list of head nodes.

If we wish to represent an $n \times m$ sparse matrix with r nonzero terms, the number of nodes needed is $\max\{n,m\} + r + 1$. Although each node may require several words of memory, the total storage needed will be less than nm for sufficiently small r.

The required node structure may be defined in Pascal using variant records:

```
type MatrixPointer = ↑MatrixNode;
     MatrixNode = record
                      down : MatrixPointer;
                      right : MatrixPointer;
                  case head : boolean of
                      true: (next : MatrixPointer);
                      false: (value : integer;
                              row : integer;
                              col : integer);
                  end;
```

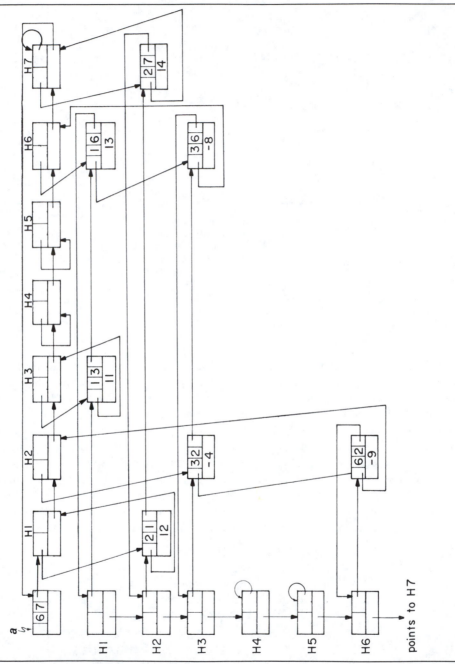

Figure 4.21: Linked representation of the sparse matrix A of Figure 4.20 (the *head* field of a node is not shown)

4.6.2   Sparse Matrix Input

The first operation we shall consider is that of reading in a sparse matrix and obtaining its linked representation. We assume that the first input line consists of n (the number of rows), m (the number of columns), and r (the number of nonzero terms). The line is followed by r lines of input; each of these is a triple of the form (i, j, a_{ij}). These triples consist of the *row*, *col*, and *value* fields of the nonzero terms of the matrix. We also assume that these triples are ordered by rows and within rows by columns.

For example, the input for the 6×7 sparse matrix of Figure 4.19, which has seven nonzero terms, would take the following form: 6,7,7; 1,3,11; 1,6,13; 2,1,12; 2,7,14; 3,2,−4; 3,6,−8; 6,2,−9. We shall not concern ourselves here with the actual format of this input on the input media (tape, disk, terminal, etc.) but shall assume that we have a mechanism to get the next triple (see Exercises for a possible input format). The procedure *mread* (Program 4.22) also makes use of an auxiliary array *hdnode*, which is assumed to be at least as large as the largest-dimensioned matrix to be input. *hdnode* [i] is a pointer to the head node for column i and hence also for row i, permitting us efficient random access to columns while the input matrix is set up. Procedure *mread* proceeds first by setting up all the head nodes and then by setting up each row list, simultaneously building the column lists. The *next* field of head node i is used initially to keep track of the last node in column i. Eventually, in line 39, the head nodes are linked together through this field.

```
 1  procedure mread (var a : MatrixPointer);
 2  {Read in a matrix and set up its linked representation.
 3   An auxiliary global array hdnode is used.}
 4  var i,m,n,p,r,rrow,ccol,val,CurrentRow : integer;
 5       x,last : MatrixPointer;

 6  begin
 7    readln(n,m,r); {matrix dimensions}
 8    if m > n then p := m else p := n;

 9    {set up head node for list of head nodes}
10    new (a); a↑.head := false ; a↑.row := n; a↑.col := m;

11    if p = 0 then a↑.right := a;
12    else begin {at least one row or column}

13    for i := 1 to p do {initialize head nodes}
14    begin
15      new (x); hdnode [i] := x;
16      with x↑ do begin head := true; right := x ; next := x; end;
17    end;
```

18    $CurrentRow := 1; last := hdnode [1];$ {last node in current row}

19   **for** $i := 1$ **to** r **do** {input triples}
20   **begin**
21   **readln**$(rrow, ccol, val);$
22   **if** $rrow > CurrentRow$
23   **then begin** {close current row}
24            $last\uparrow.right := hdnode [CurrentRow];$
25            $CurrentRow := rrow; last := hdnode [rrow];$
26   **end;**
27      $new (x);$ {node for new triple}
28   **with** $x\uparrow$ **do begin** $head := $ **false**$; row := rrow; col := ccol;$
29                $value := val;$ **end;**
30      $last\uparrow.right := x; last := x;$ {link into row list}
31   {link into column list}
32      $hdnode [ccol]\uparrow.next\uparrow.down := x; hdnode [ccol]\uparrow.next := x;$
33   **end;** {of input triples}

34   {close last row}
35    $last\uparrow.right := hdnode [CurrentRow];$

36   **for** $i := 1$ **to** m **do** {close all column lists}
37      $hdnode [i]\uparrow.next\uparrow.down := hdnode [i];$

38   {link the head nodes together}
39   **for** $i := 1$ **to** $p - 1$ **do** $hdnode [i]\uparrow.next := hdnode [i + 1];$
40    $hdnode [p]\uparrow.next := a;$
41    $a\uparrow.right := hdnode [1];$
42   **end;** {of **if** $p = 0$}
43 **end;** {of $mread$}

Program 4.22: Reading in a sparse matrix

Analysis of mread: Since *new* works in a constant amount of time, all the head nodes may be set up in $O(\max\{n,m\})$ time, where n is the number of rows and m the number of columns in the matrix being input. Each nonzero term can be set up in a constant amount of time because of the use of the variable *last* and a random access scheme for the bottommost node in each column list. Hence, the **for** loop of lines 15-28 can be carried out in $O(r)$ time. The rest of the algorithm takes $O(\max\{n,m\})$ time. The total time is therefore $O(\max\{n,m\} + r) = O(n + m + r))$. Note that this time is asymptotically better than the input time of $O(nm)$ for an $n \times m$ matrix using a two-dimensional array but slightly worse than the sequential sparse method of Section 2.3. □

4.6.3   Erasing a Sparse Matrix

All the nodes of a sparse matrix may be returned one at a time using *dispose*. A faster way to return the nodes is to set up an available-space list as was done for polynomials. Assume that *av* points to the front of this list and that this list is linked through the field *right*. Procedure *merase* (Program 4.23) solves our problem in an efficient way.

---

procedure *merase*(**var** *a* : *MatrixPointer*);
{Return all nodes of *a* to the *av* list. This list is a chain linked
 via the *right* field. *av* points to its first node.}
var *x,y* : *MatrixPointer*;
begin
   $x := a\uparrow.right; a\uparrow.right := av; av := a;$ {return *a*}
   while $x <> a$ **do** {erase by rows}
   begin
      $y := x\uparrow.right;$
      $x\uparrow.right := av;$
      $av := y;$
      $x := x\uparrow.next;$ {next row}
   end;
   $a :=$ **nil**;
end; {of *merase*}

Program 4.23: Erasing a sparse matrix

Analysis of *merase*: Since each node is in only one row list, it is sufficient to return all the row lists of the matrix *a*. Each row list is circularly linked through the field *right*. Thus, nodes need not be returned one by one, as a circular list can be erased in a constant amount of time. The computing time for the algorithm is readily seen to be $O(n + m)$. Note that even if the available-space list had been linked through the field *down*, erasing still could have been carried out in $O(n + m)$ time. □

    The subject of manipulating sparse matrix structures is studied further in the exercises. The representation studied here is rather general. For most applications this generality is not needed. A simpler representation resulting in simpler algorithms is discussed in the exercises.

EXERCISES

In Exercises 1 to 5, the sparse matrix representation described in this section is assumed.

1. Let a and b be two sparse matrices. Write an algorithm, $madd\,(a,b,c)$, to create the matrix $c = a + b$. Your algorithm should leave the matrices a and b unchanged and set up c as a new matrix in accordance with this data representation. Show that if a and b are $n \times m$ matrices with r_A and r_B nonzero terms, then this addition can be carried out in $O(n + m + r_A + r_B)$ time.

2. Let a and b be two sparse matrices. Write an algorithm, $mmul\,(a,b,c)$, to set up the structure for $c = a*b$. Show that if a is an $n \times m$ matrix with r_A nonzero terms and if b is an $m \times p$ matrix with r_B nonzero terms, then c can be computed in time $O(pr_A + nr_B)$. Can you think of a way to compute c in $O(\min\{pr_A,\ nr_B\})$?

3. Write an algorithm to write out the terms of a sparse matrix a as triples (i,j,a_{ij}). The terms are to be output by rows and within rows by columns. Show that this operation can be performed in time $O(n + r_A)$ if there are r_A nonzero terms in a and a is an $n \times m$ matrix.

4. Write an algorithm, $mtrp\,(a,b)$, to compute the matrix $b = a^T$, the transpose of the sparse matrix a. What is the computing time of your algorithm?

5. Design an algorithm to copy a sparse matrix. What is the computing time of your algorithm?

6. A simpler and more efficient representation for sparse matrices can be obtained when one is limited to the operations of addition, subtraction, and multiplication. Now, nodes have the fields $down$, $right$, row, col, and $value$. Each nonzero term is represented by a node. These nodes are linked together to form two circular lists. The first list, the row list, is made up by linking nodes by rows and within rows by columns. The linking is done via the $right$ field. The second list, the column list, is made up by linking nodes via the $down$ field. In this list, nodes are linked by columns and within columns by rows. These two lists share a common head node. In addition, a node is added to contain the dimensions of the matrix. The matrix A of Figure 4.20 has the representation shown in Figure 4.22.

   Using the same assumptions as for algorithm $mread$ (Program 4.22), write an algorithm to read in a matrix and set up its internal representation as above. How much time does your algorithm take? How much additional space is needed?

7. For the representation of Exercise 6, write algorithms to

   (a) erase a matrix

   (b) add two matrices

   (c) multiply two matrices

   (d) print out a matrix

   For each of these algorithms obtain computing times. How do these times compare with the corresponding times for the representation of this section?

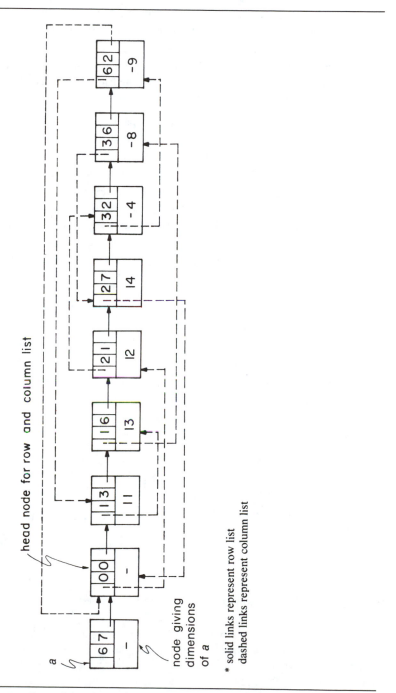

Figure 4.22: Representation of matrix *A* of Figure 4.20 using the scheme of Exercise 6

8. Compare the sparse representations of Exercise 6 and this section with respect to some other operations. For example, how much time is needed to output the entries in an arbitrary row or column?

9. [**Programming Project**] In this project, we shall implement a complete linked-list system to perform arithmetic on sparse matrices using the representation of Section 4.6. First, design a convenient node structure assuming *value* is an integer.

   Since we shall need to erase circular lists, we shall utilize the available-space list concept described in this section. So, we may begin by writing and testing the procedures associated with this list. Next, write and test the following procedures for matrix operations:

   (a) *mread* (*a*) Read matrix *a* and set it up according to the representation of this section. The first input line gives the matrix dimensions. The next several lines contain one triple, (row, column, value), each. The last triple ends the input file. These triples are in increasing order by rows. Within rows, the triples are in increasing order of columns. The data is to be read in one line at a time and converted to internal representation. The variable *a* is set to point to the head node of the circular list of head nodes (as in the text).

   (b) *mwrite*(*a*) Print out the terms of *a*. To do this, you will have to design a suitable output format. In any case, the output should be ordered by rows and within rows by columns.

   (c) *merase*(*a*) Return all nodes of the sparse matrix *a* to the available-space list.

   (d) *madd*(*a*,*b*,*c*) Create the sparse matrix *c* = *a* + *b*. *a* and *b* are to be left unaltered.

   (e) *msub*(*a*,*b*,*c*) Create the sparse matrix *c* = *a* − *b*. *a* and *b* are to be left unaltered.

   (f) *mmult*(*a*,*b*,*c*) Create the sparse matrix *c* = *a* * *b*. *a* and *b* are to be left unaltered.

   (g) *mtrp*(*a*,*b*) Create the sparse matrix *b* = *a*^t. *a* is to be left unaltered.

10. [**Programming Project**] Do Exercise 9 using the representation of Exercise 6.

4.7 DOUBLY LINKED LISTS

So far we have been working chiefly with singly linked linear lists. For some problems these would be too restrictive. One difficulty with these lists is that if we are pointing to a specific node, say *p*, then we can easily move only in the direction of the links. The only way to find the node that precedes *p* is to start at the beginning of the list. The same problem arises when one wishes to delete an arbitrary node from a singly linked list. As can be seen from Example 4.4, easy deletion of an arbitrary node requires knowing the preceding node. If we have a problem in which moving in either direction is often necessary, then it is useful to have ==doubly linked lists==. Each node now has two link fields, one linking in the forward direction and one in the backward direction.

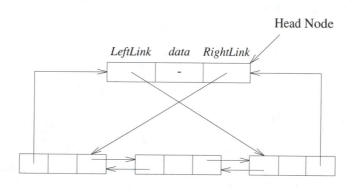

Figure 4.23: Doubly linked circular list with head node

A node in a doubly linked list has at least three fields — e.g., *data, llink* (left link), and *rlink* (right link). A doubly linked list may or may not be circular. A sample doubly linked circular list with three nodes is shown in Figure 4.23. Besides these three nodes, a special node called a head node has been added. As was true in the earlier sections, head nodes are convenient for the algorithms. The *data* field of the head node usually contains no information. Now suppose that p points to any node in a doubly linked list. In this case $p = p\uparrow.llink\uparrow.rlink = p\uparrow.rlink\uparrow.llink$. This formula reflects the essential virtue of this structure — namely, that one can go back and forth with equal ease. An empty list is not really empty, since it always has its head node and it appears as in Figure 4.24.

Figure 4.24: Empty doubly linked circular list with head node

To work with these lists we must be able to insert and delete nodes. Procedure *ddelete* (Program 4.24) deletes node x from list l. x now points to a node that is no longer part of the list l. Figure 4.25 shows how the method works on a doubly linked list with only a single node. Even though the *rlink* and *llink* fields of node x still point to the head node, this node has effectively been removed, as there is no way to access x through l. Insertion is only slightly more complex (see Program 4.25).

---

procedure *ddelete* $(x,l : dpointer)$;
begin
  if $x = l$ **then begin**
               writeln('Deletion of head node not permitted');
               halt;
          end;
  $x\uparrow.llink\uparrow.rlink := x\uparrow.rlink$;
  $x\uparrow.rlink\uparrow.llink := x\uparrow.llink$;
  dispose (x);
end; {of *ddelete*}

Program 4.24: Deletion from a doubly linked circular list

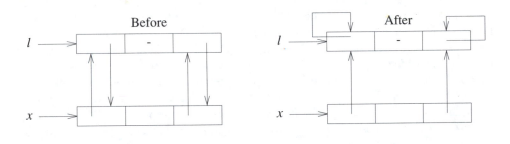

Figure 4.25: Deletion from a doubly linked circular list

EXERCISES

1. Devise a representation for a list in which insertions and deletions can be made at either end. Such a structure is called a *deque.* Write a procedure for inserting at either end.

2. Consider the operation XOR (exclusive OR, also written as $\oplus$) defined as follows (for i, j binary):

$$i \oplus j = \begin{cases} 0 & \text{if } i \text{ and } j \text{ are identical} \\ 1 & \text{otherwise} \end{cases}$$

---

procedure *dinsert* (*p,x* : *dpointer*);
{Insert node *p* to the right of node *x*.}
begin
    $p\uparrow.llink := x; p\uparrow.rlink := x\uparrow.rlink;$
    $x\uparrow.rlink\uparrow.llink := p; x\uparrow.rlink := p;$
end; {of *dinsert*}

Program 4.25: Insertion into a doubly linked circular list

This definition differs from the usual OR of logic, which is defined as

$$i \text{ OR } j = \begin{cases} 0 & \text{if } i = j = 0 \\ 1 & \text{otherwise} \end{cases}$$

The definition can be extended to the case in which *i* and *j* are binary strings (i.e., take the XOR of corresponding bits of *i* and *j*). So, for example, if $i = 10110$ and $j = 01100$, then $i \text{ XOR } j = i \oplus j = 11010$. Note that

$$a \oplus (a \oplus b) = (a \oplus a) \oplus b = b$$

and

$$(a \oplus b) \oplus b = a \oplus (b \oplus b) = a$$

This notation gives us a space-saving device for storing the right and left links of a doubly linked list. The nodes will now have only two fields: *info* and *link*. If *l* is to the left of node *x* and *r* to its right, then $link(x) = l \oplus r$ (as in the case of the storage management algorithms, we assume that available memory is an array *memory* [1 .. *n*] and that the *link* field just gives us the position of the next node in this array). For the leftmost node $l = 0$, and for the rightmost node $r = 0$. Let (l,r) be a doubly linked list so represented; *l* points to the leftmost node and *r* to the right most node in the list.

(a)   Write an algorithm to traverse the doubly linked list (l,r) from left to right, listing the contents of the *info* field of each node.

(b)   Write an algorithm to traverse the list right to left, listing the contents of the *info* field of each node.

4.8   DYNAMIC STORAGE MANAGEMENT

In a multiprocessing computer environment, several programs reside in memory at the same time. Different programs have different memory requirements. Thus, one program may require 60K of memory, another 100K, and yet another program may require 300K. Whenever the operating system needs to request memory, it must be able to allocate a block of continuous storage of the right size. When the execution of a program is complete, the program releases or frees the memory block allocated to it, and this freed block may now be allocated to another program. In a dynamic environment the sizes of memory that will be requested are not known ahead of time. Moreover, blocks of memory will, in general, be freed in some order different from that in which they were allocated.

At the start of the computer system no jobs are in memory, so the whole memory, say of size m words, is available for allocation to programs. Now jobs are submitted to the computer and requests are made for variable-size blocks of memory. Assume we start with 100,000 words of memory, and five programs, $P1$, $P2$, $P3$, $P4$, and $P5$, make requests of 10,000, 15,000, 6000, 8000, and 20,000 words respectively. Figure 4.26 indicates the status of memory after storage for $P5$ has been allocated. The unshaded area indicates the memory that is currently not in use. Assume that programs $P4$ and $P2$ complete execution, freeing the memory used by them. Figure 4.27 shows the status of memory after the blocks for $P2$ and $P4$ are freed. We now have three contiguous blocks of memory that are in use and another three that are free. To make further allocations, it is necessary to keep track of those blocks that are not in use. This problem is similar to the one encountered in previous sections where we had to maintain a list of all free nodes. The difference between the situation then and the one we have now is that the free space consists of variable-size blocks or nodes and that a request for a block of memory may now require allocation of only a portion of a node rather than the whole node.

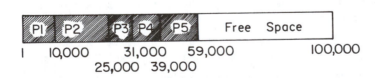

Figure 4.26: Memory after allocation to $P1$ through $P5$

One of the functions of an operating system is to maintain a list of all blocks of storage currently not in use and then to allocate storage from this unused pool as required. One can adopt the chain structure used earlier to maintain the available-space list. Now, in addition to linking all the free blocks together, it is necessary to retain in-

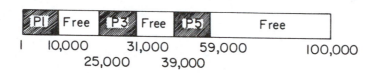

Figure 4.27: Status of memory after completion of *P* 2 and *P* 4

formation regarding the size of each block in this list of free nodes. Thus, each node on the free list has two fields in its first word, *size* and *link*. Figure 4.28 shows the free list that corresponds to Figure 4.27. The use of a head node simplifies later algorithms.

Note, however, that the storage management problem cannot be solved by defining a data type *block* with the fields *size*, *link*, and *UsableSpace* for the following reasons:

(1)   Different blocks are of different size.

(2)   We do not know how the available space in each block is to be used. In general, this space will hold programs as well as data of varying type.

(3)   The use of a particular word in memory will change with time, as this word will be a part of several different blocks as blocks continue to get allocated and freed.

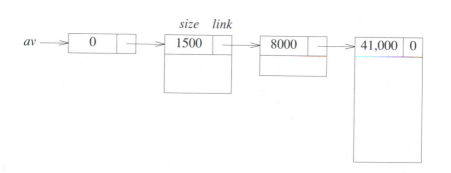

Figure 4.28: Free list with head node corresponding to Figure 4.27

Furthermore, link fields cannot be implemented as Pascal pointers because the location of these fields in memory is not known and changes in time. In addition, we shall see that in this application, it does make sense to perform arithmetic on the link fields. Without this capability, we shall have to sacrifice performance greatly.

Thus, the available memory to be managed is regarded simply as a one dimensional array of words. The array is indexed 1 through m. Each word is a sequence of bits. We shall use the following procedures and functions to set and extract the *size* and *link* fields of words:

$SetSize(i,j)$ . . . set the *size* field of word i to j
$SetLink(i,j)$ . . . set the *link* field of word i to j
$size(i)$ . . . extract the value in the *size* field of word i
$link(i)$ . . . extract the value in the *link* field of word i

Note that the *link* field contains an integer, which is the index of the first word in the next block on the available-space list. If there is no next block, then $link = 0$.

If we now receive a request for a block of memory of size n, it is necessary to search the list of free blocks finding the first block of size $\geq n$ and allocating n words out of this block. Such an allocation strategy is called *FirstFit*. Procedure *FirstFit* (Program 4.26) makes storage allocations using the first-fit strategy. An alternate strategy, *best-fit*, calls for finding a free block whose size is as close to n as possible, but not less than n. This strategy is examined in the exercises.

```
procedure FirstFit(n : integer; var p : integer);
{Allocate a block of size n using first fit. p is set to 0 if there is no
block large enough, otherwise p is the start of the allocated block.}
var q : integer; NotDone : boolean;
begin
  p := link (av); q := av ; {q trails p} NotDone := true;
  while (p <> 0) and NotDone do {examine free blocks}
    if size (p) ≥ n {block large enough}
    then begin {allocate from this block}
            SetSize (p, size (p) − n);
            if size (p) = 0 {allocate whole block}
            then SetLink (q,link (p))
            else p := p + size (p); {allocate last n words}
            NotDone := false
         end
    else begin
            q := p ; p :=link (p); {next block}
         end; {of if and while}
end; {of FirstFit}
```

Program 4.26: First-fit allocation

Program 4.26 is simple enough to understand. If only a portion of a free block is to be allocated, the allocation is made from the bottom of the block. This avoids changing links in the free list unless an entire block is allocated. There are, however, two major problems with *FirstFit*. First, experiments have shown that after some processing time, many small nodes are left in the available-space list, these nodes being smaller than any potential requests. For example, a request for 9900 words allocated from a block of size 10,000 leaves behind a block of size 100, which may be smaller than any request that will be made to the system. Retaining these small nodes on the available-space list tends to slow down the allocation process, as the time needed to make an allocation is proportional to the number of nodes on the available-space list. To avoid this problem, we choose some suitable constant ε, such that if the allocation of a portion of a node leaves behind a node of size < ε, then the entire node is allocated — i.e., we allocate more storage than requested in this case. The second problem arises from the fact that the search for a large enough node always begins at the front of the list. As a result, all the small nodes tend to collect at the front, making it is necessary to examine several nodes before allocating larger blocks. To distribute small nodes evenly along the list, one can begin searching for a new node from a different point in the list each time a request is made. To implement this, the available-space list is maintained as a circular list with a head node of size zero. *av* now points to the last node from which an allocation was made. We shall see what the new allocation algorithm looks like after we discuss what has to be done to free a block of storage.

The second operation is freeing blocks or returning nodes to *av*. Not only must we return the node, but we want to recognize if its neighbors are also free so that they can be coalesced into a single block. Looking back at Figure 4.28, we see that if *P3* is the next program to terminate, then rather than just adding this node onto the free list to get the free list of Figure 4.29, it would be better to combine the adjacent free blocks corresponding to *P2* and *P4*, obtaining the free list of Figure 4.30. This combining of adjacent free bocks to get bigger free blocks is necessary. The block-allocation algorithm splits big blocks while making allocations. As a result, sizes of available blocks become smaller and smaller. Unless recombination takes place at some point, we will no longer be able to meet large requests for memory.

With the structure we have for the available-space list, it is not easy to determine whether blocks adjacent to the block (n,p) (n = size of block, and p = starting location) being returned are free. The only way to do this, at present, is to examine all the nodes in *av* to determine whether

(1)   the left adjacent block (i.e., the block ending at $p - 1$) is free

(2)   the right adjacent block (i.e., the block beginning at $p + n$) is free

To determine (1) and (2) above without searching the available-space list, we adopt the node structure of Figure 4.31 for allocated and free nodes.

The first and last words of each block are reserved for allocation information. The first word of each free block has four fields: *llink, rlink, tag,* and *size*. Only the *tag* and *size* fields are important for a block in use. The last word in each free block has two fields: *tag* and *UpLink*. Only the *tag* field is important for a block in use. Now by just examining the tags at $p - 1$ and $p + n$, one can determine whether the adjacent blocks

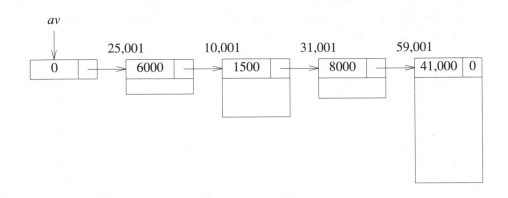

Figure 4.29: Available-space list when adjacent free blocks are not coalesced

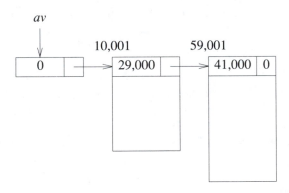

Figure 4.30: Available-space list when adjacent free blocks are coalesced

are free. The *UpLink* field of a free block points to the start of the block. The available-space list will now be a doubly linked circular list, linked through the fields *llink* and *rlink*. It will have a head node with *size* = 0. A doubly linked list is needed, as the return-block algorithm will delete nodes at random from *av*. The need for *UpLink* will become clear when we study the freeing algorithm. Since the first and last nodes of each block have *tag* fields, this system of allocation and freeing is called the *boundary tag method*.

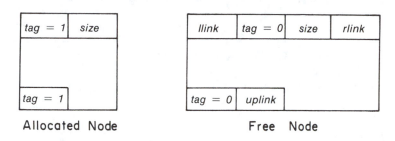

Figure 4.31: Node structure for allocated and free blocks

Note that the *tag* fields in allocated and free blocks occupy the same bit position in the first and last words, respectively. This is not obvious from Figure 4.31, where the *llink* field precedes the *tag* field in a free node. The labeling of fields in this figure has been done so as to obtain clean diagrams for the available-space list. The algorithms we shall obtain for the boundary tag method will assume that memory is numbered 1 to m and that $tag(0) = tag(m + 1) = 1$. This last requirement will enable us to free the block beginning at 1 and the one ending at m without having to test for these blocks as special cases. Such a test otherwise would have been necessary, as the first of these blocks has no left adjacent block, and the second has no right adjacent block. Although the *tag* information is all that is needed in an allocated block, it is customary to retain the size in the block as well. Hence, Figure 4.31 includes a *size* field in an allocated block.

Before presenting the allocate and free algorithms, let us study the initial condition of the system, when all memory is free. Assuming that memory begins at location 1 and ends at m, the *av* list initially looks as in Figure 4.32.

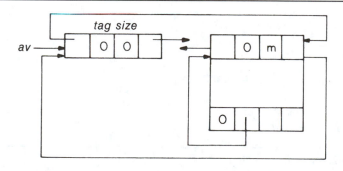

Figure 4.32: Initial configuration of *av* list

The allocate (Program 4.27) and free (Program 4.28) procedures use the following functions and procedures (the implementation of these is left unspecified):

> *setxyz* (i,j) . . . set the *xyz* field of word i to j
>
> *xyz* (i) . . . extract the value in the *xyz* field of word i

---

```
 1  procedure allocate (n : integer; var p : integer);
 2  {Use next fit to allocate a block of size at least n.
 3   No blocks of size < eps are retained on the av list.
 4   p is set as in procedure FirstFit.}
 5  label 99;
 6  var diff: integer;
 7  begin
 8      p := rlink (av); {start search at p}
 9      repeat
10        if size (p) >= n {block large enough} then
11        begin
12          diff := size (p)–n;
13          if diff < eps {allocate whole block}
14          then begin
15                  SetRlink (llink (p),rlink (p)); {delete from list}
16                  SetLlink (rlink (p),llink (p));
17                  SetTag (p,1); SetTag (p +size (p)–1,1);
18                  av := llink (p); {start next search here}
19                  goto 99;
20              end
21          else begin {allocate last n words}
22                  SetSize (p,diff); SetUpLink (p +diff −1,p);
23                  SetTag (p + diff–1,0); av := p;
24                  p := p + diff; SetSize (p,n);
25                  SetTag (p,1); SetTag (p +n −1,1);
26                  goto 99;
27              end;
28        end;
29        p := rlink (p); {examine next block}
30      until p = rlink (av);
31      p := 0; {no block large enough}
32  99: end; {of allocate}
```

Program 4.27: Next-fit allocation

Although the allocate and free procedures may appear complex, they are a direct consequence of the doubly linked list structure of the available-space list and also of the node structure in use. Notice that the use of a head node eliminates the test for an empty list in both algorithms and hence simplifies them. The use of circular linking makes it

```
 1  procedure free(p : integer);
 2  {Return a block beginning at p and of size size (p).}
 3  var n,q : integer;
 4  begin
 5    n := size (p);
 6    if (tag (p − 1) = 1) and (tag (p + n) = 1)
 7    then begin {both adjacent blocks in use}
 8            SetTag (p,0); SetTag (p +n −1,0); {free the block}
 9            SetUpLink (p +n −1,p);
10            {insert at right of av}
11            SetLlink (p,av); SetRlink (p,rlink (av));
12            SetLlink (rlink (p),p); SetRlink (av,p);
13         end
14    else if (tag (p + n) = 1) and (tag (p − 1) = 0)
15         then begin {only left block free}
16                 q := UpLink (p − 1); {start of left block}
17                 SetSize (q,size (q)+n);
18                 SetUpLink (p +n −1,q); SetTag (p +n −1,0);
19              end
20         else if (tag (p + n) = 0) and (tag (p − 1) = 1)
21              then begin {only right block free}
22                      {replace block beginning at p + n by one beginning at p}
23                      SetRlink (llink (p +n),p);
24                      SetLlink (rlink (p +n),p);
25                      SetLlink (p,llink (p +n));
26                      SetRlink (p,rlink (p +n));
27                      SetSize (p,n +size (p +n));
28                      SetUpLink (p +size (p)−1,p);
29                      SetTag (p,0);
30                      av := p;
31                   end
32              else begin {both adjacent blocks free; delete right block from av list}
33                      SetRlink (llink (p +n),rlink (p +n));
34                      SetLlink (rlink (p +n),llink (p +n));
35                      q := UpLink (p − 1);
36                      SetSize (q,size (q)+n +size (p +n));
37                      SetUpLink (q +size (q)−1,q);
38                      av := llink (p + n);
39                   end;
40  end; {of free}
```

Program 4.28: Freeing a block using boundary tags

easy to start the search for a large enough node at any point in the available-space list. The *UpLink* field in a free block is needed only when returning a block whose left adjacent block is free (see lines 16 and 35 of procedure *free*). In lines 30 and 38, *av* is ·changed so that it always points to the start of a free block rather than into the middle of a free block. One may readily verify that the algorithms work for special cases, such as when the available-space list contains only the head node.

The best way to understand the algorithms is to simulate an example. Let us start with a memory of size 5000, from which the following allocations are made: $r_1 = 300$, $r_2 = 600$, $r_3 = 900$, $r_4 = 700$, $r_5 = 1500$, and $r_6 = 1000$. At this point the memory configuration is as in Figure 4.33. This figure also depicts the different blocks of storage and the available-space list. Note that when a portion of a free block is allocated, the allocation is made from the bottom of the block to avoid unnecessary link changes in the *av* list. First, block r_1 is freed. Since $tag(5000) = tag(4700) = 1$, no coalescing takes place and the block is inserted into the *av* list (Figure 4.34(a)). Next, block r_4 is returned. Since both its left adjacent block (r_5) and its right adjacent block (r_3) are in use at this time ($tag(2500) = tag(3201) = 1$), this block is inserted into the free list to obtain the configuration of Figure 4.34(b). Block r_3 is next returned. Its left adjacent block is free ($tag(3200) = 0$), but its right adjacent block is not ($tag(4101) = 1$), so this block is attached to the end of its adjacent free block without changing any link fields (Figure 4.34(c)). Block r_5 next becomes free. Since $tag(1000) = 1$ and $tag\ (2501) = 0$, this block is coalesced with its right adjacent block, which is free, and inserted into the spot previously occupied by this adjacent free block (Figure 4.34(d)). Finally, r_2 is freed. Both its upper and lower adjacent blocks are free. The upper block is deleted from the free-space list and combined with r_2. This bigger block is appended to the end of the free block made up of r_3, r_4, and r_5 (Figure 4.34(e)).

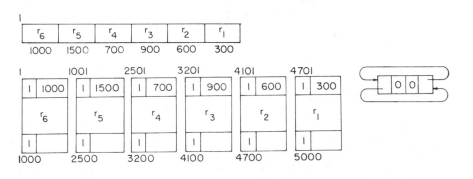

Figure 4.33: Memory configuration after the allocations $r_1, \cdots, r_6$

As for the computational complexity of the two algorithms, one may readily verify that the time required to free a block of storage is independent of the number of free blocks in *av*. Freeing a block takes a constant amount of time. To accomplish this we

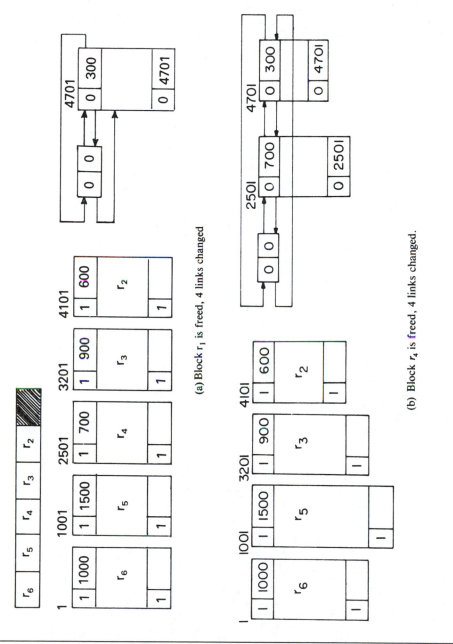

Figure 4.34: Freeing blocks in the boundary tag system (continued on next page)

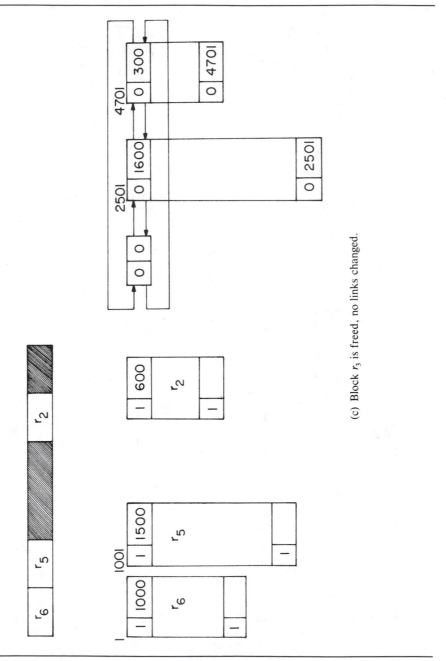

(c) Block r_3 is freed, no links changed.

Figure 4.34: Freeing blocks in the boundary tag system (continued on next page)

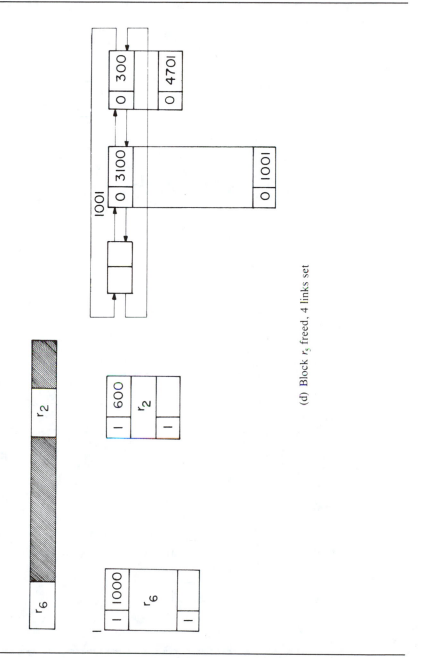

(d) Block r_5 freed, 4 links set

Figure 4.34: Freeing blocks in the boundary tag system (continued on next page)

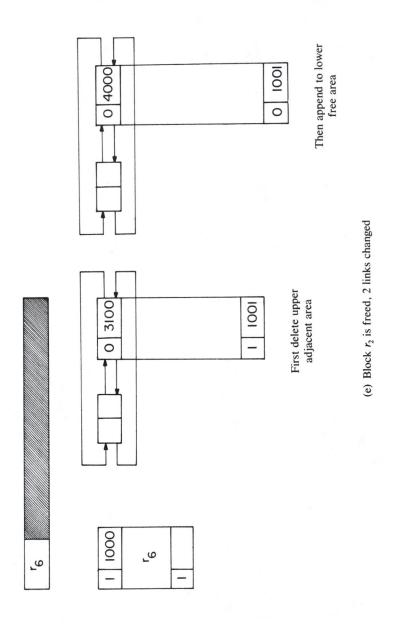

Figure 4.34: Freeing blocks in the boundary tag system

must pay a price in terms of storage. The first and last words of each block in use are reserved for *tag* information. Although additional space is needed to maintain *av* as a doubly linked list, this is of no consequence, as all storage in *av* is free in any case. The allocation of a block of storage still requires a search of the *av* list. In the worst case, all free blocks may be examined.

An alternate scheme for storage allocation, the "buddy system," is investigated in the exercises.

EXERCISES

1. (a) Write an algorithm *BestFit*(n,p) similar to algorithm *FirstFit* of Section 4.8 to allocate a block of size n using the best-fit strategy. The available-space list is a chain as in Figure 4.28. The best-fit strategy examines each block in this chain. The allocation is made from the smallest block of size $\geq n$. p is set to the starting address of the space allocated.

    (b) Which of the algorithms *BestFit* and *FirstFit* takes less time?

    (c) Give an example of a sequence of requests for memory allocation and memory freeing that can be met by *BestFit* but not by *FirstFit*.

2. Which of the two algorithms *allocate* and *free* of Section 4.8 require the condition $tag(0) = tag(m + 1) = 1$ in order to work right? Why?

3. Give an example of a sequence of requests to allocate and free memory that can be satisfied when first fit is used but not when best fit is used.

4. Give an example of a sequence of requests to allocate and free memory that can be satisfied when first fit is used but not when next fit is used.

5. Give an example of a sequence of requests to allocate and free memory that can be satisfied when best fit is used but not when first fit is used.

6. Give an example of a sequence of requests to allocate and free memory that can be satisfied when next fit is used but not when best fit is used.

7. Design a storage management scheme for the case in which all requests for memory are of the same size, say k. Is it necessary to coalesce adjacent blocks that are free? Write algorithms to free and allocate storage in this scheme.

8. Consider the dynamic storage management problem in which requests for memory are of varying sizes, as in Section 4.8. Assume that blocks of storage are freed according to the LAFF (last-allocated-first-freed) discipline.

    (a) Design a structure to represent the free space.

    (b) Write an algorithm to allocate a block of storage of size n.

    (c) Write an algorithm to free a block of storage of size n beginning at p.

9. In the case of static storage allocation, all the requests are known in advance. If there are n requests $r_1, r_2, \cdots, r_n$ and $\Sigma r_i \leq M$, where M is the total amount of memory available, then all requests can be met. So, assume $\Sigma r_i > M$.

(a)   Which of these n requests should be satisfied if we wish to maximize the number of satisfied requests?

(b)   Under the maximization criterion of (a), how small can the ratio storage allocated/M become?

(c)   Would this be a good criterion to use if jobs are charged a flat rate, say $3 per job, independent of the size of the request?

(d)   The pricing policy of (c) is unrealistic when request size can vary greatly. A more realistic policy is to charge, say, x cents per unit of request. Is the criterion of (a) good for this pricing policy? What would be a good maximization criterion for storage allocation now? Write an algorithm to determine which requests are to be satisfied. How much time does your algorithm take as a function of n, the number of requests? [If your algorithm takes a polynomial amount of time and works correctly, take it to your instructor immediately. You have made a major discovery.]

10.   [**Buddy system**] The next six exercises examine a storage management technique in which only blocks of size equal to a power of 2 are allocated. Thus, if a request for a block of size n is made, then a block of size $\lceil \log_2 n \rceil$ is allocated. As a result, all free blocks are also of a size equal to a power of 2. If the total memory size is 2^m addressed from 0 to $2^m - 1$, the possible sizes for free blocks are 2^k, $0 \le k \le m$. Free blocks of the same size are maintained in the same available-space list. Thus, this system has $m+1$ available-space lists. Each list is a doubly linked circular list and has a head node $avail[i]$, $0 \le i \le m$. Every free node has the structure of Figure 4.35. Initially all memory is free and consists of one block beginning at 0 and of size 2^m. Write an algorithm to initialize all the available-space lists.

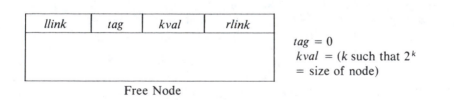

Free Node

Figure 4.35: Structure of a free node in the buddy system

11.   [**Buddy system allocation**] Using the available-space list structure of Exercise 6, write an algorithm to meet a request of size n, if possible. Note that a request of size n is to be met by allocating a block of size 2^k, $k = \lceil \log_2 n \rceil$. To do this, examine the available-space lists $avail[i]$, $k \le i \le m$, finding the smallest i for which $avail[i]$ is not empty. Remove one block from this list. Let p be the starting ad-

dress of this block. If $i > k$, then the block is too big and is broken into two blocks of size 2^{i-1} beginning at p and $p + 2^{i-1}$, respectively. The block beginning at $p + 2^{i-1}$ is inserted into the corresponding available-space list. If $i - 1 > k$, then the block is to be split further and so on. Finally, a block of size 2^k beginning at p is allocated. A block in use has the form given in Figure 4.36.

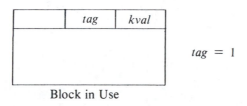

Block in Use

Figure 4.36: Structure of a block in use in buddy system

(a) Write an algorithm using the strategy outlined above to allocate a block of storage to meet a request for n units of memory.

(b) For a memory of size $2^m = 16$, draw the binary tree representing the splitting of blocks taking place to satisfy 16 consecutive requests for memory of size 1. (Note that the use of the *tag* in the allocated block does not create a problem in allocations of size 1, since memory would be allocated in units where 1 unit could be a few thousand words.) Label each node in this tree with its starting address and current *kval* (i.e., power of 2 representing its size).

12. [*Locating buddies*] Two nodes in the tree of the preceding exercise are said to be buddies iff they are sibling nodes. Prove that two nodes starting at x and y, respectively, are buddies iff:

(a) the *kval* for x and y is the same

(b) $x = y \oplus 2^k$, where $\oplus$ is the exclusive OR (XOR) operation. The $\oplus$ is done by performing the operation on all pairs of corresponding bits in the binary representation of y and 2^k.

13. [*Freeing and coalescing blocks*] When a block with *kval* k becomes free, it is to be returned to the available-space list. Free blocks are combined into bigger free blocks iff they are buddies. This combining follows the reverse process adopted during allocation. If a block beginning at p and of size k becomes free, it is to be combined with its buddy $p \oplus 2^k$ if the buddy is free. The new free block beginning at $l = \min\{p, p \oplus 2^k\}$ and of size $k + 1$ is to be combined with its buddy $l \oplus 2^{k+1}$ if free, and so on. Write an algorithm to free a block beginning at p and having *kval* $= k$, combining buddies that are free.

14. (a) Does the freeing algorithm of the preceding exercise always combine adjacent free blocks? If not, give a sequence of allocations and freeings of storage showing this to be the case.

  (b) How small can the ratio (storage requested)/(storage allocated) be for the buddy system? Storage requested = Σn_i, where n_i is the actual amount requested. Give an example approaching this ratio.

  (c) How much time does the allocation algorithm take, in the worst case, to make an allocation if the total memory size is 2^m?

  (d) How much time does the allocation algorithm take, in the worst case, to free a block of storage?

15. [*Buddy system when memory size is not a power of 2*]

  (a) How are the available-space lists to be initialized if the total storage available is not a power of 2?

  (b) What changes need to be made to the block-freeing algorithm to take care of this case? Do any changes have to be made to the allocation algorithm?

4.9 GENERALIZED LISTS

4.9.1 Representation of Generalized Lists

In Chapter 2 a linear list was defined to be a finite sequence of $n \geq 0$ elements, $\alpha_1, \cdots, \alpha_n$, which we write as $A = (\alpha_1, \cdots, \alpha_n)$. The elements of a linear list are restricted to atoms; thus, the only structural property a linear list has is that of position (i.e., α_i precedes α_{i+1}, $1 \leq i < n$). Relaxing this restriction on the elements of a list and permitting them to have a structure of their own leads to the notion of a generalized list. Now, the elements α_i, $1 \leq i \leq n$, may be either atoms or lists.

Definition: A *generalized list,* A, is a finite sequence of $n \geq 0$ elements, $\alpha_1, \cdots, \alpha_n$, where α_i is either an atom or a list. The elements α_i, $1 \leq i \leq n$, that are not atoms are said to be the *sublists* of A. □

The list A itself is written as $A = (\alpha_1, \cdots, \alpha_n)$. A is the *name* of the list $(\alpha_1, \cdots, \alpha_n)$, and n is the *length* of the list. By convention, all list names are represented by capital letters. Lowercase letters are used to represent atoms. If $n \geq 1$, then α_1 is the *head* of A, and $(\alpha_2, \cdots, \alpha_n)$ is the *tail* of A.

This definition is our first example of a recursive definition, so study it carefully. The definition is recursive because within our description of a list, we use the notion of a list. This may appear to be circular, but it is not. It is a compact way of describing a potentially large and varied structure. We will see more such definitions later. Some examples of generalized lists are

(1) $D = ()$ the null, or empty, list; its length is zero

(2) $A = (a,(b,c))$ a list of length two; its first element is the atom a,
and its second element is the linear list (b,c)

(3) $B = (A,A,())$ a list of length three whose first two elements are the list A, and
the third element is the null list

(4) $C = (a,C)$ a recursive list of length two; C corresponds to the
infinite list $C = (a, (a, (a, \ \cdots \ )$

D is the empty list. For list A, we have $head(A) = \text{'}a\text{'}$ and $tail(A) = ((b,c))$; $tail\,(A)$ also has a head and tail, which are (b,c) and $(\ )$, respectively. Looking at list B, we see that $head(B) = A$ and $tail(B) = (A,(\ ))$. Continuing, we have $head\,(tail\,(B)) = A$ and $tail\,(tail\,(B)) = ((\ ))$, both of which are lists.

Two important consequences of our definition for a list are (1) lists may be shared by other lists as in example (3), where list A makes up two of the sublists of B; and (2) lists may be recursive as in example (4). The implications of these two consequences for the data structures needed to represent lists will become evident.

First, let us restrict ourselves to the situation in which the lists being represented are neither shared nor recursive. To see where this notion of a list may be useful, consider how to represent polynomials in several variables. Suppose we need to devise a data representation for them and consider one typical example, the polynomial

$$P(x,y,z) = x^{10}y^3z^2 + 2x^8y^3z^2 + 3x^8y^2z^2 + x^4y^4z + 6x^3y^4z + 2yz$$

You can easily think of a sequential representation for P, say using nodes with four fields: *coef, expx, expy*, and *expz*. But this would mean that polynomials in a different number of variables would need a different number of fields, adding another conceptual inelegance to other difficulties we have already seen with the sequential representation of polynomials. If we used linear lists, we might conceive a node of the form

coef	*expx*	*expy*
expz	*link*	

These nodes would have to vary in size depending on the number of variables, causing difficulties in storage management. The idea of using a general list structure with nodes of fixed size arises naturally if we consider rewriting $P(x,y,z)$ as

$$((x^{10} + 2x^8)y^3 + 3x^8y^2)z^2 + ((x^4 + 6x^3)y^4 + 2y)z$$

Every polynomial can be written in this fashion, factoring out a main variable z, followed by a second variable y, and so on. Looking carefully now at $P(x,y,z)$, we see that there are two terms in the variable z, Cz^2 and Dz, where C and D are polynomials themselves, but in the variables x and y. Looking more closely at $C(x,y)$, we see that it is of the form $Ey^3 + Fy^2$, where E and F are polynomials in x. Continuing in this way, we see that every polynomial consists of a variable plus coefficient-exponent pairs. Each coefficient is itself a polynomial (in one less variable) if we regard a single numerical coefficient as a polynomial in zero variables.

We see that every polynomial, regardless of the number of variables in it, can be represented using nodes of the type *PolyNode*, defined as

$$\textbf{type } \textit{triple} = (\text{variable, ptr, no});$$
$$\textit{PolyPointer} = \uparrow\textit{PolyNode};$$
$$\textit{PolyNode} = \textbf{record}$$
$$\textit{link} : \textit{PolyPointer};$$
$$\textit{exp} : \textbf{integer};$$
$$\textbf{case } \textit{trio} : \textit{triple} \textbf{ of}$$
$$\textit{variable} : (\textit{vble} : \textbf{char});$$
$$\textit{ptr} : (\textit{dlink} : \textit{PolyPointer});$$
$$\textit{no} : \ (\textit{coef} : \textbf{integer});$$
$$\textbf{end};$$

Note that the type of the field *vble* can be changed to **integer** in case all variables are kept in a table and *vble* just gives the corresponding table index.

The polynomial $P = 3x^2y$ now takes the representation given in Figure 4.37, whereas $P(x,y,z)$ defined before has the list representation shown in Figure 4.38. For simplicity, the *trio* field is omitted from Figure 4.38. The value of this field for each node is self-evident.

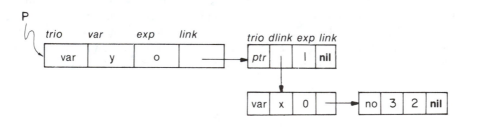

Figure 4.37: Representation of $3x^2y$

Every generalized list can be represented using the node structure

tag = true/false	data/dlink	link

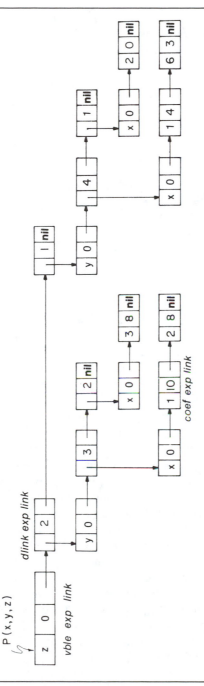

Figure 4.38: Representation of $P(x,y,z)$

This structure may be defined in Pascal as

> **type** *ListPointer* = ↑*ListNode*;
> *ListNode* = **record**
> link : *ListPointer*;
> **case** *tag* : **boolean of**
> **false** : (*data* : **char**);
> **true** : (*dlink* : *ListPointer*);
> **end**;

where the type of the *data* field changes from one application to the next. The *data*/*dlink* field holds an atom if *head*(*A*) is an atom and holds a pointer to the list representation of *head*(*A*) if *head*(*A*) is a list. Using this node structure, the example lists (1) to (4) have the representation shown in Figure 4.39.

4.9.2   Recursive Algorithms for Lists

4.9.2.1   Copying a List

Now that we have seen a particular example where generalized lists are useful, let us return to their definition. When a data object is defined recursively, it is often easy to describe algorithms that work on these objects recursively. To see how recursion is useful, let us write a procedure (Program 4.29) that produces an exact copy of a nonrecursive list *p* in which no sublists are shared. We will assume the nodes of *p* are of type *ListNode* as defined earlier.

Program 4.29 reflects exactly the definition of a list. We see immediately that *copy* works correctly for an empty list. A simple proof using induction will verify the correctness of the entire procedure. Now let us consider the computing time of this algorithm. The null list takes a constant amount of time. For the list $A = ((a,b),((c,d),e))$, which has the representation of Figure 4.40, *p* takes on the values given in Figure 4.41. The sequence of values should be read down the columns; b, r, s, t, u, v, w, and x are the addresses of the eight nodes of the list. From this example one should be able to see that nodes with *tag* = **false** will be visited twice, whereas nodes with *tag* = **true** will be visited three times. Thus, if a list has a total of *m* nodes, no more than $3m$ executions of any statement will occur. Hence, the algorithm is O(*m*), or linear, which is the best we can hope to achieve. Another factor of interest is the maximum depth of recursion or, equivalently, how many locations are needed for the recursion stack. Again, by carefully following the algorithm on the previous example, we see that the maximum depth is a combination of the lengths and depths of all sublists. However, a simple upper bound is *m*, the total number of nodes. Although this bound will be extremely large in many cases, it is achievable, for instance, if $A = (((((a)))))$.

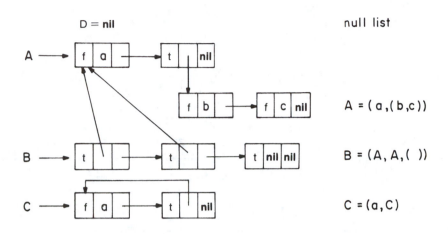

Figure 4.39: Representation of lists (1) to (4) (page 189; an *f* in the *tag* field represents the value false, whereas a *t* represents the value true

```
function copy (p: ListPointer) : ListPointer;
{Copy the nonrecursive list with no shared sublists pointed at by p.}
var q : ListPointer;
begin
  q := nil;
  if p <> nil
  then begin
          new (q); q↑.tag := p↑.tag;
          if not p↑.tag then q↑.data := p↑.data
                        else q↑.dlink := copy (p↑.dlink);
          q↑.link := copy (p↑.link);
        end;
  copy := q;
end; {of copy}
```

Program 4.29: Copying a list

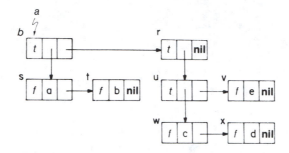

Figure 4.40: Linked representation for *A*

level of recursion	value of *p*	continuing level	*p*	continuing level	*p*
1	b	2	r	3	u
2	s	3	u	4	v
3	t	4	w	5	o
4	o	5	x	4	v
3	t	6	o	3	u
2	s	5	x	2	r
1	b	4	w	3	o
				2	r
				1	b

Figure 4.41 Values of parameters in execution of *copy* (*A*)

4.9.2.2   List Equality

Another useful procedure determines whether two lists are identical. To be identical, the lists must have the same structure and the same data in corresponding fields. Again, using the recursive definition of a list, we can write a short recursive procedure (Program 4.30) to accomplish this task.

Procedure *equal* is a function that returns the value **true** or **false**. Its computing time is clearly no more than linear when no sublists are shared, since it looks at each node of *s* and *t* no more than three times. For unequal lists the procedure terminates as soon as it discovers that the lists are not identical.

```
function equal (s,t : ListPointer) : boolean;
{s and t are nonrecursive lists.  This function has value true iff the two lists are identical.}
var x : boolean;
begin
  equal := false;
  if (s = nil) and (t = nil)
  then equal := true
  else if (s <> nil) and (t <> nil)
       then if s↑.tag = t↑.tag
            then begin
                 if not s↑.tag
                 then if s↑.data = t↑.data then x := true
                                           else x := false
                 else x := equal (s↑.dlink,t↑.dlink);
                 if x then equal := equal (s↑.link,t↑.link)
                 end;
end; {of equal}
```

Program 4.30: Determining if two lists are identical

4.9.2.3   List Depth

Another handy operation on nonrecursive lists is the function that computes the depth of a list. The depth of the empty list is defined to be zero and, in general,

$$depth(s) = \begin{cases} 0 & \text{if } s \text{ is an atom} \\ 1 + \max\{depth(x_1), \cdots, depth(x_n)\} & \text{if } s \text{ is the list } (x_1, \cdots, x_n), n \geq 1 \end{cases}$$

Function *depth* (Program 4.31) is a very close transformation of the definition, which is itself recursive. By now you have seen several programs of this type, and you should be feeling more comfortable both reading and writing recursive algorithms.

4.9.3   Reference Counts, Shared and Recursive Lists

In this section we shall consider some of the problems that arise when lists are allowed to be shared by other lists and when recursive lists are permitted. Sharing of sublists can, in some situations, result in great savings in storage used, as identical sublists occupy the same space. To facilitate specifying shared sublists, we extend the definition of a list to allow for naming of sublists. A sublist appearing within a list definition may be named

---

```
function depth (s : ListPointer) : integer;
{Compute the depth of the nonrecursive list s.}
var p : ListPointer; m,n : integer;
begin
 if s <> nil
 then begin
          p := s; m := 0;
          while p <> nil do
          begin
            if p ↑. tag
            then begin
                    n := depth (p ↑. dlink);
                    if m < n then m := n;
                end;
            p := p ↑. link;
          end;
          depth := m + 1;
        end
  else depth := 0;
end; {of depth}
```

Program 4.31: Computing the depth of a list

through the use of a list name preceding it. For example, in the list $A = (a, (b,c))$, the sublist (b,c) could be assigned the name Z by writing $A = (a,Z(b,c))$. In fact, to be consistent, we would then write $A(a,Z(b,c))$ which would define the list A as above.

Lists that are shared by other lists, such as list A of Figure 4.39, create problems when you wish to add or delete a node at the front. If the first node of A is deleted, it is necessary to change the pointers from list B to point to the second node. If a new node is added, pointers from B have to be changed to point to the new first node. However, we normally do not know all the points from which a particular list is being referenced. (Even if you did have this information, addition and deletion of nodes could require a large amount of time.) This problem is easily solved through the use of head nodes. If you expect to perform many additions and deletions at the front of lists, then the use of a head node with each list or named sublist will eliminate the need to retain a list of all pointers to any specific list. If each list is to have a head node, then lists (1) to (4) are represented as in Figure 4.42. Even in situations in which you do not wish to add or delete nodes from lists dynamically, as in the case of multivariate polynomials, head nodes prove useful in determining when the nodes of a particular structure may be returned to the storage pool. For example, let t and u be program variables pointing to the two polynomials $(3x^4 + 5x^3 + 7x)y^3$ and $(3x^4 + 5x^3 + 7x)y^6 + (6x)y$ of Figure 4.43. If *perase* is to erase a polynomial, then the invocation *perase*(*t*) should not return the nodes corresponding to the coefficient $3x^4 + 5x^3 + 7x$, since this sublist is also part of *u*.

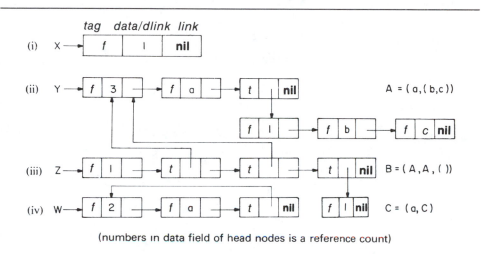

(numbers in data field of head nodes is a reference count)

Figure 4.42: Structure with head nodes for lists (1) to (4)

Thus, whenever lists are being shared by other lists, we need a mechanism to help determine whether or not the list nodes may be physically returned to the available-space list. This mechanism is generally provided through the use of a reference count maintained in the head node of each list. Since the *data* field of the head nodes is free, the reference count is maintained in this field. (Alternatively, a third variant may be introduced, with *tag* having three possible values: 0, 1, and 2.) This reference count of a list is the number of pointers (either program variables or pointers from other lists) to that list. If the lists (1) to (4) of Figure 4.42 are accessible via the program variables *x, y, z,* and *w*, then the reference counts for the lists are

(1) $ref(x) = 1$ accessible only via *x*

(2) $ref(y) = 3$ pointed to by *y* and two pointers from *z*

(3) $ref(z) = 1$ accessible only via *z*

(4) $ref(w) = 2$ two pointers to list *c*

Now a call to *lerase*(*t*) (list erase) should result only in a decrementing by 1 of the reference counter of *t*. Only if the reference count becomes zero are the nodes of *t* to be physically returned to the available-space list. The same is to be done with the sublists of *t*.

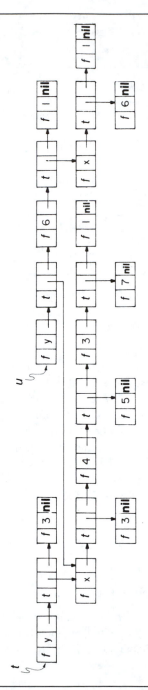

Figure 4.43: $t = (3x^4 + 5x^3 + 7x)y^3$, $u = (3x^4 + 5x^3 + 7x)y^6 + (6x)y$

Assume that the data type *ListPointer* is defined as

type *ListPointer* = ↑*ListNode*;
  three = 0..2;
  ListNode = **record**
    link : *ListPointer*;
    case *tag* : *three* **of**
      0 : (*data* : **integer**);
      1 : (*dlink* : *ListPointer*);
      2 : (*ref* : **integer**);
  end;

A recursive algorithm to erase a list *x* is given in Program 4.32. This proceeds by examining the top-level nodes of a list whose reference count has become zero. Any such sublists encountered are erased, and finally, the top-level nodes are linked into the available-space list.

```
procedure lerase (var x : ListPointer);
{Each head node has a reference count. We assume x ≠ nil.}
var y : ListPointer;
begin
  x↑.ref := x↑.ref−1; {decrement reference count}
  if x↑.ref = 0
  then begin
        y := x; {y traverses top-level of x}
        while y↑.link <> nil do
        begin
          y := y↑.link;
          if y↑.tag then lerase (y↑.dlink);
        end;
        y↑.link := av; {attach top level nodes to av list}
        av := x;
      end;
  x := nil;
end; {of lerase}
```

Program 4.32: Erasing a list recursively

A call to *lerase*(*y*) now has only the effect of decreasing the reference count of *y* to 2. Such a call followed by a call to *lerase*(*z*) results in

(1)   the reference count of *z* becomes zero

(2)   the next node is processed and *y*↑.*ref* reduces to 1

(3) $y\uparrow.ref$ becomes zero and the five nodes of list $A(a,(b,c))$ are returned to the available-space list

(4)   the top-level nodes of z are linked into the available-space list.

The use of head nodes with reference counts solves the problem of determining when nodes are to be physically freed in the case of shared sublists. However, for recursive lists, the reference count never becomes zero. $lerase(w)$ results in $w\uparrow.ref$ becoming one. The reference count does not become zero, even though this list is no longer accessible either through program variables or through other structures. The same is true in the case of indirect recursion (Figure 4.44). After calls to $lerase(r)$ and $lerase(s)$, $r\uparrow.ref=1$ and $s\uparrow.ref=2$ but the structure consisting of r and s is no longer being used, so it should have been returned to the available-space list.

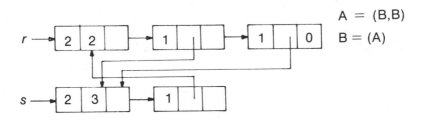

Figure 4.44: Indirect recursion of lists A and B pointed to by program variables r and s

Unfortunately, there is no simple way to supplement the list structure of Figure 4.44 so as to be able to determine when recursive lists may be physically erased. It is no longer possible to return all free nodes to the available-space list when they become free. When recursive lists are being used, it is possible to run out of available space, even though not all nodes are in use. When this happens, it is possible to collect unused nodes (i.e., garbage nodes) through a process known as garbage collection, which will be described in the next section.

EXERCISES

1.   Write a nonrecursive version of algorithm $lerase(x)$ (Program 4.32).

2.   Write a nonrecursive version of algorithm $equal(s,t)$ (Program 4.30).

3.   Write a nonrecursive version of algorithm $depth(s)$ (Program 4.31).

4.   Write a procedure that inverts an arbitrary nonrecursive list l with no shared sublists, and and all of its sublists. For example, if $l=(a,(b,c))$, then inverse $(l)=((c,b),a)$.

5. Devise a procedure that produces the list representation of an arbitrary list, given its linear form as a string of atoms, commas, blanks, and parentheses. For example, for the input $l = (a, (b,c))$, your procedure should produce the structure of Figure 4.45.

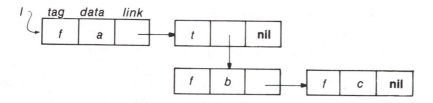

Figure 4.45: Structure for Exercise 5

6. One way to represent generalized lists is through the use of two field nodes and a symbol table that contains all atoms and list names, together with pointers to these lists. Let the two fields of each node be named *alink* and *blink*. Then *blink* either points to the next node on the same level, if there is one, or it is **nil**. The *alink* field points either to a node at a lower level or, in the case of an atom or list name, to the appropriate entry in the symbol table. For example, the list $B(A, (D,E),(\ ),B)$ would have the representation given in Figure 4.46. This figure assumes that all pointers are integer addresses.

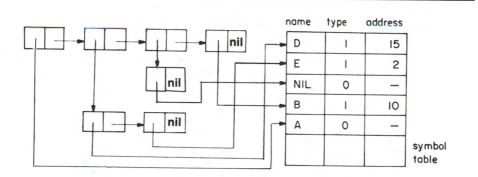

Figure 4.46: Representation for Exercise 6

(The list names D and E were already in the table at the time the list B was input. A was not in the table and is assumed to be an atom.)

The symbol table retains a type bit for each entry. This bit is 1 if the entry is a list name and 0 for an atom. The NIL atom may be in the table, or *alink* can be set to **nil** to represent the NIL atom. Write an algorithm *lread* to read in a list in parenthesis notation and to set up its linked representation as above, with *x* set to point to the first node in the list. Note that no head nodes are in use. You may need to use variant records or simulate pointers by integers (or both). The following subalgorithms may be used by *lread*:

(a) *get(a,p)* searches the symbol table for the name *a*. *p* is set to 0 if *a* is not found in the table; otherwise, *p* is set to the position of *a* in the table.

(b) *put(a,t,p)* enters *a* into the table. *p* is the position at which *a* was entered. If *a* is already in the table, then the type and address fields of the old entry are changed. *t* = **nil** to enter an atom or *t* <> **nil** to enter a list with first node *t*. (Note: This permits definition of lists using indirect recursion.)

(c) *NextToken* gets the next token in the input list. (A token may be a list name, atom, '(',')' or ','. A '#' is returned if there are no more tokens.)

(d) *new(x)* gets a node for use.

You may assume that the input list is syntactically correct. If a sublist is labeled, as in the list $C(D,E(F,G))$, the structure should be set up as in the case $C(D,(F,G))$, and *E* should be entered into the symbol table as a list with the appropriate starting address.

7. [**Wilczynski**] Following the conventions of LISP, assume nodes with two fields: *HEAD* and *TAIL*. If $A = ((a(bc)))$, then $HEAD(A) = (a(bc))$, $TAIL(A) = $ NIL, $HEAD(HEAD(A)) = a$, and $TAIL(HEAD(A)) = ((bc))$. $CONS(A,B)$ gets a new node *T*, stores *A* in its *HEAD*, *B* in its *TAIL*, and returns *T*. *B* must always be a list. If $L = a$ and $M = (bc)$, then $CONS(L,M) = (abc)$ and $CONS(M,M) = ((bc)bc)$. Three other useful functions are: $ATOM(X)$ which is true if *X* is an atom else false, $NULL(X)$ which is true if *X* is NIL else false, $EQUAL(X,Y)$ which is true if *X* and *Y* are the same atoms or equivalent lists else false.

(a) Give a sequence of *HEAD* and *TAIL* operations for extracting *a* from the lists: $((cat)), ((a)), ((mart))$, and $(((cb))a)$.

(b) Write recursive procedures for the standard LISP functions *COPY*, *REVERSE*, and *APPEND*.

(c) Implement this LISP subsystem. Store atoms in an array and write procedures *MakeList* and *ListPrint* for input and output of lists.

4.10   GARBAGE COLLECTION AND COMPACTION

4.10.1   Introduction

As remarked at the close of the last section, garbage collection is the process of collecting all unused nodes and returning them to available space. This process is carried out in two phases. In the first phase, known as the marking phase, all nodes in use are marked. In the second phase all unmarked nodes are returned to the available space list. The second phase is trivial when all nodes are of the same size. In this case, the second phase requires only the examination of each node to see if it has been marked. If there are a total of n nodes, then the second phase of garbage collection can be carried out in $O(n)$ steps. In this situation, only the first, or marking, phase is of any interest in designing an algorithm. When nodes of a variable size are in use, it is desirable to compact memory so that all free nodes form a continuous block of memory. In this case the second phase is referred to as memory compaction. Compaction of disk space to reduce average retrieval time is desirable even for nodes of fixed size. In this section we shall study two marking algorithms and one compaction algorithm.

4.10.2   Marking

To carry out the marking, we need a *mark* field in each node. It will be assumed that this *mark* field can be changed at any time by the marking algorithm. Marking algorithms mark all directly accessible nodes (i.e., nodes accessible through program variables referred to as pointer variables), as well as all indirectly accessible nodes (i.e., nodes accessible through pointer fields of nodes in accessible lists). It is assumed that a certain set of variables has been specified as pointer variables and that these variables at all times are either **nil** (i.e., point to nothing) or are valid pointers to lists. It is also assumed that the pointer fields of nodes always contain valid pointer information.

If the pointer variables are known, it is easy to mark all directly accessible nodes. The indirectly accessible nodes are marked by systematically examining all nodes reachable from these directly accessible nodes. Before examining the marking algorithms, let us review the node structure in use. Each node, regardless of its usage, will have two boolean fields: *mark* and *tag*. If *tag* = **false**, then the node contains only atomic information in a field called *data*. If *tag* = **true**, then the node has two pointer fields: *dlink* and *rlink*. Atomic information can be stored only in nodes that have *tag* = **false**. Such nodes are called *atomic* nodes. All other nodes are list nodes. This node structure is slightly different from the one used in the previous section, where a node with *tag* = **false** contained atomic information as well as a pointer. With this new node structure, the list $(a, (b))$ is represented as in Figure 4.47. The type definition for the new nodes is given below:

type *ListPointer* = ↑*ListNode*;
        ListNode = **record**
                mark : **boolean**;
                case *tag* : **boolean of**
                        true : (*dlink* : *ListPointer*;
                                rlink : *ListPointer*);
                        false : (*data* : **char**)
        end;

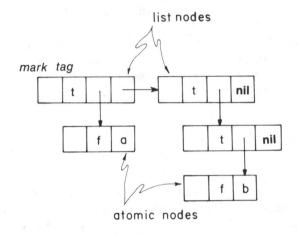

Figure 4.47: List (*a*, (*b*))

Both of the marking algorithms we shall discuss require that all nodes be initially unmarked (i.e., *x*↑.*mark* = **false** for every node *x*↑). Procedure *driver* (Program 4.33) will repeatedly call a marking algorithm to mark all nodes accessible from each of the pointer variables being used. In line 6, procedure *mark*1 (Program 4.34) is invoked. If we wish to use the second marking algorithm, then we need merely invoke *mark*2 (Program 4.35) instead of *mark*1. Both marking algorithms have been written to work on arbitrary list structures (not just generalized lists as described here).

4.10.2.1 First Marking Algorithm

The first marking algorithm, *mark*1 (Program 4.34), starts from the list node *x* and marks all nodes that can be reached from *x* via a sequence of *rlink*'s and *dlink*'s; examining all such paths results in the examination of all reachable nodes. While examining any node

```
1 procedure driver
2 begin
3 for each pointer variable x that points to an unmarked node do
4 begin
5   x↑.mark := true;
6   if x↑.tag then mark1(x); {x is a list node}
7 end;
8 end; {of driver}
```

Program 4.33: Marking all nodes in use

```
1  procedure mark1(x : ListPointer);
2  {Mark all nodes accessible from the list node x. add and delete
3   are the standard stack procedures. top points to the stack top.}
4  var p,q : ListPointer; done : boolean;
5  begin
6    top := 0; add(x); {put x on the stack}
7    while top > 0 do {stack not empty}
8    begin
9      delete(p); {unstack}; done := false;
10     repeat {move down stacking rlinks as needed}
11       q := p↑.rlink;
12       if q <> nil
13       then begin
14             if q↑.tag and not q↑.mark then add(q); {unmarked list node}
15             q↑.mark := true; {mark q}
16           end;
17       p := p↑.dlink;
18       if p <> nil then {a marked or atomic node cannot lead to new nodes}
19                       if p↑.mark or not p↑.tag then done := true
20                                            else p↑.mark := true
21               else done := true;
22     until done;
23     if p <> nil then p↑.mark := true;
24   end; {of while}
25 end; {of mark1}
```

Program 4.34: First marking algorithm

of type list, we have a choice to move to the *dlink* or to the *rlink*. *mark*1 moves to the *dlink* but at the same time places the *rlink* on a stack if the *rlink* is a list node not yet marked. The use of this stack enables us to return at a later point to the *rlink* and examine all paths from there. This strategy is similar to the one used in the previous section for *lerase* (Program 4.32).

Analysis of *mark1*: In lines 12 to 14 of *mark*1 we check to see if $q = p\uparrow.rlink$ can lead to other unmarked accessible nodes. If so, q is stacked. The examination of nodes continues with the node at $p\uparrow.dlink$. When we have moved down as far as possible, we exit from the loop of lines 10 to 22. At this point we try out one of the alternative moves from the stack, line 9. You may verify that *mark*1 does indeed mark all previously unmarked nodes that are accessible from x.

In analyzing the computing time of this algorithm we observe that on each iteration (except for the last) of the loop of lines 10 to 22, at least one previously unmarked node gets marked (line 20). Thus, if the **while** loop, lines 7 to 24, is iterated r times and the total number of iterations of the **repeat** loop, lines 10 to 22, is u, then at least $w = u - r$ previously unmarked nodes get marked by the algorithm. Let m be the number of new nodes marked. Then $m \geq w = u - r$. Also, the number of iterations of the loop of lines 7 to 24 is one, plus the number of nodes that get stacked. The only nodes that can be stacked are those previously unmarked (line 14). Once a node is stacked it gets marked (line 15). Hence, $r \leq m + 1$. From this and the knowledge that $m \geq u - r$, we conclude that $u \leq 2m + 1$. The computing time of the algorithm is $O(u + r)$. Substituting for u and r, we obtain $O(m)$ as the computing time. The time is linear in the number of new nodes marked. Since any algorithm to mark nodes must spend at least one unit of time on each new node marked, there is no algorithm with a time less than $O(m)$. Hence, *mark*1 is optimal to within a constant factor (recall that $2m = O(m)$ and $10m = O(m)$). □

Having observed that *mark*1 is optimal to within a constant factor, you may be tempted to sit back in your arm chair and relish a moment of smugness. There is, unfortunately, a serious flaw with *mark*1. This flaw is sufficiently serious to make the algorithm of little use in many garbage collection applications. Garbage collectors are invoked only when we have run out of space. This means that at the time *mark*1 is to operate, we do not have an unlimited amount of space available in which to maintain the stack. In some applications each node might have a free field that can be used to maintain a linked stack. In fact, if nodes of variable size are in use and storage compaction is to be carried out, then such a field will be available (see the compaction algorithm *compact* (Program 4.39). When fixed-size nodes are in use, compaction can be carried out efficiently without this additional field, so we will not be able to maintain a linked stack (see exercises for another special case permitting the growth of a linked stack). Realizing this deficiency in *mark*1, let us proceed to another marking algorithm, *mark*2. *mark*2 does not require additional space in which to maintain a stack. Its computing time is also $O(m)$, but the constant factor here is larger than that for *mark*1.

4.10.2.2   Second Marking Algorithm

Unlike *mark*1, which does not alter any of the links in the list *x*, our second marking algorithm, *mark*2 (Program 4.35), modifies some of these links. However, by the time *mark*2 finishes its task, the list structure is restored to its original form. Starting from a list node *x*, *mark*2 traces all possible paths made up of *dlink*'s and *rlink*'s. Whenever a choice is to be made, the *dlink* direction is explored first. Instead of maintaining a stack of alternative choices (as was done by *mark*1), we now maintain the path taken from *x* to the node *p* that is currently being examined. This path is maintained by changing some of the links along the path from *x* to *p*.

Consider the example list of Figure 4.48(a). Initially all nodes except node *A* are unmarked, and only node *E* is atomic. From node *A* we can move either down to node *B* or right to node *I*. *mark*2 always moves down when faced with such a choice. We shall use *p* to point to the node currently being examined and *t* to point to the node preceding *p* in the path from *x* to *p*. The path *t* to *x* is maintained as a chain comprised of the nodes on this *t*−*x* path (read as "*t* to *x*"). If we advance from node *p* to node *q*, then either $q = p\uparrow.rlink$ or $q = p\uparrow.dlink$, and *q* becomes the node currently being examined. The node preceding *q* on the *x*−*q* path is *p*, so the path list must be updated to represent the path from *p* to *x*. This is done simply by adding node *p* to the *t*−*x* path already constructed. Nodes are linked onto this path through either their *dlink* or their *rlink* field. Only list nodes are placed onto this path chain. When node *p* is being added to the path chain, *p* is linked to *t* via its *dlink* field if $q = p\uparrow.dlink$. When $q = p\uparrow.rlink$, *p* is linked to *t* via its *rlink* field. To determine whether a node on the *t*−*x* path list is linked through its *dlink* or *rlink* field, we make use of the *tag* field. Notice that since the *t*−*x* path list contains only list nodes, the tag on each of these nodes is **true**. When the *dlink* field is used for linking, this tag is changed to **false**. Thus, for nodes on the *t*−*x* path,

$$tag = \begin{cases} \textbf{false} \text{ if the node is linked via its } dlink \text{ field} \\ \textbf{true} \text{ if the node is linked via its } rlink \text{ field} \end{cases}$$

The tag is reset to true when the node gets off the *t*−*x* path list. (Although this use of the *tag* field represents a slight abuse of the language, it is preferable to introducing an additional field.)

Figure 4.48(b) shows the *t*−*x* path list when node *p* is being examined. Nodes *A*, *B*, and *C* have a tag of zero (for false), indicating that linking on these nodes is via the *dlink* field. This also implies that in the original list structure, $B = A\uparrow.dlink$, $C = B\uparrow.dlink$, and $D = p = C\uparrow.dlink$. Thus, the link information destroyed while creating the *t*−*x* path list is present in the path list. Nodes *B*, *C*, and *D* have already been marked by the algorithm. In exploring *p*, first we attempt to move down to $q = p\uparrow.dlink = E$. *E* is an atomic node, so it gets marked, and then we attempt to move right from *p*. Now, $q = p\uparrow.rlink = F$. This is an unmarked list node. So, we add *p* to the path list and proceed to explore *q*. Since *p* is linked to *q* by its *rlink* field, the linking of *p* onto the *t*−*x* path is made through its *rlink* field. Figure 4.48(c) shows the list structure at

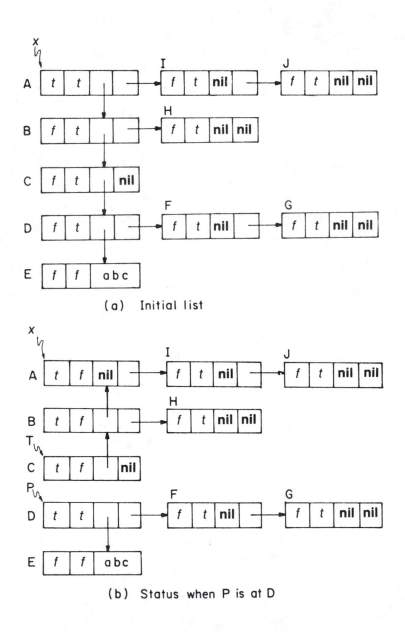

(a)   Initial list

(b)   Status when P is at D

Figure 4.48: Example list for *mark2* (continued on next page)

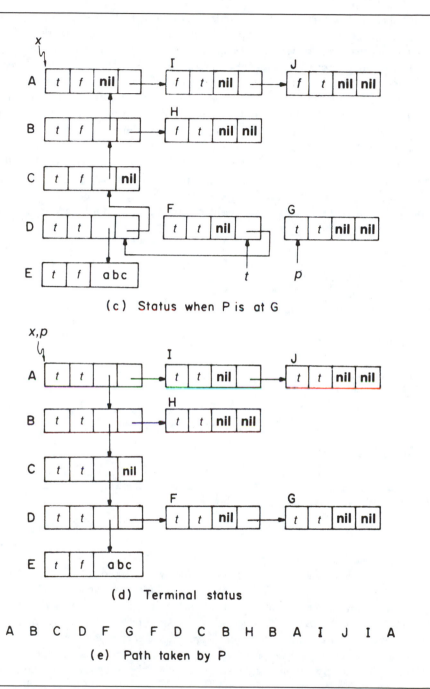

(c) Status when P is at G

(d) Terminal status

A B C D F G F D C B H B A I J I A

(e) Path taken by P

Figure 4.48: Example list for *mark2*

the time node G is being examined. Node G is a dead end. We cannot move further down or right. At this time we move backward on the $x-t$ path, resetting *link* and *tag* fields until we reach a node whose *rlink* has not yet been examined. The marking continues from this node. Because nodes are removed from the $t-x$ path list in the reverse order in which they were added to it, this list behaves as a stack. The remaining details of *mark 2* are spelled out in Program 4.35. The same driver as for *mark 1* is assumed.

The procedure *mark2* given in Program 4.35 makes use of three other procedures, which are given in Programs 4.36 to 4.38. These procedures are to be placed between the **var** and first **begin** statement of *mark2*. Procedure *mark2* first attempts to move p one node down. If it cannot, then it attempts to move p one node to the right. If this cannot be done, then we attempt to move backward on the $t-x$ list and move p to a node from which a move to the right may be possible. When even this backward movement is not possible, *mark2* terminates. The correctness of the procedures of Programs 4.35 to 4.38 is easily established.

```
procedure mark2(x : ListPointer);
{Same function as mark1 (Program 4.34).}
var p, q, t : ListPointer; failure : boolean;
begin
    p := x; t := nil; {initialize t −x path list}
    repeat
      MoveDown ;
      if failure then begin
                        MoveRight;
                        if failure then backup;
                  end;
    until failure;
end; {of mark2}
```

Program 4.35: Second marking algorithm

Analysis of *mark2*: Figure 4.48(e) shows the path taken by p on the list of Figure 4.48(a). It should be clear that a list node previously unmarked gets visited at most three times. Except for node x, each time a node already marked is reached, at least one previously unmarked node is also examined (i.e., the one that led to this marked node). Hence the computing time of *mark2* is $O(m)$, where m is the number of newly marked nodes. The constant factor associated with m is, however, larger than that for *mark1*, but *mark2* does not require the stack space needed by *mark1*. A faster marking algorithm can be obtained by judiciously combining the strategies of *mark1* and *mark2* (see the exercises).

When the node structure of Section 4.9 is in use, an additional boolean field in each node is needed to implement the strategy of *mark2*. This field is used to distinguish

procedure *MoveDown*;
{Attempt to move *p* one node down.}
begin
　q := *p*↑.*dlink*; {go down list}; *failure* := **true**;
　if *q* <> **nil**
　then if not *q*↑.*mark* **and** *q* ↑.*tag*
　　　then begin {unmarked list node}
　　　　　q↑.*mark* := **true**; *p* ↑.*tag* := **false**;
　　　　　p ↑.*dlink* := *t*; *t* := *p*; {add *p* to *t*−*x* path list}
　　　　　p := *q*; *failure* := **false**;
　　　　end
　　　else *q*↑.*mark* := **true**;
end; {of *MoveDown*}

Program 4.36: Moving down one node

procedure *MoveRight*;
{Attempt to move *p* one node right.}
begin
　q := *p* ↑.*rlink*; {move right}; *failure* := **true**;
　if *q* <> **nil**
　then if not *q*↑.*mark* **and** *q* ↑.*tag*
　　　then begin {unmarked list node}
　　　　　q↑.*mark* := **true**; *p* ↑.*rlink* := *t*;
　　　　　t := *p*; *p* := *q*; *failure* := **false**;
　　　　end
　　　else *q*↑.*mark* := **true**;
end; {of *MoveRight*}

Program 4.37: Moving right one node

between the case when a *dlink* is used to link into the path list and when an *rlink* is used. The existing *tag* field cannot be used, as some of the nodes on the *t*−*x* path list originally have *tag* = **true**, whereas others have *tag* = **false**, so it is not possible to reset *tag* values correctly when nodes are removed from the *t*−*x* list. □

```
procedure backup;
{Attempt to move backward on t−x list.}
begin
    failure := true;
    while (t <> nil) and failure do
    begin
        q := t;
        if not q↑.tag
        then begin {linked via dlink}
                t := q↑.dlink; q↑.dlink := p;
                q↑.tag := true; p := q;
                MoveRight;
            end
        else begin {linked via rlink}
                {p is to right of q}
                t := q↑.rlink; q↑.rlink := p;
                p := q;
            end;
    end; {of while}
end; {of backup}
```

Program 4.38: Moving backward on the t−x list

4.10.3   Storage Compaction

When all requests for storage are of a fixed size, it is enough just to link all unmarked (i.e., free) nodes together into an available-space list. However, when storage requests may be for blocks of varying sizes, it is desirable to compact storage so that all the free space forms one continuous block. Consider the memory configuration of Figure 4.49. Nodes in use have a *mark* field = t (for true), while free nodes have a *mark* field = f (for false). The nodes are labeled 1 through 8, with n_i, $1 \le i \le 8$, being the size of the *i*th node.

The free nodes could be linked together to obtain the available-space list of Figure 4.50. Although the total amount of memory available is $n_1 + n_3 + n_5 + n_8$, a request for this much memory cannot be met since the memory is fragmented into four nonadjacent nodes. Further, with more and more use of these nodes, the size of free nodes becomes smaller and smaller. Ultimately, it is impossible to meet requests for all but the smallest of nodes. To overcome this, it is necessary to reallocate the storage of the nodes in use so that the used part of memory (and hence also the free portion) forms a continuous block at one end, as in Figure 4.51. This reallocation of storage resulting in a partitioning of memory into two continuous blocks (one used, the other free) is referred to as

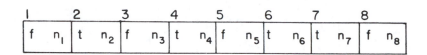

Figure 4.49: Memory configuraton after marking; free nodes have *mark* field = f

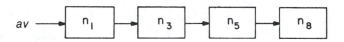

Figure 4.50: Available-space list corresponding to Figure 4.49

storage compaction. Since there will, in general, be links from one node to another, storage compaction must update these links to point to the relocated address of the respective node. If node n_i starts at location l_i before compaction and at l_i' after compaction, then all link references to l_i must also be changed to l_i' in order not to disrupt the linked-list structures existing in the system. Figure 4.52(a) shows a possible link configuration at the time the garbage collection process is invoked. Links are shown only for those nodes that were marked during the marking phase. It is assumed that there are only two links per node. Figure 4.52(b) shows the configuration following compaction. Note that the list structure is unchanged even though the actual addresses represented by the links have been changed.

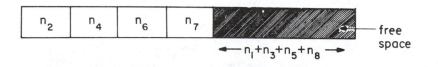

Figure 4.51: Memory configuraton after reallocating storage to nodes in use

With storage compaction we may identify three tasks: (1) determining new addresses for nodes in use, (2) updating all links in nodes in use, and (3) relocating nodes to new addresses. Our storage compaction algorithm, *compact* (Program 4.39), is fairly straightforward, implementing each of these three tasks in a separate scan of memory.

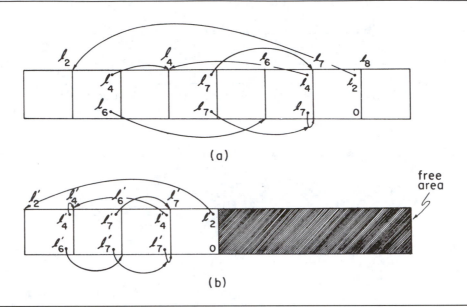

Figure 4.52: Configurations before and after compaction

The algorithm assumes that each node, free or in use, has a *size* field giving the length of the node and an additional field, *NewAddr*, which may be used to store the relocated address of the node. Further, it is assumed that each node has two pointer fields, *link*1 and *link*2. The extension of the algorithm to the most general situation, in which nodes have a variable number of links, is simple and requires only a modification of the second phase. As in the case of the dynamic storage management algorithms of Section 4.8, the pointer fields contain integer values that give us the index of the first word in the node pointed at. Zero denotes a **nil** link. The fields in a node may be set and extracted using appropriate procedures and functions. In addition, we assume that the memory to be compacted is the array *memory* [1..*m*].

In analyzing this algorithm, we see that if the number of nodes in memory is n, then phases I and II each require n iterations of their respective **while** loops. Since each iteration of these loops takes $O(1)$ time, the time for these two phases is $O(n)$. Phase III, however, will, in general, be more expensive. Although the **while** loop of this phase is also executed only n times, the time per iteration depends on the size of the node being relocated. If s is the amount of memory in use, then the time for this phase is $O(n + s)$. The overall computing time is, therefore, $O(n + s)$. The value of av at the end of phase I marks the beginning of the free space. At the termination of the algorithm, the space *memory*[av] to *memory*[m] is free space. Finally, the physical relocation of nodes in phase III can be carried out using a long shift if your computer has this facility.

---

procedure *compact*;
{Compact the array *memory* [1..*m*]. Every node that is in use has *mark* = **true**, a *NewAddr* field, and two pointer fields. *size* (*i*) = number of words in the node.}
var *i,j,k* : **integer**;
begin
　{Phase I: Scan memory left to right, assigning new addresses to nodes in use.
　av = next available word.}
　av := 1; *i* := 1;
　while *i* <= *m* **do**
　begin
　　if *mark*(*i*) **then begin** {assign new addresses}
　　　　　　　　SetNewAddr (*i*) := *av*;
　　　　　　　　av := *av* + *size* (*i*);
　　　　　　　end;
　　i := *i* +*size* (*i*); {next node}
　end;
　{Phase II: Update all links. Assume that *NewAddr* (0) = 0.}
　i := 1;
　while *i* <= *m* **do**
　begin
　　if *mark*(*i*) **then begin**
　　　　　　　　SetLink 1(*i*,*NewAddr* (*link* 1(*i*)));
　　　　　　　　SetLink 2(*i*,*NewAddr* (*link* 2(*i*)));
　　　　　　　end;
　　i := *i* + *size* (*i*);
　end;
　{Phase III: Relocate nodes.}
　i := 1;
　while *i* <= *m* **do**
　　if *mark*(*i*) **then begin**
　　　　　　　　k := *i* −*NewAddr* (*i*); *l* := *NewAddr* (*i*);
　　　　　　　　for *j* := *i* **to** *i* + *size* (*i*) − 1 **do**
　　　　　　　　　memory [*j* − *k*] := *memory* [*j*];
　　　　　　　　i := *i* + *size* (*l*);
　　　　　　　end
　　　　　　else *i* := *i* + *size* (*i*);
end; {of *compact*}

Program 4.39: Memory compaction

In conclusion, we remark that both marking and storage compaction are slow processes. The time for the former is O(number of nodes); the time for the latter is O(number of nodes + Σ(size of nodes relocated)). In the case of generalized lists, garbage collection is necessitated by the absence of other efficient means to free storage when needed. Garbage collection has found use in some programming languages where it is desirable to free the user from the task of returning storage. In both situations, a disciplined use of pointer variables and pointer fields is required. Clever coding tricks involving illegal use of pointer fields could result in chaos during marking and compaction.

Although presented here primarily for use with generalized list systems using nodes of variable size, compaction can also be used in other environments, such as the dynamic storage allocation environment of Section 4.8. Even though coalescing of adjacent free blocks takes place in algorithm *free* of Section 4.8, it is still possible to have several small nonadjacent blocks of memory free. The total size of these blocks may be large enough to meet a request, and it may then be desirable to compact storage. The compaction algorithm in this case is simpler than the one described here. Since all addresses used within a block will be relative to the starting address rather than the absolute address, no updating of links within a block is required. Phases I and III can, therefore, be combined into one phase and phase II eliminated altogether. Since compaction is very slow, one would like to minimize the number of times it is carried out. With the introduction of compaction, several alternative schemes for dynamic storage management become viable. The exercises explore some of these alternatives.

EXERCISES

1. Rewrite algorithm *mark*1 (Program 4.34) using the conventions of the preceding section for a *tag* field.

2. Rewrite algorithm *mark*1 for the case when each list and sublist has a head node. Assume that the *dlink* field of each head node is free and so may be used to maintain a linked stack without using any additional space. Show that the computing time is still $O(m)$.

3. When the *dlink* field of a node is used to retain atomic information, implementing the marking strategy of *mark*2 (Program 4.35) requires an additional bit in each node. In this exercise we shall explore a marking strategy that does not require this additional bit. Its worst-case computing time will, however, be $O(mn)$, where m is the number of nodes marked and n the total number of nodes in the system. Write a marking algorithm using the node structure and conventions of this section. Each node has the following fields: *mark*, *tag*, *dlink*, and *rlink*. Your marking algorithm will use variable p to point to the node currently being examined and *next* to point to the next node to be examined. If l is the address of the as-yet-unexplored list node with least address and p the address of the node currently being examined, then the value of *next* will be min$\{l, p + 1\}$. Show that the computing time of your algorithm is $O(mn)$.

4. Prove that *mark* $2(x)$ marks all unmarked nodes accessible from x.

5. Write a composite marking algorithm using *mark*1, *mark*2, and a fixed amount m of stack space. Stack nodes as in *mark*1 until the stack is full. When the stack becomes full, revert to the strategy of *mark*2. On completion of *mark*2, pick up a node from the stack and explore it using the composite algorithm. If the stack never overflows, the composite algorithm will be as fast as *mark*1. When $m = 0$, the algorithm essentially becomes *mark*2. The computing time will, in general, be somewhere in between that of *mark*1 and *mark*2.

6. Write a storage compaction algorithm to be used following the marking phase of garbage collection. Assume that all nodes are of a fixed size and can be addressed as *node* $[i]$, $1 \leq i \leq m$. Show that this can be done in two phases, where in the first phase a left-to-right scan for free nodes and a right-to-left scan for nodes in use is carried out. During this phase, used nodes from the right end of memory are moved to free positions at the left end. The relocated address of such nodes is noted in one of the fields of the old address. At the end of this phase all nodes in use occupy a continuous chunk of memory at the left end. In the second phase, links to relocated nodes are updated.

7. Design a dynamic storage management system in which blocks of variable size are to be freed and allocated. Blocks are to be returned to the available-space list only during compaction. At all other times, a *tag* is set to indicate the block has become free. Assume that initially all of memory is free and available as one block. Let memory be addressed 1 through m. For your design, write the following algorithms:

    (a) *allocate*(n,p) allocates a block of size n; p is set to its starting address. Assume that size n includes any space needed for control fields in your design.

    (b) *free*(n,p) frees a block of size n beginning p.

    (c) *compact* compacts memory and reinitializes the available-space list. You may assume that all address references within a block are relative to the start of the block, so no pointer fields within blocks need to be changed. Also, there are no interblock references.

4.11 REFERENCES AND SELECTED READINGS

More list copying and marking algorithms may be found in ''Copying list structures using bounded workspace,'' by G. Lindstrom, *CACM*, 17:4, 1974, pp. 198-202; ''A nonrecursive list moving algorithm,'' by E. Reingold, *CACM*, 16:5, 1973, pp. 305-307; and ''Bounded workspace garbage collection in an address-order preserving list processing environment,'' by D. Fisher, *Information Processing Letters*, 3:1, 1974, pp. 29-32.

CHAPTER 5

TREES

5.1 INTRODUCTION

5.1.1 Terminology

In this chapter we shall study a very important data object, the tree. Intuitively, a tree structure means that the data are organized so that items of information are related by branches. One very common place where such a structure arises is in the investigation of genealogies. There are two types of genealogical charts that are used to present such data: the *pedigree* and the *lineal* chart. Figure 5.1 gives an example of each.

The pedigree chart of Figure 5.1(a) shows someone's ancestors, in this case those of Dusty, whose two parents are Honey Bear and Brandy. Brandy's parents are Coyote and Nugget, who are Dusty's grandparents on her father's side. The chart continues one more generation back to the great-grandparents. By the nature of things, we know that the pedigree chart is normally two-way branching, though this does not allow for inbreeding. When inbreeding occurs, we no longer have a tree structure unless we insist that each occurrence of breeding is separately listed. Inbreeding may occur frequently when describing family histories of flowers or animals.

The lineal chart of Figure 5.1(b), though it has nothing to do with people, is still a genealogy. It describes, in somewhat abbreviated form, the ancestry of the modern European languages. Thus, this is a chart of descendants rather than ancestors, and each item can produce several others. Latin, for instance, is the forebear of Spanish, French,

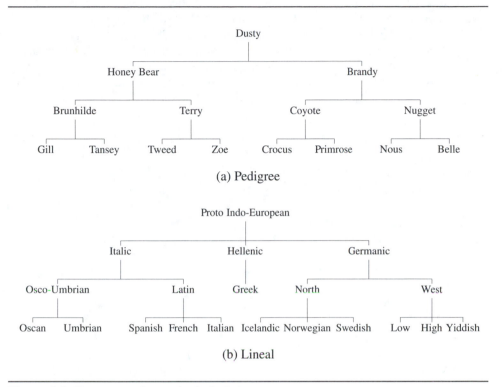

Figure 5.1: Two types of genealogical charts

and Italian. Proto Indo-European is a prehistoric language presumed to have existed in the fifth millenium B.C. This tree does not have the regular structure of the pedigree chart, but it is a tree structure nevertheless.

With these two examples as motivation, let us define formally what we mean by a tree.

Definition: A *tree* is a finite set of one or more nodes such that

(1)   There is a specially designated node called the *root.*

(2)   The remaining nodes are partitioned into $n \geq 0$ disjoint sets $T_1, \cdots, T_n$, where each of these sets is a tree. $T_1, \cdots, T_n$ are called the *subtrees* of the root. $\square$

Notice that we have an instance of a recursive definition. If we return to Figure 5.1, we see that the roots of the trees are Dusty and Proto Indo-European. Tree (a) has two subtrees, whose roots are Honey Bear and Brandy; tree (b) has three subtrees, with roots Italic, Hellenic, and Germanic. The condition that $T_1, \cdots, T_n$ be disjoint sets prohibits subtrees from ever connecting together (i.e., there is no cross-breeding). It follows that every item in a tree is the root of some subtree of the whole. For instance, Osco-Umbrian is the root of a subtree of Italic, which itself has two subtrees with the roots Oscan and Umbrian. Umbrian is the root of a tree with no subtrees.

There are many terms that are often used when referring to trees. A *node* stands for the item of information plus the branches to other nodes. Consider the tree in Figure 5.2. This tree has 13 nodes, each item of data being a single letter for convenience. The root is *A*, and we will normally draw trees with the root at the top.

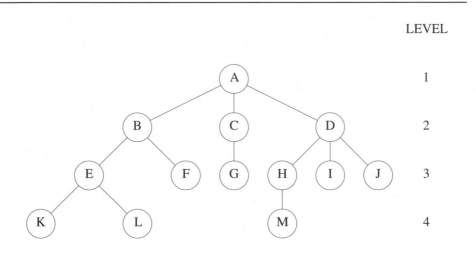

LEVEL

Figure 5.2: A sample tree

The number of subtrees of a node is called its *degree*. The degree of *A* is 3, of *C* is 1, and of *F* is zero. Nodes that have degree zero are called *leaf* or *terminal* nodes. {*K,L,F,G,M,I,J*} is the set of leaf nodes. Consequently, the other nodes are referred to as *nonterminals*. The roots of the subtrees of a node *X* are the *children* of *X*. *X* is the *parent* of its children. Thus, the children of *D* are *H, I*, and *J*; the parent of *D* is *A*. Children of the same parent are said to be *siblings*. *H, I*, and *J* are siblings. We can extend this terminology if we need to so that we can ask for the grandparent of *M*, which is *D*, and so on. The *degree of a tree* is the maximum of the degree of the nodes in the tree. The tree of Figure 5.2 has degree 3. The *ancestors* of a node are all the nodes along the path from the root to that node. The ancestors of *M* are *A, D*, and *H*.

The *level* of a node is defined by letting the root be at level one. If a node is at level *l*, then its children are at level *l* + 1. Figure 5.2 shows the levels of all nodes in that tree. The *height* or *depth of a tree* is defined to be the maximum level of any node in the tree. Thus, the depth of the tree in Figure 5.2 is 4.

5.1.2 Representation of Trees

5.1.2.1 List Representation

There are several ways to draw a tree besides the one presented in Figure 5.2. One useful way is as a list. The tree of Figure 5.2 could be written as the list

$$(A \, (B \, (E \, (K,L),F),C \, (G),D \, (H \, (M),I,J)))$$

The information in the root node comes first, followed by a list of the subtrees of that node. This way of drawing trees leads to a memory representation of trees that is the same as that used for generalized lists in Chapter 4. Figure 5.3 shows the resulting memory representation for the tree of Figure 5.2. If we use this representation, we can make use of many of the general procedures that we originally wrote for handling lists.

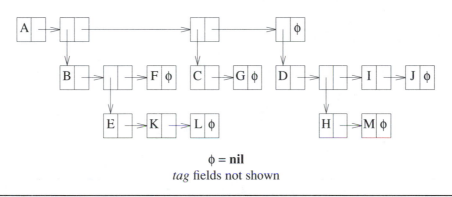

$\phi = $ **nil**

tag fields not shown

Figure 5.3: List representation of the tree of Figure 5.2

For several applications it is desirable to have a representation that is specialized to trees. One possibility is to represent each tree node by a memory node that has fields for the data and pointers to the tree node's children. Since the degree of each tree node may be different, we may be tempted to use memory nodes with a varying number of pointer fields. However, as it is often easier to write algorithms for a data representation when the node size is fixed, in practice one uses only nodes of a fixed size to represent tree nodes. For a tree of degree k, we could use the node structure of Figure 5.4. Each child field is used to point to a subtree. Lemma 5.1 shows that using this node structure is very wasteful of space.

Lemma 5.1: If T is a k-ary tree (i.e., a tree of degree k) with n nodes, each having a fixed size as in Figure 5.4, then $n \, (k - 1) + 1$ of the nk child fields are **nil**, $n \geq 1$.

| DATA | CHILD 1 | CHILD 2 | ... | CHILD k |

Figure 5.4: Possible node structure for a tree of degree k

Proof: Since each non-**nil** child field points to a node and there is exactly one pointer to each node other than the root, the number of non-**nil** child fields in an n-node tree is exactly $n - 1$. The total number of child fields in a k-ary tree with n nodes is nk. Hence, the number of **nil** fields is $nk - (n - 1) = n(k - 1) + 1$. $\square$

We shall develop two specialized fixed-node-size representations for trees. Both of these require exactly two link, or pointer, fields per node.

5.1.2.2 Left Child-Right Sibling Representation

Figure 5.5 shows the node structure used in the left child–right sibling representation.

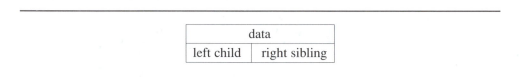

Figure 5.5: Left child-right sibling node structure

To convert the tree of Figure 5.2 into this representation, we first note that every node has at most one leftmost child and at most one closest right sibling. For example, in Figure 5.2, the leftmost child of A is B, and the leftmost child of D is H. Similarly, the closest right sibling of B is C, and the closest right sibling of H is I. Strictly speaking, since the order of children in a tree is not important, any of the children of a node could be the leftmost child, and any of its siblings could be the closest right sibling. For the sake of definiteness, we choose the nodes based on how the tree is drawn. The *left child* field of each node points to its leftmost child (if any), and the *right sibling* field points to its closest right sibling (if any). Figure 5.6 shows the tree of Figure 5.2 redrawn using the left child-right sibling representation.

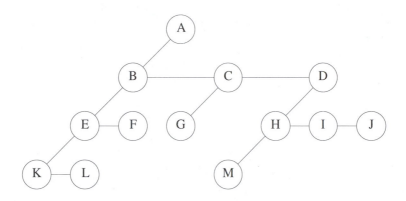

Figure 5.6: Left child-right sibling representation of tree of Figure 5.2

5.1.2.3   Representation as a Degree-Two Tree

To obtain the degree-two tree representation of a tree, we simply rotate the right-sibling pointers in a left child-right sibling tree clockwise by 45 degrees. This gives us the degree-two tree displayed in Figure 5.7. In the degree-two representation, we refer to the two children of a node as the left and right children. Notice that the right child of the root node of the tree is empty. This is always the case since the root of the tree we are transforming can never have a sibling. Figure 5.8 shows two additional examples of trees represented as left child-right sibling trees and as left child-right child (or degree-two) trees. Left child-right child trees are also known as *binary trees*.

EXERCISES

1. Write a procedure that reads in a tree represented as a list and creates its internal representation using nodes with three fields: *tag*, *data*, and *link*.

2. Write a procedure that reverses the process in Exercise 1 and takes a pointer to a tree and prints out its list representation.

3. [***Programming Project***] Assume that we represent trees using the list representation described in this section. Write Pascal subprograms that

    (a)   accept a tree represented as a parenthesized list as input and create the generalized list representation of the tree (see Figure 5.3)

    (b)   copy a tree represented as a generalized list

    (c)   test for equality between two trees represented as generalized lists

    (d)   erase a tree represented as a generalized list

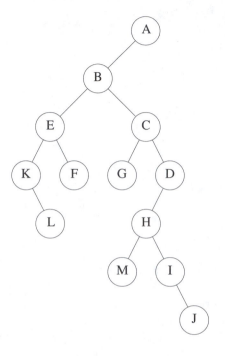

Figure 5.7: Left child-right child tree representation of tree of Figure 5.2

(e)   output a tree in its parenthesized list notation

Test the correctness of your subprograms using suitable test data.

5.2   BINARY TREES

5.2.1   The Abstract Data Type

We have seen that we can represent any tree as a binary tree. In fact, binary trees are an important type of tree structure that occurs very often. Binary trees are characterized by the fact that any node can have at most two branches (i.e., there is no node with degree greater than two). For binary trees we distinguish between the subtree on the left and that on the right, whereas for trees the order of the subtrees is irrelevant. Also, a binary tree may have zero nodes. Thus, a binary tree is really a different object from a tree.

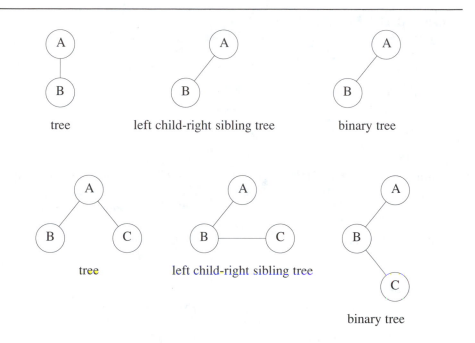

tree   left child-right sibling tree   binary tree

tree   left child-right sibling tree   binary tree

Figure 5.8: Tree representations

Definition: A *binary tree* is a finite set of nodes that either is empty or consists of a root and two disjoint binary trees called the *left subtree* and the *right subtree*. □

    Structure 5.1 contains the specification for the binary tree ADT. This structure defines only a minimal set of operations on binary trees, which we use as a foundation on which to build additional operations.

    Let us carefully review the distinctions between a binary tree and a tree. First, there is no tree having zero nodes, but there is an empty binary tree. Second, in a binary tree we distinguish between the order of the children; in a tree we do not. Thus, the two binary trees of Figure 5.9 are different, since the first binary tree has an empty right subtree, while the second has an empty left subtree. Viewed as trees, however, they are the same, despite the fact that they are drawn slightly differently.

    Figure 5.10 shows two special kinds of binary trees. The first is a *skewed* tree, skewed to the left, and there is a corresponding tree that skews to the right. The tree of Figure 5.10(b) is called a *complete* binary tree. This kind of binary tree will be defined formally later. Notice that all terminal nodes are on adjacent levels. The terms that we introduced for trees such as degree, level, height, leaf, parent, and child all apply to binary trees in the natural way.

structure *BinaryTree* (abbreviated *BinTree*) is

 objects: A finite set of nodes either empty or consisting of a root node, left *BinaryTree*, and right *BinaryTree*.

 functions:

   for all *bt,bt1,bt2* ∈ *BinTree*, *item* ∈ *element*

Create ( ) : *BinTree*	::=	creates an empty binary tree
IsEmpty (*bt*) : **boolean**	::=	**if** *bt* is an empty binary tree **then** *IsEmpty* := **true** **else** *IsEmpty* := **false**
MakeBT (*bt*1, *item*, *bt*2) : *BinTree*	::=	*MakeBT* is a binary tree whose left subtree is *bt*1, whose right subtree is *bt*2, and whose root node contains the data *item*
Lchild (*bt*) : *BinTree*	::=	**if** *IsEmpty* (*bt*) **then** *Lchild* := error **else** *Lchild* := the left subtree of *bt*
Data (*bt*) : *element*	::=	**if** *IsEmpty* (*bt*) **then** *Data* := error **else** *data* := the data in the root node of *bt*
Rchild (*bt*) : *BinTree*	::=	**if** *IsEmpty* (*bt*) **then** *Rchild* := error **else** *Rchild* := the right subtree of *bt*

Structure 5.1: Abstract data type *BinaryTree*

Figure 5.9: Two different binary trees

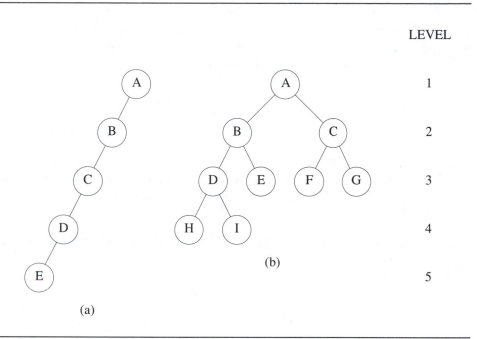

Figure 5.10: Skewed and complete binary trees

5.2.2 Properties of Binary Trees

Before examining data representations for binary trees, let us make some observations about such trees. In particular, we want to determine the maximum number of nodes in a binary tree of depth k and the relationship between the number of leaf nodes and the number of degree-two nodes in a binary tree.

Lemma 5.2 [*Maximum number of nodes*]:

(1)   The maximum number of nodes on level i of a binary tree is 2^{i-1}, $i \geq 1$.

(2)   The maximum number of nodes in a binary tree of depth k is $2^k - 1$, $k \geq 1$.

Proof:

(1) The proof is by induction on i.

Induction Base: The root is the only node on level $i = 1$. Hence, the maximum number of nodes on level $i = 1$ is $2^{i-1} = 2^0 = 1$.

Induction Hypothesis: Let i be an arbitrary positive integer greater than 1. Assume that the maximum number of nodes on level $i - 1$ is 2^{i-2}.

Induction Step: The maximum number of nodes on level $i - 1$ is 2^{i-2} by the induction hypothesis. Since each node in a binary tree has a maximum degree of 2, the maximum number of nodes on level i is two times the maximum number of nodes on level $i-1$, or 2^{i-1}.

(2) The maximum number of nodes in a binary tree of depth k is

$$\sum_{i=1}^{k} (\text{maximum number of nodes on level } i) = \sum_{i=1}^{k} 2^{i-1} = 2^k - 1 \ \square$$

Lemma 5.3 [*Relation between number of leaf nodes and degree-2 nodes*]: For any nonempty binary tree, T, if n_0 is the number of leaf nodes and n_2 the number of nodes of degree 2, then $n_0 = n_2 + 1$.

Proof: Let n_1 be the number of nodes of degree one and n the total number of nodes. Since all nodes in T are at most of degree two, we have

$$n = n_0 + n_1 + n_2 \tag{5.1}$$

If we count the number of branches in a binary tree, we see that every node except the root has a branch leading into it. If B is the number of branches, then $n = B + 1$. All branches stem from a node of degree one or two. Thus, $B = n_1 + 2n_2$. Hence, we obtain

$$n = B + 1 = n_1 + 2n_2 + 1 \tag{5.2}$$

Subtracting Eq. (5.2) from Eq. (5.1) and rearranging terms, we get

$$n_0 = n_2 + 1 \ \square$$

In Figure 5.10(a), $n_0 = 1$ and $n_2 = 0$; in Figure 5.10(b), $n_0 = 5$ and $n_2 = 4$.

We are now ready to define full and complete binary trees.

Definition: A *full binary tree* of depth k is a binary tree of depth k having $2^k - 1$ nodes, $k \geq 0$. $\square$

By Lemma 5.2, $2^k - 1$ is the maximum number of nodes in a binary tree of depth k. Figure 5.11 shows a full binary tree of depth 4. Suppose we number the nodes in a full binary tree starting with the root on level 1, continuing with the nodes on level 2, and so on. Nodes on any level are numbered from left to right. This numbering scheme gives us the definition of a complete binary tree.

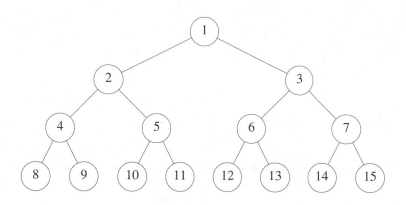

Figure 5.11: Full binary tree of depth 4 with sequential node numbers

Definition: A binary tree with n nodes and depth k is *complete* iff its nodes correspond to the nodes numbered from 1 to n in the full binary tree of depth k. □

From Lemma 5.2, it follows that the height of a complete binary tree with n nodes is $\lceil \log_2(n + 1) \rceil$.

5.2.3   Binary Tree Representations

5.2.3.1   Array Representation

The numbering scheme used in Figure 5.11 suggests our first representation of a binary tree in memory. Since the nodes are numbered from 1 to n, we can use a one-dimensional array to store the nodes. Using Lemma 5.4 we can easily determine the locations of the parent, left child, and right child of any node, i, in the binary tree.

Lemma 5.4: If a complete binary tree with n nodes is represented sequentially, then for any node with index i, $1 \leq i \leq n$, we have

(1)   *parent* (i) is at $\lfloor i/2 \rfloor$ if $i \neq 1$. If $i = 1$, i is at the root and has no parent.

(2)   *LeftChild* (i) is at $2i$ if $2i \leq n$. If $2i > n$, then i has no left child.

(3)   *RightChild* (i) is at $2i + 1$ if $2i + 1 \leq n$. If $2i + 1 > n$, then i has no right child.

Proof: We prove (2). (3) is an immediate consequence of (2) and the numbering of nodes on the same level from left to right. (1) follows from (2) and (3). We prove (2) by induction on i. For $i = 1$, clearly the left child is at 2 unless $2 > n$, in which case i has no left child. Now assume that for all j, $1 \leq j \leq i$, *LeftChild* (j) is at $2j$. Then the two nodes immediately preceding *LeftChild* $(i + 1)$ are the right and left children of i. The left child is at $2i$. Hence, the left child of $i + 1$ is at $2i + 2 = 2(i + 1)$ unless $2(i + 1) > n$, in which case $i + 1$ has no left child. $\square$

This representation can clearly be used for all binary trees, though in most cases there will be a lot of unutilized space. Figure 5.12 shows the array representation for both trees of Figure 5.10. For complete binary trees such as the one in Figure 5.10(b), the representation is ideal, as no space is wasted. For the skewed tree of Figure 5.10(a), however, less than half the array is utilized. In the worst case a skewed tree of depth k will require $2^k - 1$ spaces. Of these, only k will be used.

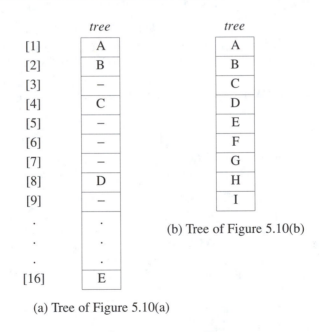

(a) Tree of Figure 5.10(a)

(b) Tree of Figure 5.10(b)

Figure 5.12: Array representation of the binary trees of Figure 5.10

5.2.3.2   Linked Representation

Although the array representation is good for complete binary trees, it is wasteful for many other binary trees. In addition, the representation suffers from the general inadequacies of sequential representations. Insertion and deletion of nodes from the middle of a tree require the movement of potentially many nodes to reflect the change in level number of these nodes. These problems can be overcome easily through the use of a linked representation. Each node has three fields, *LeftChild*, *data*, and *RightChild*, and is defined in Pascal as

type *TreePointer* = ↑*TreeRecord* ;
  TreeRecord = **record**
        LeftChild : *TreePointer* ;
        data : **char**;
        RightChild : *TreePointer* ;
      end;

We shall draw such a node using either of the representations of Figure 5.13.

Figure 5.13: Node representations

Although with this node structure it is difficult to determine the parent of a node, we shall see that for most applications, this structure is adequate. If it is necessary to be able to determine the parent of random nodes, then a fourth field, *parent*, may be included. The representation of the binary trees of Figure 5.10 using this node structure is given in Figure 5.14. A tree is referred to by the variable that points to its root.

EXERCISES

1. For the binary tree of Figure 5.15, list the terminal nodes, the nonterminal nodes, and the level of each node.

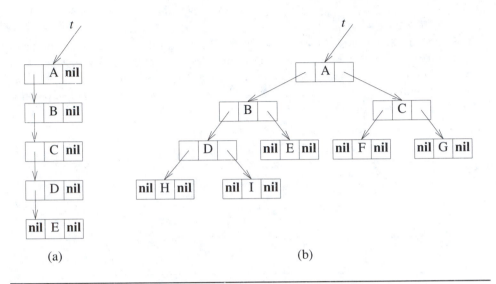

Figure 5.14: Linked representation for the binary trees of Figure 5.10

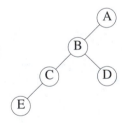

Figure 5.15: Binary tree for Exercise 1

2. What is the maximum number of nodes in a k-ary tree of height h? Prove your answer.

3. Draw the internal memory representation of the binary tree of Figure 5.15 using (a) sequential and (b) linked representations.

5.3   BINARY TREE TRAVERSAL

5.3.1   Introduction

There are many operations that we often want to perform on trees. One notion that arises frequently is the idea of traversing a tree or visiting each node in the tree exactly once. When a node is visited, some operation (such as outputting its *data* field) is performed on it. A full traversal produces a linear order for the nodes in a tree. This linear order, given by the order in which the nodes are visited, may be familiar and useful. When traversing a binary tree, we want to treat each node and its subtrees in the same fashion. If we let *L*, *V*, and *R* stand for moving left, visiting the node, and moving right when at a node, then there are six possible combinations of traversal: *LVR, LRV, VLR, VRL, RVL*, and *RLV*. If we adopt the convention that we traverse left before right, then only three traversals remain: *LVR, LRV*, and *VLR*. To these we assign the names *inorder, postorder*, and *preorder*, respectively, because of the position of the *V* with respect to the *L* and the *R*. For example, in postorder, we visit a node after we have traversed its left and right subtrees, whereas in preorder the visiting is done before the traversal of these subtrees.

There is a natural correspondence between these traversals and producing the infix, postfix, and prefix forms of an expression. Consider the binary tree of Figure 5.16. This tree contains an arithmetic expression with the binary operators add (+), multiply (*), and divide (/) and the variables *A, B, C, D*, and *E*. For each node that contains an operator, its left subtree gives the left operand and its right subtree the right operand. We will not worry for now how this binary tree was formed but assume that it is available. We use this tree to illustrate each of the traversals.

5.3.2   Inorder Traversal

Informally, *inorder traversal* calls for moving down the tree toward the left until you can go no farther. Then you "visit" the node, move one node to the right and continue. If you cannot move to the right, go back one more node. A precise way of describing this traversal is to write it as a recursive procedure as in Program 5.1. This procedure assumes that when a node is visited, we write out its *data* field (line 9). In other applications of inorder traversal, this line may be replaced by code to perform some other function on the node being visited.

Recursion is an elegant device for describing this traversal. Figure 5.17 is a trace of how procedure *inorder* (Program 5.1) works on the tree of Figure 5.16. Read down the left column first and then the right one. Including the initial invocation, the procedure is invoked a total of 19 times. The elements get output in the following order:

$$A \, / \, B * C * D + E$$

which is the *in*fix form of the expression.

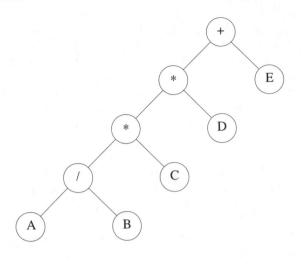

Figure 5.16: Binary tree with arithmetic expression

```
 1 procedure inorder (CurrentNode : TreePointer );
 2 {CurrentNode is a pointer to a node in a binary tree. For full
 3   tree traversal, pass inorder the pointer to the top of the tree.}
 4 begin
 5   if CurrentNode < > nil
 6   then
 7   begin
 8     inorder (CurrentNode ↑. LeftChild);
 9     write(CurrentNode ↑. data);
10     inorder (CurrentNode ↑. RightChild);
11   end
12 end; {of inorder}
```

Program 5.1: Inorder traversal of a binary tree

5.3.3   Preorder Traversal

The Pascal code for the second form of traversal, *preorder*, is given in Program 5.2. In words, we would say "visit a node, traverse left, and continue. When you cannot continue, move right and begin again or move back until you can move right and resume."

Call of *inorder*	Value in root	Action	Call of *inorder*	Value in root	Action
MAIN	+		10	C	
1	*		11	**nil**	
2	*		10	C	write('C')
3	/		12	**nil**	
4	A		1	*	write('*')
5	**nil**		13	D	
4	A	write('A')	14	**nil**	
6	**nil**		13	D	write('D')
3	/	write('/')	15	**nil**	
7	B		MAIN	+	write('+')
8	**nil**		16	E	
7	B	write ('B')	17	**nil**	
9	**nil**		16	E	write('E')
2	*	write('*')	18	**nil**	

Figure 5.17: Trace of Program 5.1

The nodes of Figure 5.16 would be output in *pre*order as

$$+ * * / A\ B\ C\ D\ E$$

which we recognize as the *pre*fix form of the expression.

5.3.4 Postorder Traversal

The code for *postorder* traversal is given in Program 5.3. On the tree of Figure 5.16, this procedure produces the following output:

$$A\ B\ /\ C * D * E +$$

which is the *post*fix form of our expression.

```
 1 procedure preorder (CurrentNode : TreePointer);
 2 {CurrentNode is a pointer to a node in a binary tree. For full
 3   tree traversal, pass preorder the pointer to the top of the tree.}
 4 begin
 5   if CurrentNode < > nil
 6   then
 7   begin
 8    write(CurrentNode↑.data);
 9    preorder (CurrentNode↑.LeftChild);
10    preorder (CurrentNode↑.RightChild);
11   end {of if}
12 end; {of preorder}
```

Program 5.2: Preorder traversal of a binary tree

```
 1 procedure postorder (CurrentNode : TreePointer);
 2 {CurrentNode is a pointer to a node in a binary tree. For full
 3   tree traversal, pass postorder the pointer to the top of the tree.}
 4 begin
 5   if CurrentNode < > nil
 6   then
 7   begin
 8    postorder (CurrentNode↑.LeftChild);
 9    postorder (CurrentNode↑.RightChild);
10    write(CurrentNode↑.data);
11   end {of if}
12 end; {of postorder}
```

Program 5.3: Postorder traversal of a binary tree

5.3.5   Iterative Inorder Traversal

Although we have written the code for the three traversal methods using recursion, it is very easy to produce equivalent nonrecursive versions. Such a version for inorder traversal is given in Program 5.4. This program uses procedures *add* (Program 3.1) and *delete* (Program 3.2) to add an element to a sequential stack and to delete an element from such a stack, respectively.

```
 1 procedure NonrecInorder (CurrentNode : TreePointer);
 2 {Nonrecursive inorder traversal using a stack of size MaxStackSize.}
 3 const MaxStackSize = 100;
 4 var done : boolean;
 5     StackPointer : integer;
 6     NodeStack : array [1..MaxStackSize] of TreePointer ;
 7 begin
 8   StackPointer := 0; {initialize stack}
 9   done := false; {initialize loop condition}
10   repeat
11     while CurrentNode <> nil do {move down LeftChild fields}
12     begin
13       add (CurrentNode ); {add to stack}
14       CurrentNode := CurrentNode↑.LeftChild;
15     end; {of while}
16     if StackPointer <> 0
17     then begin
18         delete (CurrentNode ); {delete from stack}
19         write(CurrentNode↑.data );
20         CurrentNode := CurrentNode↑.RightChild ;
21       end
22     else done := true;
23   until done;
24 end; {of NonrecInorder}
```

Program 5.4: Nonrecursive inorder traversal

Analysis of *NonrecInorder:* Let n be the number of nodes in the tree. If we consider the action of Program 5.4, we note that every node of the tree is placed on the stack once. Thus, the statements on lines 13 to 14 and 18 to 20 are executed n times. Moreover, *CurrentNode* will equal **nil** once for every **nil** link in the tree, which is exactly

$$2n_0 + n_1 = n_0 + n_1 + n_2 + 1 = n + 1$$

Every step will be executed no more than some constant times n, so the time complexity is $O(n)$. The run time can be reduced by a constant factor by eliminating some of the unneccessary stacking (see exercises). The space required for the stack is equal to the depth of the tree. This is at most n. □

5.3.6 Level-Order Traversal

Whether written iteratively or recursively, the inorder, preorder, and postorder traversals all require a stack. We now turn to a traversal that requires a queue. This traversal, called *level-order traversal*, visits the nodes using the ordering scheme suggested in Figure 5.11. Thus, we visit the root first, then the root's left child, followed by the root's right child. We continue in this manner, visiting the nodes at each new level from the leftmost node to the rightmost node.

The code for this traversal, given in Program 5.5, assumes a circular queue as in Chapter 3. Procedure *addq* differs from the corresponding one of Chapter 3 (Program 3.5) only in that the data type of the elements in the queue is different. Similarly, the procedure *deleteq* (compare Program 3.6) used in Program 5.5 returns a value of type *TreePointer* rather than of type element. It returns **nil** if the queue is empty.

```
procedure LevelOrder (CurrentNode : TreePointer);
{Traverse the binary tree CurrentNode in level order.}
begin
    front := 0; rear := 0; {initialize queue}
    while CurrentNode <> nil do
    begin
        write(CurrentNode↑.data);
        if CurrentNode↑.LeftChild <> nil then addq (CurrentNode↑.LeftChild);
        if CurrentNode↑.RightChild <> nil then addq (CurrentNode↑.RightChild);
        deleteq (CurrentNode);
    end;
end; {of LevelOrder}
```

Program 5.5: Level-order traversal of a binary tree

We begin by adding the root to the queue. The traversal works by deleting the node at the front of the queue, writing out the node's *data* field, and adding the node's left and right children to the queue (unless they are **nil**). Since a node's children are at the next lower level, and we add the left child before the right child, the nodes are output using the ordering scheme found in Figure 5.11. The level-order traversal of the tree in Figure 5.16 is

$$+ * E * D / C A B$$

5.3.7   Traversal without a Stack

Before we leave the topic of tree traversal, we shall consider one final question. Is inorder traversal of binary trees possible without the use of extra space for a stack? One simple solution is to add a *parent* field to each node. Then we can trace our way back up to any root and down again. Another solution, which requires two bits per node, represents binary trees as threaded binary trees. We study this in Section 5.5. If the allocation of this extra space is too costly, then we can use the method of algorithm *mark2* of Chapter 4 (Program 4.35). No extra storage is required, since during processing the *LeftChild* and *RightChild* fields are used to maintain the paths back to the root. The stack of addresses is stored in the leaf nodes. The exercises examine this algorithm more closely.

EXERCISES

1. Write out the inorder, preorder, postorder, and level-order traversals for the binary trees of Figure 5.10.
2. Do Exercise 1 for the binary tree of Figure 5.11.
3. Do Exercise 1 for the binary tree of Figure 5.15.
4. Write a nonrecursive version of procedure *preorder* (Program 5.2).
5. Write a nonrecursive version of procedure *postorder* (Program 5.3) that does not use the **goto** statement.
6. Rework *NonrecInorder* (Program 5.4) so that it is as fast as possible. (Hint: Minimize the stacking and the testing within the loop.)
7. Program 5.6 performs an inorder traversal without using threads, a stack, or a *parent* field. Verify that the algorithm is correct by running it on a variety of binary trees that cause every statement to execute at least once. Before attempting to study this algorithm, be sure you understand *mark2* of Chapter 4 (Program 4.35).

```
1  procedure NoStackInorder (CurrentNode : TreePointer);
2  {Inorder traversal of binary tree CurrentNode using a fixed
3  amount of additional storage.}
4  label 1, 80, 99;
5  var top, LastRight : TreePointer ;
6       p, q, r, av, r1 : TreePointer ;
7  begin
8  if CurrentNode = nil then goto 99; {empty binary tree}
9  top := nil; LastRight := nil; p := CurrentNode ; q := CurrentNode ;
10 repeat
11     repeat
12         if (p↑.LeftChild = nil) and (p↑.RightChild = nil
```

```
13              then {cannot move down}
14                  begin
15                      writeln(p↑.data); goto 1
16                  end
17              else if p↑.LeftChild = nil then {move to p↑.RightChild}
18                              begin
19                                  writeln(p↑.data);
20                                  r := p↑.RightChild; p↑.RightChild := q;
21                                  q := p; p := r;
22                              end
23                                  else {move to p↑.LeftChild}
24                                      begin
25                                          r :=p↑.LeftChild; p↑.LeftChild := q;
26                                          q :=p; p := r;
27                                      end
28          until false;
29  {p is a leaf node, move upward to a node whose right
30   subtree has not yet been examined}
31  1: av := p;
32      repeat
33              if p = t then goto 99;
34              if q↑.LeftChild = nil
35              then begin
36                      r := q↑.RightChild; q↑.RightChild := p;
37                      p := q; q := r;
38                  end
39              else if q↑.RightChild = nil
40                  then  begin {q is linked via LeftChild}
41                      r := q↑.LeftChild;q↑.LeftChild := p;
42                      p := q; q := r; writeln(p↑.data);
43                          end
44              else {check if p is RightChild of q}
45              if q = LastRight then begin
46                      r := top; LastRight := r↑.LeftChild;
47                      top := r↑.RightChild;    {unstack}
48                      r↑.LeftChild := nil; r↑.RightChild := nil;
49                      r :=q↑.RightChild; q↑.RightChild :=p;
50                      p := q; q :=r; end
51              else begin {p is LeftChild of q}
52                  writeln(q↑.data) {visit q}
53                  av↑.LeftChild := LastRight; av↑.RightChild := top;
54                  top := av; LastRight := q;
55                  r :=q↑.LeftChild; q↑.LeftChild := p; {restore link to p}
56                  r1 := q↑.RightChild; q↑.RightChild := r;
```

```
57                   p := r1; goto 80;
58                      {move right}
59                         end
60      until false;
61  80: {dummy statement}
62  until false;
63  99: end; {of NoStackInorder}
```

Program 5.6: O(1) space inorder traversal

8. Write a nonrecursive version of procedure *postorder* (Program 5.3) using only a fixed amount of additional space. (Use the ideas of the previous exercise.)

9. Do the preceding exercise for the case of *preorder* (Program 5.2).

5.4   ADDITIONAL BINARY TREE OPERATIONS

5.4.1   Copying Binary Trees

Using the definition of a binary tree and the recursive version of the traversals, we can easily write other routines for working with binary trees. For instance, if we want to produce an exact copy of a given binary tree, we can modify the postorder traversal algorithm only slightly to get Program 5.7.

```
function copy (OriginalTree : TreePointer) : TreePointer ;
{This function returns a pointer to an exact copy of the binary tree OriginalTree.}
var TempTree : TreePointer ;
begin
 if OriginalTree <> nil
 then begin
         new(TempTree);
         TempTree↑.LeftChild := copy (OriginalTree↑.LeftChild);
         TempTree↑.RightChild := copy(OriginalTree↑.RightChild);
         TempTree↑.data := OriginalTree↑.data ;
         copy := TempTree ;
 end
 else copy := nil;
end {of copy}
```

Program 5.7: Copying a binary tree

5.4.2   Testing Equality

Another problem that is especially easy to solve using recursion is determining the equivalence of two binary trees. Binary trees are equivalent if they have the same topology and the information in corresponding nodes is identical. By the same topology we mean that every branch in one tree corresponds to a branch in the second in the same order and vice versa. Function *equal* (Program 5.8) traverses the binary trees in preorder, though any order could be used.

---

function *equal* (*FirstTree*, *SecondTree* : *TreePointer*) : **boolean**;
{This procedure returns **false** if the binary trees *FirstTree* and *SecondTree* are not equivalent. Otherwise, it will return **true**.}
begin
  equal := **false**; {initialize answer}
  if (*FirstTree* = **nil**) **and** (*SecondTree* = **nil**)
  then *equal* := **true**
  else
    if (*FirstTree* < > **nil**) **and** (*SecondTree* < > **nil**)
    then if *FirstTree* ↑. *data* = *SecondTree* ↑. *data*
        then *equal* := *equal* (*FirstTree* ↑. *RightChild*, *SecondTree* ↑. *RightChild*);
end; {of *equal*}

Program 5.8: Binary tree equivalence

5.4.3   The Satisfiability Problem

Consider the set of formulas we can construct by taking variables $x_1, x_2, x_3, \cdots$, and the operators ∧ (**and**), ∨ (**or**), and ¬ (**not**). These variables can hold only one of two possible values, *true* or *false*. The set of expressions that can be formed using these variables and operators is defined by the following rules:

(1)   a variable is an expression

(2)   if x and y are expressions then $x \wedge y$, $x \vee y$, and $\neg x$ are expressions

(3)   parentheses can be used to alter the normal order of evaluation, which is **not** before **and** before **or**.

This set defines the formulas of the *propositional calculus* (other operations such as implication can be expressed using ∧, ∨, and ¬). The expression

$$x_1 \vee (x_2 \wedge \neg x_3)$$

is a formula (read "x_1 or x_2 and not x_3"). If x_1 and x_3 are *false* and x_2 is *true*, then the value of this expression is

$$false \lor (true \land \neg false)$$

$$= false \lor true$$

$$= true$$

The *satisfiability problem* for formulas of propositional calculus asks if there is an assignment of values to the variables that causes the value of the expression to be true.

Again, let us assume that our formula is already in a binary tree, say

$$(x_1 \land \neg x_2) \lor (\neg x_1 \land x_3) \lor \neg x_3$$

in the tree of Figure 5.18. The inorder traversal of this tree is

$$x_1 \land \neg x_2 \lor \neg x_1 \land x_3 \lor \neg x_3$$

which is the infix form of the expression. The most obvious algorithm to determine satisfiability is to let (x_1, x_2, x_3) take on all possible combinations of *true* and *false* values and to check the formula for each combination. For n variables there are 2^n possible combinations of *true* $= t$ and *false* $= f$. For example, for $n = 3$, the eight combinations are: (t,t,t), (t,t,f), (t,f,t), (t,f,f), (f,t,t), (f,t,f), (f,f,t), (f,f,f). The algorithm will take $O(g\ 2^n)$, or exponential time, where g is the time to substitute values for $x_1, x_2, \cdots, x_n$ and evaluate the expression.

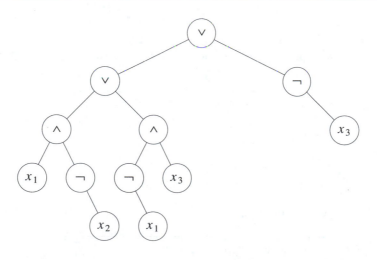

Figure 5.18: Propositional formula in a binary tree

To evaluate an expression we can traverse its tree in postorder, evaluating subtrees until the entire expression is reduced to a single value. This corresponds to the postfix evaluation of an arithmetic expression that we saw earlier. Viewing this from the perspective of the tree representation, for every node we reach, the values of its arguments (or children) have already been computed. So when we reach the $\vee$ node on level 2, the values of $x_1 \wedge \neg x_2$ and $\neg x_1 \wedge x_3$ will already be available to us, and we can apply the rule for **or**. Notice that a node containing $\neg$ has only a right branch, since **not** is a unary operator.

For the purposes of our evaluation algorithm, we assume each node has four fields:

LeftChild	data	value	RightChild

where *LeftChild*, *data*, and *RightChild* are as described earlier and *value* is of type boolean. This node structure may be defined in Pascal as

```
type TypesOfData = (LogicalNot, LogicalAnd, LogicalOr, LogicalTrue,
                    LogicalFalse);
     TreePointer = ↑TreeRecord;
     TreeRecord = record
                       LeftChild   : TreePointer;
                       data        : TypesOfData;
                       value       : boolean;
                       RightChild  : TreePointer;
                  end;
```

Also we assume that for leaf nodes, $t\uparrow.data$ contains the current value (i.e., *LogicalTrue* or *LogicalFalse*) of the variable represented at the node. The first version of our algorithm for the satisfiability problem is Program 5.9. In this, *n* is the number of variables in the formula and *formula* points to the root of the binary tree that represents the formula.

```
for all 2ⁿ possible truth value combinations for the n variables do
begin
    generate the next combination;
    replace the variables by their values;
    evaluate formula by traversing the tree it points to in postorder;
    if formula↑.value then output combination and stop
end
writeln ("no satisfiable combination")
```

Program 5.9: First version of satisfiability algorithm

We can evaluate a formula using Program 5.10, which is a modified version of procedure *postorder* (Program 5.3).

```
 1  procedure PostOrderEval (formula : TreePointer )
 2  begin
 3    if formula < > nil
 4    then
 5    begin
 6      PostOrderEval (formula↑.LeftChild);
 7      PostOrderEval (formula↑.RightChild);
 8      case formula↑.data of
 9        LogicalNot    : formula↑.value := not formula↑.RightChild↑.value;
10        LogicalAnd    : formula↑.value := formula↑.LeftChild↑.value and
11                                 formula↑.RightChild↑.value ;
12        LogicalOr     : formula↑.value := formula↑.LeftChild↑.value or
13                                 formula↑.RightChild↑.value ;
14        LogicalTrue   : formula↑.value := true;
15        LogicalFalse  : formula↑.value := false;
16      end; {of case}
17    end; {of if}
18  end; {of PostOrderEval}
```

Program 5.10: Evaluating a formula

EXERCISES

1. Write a Pascal function to count the number of leaf nodes in a binary tree, *T*. What is its computing time?

2. Write an algorithm, *SwapTree* (*t*), that takes a binary tree and swaps the left and right children of every node. An example is given in Figure 5.19.

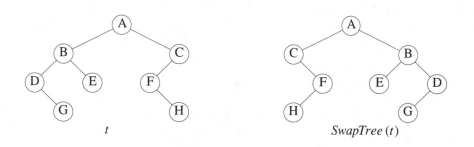

Figure 5.19: A *SwapTree* example

3. [***Programming Project***] Devise an external representation for the formulas in propositional calculus. Write a procedure that reads such a formula and creates its binary tree representation. What is the complexity of your procedure?

4. What is the computing time for *PostOrderEval* (Program 5.10)?

5.5 THREADED BINARY TREES

5.5.1 Threads

If we look carefully at the linked representation of any binary tree, we notice that there are more null links than actual pointers. As we saw before, there are $n + 1$ null links and $2n$ total links. A clever way to make use of these null links has been devised by A. J. Perlis and C. Thornton. Their idea is to replace the null links by pointers, called threads, to other nodes in the tree. These threads are constructed using the following rules:

(1) A null *RightChild* field in node *p* is replaced by a pointer to the node that would be visited after *p* when traversing the tree in inorder. That is, it is replaced by the inorder successor of *p*.

(2) A null *LeftChild* link at node *p* is replaced by a pointer to the node that immediately precedes node *p* in inorder (i.e., it is replaced by the inorder predecessor of *p*).

Figure 5.20 shows the binary tree of Figure 5.10(b) with its new threads drawn in as broken lines. This tree has 9 nodes and 10 null links, which have been replaced by threads. If we traverse the tree in inorder, the nodes will be visited in the order *H, D, I, B, E, A, F, C, G*. For example, node *E* has a predecessor thread that points to *B* and a successor thread that points to *A*.

In the memory representation we must be able to distinguish between threads and normal pointers. This is done by adding two boolean fields, *LeftThread* and *Right-Thread*, to the record. If $tree\uparrow.LeftThread =$ **true**, then $tree\uparrow.LeftChild$ contains a thread; otherwise it contains a pointer to the left child. Similarly if $tree\uparrow.RightThread =$ true, then $tree\uparrow.RightChild$ contains a thread; otherwise it contains a pointer to the right child. This node structure is now given by the following Pascal type declaration:

```
type ThreadedPointer = ↑ThreadedTree ;
     ThreadedTree = record
                      LeftThread  : boolean;
                      LeftChild   : ThreadedPointer ;
                      data        : char;
                      RightChild  : ThreadedPointer ;
                      RightThread : boolean;
                    end;
```

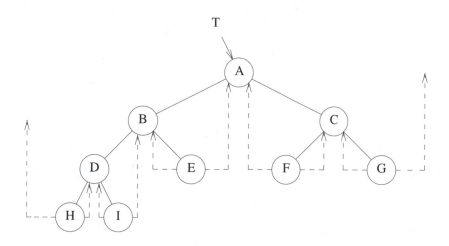

Figure 5.20: Threaded tree corresponding to Figure 5.10(b)

In Figure 5.20 we see that two threads have been left dangling. One is the *LeftChild* of *H* and the other the *RightChild* of *G*. In order that we leave no loose threads, we will assume a head node for all threaded binary trees. The original tree is the left subtree of the head node. An empty binary tree is represented by its head node as in Figure 5.21. The complete memory representation for the tree of Figure 5.20 is shown in Figure 5.22.

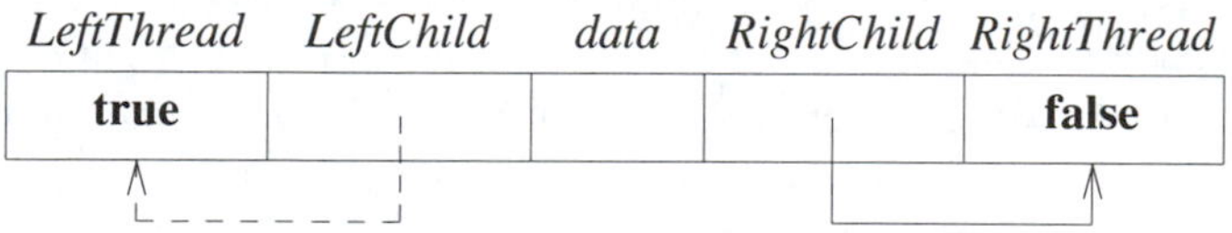

LeftThread	LeftChild	data	RightChild	RightThread
true				**false**

Figure 5.21: An empty threaded binary tree

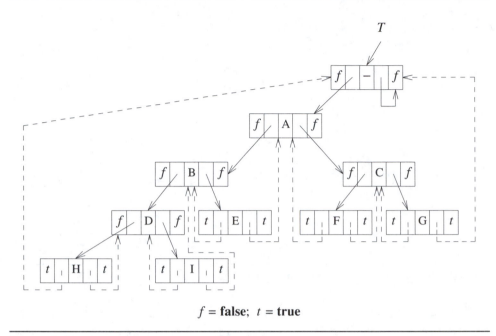

f = **false**; t = **true**

Figure 5.22: Memory representation of threaded tree

5.5.2   Inorder Traversal of a Threaded Binary Tree

By using the threads, we can perform an inorder traversal without making use of a stack. Observe that for any node x in a binary tree, if $x\uparrow.RightThread$ = **true**, then the inorder successor of x is $x\uparrow.RightChild$ by definition of threads. Otherwise the inorder successor of x is obtained by following a path of left-child links from the right child of x until a node with $LeftThread$ = **true** is reached. Procedure $InorderSuc$ (Program 5.11) finds the inorder successor of any node x in a threaded binary tree.

The interesting thing to note about procedure $InorderSuc$ is that it is now possible to find the inorder successor of any arbitrary node in a threaded binary tree without using an additional stack. If we wish to list the nodes in a threaded binary tree in inorder, then we can make repeated calls to procedure $InorderSuc$. Since the tree is the left subtree of the head node and because of the choice of $RightThread$ = **false** for the head node, the inorder sequence of nodes in the original binary tree is obtained by procedure $ThreadedInorder$ (Program 5.12). The computing time of this procedure is readily seen to be O(n) for an n-node tree.

We have seen how to use the threads of a threaded binary tree for inorder traversal. These threads also simplify the algorithms for preorder and postorder traversal.

```
 1 function InorderSuc (tree : ThreadedPointer) : ThreadedPointer ;
 2 {Find the inorder successor of tree in a threaded binary tree.}
 3 var temp : ThreadedPointer ;
 4 begin
 5     temp := tree↑.RightChild ;
 6     if not tree↑.RightThread
 7     then while not temp↑.LeftThread do
 8             temp := temp↑.LeftChild;
 9     InorderSuc := temp ;
10 end; {of InorderSuc}
```

Program 5.11: Finding the inorder successor in a threaded binary tree

```
 1 procedure ThreadedInorder (tree : ThreadedPointer);
 2 {tree is the head node of the threaded binary tree.}
 3 var temp : ThreadedPointer ;
 4 begin
 5     temp := tree ;
 6     repeat
 7         temp := InorderSuc (temp);
 8         if temp <> tree
 9         then write(temp↑.data);
10     until temp = tree ;
11 end; {of ThreadedInorder}
```

Program 5.12: Inorder traversal of threaded binary tree

5.5.3   Inserting a Node into a Threaded Binary Tree

We now examine how to make insertions into a threaded tree. This will give us a procedure for growing threaded trees. We shall study only the case of inserting a node r as the right child of a node s. The case of insertion of a left child is given as an exercise. The cases for insertion are

(1)   If s has an empty right subtree, then the insertion is simple and diagrammed in Figure 5.23(a).

(2)   If the right subtree of s is not empty, then this right subtree is made the right subtree of r after insertion. When this is done, r becomes the inorder predecessor of a node that has a *LeftThread* = **true** field, and consequently there is a thread which

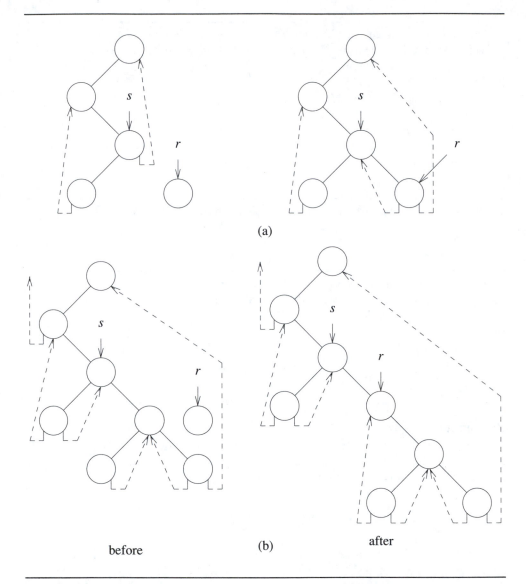

before   (b)   after

Figure 5.23: Insertion of r as a right child of s in a threaded binary tree

has to be updated to point to r. The node containing this thread was previously the inorder successor of s. Figure 5.23(b) illustrates the insertion for this case.

In both cases s is the inorder predecessor of r. The details are given out in procedure *InsertRight* (Program 5.13).

```
 1 procedure InsertRight (s, r : ThreadedPointer);
 2 {Insert node r as the right child of s in a threaded binary
 3 tree.}
 4 var temp : ThreadedPointer ;
 5 begin
 6     r↑.RightChild := s↑.RightChild ;
 7     r↑.RightThread := s↑.RightThread ;
 8     r↑.LeftChild := s ;
 9     r↑.LeftThread := true; {LeftChild is a thread}
10     s↑.RightChild := r; {attach r to s}
11     s↑.RightThread := false;
12     if not r↑.RightThread
13     then begin
14             temp := InorderSuc (r);
15             temp↑.LeftChild := r ;
16         end;
17 end; {of InsertRight}
```

Program 5.13: Inserting *r* as the right child of *s*

EXERCISES

1. Write an algorithm that inserts a new node *l* as the left child of node *s* in a threaded binary tree. The left subtree of *s* becomes the left subtree of *l*.

2. Write a procedure to traverse a threaded binary tree in postorder. What are the time and space requirements of your procedure?

3. Write an algorithm for traversing a threaded binary tree in preorder. What are the time and space requirements of your method?

4. Consider threading a binary tree using preorder threads rather than inorder threads as in the text. Which of the traversals can be done without the use of a stack? For those that can be performed without a stack, write an algorithm and analyze its space complexity.

5. Consider threading a binary tree using postorder threads rather than inorder threads as in the text. Which of the traversals can be done without the use of a stack? For those that can be performed without a stack, write an algorithm and analyze its space complexity.

5.6   HEAPS

5.6.1   Definitions

In Section 5.2.2, we defined a complete binary tree. In this section we present a special form of a complete binary tree that is useful in many applications.

Definition: A *max (min) tree* is a tree in which the key value in each node is no smaller (larger) than the key values in its children (if any). A *max heap* is a complete binary tree that is also a max tree. A *min heap* is a complete binary tree that is also a min tree. □

Some examples of max heaps and min heaps are shown in Figures 5.24 and 5.25, respectively.

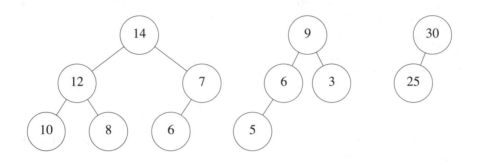

Figure 5.24: Max heaps

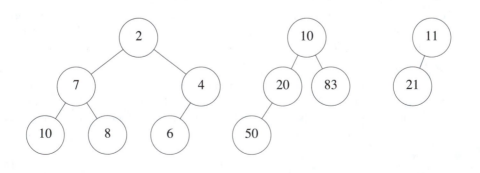

Figure 5.25: Min heaps

From the definitions, it follows that the key in the root of a min tree is the smallest key in the tree, whereas that in the root of a max tree is the largest. When viewed as an ADT, a max heap is very simple. The basic operations are

(1)   creation of an empty heap

(2)   insertion of a new element into the heap

(3)   deletion of the largest element from the heap

These operations are defined in Structure 5.2.

---

structure *MaxHeap* is

    objects: A complete binary tree of $n > 0$ elements organized so that the value in each node is at least as large as those in its children.

    functions:

      for all *heap* $\in$ *MaxHeap*, *item* $\in$ *Element*, *n*, *MaxSize* $\in$ **integer**

Create(MaxSize) : MaxHeap	::=	create an empty heap that can hold a maximum of *MaxSize* elements
HeapFull (*heap*, *n*) : **boolean**	::=	**if** $n = MaxSize$ **then** *HeapFull* := **true** **else** *HeapFull* := **false**
Insert (*heap*, *item*, *n*)	::=	**if** *HeapFull* (*heap*, *n*) **then** error **else** insert *item* into *heap* and increment *n* by one
HeapEmpty (*heap*, *n*) : **boolean**	::=	**if** $n = 0$ **then** *HeapEmpty* := **true** **else** *HeapEmpty* := **false**
Delete (*heap*, *n*) : *Element*	::=	**if** *HeapEmpty* (*heap*, *n*) **then** error **else** one instance of the largest element in the heap is deleted and *Delete* is set to this. *n* incremented by one

---

Structure 5.2: Abstract data type *MaxHeap*

5.6.2   Priority Queues

Heaps are frequently used to implement *priority queues.* In this kind of queue, the element to be deleted is the one with highest (or lowest) priority. At any time, an element with arbitrary priority can be inserted into the queue. In applications in which an element with highest (lowest) priority is to be deleted each time, a max (min) heap may be used.

Example 5.1: Suppose that we are selling the services of a machine. Each user pays a fixed amount per use. However, the time needed by each user is different. We wish to maximize the returns from this machine under the assumption that the machine is not to be kept idle unless no user is available. This can be done by maintaining a priority queue of all persons waiting to use the machine. Whenever the machine becomes available, the user with the smallest time requirement is selected. Hence, a min heap is required. When a new user requests the machine, his/her request is put into the heap.

If each user needs the same amount of time on the machine but people are willing to pay different amounts for the service, then a priority queue based on the amount of payment can be maintained. Whenever the machine becomes available, the user paying the most is selected. This requires a max heap. □

Example 5.2: Suppose that we are simulating a large factory. This factory has many machines and many jobs that require processing on some of the machines. An *event* is said to occur whenever a machine completes the processing of a job. When an event occurs, the job has to be moved to the queue for the next machine (if any) that it needs. If this queue is empty, the job can be assigned to the machine immediately. Also, a new job can be scheduled on the machine that has become idle (provided that its queue is not empty).

To determine the occurrence of events, a priority queue is used. This queue contains the finish time of all jobs that are presently being worked on. The next event occurs at the least time in the priority queue. So, a min heap can be used in this application. □

Before developing procedures to add to and delete from a heap, let us examine some other representations for a priority queue. We shall assume that each deletion removes the element with largest key value from the queue. The conclusions we draw are the same when the smallest element is to be deleted.

The simplest way to represent a priority queue is as an unordered linear list. Suppose that we have n elements in this queue. If the list is represented sequentially, additions are most easily performed at the end of this list. Hence, the insert time is $\Theta(1)$. A deletion requires a search for the element with largest key, followed by its deletion. Since it takes $\Theta(n)$ time to find the largest element in an n-element unordered list, the delete time is $\Theta(n)$. If a chain is used, additions can be performed at the front of the chain in $\Theta(1)$ time. Each deletion takes $\Theta(n)$ time. An alternative is to use an ordered linear list. The elements are in nondecreasing order if a sequential representation is used and in nonincreasing order if an ordered chain is used. The delete time for each representation is $\Theta(1)$ and the insert time $O(n)$. As we shall see shortly, when a max heap is used, both additions and deletions can be performed in $O(\log n)$ time.

5.6.3 Insertion into a Max Heap

A max heap with five elements is shown in Figure 5.26(a). When an element is added to this heap, the resulting six-element heap must have the structure shown in Figure 5.26(b), because a heap is a complete binary tree. If the element to be inserted has key value 1, it may be inserted as the left child of 2. If instead, the key value of the new element is 5, then this cannot be inserted as the left child of 2 (as otherwise, we will not have a max heap following the insertion). So, the 2 is moved down to its left child (Figure 5.26(c)), and we determine if placing the 5 at the old position of 2 results in a max heap. Since the parent element (20) is at least as large as the element being inserted (5), it is all right to insert the new element at the position shown in the figure. Next, suppose that the new element has value 21 rather than 5. In this case, the 2 moves down to its left child as in Figure 5.26(c). The 21 cannot be inserted into the old position occupied by the 2, as the parent of this position is smaller than 21. Hence, the 20 is moved down to its right child and the 21 inserted into the root of the heap (Figure 5.26(d)).

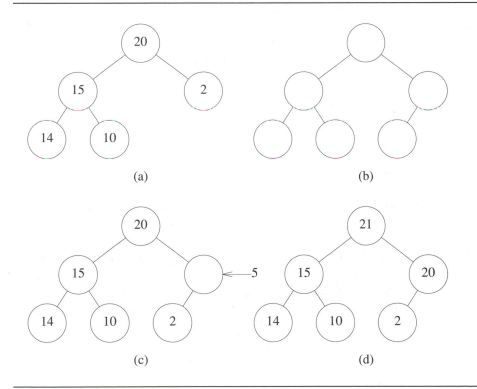

Figure 5.26: Insertion into a max heap

To implement the insertion strategy just described, we need to go from an element to its parent. If a linked representation is used, an additional *parent* field is to be added to each node. However, since a heap is a complete binary tree, the formula-based representation can be used. Lemma 5.4 enables us to locate the parent of any element easily. Program 5.14 performs an insertion into a max heap that contains n elements. This assumes that *heap* is an array with allowable indices in the range $1..MaxElements$. Further, it is assumed that the type *element* is a record with a *key* field in addition to other fields.

---

procedure *InsertMaxHeap* (x : *element*);
{Insert x into the global max heap *heap* [1..*MaxElements*]. n is the present size of the heap.}
var i : **integer**; *NotDone* : **boolean**;
begin
  if $n = MaxElements$ **then** *HeapFull*
  else begin
        $n := n + 1$; $i := n$; *NotDone* := **true**;
        while *NotDone* **do**
            if $i = 1$ **then** *NotDone* := **false** {at root}
            else if $x.key <= heap$ [i **div** 2].*key* **then** *NotDone* := **false**
                else begin {move from parent to i}
                      heap [i] := *heap* [i **div** 2];
                      $i := i$ **div** 2;
                end;
      heap [i] := x;
    end; {of **if** $n = MaxElemenets$}
end; {of *InsertMaxHeap*}

Program 5.14: Insertion into a max heap

Analysis of *InsertMaxHeap*: The insertion procedure begins at a leaf of a compiete binary tree and moves up toward the root. At each node on this path, O(1) amount of work is done. Since a complete binary tree with n elements has a height $\lceil \log_2(n+1) \rceil$, the **while** loop of the insertion procedure is iterated O(log n) times. Hence, the complexity of procedure *InsertMaxHeap* is O(log n). □

5.6.4 Deletion from a Max Heap

When an element is to be deleted from a max heap, it is taken from the root of the heap. For instance, a deletion from the heap of Figure 5.26(d) results in the removal of the element 21. Since the resulting heap has only five elements in it, the binary tree of Figure 5.26(d) needs to be restructured to correspond to a complete binary tree with five elements. To do this, we remove the element in position 6 (i.e., the element 2). Now we have the right structure (Figure 5.27(a)), but the root is vacant and the element 2 is not in the heap. If the 2 is inserted into the root, the resulting binary tree is not a max heap. The element at the root should be the largest from among the 2 and the elements in the left and right children of the root. This element is 20. It is moved into the root, thereby creating a vacancy in position 3. Since this position has no children, the 2 may be inserted here. The resulting heap is shown in Figure 5.26(a).

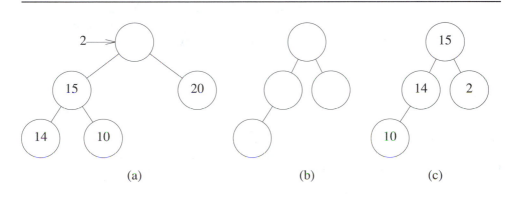

Figure 5.27: Deletion from a heap

Now, suppose we wish to perform another deletion. The 20 is to be deleted. Following the deletion, the heap has the binary tree structure shown in Figure 5.27(b). To get this structure, the 10 is removed from position 5. It cannot be inserted into the root, as it is not large enough. The 15 moves to the root, and we attempt to insert the 10 into position 2. This is, however, smaller than the 14 below it. So, the 14 is moved up and the 10 inserted into position 4. The resulting heap is shown in Figure 5.27(c).

Program 5.15 implements this strategy to delete from a heap.

Analysis of *DeleteMaxHeap*: Once again, since the height of a heap with n elements is $\lceil \log_2(n+1) \rceil$, the **while** loop of this procedure is iterated $O(\log n)$ times. Each iteration of this while loop takes $O(1)$ time. Hence, the complexity of procedure *DeleteMaxHeap* is $O(\log n)$. □

---

procedure *DeleteMaxHeap* (**var** *x* : *element*);
{Delete from the max heap *heap* [1..*MaxElements*]. *n* is the current heap size.}
var *i, j* : **integer**; *k* : *element*; *NotDone* : **boolean**;
begin
  if *n* = 0 **then** *HeapEmpty*
  else begin
       NotDone := **true**; *x* := *heap* [1]; *k* := *heap* [*n*]; *n* := *n* − 1;
       i := 1; *j* := 2; {*j* is left child of *i*}
       while (*j* <= *n*) **and** *NotDone* **do**
       begin
         if *j* < *n* **then if** *heap* [*j*].*key* < *heap* [*j* +1].*key* **then** *j* := *j* +1;
         {*j* points to larger child}
         if *k.key* >= *heap* [*j*].*key* **then** *NotDone* := **false**
                   else begin
                       heap [*i*] := *heap* [*j*]; {move child up}
                       {move *i* and *j* down}
                       i := *j*; *j* := 2*j*;
                   end;
     end;
     heap [*i*] := *k*;
   end;
end; {of *DeleteMaxHeap*}

Program 5.15: Deletion from a max heap

EXERCISES

1. Compare the run-time performance of max heaps with that of unordered and or-dered linear lists as a representation for priority queues. For this comparison, pro-gram the max heap insertion and deletion algorithms, as well as algorithms to per-form these tasks on unordered and ordered linear lists that are maintained as sequential lists in a one-dimensional array. Generate a random sequence of *n* values and insert these into the priority queue. Next, perform a random sequence of *m* inserts and deletes starting with the initial queue of *n* values. This sequence is to be generated so that the next operation in the sequence has an equal chance of being either an insert or a delete. Care should be taken so that the sequence does not cause the priority queue to become empty at any time. Measure the time taken for the sequence of *m* operations using both a max heap and an unordered list. Divide the total time by *m* and plot the times as a function of *n*. Do this for *n* = 100, 500, 1000, 2000, 3000, and 4000. Set *m* to be 1000. Make some qualitative statements about the relative performance of the two representations for a priority queue.

2. Write an algorithm to insert into a min heap. Use the notation of Program 5.14. The complexity of your algorithm should be $O(\log n)$. Show that this is the case.

3. Write an algorithm to delete the smallest item from a min heap. Use the notation of Program 5.15. The complexity of your algorithm should be $O(\log n)$. Show that this is the case.

4. The worst-case number of comparisons performed during an insertion into a max heap can be reduced to $O(\log\log n)$ by performing a binary search on the path from the new leaf to the root. This does not affect the number of data moves though. Write an insertion algorithm that uses this strategy. Redo Exercise 1 using this insertion algorithm. Based on your experiments, what can you say about the value of this strategy over the one used in Program 5.14?

5.7 BINARY SEARCH TREES

5.7.1 Definition

Although a heap is well suited for applications that require priority queues, it is not suited for applications in which arbitrary elements are to be deleted from the element list. Deletion of an arbitrary element from an n-element heap takes $O(n)$ time (it takes this much time just to locate the element to be deleted). This is no better than the time needed for arbitrary deletions from an unordered linear list.

A *binary search tree* has a better performance than any of the data structures studied so far when the functions to be performed are search, insert, and delete. In fact, with a binary search tree, these functions can be performed both by key value and by rank (i.e., find an element with key x; find the fifth smallest element; delete the element with key x; delete the fifth smallest element; insert an element and determine its rank; and so on).

Definition: A *binary search tree* is a binary tree. It may be empty. If it is not empty then it satisfies the following properties:

(1) Every element has a key and no two elements have the same key (i.e., the keys are distinct).

(2) The keys (if any) in the left subtree are smaller than the key in the root.

(3) The keys (if any) in the right subtree are larger than the key in the root.

(4) The left and right subtrees are also binary search trees. □

There is some redundancy in this definition. Properties (2), (3), and (4) together imply that the keys must be distinct. So, property (1) can be replaced by the property: The root has a key.

Some examples of binary trees in which the elements have distinct keys are shown in Figure 5.28. The tree of Figure 5.28(a) is not a binary search tree, despite the fact that it satisfies properties (1), (2), and (3). The right subtree fails to satisfy property (4). This subtree is not a binary search tree, as its right subtree has a key value (22) that is smaller than that in the subtree's root (25). The binary trees of Figures 5.28(b) and (c) are binary search trees.

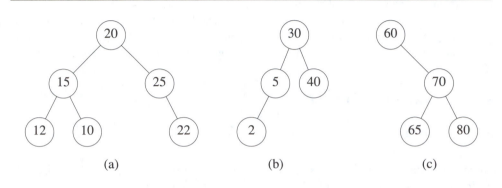

Figure 5.28: Binary trees

5.7.2 Searching a Binary Search Tree

Since the definition of a binary search tree is recursive, it is easiest to describe a recursive search method. Suppose we wish to search for an element with key x. We begin at the root. If the root is **nil**, then the search tree contains no elements and the search is unsuccessful. Otherwise, we compare x with the key in the root. If x equals this key, then the search terminates successfully. If x is less than the key in the root, then no element in the right subtree can have key value x, and only the left subtree is to be searched. If x is larger than the key in the root, only the right subtree needs to be searched. The subtrees may be searched recursively as in Program 5.16. This function assumes a linked representation for the search tree. Each node has the three fields: *LeftChild*, *RightChild*, and *data*. *data* is of type *element* and has at least the field *key*, which is of type **integer**. The recursion of Program 5.16 is easily replaced by a **while** loop, as in Program 5.17.

If we wish to search by rank, each node should have an additional field *LeftSize*, which is one plus the number of elements in the left subtree of the node. For the search tree of Figure 5.28(b), the nodes with keys 2, 5, 30, and 40, respectively, have *LeftSize* equal to 1, 2, 3, and 1. Program 5.18 searches for the kth smallest element.

As can be seen, a binary search tree of height h can be searched by key as well as by rank in O(h) time.

---

function *search* (*t* : *TreePointer* ; *x* : **integer**): *TreePointer*;
{Search the binary search tree *t* for an element with key *x*. If such an element is found,
return a pointer to the node that contains it. Return **nil** otherwise.}
begin
  if *t* = **nil then** *search* := **nil**
  else if *x* = *t* ↑ . *data*.*key* **then** *search* := *t*
    else if *x* < *t* ↑ . *data*.*key* **then** *search* := *search* (*t* ↑ . *LeftChild*, *x*)
      else *search* := *search* (*t* ↑ . *RightChild*, *x*);
end; {of *search*}

Program 5.16: Recursive search of a binary search tree

---

function *search* (*t* : *TreePointer* ; *x* : **integer**): *TreePointer*;
{Search the binary search tree *t* for an element with key *x*.}
var *NotFound* : **boolean**;
begin
  NotFound := **true**;

  while (*t* < > **nil**) **and** *NotFound* **do**
    if *x* = *t* ↑ . *data*.*key* **then** *NotFound* := **false**
    else if *x* < *t* ↑ . *data*.*key* **then** *t* := *t* ↑ . *LeftChild*
      else *t* := *t* ↑ . *RightChild*;

  if *NotFound* **then** *search* := **nil**
    else *search* := *t*;
end; {of *search*}

Program 5.17: Iterative search of a binary search tree

5.7.3 Insertion into a Binary Search Tree

To insert a new element *x*, we must first verify that its key is different from those of existing elements. To do this, a search is carried out. If the search is unsuccessful, then the
element is inserted at the point the search terminated. For instance, to insert an element
with key 80 into the tree of Figure 5.28(b), we first search for 80. This search terminates
unsuccessfully, and the last node examined is the one with key 40. The new element is
inserted as the right child of this node. The resulting search tree is shown in Figure
5.29(a). Figure 5.29(b) shows the result of inserting the key 35 into the search tree of
Figure 5.29(a).

```
function search (t : TreePointer ; k : integer): TreePointer;
{Search the binary search tree t for the kth smallest element.}
var NotFound : boolean;
begin
    NotFound := true;

    while (t < > nil) and NotFound do
        if k = t↑.LeftSize then NotFound := false
        else if  k < t↑.LeftSize then t := t↑.LeftChild
            else begin
                    k := k − LeftSize; {search for ith in right subtree}
                    t := t↑.RightChild;
                end;

    if NotFound then search := nil
                else search := t;
end; {of search}
```

Program 5.18: Searching a binary search tree by rank

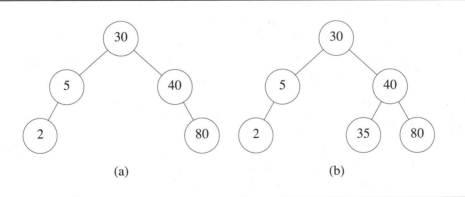

(a)   (b)

Figure 5.29: Inserting into a binary search tree

Program 5.19 implements the insert strategy just described. If a node has a *Left-Size* field, then this is to be updated too. Regardless, the insertion can be performed in $O(h)$ time, where h is the height of the search tree.

```
procedure insert (var t : TreePointer ; x : element ; var success : boolean);
{Insert x into the binary search tree t.}
var p, q : TreePointer; NotFound : boolean;
begin
    {Search for x.key.  q is parent of p}
    q := nil; p := t; NotFound := true;
    while (p < > nil) and NotFound do
    begin
        q := p; {save p}
        if x.key = p↑.data.key then NotFound := false
        else if x.key < p↑.data.key then p :=p ↑.LeftChild
                                    else p := p↑.RightChild;
    end;

    {Perform insertion}
    if NotFound then success := false {x.key already in t}
    else begin {insert into t}
            new (p);
            with p↑ do begin
                            LeftChild := nil; RightChild := nil; data := x;
                        end;
            if t = nil then t := p
                        else if x.key < q↑.data.key then q↑.LeftChild := p
                                                    else q↑.RightChild := p;
            success := true;
        end;
end; {of insert}
```

Program 5.19: Insertion into a binary search tree

5.7.4   Deletion from a Binary Search Tree

Deletion of a leaf element is quite easy. For example, to delete 35 from the tree of Figure 5.29(b), the left-child field of its parent is set to **nil** and the node disposed. This gives us the tree of Figure 5.29(a). To delete the 80 from this tree, the right-child field of 40 is set to **nil**, obtaining the tree of Figure 5.28(b), and the node containing 80 is disposed.

The deletion of a nonleaf element that has only one child is also easy. The node containing the element to be deleted is disposed, and the single-child takes the place of the disposed node. So, to delete the element 5 from the tree of Figure 5.29(a), we simply change the pointer from the parent node (i.e., the node containing 30) to the single-child node (i.e., the node containing 2).

When the element to be deleted is in a nonleaf node that has two children, the element is replaced by either the largest element in its left subtree or the smallest one in its right subtree. Then we proceed to delete this replacing element from the subtree from which it was taken. For instance, if we wish to delete the element with key 30 from the tree of Figure 5.29(b), then we replace it by either the largest element, 5, in its left subtree or the smallest element, 35, in its right subtree. Suppose we opt for the largest element in the left subtree. The 5 is moved into the root, and the tree of Figure 5.30(a) is obtained. Now we must delete the second 5. Since this node has only one child, the pointer from its parent is changed to point to this child. The tree of Figure 5.30(b) is obtained. One may verify that regardless of whether the replacing element is the largest in the left subtree or the smallest in the right subtree, it is originally in a node with a degree of at most one. So, deleting it from this node is quite easy. We leave the writing of the deletion procedure as an exercise. It should be evident that a deletion can be performed in O(h) time if the search tree has a height of h.

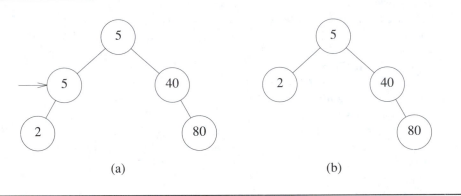

(a) (b)

Figure 5.30: Deletion from a binary search tree

5.7.5 Joining and Splitting Binary Trees

Although search, insert, and delete are the operations most frequently performed on a binary search tree, the following additional operations are useful in certain applications:

(a) *ThreeWayJoin* (A,x,B,C): This creates a new binary search tree C consisting of the elements initially in the binary search trees A and B, as well as the single element x. It is assumed that each element in A has a smaller key than x.*key* and that each element in B has a larger key than x.*key*. The join operation may destroy both A and B.

(b)   *TwoWayJoin* (A,B,C): This joins the two binary search trees A and B to obtain a single binary search tree C that contains all the elements originally in A and B. It is assumed that all keys of A are smaller than all keys of B and that the join operation is to destroy both A and B.

(c)   *Split* (A,i,B,x,C): The binary search tree A is split into three parts. B is a binary search tree that contains all elements of A that have key less than i; if A contains a record with key i, then x is set to this record (otherwise, x . *key* is set to some value other than i to indicate that there is no record in A with key i); C is a binary search tree that contains all records of A that have key larger than i. The split operation may destroy A.

A three-way join operation is particularly easy to perform. We simply obtain a new node and set its data field to x, its left-child pointer to A, and its right-child pointer to B. The time taken for this operation is O(1), and the height of the new tree C is max$\{height(A), height(B)\} + 1$.

Consider the two-way join operation. If either A or B is empty, the result is C. When neither is empty, we may first delete from A the record x with the largest key. Let the resulting binary search tree be A'. To complete the operation, we perform the three-way join operation *ThreeWayJoin* (A',x,B,C). The overall time required to perform the two-way join operation is O($height(A)$), and the height of C is max$\{height(A), height(B)\} + 1$. The run time can be made O(min$\{height(A), height(B)\}$) if we retain with each tree its height. Then we delete the record with the largest key value from A if the height of A is no more than that of B; otherwise, we delete from B the record with the smallest key value. This is followed by a three-way join operation.

To perform a split, we first note that splitting at the root (i.e., $i = A\uparrow.data.key$) is particularly easy. In this case, B is the left subtree of A, x is the record in the root, and C is the right subtree of A. If i is smaller than the key at the root, then the root together with its right subtree is to be in C. When i is larger than the key at the root, the root together with its left subtree is to be in B. Using these observations, we can perform a split by moving down the search tree A searching for a record with key i. As we move down, we construct the two search trees B and C. The algorithm for this is given in Program 5.20. To simplify the code, we begin with two head nodes Y and Z for B and C, respectively. B is grown as the right subtree of Y; C is grown as the left subtree of Z. L (R) points to the node of Y (Z) at which further subtrees of A that are to be part of B (C) may be attached. Attaching a subtree to B (C) is done as the right (left) child of L (R).

Analysis of *split*: The **while** loop maintains the invariant that all keys in the subtree with root p are larger than those in Y and smaller than those in Z. The correctness of the procedure is easy to establish, and its complexity is seen to be O($height(A)$). One may verify that neither B nor C has a height larger than that of A. □

---

procedure *split* (**var** *A* : *TreePointer* ; *i* : **integer**; **var** *B* : *TreePointer* ;
                    var *x* : *element* ; **var** *C* : *TreePointer*);
{Split the binary search tree *A* with respect to the key *i*.}
var *Y, Z, L, R* : *TreePointer* ;
begin
  x . *key* := *i* + 1;
  if *A* = **nil then begin** {empty tree} *B* := **nil**; *C* := **nil**; **end**
  else begin
      {create head nodes for *B* and *C*}
      new (*Y*); *L* := *Y*; *new* (*Z*); *R* := *Z*;

      {search for *i* constructing *B* and *C*}
      while *A* < > **nil do**
        if *i* = *A* ↑ . *data* . *key* **then begin** {split at *A*}
                          L ↑ . *RightChild* := *A* ↑ . *LeftChild*;
                          R ↑ . *LeftChild* := *A* ↑ . *RightChild*;
                          x := *A* ↑ . *data*; *A* := **nil**;
                  end
        else if *i* < *A* ↑ . *data* . *key* **then begin**
                        R ↑ . *LeftChild* := *A*;
                        R := *A*; *A* := *A* ↑ . *LeftChild*;
                  end
        else begin
                  L ↑ . *RightChild* := *A*;
                  L := *A*; *A* := *A* ↑ . *RightChild*;
                end;

      {Set **nil** tree pointers and delete head nodes}
      if *x* . *key* < > *i* **then begin**
                  L ↑ . *RightChild* := **nil**;
                  R ↑ . *LeftChild* := **nil**;
                end;
      B := *Y* ↑ . *RightChild* ; *dispose* (*Y*);
      C := *Z* ↑ . *LeftChild* ; *dispose* (*Z*);
    end;
end; {of *split*}

Program 5.20 Splitting a binary search tree

5.7.6   Height of a Binary Search Tree

Unless care is taken, the height of a binary search tree with n elements can become as large as n. This is the case, for instance, when Program 5.19 is used to insert the keys [1, 2, 3, . . ., n], in this order, into an initially empty binary search tree. It can, however, be shown that when insertions and deletions are made at random using the procedures given here, the height of the binary search tree is $O(\log n)$ on the average.

Search trees with a worst-case height of $O(\log n)$ are called *balanced search trees.* Balanced search trees that permit searches, inserts, and deletes to be performed in $O(h)$ time exist. Most notable among these are AVL, 2-3, 2-3-4, red/black, and B trees. These are discussed in Chapter 10.

EXERCISES

1. Write a Pascal procedure to delete an element X from a binary search tree T. What is the time complexity of your algorithm?

2. Write a program to start with an initially empty binary search tree and make n random insertions. Use a uniform random number generator to obtain the values to be inserted. Measure the height of the resulting binary search tree and divide this height by $\log_2 n$. Do this for $n = 100, 500, 1000, 2000, 3000, \cdots, 10,000$. Plot the ratio *height* $/\log_2 n$ as a function of n. The ratio should be approximately constant (around 2). Verify that this is so.

3. Suppose that each node in a binary search tree also has the field *LeftSize* as described in the text. Write a procedure to insert an element x into such a binary search tree. The complexity of your algorithm should be $O(h)$, where h is the height of the search tree. Show that this is the case.

4. Do Exercise 3, but this time write a procedure to delete the element with kth smallest key in the binary search tree.

5. Write a Pascal procedure that implements the three-way join operation in $O(1)$ time.

6. Write a Pascal procedure that implements the two-way join operation in $O(height(A))$ time, where A is one of the two trees being joined.

7. Any algorithm that merges together two sorted lists of size n and m, respectively, must make at least $n + m - 1$ comparisons in the worst case. What implications does this result have on the time complexity of any comparison-based algorithm that combines two binary search trees that have n and m elements, respectively?

8. In Chapter 7, we shall see that every comparison-based algorithm to sort n elements must make $O(n\log n)$ comparisons in the worst case. What implications does this result have on the complexity of initializing a binary search tree with n elements?

9. Notice that a binary search tree can be used to implement a priority queue.

(a) Write a Pascal procedure to delete the largest element in a binary search tree. Your procedure should have complexity $O(h)$, where h is the height of the search tree. Since h is $O(\log n)$ on average, we can perform each of the priority queue operations in average time $O(\log n)$.

(b) Compare the actual performance of heaps and binary search trees as data structures for priority queues. For this comparison, generate random sequences of insert and delete max operations and measure the total time taken for each sequence by each of these data structures.

5.8 SELECTION TREES

5.8.1 Introduction

Suppose we have k ordered sequences, called *runs*, that are to be merged into a single ordered sequence. Each run consists of some records and is in nondecreasing order of a designated field called the *key*. Let n be the number of records in all k runs together. The merging task can be accomplished by repeatedly outputting the record with the smallest key. The smallest has to be found from k possibilities, and it could be the leading record in any of the k runs. The most direct way to merge k runs is to make $k - 1$ comparisons to determine the next record to output. For $k > 2$, we can achieve a reduction in the number of comparisons needed to find the next smallest element by using the data structure *selection tree*. There are two kinds of selection trees: *winner trees* and *loser trees*.

5.8.2 Winner Trees

A *winner tree* is a complete binary tree in which each node represents the smaller of its two children. Thus, the root node represents the smallest node in the tree. Figure 5.31 illustrates a winner tree for the case $k = 8$.

The construction of this winner tree may be compared to the playing of a tournament in which the winner is the record with the smaller key. Then, each nonleaf node in the tree represents the winner of a tournament, and the root node represents the overall winner, or the smallest key. Each leaf node represents the first record in the corresponding run. Since the records being merged are generally large, each node will contain only a pointer to the record it represents. Thus, the root node contains a pointer to the first record in run 4.

A winner tree may be represented using the sequential allocation scheme for binary trees that results from Lemma 5.4. The number above each node in Figure 5.31 is the address of the node in this sequential representation. The record pointed to by the

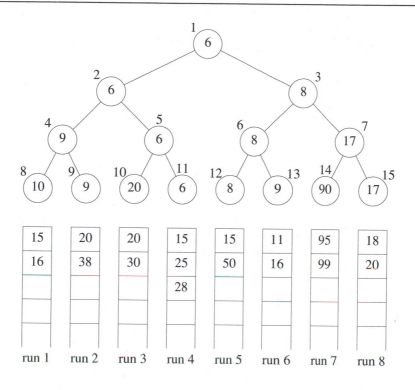

Figure 5.31: Winner tree for $k = 8$, showing the first three keys in each of the eight runs

root has the smallest key and so may be output. Now, the next record from run 4 enters the winner tree. It has a key value of 15. To restructure the tree, the tournament has to be replayed only along the path from node 11 to the root. Thus, the winner from nodes 10 and 11 is again node 11 ($15 < 20$). The winner from nodes 4 and 5 is node 4 ($9 < 15$). The winner from 2 and 3 is node 3 ($8 < 9$). The new tree is shown in Figure 5.32. The tournament is played between sibling nodes and the result put in the parent node. Lemma 5.4 may be used to compute the address of sibling and parent nodes efficiently. Each new comparison takes place at the next higher level in the tree.

Analysis of merging runs using winner trees: The number of levels in the tree is $\lceil \log_2(k + 1) \rceil$. So, the time to restructure the tree is $O(\log_2 k)$. The tree has to be restructured each time a record is merged into the output file. Hence, the time required to merge all n records is $O(n \log_2 k)$. The time required to set up the selection tree the first time is $O(k)$. Thus, the total time needed to merge the k runs is $O(n \log_2 k)$. $\square$

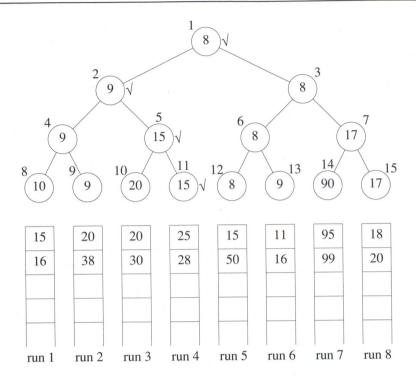

Figure 5.32: Winner tree of Figure 5.31 after one record has been output and the tree restructured (nodes that were changed are labeled √)

5.8.3   Loser Trees

After the record with the smallest key value is output, the winner tree of Figure 5.31 is to be restructured. Since the record with the smallest key value is in run 4, this restructuring involves inserting the next record from this run into the tree. The next record has key value 15. Tournaments are played between sibling nodes along the path from node 11 to the root. Since these sibling nodes represent the losers of tournaments played earlier, we can simplify the restructuring process by placing in each nonleaf node a pointer to the record that loses the tournament rather than to the winner of the tournament. A selection tree in which each nonleaf node retains a pointer to the loser is called a *loser tree*. Figure 5.33 shows the loser tree that corresponds to the winner tree of Figure 5.31. For convenience, each node contains the key value of a record rather than a pointer to the record represented. The leaf nodes represent the first record in each run.

An additional node, node 0, has been added to represent the overall winner of the tournament. Following the output of the overall winner, the tree is restructured by playing tournaments along the path from node 11 to node 1. The records with which these tournaments are to be played are readily available from the parent nodes. As a result, sibling nodes along the path from 11 to 1 are not accessed.

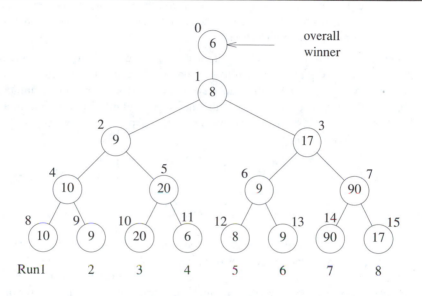

Figure 5.33: Loser tree corresponding to winner tree of Figure 5.31

EXERCISES

1. Write a procedure to construct a winner tree for records R_i, $1 \le i \le k$, with key values K_i, $1 \le i \le k$. Let the tree nodes be T_i, $1 \le i < k$, with T_i, $1 \le i < k$, a pointer to the winner of a tournament. Assume that k is a power of 2. Show that this construction can be carried out in time $O(k)$.

2. Do Exercise 1 for the case when k is not restricted to being a power of 2.

3. Write a procedure to construct a loser tree for records R_i, $1 \le i \le k$, with key values K_i, $1 \le i \le k$. Let the tree nodes be T_i, $0 \le i < k$, with T_i, $1 \le i < k$, a pointer to the loser of a tournament and T_0 a pointer to the overall winner. Show that this construction can be carried out in time $O(k)$. Assume that k is a power of 2.

4. Do Exercise 3 for the case when k is not restricted to being a power of 2.

5. Write an algorithm, using a tree of losers, to carry out a k-way merge of k runs, $k \geq 2$. Use the data structures of Exercise 3 and assume the existence of a procedure to initialize the loser tree. This initialization procedure runs in linear time. Show that if there are n records in all k runs together, then the computing time is $O(n \log_2 k)$.

6. Do the previous exercise for the case in which a tree of winners is used. This time use the data structures of Exercise 1 and assume the existence of a linear-time procedure to initialize the winner tree.

7. Compare the performance of your algorithms for the preceding two exercises for the case $k = 8$. Generate eight runs of data, each having 100 records. Use a random number generator for this (the keys obtained from the random number generator will need to be sorted before the merge can begin). Measure the time taken to merge the eight runs using the two strategies. Approximately how much faster is the loser-tree scheme?

5.9 FORESTS

Definition: A *forest* is a set of $n \geq 0$ disjoint trees. $\square$

A three-tree forest is shown in Figure 5.34. The concept of a forest is very close to that of a tree because if we remove the root of a tree, we obtain a forest. For example, removing the root of any binary tree produces a forest of two trees. In this section, we briefly consider several forest operations, including transforming a forest into a binary tree and forest traversals. In the next section, we use forests to represent disjoint sets.

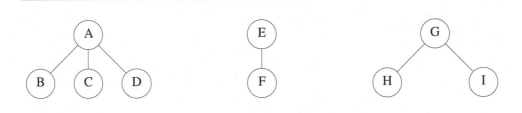

Figure 5.34: Three-tree forest

5.9.1 Transforming a Forest into a Binary Tree

To transform a forest into a single binary tree, we first obtain the binary tree representation of each of the trees in the forest and then link these binary trees together through the *RightChild* field of the root nodes. Using this transformation, the forest of Figure 5.34 becomes the binary tree of Figure 5.35.

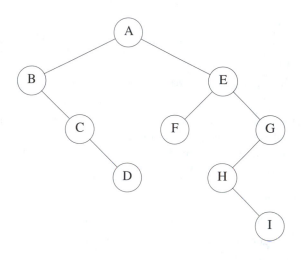

Figure 5.35: Binary tree representation of forest of Figure 5.34

We can define this transformation in a formal way as follows:

Definition: If T_1, $\cdots$, T_n is a forest of trees, then the binary tree corresponding to this forest, denoted by $B(T_1, \cdots, T_n)$,

(1)   is empty if $n = 0$

(2)   has root equal to root (T_1); has left subtree equal to $B(T_{11}, T_{12}, \cdots, T_{1m})$, where $T_{11}, \cdots, T_{1m}$ are the subtrees of root(T_1); and has right subtree $B(T_2, \cdots, T_n)$.
       $\square$

5.9.2 Forest Traversals

Preorder and inorder traversals of the corresponding binary tree T of a forest F have a natural correspondence to traversals on F. Preorder traversal of T is equivalent to visiting the nodes of F in *forest preorder*, which is defined as follows:

(1) If F is empty then return.

(2) Visit the root of the first tree of F.

(3) Traverse the subtrees of the first tree in forest preorder.

(4) Traverse the remaining trees of F in forest preorder.

Inorder traversal of T is equivalent to visiting the nodes of F in *forest inorder*, which is defined as follows:

(1) If F is empty then return.

(2) Traverse the subtrees of the first tree in forest inorder.

(3) Visit the root of the first tree.

(4) Traverse the remaining trees in forest inorder.

The proofs that preorder and inorder on the corresponding binary tree are the same as preorder and inorder on the forest are left as exercises. There is no natural analog for postorder traversal of the corresponding binary tree of a forest. Nevertheless, we can define the *postorder traversal of a forest* as follows:

(1) If F is empty then return.

(2) Traverse the subtrees of the first tree of F in forest postorder.

(3) Traverse the remaining trees of F in forest postorder.

(4) Visit the root of the first tree of F.

In a *level-order traversal of a forest*, nodes are visited by level, beginning with the roots of each tree in the forest. Within each level, nodes are visited from left to right. One may verify that the level-order traversal of a forest and that of its associated binary tree do not necessarily yield the same result.

EXERCISES

1. Define the inverse transformation of the one that creates the associated binary tree from a forest. Are these transformations unique?

2. Prove that the preorder traversal of a forest and the preorder traversal of its associated binary tree give the same result.

3. Prove that the inorder traversal of a forest and the inorder traversal of its associated binary tree give the same result.

4. Prove that the postorder traversal of a forest and that of its corresponding binary tree do not necessarily yield the same result.

5. Prove that the level-order traversal of a forest and that of its corresponding binary tree do not necessarily yield the same result.

6. Write a nonrecursive procedure to traverse the associated binary tree of a forest in forest postorder. What are the time and space complexities of your procedure?

7. Do the preceding exercise for the case of forest level-order traversal.

5.10 SET REPRESENTATION

5.10.1 Introduction

In this section we study the use of trees in the representation of sets. We shall assume that the elements of the sets are the numbers $1, 2, 3, \cdots, n$. These numbers might, in practice, be indices into a symbol table where the actual names of the elements are stored. We shall assume that the sets being represented are pairwise disjoint (i.e., if S_i and S_j, $i \neq j$, are two sets, then there is no element that is in both S_i and S_j). For example, when $n = 10$, the elements may be partitioned into three disjoint sets, $S_1 = \{1, 7, 8, 9\}$, $S_2 = \{2, 5, 10\}$, and $S_3 = \{3, 4, 6\}$. Figure 5.36 shows one possible representation for these sets. In this representation, each set is represented as a tree. Notice that for each set we have linked the nodes from the children to the parent, rather than our usual method of linking from the parent to the children. The reason for this change in linkage will become apparent when we discuss the implementation of set operations.

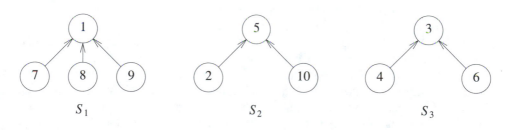

Figure 5.36: Possible tree representation of sets

The operations we wish to perform on these sets are:

(1) *Disjoint set union.* If S_i and S_j are two disjoint sets, then their union $S_i \cup S_j = \{$all elements x such that x is in S_i or $S_j\}$. Thus, $S_1 \cup S_2 = \{1, 7, 8, 9, 2, 5, 10\}$. Since we have assumed that all sets are disjoint, we can assume that following the union of S_i and S_j, the sets S_i and S_j do not exist independently; that is, they are replaced by $S_i \cup S_j$ in the collection of sets.

(2) *Find(i).* Find the set containing element i. Thus, 4 is in set S_3, and 9 is in set S_1.

5.10.2   Union and Find Operations

Let us consider the union operation first. Suppose that we wish to obtain the union of S_1 and S_2 (see Figure 5.36). Since we have linked the nodes from children to parent, we simply make one of the trees a subtree of the other. $S_1 \cup S_2$ could then have one of the representations of Figure 5.37.

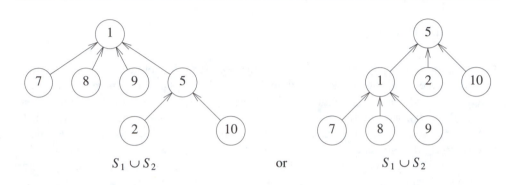

$S_1 \cup S_2$ or $S_1 \cup S_2$

Figure 5.37: Possible representations of $S_1 \cup S_2$

To obtain the union of two sets, all that has to be done is to set the parent field of one of the roots to the other root. This can be accomplished easily if, with each set name, we keep a pointer to the root of the tree representing that set. If, in addition, each root has a pointer to the set name, then to determine which set an element is currently in, we follow parent links to the root of its tree and use the pointer to the set name. The data representation for S_1, S_2, and S_3 may then take the form shown in Figure 5.38.

In presenting the union and find algorithms we shall ignore the actual set names and just identify sets by the roots of the trees representing them. This will simplify the discussion. The transition to set names is easy. If we determine that element i is in a tree with root j, and j has a pointer to entry k in the set name table, then the set name is just *name*[k]. If we wish to unite sets S_i and S_j, then we wish to unite the trees with roots *FindPointer*(S_i) and *FindPointer*(S_j). Here *FindPointer* is a function that takes a set name and determines the root of the tree that represents it. This is done by an examination of the [set name, pointer] table. As we shall see, in many applications the set name is just the element at the root. The operation of *find*(i) now becomes: Determine the root of the tree containing element i. The function *union*(i, j) requires two trees with roots i and j to be joined. Another simplifying assumption we shall make is that the set elements are the numbers 1 through n.

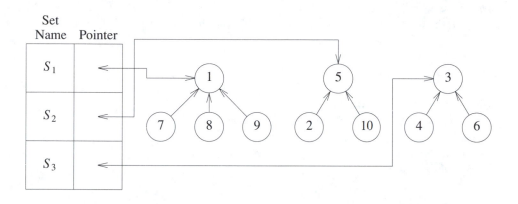

Figure 5.38: Data representation for $S_1, S_2,$ and S_3

Since the set elements are numbered 1 through n, we represent the tree nodes using an array *parent*[*MaxElements*], where *MaxElements* is the maximum number of elements. The *i*th element of this array represents the tree node that contains element i. This array element gives the parent pointer of the corresponding tree node. Figure 5.39 shows this representation of the sets, $S_1, S_2,$ and S_3 of Figure 5.36. Notice that root nodes have a parent of 0.

i	[1]	[2]	[3]	[4]	[5]	[6]	[7]	[8]	[9]	[10]
parent	0	5	0	3	0	3	1	1	1	5

Figure 5.39: Array representation of $S_1, S_2,$ and S_3 of Figure 5.36

We can now implement *find*(i) by simply following the indices starting at i and continuing until we reach a node with parent value 0. For example, *find*(6) starts at 6 and then moves to 6's parent, 3. Since *parent* [3] = 0, we have reached the root. The operation *union*(i, j) is equally simple. We pass in two trees with roots i and j. Assuming that we adopt the convention that the first tree becomes a subtree of the second, the statement *parent* [i] := j accomplishes the union. Program 5.21 implements the union and find operations as just discussed.

Analysis of *SimpleUnion* and *SimpleFind*: Although these two algorithms are very easy to state, their performance characteristics are not very good. For instance, if we

---

procedure *SimpleUnion* (*i*,*j* : **integer**);
{Replace the disjoint sets with roots *i* and *j*, *i* ≠ *j* with their union.}
begin
    parent [*i*] := *j* ;
end; {of *SimpleUnion*}

function *SimpleFind* (*i* : **integer**) : **integer**;
{Find the root of the tree containing element *i*.}
begin
    while *parent* [*i*] > 0 **do**
        i := *parent* [*i*];
    SimpleFind := *i* ;
end; {of *SimpleFind*}

Program 5.21: Simple algorithms for union and find

start off with p elements each in a set of its own (i.e., $S_i = \{i\}$, $1 \le i \le p$), then the initial configuration consists of a forest with p nodes, and *parent* [*i*] = 0, $1 \le i \le p$. Now let us process the following sequence of *union-find* operations:

$$union(1,2), \ union(2,3), \ union(3,4), \ union(4,5), \ \cdots, union(n-1,n)$$
$$find(1), find(2), \ \cdots, find(n)$$

This sequence results in the degenerate tree of Figure 5.40. Since the time taken for a union is constant, the $n - 1$ unions can be processed in time O(n). However, each find requires following a sequence of *parent* pointers from the element to be found to the root. Since the time required to process a find for an element at level i of a tree is O(i), the total time needed to process the n finds is O($\Sigma_{i=1}^{n} i$) = O(n^2). □

We can improve the performance of our union and find algorithms by avoiding the creation of degenerate trees. In order to accomplish this we shall make use of a weighting rule for *union*(*i*,*j*).

Definition [*Weighting rule for union(i,j)*]: If the number of nodes in the tree with root i is less than the number in the tree with root j, then make j the parent of i; otherwise make i the parent of j. □

When we use the weighting rule to perform the sequence of set unions given before, we obtain the trees of Figure 5.41. In this figure, the unions have been modified so that the input parameter values correspond to the roots of the trees to be combined.

To implement the weighting rule, we need to know how many nodes there are in every tree. To do this easily, we maintain a *count* field in the root of every tree. If i is a

Figure 5.40: Degenerate tree

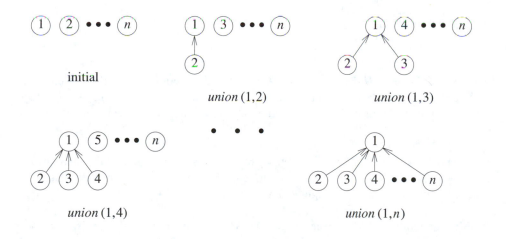

Figure 5.41: Trees obtained using the weighting rule

root node, then *count*[*i*] equals the number of nodes in that tree. Since all nodes other than the roots of trees have a positive number in the *parent* field, we can maintain the count in the *parent* field of the roots as a negative number. Using this convention, we obtain the union procedure of Program 5.22.

```
procedure WeightedUnion(i, j : integer);
{Union sets with roots i and j, i≠j, using the weighting rule. parent [i ] = − count [i ] and
parent [j ] = −count [j ].}
var temp : integer;
begin
    temp := parent [i ] + parent [j ];
    if parent [i ] > parent [j ]
    then begin {i has fewer nodes}
            parent [i ] := j ;
            parent [j ] := temp ;
         end
    else begin {j has fewer nodes}
            parent [j ] := i ;
            parent [i ] := temp ;
         end;
end; {of WeightedUnion}
```

Program 5.22: Union algorithm with weighting rule

Analysis of *WeightedUnion* and *SimpleFind*: The time required to perform a union has increased somewhat but is still bounded by a constant (i.e., it is $O(1)$). The find algorithm remains unchanged. The maximum time to perform a find is determined by Lemma 5.5.

Lemma 5.5: Assume that we start with a forest of trees, each having one node. Let T be a tree with m nodes created as a result of a sequence of unions each performed using procedure *WeightedUnion*. The height of T is no greater than $\lfloor \log_2 m \rfloor + 1$.

Proof: The lemma is clearly true for $m = 1$. Assume it is true for all trees with i nodes, $i \leq m - 1$. We shall show that it is also true for $i = m$. Let T be a tree with m nodes created by procedure *WeightedUnion*. Consider the last union operation performed, *union*(k, j). Let a be the number of nodes in tree j and $m - a$ the number in k. Without loss of generality we may assume $1 \leq a \leq m/2$. Then the height of T is either the same as that of k or is one more than that of j. If the former is the case, the height of T is $\leq \lfloor \log_2 (m - a) \rfloor + 1 \leq \lfloor \log_2 m \rfloor + 1$. If the latter is the case, the height of T is $\leq \lfloor \log_2 a \rfloor + 2 \leq \lfloor \log_2 m/2 \rfloor + 2 \leq \lfloor \log_2 m \rfloor + 1$. $\square$

Example 5.3 shows that the bound of Lemma 5.5 is achievable for some sequence of unions.

Example 5.3: Consider the behavior of procedure *WeightedUnion* on the following sequence of unions starting from the initial configuration $parent[i] = -count[i] = -1, 1 \leq i \leq n = 8$:

$$union(1,2), \quad union(3,4), \quad union(5,6), \quad union(7,8),$$
$$union(1,3), \quad union(5,7), \quad union(1,5)$$

The trees of Figure 5.42 are obtained. As is evident, the height of each tree with m nodes is $\lfloor \log_2 m \rfloor + 1$. $\square$

From Lemma 5.5, it follows that the time to process a find is $O(\log m)$ if there are m elements in a tree. If an intermixed sequence of $u - 1$ union and f find operations is to be processed, the time becomes $O(u + f \log u)$, as no tree has more than u nodes in it. Of course, we need $O(n)$ additional time to initialize the n-tree forest. $\square$

Surprisingly, further improvement is possible. This time the modification will be made in the find algorithm using the *collapsing rule*.

Definition [*Collapsing rule*]: If j is a node on the path from i to its root and $parent[i] \neq root(i)$, then set $parent[j]$ to $root(i)$. $\square$

Function *CollapsingFind* (Program 5.23) incorporates the collapsing rule.

Example 5.4: Consider the tree created by procedure *WeightedUnion* on the sequence of unions of Example 5.3. Now process the following eight finds:

$$find(8), find(8), \cdots, find(8)$$

If *SimpleFind* is used, each *find*(8) requires going up three parent link fields for a total of 24 moves to process all eight finds. When *CollapsingFind* is used, the first *find*(8) requires going up three links and then resetting two links. Note that even though only two parent links need to be reset, procedure *CollapsingFind* will actually reset three (the parent of 5 is reset to 1). Each of the remaining seven finds requires going up only one link field. The total cost is now only 13 moves. $\square$

Analysis of *WeightedUnion* and *CollapsingFind*: Use of the collapsing rule roughly doubles the time for an individual find. However, it reduces the worst-case time over a sequence of finds. The worst-case complexity of processing a sequence of unions and finds using *WeightedUnion* and *CollapsingFind* is stated in Lemma 5.6. This lemma makes use of a function $\alpha(p,q)$ that is related to a functional inverse of Ackermann's function $A(i,j)$. These functions are defined as follows:

(a) Initial height-1 trees

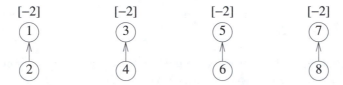

(b) Height-2 trees following *union* (1,2), (3,4), (5,6), and (7,8)

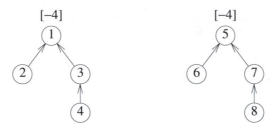

(c) Height-3 trees following *union* (1,3) and (5,7)

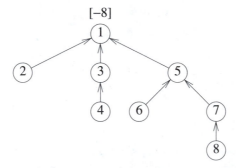

(d) Height-4 tree following *union* (1,5)

Figure 5.42: Trees achieving worst-case bound

```
function CollapsingFind (i : integer) : integer;
{Find the root of the tree containing element i. Use the collapsing rule collapse all nodes
from i to the root.}
var r, s : integer;
begin
  r := i;
  while parent [r] > 0 do {find root}
    r := parent [r];
  while i <> r do {collapse}
  begin
    s := parent [i];
    parent [i] := r;
    i := s;
  end;
  CollapsingFind := r;
end; {of CollapsingFind}
```

Program 5.23: Find algorithm with collapsing rule

$$A(1,j) = 2^j, \qquad\qquad \text{for } j \geq 1$$
$$A(i, 1) = A(i-1,2) \qquad \text{for } i \geq 2$$
$$A(i,j) = A(i-1,A(i,j-1)) \quad \text{for } i,j \geq 2$$

$$\alpha(p,q) = \min\{z \geq 1 \mid A(z, \lfloor p/q \rfloor) > \log_2 q\}, \ p \geq q \geq 1$$

The function $A(i,j)$ is a very rapidly growing function. Consequently, α grows very slowly as p and q are increased. In fact, since $A(3,1) = 16$, $\alpha(p,q) \leq 3$ for $q < 2^{16} = 65{,}536$ and $p \geq q$. Since $A(4,1)$ is a very large number and in our application q will be the number, n, of set elements and p will be $n + f$ (f is the number of finds), $\alpha(p,q) \leq 4$ for all practical purposes.

Lemma 5.6 [*Tarjan and Van Leeuwen*]: Assume that we start with a forest of trees, each having one node. Let $T(f,u)$ be the maximum time required to process any inter-mixed sequence of f finds and u unions. Assume that $u \geq n/2$. Then

$$k_1(n + f\,\alpha(f+n,n)) \leq T(f,u) \leq k_2(n + f\,\alpha(f+n,n))$$

for some positive constants k_1 and k_2. $\square$

The requirement that $u \geq n/2$ in Lemma 5.6, is really not significant, as when $u < n/2$, some elements are involved in no union operation. These elements remain in singleton sets throughout the sequence of union and find operations and can be eliminated from consideration, as find operations that involve these can be done in O(1) time each. Even though the function $\alpha(f,u)$ is a very slowly growing function, the complexity of our solution to the set representation problem is not linear in the number of unions and finds. The space requirements are one node for each element. □

In the exercises, we explore alternatives to the weight rule and the collapsing rule that preserve the time bounds of Lemma 5.6.

5.10.3   Application to Equivalence Classes

Consider the equivalence pairs processing problem of Section 4.5. The equivalence classes to be generated may be regarded as sets. These sets are disjoint, as no polygon can be in two equivalence classes. Initially, all n polygons are in an equivalence class of their own; thus $parent\,[i\,] = -1, 1 \leq i \leq n$. If an equivalence pair, $i \equiv j$, is to be processed, we must first determine the sets containing i and j. If these are different, then the two sets are to be replaced by their union. If the two sets are the same, then nothing is to be done, as the relation $i \equiv j$ is redundant; i and j are already in the same equivalence class. To process each equivalence pair we need to perform two finds and at most one union. Thus, if we have n polygons and m equivalence pairs, we need to spend O(n) time to set up the initial n-tree forest, and then we need to process $2m$ finds and at most $\min\{n - 1, m\}$ unions. (Note that after $n - 1$ unions, all n polygons will be in the same equivalence class and no more unions can be performed.) If we use *WeightedUnion* and *CollapsingFind*, the total time to process the equivalence relations is O($n + m\alpha(2m, \min\{n-1, m\})$). Although this is slightly worse than the algorithm of Section 4.5, it needs less space and is line. By ''on line,'' we mean that as each equivalence is processed, we can tell which equivalence class each polygon is in.

Example 5.5: Consider the equivalence pairs example of Chapter 4. Initially, there are 12 trees, one for each variable. $parent[i] = -1$, $1 \leq i \leq 12$. The tree configuration following the processing of each equivalence pair is shown in Figure 5.43. Each tree represents an equivalence class. It is possible to determine if two elements are currently in the same equivalence class at each stage of the processing simply by making two finds. □

EXERCISES

1. Suppose we start with n sets, each containing a distinct element.

    (a) Show that if u unions are performed, then no set contains more than $u + 1$ elements.

    (b) Show that at most $n - 1$ unions can be performed before the number of sets becomes 1.

    (c) Show that if fewer than $\lceil n/2 \rceil$ unions are performed, then at least one set with a single element in it remains.

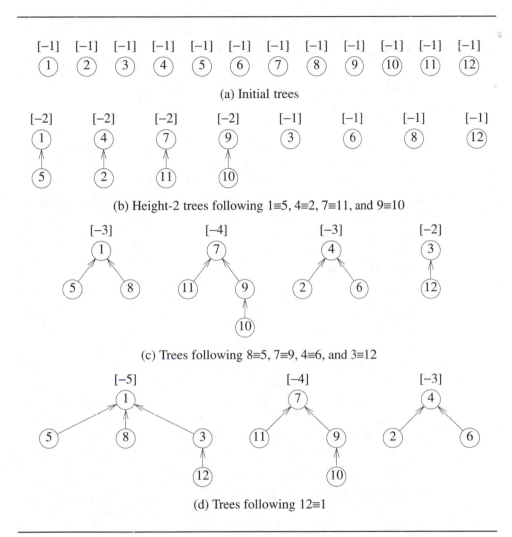

(a) Initial trees

(b) Height-2 trees following 1≡5, 4≡2, 7≡11, and 9≡10

(c) Trees following 8≡5, 7≡9, 4≡6, and 3≡12

(d) Trees following 12≡1

Figure 5.43: Trees for Example 5.5

    (d)   Show that if *u* unions are performed, then at least max{*n* − 2*u*, 0} singleton sets remain.

2. Using the result of Example 5.5, draw the trees after processing the instruction *union*(12,10).

3. Experimentally compare the performance of *SimpleUnion* and *SimpleFind* (Program 5.21) with *WeightedUnion* (Program 5.22) and *CollapsingFind* (Program 5.23). For this, generate a random sequence of union and find operations.

4. (a) Write a procedure *HeightUnion* that uses the *height rule* for union operations instead of the weighting rule. This rule is defined below:

   Definition [*Height Rule*]: If the height of tree i is less than that of tree j, then make j the parent of i, otherwise make i the parent of j. □

   Your procedure must run in $O(1)$ time and should maintain the height of each tree as a negative number in the *parent* field of the root.

   (b) Show that the height bound of Lemma 5.5 applies to trees constructed using the height rule.

   (c) Give an example of a sequence of unions that start with singleton sets and create trees whose height equals the upper bound given in Lemma 5.5. Assume that each union is performed using the height rule.

   (d) Experiment with procedures *WeightedUnion* (Program 5.22) and *HeightUnion* to determine which one produces better results when used in conjunction with function *CollapsingFind* (Program 5.23).

5. (a) Write a function *SplittingFind* that uses *path splitting* for the find operations instead of path collapsing. This is defined below:

   Definition [*Path Splitting*]: In path splitting, the parent pointer in each node (except the root and its child) on the path from i to the root is changed to point to the node's grandparent. □

   Note that when path splitting is used, a single pass from i to the root suffices. Tarjan and Van Leeuwen have shown that Lemma 5.6 holds when path splitting is used in conjunction with either the weight or height rule for unions.

   (b) Experiment with functions *CollapsingFind* (Program 5.23) and *SplittingFind* to determine which produces better results when used in conjunction with procedure *WeightedUnion* (Program 5.22).

6. (a) Write a function *HalvingFind* that uses *path halving* for the find operations instead of path collapsing. This is defined below:

   Definition [*Path Halving*]: In path halving, the parent pointer of every other node (except the root and its child) on the path from i to the root is changed to point to the nodes grandparent. □

   Note that path halving, like path splitting (Exercise 5) can be implemented with a single pass from i to the root. However, in path halving, only half as many pointers are changed as in path splitting. Tarjan and Van Leeuwen have shown that Lemma 5.6 holds when path halving is used in conjunction with either the weight or height rule for unions.

   (b) Experiment with functions *CollapsingFind* and *HalvingFind* to determine which one produces better results when used in conjunction with procedure *WeightedUnion*.

5.11 COUNTING BINARY TREES

As a conclusion to our chapter on trees, we consider three disparate problems that amazingly have the same solution. We wish to determine the number of distinct binary trees having n nodes, the number of distinct permutations of the numbers from 1 through n obtainable by a stack, and the number of distinct ways of multiplying $n + 1$ matrices. Let us begin with a quick look at these problems.

5.11.1 Distinct Binary Trees

We know that if $n = 0$ or $n = 1$, there is only one binary tree. If $n = 2$, then there are two distinct trees (Figure 5.44), and if $n = 3$, there are five such trees (Figure 5.45). How many distinct trees are there with n nodes? Before deriving a solution, we will examine the two remaining problems. You might attempt to sketch out a solution of your own before reading further.

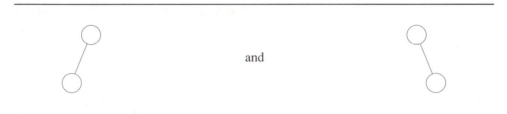

Figure 5.44: Distinct binary trees with $n = 2$

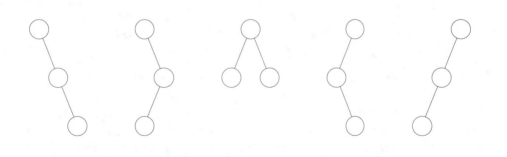

Figure 5.45: Distinct binary trees with $n = 3$

5.11.2   Stack Permutations

In Section 5.3, we introduced preorder, inorder, and postorder traversals and indicated that each traversal requires a stack. Suppose we have the preorder sequence *A B C D E F G H I* and the inorder sequence *B C A E D G H F I* of the same binary tree. Does such a pair of sequences uniquely define a binary tree? Put another way, can this pair of sequences come from more than one binary tree?

To construct the binary tree from these sequences, we look at the first letter in the preorder sequence, *A*. This letter must be the root of the tree by definition of the preorder traversal (*VLR*). We also know by definition of the inorder traversal (*LVR*) that all nodes preceding *A* in the inorder sequence (*B C*) are in the left subtree, and the remaining nodes (*E D G H F I*) are in the right subtree. Figure 5.46(a) is our first approximation to the correct tree.

Moving right in the preorder sequence, we find *B* as the next root. Since no node precedes *B* in the inorder sequence, *B* has an empty left subtree, which means that *C* is in its right subtree. Figure 5.46(b) is the next approximation. Continuing in this way, we arrive at the binary tree of Figure 5.47(a). By formalizing this argument (see the exercises), we can verify that every binary tree has a unique pair of preorder/inorder sequences.

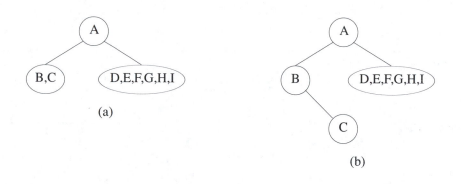

(a)

(b)

Figure 5.46: Constructing a binary tree from its inorder and preorder sequences

Let the nodes of an *n*-node binary tree be numbered from 1 through *n*. The inorder permutation defined by such a binary tree is the order in which its nodes are visited during an inorder traversal of the tree. A preorder permutation is similarly defined.

As an example, consider the binary tree of Figure 5.47(a) with the node numbering of Figure 5.47(b). Its preorder permutation is 1, 2, $\cdots$, 9, and its inorder permutation is 2, 3, 1, 5, 4, 7, 8, 6, 9.

If the nodes of the tree are numbered such that its preorder permutation is 1, 2, $\cdots$, *n*, then from our earlier discussion it follows that distinct binary trees define distinct

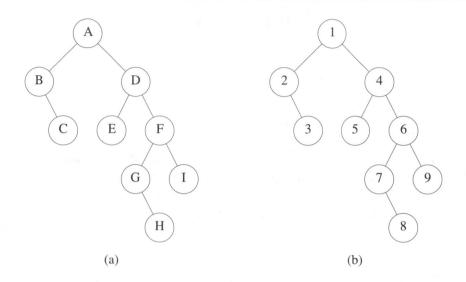

(a)   (b)

Figure 5.47: Binary tree constructed from its inorder and preorder sequences

inorder permutations. Thus, the number of distinct binary trees is equal to the number of distinct inorder permutations obtainable from binary trees having the preorder permutation, $1, 2, \cdots, n$.

Using the concept of an inorder permutation, we can show that the number of distinct permutations obtainable by passing the numbers 1 through n through a stack and deleting in all possible ways is equal to the number of distinct binary trees with n nodes (see the exercises). If we start with the numbers 1, 2, and 3, then the possible permutations obtainable by a stack are

$$(1, 2, 3)\ (1, 3, 2)\ (2, 1, 3)\ (2, 3, 1)\ (3, 2, 1)$$

Obtaining (3, 1, 2) is impossible. Each of these five permutations corresponds to one of the five distinct binary trees with three nodes (Figure 5.48).

5.11.3   Matrix Multiplication

Another problem that surprisingly has a connection with the previous two involves the product of n matrices. Suppose that we wish to compute the product of n matrices:

$$M_1 * M_2 * \cdots * M_n$$

Since matrix multiplication is associative, we can perform these multiplications in any order. We would like to know how many different ways we can perform these multipli-

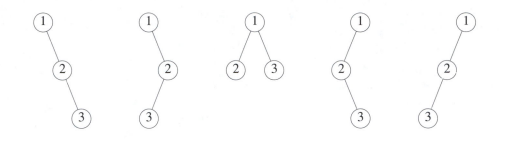

Figure 5.48: Binary trees corresponding to five permutations

cations. For example, if $n = 3$, there are two possibilities:

$$(M_1 * M_2) * M_3$$
$$M_1 * (M_2 * M_3)$$

and if $n = 4$, there are five:

$$((M_1 * M_2) * M_3) * M_4$$
$$(M_1 * (M_2 * M_3)) * M_4$$
$$M_1 * ((M_2 * M_3) * M_4)$$
$$(M_1 * (M_2 * (M_3 * M_4)))$$
$$((M_1 * M_2) * (M_3 * M_4))$$

Let b_n be the number of different ways to compute the product of n matrices. Then $b_2 = 1$, $b_3 = 2$, and $b_4 = 5$. Let M_{ij}, $i \leq j$, be the product $M_i * M_{i+1} * \cdots * M_j$. The product we wish to compute is M_{1n}. We may compute M_{1n} by computing any one of the products $M_{1i} * M_{i+1,n}$, $1 \leq i \leq n$. The number of distinct ways to obtain M_{1i} and $M_{i+1,n}$ are b_i and b_{n-i}, respectively. Therefore, letting $b_1 = 1$, we have

$$b_n = \sum_{i=1}^{n-1} b_i \, b_{n-i}, n > 1$$

If we can determine the expression for b_n only in terms of n, then we have a solution to our problem.

Now instead let b_n be the number of distinct binary trees with n nodes. Again an expression for b_n in terms of n is what we want. Then we see that b_n is the sum of all the possible binary trees formed in the following way: a root and two subtrees with b_i and b_{n-i-1} nodes, for $0 \leq i < n$ (Figure 5.49). This explanation says that

$$b_n = \sum_{i=0}^{n-1} b_i \, b_{n-i-1} , n \geq 1 , \text{ and } b_0 = 1 \tag{5.3}$$

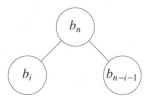

Figure 5.49: Decomposing b_n

This formula and the previous one are essentially the same. Therefore, the number of binary trees with n nodes, the number of permutations of 1 to n obtainable with a stack, and the number of ways to multiply $n + 1$ matrices are all equal.

5.11.4 Number of Distinct Binary Trees

To obtain the number of distinct binary trees with n nodes, we must solve the recurrence of Eq. (5.3). To begin we let

$$B(x) = \sum_{i \geq 0} b_i \, x^i \qquad (5.4)$$

which is the generating function for the number of binary trees. Next observe that by the recurrence relation we get the identity

$$xB^2(x) = B(x) - 1$$

Using the formula to solve quadratics and the fact that $B(0) = b_0 = 1$ (Eq.(5.3)), we get

$$B(x) = \frac{1 - \sqrt{1-4x}}{2x}$$

We can use the binomial theorem to expand $(1 - 4x)^{1/2}$ to obtain

$$B(x) = \frac{1}{2x}\left[1 - \sum_{n \geq 0} \binom{1/2}{n}(-4x)^n\right] = \sum_{m \geq 0}\binom{1/2}{m+1}(-1)^m \, 2^{2m+1} \, x^m \qquad (5.5)$$

Comparing Eqs. (5.4) and (5.5), we see that b_n, which is the coefficient of x^n in $B(x)$, is

$$\binom{1/2}{n+1}(-1)^n \, 2^{2n+1}$$

Some simplification yields the more compact form

$$b_n = \frac{1}{n+1} \begin{bmatrix} 2n \\ n \end{bmatrix}$$

which is approximately

$$b_n = O(4^n / n^{3/2})$$

EXERCISES

1. Prove that every binary tree is uniquely defined by its preorder and inorder sequences.

2. Do the inorder and postorder sequences of a binary tree uniquely define the binary tree? Prove your answer.

3. Do the inorder and preorder sequences of a binary tree uniquely define the binary tree? Prove your answer.

4. Do the inorder and level-order sequences of a binary tree uniquely define the binary tree? Prove your answer.

5. Write an algorithm to construct the binary tree with given preorder and inorder sequences.

6. Repeat Exercise 5 with the inorder and postorder sequences.

7. Prove that the number of distinct permutations of $1, 2, \cdots, n$ obtainable by a stack is equal to the number of distinct binary trees with n nodes. (Hint: Use the concept of an inorder permutation of a tree with preorder permutation $1, 2, \cdots, n$).

5.12   REFERENCES AND SELECTED READINGS

For other representations of trees, see *The Art of Computer Programming: Fundamental Algorithms*, Second Edition, by D. Knuth, Addison-Wesley, Reading, MA, 1973.

For the use of trees in generating optimal compiled code, see *Compilers: Principles, Techniques, and Tools*, by A. Aho, R. Sethi, and J. Ullman, Addison-Wesley, Reading, MA, 1986.

Tree traversal algorithms may be found in "Scanning list structures without stacks and tag bits," by G. Lindstrom, *Information Processing Letters*, 2:2, 1973, pp. 47-51, and "Simple algorithms for traversing a tree without an auxiliary stack," by B. Dwyer, *Information Processing Letters*, 2:5, 1973, pp. 143-145.

For more on data structures for the set representation problems see "Worst case analysis of set union algorithms," by R. Tarjan and J. Van Leeuwen, *Journal of the ACM*, 31:2, 1984, pp. 245-281.

CHAPTER 6

GRAPHS

6.1 THE GRAPH ABSTRACT DATA TYPE

6.1.1 Introduction

The first recorded evidence of the use of graphs dates back to 1736, when Leonhard Euler used them to solve the now classical Königsberg bridge problem. In the town of Königsberg (now Kaliningrad) the river Pregel (Pregolya) flows around the island Kneiphof and then divides into two. There are, therefore, four land areas that have this river on its borders (see Figure 6.1(a)). These land areas are interconnected by seven bridges labeled $a-g$. The land areas themselves are labeled $A-D$. The Königsberg bridge problem is to determine whether, starting at one land area, it is possible to walk across all the bridges exactly once in returning to the starting land area. One possible walk is

- start from land area B
- walk across bridge a to island A
- take bridge e to area D
- take bridge g to C
- take bridge d to A

- take bridge b to B
- take bridge f to D

This walk does not go across all bridges exactly once, nor does it return to the starting land area B. Euler answered the Königsberg bridge problem in the negative: The people of Königsberg will not be able to walk across each bridge exactly once and return to the starting point. He solved the problem by representing the land areas as vertices and the bridges as edges in a graph (actually a multigraph) as in Figure 6.1(b). His solution is elegant and applies to all graphs. Defining the *degree* of a vertex to be the number of edges incident to it, Euler showed that there is a walk starting at any vertex, going through each edge exactly once and terminating at the start vertex iff the degree of each vertex is even. A walk that does this is called *Eulerian*. There is no Eulerian walk for the Königsberg bridge problem, as all four vertices are of odd degree.

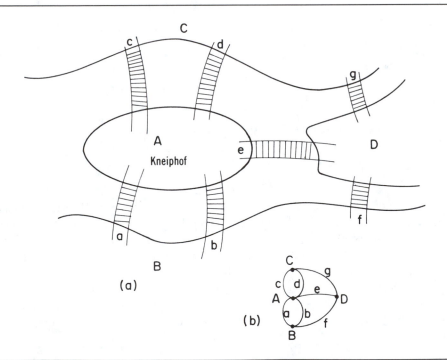

Figure 6.1: Section of the river Pregel in Königsberg and Euler's graph

Since this first application, graphs have been used in a wide variety of applications. Some of these applications are: analysis of electrical circuits, finding shortest routes, project planning, identification of chemical compounds, statistical mechanics, genetics, cybernetics, linguistics, social sciences, and so on. Indeed, it might well be said that of all mathematical structures, graphs are the most widely used.

6.1.2 Definitions

A graph, G, consists of two sets, V and E. V is a finite, nonempty set of *vertices*. E is a set of pairs of vertices; these pairs are called *edges*. $V(G)$ and $E(G)$ will represent the sets of vertices and edges, respectively, of graph G. We will also write $G = (V,E)$ to represent a graph. In an *undirected graph* the pair of vertices representing any edge is unordered. Thus, the pairs (u,v) and (v,u) represent the same edge. In a *directed graph* each edge is represented by a directed pair $<u,v>$; u is the *tail* and v the *head* of the edge. Therefore, $<v,u>$ and $<u,v>$ represent two different edges. Figure 6.2 shows three graphs: G_1, G_2, and G_3. The graphs G_1 and G_2 are undirected. G_3 is a directed graph.

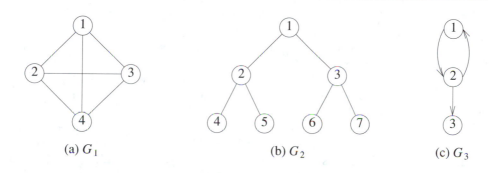

(a) G_1 (b) G_2 (c) G_3

Figure 6.2: Three sample graphs

The set representation of each of these graphs is

$V(G_1) = \{1,2,3,4\};$ $E(G_1) = \{(1,2),(1,3),(1,4),(2,3),(2,4),(3,4)\}$

$V(G_2) = \{1,2,3,4,5,6,7\};$ $E(G_2) = \{(1,2),(1,3),(2,4),(2,5),(3,6),(3,7)\}$

$V(G_3) = \{1,2,3\};$ $E(G_3) = \{<1,2>,<2,1>,<2,3>\}.$

Notice that the edges of a directed graph are drawn with an arrow from the tail to the head. The graph G_2 is a tree; the graphs G_1 and G_3 are not.

Since we define the edges and vertices of a graph as sets, we impose the following restrictions on graphs:

(1) A graph may not have an edge from a vertex, v, back to itself. That is, edges of the form (v, v) and $<v, v>$ are not legal. Such edges are known as *self edges* or *self loops*. If we permit self edges, we obtain a data object referred to as a *graph with self edges*. An example is shown in Figure 6.3(a).

(2)   A graph may not have multiple occurrences of the same edge. If we remove this restriction, we obtain a data object referred to as a *multigraph* (see Figure 6.3(b)).

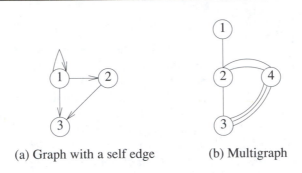

(a) Graph with a self edge   (b) Multigraph

Figure 6.3: Examples of graphlike structures

The number of distinct unordered pairs (u,v) with $u \neq v$ in a graph with n vertices is $n(n-1)/2$. This is the maximum number of edges in any n-vertex, undirected graph. An n-vertex, undirected graph with exactly $n(n-1)/2$ edges is said to be *complete*. The graph G_1 of Figure 6.2(a) is the complete graph on four vertices, whereas G_2 and G_3 are not complete graphs. In the case of a directed graph on n vertices, the maximum number of edges is $n(n-1)$.

If (u,v) is an edge in $E(G)$, then we shall say the vertices u and v are *adjacent* and that the edge (u,v) is *incident* on vertices u and v. The vertices adjacent to vertex 2 in G_2 are 4, 5, and 1. The edges incident on vertex 3 in G_2 are (1,3), (3,6), and (3,7). If $<u,v>$ is a directed edge, then vertex u is *adjacent to* v, and v is *adjacent from* u. The edge $<u,v>$ is incident to u and v. In G_3, the edges incident to vertex 2 are $<1,2>$, $<2,1>$, and $<2,3>$.

A *subgraph* of G is a graph G' such that $V(G') \subseteq V(G)$ and $E(G') \subseteq E(G)$. Figure 6.4 shows some of the subgraphs of G_1 and G_3.

A *path* from vertex u to vertex v in graph G is a sequence of vertices $u, i_1, i_2, \cdots, i_k, v$ such that $(u, i_1), (i_1, i_2), \cdots, (i_k, v)$ are edges in $E(G)$. If G' is directed, then the path consists of $<u, i_1>, <i_1, i_2>, \cdots, <i_k, v>$ edges in $E(G')$. The *length* of a path is the number of edges on it. A *simple path* is a path in which all vertices except possibly the first and last are distinct. A path such as (1,2), (2,4), (4,3), is also written as 1,2,4,3. Paths 1,2,4,3 and 1,2,4,2 of G_1 are both of length 3. The first is a simple path; the second is not. 1,2,3 is a simple directed path in G_3. 1,2,3,2 is not a path in G_3, as the edge $<3,2>$ is not in $E(G_3)$.

A *cycle* is a simple path in which the first and last vertices are the same. 1,2,3,1 is a cycle in G_1. 1,2,1 is a cycle in G_3. For the case of directed graphs we normally add the prefix ''directed'' to the terms cycle and path.

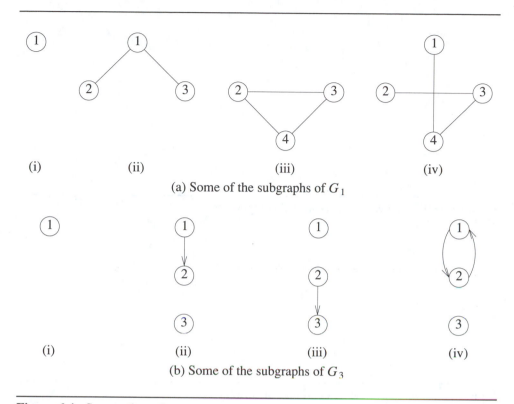

(a) Some of the subgraphs of G_1

(b) Some of the subgraphs of G_3

Figure 6.4: Some subgraphs

In an undirected graph, G, two vertices u and v are said to be *connected* iff there is a path in G from u to v (since G is undirected, this means there must also be a path from v to u). An undirected graph is said to be connected iff for every pair of distinct vertices u and v in $V(G)$ there is a path from u to v in G. Graphs G_1 and G_2 are connected, whereas G_4 of Figure 6.5 is not. A *connected component* (or simply a component), H, of an undirected graph is a *maximal* connected subgraph. By maximal, we mean that G contains no other subgraph that is both connected and properly contains H. G_4 has two components, H_1 and H_2 (see Figure 6.5).

A *tree* is a connected acyclic (i.e., has no cycles) graph.

A directed graph G is said to be *strongly connected* iff for every pair of distinct vertices u and v in $V(G)$, there is a directed path from u to v and also from v to u. The graph G_3 is not strongly connected, as there is no path from vertex 3 to 2. A *strongly connected component* is a maximal subgraph that is strongly connected. G_3 has two strongly connected components (see Figure 6.6).

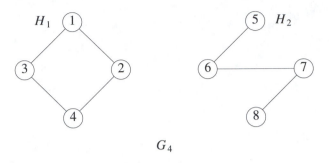

Figure 6.5: A graph with two connected components

Figure 6.6: Strongly connected components of G_3

The degree of a vertex is the number of edges incident to that vertex. The degree of vertex 1 in G_1 is 3. If G is a directed graph, we define the *in-degree* of a vertex v to be the number of edges for which v is the head. The *out-degree* is defined to be the number of edges for which v is the tail. Vertex 2 of G_3 has in-degree 1, out-degree 2, and degree 3. If d_i is the degree of vertex i in a graph G with n vertices and e edges, then the number of edges is

$$e = (\sum_{i=1}^{n} d_i)/2$$

In the remainder of this chapter, we shall refer to a directed graph as a *digraph*. When we use the term *graph*, we assume that it is an undirected graph. Now that we have defined all the terminology we will need, let us consider the graph as an ADT. The resulting specification is given in Structure 6.1.

The operations in Structure 6.1 are a basic set in that they allow us to create any arbitrary graph and do some elementary tests. In later sections of this chapter we will

---

structure *Graph* **is**

    objects: A nonempty set of vertices and a set of undirected edges, where each edge is a pair of vertices.

    functions:

        for all *graph* ∈ *Graph*, *u* and *v* ∈ *Vertices*

Create ( ) : *Graph*	::=	*Create* := an empty graph
InsertVertex (*graph*, *v*) : *Graph*	::=	*InsertVertex* := *graph* with *v* inserted, *v* has no incident edges
InsertEdge (*graph*, *u*, *v*) : *Graph*	::=	*InsertEdge* := *graph* with a new edge between *u* and *v*
DeleteVertex (*graph*, *v*) : *Graph*	::=	*DeleteVertex* := *graph* with *v* and all edges incident to it removed
DeleteEdge (*graph*, *u*, *v*) : *Graph*	::=	*DeleteEdge* := *graph* with edge (*u*, *v*) removed
IsEmpty (*graph*) : *Boolean*	::=	**if** *graph* has no vertices **then** *IsEmptyGraph* := **true** **else** *IsEmptyGraph* := **false**
Adjacent (*graph*, *v*) : *List*	::=	*Adjacent* := a list of all vertices that are adjacent to *v*

Structure 6.1: Abstract data type *Graph*

see procedures that traverse a graph (depth-first or breadth-first search) and that determine if a graph has special properties (e.g., connected, biconnected, or planar).

6.1.3 Graph Representations

Although several representations for graphs are possible, we shall study only the three most commonly used: adjacency matrices, adjacency lists, and adjacency multilists. Once again, the choice of a particular representation will depend upon the application one has in mind and the functions one expects to perform on the graph.

6.1.3.1 Adjacency Matrix

Let $G = (V, E)$ be a graph with n vertices, $n \geq 1$. The adjacency matrix of G is a two-dimensional $n \times n$ array, say A, with the property that $A[i, j] = 1$ iff the edge (i, j) ($<i, j>$ for a directed graph) is in $E(G)$. $A[i, j] = 0$ if there is no such edge in G. The adjacency matrices for the graphs G_1, G_3, and G_4 are shown in Figure 6.7. The adjacency matrix for an undirected graph is symmetric, as the edge (i, j) is in $E(G)$ iff the edge (j, i) is also in $E(G)$. The adjacency matrix for a directed graph may not be symmetric (as is the case for G_3). The space needed to represent a graph using its adjacency matrix is n^2 bits. About half this space can be saved in the case of undirected graphs by storing only the upper or lower triangle of the matrix.

	1	2	3	4
1	0	1	1	1
2	1	0	1	1
3	1	1	0	1
4	1	1	1	0

(a) G_1

	1	2	3
1	0	1	0
2	1	0	1
3	0	0	0

(b) G_3

	1	2	3	4	5	6	7	8
1	0	1	1	0	0	0	0	0
2	1	0	0	1	0	0	0	0
3	1	0	0	1	0	0	0	0
4	0	1	1	0	0	0	0	0
5	0	0	0	0	0	1	0	0
6	0	0	0	0	1	0	1	0
7	0	0	0	0	0	1	0	1
8	0	0	0	0	0	0	1	0

(c) G_4

Figure 6.7: Adjacency matrices

From the adjacency matrix, one may readily determine if there is an edge connecting any two vertices i and j. For an undirected graph the degree of any vertex i is its row sum:

$$\sum_{j=1}^{n} A[i, j]$$

For a directed graph the row sum is the out-degree, and the column sum is the in-degree.

Suppose we want to answer a nontrivial question about graphs, such as, How many edges are there in G? or Is G connected? Adjacency matrices will require at least $O(n^2)$ time, as $n^2 - n$ entries of the matrix (diagonal entries are zero) have to be examined. When graphs are sparse (i.e., most of the terms in the adjacency matrix are zero) one would expect that the former question could be answered in significantly less time, say $O(e + n)$, where e is the number of edges in G, and $e << n^2/2$. Such a speed-up can be made possible through the use of a representation in which only the edges that are in G are explicitly stored. This leads to the next representation for graphs, adjacency lists.

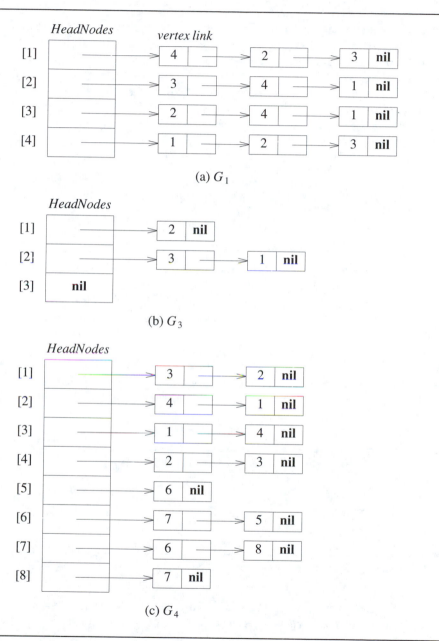

Figure 6.8: Adjacency lists

6.1.3.2   Adjacency Lists

In this representation of graphs, the n rows of the adjacency matrix are represented as n linked lists. There is one list for each vertex in G. The nodes in list i represent the vertices that are adjacent from vertex i. Each node has at least two fields: *vertex* and *link*. The *vertex* fields contain the indices of the vertices adjacent to vertex i. The adjacency lists for G_1, G_3, and G_4 are shown in Figure 6.8. Notice that the vertices in each list are not required to be ordered. Each list has a head node. The head nodes are sequential, providing easy random access to the adjacency list for any particular vertex. The declarations in Pascal for the adjacency list representation are

$$\textbf{type } NextNode = \uparrow node;$$
$$node = \textbf{record}$$
$$vertex : \textbf{integer};$$
$$link : NextNode;$$
$$\textbf{end};$$
$$\textbf{var } HeadNodes : \textbf{array}[1..n] \textbf{ of } NextNode;$$

For an undirected graph with n vertices and e edges, this representation requires n head nodes and $2e$ list nodes. Each list node has two fields. In terms of the number of bits of storage needed, this count should be multiplied by $\log n$ for the head nodes and $\log n + \log e$ for the list nodes, as it takes $O(\log m)$ bits to represent a number of value m. Often, you can sequentially pack the nodes on the adjacency lists, thereby eliminating the use of pointers. In this case, an array $node[1..n + 2e + 1]$ may be used. $node[i]$ gives the starting point of the list for vertex i, $1 \le i \le n$, and $node[n+1]$ is set to $n + 2e + 2$. The vertices adjacent from vertex i are stored in $node[i]$, $\cdots$, $node[i + 1] - 1$, $1 \le i \le n$. Figure 6.9 shows the representation for the graph G_4 of Figure 6.5.

---

var *nodes* : **array**[1 .. n + 2*e + 1] **of integer**;

1	2	3	4	5	6	7	8	9	10	11	12	13	14	15	16	17	18	19	20	21	22	23
10	12	14	16	18	19	21	23	24	3	2	4	1	1	4	2	3	6	7	5	6	8	7

Figure 6.9: Sequential representation of graph G_4

The degree of any vertex in an undirected graph may be determined by just counting the number of nodes in its adjacency list. So, the number of edges in G may be determined in $O(n + e)$ time.

For a digraph, the number of list nodes is only e. The out-degree of any vertex may be determined by counting the number of nodes on its adjacency list. Hence, the total number of edges in G can be determined in $O(n + e)$ time. Determining the in-degree of a vertex is a little more complex. If there is a need to access repeatedly all vertices adjacent to another vertex, then it may be worth the effort to keep another set of lists in addition to the adjacency lists. This set of lists, called *inverse adjacency lists*, will contain one list for each vertex. Each list will contain a node for each vertex adjacent to the vertex it represents (see Figure 6.10).

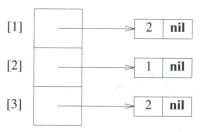

Figure 6.10: Inverse adjacency lists for G_3 (Figure 6.2(c))

Alternatively, one can adopt a simplified version of the list structure used for sparse matrix representation in Chapter 4. Each node now has four fields and represents one edge. The node structure is

tail	head	column link for head	row link for tail

Figure 6.11 shows the resulting structure for the graph G_3 of Figure 6.2(c). The head nodes are stored sequentially.

6.1.3.3 Adjacency Multilists

In the adjacency-list representation of an undirected graph, each edge (u,v) is represented by two entries, one on the list for u and the other on the list for v. As we shall see, in some situations it is necessary to be able to determine the second entry for a particular edge and mark that edge as having been examined. This can be accomplished easily if the adjacency lists are actually maintained as multilists (i.e., lists in which nodes may be shared among several lists). For each edge there will be exactly one node, but this node will be in two lists (i.e., the adjacency lists for each of the two nodes to which it is incident). The new node structure is

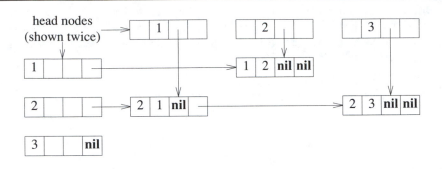

Figure 6.11: Orthogonal list representation for G_3 of Figure 6.2(c)

m	vertex 1	vertex 2	list 1	list 2

where m is a one-bit mark field that may be used to indicate whether or not the edge has been examined. The Pascal declarations are

$$\textbf{type } NextEdges = \uparrow edge;$$
$$edge = \textbf{record}$$
$$m : \textbf{boolean};$$
$$vertex\ 1 : \textbf{integer};$$
$$vertex\ 2 : \textbf{integer};$$
$$path\ 1 : NextEdges;$$
$$path\ 2 : NextEdges;$$
$$\textbf{end};$$
$$\textbf{var } HeadNodes : \textbf{array}[1\ ..\ n\ ] \textbf{ of } NextEdges;$$

The storage requirements are the same as for normal adjacency lists, except for the addition of the mark bit m. Figure 6.12 shows the adjacency multilists for G_1 of Figure 6.2(a).

6.1.3.4 Weighted Edges

In many applications, the edges of a graph have weights assigned to them. These weights may represent the distance from one vertex to another or the cost of going from one vertex to an adjacent vertex. In these applications, the adjacency matrix entries $A[i,j]$ would keep this information too. When adjacency lists are used, the weight information may be kept in the list nodes by including an additional field, *weight*. A graph with weighted edges is called a *network*.

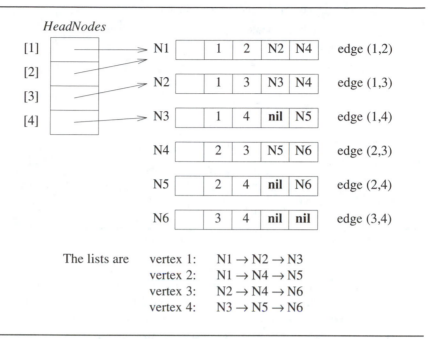

The lists are   vertex 1:   N1 → N2 → N3
                 vertex 2:   N1 → N4 → N5
                 vertex 3:   N2 → N4 → N6
                 vertex 4:   N3 → N5 → N6

Figure 6.12: Adjacency multilists for G_1 of Figure 6.2(a)

EXERCISES

1. Does the multigraph of Figure 6.13 have an Eulerian walk? If so, find one.

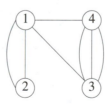

Figure 6.13: A multigraph

2. For the digraph of Figure 6.14 obtain
   (a)   the in-degree and out-degree of each vertex
   (b)   its adjacency-matrix

(c)   its adjacency-list representation

(d)   its adjacency-multilist representation

(e)   its strongly connected components

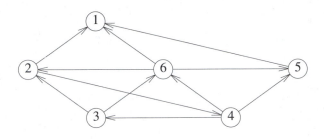

Figure 6.14: A digraph

3. Devise a suitable representation for graphs so that they can be stored on disk. Write an algorithm that reads in such a graph and creates its adjacency matrix. Write another algorithm that creates the adjacency lists from the disk input.

4. Draw the complete undirected graphs on one, two, three, four, and five vertices. Prove that the number of edges in an n-vertex complete graph is $n(n-1)/2$.

5. Is the directed graph of Figure 6.15 strongly connected? List all the simple paths.

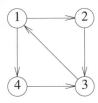

Figure 6.15: A directed graph

6. Obtain the adjacency-matrix, adjacency-list, and adjacency-multilist representations of the graph of Figure 6.15.

7. Show that the sum of the degrees of the vertices of an undirected graph is twice the number of edges.

8. (a) Let G be a connected, undirected graph on n vertices. Show that G must have at least $n-1$ edges and that all connected, undirected graphs with $n-1$ edges are trees.

   (b) What is the minimum number of edges in a strongly connected digraph on n vertices? What form do such digraphs have?

9. For an undirected graph G with n vertices, prove that the following are equivalent:

   (a) G is a tree

   (b) G is connected, but if any edge is removed the resulting graph is not connected

   (c) For any two distinct vertices $u \in V(G)$ and $v \in V(G)$, there is exactly one simple path from u to v

   (d) G contains no cycles and has $n-1$ edges

10. Write a Pascal procedure to input the number of vertices in an undirected graph and its edges one by one and to set up the linked adjacency-list representation of the graph. You may assume that no edge is input twice. What is the run time of your procedure as a function of the number of vertices and the number of edges?

11. Do the preceding exercise but this time set up the multilist representation.

12. Let G be an undirected, connected graph with at least one vertex of odd degree. Show that G contains no Eulerian walk.

6.2 ELEMENTARY GRAPH OPERATIONS

When we discussed binary trees in Chapter 5, we indicated that tree traversals were among the most frequently used tree operations. Thus, we defined and implemented preorder, inorder, postorder, and level-order tree traversals. An analogous situation occurs in the case of graphs. Given a graph $G = (V, E)$ and a vertex v in $V(G)$, we wish to visit all vertices in G that are reachable from v (i.e., all vertices that are connected to v). We shall look at two ways of doing this: *depth-first search* and *breadth-first search*. Although these methods work on both directed and undirected graphs, the following discussion assumes that the graphs are undirected.

6.2.1 Depth-First Search

We begin by visiting the start vertex v. Next an unvisited vertex w adjacent to v is selected, and a depth-first search from w is initiated. When a vertex u is reached such that all its adjacent vertices have been visited, we back up to the last vertex visited that has an unvisited vertex w adjacent to it and initiate a depth-first search from w. The search terminates when no unvisited vertex can be reached from any of the visited vertices. This procedure is best described recursively as in Program 6.1. The procedure assumes a global array *visited*[1 .. *n*] of type boolean that is initialized to **false**.

---

procedure *dfs*(*v* : **integer**);
{Given an undirected graph $G = (V,E)$ with *n* vertices and an array *visited*[*n*] initially set to **false**, this algorithm visits all vertices reachable from *v*. The array *visited* is global.}
var *w* : *integer* ;
begin
    visited [*v*] := **true**;
    for each vertex *w* adjacent to *v* **do**
      if not *visited* [*w*] **then** *dfs*(*w*);
end; {of *dfs*}

Program 6.1: Depth-first search

Example 6.1: Consider the graph *G* of Figure 6.16(a), which is represented by its adjacency lists as in Figure 6.16(b). If a depth-first search is initiated from vertex 1, then the vertices of *G* are visited in the following order: 1, 2, 4, 8, 5, 6, 3, 7. Since *dfs*(1) visits all vertices that can be reached from 1, the vertices visited, together with all edges in *G* incident to these vertices, form a connected component of *G*. □

Analysis of *dfs*: When *G* is represented by its adjacency lists, the vertices *w* adjacent to *v* can be determined by following a chain of links. Since *dfs* examines each node in the adjacency lists at most once, and there are 2*e* list nodes, the time to complete the search is O(*e*). If *G* is represented by its adjacency matrix, then the time to determine all vertices adjacent to *v* is O(*n*). Since at most *n* vertices are visited, the total time is O(n^2). □

6.2.2   Breadth-First Search

In a breadth-first search, we begin by visiting the start vertex *v*. Next, all unvisited vertices adjacent to *v* are visited. Unvisited vertices adjacent to these newly visited vertices are then visited, and so on. Algorithm *bfs* (Program 6.2) gives the details.

Example 6.2: Consider the graph of Figure 6.16(a). If a breadth-first search is performed beginning at vertex 1, then we first visit vertex 1. Next, vertices 2 and 3 are visited. Then vertices 4, 5, 6, and 7, and finally 8, are visited. □

Analysis of *bfs*: Each visited vertex enters the queue exactly once. So, the **while** loop is iterated at most *n* times. If an adjacency matrix is used, the loop takes O(*n*) time for each vertex visited. The total time is, therefore, O(n^2). If adjacency lists are used, the

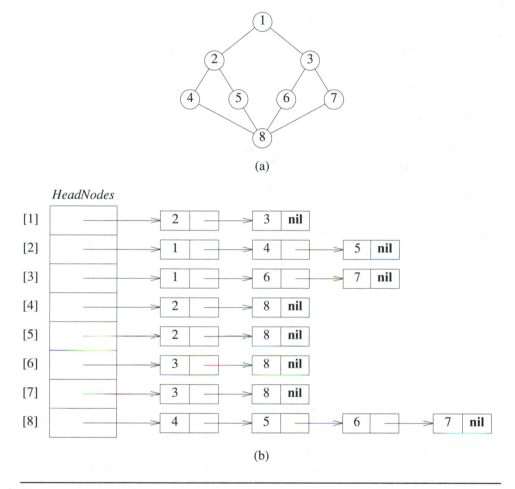

Figure 6.16: Graph G and its adjacency lists

loop has a total cost of $d_1 + \cdots + d_n = O(e)$, where d_i is the degree of vertex i. As in the case of *dfs*, all visited vertices, together with all edges incident to them, form a connected component of G. □

---

procedure *bfs* (*v* : **integer**);
{A breadth-first search of *G* is carried out beginning at vertex *v*. All vertices visited are marked as *visited* [*i*] := **true**. The graph *G* and array *visited* are global, and *visited* is initialized to **false**. *InitializeQueue*, *AddQueue*, *EmptyQueue*, and *DeleteQueue* are procedures/functions to handle queue operations.}
var *w* : **integer**; *q* : *queue*;
begin
   visited [*v*] := **true**;
   InitializeQueue (*q*);   {*q* is a queue}
   AddQueue (*q*,*v*);   {add vertex to queue}
   while not *EmptyQueue* (*q*) **do**
   begin
     DeleteQueue (*q*,*v*):   {remove from queue vertex *v*}
     for all vertices *w* adjacent to *v* **do**
      if not *visited* [*w*] **then begin**
                       AddQueue (*q*,*w*);
                       visited [*w*] := **true**;
                   end; {of **if** and **for**}
  end; {of **while**}
end; {of *bfs*}

Program 6.2: Breadth-first search

6.2.3   Connected Components

If *G* is an undirected graph, then one can determine whether or not it is connected by simply making a call to either *dfs* or *bfs* and then determining if there is any unvisited vertex. The connected components of a graph may be obtained by making repeated calls to either *dfs*(*v*) or *bfs*(*v*), with *v* a vertex not yet visited. This leads to procedure *comp* (Program 6.3), which determines the connected components of *G*. The algorithm uses *dfs* (*bfs* may be used instead if desired). The computing time is not affected. Procedure *OutputNewComponent* outputs all vertices visited in the most recent invocation of *dfs*, together with all edges incident on these vertices.

Analysis of *comp*: If *G* is represented by its adjacency lists, then the total time taken by *dfs* is O(*e*). The output can be completed in time O(*e*) if *dfs* keeps a list of all newly visited vertices. Since the **for** loops take O(*n*) time, the total time to generate all the connected components is O(*n* + *e*). If adjacency matrices are used instead, the time required is O(n^2). $\square$

```
procedure comp (g : UndirectedGraph );
{Determine the connected components of g. g has n ≥ 1 vertices.}
var visited : array [1 .. n] of boolean;
    i : integer;
begin
   for i := 1 to n do
      visited [i] := false; {initialize all vertices as unvisited}
   for i := 1 to n do
      if not visited [i] then begin
                           dfs(i); {find a component}
                           OutputNewComponent ;
                        end; {of if and for}
end; {of comp}
```

Program 6.3: Determining connected components

6.2.4 Spanning Trees

When the graph G is connected, a depth-first or breadth-first search starting at any vertex visits all the vertices in G. In this case the edges of G are partitioned into two sets, T (for tree edges) and N (for nontree edges), where T is the set of edges used or traversed during the search and N the set of remaining edges. The set T may be determined by inserting the statement $T := T \cup \{(v,w)\}$ in the **then** clauses of *dfs* and *bfs*. The edges in T form a tree that includes all the vertices of G. Any tree consisting solely of edges in G and including all vertices in G is called a *spanning tree.* Figure 6.17 shows a graph and some of its spanning trees.

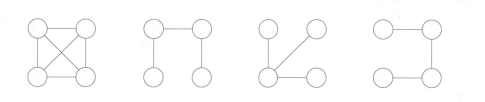

Figure 6.17: A complete graph and three of its spanning trees

As indicated earlier, a spanning tree may be constructed using either a depth-first or a breadth-first search. The spanning tree resulting from a depth-first search is known as a *depth-first spanning tree.* When a breadth-first search is used, the spanning tree is called a *breadth-first spanning tree.* Figure 6.18 shows the spanning trees resulting from a depth-first and breadth-first search starting at vertex 1 of the graph of Figure 6.16.

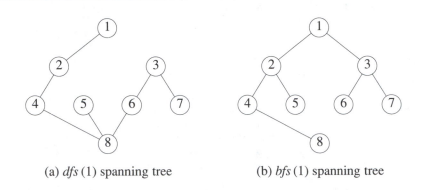

(a) *dfs* (1) spanning tree   (b) *bfs* (1) spanning tree

Figure 6.18: Depth-first and breadth-first spanning trees for graph of Figure 6.16

If a nontree edge (v, w) is introduced into any spanning tree T, then a cycle is formed. This cycle consists of the edge (v,w) and all the edges on the path from w to v in T. For example, if the edge $(8,7)$ is introduced into the *dfs* spanning tree of Figure 6.18(a), then the resulting cycle is 8,7,3,6,8. We can use this property of spanning trees to obtain an independent set of circuit equations for an electrical network.

Example 6.3 [*Creation of circuit equations*]: To obtain the circuit equations, we must first obtain a spanning tree for the electrical network. Then we introduce the nontree edges into the spanning tree one at a time. The introduction of each such edge produces a cycle. Next we use Kirchhoff's second law on this cycle to obtain a circuit equation. The cycles obtained in this way are independent (we cannot obtain any of these cycles by taking a linear combination of the remaining cycles), since each contains a nontree edge that is not contained in any other cycle. Thus, the circuit equations are also independent. In fact, we can show that the cycles obtained by introducing the nontree edges one at a time into the spanning tree form a cycle basis. This means that we can construct all other cycles in the graph by taking a linear combination of the cycles in the basis. (For further details, see the Harary text cited in the References and Selected Readings section.) □

Let us examine a second property of spanning trees. A spanning tree is a *minimal subgraph*, G', of G such that $V(G') = V(G)$, and G' is connected. We define a minimal subgraph as one with the fewest number of edges. Any connected graph with n vertices must have at least $n - 1$ edges, and all connected graphs with $n - 1$ edges are trees. Therefore, we conclude that a spanning tree has $n - 1$ edges. (The exercises explore this property more fully.)

Constructing minimal subgraphs finds frequent application in the design of communication networks. Suppose that the vertices of a graph G represent cities, and the edges represent communication links between cities. The minimum number of links needed to connect n cities is $n - 1$. Constructing the spanning trees of G produces all feasible choices. However, we know that the cost of constructing communication links between cities is rarely the same. Therefore, in practical applications, we assign weights to the edges. These weights might represent the cost of constructing the communication link or the length of the link. Given such a weighted graph, we would like to select the spanning tree that represents either the lowest total cost or the lowest overall length. We assume that the cost of a spanning tree is the sum of the costs of the edges of that tree. Algorithms to obtain minimum-cost spanning trees are studied in Section 6.3.

6.2.5   Biconnected Components

The operations that we have implemented thus far are simple extensions of depth-first and breadth-first searches. The next operation we implement is more complex and requires the introduction of additional terminology. We begin by assuming that G is an undirected, connected graph.

Definition: A vertex v of G is an *articulation point* iff the deletion of v, together with the deletion of all edges incident to v, leaves behind a graph that has at least two connected components. □

Vertices 2, 4, 6, and 8 are the articulation points of the connected graph of Figure 6.19(a).

Definition: A *biconnected graph* is a connected graph that has no articulation points. □

The graph of Figure 6.19 is not biconnected, and that of Figure 6.16(a) is. Articulation points are undesirable in graphs that represent communication networks. In such graphs the vertices represent communication stations, and the edges represent communication links. The failure of a communication station that is an articulation point results in a loss of communication to stations other than the one that failed. If the communication graph is biconnected, then the failure of a single station results in a loss of communication to and from only that station.

Definition: A *biconnected component* of a connected graph G is a maximal biconnected subgraph H of G. By maximal, we mean that G contains no other subgraph that is both biconnected and properly contains H. □

The graph of Figure 6.19(a) contains six biconnected components. These are shown in Figure 6.19(b). Note that a biconnected graph has just one biconnected com-

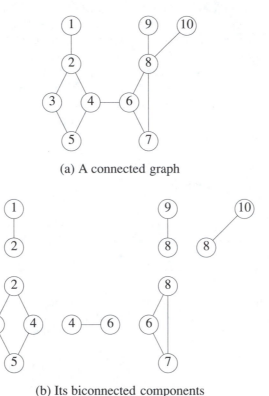

(a) A connected graph

(b) Its biconnected components

Figure 6.19: A connected graph and its biconnected components

ponent: the whole graph. It is easy to verify that two biconnected components of the same graph can have at most one vertex in common. From this it follows that no edge can be in two or more biconnected components. Hence, the biconnected components of G partition the edges of G.

The biconnected components of a connected, undirected graph G can be found by using any depth-first spanning tree of G. For the graph of Figure 6.19(a) a depth-first spanning tree with root 4 is shown in Figure 6.20(a). This tree is redrawn in Figure 6.20(b) to better reveal the tree structure. This figure also shows the nontree edges of G by broken lines. The numbers outside the vertices give the sequence in which the vertices are visited during the depth-first search. This number is called the *depth-first number*, *dfn*, of the vertex. So, $dfn(1) = 5$, and $dfn(10) = 9$. Note that if u and v are two vertices such that u is an ancestor of v in the depth-first spanning tree, then $dfn(u) < dfn(v)$.

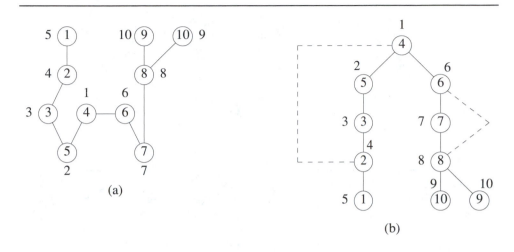

Figure 6.20: Depth-first spanning tree of Figure 6.19(a)

The broken lines in Figure 6.20(b) represent nontree edges. A nontree edge (u, v) is a *back edge* with respect to a spanning tree T iff either u is an ancestor of v or v is an ancestor of u. A nontree edge that is not a back edge is called a *cross edge*. The nontree edges (4, 2) and (6, 8) are back edges. From the definition of a depth-first search, one can show that no graph can have cross edges with respect to any of its depth-first spanning trees. From this, it follows that the root of the depth-first spanning tree is an articulation point iff it has at least two children. Further, any other vertex u is an articulation point iff it has at least one child w such that it is not possible to reach an ancestor of u using a path composed solely of w, descendants of w, and a single back edge. These observations lead us to define a value *low* for each vertex of G such that $low(u)$ is the lowest depth-first number that can be reached from u using a path of descendants followed by, at most, one back edge. $low(u)$ is given by the equation

$$low(u) = \min\{dfn(u), \min\{low(w) \mid w \text{ is a child of } u\},$$
$$\min\{dfn(w) \mid (u, w) \text{ is a back edge}\}\}$$

From the preceding discussion it follows that u is an articulation point iff u is either the root of the spanning tree and has two or more children or u is not the root and u has a child w such that $low(w) \geq dfn(u)$. Figure 6.21 gives the *dfn* and *low* values for each vertex of the spanning tree of Figure 6.20(b).

Procedure *dfs* is easily modified to compute *dfn* and *low* for each vertex of a connected graph. The result is procedure *DfnLow* (Program 6.4). This procedure uses the function *min 2*, which returns the smaller of its two parameters. The procedure is invoked as *DfnLow* $(x, 0)$, where x is the start vertex for the depth-first search.

vertex	1	2	3	4	5	6	7	8	9	10
dfn	5	4	1	1	1	6	6	8	10	9
low	5	4	1	1	1	6	6	8	10	9

Figure 6.21: *dfn* and *low* values for the spanning tree of Figure 6.20(b)

---

procedure *DfnLow* (*u*, *v* : **integer**);
{Compute *dfn* and *low* while performing a depth-first search beginning at vertex *u*. *v* is the parent (if any) of *u* in the resulting spanning tree. It is assumed that *dfn* [1 .. *n*] is initialized to zero and that *num* initially is 1.}
var *w* : **integer**;
begin
  dfn [*u*] := *num*; *low* [*u*] := *num*; *num* := *num* + 1;
  for each vertex *w* adjacent from *u* **do**
    if *dfn* [*w*] = 0 **then begin**
                  DfnLow (*w*, *u*); {*w* is an unvisited vertex}
                  low [*u*] := *min* 2(*low* [*u*], *low* [*w*]);
           end
          else if *w* < > *v* **then** *low* [*u*] := *min* 2(*low* [*u*], *dfn* [*w*]);
end; {of *DfnLow*}

Program 6.4: Computing *dfn* and *low*

The edges of the connected graph may be partitioned into their biconnected components by adding some code to procedure *DfnLow*. First, note that following the return from *DfnLow* (*w*, *u*), *low* [*w*] has been computed. If *low* [*w*] ≥ *dfn* [*u*], then a new biconnected component has been identified. By using a stack to save edges when they are first encountered, we can output all edges in a biconnected component, as in procedure *bicon* (Program 6.5).

Establishing the correctness of procedure *bicon* is left as an exercise. Its complexity is O(*n* +*e*). Note that procedure *bicon* assumes that the input connected graph has at least two vertices. Connected graphs with just one vertex contain no edges. By convention these graphs are biconnected, and a proper biconnected components procedure should handle them as a special case, producing a single biconnected component as output.

---

procedure *bicon* (*u*, *v* : **integer**);
{Compute *dfn* and *low* and output the edges of *G* by their biconnected components. *v* is the parent (if any) of *u* in the resulting spanning tree. It is assumed that *dfn* [1 .. *n*] is initialized to zero and that *num* initially is 1. *S* is a global stack that initially is empty.
var *w* : **integer**;
begin
  dfn [*u*] := *num*; *low* [*u*] := *num*; *num* := *num* + 1;
  for each vertex *w* adjacent from *u* **do**
  begin
    if (*v* < > *w*) **and** (*dfn* (*w*) < *dfn* (*u*)) **then** add (*u*, *w*) to stack *S*;
    if *dfn* [*w*] = 0 **then begin**
               bicon (*w*, *u*); {*w* is an unvisited vertex}
               low [*u*] := *min* 2(*low* [*u*], *low* [*w*]);
               if *low* [*w*] >= *dfn* [*u*]
               then begin
                    writeln('New biconnected component');
                    repeat
                      delete an edge from the stack *S*;
                      let this edge be (*x*, *y*);
                      writeln(*x*, ', ',*y*);
                    until (*x*, *y*) and (*u*, *w*) are the same edge;
                  end;
          end
          else if *w* < > *v* **then** *low* [*u*] := *min* 2(*low* [*u*], *dfn* [*w*]);
  end; {of **for**}
end; {of *bicon*}

Program 6.5: Outputting biconnected components when *n* > 1

EXERCISES

1. Apply depth-first and breadth-first searches to the complete graph on four vertices. List the vertices in the order they would be visited.

2. Write a complete Pascal procedure for depth-first search under the assumption that graphs are represented using adjacency matrices. Test the correctness of your procedure using suitable graphs.

3. Write a complete Pascal procedure for depth-first search under the assumption that graphs are represented using adjacency lists. Test the correctness of your procedure using suitable graphs.

4. Write a complete Pascal procedure for breadth-first search under the assumption that graphs are represented using adjacency matrices. Test the correctness of your procedure using suitable graphs.

5. Write a complete Pascal procedure for breadth-first search under the assumption that graphs are represented using adjacency lists. Test the correctness of your procedure using suitable graphs.

6. Show how to modify procedure *dfs* (Program 6.1), as it is used in *comp* (Program 6.3), to produce a list of all newly visited vertices.

7. Prove that when procedure *dfs* is applied to a connected graph, the edges of T form a tree.

8. Prove that when procedure *bfs* (Program 6.2) is applied to a connected graph, the edges of T form a tree.

9. Show that if T is a spanning tree for the undirected graph G, then the addition of an edge e, $e \notin E(T)$ and $e \in E(G)$, to T creates a unique cycle.

10. Show that the number of spanning trees in a complete graph with n vertices is at least $2^{n-1} - 1$.

11. Let G be a connected graph and let T be any of its depth-first spanning trees. Show that G has no cross edges relative to T.

12. Prove that procedure *bicon* (Program 6.5) correctly partitions the edges of a connected graph into the biconnected components of the graph.

13. Let G be a connected, undirected graph. Show that no edge of G can be in two or more biconnected components of G.

6.3 MINIMUM-COST SPANNING TREES

The *cost* of a spanning tree of a weighted, undirected graph is the sum of the costs (weights) of the edges in the spanning tree. A *minimum-cost spanning tree* is a spanning tree of least cost. Three different algorithms can be used to obtain a minimum-cost spanning tree of a connected, undirected graph. All three use a design strategy called the *greedy method*. We shall refer to the three algorithms as Kruskal's, Prim's, and Sollin's algorithms, respectively.

In the greedy method, we construct an optimal solution in stages. At each stage, we make the best decision (using some criterion) possible at the time. Since we cannot change this decision later, we make sure that the decision will result in a feasible solution. The greedy method can be applied to a wide variety of programming problems. Typically, the selection of an item at each stage is based on either a least-cost or a highest profit criterion. A feasible solution is one that works within the constraints specified by the problem.

To construct minimum-cost spanning trees, we use a least-cost criterion. Our solution must satisfy the following constraints:

(1)   We must use only edges within the graph.

(2)   We must use exactly $n - 1$ edges.

(3)   We may not use edges that produce a cycle.

6.3.1   Kruskal's Algorithm

Kruskal's algorithm builds a minimum-cost spanning tree T by adding edges to T one at a time. The algorithm selects the edges for inclusion in T in nondecreasing order of their cost. An edge is added to T if it does not form a cycle with the edges that are already in T. Since G is connected and has $n > 0$ vertices, exactly $n - 1$ edges will be selected for inclusion in T.

Example 6.4: We will construct a minimum-cost spanning tree of the graph of Figure 6.22(a). We begin with no edges selected. Figure 6.22(b) shows the current graph with no edges selected. Edge (1,6) is the first edge considered. It is included in the spanning tree being built. This yields the graph of Figure 6.22(c).

Next, the edge (3,4) is selected and included in the tree (Figure 6.22(d)). The next edge to be considered is (2,7). Its inclusion in the tree being built does not create a cycle, so we get the graph of Figure 6.22(e). Edge (2,3) is considered next and included in the tree (Figure 6.22(f)). Of the edges not yet considered, (7,4) has the least cost. It is considered next. Its inclusion in the tree results in a cycle, so this edge is discarded. Edge (5,4) is the next edge to be added to the tree being built. This results in the configuration of Figure 6.22(g). The next edge to be considered is the edge (7,5). It is discarded, as its inclusion creates a cycle. Finally, edge (6,5) is considered and included in the tree being built. This completes the spanning tree. The resulting tree (Figure 6.22(h)) has cost 99. □

It is somewhat surprising that this straightforward approach should always result in a minimum-cost spanning tree. We shall soon prove, however, that this is indeed the case. First, let us look into the details of the algorithm. For clarity, Kruskal's algorithm is written out more formally in Program 6.6. Initially, E is the set of all edges in G. The only functions we wish to perform on this set are

(1)   determine an edge with minimum cost (line 3)

(2)   delete this edge (line 4)

Both these functions can be performed efficiently if the edges in E are maintained as a sorted sequential list. In Chapter 7 we shall see how to sort these edges into nondecreasing order in time $O(e \log e)$, where e is the number of edges in E. It is not essential to sort all the edges, as long as the next edge for line 3 can be determined easily. This is an instance where a min heap is ideal, as it permits the next edge to be determined and deleted in $O(\log e)$ time. The construction of the heap itself takes $O(e)$ time.

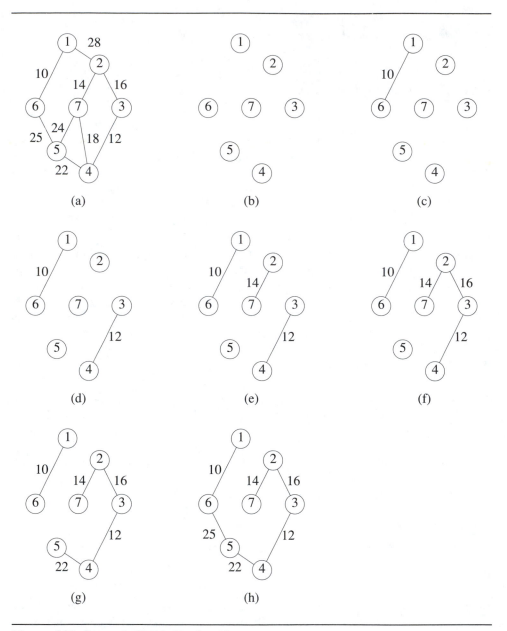

Figure 6.22: Stages in Kruskal's algorithm

```
1  T := ∅;
2  while T contains less than n − 1 edges and E not empty do begin
3      choose an edge (v,w) from E of lowest cost;
4      delete (v,w) from E;
5      if (v,w) does not create a cycle in T
6          then add (v,w) to T
7          else discard (v,w);
8  end;
9  if T contains fewer than n − 1 edges then writeln ('no spanning tree');
```

Program 6.6: Kruskal's algorithm

To perform lines 5 and 6 of Program 6.6 efficiently, the vertices in G should be grouped together in such a way that one may easily determine if the vertices v and w are already connected by the earlier selection of edges. If they are, then the edge (v,w) is to be discarded. If they are not, then (v,w) is to be added to T. One possible grouping is to place all vertices in the same connected component of T into a set (all connected components of T will also be trees). Then, two vertices v and w are connected in T iff they are in the same set. For example, when the edge $(4, 7)$ is to be considered, the sets would be $\{1, 6\}$, $\{2, 3, 4, 7\}$, and $\{5\}$. Vertices 4 and 7 are already in the same set, so the edge $(4, 7)$ is rejected. The next edge to be considered is $(4, 5)$. Since vertices 4 and 5 are in different sets, the edge is accepted. This edge connects the two components $\{2, 3, 4, 7\}$ and $\{5\}$, so these two sets should be unioned to obtain the set representing the new component. Using the set representation scheme of Chapter 5, we can obtain an efficient implementation of lines 5 and 6. The computing time is, therefore, determined by the time for lines 3 and 4, which in the worst case is O($e \log e$). We leave the writing of the resulting algorithm as an exercise. Theorem 6.1 proves that the algorithm resulting from Program 6.6 does yield a minimum-cost spanning tree of G.

Theorem 6.1: Let G be any undirected, connected graph. Kruskal's algorithm generates a minimum-cost spanning tree.

Proof: We shall show the following: (a) Kruskal's method results in a spanning tree whenever a spanning tree exists; and (b) the spanning tree generated is of minimum cost.

For (a), we note that the only edges that get discarded in Kruskal's method are those that result in a cycle. The deletion of a single edge that is on a cycle of a connected graph results in a graph that is also connected. Hence, if G initially is connected, the set of edges in T and E always form a connected graph. Consequently, if G initially is connected, the algorithm cannot terminate with $E = \emptyset$ and $|T| < n − 1$.

Now, let us proceed to establish that the constructed spanning tree, T, is of minimum cost. Since G has a finite number of spanning trees, it must have at least one of minimum cost. Let U be a minimum-cost spanning tree. Both T and U have exactly $n-1$ edges. If $T = U$, then T is of minimum cost, and we have nothing to prove. So, assume that $T \neq U$. Let $k, k > 0$, be the number of edges in T that are not in U. Note that k is also the number of edges in U that are not in T.

We shall show that T and U have the same cost by transforming U into T. This transformation will be done in k steps. At each step, the number of edges in T that are not in U will be reduced by exactly 1. Further, the cost of U will not change as a result of the transformation. As a result, U after k steps of transformation will have the same cost as the initial U and will consist of exactly those edges that are in T. This implies that T is of minimum cost.

Each step of the transformation involves adding to U one edge, e, from T and removing one edge, f, from U. The edges e and f are selected in the following way:

(1)   Let e be the least-cost edge in T that is not in U. Such an edge must exist as $k > 0$.

(2)   When e is added to U, a unique cycle is created. Let f be any edge on this cycle that is not in T. Note that at least one of the edges on this cycle is not in T, as T contains no cycles.

From the way e and f are selected, it follows that $V = U + \{e\} - \{f\}$ is a spanning tree and that T has exactly $k-1$ edges that are not in V. We need to show that the cost of V is the same as that of U. Clearly, the cost of V is the cost of U plus the cost of the edge e minus the cost of the edge f. The cost of e cannot be less than the cost of f, as otherwise the spanning tree V has a smaller cost than the tree U, which is impossible. If e has a higher cost than f, then f is considered before e by Kruskal's algorithm. Since f is not in T, Kruskal's algorithm must have discarded this edge at this time. Hence, f, together with edges in T having a cost less than or equal to the cost of f, must form a cycle. By the choice of e, all these edges are also in U. Hence, U must also contain a cycle. But it does not, as it is a spanning tree. So, the assumption that e is of higher cost than f leads to a contradiction. The only possibility that remains is that e and f have the same cost. Hence, V has the same cost as U. $\square$

6.3.2   Prim's Algorithm

Prim's algorithm, like Kruskal's, constructs the minimum-cost spanning tree edge by edge. However, at all times during the algorithm, the set of selected edges forms a tree. (By contrast, the set of selected edges in Kruskal's algorithm forms a forest at all times.) Prim's algorithm begins with a tree T that contains a single vertex. This vertex can be any of the vertices in the original graph. Then we add a least-cost edge (u, v) to T such that $T \cup \{(u, v)\}$ is also a tree. This edge-addition step is repeated until T contains $n-1$ edges. Notice that edge (u, v) is always such that exactly one of u and v is in T. A high-level description of Prim's algorithm is provided in Program 6.7. This description also provides for the possibility that the input graph may not be connected. In this case there is no spanning tree. Figure 6.23 shows the progress of Prim's algorithm on the graph of Figure 6.22(a).

{Assume that G has at least one vertex.}
$T := \emptyset$; $TV := \{1\}$; {start with vertex 1 and no edges}
done := **false**;
while T contains fewer than $n-1$ edges **and not** *done* **do**
begin
    Let (u, v) be a least-cost edge such that $u \in TV$ and $v \notin TV$;
    if there is no such edge **then** *done* := **true**
                            else add v to TV and (u, v) to T;
end;
if T contains fewer than $n-1$ edges **then writeln** ('no spanning tree');

Program 6.7: Prim's algorithm

Prim's algorithm can be implemented to have a time complexity $O(n^2)$ if we associate with each vertex v not in TV a vertex *near*(v) such that *near*$(v) \in TV$ and *cost*$(near(v), v)$ is the minimum over all such choices for *near*(v) (we assume that *cost*$(v, w) = \infty$ if $(v, w) \notin E$). The next edge to add to T is such that *cost*$(near(v), v)$ is the minimum and $v \notin TV$. Asymptotically faster implementations are also possible. One of these results from the use of Fibonacci heaps, which are studied in Chapter 9. A reference pertaining to the application of Fibonacci heaps to the implementation of Prim's algorithm is provided at the end of Chapter 9. Establishing the correctness of Prim's algorithm is left as an exercise.

6.3.3 Sollin's Algorithm

Sollin's algorithm selects several edges at each stage. At the start of a stage, the selected edges, together with all n graph vertices, form a spanning forest. During a stage we select one edge for each tree in this forest. This edge is a minimum-cost edge that has exactly one vertex in the tree. The selected edges are added to the spanning tree being constructed. Note that it is possible for two trees in the forest to select the same edge. So, multiple copies of the same edge are to be eliminated. Also, when the graph has several edges with the same cost, it is possible for two trees to select two different edges that connect them together. These edges will, of course, have the same cost; only one of these should be retained. At the start of the first stage, the set of selected edges is empty. The algorithm terminates when there is only one tree at the end of a stage or when no edges remain to be selected.

Figure 6.24 shows the stages in Sollin's algorithm when it begins with the graph of Figure 6.22(a). The initial configuration of zero selected edges is the same as that shown

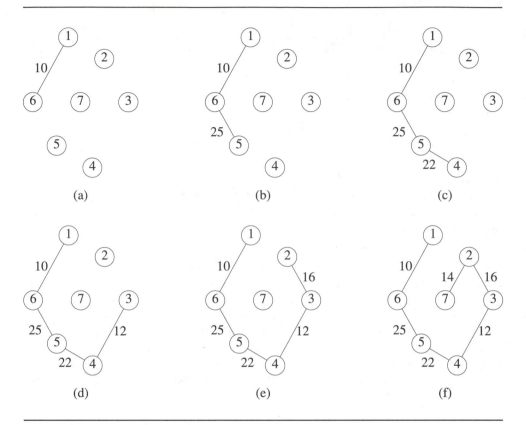

Figure 6.23: Stages in Prim's algorithm

in Figure 6.22(b). Each tree in this spanning forest is a single vertex. The edges selected by vertices 1, 2, $\cdots$, 7 are, respectively, (1, 6), (2, 7), (3, 4), (4, 3), (5, 4), (6, 1), and (7, 2). The distinct edges in this selection are (1, 6), (2, 7), (3, 4), and (5, 4). Adding these to the set of selected edges results in the configuration of Figure 6.24(a). In the next stage, the tree with vertex set {1, 6} selects the edge (6, 5), and the remaining two trees select the edge (2, 3). Following the addition of these two edges to the set of selected edges, construction of the spanning tree is complete. The resulting spanning tree is shown in Figure 6.24(b). The development of Sollin's algorithm into a Pascal procedure and its correctness proof are left as exercises.

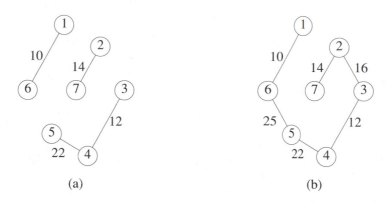

Figure 6.24: Stages in Sollin's algorithm

EXERCISES

1. Write out Kruskal's minimum-cost spanning tree algorithm (Program 6.6) as a complete program. You may use as procedures the algorithms *WeightedUnion* (Program 5.22) and *CollapsingFind* (Program 5.23). Use algorithm *sort* (Program 1.2) to sort the edges into nondecreasing order by weight.

2. Prove that Prim's algorithm finds a minimum-cost spanning tree for every connected, undirected graph.

3. Refine Program 6.7 into a Pascal procedure to find a minimum-cost spanning tree. The complexity of your procedure should be $O(n^2)$, where n is the number of vertices in the input graph. Show that this is the case.

4. Prove that Sollin's algorithm finds a minimum-cost spanning tree for every connected, undirected graph.

5. What is the maximum number of stages in Sollin's algorithm? Give this as a function of the number of vertices n in the graph.

6. Obtain a Pascal procedure to find a minimum-cost spanning tree using Sollin's algorithm. What is the complexity of your procedure?

6.4   SHORTEST PATHS AND TRANSITIVE CLOSURE

Graphs may be used to represent the highway structure of a state or country with vertices representing cities and edges representing sections of highway. The edges may then be assigned weights, which might be the distance between the two cities connected by the edge or the average time to drive along that section of highway. A motorist wishing to drive from city A to city B would be interested in answers to the following questions:

(1)   Is there a path from A to B?

(2)   If there is more than one path from A to B, which is the shortest path?

The problems defined by (1) and (2) above are special cases of the path problems we shall be studying in this section. An edge weight is also referred to as an edge length or edge cost. We shall use the terms weight, cost, and length interchangeably. The length (cost, weight) of a path is now defined to be the sum of the lengths (costs, weights) of the edges on that path, rather than the number of edges. The starting vertex of the path will be referred to as the *source* and the last vertex the *destination*. The graphs will be digraphs to allow for one-way streets.

6.4.1   Single Source/All Destinations: Nonnegative Edge Costs

In this problem we are given a directed graph $G = (V,E)$, a length function *length* (i,j), *length* $(i,j) \geq 0$, for the edges of G, and a source vertex v. The problem is to determine a shortest path from v to each of the remaining vertices of G. As an example, consider the directed graph of Figure 6.25(a). The numbers on the edges are the edge lengths. If vertex 1 is the source vertex, then the shortest path from 1 to 2 is 1, 4, 5, 2. The length of this path is $10 + 15 + 20 = 45$. Even though there are three edges on this path, it is shorter than the path 1, 2, which is of length 50. There is no path from 1 to 6. Figure 6.25(b) lists the shortest paths from 1 to 2, 3, 4, and 5. The paths have been listed in nondecreasing order of path length. A greedy algorithm will generate the shortest paths in this order.

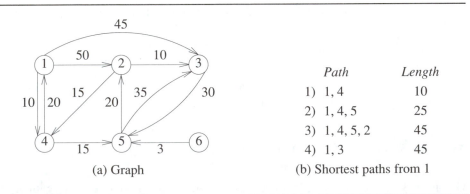

	Path	Length
1)	1, 4	10
2)	1, 4, 5	25
3)	1, 4, 5, 2	45
4)	1, 3	45

(a) Graph   (b) Shortest paths from 1

Figure 6.25: Graph and shortest paths from vertex 1 to all destinations

Let S denote the set of vertices (including the source v) to which the shortest paths have already been found. For w not in S, let $dist[w]$ be the length of the shortest path starting from v, going through only the vertices that are in S, and ending at w. We observe that when paths are generated in nondecreasing order of length,

(1) If the next shortest path is to vertex u, then the path begins at v, ends at u, and goes through only vertices that are in S. To prove this we must show that all of the intermediate vertices on the shortest path to u must be in S. Assume there is a vertex w on this path that is not in S. Then, the v-to-u path also contains a path from v to w that is of length less than that of the v-to-u path. By assumption, the shortest paths are being generated in nondecreasing order of path length, so the shorter path from v to w has been generated already. Hence, there is no intermediate vertex that is not in S.

(2) The destination of the next path generated must be the vertex u that has the minimum distance, $dist[u]$, among all vertices not in S. This follows from the definition of $dist$ and observation (1). If there are several vertices not in S with the same $dist$, then any of these may be selected.

(3) The vertex u selected in (2) becomes a member of S. The shortest v-to-u path is obtained from the selection process of (2). At this point, the length of the shortest paths starting at v, going through vertices only in S, and ending at a vertex w not in S may decrease (i.e., the value of $dist[w]$ may change). If it does change, then the change must be due to a shorter path starting at v going to u and then to w. The intermediate vertices on the v-to-u path and the u to w path must all be in S. Further, the v-to-u path must be the shortest such path; otherwise $dist[w]$ is not defined properly. Also, the u-to-w path can be chosen so that it does not contain any intermediate vertices. Therefore, we may conclude that if $dist[w]$ changes (i.e., decreases), then the change is due to the path from v to u to w, where the path from v to u is the shortest such path and the path from u to w is the edge $<u,w>$. The length of this path is $dist[u] + length(<u,w>)$.

The algorithm *ShortestPath*, as first given by Edsger Dijkstra makes use of these observations to determine the length of the shortest paths from v to all other vertices in G. The generation of the paths is a minor extension of the algorithm and is left as an exercise. It is assumed that the n vertices of G are numbered 1 through n. The set S is maintained as a boolean array with $s[i] = $ **false** if vertex i is not in S and $s[i] = $ **true** if it is. It is assumed that the graph itself is represented by its length-adjacency matrix, with $length[i,j]$ being the length of the edge $<i,j>$. If $<i, j>$ is not an edge of the graph and $i \neq j$, $length[i,j]$ may be set to some large number. The choice of this number is arbitrary, although we make two stipulations regarding its value:

(1)   The number must be larger than any of the values in the length matrix.

(2)   The number must be chosen so that the statement $dist[u] + length[u, w]$ does not produce an overflow.

Restriction (2) makes **maxint** a poor choice for nonexistent edges. For $i = j$, $length[i,j]$ may be set to any nonnegative number without affecting the outcome of the algorithm.

Program 6.8 describes the algorithm. The data types *AdjacencyMatrix* and *distance* are defined as follows:

$$\textbf{type } AdjacencyMatrix = \textbf{array } [1..maxn, 1..maxn] \textbf{ of integer};$$
$$distance = \textbf{array } [1..maxn] \textbf{ of integer};$$

```
1  procedure ShortestPath (v : integer; length : AdjacencyMatrix ;
2                            var dist : distance ; n : integer);
3  {dist [j], 1 ≤ j ≤n, is set to the length of the shortest path from vertex v to vertex j
4  in a digraph G with n vertices and edge lengths given by length [i,j].}
5  var s : array [1..maxn] of boolean;
6      i, u, w : integer;
7  begin
8     for i := 1 to  n do {initialize set S to empty}
9     begin
10       s [i ] := false;
11       dist [i ] := length [v,i ];
12    end;
13    s [v ] := true;
14    dist [v ] := 0;
15    for i := 1 to n − 2 do {determine n − 1 paths from vertex v}
16    begin
17       u := choose (dist, n); {choose returns a value u:
18                  dist [u ] = min{dist [w ] | s [w ] = false}
19       s [u ] := true;
20       for w := 1 to n do
21           if not s [w ] then
22              if dist [u ] + length [u,w ] < dist [w ]
23                       then dist [w ] := dist [u ] + length [u,w ];
24    end; {of for i}
25 end; {of ShortestPath}
```

Program 6.8: Determining the shortest paths

Analysis of *ShortestPath*: From our earlier discussion, it is easy to see that the algorithm works. The time taken by the algorithm on a graph with n vertices is $O(n^2)$. To see this, note that the **for** loop of line 8 takes $O(n)$ time. The **for** loop of line 15 is executed $n − 2$ times. Each execution of this loop requires $O(n)$ time at line 17 to select the next vertex and again in lines 20 to 23 to update *dist*. So, the total time for this loop is $O(n^2)$. If a list of T vertices currently not in S is maintained, then the number of nodes on this list would at any time be $n − i$. This would speed up lines 17 and 20 to 23, but the asympototic time would remain $O(n^2)$. This and other variations of the algorithm are explored in the exercises.

Any shortest-path algorithm must examine each edge in the graph at least once, since any of the edges could be in a shortest path. Hence, the minimum possible time for such an algorithm would be $O(e)$. Since length-adjacency matrices were used to represent the graph, it takes $O(n^2)$ time just to determine which edges are in G, so any shortest-path algorithm, that uses this representation must take $O(n^2)$. For this representation, then, algorithm *ShortestPath* is optimal to within a constant factor. Even if a change to adjacency lists is made, only the overall time for the **for** loop of lines 20 to 23 can be brought down to $O(e)$ (since the *dist* can change only for vertices that are adjacent from u). The total time for line 17 remains $O(n^2)$. By using Fibonacci heaps (see Chapter 9) and adjacency lists, the greedy algorithm for the single-source/all-destinations problem can be implemented to have complexity $O(n\log n + e)$. For sparse graphs, this implementation is superior to that of Program 6.8. $\square$

Example 6.5: Consider the eight-vertex digraph of Figure 6.26(a) with length-adjacency matrix as in Figure 6.26(b). Suppose that the source vertex is Boston. The values of *dist* and the vertex u selected in each iteration of the **for** loop of lines 15 to 24 (Program 6.8) are shown in Figure 6.27. Note that the algorithm terminates when only seven of the eight vertices are in S. By the definition of *dist*, the distance of the last vertex, in this case Los Angeles, is correct, as the shortest path from Boston to Los Angeles can go through only the remaining six vertices. $\square$

6.4.2 Single Source/All Destinations: General Weights

We now consider the general case when some or all of the edges of the directed graph G may have negative length. To see that procedure *ShortestPath* (Program 6.8) does not necessarily give the correct results on such graphs, consider the graph of Figure 6.28. Let $v = 1$ be the source vertex. Since $n = 3$, the loop of lines 15 to 24 is iterated just once. $u = 3$ in line 17, and no changes are made to *dist*. The procedure terminates with *dist* $[2] = 7$ and *dist* $[3] = 5$. The shortest path from 1 to 3 is 1, 2, 3. This path has length 2, which is less than the computed value of *dist* $[3]$.

When negative edge lengths are permitted, we require that the graph have no cycles of negative length. This is necessary so as to ensure that shortest paths consist of a finite number of edges. For example, consider the graph of Figure 6.29. The length of the shortest path from vertex 1 to vertex 3 is $-\infty$, as the length of the path

$$1, 2, 1, 2, 1, 2, \cdots, 1, 2, 3$$

can be made arbitrarily small. This is so because of the presence of the cycle 1, 2, 1, which has a length of -1.

When there are no cycles of negative length, there is a shortest path between any two vertices of an n-vertex graph that has at most $n - 1$ edges on it. To see this, observe

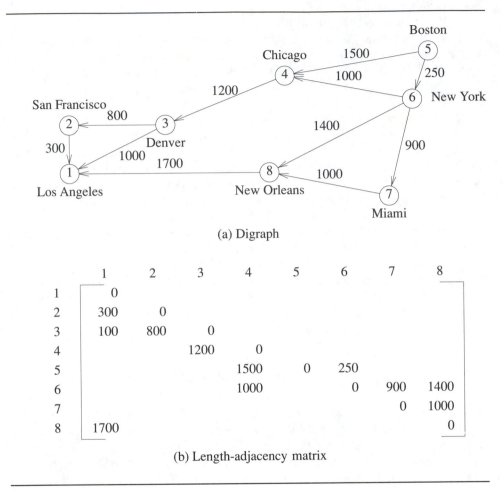

(a) Digraph

(b) Length-adjacency matrix

Figure 6.26: Digraph for Example 6.5

that a path that has more than $n-1$ edges must repeat at least one vertex and hence must contain a cycle. Elimination of the cycles from the path results in another path with the same source and destination. This path is cycle-free and has a length that is no more than that of the original path, as the length of the eliminated cycles was at least zero. We can use this observation on the maximum number of edges on a cycle-free shortest path to obtain an algorithm to determine a shortest path from a source vertex to all remaining vertices in the graph. As in the case of procedure *ShortestPath* (Program 6.8), we shall compute only the length, *dist* [*u*], of the shortest path from the source vertex *v* to *u*. An exercise examines the extension needed to construct the shortest paths.

			Distance							
Iteration	S	Vertex selected	LA [1]	SF [2]	DEN [3]	CHI [4]	BOST [5]	NY [6]	MIA [7]	NO [8]
Initial	--	----	$+\infty$	$+\infty$	$+\infty$	1500	0	250	$+\infty$	$+\infty$
1	{5}	6	$+\infty$	$+\infty$	$+\infty$	1250	0	250	1150	1650
2	{5,6}	7	$+\infty$	$+\infty$	$+\infty$	1250	0	250	1150	1650
3	{5,6,7}	4	$+\infty$	$+\infty$	2450	1250	0	250	1150	1650
4	{5,6,7,4}	8	3350	$+\infty$	2450	1250	0	250	1150	1650
5	{5,6,7,4,8}	3	3350	3250	2450	1250	0	250	1150	1650
6	{5,6,7,4,8,3}	2	3350	3250	2450	1250	0	250	1150	1650
	{5,6,7,4,8,3,2}									

Figure 6.27: Action of *ShortestPath* on digraph of Figure 6.26

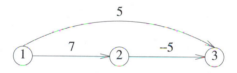

Figure 6.28: Directed graph with a negative-length edge

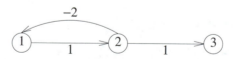

Figure 6.29: Directed graph with a cycle of negative length

Let $dist^l[u]$ be the length of a shortest path from the source vertex v to vertex u under the constraint that the shortest path contains at most l edges. Then, $dist^1[u] = length[v,u]$, $1 \leq u \leq n$. As noted earlier, when there are no cycles of negative length, we can limit our search for shortest paths to paths with at most $n-1$ edges. Hence, $dist^{n-1}[u]$ is the length of an unrestricted shortest path from v to u.

Our goal then is to compute $dist^{n-1}[u]$ for all u. This can be done using the dynamic programming methodology. First, we make the following observations:

(1) If the shortest path from v to u with at most k, $k > 1$, edges has no more than $k-1$ edges, then $dist^k[u] = dist^{k-1}[u]$.

(2) If the shortest path from v to u with at most k, $k > 1$, edges has exactly k edges, then it is comprised of a shortest path from v to some vertex j followed by the edge $<j,u>$. The path from v to j has $k-1$ edges, and its length is $dist^{k-1}[j]$. All vertices i such that the edge $<i,u>$ is in the graph are candidates for j. Since we are interested in a shortest path, the i that minimizes $dist^{k-1}[i] + length[i,u]$ is the correct value for j.

These observations result in the following recurrence for $dist$:

$$dist^k[u] = \min\{dist^{k-1}[u], \min_i\{dist^{k-1}[i] + length[i,u]\}\}$$

This recurrence may be used to compute $dist^k$ from $dist^{k-1}$, for $k = 2, 3, \cdots, n-1$.

Example 6.6: Figure 6.30 gives a seven-vertex graph, together with the arrays $dist^k$, $k = 1, \cdots, 6$. These arrays were computed using the equation just given. $\square$

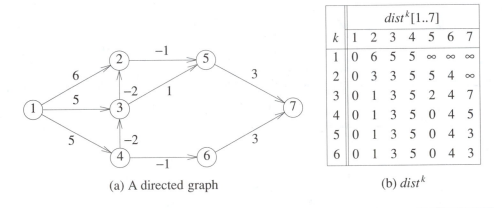

			$dist^k[1..7]$				
k	1	2	3	4	5	6	7
1	0	6	5	5	∞	∞	∞
2	0	3	3	5	5	4	∞
3	0	1	3	5	2	4	7
4	0	1	3	5	0	4	5
5	0	1	3	5	0	4	3
6	0	1	3	5	0	4	3

(a) A directed graph

(b) $dist^k$

Figure 6.30: Shortest paths with negative edge lengths

An exercise shows that if we use the same memory location $dist[u]$ for $dist^k[u]$, $k = 1, \cdots, n-1$, then the final value of $dist[u]$ is still $dist^{n-1}[u]$. Using this fact and the recurrence for $dist$ shown above, we arrive at the algorithm of Program 6.9 to compute the length of the shortest path from vertex v to each other vertex of the graph. This algorithm is referred to as the Bellman and Ford algorithm.

```
 1  procedure BellmanFord (v : integer; length : AdjacencyMatrix ;
 2                                var dist : distance ; n : integer);
 3  {Single-source/all-destinations shortest paths with negative edge lengths.}
 4  var i,u,k : integer;
 5  begin
 6    for i := 1 to  n do {initialize dist}
 7      dist [i ] := length [v,i ];
 8    for k := 2 to n − 1 do
 9      for each u such that u < > v and u has at least one incoming edge do
10        for each <i,u > in the graph do
11          if dist [u ] > dist [i ] + length [i,u ] then dist [u ] := dist [i ] + length [i,u ];
12  end; {of BellmanFord}
```

Program 6.9: Bellman and Ford algorithm to compute shortest paths

Analysis of *BellmanFord*: Each iteration of the **for** loop of lines 8 to 11 takes $O(n^2)$ time if adjacency matrices are used and $O(e)$ time if adjacency lists are used. The overall complexity is $O(n^3)$ when adjacency matrices are used and $O(ne)$ when adjacency lists are used. The observed complexity of the shortest-path algorithm can be reduced by noting that if none of the *dist* values change on one iteration of the **for** loop of lines 8 to 11, then none will change on successive iterations. So, this loop may be rewritten to terminate either after $n − 1$ iterations or after the first iteration in which no *dist* values are changed, whichever occurs first. Another possibility is to maintain a queue of vertices *i* whose *dist* value changed on the previous iteration of the **for** loop. These are the only values for *i* that need to be considered in line 10 during the next iteration. When a queue of these values is maintained, we can rewrite the loop of lines 8 to 11 so that on each iteration, a vertex *i* is removed from the queue, and the *dist* values of all vertices adjacent from *i* are updated as in line 11. Vertices whose *dist* value decreases as a result of this are added to the end of the queue unless they are already on it. The loop terminates when the queue becomes empty. These two strategies to improve the performance of procedure *BellmanFord* are considered in the exercises. Other strategies for improving performance are discussed in the References and Selected Readings section. □

6.4.3 All-Pairs Shortest Paths

In the *all-pairs shortest-path problem*, we are to find the shortest paths between all pairs of vertices *u* and *v*, $u \neq v$. This problem can be solved as *n* independent single-source/all-destinations problems using each of the *n* vertices of *G* as a source vertex. If we use this approach on graphs with nonnegative edges, the total time taken would be $O(n^3)$ (or $O(n^2 \log n + ne)$ if Fibonacci heaps are used). On graphs with negative edges the run time will be $O(n^4)$ if adjacency matrices are used and $O(n^2 e)$ if adjacency lists are used.

Using the dynamic programming approach to the design of algorithms, we can obtain a conceptually simpler algorithm that has complexity $O(n^3)$ and works even when G has edges with negative length. Like the Bellman and Ford algorithm, this algorithm requires that G have no cycles with negative length. This algorithm is faster for graphs with negative edges, as long as the graphs have at least $c*n$ edges for some suitable constant c. Its observed run time is also less for dense graphs with nonnegative edge lengths. However, for sparse graphs with nonnegative edge lengths, using the single-source algorithm and Fibonacci heaps results in a faster algorithm for the all-pairs problem.

The graph G is represented by its length-adjacency matrix as described for procedure *ShortestPath* (Program 6.8). Define $A^k[i,j]$ to be the length of the shortest path from i to j going through no intermediate vertex of index greater than k. Then, $A^n[i,j]$ will be the length of the shortest i-to-j path in G, since G contains no vertex with index greater than n. $A^0[i,j]$ is just *length* $[i,j]$, since the only i-to-j paths allowed can have no intermediate vertices on them.

The basic idea in the all-pairs algorithm is to successively generate the matrices $A^0, A^1, A^2, \cdots, A^n$. If we have already generated A^{k-1}, then we may generate A^k by realizing that for any pair of vertices i and j, one of the following applies:

(1)   The shortest path from i to j going through no vertex with index greater than k does not go through the vertex with index k, so its length is $A^{k-1}[i,j]$.

(2)   The shortest path goes through vertex k. In this case, the path consists of a subpath from i to k and another one from k to j. These subpaths must be the shortest paths from i to k and from k to j going through no vertex with index greater than $k-1$, so their lengths are $A^{k-1}[i,k]$ and $A^{k-1}[k,j]$. Note that this is true only if G has no cycle with negative length containing vertex k. When cycles of negative length are present, the shortest i-to-j path going through no vertices of index greater than k may make several cycles from k to k and thus have a length substantially less than $A^{k-1}[i,k] + A^{k-1}[k,j]$.

The preceding rules yield the following formulas for $A^k[i,j]$:

$$A^k[i,j] = \min\{A^{k-1}[i,j], A^{k-1}[i,k] + A^{k-1}[k,j]\}, k \geq 1$$

and

$$A^0[i,j] = length[i,j]$$

The algorithm *AllLengths* (Program 6.10) computes $A^n[i,j]$. The computation is done in place using the array a. The reason this computation can be carried out in place is that $A^k[i,k] = A^{k-1}[i,k]$ and $A^k[k,j] = A^{k-1}[k,j]$, so the in-place computation does not alter the outcome.

```
 1  procedure AllLengths (var length, a : AdjacencyMatrix; n : integer);
 2  {length [1 ..n, 1 .. n ] is the length-adjacency matrix of a graph with n
 3  vertices; a [i,j] is the length of the shortest path between vertices i and j.}
 4  var i, j, k : integer;
 5  begin
 6     for i := 1 to n do
 7        for j := 1 to n do
 8           a [i,j] := length [i,j]; {copy length into a}
 9        for k := 1 to n do {for a path with highest-vertex index k}
10           for i := 1 to n do {for all possible pairs of vertices}
11              for j := 1 to n do
12                 if (a [i,k] + a [k,j]) < a [i,j] then a [i,j] := a [i,k] + a [k,j];
13  end; {of AllLengths}
```

Program 6.10: All-pairs shortest paths

Analysis of *AllLengths*: This algorithm is especially easy to analyze because the loop-ing is independent of the data in the matrix a. The total time for procedure *AllLengths* is $O(n^3)$. An exercise examines the extensions needed to obtain the (i,j) paths with these lengths. Some speed-up can be obtained by noticing that the innermost **for** loop needs be executed only when $a [i,k]$ is not equal to **maxint**. □

Example 6.7: For the digraph of Figure 6.31(a), the initial a matrix, A^0, plus its value after each of three iterations, A^1, A^2, and A^3, is also given in Figure 6.31. □

6.4.4 Transitive Closure

We end this section by studying a problem that is closely related to the all-pairs shortest-path problem. Assume that we have a graph G with unweighted edges. We want to determine if there is a path from i to j for all values of i and j. Two cases are of interest. The first case requires positive path lengths; the second requires only nonnega-tive path lengths. These cases are known as the *transitive closure* and *reflexive transitive closure* of a graph, respectively. We define them as follows:

Definition: The *transitive closure matrix*, denoted A^+, of a graph, G, is a matrix such that $A^+[i,j] = 1$ if there is a path of length > 0 from i to j; otherwise, $A^+[i,j] = 0$. □

Definition: The *reflexive transitive closure matrix*, denoted A^*, of a graph, G, is a matrix such that $A^*[i,j] = 1$ if there is a path of length ≥ 0 from i to j; otherwise, $A^*[i,j] = 0$. □

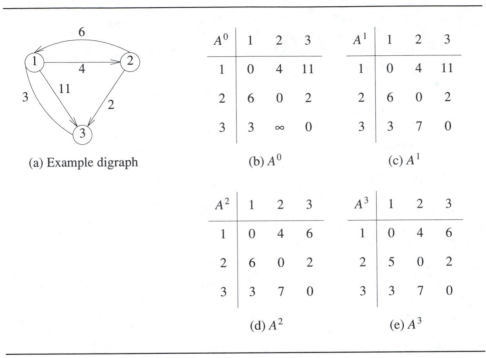

A^0	1	2	3
1	0	4	11
2	6	0	2
3	3	∞	0

A^1	1	2	3
1	0	4	11
2	6	0	2
3	3	7	0

(a) Example digraph   (b) A^0 (c) A^1

A^2	1	2	3
1	0	4	6
2	6	0	2
3	3	7	0

A^3	1	2	3
1	0	4	6
2	5	0	2
3	3	7	0

(d) A^2 (e) A^3

Figure 6.31: Example for all-pairs shortest-paths problem

Figure 6.32 shows A^+ and $A*$ for a digraph. Clearly, the only difference between $A*$ and A^+ is in the terms on the diagonal. $A^+[i,i] = 1$ iff there is a cycle of length >1 containing vertex i, whereas $A*[i,i]$ is always one, as there is a path of length 0 from i to i.

We can use procedure *AllLengths* (Program 6.10) to compute A^+. We begin with *length* $[i,j] = 1$ if $<i,j>$ is an edge in G and *length* $[i,j] = +\infty$ if $<i,j>$ is not in G. When *AllLengths* terminates, we can obtain A^+ from the final matrix a by letting $A^+[i,j] = 1$ iff $a[i,j] < +\infty$. $A*$ can be obtained from A^+ by setting all diagonal elements equal to 1. The total time is $O(n^3)$.

Some simplification is achieved by slightly modifying procedure *AllLengths*. In this modification, we make *length* and a boolean arrays. Initially, *length* $[i,j] = $ **true** iff $<i,j>$ is an edge of G. That is, *length* is the adjacency matrix of the graph. Line 12 of *AllLengths* is replaced by

$$a[i,j] := a[i,j] \text{ or } (a[i,k] \text{ and } a[k,j])$$

Upon termination of *AllLengths*, the final matrix a is A^+.

The transitive closure of an undirected graph G can be found more easily from its connected components. From the definition of a connected component, it follows that

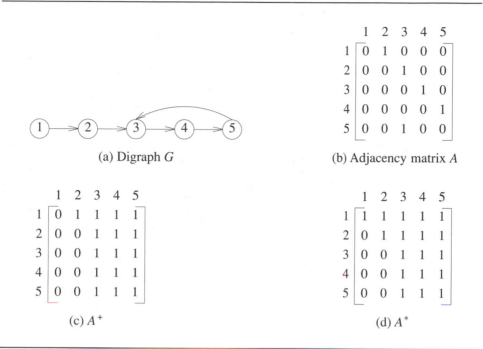

$$\begin{array}{c} \\ \\ 1 \\ 2 \\ 3 \\ 4 \\ 5 \end{array} \begin{array}{ccccc} 1 & 2 & 3 & 4 & 5 \\ \left[\begin{array}{ccccc} 0 & 1 & 0 & 0 & 0 \\ 0 & 0 & 1 & 0 & 0 \\ 0 & 0 & 0 & 1 & 0 \\ 0 & 0 & 0 & 0 & 1 \\ 0 & 0 & 1 & 0 & 0 \end{array}\right] \end{array}$$

(a) Digraph G (b) Adjacency matrix A

$$\begin{array}{c} \\ \\ 1 \\ 2 \\ 3 \\ 4 \\ 5 \end{array} \begin{array}{ccccc} 1 & 2 & 3 & 4 & 5 \\ \left[\begin{array}{ccccc} 0 & 1 & 1 & 1 & 1 \\ 0 & 0 & 1 & 1 & 1 \\ 0 & 0 & 1 & 1 & 1 \\ 0 & 0 & 1 & 1 & 1 \\ 0 & 0 & 1 & 1 & 1 \end{array}\right] \end{array}$$

(c) A^+

$$\begin{array}{c} \\ \\ 1 \\ 2 \\ 3 \\ 4 \\ 5 \end{array} \begin{array}{ccccc} 1 & 2 & 3 & 4 & 5 \\ \left[\begin{array}{ccccc} 1 & 1 & 1 & 1 & 1 \\ 0 & 1 & 1 & 1 & 1 \\ 0 & 0 & 1 & 1 & 1 \\ 0 & 0 & 1 & 1 & 1 \\ 0 & 0 & 1 & 1 & 1 \end{array}\right] \end{array}$$

(d) A^*

Figure 6.32: Graph G and its adjacency matrix A, A^+, and A^*

there is a path between every pair of vertices in the component and there is no path in G between two vertices that are in different components. Hence, if A is the adjacency matrix of an undirected graph (i.e., A is symmetric) then its transitive closure A^+ may be determined in $O(n^2)$ time by first determining the connected components of the graph. $A^+[i,j] = 1$ iff there is a path from vertex i to j. For every pair of distinct vertices in the same component, $A^+[i,j] = 1$. On the diagonal, $A^+[i,i] = 1$ iff the component containing i has at least two vertices.

EXERCISES

1. Let T be a tree with root v. The edges of T are undirected. Each edge in T has a nonnegative length. Write an algorithm to determine the length of the shortest paths from v to the remaining vertices of T. Your algorithm should have complexity $O(n)$, where n is the number of vertices in T. Show that this is the case.

2. Let G be a directed, acyclic graph with n vertices. Assume that the vertices are numbered 1 through n such that all edges are of the form $<i,j>$, where $i < j$. Assume that the graph is available as a set of adjacency lists and that each edge has a length (which may be negative) associated with it. Write an algorithm to deter-

mine the length of the shortest paths from vertex 1 to the remaining vertices. The complexity of your algorithm should be $O(n + e)$, where e is the number of edges in the graph. Show that this is the case.

3. (a) Do the previous exercise, but this time find the length of the longest paths instead of the shortest paths.

   (b) Extend your algorithm of (a) to determine a longest path from vertex 1 to each of the remaining vertices.

4. Using the idea of algorithm *ShortestPath* (Program 6.8), give an algorithm to find a minimum-cost spanning tree whose worst-case time is $O(n^2)$.

5. Use algorithm *ShortestPath* to obtain, in nondecreasing order, the lengths of the shortest paths from vertex 1 to all remaining vertices in the digraph of Figure 6.33.

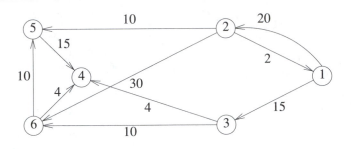

Figure 6.33: A digraph

6. Rewrite algorithm *ShortestPath* under the following assumptions:

   (a) G is represented by its adjacency lists, where each node has three fields: *vertex*, *length*, and *link*. *length* is the length of the corresponding edge and n the number of vertices in G.

   (b) Instead of S (the set of vertices to which the shortest paths have already been found), the set $T = V(G) - S$ is represented using a linked list.

   What can you say about the computing time of your new algorithm relative to that of *ShortestPath*?

7. Modify algorithm *ShortestPath* so that it obtains the shortest paths, in addition to the lengths of these paths. What is the computing time of your algorithm?

8. Using the directed graph of Figure 6.34, explain why *ShortestPath* will not work properly. What is the shortest path between vertices 1 and 7?

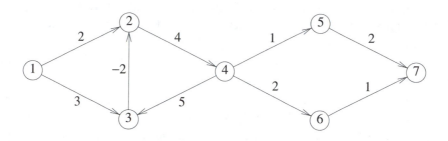

Figure 6.34: Directed graph on which *ShortestPath* does not work properly

9. Prove the correctness of procedure *BellmanFord* (Program 6.9). Note that this procedure does not faithfully implement the computation of the recurrence for $dist^k$. In fact, for $k < n-1$, the *dist* values following iteration k of the **for** loop of lines 8 to 11 may not be $dist^k$.

10. Transform procedure *BellmanFord* into a Pascal procedure. Assume that graphs are represented using adjacency lists in which each node has an additional field called *length* that gives the length of the edge represented by that node. As a result of this, there is no length-adjacency matrix. Generate some test graphs and test the correctness of your procedure.

11. Rewrite procedure *BellmanFord* so that the loop of lines 8 to 11 terminates either after $n-1$ iterations or after the first iteration in which no *dist* values are changed, whichever occurs first.

12. Rewrite procedure *BellmanFord* by replacing the loop of lines 8 to 11 with code that uses a queue of vertices that may potentially result in a reduction of other *dist* vertices. This queue initially contains all vertices that are adjacent from the source vertex v. On each successive iteration of the new loop, a vertex i is removed from the queue (unless the queue is empty), and the *dist* values to vertices adjacent from i are updated as in line 11 of Program 6.9. When the *dist* value of a vertex is reduced because of this, it is added to the queue unless it is already on the queue.

    (a) Prove that the new procedure produces the same results as the original one.

    (b) Show that the complexity of the new procedure is no more than that of the original one.

13. Compare the run-time performance of the Bellman and Ford procedures of the preceding two exercises and that of Program 6.9. For this, generate test graphs that will expose the relative performance of the three procedures.

14. Modify procedure *BellmanFord* so that it obtains the shortest paths, in addition to the lengths of these paths. What is the computing time of your procedure?

15. Modify procedure *AllLengths* (Program 6.10) so that it obtains a shortest path for all pairs of vertices. What is the computing time of your new procedure?

16. Use procedure *AllLengths* to obtain the lengths of the shortest paths between all pairs of vertices in the graph of Figure 6.33. Does *AllLengths* give the right answers? Why?

17. By considering the complete graph with n vertices, show that the maximum number of simple paths between two vertices is $O((n-1)!)$.

18. Show that $A^+ = A^* \times A$, where matrix multiplication of the two matrices is defined as $a_{ij}^+ = \vee_{k=1}^{n} a_{ik}^* \wedge a_{kj}$. $\vee$ is the logical **or** operation, and $\wedge$ is the logical **and** operation.

19. Obtain the matrices A^+ and A^* for the digraph of Figure 6.15.

6.5   ACTIVITY NETWORKS

6.5.1   Activity-on-Vertex (AOV) Networks

All but the simplest of projects can be subdivided into several subprojects called activities. The successful completion of these activities results in the completion of the entire project. A student working toward a degree in computer science must complete several courses successfully. The project in this case is to complete the major, and the activities are the individual courses that have to be taken. Figure 6.35 lists the courses needed for a computer science major at a hypothetical university. Some of these courses may be taken independently of others; other courses have prerequisites and can be taken only if all the prerequisites have already been taken. The data structures course cannot be started until certain programming and math courses have been completed. Thus, prerequisites define precedence relations between courses. The relationships defined may be more clearly represented using a directed graph in which the vertices represent courses and the directed edges represent prerequisites.

Definition: A directed graph G in which the vertices represent tasks or activities and the edges represent precedence relations between tasks is an *activity-on-vertex network* or AOV network. □

Figure 6.35(b) is the AOV network corresponding to the courses of Figure 6.35(a). Each edge $<i, j>$ implies that course i is a prerequisite of course j.

Definition: Vertex i in an AOV network G is a *predecessor* of vertex j iff there is a directed path from vertex i to vertex j. i is an *immediate predecessor* of j iff $<i,j>$ is an

Course number	Course name	Prerequisites
C1	Programming I	None
C2	Discrete Mathematics	None
C3	Data Structures	C1, C2
C4	Calculus I	None
C5	Calculus II	C4
C6	Linear Algebra	C5
C7	Analysis of Algorithms	C3, C6
C8	Assembly Language	C3
C9	Operating Systems	C7, C8
C10	Programming Languages	C7
C11	Compiler Design	C10
C12	Artificial Intelligence	C7
C13	Computational Theory	C7
C14	Parallel Algorithms	C13
C15	Numerical Analysis	C5

(a) Courses needed for a computer science degree at a hypothetical university

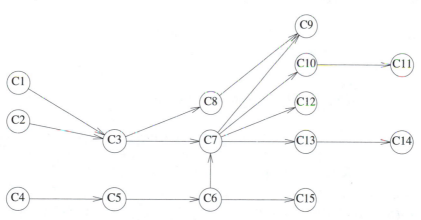

(b) AOV network representing courses as vertices and prerequisites as edges

Figure 6.35: An activity-on-vertex (AOV) network

edge in G. If i is a predecessor of j, then j is a *successor* of i. If i is an immediate predecessor of j, then j is an *immediate successor* of i. □

C3 and C6 are immediate predecessors of C7. C9, C10, C12, and C13 are immediate successors of C7. C14 is a successor, but not an immediate successor, of C3.

Definition: A relation $\cdot$ is *transitive* iff it is the case that for all triples i,j,k, $i \cdot j$ and $j \cdot k \Rightarrow i \cdot k$. A relation $\cdot$ is *irreflexive* on a set S if for no element x in S it is the case that $x \cdot x$. A precedence relation that is both transitive and irreflexive is a *partial order*. $\square$

Notice that the precedence relation defined by course prerequisites is transitive. That is, if course i must be taken before course j (as i is a prerequiste of j), and if j must be taken before k, then i must be taken before k. This fact is not obvious from the AOV network. For example, <C4, C5> and <C5, C6> are edges in the AOV network of Figure 6.35(b). However, <C4, C6> is not. Generally, AOV networks are incompletely specified, and the edges needed to make the precedence relation transitive are implied.

If the precedence relation defined by the edges of an AOV network is not irreflexive, then there is an activity that is a predecessor of itself and so must be completed before it can be started. This is clearly impossible. When there are no inconsistencies of this type, the project is feasible. Given an AOV network, one of our concerns would be to determine whether or not the precedence relation defined by its edges is irreflexive. This is identical to determining whether or not the network contains any directed cycles. A directed graph with no directed cycles is an *acyclic* graph. Our algorithm to test an AOV network for feasibility will also generate a linear ordering, $v_1, v_2, \cdots, v_n$, of the vertices (activities). This linear ordering will have the property that if vertex i is a predecessor of j in the network, then i precedes j in the linear ordering. A linear ordering with this property is called a *topological order*.

Definition: A *topological order* is a linear ordering of the vertices of a graph such that, for any two vertices i and j, if i is a predecessor of j in the network, then i precedes j in the linear ordering. $\square$

There are several possible topological orders for the network of Figure 6.35(b). Two of these are

        C1, C2, C4, C5, C3, C6, C8, C7, C10, C13, C12, C14, C15, C11, C9

and

        C4, C5, C2, C1, C6, C3, C8, C15, C7, C9, C10, C11, C12, C13, C14

If a student were taking just one course per term, then she or he would have to take them in topological order. If the AOV network represented the different tasks involved in assembling an automobile, then these tasks would be carried out in topological order on an assembly line. The algorithm to sort the tasks into topological order is straightforward and proceeds by listing a vertex in the network that has no predecessor. Then, this vertex together with all edges leading out from it is deleted from the network. These two steps are repeated until all vertices have been listed or all remaining vertices in the network have predecessors, and so none can be removed. In this case there is a cycle in the network, and the project is infeasible. The algorithm is stated more formally in Program 6.11.

---

1 Input the AOV network. Let n be the number of vertices.
2 **for** $i := 1$ **to** n **do** {output the vertices}
3 **begin**
4   **if** every vertex has a predecessor
5   **then** [the network has a cycle and is infeasible. **halt**];
6   pick a vertex v that has no predecessors;
7   output v;
8   delete v and all edges leading out of v from the network;
9 **end**;

Program 6.11: Design of a topological sorting algorithm

Example 6.8: Let us try out our topological sorting algorithm on the network of Figure 6.36(a). The first vertex to be picked in line 6 is 1, as it is the only one with no predecessors. Vertex 1 and the edges <1, 2>, <1, 3>, and <1, 4> are deleted. In the resulting network (Figure 6.36(b)), vertices 2, 3, and 4 have no predecessor. Any of these can be the next vertex in the topological order. Assume that 4 is picked. Deletion of vertex 4 and the edges <4, 6> and <4, 5> results in the network of Figure 6.36(c). Either 2 or 3 may next be picked. Figure 6.36 shows the progress of the algorithm on the network. □

To obtain a complete algorithm that can be easily translated into a computer program, it is necessary to specify the data representation for the AOV network. The choice of a data representation, as always, depends on the functions you wish to perform. In this problem, the functions are

(1)   decide whether a vertex has any predecessors (line 4)

(2)   delete a vertex together with all its incident edges

To perform the first function efficiently, we maintain a count of the number of immediate predecessors each vertex has. The second function is easily implemented if the network is represented by its adjacency lists. Then the deletion of all edges leading out of vertex v can be carried out by decreasing the predecessor count of all vertices on its adjacency list. Whenever the count of a vertex drops to zero, that vertex can be placed onto a list of vertices with a zero count. Then the selection in line 6 just requires removal of a vertex from this list.

As a result of the preceding analysis, we represent the AOV network using adjacency lists. The head nodes of these lists contain two fields: *count* and *link*. The data types needed are

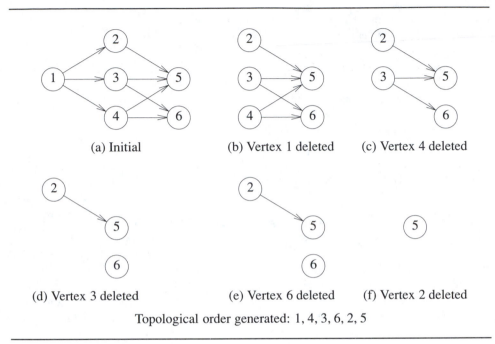

(a) Initial   (b) Vertex 1 deleted   (c) Vertex 4 deleted

(d) Vertex 3 deleted   (e) Vertex 6 deleted   (f) Vertex 2 deleted

Topological order generated: 1, 4, 3, 6, 2, 5

Figure 6.36: Action of Program 6.11 on an AOV network

```
type NextNode = ↑node;
     node = record
              vertex : integer;
              link : NextNode;
            end;
     HeadNodes = record
                   count : integer;
                   link : NextNode;
                 end;
     AdjacencyLists = array [1 .. n] of HeadNodes;
```

The *count* field of a head node contains the in-degree of the vertex, and *link* is a pointer to the first node on the adjacency list. Each list node has two fields: *vertex* and *link*. *count* fields can be set up easily at the time of input. When edge $<i,j>$ is input, the count of vertex j is incremented by 1. Figure 6.37(a) shows the internal representation of the network of Figure 6.36(a).

Inserting these details into the algorithm of Program 6.11, we obtain the Pascal program *TopologicalOrder* (Program 6.12). The list of vertices with zero count is maintained as a stack. A queue could have been used instead, but a stack is slightly simpler.

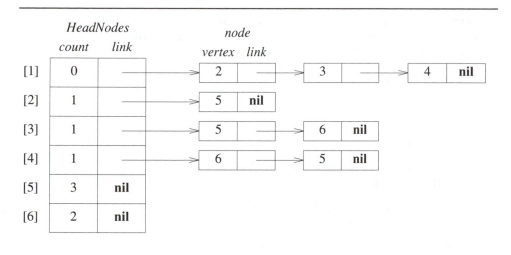

Figure 6.37: Internal representation used by topological sorting algorithm

The stack is linked through the *count* field of the head nodes, since this field is of no use after the count has become zero.

Analysis of *TopologicalOrder*: As a result of a judicious choice of data structures, the algorithm is very efficient. For a network with n vertices and e edges, the loop of lines 10 to 14 takes $O(n)$ time; lines 17 to 23 take $O(n)$ time over the entire algorithm; and the **while** loop of lines 24 to 33 takes time $O(d_i)$ for each vertex i, where d_i is the out-degree of vertex i. Since this loop is encountered once for each vertex output, the total time for this part of the algorithm is $O((\Sigma_{i=1}^{n}d_i)+n) = O(e + n)$. Hence, the asymptotic computing time of the algorithm is $O(e+n)$. It is linear in the size of the problem! $\square$

6.5.2 Activity-on-Edge (AOE) Networks

An activity network closely related to the AOV network is the *activity-on-edge*, or *AOE, network*. The tasks to be performed on a project are represented by directed edges. Vertices in the network represent events. Events signal the completion of certain activities. Activities represented by edges leaving a vertex cannot be started until the event at that vertex has occurred. An event occurs only when all activities entering it have been completed. Figure 6.38(a) is an AOE network for a hypothetical project with 11 tasks or activities: $a_1, \cdots, a_{11}$. There are nine events: $1, 2, \cdots, 9$. The events 1 and 9 may be interpreted as "start project" and "finish project," respectively. Figure 6.38(b) gives interpretations for some of the nine events. The number associated with each activity is

```
 1 procedure TopologicalOrder (var AdList : AdjacencyLists ; n : integer);
 2 {The n vertices of an AOV network are listed in topological order.
 3 The network is represented as a set of adjacency lists with
 4 AdList [i ].count = the in-degree of vertex i.}
 5 var i, j, k, top : integer;
 6     ptr : NextNode;
 7     done : boolean;
 8 begin
 9    top := 0; {initialize stack}
10    for i := 1 to n do {create a linked stack of vertices with}
11      if AdList [i ].count = 0 {no predecessors}
12      then begin
13              AdList [i ].count := top; top := i;
14           end;
15    i := 1; done := false;
16    while ((i <= n) and not done) do
17      if top = 0 then begin
18                      writeln('network has a cycle'); done := true;
19                  end
20              else begin
21                      j := top; top := AdList [top ].count ; {unstack a vertex}
22                      writeln (j);
23                      ptr := AdList [j ].link;
24                      while ptr < > nil do
25                      begin {decrease the count of the successor vertices of j}
26                        k := ptr ↑. vertex ; {k is a successor of j}
27                        AdList [k ].count := AdList [k ].count − 1; {decrease count}
28                        if AdList [k ].count = 0
29                        then begin {add vertex k to stack}
30                                AdList [k ].count := top; top := k;
31                             end; {of if};
32                        ptr := ptr ↑. link ;
33                      end; {of while ptr < > nil}
34                      i := i + 1;
35                  end; {of while (i <= n) and not done}
36 end; {of TopologicalOrder}
```

Program 6.12: Topological order

the time needed to perform that activity. Thus, activity a_1 requires 6 days, whereas a_{11} requires 4 days. Usually, these times are only estimates. Activities a_1, a_2, and a_3 may be carried out concurrently after the start of the project. Activities a_4, a_5, and a_6 cannot be started until events 2, 3, and 4, respectively, occur. Activities a_7 and a_8 can be carried out concurrently after the occurrence of event 5 (i.e., after a_4 and a_5 have been completed). If additional ordering constraints are to be put on the activities, dummy activities whose time is zero may be introduced. Thus, if we desire that activities a_7 and a_8 not start until both events 5 and 6 have occurred, a dummy activity a_{12} represented by an edge <6,5> may be introduced.

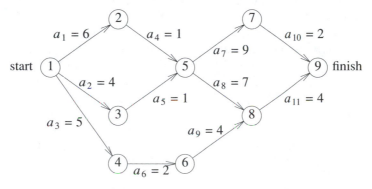

(a) Activity network of a hypothetical project

event	interpretation
1	start of project
2	completion of activity a_1
5	completion of activities a_4 and a_5
8	completion of activities a_8 and a_9
9	completion of project

(b) Interpretation of some of the events in the network of (a)

Figure 6.38: An AOE network

Activity networks of the AOE type have proved very useful in the performance evaluation of several types of projects. This evaluation includes determining such facts about the project as what is the least amount of time in which the project may be completed (assuming there are no cycles in the network), which activities should be speeded to reduce project length, and so on.

Since the activities in an AOE network can be carried out in parallel, the minimum time to complete the project is the length of the longest path from the start vertex to the finish vertex (the length of a path is the sum of the times of activities on this path). A path of longest length is a *critical path*. The path 1, 2, 5, 7, 9 is a critical path in the network of Figure 6.38(a). The length of this critical path is 18. A network may have more than one critical path (the path 1, 2, 5, 8, 9 is also critical).

The *earliest time* that an event i can occur is the length of the longest path from the start vertex 1 to the vertex i. The earliest time that event v_5 can occur is 7. The earliest time an event can occur determines the *earliest start time* for all activities represented by edges leaving that vertex. Denote this time by $e(i)$ for activity a_i. For example, $e(7)=e(8)=7$.

For every activity a_i, we may also define the *latest time*, $l(i)$, that an activity may start without increasing the project duration (i.e., length of the longest path from start to finish). In Figure 6.38(a) we have $e(6)=5$ and $l(6)=8$, $e(8)=7$ and $l(8)=7$.

All activities for which $e(i)=l(i)$ are called *critical activities*. The difference $l(i)-e(i)$ is a measure of the criticality of an activity. It gives the time by which an activity may be delayed or slowed without increasing the total time needed to finish the project. If activity a_6 is slowed down to take 2 extra days, this will not affect the project finish time. Clearly, all activities on a critical path are strategic, and speeding up noncritical activities will not reduce the project duration.

The purpose of critical-path analysis is to identify critical activities so that resources may be concentrated on these activities in an attempt to reduce project finish time. Speeding a critical activity will not result in a reduced project length unless that activity is on all critical paths. In Figure 6.38(a) the activity a_{11} is critical, but speeding it up so that it takes only 3 days instead of 4 does not reduce the finish time to 17 days. This is so because there is another critical path (1, 2, 5, 7, 9) that does not contain this activity. The activities a_1 and a_4 are on all critical paths. Speeding a_1 by 2 days reduces the critical path length to 16 days. Critical-path methods have proved very valuable in evaluating project performance and identifying bottlenecks.

Critical-path analysis can also be carried out with AOV networks. The length of a path would now be the sum of the activity times of the vertices on that path. By analogy, for each activity or vertex we could define the quantities $e(i)$ and $l(i)$. Since the activity times are only estimates, it is necessary to reevaluate the project during several stages of its completion as more accurate estimates of activity times become available. These changes in activity times could make previously noncritical activities critical, and vice versa.

Before ending our discussion on activity networks, let us design an algorithm to calculate $e(i)$ and $l(i)$ for all activities in an AOE network. Once these quantities are known, then the critical activities may easily be identified. Deleting all noncritical activities from the AOE network, all critical paths may be found by just generating all paths from the start-to-finish vertex (all such paths will include only critical activities and so must be critical, and since no noncritical activity can be on a critical path, the network with noncritical activities removed contains all critical paths present in the original network).

6.5.2.1   Calculation of Early Activity Times

When computing the early and late activity times, it is easiest first to obtain the earliest event time, $ee[j]$, and latest event time, $le[j]$, for all events, j, in the network. Thus if activity a_i is represented by edge $<k,l>$, we can compute $e(i)$ and $l(i)$ from the following formulas:

$$e(i)=ee[k]$$

and $\hspace{11cm}$ (6.1)

$$l(i)=le[l]-\text{duration of activity } a_i$$

The times $ee[j]$ and $le[j]$ are computed in two stages: a forward stage and a backward stage. During the forward stage we start with $ee[1]=0$ and compute the remaining early start times, using the formula

$$ee[j]=\max_{i\in P(j)}\{ee[i]+\text{duration of}<i,j>\}\hspace{2cm}(6.2)$$

where $P(j)$ is the set of all vertices adjacent to vertex j. If this computation is carried out in topological order, the early start times of all predecessors of j would have been computed prior to the computation of $ee[j]$. The algorithm to do this is obtained easily from algorithm *TopologicalOrder* (Program 6.12) by inserting the step

$$\textbf{if } ee[k] < ee[j] + ptr\uparrow.dur \textbf{ then } ee[k] := ee[j] + ptr\uparrow.dur;$$

between lines 26 and 27. It is assumed that the array ee is initialized to zero and that dur is another field in the adjacency-list nodes that contains the activity duration. This modification results in the evaluation of Eq. (6.2) in parallel with the generation of a topological order. $ee(j)$ is updated each time the $ee(i)$ of one of its predecessors is known (i.e., when i is ready for output). The step **writeln**(j) of line 22 may be omitted.

To illustrate the working of the modified *TopologicalOrder* algorithm, let us try it out on the network of Figure 6.38(a). The adjacency lists for the network are shown in Figure 6.39(a). The order of nodes on these lists determines the order in which vertices will be considered by the algorithm. At the outset, the early start time for all vertices is 0, and the start vertex is the only one in the stack. When the adjacency list for this vertex is processed, the early start time of all vertices adjacent from 1 is updated. Since vertices 2, 3, and 4 are now in the stack, all their predecessors have been processed, and Eq. (6.2) has been evaluated for these three vertices. $ee[6]$ is the next one determined. When vertex 6 is being processed, $ee[8]$ is updated to 11. This, however, is not the true value for $ee[8]$, since Eq. (6.2) has not been evaluated over all predecessors of 8 (v_5 has not yet been considered). This does not matter, as 8 cannot get stacked until all its predecessors have been processed. $ee[5]$ is next updated to 5 and finally to 7. At this point $ee[5]$ has been determined, as all the predecessors of 5 have been examined. The values of $ee[7]$ and $ee[8]$ are next obtained. $ee[9]$ is ultimately determined to be 18, the

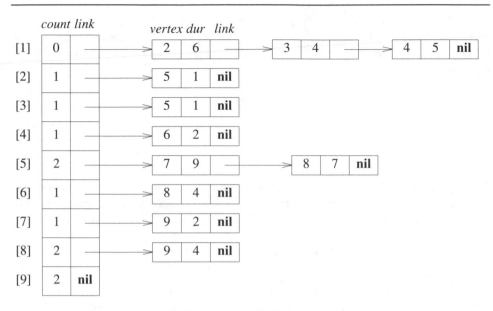

(a) Adjacency lists for Figure 6.38(a)

ee	[1]	[2]	[3]	[4]	[5]	[6]	[7]	[8]	[9]	Stack
initial	0	0	0	0	0	0	0	0	0	[1]
output 1	0	6	4	5	0	0	0	0	0	[4, 3, 2]
output 4	0	6	4	5	0	7	0	0	0	[6, 3, 2]
output 6	0	6	4	5	0	7	0	11	0	[3, 2]
output 3	0	6	4	5	5	7	0	11	0	[2]
output 2	0	6	4	5	7	7	0	11	0	[5]
output 5	0	6	4	5	7	7	16	14	0	[8, 7]
output 8	0	6	4	5	7	7	16	14	18	[7]
output 7	0	6	4	5	7	7	16	14	18	[9]
output 9										

(b) Computation of *ee*

Figure 6.39: Computing *ee* using modified *TopologicalOrder* (Program 6.12)

length of a critical path. You may readily verify that when a vertex is put into the stack, its early time has been correctly computed. The insertion of the new statement does not change the asymptotic computing time; it remains O($e + n$).

6.5.2.2 Calculation of Late Activity Times

In the backward stage the values of $le[i]$ are computed using a procedure analogous to that used in the forward stage. We start with $le[n]=ee[n]$ and use the equation

$$le[j] = \min_{i \in S(j)} \{le[i] - \text{duration of} <j,i>\} \qquad (6.3)$$

where $S(j)$ is the set of vertices adjacent from vertex j. The initial values for $le[i]$ may be set to $ee[n]$. Basically, Eq. (6.3) says that if $<j,i>$ is an activity and the latest start time for event i is $le[i]$, then event j must occur no later than $le[i]$ – duration of $<j,i>$. Before $le[j]$ can be computed for some event j, the latest event time for all successor events (i.e., events adjacent from j) must be computed. These times can be obtained in a manner identical to the computation of the early times by using inverse adjacency lists and inserting the step $le[k] := \min\{le[k], le[j] - ptr\uparrow.dur\}$ at the same place as before in algorithm *TopologicalOrder* (Program 6.12). The *count* field of a head node initially is the out-degree of the vertex.

Figure 6.40 describes the process on the network of Figure 6.38(a). If the forward stage has already been carried out and a topological ordering of the vertices obtained, then the values of $le[i]$ can be computed directly, using Eq. (6.3), by performing the computations in the reverse topological order. The topological order generated in Figure 6.39(b) is 1, 4, 6, 3, 2, 5, 8, 7, 9. We may compute the values of $le[i]$ in the order 9, 7, 8, 5, 2, 3, 6, 4, 1, as all successors of an event precede that event in this order. This is done in Figure 6.40(c). In practice, one would usually compute both *ee* and *le*. The procedure would then be to compute *ee* first, using algorithm *TopologicalOrder*, modified as discussed for the forward stage, and then to compute *le* directly from Eq. (6.3) in reverse topological order.

Using the values of *ee* (Figure 6.39) and of *le* (Figure 6.40), and Eq. (6.1), we may compute the early and late times $e(i)$ and $l(i)$ and the degree of criticality (also called slack) of each task. Figure 6.41 gives the values. The critical activities are a_1, a_4, a_7, a_8, a_{10}, and a_{11}. Deleting all noncritical activities from the network, we get the directed graph or critical network of Figure 6.42. All paths from 1 to 9 in this graph are critical paths, and there are no critical paths in the original network that are not paths in this graph.

As a final remark on activity networks, we note that the algorithm *Topological Order* detects only directed cycles in the network. There may be other flaws, such as vertices not reachable from the start vertex (Figure 6.43). When a critical-path analysis is carried out on such networks, there will be several vertices with $ee[i] = 0$. Since all activity times are assumed > 0, only the start vertex can have $ee[i] = 0$. Hence, critical-path analysis can also be used to detect this kind of fault in project planning.

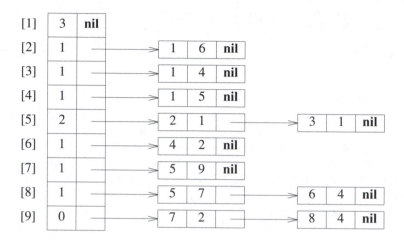

(a) Inverse adjacency lists for Figure 6.38(a)

le	[1]	[2]	[3]	[4]	[5]	[6]	[7]	[8]	[9]	Stack
initial	18	18	18	18	18	18	18	18	18	[9]
output 9	18	18	18	18	18	18	16	14	18	[8,7]
output 8	18	18	18	18	7	10	16	14	18	[6,7]
output 6	18	18	18	8	7	10	16	14	18	[4,7]
output 4	3	18	18	8	7	10	16	14	18	[7]
output 7	3	18	18	8	7	10	16	14	18	[5]
output 5	3	6	6	8	7	10	16	14	18	[3,2]
output 3	2	6	6	8	7	10	16	14	18	[2]
output 2	0	6	6	8	7	10	16	14	18	[1]

(b) Computation of *le*

Figure 6.40: Computing *le* for the AOE network of Figure 6.38(a) (continued on next page)

EXERCISES

1. Does the following set of precedence relations ($<$) define a partial order on the elements 1 thru 5? Why?

$$1 < 2; \ 2 < 4; \ 2 < 3; \ 3 < 4; \ 3 < 5; \ 5 < 1$$

$le\,[9] = ee\,[9] = 18$
$le\,[7] = \min\{le\,[9] - 2\} = 16$
$le\,[8] = \min\{le\,[9] - 4\} = 14$
$le\,[5] = \min\{le\,[7] - 9,\ le\,[8] - 7\} = 14$
$le\,[2] = \min\{le\,[5] - 1\} = 6$
$le\,[3] = \min\{le\,[5] - 1\} = 6$
$le\,[6] = \min\{le\,[8] - 4\} = 10$
$le\,[4] = \min\{le\,[6] - 2\} = 8$
$le\,[1] = \min\{le\,[2] - 6,\ le\,[3] - 4,\ le\,[4] - 5\} = 0$

(c) Computation of le using a reverse topological order

Figure 6.40: Computing le for the AOE network of Figure 6.38(a)

activity	early time e	late time l	slack $l - e$	critical $l - e = 0$
a_1	0	0	0	Yes
a_2	0	2	2	No
a_3	0	3	3	No
a_4	6	6	0	Yes
a_5	4	6	2	No
a_6	5	8	3	No
a_7	7	7	0	Yes
a_8	7	7	0	Yes
a_9	7	10	3	No
a_{10}	16	16	0	Yes
a_{11}	14	14	0	Yes

Figure 6.41: Early, late, and criticality values

2. (a) For the AOE network of Figure 6.44 obtain the early, $e(\ )$, and late, $l(\ )$, start times for each activity. Use the forward-backward approach.

(b) What is the earliest time the project can finish?

(c) Which activities are critical?

(d) Is there any single activity whose speed-up would result in a reduction of the project length?

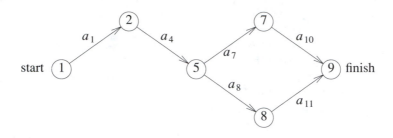

Figure 6.42: Graph obtained after deleting all noncritical activities

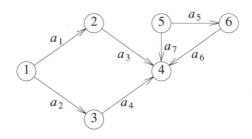

Figure 6.43: AOE network with some nonreachable activities

3. Define a critical AOE network to be an AOE network in which all activities are critical. Let G be the undirected graph obtained by removing the directions and weights from the edges of the network.

   (a) Show that the project length can be decreased by speeding up exactly one activity if there is an edge in G that lies on every path from the start vertex to the finish vertex. Such an edge is called a bridge. Deletion of a bridge from a connected graph separates the graph into two connected components.

   (b) Write an $O(n + e)$ algorithm using adjacency lists to determine whether the connected graph G has a bridge. If G has a bridge, your algorithm should output one such bridge.

4. Write a Pascal program that inputs an AOE network and outputs the following:

   (a) A table of all events together with their earliest and latest times.

   (b) A table of all activities together with their early and late times. This table

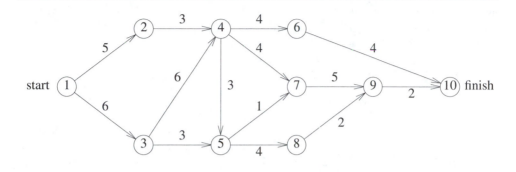

Figure 6.44: An AOE network

should also list the slack for each activity and identify all critical activities (see Figure 6.41).

(c)   The critical network.

(d)   Whether or not the project length can be reduced by speeding a single activity. If so, then by how much?

6.6   REFERENCES AND SELECTED READINGS

Euler's original paper on the Königsberg bridge problem makes interesting reading. This paper has been reprinted in: ''Leonhard Euler and the Königsberg bridges,'' *Scientific American*, 189:1, 1953, pp. 66-70.

The biconnected-component algorithm is due to Robert Tarjan. This, together with a linear-time algorithm to find the strongly connected components of a directed graph, appears in the paper ''Depth-first search and linear graph algorithms,'' by R. Tarjan, *SIAM Journal on Computing*, 1:2, 1972, pp. 146-159.

Prim's minimum-cost spanning tree algorithm was actually first proposed by Jarnik in 1930 and rediscovered by Prim in 1957. Since virtually all references to this algorithm give credit to Prim, we continue to refer to it as Prim's algorithm. Similarly, the algorithm we refer to as Sollin's algorithm was first proposed by Boruvka in 1926 and rediscovered by Sollin several years later. For an interesting discussion of the history of the minimum spanning tree problem, see ''On the history of the minimum spanning tree problem,'' by R. Graham and P. Hell, *Annals of the History of Computing*, 7:1, 1985, pp. 43-57.

Further algorithms on graphs may be found in *The Design and Analysis of Computer Algorithms*, by A. Aho, J. Hopcroft, and J. Ullman, Addison-Wesley, Reading, MA, 1974; *Graph Theory with Applications to Engineering and Computer Science*, by

N. Deo, Prentice-Hall, Englewood Cliffs, NJ, 1974; *Combinatorial Optimization*, by E. Lawler, Holt, Reinhart and Winston, New York, 1976; *Flows in Networks*, by L. Ford and D. Fulkerson, Princeton University Press, Princeton, NJ, 1962; and *Integer Programming and Network Flows*, by T. C. Hu, Addison-Wesley, Reading, MA, 1970.

6.7 ADDITIONAL EXERCISES

1. Program 6.13 was obtained by Stephen Barnard to find an Eulerian walk in a connected, undirected graph that has no vertices with odd degree.

```
    function euler (v : vertex) : path;
1   begin
2      path := {Ø};
3      for all vertices w  adjacent to v and edge (v,w) not yet used do begin
4         mark edge (v,w) as used;
5         path := {(v,w)} ∪ euler (w) ∪ path;
6      end;
7         euler := path;
8   end; {of euler}
```

Program 6.13: Finding an Eulerian walk

(a) Show that if G is represented by its adjacency multilists and *path* by a linked list, then function *euler* works in time $O(n + e)$.

(b) Prove by induction on the number of edges in G that this algorithm does obtain an Eulerian walk for all graphs G having such a walk. The initial call to *euler* can be made with any vertex v.

(c) At termination, what has to be done to determine whether or not G has an Eulerian walk?

2. A *bipartite graph* $G = (V, E)$ is an undirected graph whose vertices can be partitioned into two disjoint sets, A and $B = V - A$, with the following properties: (1) No two vertices in A are adjacent in G, and (2) no two vertices in B are adjacent in G. The graph G_4 of Figure 6.5 is bipartite. A possible partitioning of V is $A = \{1,4,5,7\}$ and $B = \{2,3,6,8\}$. Write an algorithm to determine whether a graph G is bipartite. If G is bipartite your algorithm should obtain a partitioning of the vertices into two disjoint sets, A and B, satisfying properties (1) and (2) above. Show that if G is represented by its adjacency lists, then this algorithm can be made to work in time $O(n + e)$, where $n = |V|$ and $e = |E|$.

3. Show that every tree is a bipartite graph.

4. Prove that a graph G is bipartite iff it contains no cycles of odd length.

5. The *radius* of a tree is the maximum distance from the root to a leaf. Given a connected, undirected graph, write a procedure to find a spanning tree of minimum radius. (Hint: Use breadth-first search.) Prove that your algorithm is correct.

6. The *diameter* of a tree is the maximum distance between any two vertices. Given a connected, undirected graph, write an algorithm for finding a spanning tree of minimum diameter. Prove the correctness of your algorithm.

7. Let $G[1..n, 1..n]$ be a wiring grid. $G[i,j] > 0$ represents a grid position that is blocked; $G[i,j] = 0$ represents an unblocked position. Assume that positions $[a,b]$ and $[c,d]$ are blocked positions. A path from $[a,b]$ to $[b,c]$ is a sequence of grid positions such that

    (a) $[a,b]$ and $[c,d]$ are, respectively, the first and last positions on the path

    (b) successive positions of the sequence are vertically or horizontally adjacent in the grid

    (c) all positions of the sequence other than the first and last are unblocked positions

    The length of a path is the number of grid positions on the path. We wish to connect positions $[a,b]$ and $[c,d]$ by a wire of shortest length. The wire path is a shortest grid path between these two vertices. Lee's algorithm for this works in the following steps:

    (a) [Forward step] Start a breadth-first search from position $[a,b]$, labeling unblocked positions by their shortest distance from $[a,b]$. To avoid conflicts with existing labels, use negative labels. The labeling stops when the position $[c,d]$ is reached.

    (b) [Backtrace] Use the labels of (a) to label the shortest path between $[a,b]$ and $[c,d]$, using the unique label $w > 0$ for the wire. For this, start at position $[c,d]$.

    (c) [Clean-up] Change the remaining negative labels to 0.

    Write algorithms for each of the three steps of Lee's algorithm. What is the complexity of each step?

8. Another way to represent a graph is by its incidence matrix, INC. There is one row for each vertex and one column for each edge. Then $INC[i,j] = 1$ if edge j is incident to vertex i. The incidence matrix for the graph of Figure 6.16(a) is given in Figure 6.45. The edges of Figure 6.16(a) have been numbered from left to right and top to bottom. Rewrite procedure *dfs* (Program 6.1) so that it works on a graph represented by its incidence matrix.

9. If ADJ is the adjacency matrix of a graph $G = (V,E)$, and INC is the incidence matrix, under what conditions will $ADJ = INC \times INC^T - I$, where INC^T is the transpose of matrix INC? I is the identity matrix, and the matrix product $C = A \times B$,

	1 2 3 4 5 6 7 8 9 10
1	1 1 0 0 0 0 0 0 0 0
2	1 0 1 1 0 0 0 0 0 0
3	0 1 0 0 1 1 0 0 0 0
4	0 0 1 0 0 0 1 0 0 0
5	0 0 0 1 0 0 0 1 0 0
6	0 0 0 0 1 0 0 0 1 0
7	0 0 0 0 0 1 0 0 0 1
8	0 0 0 0 0 0 1 1 1 1

Figure 6.45: Incidence matrix of graph of Figure 6.16(a)

where all matrices are $n \times n$, is defined as $c_{ij} = \vee_{k=1}^{n} a_{ik} \wedge b_{kj}$. $\vee$ is the logical **or** operation, and $\wedge$ is the logical **and** operation.

10. An edge (u, v) of a connected, undirected graph G is a *bridge* iff its deletion from G results in a graph that is not connected. In the graph of Figure 6.19, the edges $(1, 2)$, $(4, 6)$, $(8, 9)$, and $(8, 10)$ are bridges. Write an algorithm that runs in $O(n + e)$ time to find the bridges of G. n and e are, respectively, the number of vertices and edges of G. (Hint: Use the ideas in procedure *bicon* (Program 6.5).)

11. Write a set of computer programs for manipulating graphs. Such a collection should allow input and output of arbitrary graphs, determining connected components, spanning trees, minimum-cost spanning trees, biconnected components, shortest paths, and so on. The capabililty of attaching weights to the edges should also be provided. Test the correctness of your program suite using suitable test data.

CHAPTER 7

SORTING

7.1 MOTIVATION

In this chapter, we use the term *list* to mean a collection of records, each record having one or more fields. The fields used to distinguish among the records are known as *keys*. Since the same list may be used for several different applications, the key fields for record identification depend on the particular application. For instance, we may regard a telephone directory as a list, each record having three fields: name, address, and phone number. The key is usually the person's name. However, we may wish to locate the record corresponding to a given number, in which case the phone number field would be the key. In yet another application we may desire the phone number at a particular address, so the address field could also be the key.

Once we have a collection of records, there are at least two ways in which to store them: sequentially or nonsequentially. For the time being let us assume we have a sequential list f, and we wish to retrieve a record with a certain key value k. If f has n records with $f[i].key$ the key value for record i, then we may carry out the retrieval by examining the key values $f[n].key, \cdots, f[1].key$, in that order, until the correct record is located. Such a search is known as a sequential search, since the records are examined sequentially. Program 7.1 gives a sequential search procedure that uses the following data types:

type *records* = **record**
        key : **integer**;
        other : *fields*;
   end;
alist = **array** [0 .. *MaxSize*] **of** *records*;

---

procedure *SeqSearch* (**var** f : *alist*; **var** i : **integer**; n, k : **integer**);
{Search a list f with key values $f[1].key$, $\cdots$, $f[n].key$ for a record such that $f[i].key = k$. If there is no such record, i is set to 0.}
begin
  $f[0].key := k$;
  $i := n$;
  while $f[i].key <> k$ **do**
    $i := i - 1$;
end; {of *SeqSearch*}

Program 7.1: Sequential search

Note that the introduction of the dummy record 0 with $f[0].key = k$ simplifies the search by eliminating the need for an end-of-list test ($i < 1$) in the **while** loop. Although this might appear to be a minor improvement, it actually reduces the run time considerably for large n. If no record in the list has key value k, then $i = 0$, and the above procedure requires $n + 1$ comparisons. The number of key comparisons made in the case of a successful search depends on the position of the key in the list. If all keys are distinct and key $f[i].key$ is being searched for, then $n - i + 1$ key comparisons are made. The average number of comparisons for a successful search is, therefore,

$$\sum_{1 \le i \le n} (n - i + 1)/n = (n + 1)/2.$$

It is possible to do much better when looking up phone numbers. The fact that the entries in the list (i.e., the telephone directory) are in lexicographic order (on the name key) enables one to look up a number while examining only a very few entries in the list. Binary search (see Chapter 1) is one of the better-known methods for searching an ordered, sequential list. A binary search takes only O($\log n$) time to search a list with n records. This is considerably better than the O(n) time required by a sequential search. We note that when a sequential search is performed on an ordered list, the conditional of the **while** loop of *SeqSearch* can be changed to $f[i].key > x$. This improves the performance for the case of unsuccessful searches.

Getting back to our example of the telephone directory, we notice that neither a sequential nor a binary search strategy corresponds to the search method actually employed by humans. If we are looking for a name that begins with the letter W, we start the search toward the end of the directory rather than at the middle. A search method based on this interpolation scheme would begin by comparing $f[i].key$ with

$i = ((k - f[l].key)/(f[u].key - f[l].key)) * n$, where $f[l].key$ and $f[u].key$ are the values of the smallest and largest keys in the list. An interpolation search can be used only when the list is ordered. The behavior of such a search depends on the distribution of the keys in the list.

We have seen that as far as the searching problem is concerned, something is to be gained by maintaining the list in an ordered manner if the list is to be searched repeatedly. Let us now look at another example in which the use of ordered lists greatly reduces the computational effort. The problem we are now concerned with is that of comparing two lists of records containing data that are essentially the same but have been obtained from two different sources. Such a problem could arise, for instance, in the case of the United States Internal Revenue Service (IRS), which might receive millions of forms from various employers stating how much they paid their employees and then another set of forms from individual employees stating how much they received. So we have two lists of records, and we wish to verify that there is no discrepancy between the two sets of information. Since the forms arrive at the IRS in a random order, we may assume a random arrangement of the records in the lists. The keys here are the social security numbers of the employees.

Let the two lists be $F1$ and $F2$ with keys $F1[i].key$ and $F2[i].key$. We make the following assumptions about the required verification:

(1)   If there is no record in the employee list corresponding to a key $F1[i].key$ in the employer list, a message is to be sent to the employee.

(2)   If the reverse is true, then a message is to be sent to the employer.

(3)   If there is a discrepancy between two records with the same key, a message to this effect is to be output.

Procedure *verify*1 (Program 7.2) solves the verification problem by directly comparing the two unsorted lists. Its complexity is $O(mn)$. On the other hand, if we first sort the two lists and then do the comparison, we can carry out the verification task in time $O(t_{sort}(n) + t_{sort}(m) + n + m)$, where $t_{sort}(n)$ is the time needed to sort a list of n records. As we shall see, it is possible to sort n records in $O(n \log n)$ time, so the computing time becomes $O(\max\{n \log n, m \log m\})$. Procedure *verify*2 (Program 7.3) achieves this time.

We have seen two important uses of sorting: (1) as an aid in searching and (2) as a means for matching entries in lists. Sorting also finds application in the solution of many other more complex problems, e.g., from operations research and job scheduling. In fact, it is estimated that over 25 percent of all computing time is spent on sorting, with some installations spending more than 50 percent of their computing time sorting lists. Consequently, the problem of sorting has great relevance in the study of computing. Unfortunately, no one method is the best for all initial orderings of the list being sorted. We shall therefore study several methods, indicating when one is superior to the others.

First let us formally state the problem we are about to consider. We are given a list of records $(R_1, R_2, \cdots, R_n)$. Each record, R_i, has key value K_i. In addition, we assume an ordering relation $(<)$ on the keys so that for any two key values x and y, $x = y$ or

---

```
procedure verify1(F1, F2 : alist; n, m : integer);
{Compare two unordered lists F1 and F2 of size n and m, respectively.}
var i, j : integer;
    marked : array[1 .. MaxSize] of boolean;
begin
  for i := 1 to m do marked [i] := false;
  for i := 1 to n do
  begin
    SeqSearch (F2, j, m, F1[i].key);
    if j = 0 then writeln(F1[i].key, 'not in F2.') {satisfies (1)}
    else begin
            if F1[i].other < > F2[j].other
            then {satisfies (3)}
                writeln('discrepancy in ', F1[i].key, F1[i].other, F2[j].other);
            marked [j] :=true; {mark the record in F2[j] as being seen}
        end;
  end;
  for i := 1 to m do
      if not marked [i] then writeln (F2[i].key, 'not in F1.'); {satisfies (2)}
end; {of verify1}
```

Program 7.2: Verifying two lists using a sequential search

$x < y$ or $y < x$. The ordering relation ($<$) is assumed to be transitive (i.e., for any three values x, y, and z, $x < y$ and $y < z$ implies $x < z$). The sorting problem then is that of finding a permutation, σ, such that $K_{\sigma(i)} \leq K_{\sigma(i+1)}$, $1 \leq i \leq n - 1$. The desired ordering is $(R_{\sigma(1)}, R_{\sigma(2)}, \cdots, R_{\sigma(n)})$.

Note that when the list has several key values that are identical, the permutation, σ, is not unique. We shall distinguish one permutation, σ_s, from the others that also order the list. Let σ_s be the permutation with the following properties:

(1) $K_{\sigma_s(i)} \leq K_{\sigma_s(i+1)}$, $1 \leq i \leq n - 1$.

(2)   If $i < j$ and $K_i = K_j$ in the input list, then R_i precedes R_j in the sorted list.

A sorting method that generates the permutation σ_s is *stable*.

We characterize sorting methods into two broad categories: (1) internal methods (i.e., methods to be used when the list to be sorted is small enough so that the entire sort can be carried out in main memory) and (2) external methods (i.e., methods to be used on larger lists). The following internal sorting methods will be developed: insertion sort, quick sort, merge sort, heap sort, and radix sort. This development will be followed by a discussion of external sorting.

```
procedure verify2(var F1,F2 : alist; n, m : integer);
{Same task as verify1. However, this time sort F1 and F2 so that the keys are in
increasing order in each list.  We assume that the keys in each list are distinct.}
  var i, j : integer;
  begin
    sort (F1, n); {sort the list by key}
    sort (F2, m);
    i := 1; j := 1;
    while ((i <= n) and (j <= m)) do
        case compare (F1[i] . key, F2[j] . key) of
        '<' : begin
                writeln(F1[i] . key, 'not in F2.');
                i := i + 1;
            end
        '=' : begin
                if F1[i] . other < > F2[j] . other
                then writeln ('discrepancy in ', F1[i] . other, F2[j] . other);
                i := i + 1; j := j + 1;
            end;
        '>' : begin
                writeln (F2[j] . key, 'not in F1.');
                j := j + 1;
            end;
        end; {of case and while}
    if i <= n then PrintRest (F1, i, n, 1) {print records i through n of F1}
    else if j <= m then PrintRest (F2, j, m, 2);
  end; {of verify2}
```

Program 7.3: Fast verification of two lists

7.2   INSERTION SORT

The basic step in this method is to insert a record R into a sequence of ordered records, $R_1, R_2, \cdots, R_i \ (K_1 \le K_2, \cdots, \le K_i)$ in such a way that the resulting sequence of size $i + 1$ is also ordered. Procedure *insert* (Program 7.4) accomplishes this insertion. It assumes the existence of an artificial record R_0 with key $K_0 = -$**maxint** (i.e, all keys are $\ge K_0$). Also the type *alist* is defined as

$$\textbf{type } \textit{alist} = \textbf{array } [0 .. \textit{MaxSize}] \textbf{ of } \textit{records};$$

The use of R_0 enables us to simplify the **while** loop, avoiding a test for end of list (i.e., $j < 1$). In insertion sort, we begin with the ordered sequence R_0, R_1 and succes-

---

procedure *insert* (*r* : *records* ; **var** *list* : *alist*; *i* : **integer**);
{Insert record *r* with key *r* . *key* into the ordered sequence *list* [0], $\cdots$, *list* [*i*] such that
the resulting sequence is also ordered. Assume that *r* . *key* ≥ *list* [0] . *key*.}
begin
  while *r* . *key* < *list* [*i*] . *key* **do**
  begin
    list [*i* + 1] := *list* [*i*];
    i := *i* − 1;
  end;
  list [*i* + 1] := *r*;
end; {of *insert*}

Program 7.4: Insertion into a sorted list

sively insert the records $R_2, R_3, \cdots, R_n$. Since each insertion leaves the resultant sequence ordered, the list with *n* records can be ordered making *n* − 1 insertions. The details are given in procedure *InsertionSort* (Program 7.5).

---

procedure *InsertionSort*(**var** *list* : *alist*; *n* : **integer**);
{Sort *list* in nondecreasing order of *key*.}
var *j* : **integer**;
begin
  list [0] . *key* := −**maxint**;
  for *j* := 2 **to** *n* **do**
    insert (*list* [*j*], *list*, *j* − 1);
end; {of *InsertionSort*}

Program 7.5: Insertion sort

Analysis of *InsertionSort*: In the worst case *insert* (*r*, *list*, *i*) makes *i* + 1 comparisons before making the insertion. Hence its complexity is O(*i*). *InsertionSort* invokes *insert* for *i* = *j* − 1 = 1, 2, $\cdots$, *n* − 1. So, the worst-case time is

$$O(\sum_{i=1}^{n-1} (i+1)) = O(n^2).$$

We can also obtain an estimate of the computing time of this method based on the relative disorder in the input list. Record R_i is *left out of order* (LOO) iff $R_i < \max_{1 \le j < i}\{R_j\}$. The insertion step has to be carried out only for those records that are LOO. If *k* is the number of LOO records, the computing time is $O((k + 1)n)$. The worst-case time is still $O(n^2)$. We can also show that the average time is $O(n^2)$. □

Example 7.1: Assume that $n = 5$ and the input key sequence is 5, 4, 3, 2, 1. After each insertion we have

j	[1]	[2]	[3]	[4]	[5]
–	**5**	4	3	2	1
2	**4**	**5**	3	2	1
3	**3**	**4**	**5**	2	1
4	**2**	**3**	**4**	**5**	1
5	**1**	**2**	**3**	**4**	**5**

For convenience, only the key field of each record is displayed, and the sorted part of the list is shown in bold. Since the input list is in reverse order, as each new record R_i is inserted into the ordered sublist $R_1, \cdots, R_{i-1}$, the entire sublist is shifted right by one position. Thus, this input sequence exhibits the worst-case behavior of insertion sort. □

Example 7.2: Assume that $n = 5$ and the input key sequence is 2, 3, 4, 5, 1. After each iteration we have

j	[1]	[2]	[3]	[4]	[5]
–	**2**	3	4	5	1
2	**2**	**3**	4	5	1
3	**2**	**3**	**4**	5	1
4	**2**	**3**	**4**	**5**	1
5	**1**	**2**	**3**	**4**	**5**

In this example, only R_5 is LOO, and the time for each $j = 2$, 3, and 4 is $O(1)$, whereas for $j = 5$ it is $O(n)$. □

It should be fairly obvious that *InsertionSort* is stable. The fact that the computing time is $O((k + 1)n) = O(kn)$ makes this method very desirable in sorting sequences in which only a very few records are LOO (i.e., $k<<n$). The simplicity of this scheme makes it about the fastest sorting method for $n \leq 20$ (for example).

Variations

1. **Binary insertion sort:** We can reduce the number of comparisons made in an insertion sort by replacing the sequential searching technique used in *insert* (Program 7.4) with binary search. The number of record moves remains unchanged.

2. *List insertion sort:* The elements of the list are represented as a linked list rather than as an array. The number of record moves becomes zero because only the link fields require adjustment. However, we must retain the sequential search used in *insert*.

EXERCISES

1. Write the status of the list $F = (12, 2, 16, 30, 8, 28, 4, 10, 20, 6, 18)$ at the end of each phase of *InsertionSort* (Program 7.5).

2. Write a Pascal procedure that implements binary insertion sort. What is the worst-case number of comparisons made by your sort procedure? What is the worst-case number of record moves made? How do these compare with the corresponding numbers for Program 7.5?

3. Write a Pascal procedure that implements linked insertion sort. What is the worst-case number of comparisons made by your sort procedure? What is the worst-case number of record moves made? How do these compare with the corresponding numbers for Program 7.5?

7.3 QUICK SORT

We now turn our attention to a sorting scheme with very good average behavior. The quick-sort scheme developed by C. A. R. Hoare has the best average behavior among the sorting methods we shall be studying. In insertion sort the pivot key K_i currently controlling the insertion is placed into the correct spot with respect to the sorted sublist (R_1, $\cdots, R_{i-1}$). Quick sort differs from insertion sort in that the pivot key K_i is placed at the correct spot with respect to the whole list. Thus, if key K_i is placed in position $s(i)$, then $K_j \leq K_{s(i)}$ for $j < s(i)$, and $K_j \geq K_{s(i)}$ for $j > s(i)$. Hence, after this positioning has been done, the original list is partitioned into two sublists, one consisting of records $R_1, \cdots, R_{s(i)-1}$ and the other of records $R_{s(i)}+1, \cdots, R_n$. Since in the sorted sequence all records in the first sublist may appear to the left of $s(i)$ and all in the second sublist to the right of $s(i)$, these two sublists may be sorted independently.

Procedure *QuickSort* (Program 7.6) is the resulting procedure. Procedure *InterChange* (x, y) performs $t := x$; $x := y$; $y := t$. To sort elements 1 through n of a list *list*, the procedure invocation is *QuickSort* (*list*, 1, n). Procedure *QuickSort* assumes that *list* $[n + 1]$ has been set to have a key at least as large as the remaining keys.

Example 7.3: The input list has 10 records with keys (26, 5, 37, 1, 61, 11, 59, 15, 48, 19). Figure 7.1 gives the status of the list at each call of *QuickSort*. Square brackets indicate sublists yet to be sorted. □

Analysis of *QuickSort*: The worst-case behavior of *QuickSort* is examined in Exercise 2 and shown to be $O(n^2)$. However, if we are lucky, then each time a record is correctly positioned, the sublist to its left will be of the same size as that to its right. This would

---

procedure *QuickSort*(**var** *list* : *alist*; *l, r* : **integer**);
{Sort records *list* [*l*], $\cdots$, *list* [*r*] into nondecreasing order on field *key*. Key *pivot* = *list* [*l*] . *key* is arbitrarily chosen as the pivot key. Pointers *i* and *j* are used to partition the sublist so that at any time *list* [*m*] . *key* $\leq$ *pivot*, *m* < *i*, and *list* [*m*] . *key* $\geq$ *pivot*, *m* > *j*. It is assumed that *list* [*l*] . *key* $\leq$ *list* [*r* + 1] . *key*.}
var *i, j, pivot* : **integer**;
begin
  if *l* < *r* **then begin**
                i := *l*; *j* := *r* + 1; *pivot* := *list* [*l*] . *key*;
                repeat
                  repeat
                    i := *i* + 1;
                  until *list* [*i*] . *key* >= *pivot*;
                  repeat
                    j := *j* – 1;
                  until *list* [*j*] . *key* <= *pivot*;
                  if *i* < *j* **then** *InterChange* (*list* [*i*], *list* [*j*]);
                until *i* >= *j*;
                InterChange (*list* [*l*], *list* [*j*]);
                QuickSort (*list*, *l, j* – 1);
                QuickSort (*list*, *j* + 1, *r*);
             end; {of **if** *l* < *r*}
end; {of *QuickSort*}

Program 7.6: Quick sort

leave us with the sorting of two sublists, each of size roughly *n*/2. The time required to position a record in a list of size *n* is O(*n*). If *T* (*n*) is the time taken to sort a list of *n* records, then when the list splits roughly into two equal parts each time a record is positioned correctly, we have

$$T(n) \leq cn + 2T(n/2), \text{ for some constant } c$$

$$\leq cn + 2(cn/2 + 2T(n/4))$$

$$\leq 2cn + 4T(n/4)$$

$$\cdot$$
$$\cdot$$
$$\cdot$$

$$\leq cn \log_2 n + nT(1) = O(n \log n)$$

R_1	R_2	R_3	R_4	R_5	R_6	R_7	R_8	R_9	R_{10}	m	n
[26	5	37	1	61	11	59	15	48	19]	1	10
[11	5	19	1	15]	26	[59	61	48	37]	1	5
[1	5]	11	[19	15]	26	[59	61	48	37	1	2
1	5	11	[19	15]	26	[59	61	48	37]	4	5
1	5	11	15	19	26	[59	61	48	37]	7	10
1	5	11	15	19	26	[48	37]	59	[61]	7	8
1	5	11	15	19	26	37	48	59	[61]	10	10
1	5	11	15	19	26	37	48	59	61		

Figure 7.1: Quick-sort example

Lemma 7.1 shows that the average computing time for procedure *QuickSort* is $O(n \log n)$. Moreover, experimental results show that as far as average computing time is concerned, quick sort is the best of the internal sorting methods we shall be studying.

Lemma 7.1: Let $T_{avg}(n)$ be the expected time for procedure *QuickSort* to sort a list with n records. Then there exists a constant k such that $T_{avg}(n) \le kn\log_e n$ for $n \ge 2$.

Proof: In the call to *QuickSort* $(1, n)$, K_1 gets placed at position j. This leaves us with the problem of sorting two sublists of size $j - 1$ and $n - j$. The expected time for this is $T_{avg}(j - 1) + T_{avg}(n - j)$. The remainder of the algorithm clearly takes at most cn time for some constant c. Since j may take on any of the values 1 to n with equal probability, we have

$$T_{avg}(n) \le cn + \frac{1}{n}\sum_{j=1}^{n}(T_{avg}(j - 1) + T_{avg}(n - j)) = cn + \frac{2}{n}\sum_{j=0}^{n-1}T_{avg}(j), \ n \ge 2 \quad (7.1)$$

We may assume $T_{avg}(0) \le b$ and $T_{avg}(1) \le b$ for some constant b. We shall now show $T_{avg}(n) \le kn\log_e n$ for $n \ge 2$ and $k = 2(b + c)$. The proof is by induction on n.

Induction base: For $n = 2$, Eq. (7.1) yields $T_{avg}(2) \le 2c + 2b \le kn\log_e 2$.

Induction hypothesis: Assume $T_{avg}(n) \le kn\log_e n$ for $1 \le n < m$.

Induction step: From Eq. (7.1) and the induction hypothesis we have

$$T_{avg}(m) \le cm + \frac{4b}{m} + \frac{2}{m}\sum_{j=2}^{m-1}T_{avg}(j) \le cm + \frac{4b}{m} + \frac{2k}{m}\sum_{j=2}^{m-1}j\log_e j \quad (7.2)$$

Since $j\log_e j$ is an increasing function of j, Eq. (7.2) yields

$$T_{avg}(m) \leq cm + \frac{4b}{m} + \frac{2k}{m}\int_2^m x\log_e x \, dx = cm + \frac{4b}{m} + \frac{2k}{m}\left[\frac{m^2\log_e m}{2} - \frac{m^2}{4}\right]$$

$$= cm + \frac{4b}{m} + km\log_e m - \frac{km}{2} \leq km\log_e m, \quad \text{for } m \geq 2 \quad \square$$

Unlike insertion sort, where the only additional space needed was for one record, quick sort needs stack space to implement the recursion. If the lists split evenly, as in the above analysis, the maximum recursion depth would be $\log n$, requiring a stack space of $O(\log n)$. The worst case occurs when the list is split into a left sublist of size $n - 1$ and a right sublist of size 0 at each level of recursion. In this case, the depth of recursion becomes n, requiring stack space of $O(n)$. The worst-case stack space can be reduced by a factor of 4 by realizing that right sublists of size less than 2 need not be stacked. An asymptotic reduction in stack space can be achieved by sorting smaller sublists first. In this case the additional stack space is at most $O(\log n)$. $\square$

Variation

Quick sort using a median of three: Our version of quick sort always picked the key of the first record in the current sublist as the pivot. A better choice for this pivot is the median of the first, middle, and last keys in the current sublist. Thus, *pivot = median* $\{K_1, K_{(l+r)/2}, K_r\}$. For example, *median*$\{10, 5, 7\} = 7$ and *median*$\{10, 7, 7\} = 7$.

EXERCISES

1. Write the status of the list $F = (12, 2, 16, 30, 8, 28, 4, 10, 20, 6, 18)$ at the end of each phase of *QuickSort* (Program 7.6).

2. (a) Show that *QuickSort* takes $O(n^2)$ time when the input list is already in sorted order.

   (b) Show that the worst-case time complexity of *QuickSort* is $O(n^2)$.

   (c) Why is *list* $[l]$. *key* $\leq$ *list* $[r + 1]$. *key* required in *QuickSort*?

3. (a) Write a nonrecursive version of *QuickSort* incorporating the median-of-three rule to determine the pivot key.

   (b) Show that this procedure takes $O(n \log n)$ time on an already sorted list.

4. Show that if smaller sublists are sorted first, then the recursion in *QuickSort* can be simulated by a stack of depth $O(\log n)$.

5. Quick sort is an unstable sorting method. Give an example of an input list in which the order of records with equal keys is not preserved.

7.4   HOW FAST CAN WE SORT?

Both of the sorting methods we have seen so far have a worst-case behavior of O(n^2). It is natural at this point to ask the question, What is the best computing time for sorting that we can hope for? The theorem we shall prove shows that if we restrict our question to sorting algorithms in which the only operations permitted on keys are comparisons and interchanges, then O($n \log n$) is the best possible time.

The method we use is to consider a tree that describes the sorting process. Each vertex of the tree represents a key comparison, and the branches indicate the result. Such a tree is called a *decision tree*. A path through a decision tree represents a sequence of computations that an algorithm could produce.

Example 7.4: Let us look at the decision tree obtained for insertion sort working on a list with three records (Figure 7.2). The input sequence is R_1, R_2, and R_3, so the root of the tree is labeled [1, 2, 3]. Depending on the outcome of the comparison between keys K_1 and K_2, this sequence may or may not change. If $K_2 < K_1$, then the sequence becomes [2, 1, 3]; otherwise it stays [1, 2, 3]. The full tree resulting from these comparisons is given in Figure 7.2.

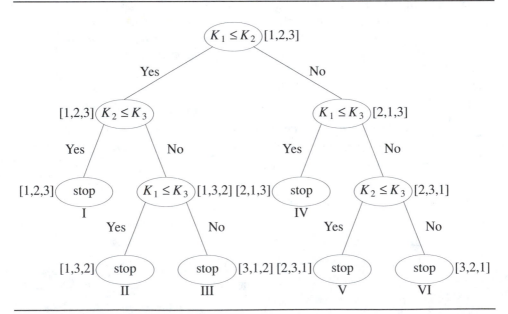

Figure 7.2: Decision tree for insertion sort

The leaf nodes are labeled I to VI. These are the only points at which the algorithm may terminate. Hence, only six permutations of the input sequence are obtainable from this algorithm. Since all six of these are different, and 3! = 6, it follows that this algorithm has enough leaves to constitute a valid sorting algorithm for three records. The maximum depth of this tree is 3. Figure 7.3 gives six different orderings of the key values 7, 9, and 10, which show that all six permutations are possible. $\square$

leaf	permutation	sample input key values that give the permutation
I	1 2 3	[7, 9, 10]
II	1 3 2	[7, 10, 9]
III	3 1 2	[9, 10, 7]
IV	2 1 3	[9, 7, 10]
V	2 3 1	[10, 7, 9]
VI	3 2 1	[10, 9, 7]

Figure 7.3: Sample input permutations

Theorem 7.1: Any decision tree that sorts n distinct elements has a height of at least $\log_2(n!) + 1$.

Proof: When sorting n elements, there are $n!$ different possible results. Thus, every decision tree for sorting must have at least $n!$ leaves. But a decision tree is also a binary tree, which can have at most 2^{k-1} leaves if its height is k. Therefore, the height must be at least $\log_2 n! + 1$. $\square$

Corollary: Any algorithm that sorts only by comparisons must have a worst-case computing time of $\Omega(n \log n)$.

Proof: We must show that for every decision tree with $n!$ leaves, there is a path of length $cn\log_2 n$, where c is a constant. By the theorem, there is a path of length $\log_2 n!$. Now

$$n! = n(n-1)(n-2) \cdots (3)(2)(1) \geq (n/2)^{n/2}$$

So, $\log_2 n! \geq (n/2)\log_2(n/2) = \Omega(n\log n)$. $\square$

Using a similar argument and the fact that binary trees with 2^n leaves must have an average root-to-leaf path length of $\Omega(n \log n)$, we can show that the average complexity of comparison-based sorting methods is $\Omega(n \log n)$.

7.5 MERGE SORT

7.5.1 Merging

Before looking at the merge-sort method to sort n records, let us see how one may merge two sorted lists to get a single sorted list. We shall examine two different algorithms. The first one, Program 7.7, is very simple and uses $O(n)$ additional space. The two lists to be merged are $(x_l, \cdots, x_m)$ and $(x_{m+1}, \cdots, x_n)$. The resulting merged list is $(z_l, \cdots, z_n)$.

```
procedure merge(var x, z : alist; l, m, n : integer);
{(x [l], ⋯, x [m]) and (x [m + 1], ⋯, x [n]) are sorted lists with keys
x [l] . key ≤ ⋯ ≤ x [m] . key and x [m + 1] . key ≤ ⋯ ≤ x [n] . key. These lists are
merged to obtain the sorted list (z [l], ⋯, z [n]), z [l] . key ≤ ⋯ ≤ z [n] . key.}
var i, j, k, t : integer;
begin
    i := l; k := l; j := m + 1; {i, j, and k are positions in the three lists}
    while ((i <= m) and (j <= n)) do
    begin
        if x [i] . key <= x [j] . key then begin
                                z [k] := x [i];
                                i := i + 1;
                            end
                        else begin
                                z [k] := x [j];
                                j := j + 1;
                            end;
        k := k + 1;
    end; {of while}
    if i > m then      {(z_k, ⋯, z_n) := (x_j, ⋯, x_n)}
            for t := j to n do z [k + t − j] :=x [t]
        else      {(z_k, ⋯, z_m) := (x_j, ⋯, x_m)}
            for t := i to m do z [k + t − i] := x [t];
end; {of merge}
```

Program 7.7: Merging two sorted lists

Analysis of *merge*: At each iteration of the **while** loop, k increases by 1. The total increment in k is $n − l + 1$. Hence, the **while** loop is iterated at most $n − l + 1$ times. The **if** statement moves at most one record per iteration. The total time is therefore $O(n − l + 1)$.

If each record has a size s, then the time is $O(s(n - l + 1))$. When s is greater than 1, we can use linked lists for $(x_1, \cdots, x_m)$ and $(x_{m+1}, \cdots, x_n)$ and obtain a new sorted linked list containing these $n - l + 1$ records. Now, we will not need the additional space for $n - l + 1$ records as needed in *merge* for the array z. Instead, space for $n - l + 1$ links is needed. The merge time becomes $O(n - l + 1)$ and is independent of s. Note that $n - l + 1$ is the number of records being merged. $\square$

The second merging algorithm we shall consider is more complex. However, it requires only $O(1)$ additional space. We assume that $l = 1$. With this assumption the total number of records in the two lists being merged is n. Our discussion will make the further simplifying assumptions that n is a perfect square and that the number of records in each of the two lists to be merged is a multiple of $\sqrt{n}$. The development of the full algorithm with these assumptions removed is left as an exercise.

Suppose that $n = 36$ and that each of the two lists to be merged has 18 records. The first line of Figure 7.4 gives an example. Only the record keys are shown. We assume that the sorted key sequence is 0, 1, . . ., a, b, . . ., z. The vertical bar separates the two sorted lists of size 18 each. Each list can be thought of as consisting of sorted blocks of size $\sqrt{n} = 6$. The first step in the $O(1)$ merge is to create a block that consists of the $\sqrt{n}$ records with the largest keys. This is done by scanning the two sorted lists from the right end to the left end. From this scan we discover that the $\sqrt{n}$ largest keys are those that are boxed in line 2 of Figure 7.4.

Next, the records from the second list that are in the set of $\sqrt{n}$ records with largest keys are exchanged with the same number of records just to the left of those in the first list that are in this set. This exchange results in the configuration of line 3 of the figure. The vertical bars partition the n records into blocks of $\sqrt{n}$ consecutive records. Notice that the $\sqrt{n}$ records with largest keys form a single block. This block is now swapped with the leftmost block, and the rightmost block is sorted to get line 4. The $\sqrt{n} - 1$ blocks, excluding the one with the largest keys, are sorted by their rightmost records to get line 5. This completes the preprocessing needed to commence the merge.

The merge consists of several merge substeps, in each of which two segments of records are merged together. The first segment is the longest sorted sequence of records beginning at block two. Observe that this will always end at a block boundary. The second sequence consists solely of the next block. In the case of line 5, both of these sequences consist of exactly one block. A merge substep uses three place markers, which are depicted in line 5 by the symbol •. The leftmost marker indicates the position where the next merged record is to go. The second marker points to the next unmerged record of the first segment, and the third marker points to the next unmerged record of the second segment. Initially these are, respectively, positioned at the first records of the leftmost block, segment one, and segment two. The two segments are merged by comparing the two keys indicated by the second and third markers and exchanging the record with smaller key (in case of a tie, the record in the first segment is used) with the record indicated by the first marker. Following the first such exchange, we get line 6. Lines 7 and 8 show the configuration following each of the next two exchanges. This merge exchanging continues until all of the first segment has been merged. In our example, eight

0 2 4 6 8 a c e g i j k *l* m n t w z | 1 3 5 7 9 b d f h o p q r s u v x y

0 2 4 6 8 a c e g i j k *l* m n t [w z] 1 3 5 7 9 b d f h o p q r s [u v x y]

0 2 4 6 8 a | c e g i j k | u v x y w z | 1 3 5 7 9 b | d f h o p q | r s *l* m n t

u v x y w z | c e g i j k | 0 2 4 6 8 a | 1 3 5 7 9 b | d f h o p q | *l* m n r s t

u v x y w z 0 2 4 6 8 a | 1 3 5 7 9 b | c e g i j k | d f h o p q | *l* m n r s t

0 v x y w z u 2 4 6 8 a | 1 3 5 7 9 b | c e g i j k | d f h o p q | *l* m n r s t

0 1 x y w z u 2 4 6 8 a | v 3 5 7 9 b | c e g i j k | d f h o p q | *l* m n r s t

0 1 2 y w z u x 4 6 8 a | v 3 5 7 9 b | c e g i j k | d f h o p q | *l* m n r s t

Figure 7.4: First eight lines for O(1) space merge example

more records are merged before the current merge substep terminates. Line 1 of Figure 7.5 shows the configuration after the records with keys 3, 4, and 5 have been merged; line 2 shows the configuration following the merging of the records with keys 6, 7, and 8; and line 3 shows the status after segment one has been fully merged.

The following observations allow us to conclude that the merge of a merge substep can always be done as just described without using extra space beyond that needed to exchange two records:

(1)   There are $\sqrt{n}$ records from the initial position of the first marker to that of the second marker.

(2)   The second segment has $\sqrt{n}$ records.

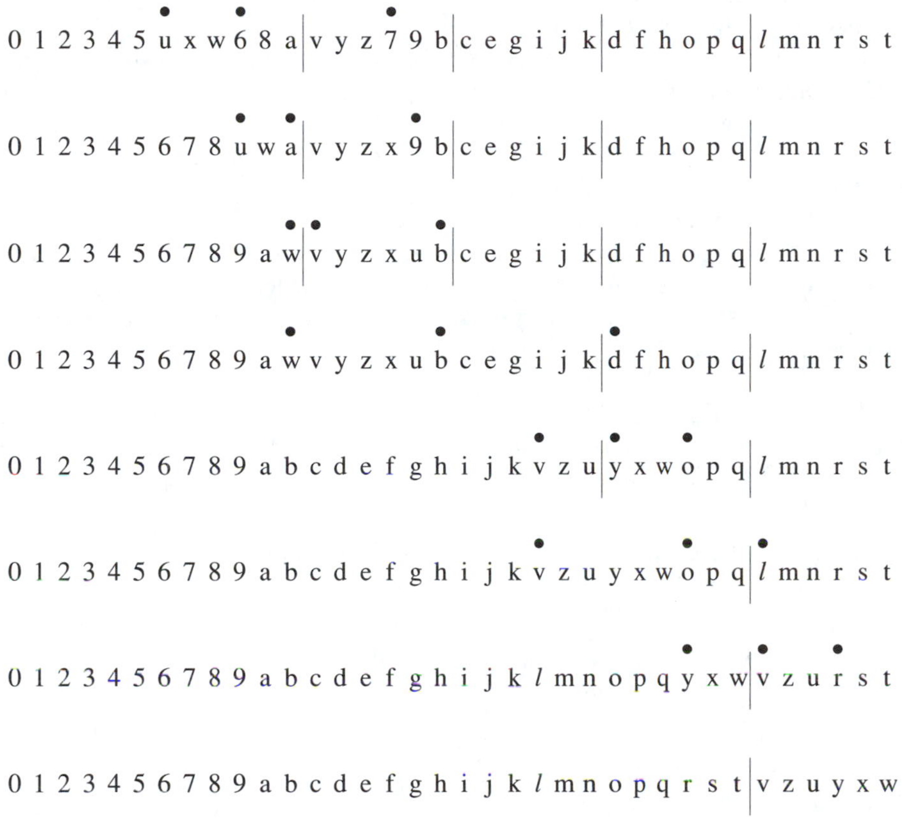

0 1 2 3 4 5 u x w 6 8 a|v y z 7 9 b|c e g i j k|d f h o p q‖l m n r s t

0 1 2 3 4 5 6 7 8 u w a|v y z x 9 b|c e g i j k|d f h o p q‖l m n r s t

0 1 2 3 4 5 6 7 8 9 a w|v y z x u b|c e g i j k|d f h o p q‖l m n r s t

0 1 2 3 4 5 6 7 8 9 a w v y z x u b c e g i j k|d f h o p q‖l m n r s t

0 1 2 3 4 5 6 7 8 9 a b c d e f g h i j k v z u|y x w o p q‖l m n r s t

0 1 2 3 4 5 6 7 8 9 a b c d e f g h i j k v z u y x w o p q‖l m n r s t

0 1 2 3 4 5 6 7 8 9 a b c d e f g h i j k l m n o p q y x w|v z u r s t

0 1 2 3 4 5 6 7 8 9 a b c d e f g h i j k l m n o p q r s t|v z u y x w

Figure 7.5: Last eight lines for O(1) space merge example

(3)   Because of the tie breaker rule and the initial ordering of blocks by their last records, the first segment will be fully merged before the second.

When a merge substep is complete, the $\sqrt{n}$ records with largest keys are contiguous, and the first marker points to the first of these records. The third marker points to the first unmerged record in the second segment. The first segment for the next merge substep is the longest sorted segment that begins at the third marker. This segment always ends at a block boundary. The next block forms the second segment. In the case of our example, the first segment begins at the record with key b and the second begins at the record with key d. Line 4 of Figure 7.5 shows the initial positions of the three markers. Line 5 shows the configuration after the first segment has been fully merged.

The first segment for the next merge substep begins at the record pointed at by the third marker. We find a longest sorted sequence that begins here. This consists of just three records. The next block forms the second sequence. The initial positions of the three markers for the third sort substep are shown in line 6 of the figure. Line 7 shows the status after this substep is complete. Now the longest sorted sequence that begins at the third marker consists of the records with keys r, s, and t. Since there is no next block, the second segment is empty. The last merge substep results in the configuration of line 8. Since the second segment is empty to begin with, the last merge substep can be performed using just two markers that move to the right one position at a time. We simply exchange the records indicated by these two markers.

Once the merge substeps have been performed, the block of records with largest keys is at the right end and may be sorted using an O(1) space sorting algorithm such as insertion sort. The steps involved in the O(1) space merge algorithm just described are summarized in Program 7.8.

{Steps in an O(1) space merge when the total number of records, n, is a perfect square, and the number of records in each of the lists to be merged is a multiple of $\sqrt{n}$.}

Step 1: Identify the $\sqrt{n}$ records with largest keys. This is done by following right to left along the two lists to be merged.

Step 2: Exchange the records of the second list that were identified in Step 1 with those just to the left of those identified from the first list so that the $\sqrt{n}$ records with largest keys are contiguous.

Step 3: Swap the block of $\sqrt{n}$ largest records with the leftmost block (unless it is already the leftmost block). Sort the rightmost block.

Step 4: Reorder the blocks, excluding the block of largest records, into nondecreasing order of the last key in the blocks.

Step 5: Perform as many merge substeps as needed to merge the $\sqrt{n} - 1$ blocks, other than the block with the largest keys.

Step 6: Sort the block with the largest keys.

Program 7.8: O(1) space merge

Analysis of O(1) space merge: For the complexity analysis, we see that Steps 1 and 2 and the swapping of Step 3 each take O($\sqrt{n}$) time and O(1) space. The sort of Step 3 can be done in O(n) time and O(1) space using insertion sort. Step 4 can be done in O(n) time and O(1) space using a selection sort (see Chapter 1). Note that selection sort sorts m records using O(m^2) key comparisons and O(m) record moves. When selection sort is used to implement Step 4 of Program 7.8, each block of $\sqrt{n}$ records is regarded as a single record with key equal to that of the last record in the block. So, each record move of selection sort actually moves a block of size $\sqrt{n}$. The number of key comparisons is $O(n)$, and although the number of block moves is $O(\sqrt{n})$, the time needed for these moves is $O(n)$. Note that if insertion sort is used in place of selection sort, the time becomes $O(n^{1.5})$, as insertion sort makes $O(m^2)$ record moves when sorting m records. So, in this application insertion sort is inferior to selection sort. The total number of merge substeps is at most $\sqrt{n} - 1$. The end point of the first segment for each merge substep can be found in time proportional to the number of blocks in the segment, as we need merely find the first block whose last key is greater than the first key of the next block. The time for each substep is therefore linear in the number of records merged. Hence, the total time for Step 5 is $O(n)$. The sort of Step 6 can be done in $O(n)$ time using either a selection or an insertion sort. When the steps of Program 7.8 are implemented as described here, the total time is $O(n)$, and the additional space used is $O(1)$. □

7.5.2 Iterative Merge Sort

This version begins by interpreting the input as n sorted lists, each of length 1. These lists are merged by pairs to obtain $n/2$ lists, each of size 2 (if n is odd, then one list is of size 1). These $n/2$ lists are then merged by pairs, and so on until we are left with only one list. The example below illustrates the process.

Example 7.5: The input list is (26, 5, 77, 1, 61, 11, 59, 15, 48, 19). The tree of Figure 7.6 illustrates the sublists being merged at each pass. □

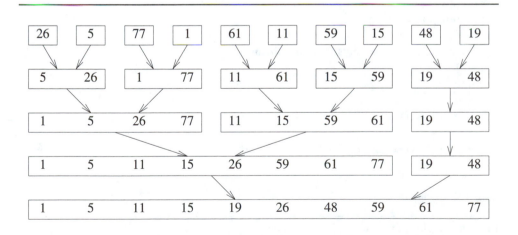

Figure 7.6: Merge tree

Since a merge sort consists of several merge passes, it is convenient first to write a procedure (Program 7.9) for this. Now the sort can be done by repeatedly invoking this procedure as in Program 7.10.

---

procedure *MergePass*(**var** *x*, *y* : *alist*; *n*, *l* : **integer**);
{One pass of merge sort. Adjacent pairs of sublists of length *l* are merged from list *x* to list *y*. *n* is the number of records in *x*.}
var *i*, *t* : **integer**;
begin
  i := 1;
  while *i* <= ($n - 2*l + 1$) **do**
  begin
    merge (*x*, *y*, *i*, $i + l - 1$, $i + 2*l - 1$);
    i := $i + 2*l$;
  end;
  {merge remaining list of length $< 2*l$}
  if ($i + l - 1$) $< n$ **then** *merge* (*x*, *y*, *i*, $i + l - 1$, *n*)
  else for *t* := *i* **to** *n* **do** *y* [*t*] := *x* [*t*];
end; {of *MergePass*}

Program 7.9: Merge pass

---

procedure *MergeSort*(**var** *x* : *alist*; *n* : **integer**);
{Sort list *x* into nondecreasing order of the keys *x* [1] . *key*, $\cdots$, *x* [*n*] . *key*.}
var *l* : **integer**; *y* : *alist*;
begin
  {*l* is the length of the sublist currently being merged}
  l := 1;
  while *l* $< n$ **do**
  begin
    MergePass (*x*, *y*, *n*, *l*);
    l := $2 * l$;
    MergePass (*y*, *x*, *n*, *l*); {interchange role of *x* and *y*}
    l := $2 * l$;
  end
end; {of *MergeSort*}

Program 7.10: Merge sort

Analysis of *MergeSort*: Procedure *MergeSort* makes several passes over the records being sorted. In the first pass, lists of size 1 are merged. In the second, the size of the lists being merged is 2. On the ith pass the lists being merged are of size 2^{i-1}. Consequently, a total of $\lceil \log_2 n \rceil$ passes are made over the data. Since two lists can be merged in linear time (procedure *merge*), each pass of merge sort takes O(n)time. The total computing time is O($n \log n$). $\square$

It is easy to verify that *MergeSort* results in a stable sorting procedure.

7.5.3   Recursive Merge Sort

In the recursive formulation we divide the list to be sorted into two roughly equal parts called the left and the right sublists. These sublists are sorted recursively, and the sorted sublists are merged.

Example 7.6: The input list (26, 5, 77, 1, 61, 11, 59, 15, 49, 19) is to be sorted using the recursive formulation of merge sort. If the sublist from l to u is currently to be sorted, then its two sublists are indexed from l to $\lfloor (l + u)/2 \rfloor$ and from $\lfloor (l + u)/2 \rfloor + 1$ to u. The sublist partitioning that takes place is described by the binary tree of Figure 7.7. Note that the sublists being merged are different from those being merged in *MergeSort*. $\square$

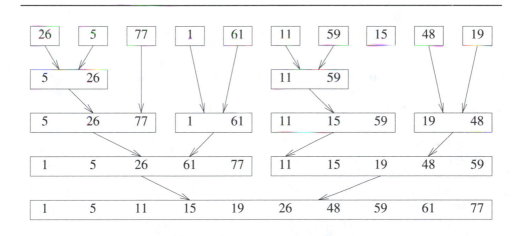

Figure 7.7: Sublist partitioning for recursive merge sort

From the preceding example, we see that if procedure *merge* (Program 7.7) is used to merge sorted sublists from one array into another, then it is necessary to copy sublists. For example to merge [5, 26] and [77], we would have to copy [77] into the same array as [5, 26]. To avoid this unnecessary copying of sublists, we look to a linked list representation for sublists. This results in an efficient recursive version of merge sort.

Each record is assumed to have three fields: *link*, *key*, and *other*. The record structure is defined as

$$\textbf{type } records = \textbf{record}$$
$$key : \textbf{integer};$$
$$other : fields;$$
$$link : \textbf{integer};$$
$$\textbf{end};$$
$$alist = \textbf{array } [0 .. MaxSize] \textbf{ of } records;$$

$r[i].link$ and $r[i].key$ are the link and key value fields in record i, $1 \le i \le n$. Note that for this application, the *link* fields are of type **integer** and not of type **pointer**. We assume that initially $alist[i].link = 0$, $1 \le i \le n$. Thus, each record is initially in a chain containing only itself. Let q and r be pointers to two chains of records. The records on each chain are assumed linked in nondecreasing order of the key field. Let *ListMerge* (q, r, p) be a procedure to merge two chains q and r to obtain chain p that is linked in nondecreasing order of key values. The recursive version of merge sort is given by procedure *rMergeSort* (Program 7.11). To sort the list $x_1, \cdots, x_n$ this procedure is invoked as *rMergeSort* (x,l,n,p). p is returned as the start of a chain ordered as described earlier. If the list is to be physically rearranged into this order, one of the schemes discussed in Section 7.8 may be used. Procedure *ListMerge* is given in Program 7.12.

---

procedure *rMergeSort*(**var** x : *alist*; l, u : **integer**; **var** p : **integer**);
{List $x = (x[l], \cdots, x[u])$ is to be sorted on the field *key*. *link* is a link field in each record that is initially 0. The sorted list is a chain beginning at p. $x[0]$ is a record for intermediate results used only in *ListMerge*.}
var *mid*, q, r : **integer**;
begin
  if $l >= u$ **then** $p := l$
  else begin
       mid := $(l + u)$ **div** 2;
       rMergeSort (x, l, mid, q);
       rMergeSort $(x, mid+1, u, r)$;
       ListMerge (x, q, r, p);
    end; {of **if**}
end; {of *rMergeSort*}

Program 7.11: Recursive merge sort

Analysis of *rMergeSort*: It is easy to see that the recursive merge sort is stable, and its computing time is O($n \log n$). $\square$

procedure *ListMerge* (**var** *x* : *alist*; *u, y* : **integer**; **var** *z* : **integer**);
{The sorted linked lists *u* and *y* are merged to obtain the sorted linked list *z*. Integer
links are assumed. The list of records is named *x* and is of type *alist*.}
var *i* ,*j* : **integer**;
begin
　　i := *u*; *j* := *y*; *z* := 0;
　　while ((*i* < > 0) **and** (*j* < > 0)) **do**
　　　if *x* [*i*] . *key* <= *x* [*j*] . *key*
　　　then begin
　　　　　　x [*z*] . *link* := *i*;
　　　　　　z := *i*; *i* := *x* [*i*] . *link*;
　　　　　end
　　　else begin
　　　　　　x [*z*] . *link* := *j*;
　　　　　　z := *j*; *j* := *x* [*j*] . *link*;
　　　　　end;
　　{move remainder}
　　if *i* = 0 **then** *x* [*z*] . *link* := *j*
　　　　　else *x* [*z*] . *link* := *i*;
　　z := *x* [0] . *link*;
end; {of *ListMerge*}

Program 7.12: Merging linked lists

Variation

Natural merge sort: We can modify *MergeSort* to take into account the prevailing order
within the input list. In this implementation we make an initial pass over the data to
determine the sublists of records that are in order. The merge sort then uses these initially ordered sublists for the remainder of the passes. Figure 7.8 shows natural merge sort
using the input sequence of Example 7.6.

EXERCISES

1.　Write a procedure to shift the records $(x_1, \cdots, x_n)$ circularly to the right by p, $0 \le$
　　$p \le n$, positions. Your procedure should have time complexity $O(n)$ and space
　　complexity $O(1)$. (Hint: Use three calls to a segment reversal procedure.)

2.　The two sorted lists $(x_1, \cdots, x_m)$ and $(x_{m+1}, \cdots, x_n)$ are to be merged to get the
　　sorted list $(x_l, \cdots, x_n)$. Let $s = \lfloor \sqrt{n} \rfloor$.

　　(a)　Assume that one of these lists has fewer than s records. Write a procedure to
　　　　merge the two sorted lists in $O(n)$ time while using only $O(1)$ additional

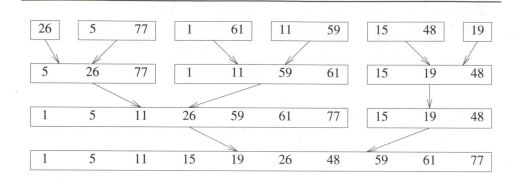

Figure 7.8: Natural merge sort

space. Show that your procedure actually has these complexities. (Hint: If the first list has fewer than s elements, then find the position, q, in the merged list of the first element of the first list; perform a circular shift of $q-1$ as in the preceding exercise. This circular shift involves only the records of the first list and the first $q-1$ records of the second. Following the circular shift, the first q records are in their final merged positions. Repeat this process for the second, third, and remaining elements of the initial first list.)

(b) Assume that both lists have at least s elements. Write a merge procedure with the same asymptotic complexity as that for (a). Show that your procedure actually has this complexity. (Hint: Partition the first list such that the first block has $s_1, 0 \le s_1 < s$, records and the remainder have s records. Partition the second list so that the last block has $s_2, 0 \le s_2 < s$ records. If $s_1 \ne 0$, then compare the first blocks of the two lists to identify the s_1 records with smallest key. Perform a swap as in Step 2 of Program 7.8 so that these s_1 records are in the leftmost block of the first list. If $s_2 \ne 0$, then using a similar process, we can get the s_2 records with largest keys into the rightmost block of the second list. Now, the leftmost block of size s_1 and the rightmost block of size s_2 are sorted. Following this, we may forget about them. The remaining blocks of the first and second lists may be arranged in sorted order using the merge procedure of part (a). Next, Program 7.8 may be used to merge them.)

(c) Use the procedures for (a) and (b) to obtain an O(n) time and O(1) space procedure to merge two lists of arbitrary size.

(d) Compare the run time of the merge procedure of (c) with that of Program 7.7. Use $m = n/2$ and the values $n = 100, 250, 500, 1000, 2000, 5000,$ and

10,000. For each value of n use ten randomly generated pairs of sorted lists and compute the average merge time. Plot these for the two merge procedures. What conclusions can you draw?

(e) Modify your procedure for part (b) so that it does not use the procedure of (a) to rearrange records in the first and second lists into sorted order. Rather, the last and first blocks of the first and second lists, respectively, are sorted. To find the largest s records we need to look at the last two blocks of the first list and the last block of the second list. Program this procedure and obtain run times using the data of (d). Add these to your plot of (d).

(f) Program the $O(1)$ space merge procedure as described by Huang and Langston in their paper cited in the References and Selected Readings section. This procedure begins by partitioning the first list as in (b). The second list is partitioned into blocks of size s, except for the last block whose size s_2 is such that $s \leq s_2 < 2*s$. The largest s records are found and placed in the rightmost block of the first list. This is called the merge buffer. The rightmost block of the second list (i.e., the one with size s_2) is sorted. If $s_1 > 0$, the leftmost block of the first list is merged with the leftmost block of the second list using the last s_1 positions of the merge buffer. A swap of the leftmost s_1 records and those in the rightmost s_1 positions of the merge buffer results in moving the s_1 smallest records to their final place and also restores the merge buffer to contain the largest s records. Now we can forget about the first s_1 records and proceed to move the merge buffer to the leftmost block of size s and sort the remaining blocks by their last records. One of these blocks is of size s_2, and the sort should take this into account. Obtain the run times for this procedure using the data of (d). Add these results to your plot of (d). What conclusions can you draw?

3. Write the status of the list $F = (12, 2, 16, 30, 8, 28, 4, 10, 20, 6, 18)$ at the end of each phase of *MergeSort* (Program 7.10).

4. Suppose we use Program 7.8 to obtain a merge sort procedure. Is the resulting procedure a stable sort?

5. Prove that *MergeSort* is stable.

6. Write an iterative natural merge sort procedure using arrays as in procedure *MergeSort*. How much time does this procedure take on an initially sorted list? Note that *MergeSort* takes $O(n \log n)$ on such an input list. What is the worst-case computing time of the new procedure? How much additional space is needed?

7. Do the previous exercise using linked lists.

7.6 HEAP SORT

Although the merge sort scheme discussed in the previous section has a computing time of O(n log n) both in the worst case and as average behavior, it requires additional storage proportional to the number of records in the file being sorted. By using the O(1) space merge algorithm, the space requirements can be reduced to O(1). The resulting sort algorithm is significantly slower than the original one. The sorting method, heap sort, we are about to study requires only a fixed amount of additional storage and at the same time has as its worst-case and average computing time O(n log n). Although heap sort is slightly slower than merge sort using O(n) additional space, it is faster than merge sort using O(1) additional space.

In heap sort, we utilize the max-heap structure introduced in Chapter 5. The deletion and insertion procedures associated with max heaps directly yield an O(n log n) sorting method. The n records are first inserted into an initially empty heap. Next, the records are extracted from the heap one at a time. It is possible to create the heap of n records faster by using the procedure *adjust* (Program 7.13). This procedure takes a binary tree T, whose left and right subtrees satisfy the heap property but whose root may not, and adjusts T so that the entire binary tree satisfies the heap property. If the depth of the tree with root i is d, then the **while** loop is executed at most d times. Hence the computing time of *adjust* is O(d).

To sort the list, first we create a max heap by using *adjust* repeatedly, as in the first **for** loop of procedure *HeapSort* (Program 7.14). Next, we make $n - 1$ passes over the list. On each pass, we exchange the first record in the heap with the last record. Since the first record always contains the highest key, this record is now in its sorted position. We then decrement the heap size and readjust the heap. For example, on the first pass, we place the record with the highest key in the nth position; on the second pass, we place the record with the second highest key in position $n - 1$; and on the ith pass, we place the record with the ith highest key in position $n - i + 1$. The invocation is *HeapSort(list, n)*.

Example 7.7: The input list is (26, 5, 77, 1, 61, 11, 59, 15, 48, 19). If we interpret this list as a binary tree, we get the tree of Figure 7.9(a). Figure 7.9(b) depicts the max heap after the first **for** loop of *HeapSort*. Figure 7.10 shows the array of records following each of the first seven iterations of the second **for** loop. The portion of the array that still represents a max heap is shown as a binary tree; the sorted part of the array is shown as an array. □

Analysis of *HeapSort*: Suppose $2^{k-1} \leq n < 2^k$, so the tree has k levels and the number of nodes on level i is $\leq 2^{i-1}$. In the first **for** loop, *adjust* (Program 7.13) is called once for each node that has a child. Hence, the time required for this loop is the sum, over each level, of the number of nodes on a level multiplied by the maximum distance the node can move. This is no more than

$$\sum_{1 \leq i \leq k} 2^{i-1}(k-i) = \sum_{1 \leq i \leq k-1} 2^{k-i-1} i \leq n \sum_{1 \leq i \leq k-1} i/2^i < 2n = O(n)$$

```
procedure adjust(var tree : alist; i,n : integer);
{Adjust the binary tree with root i to satisfy the heap property.  The left and right
subtrees of i already satisfy the heap property.  No node has index greater than n.}
var j, k : integer; r : records; done : boolean;
begin
   done := false;
   r := tree [i ];
   k := tree [i ] . key;
   j := 2 * i;
   while ((j <= n) and not done) do
   begin {first find max of left and right child}
      if j < n then if  tree [j ] . key < tree [j + 1] . key then j := j + 1;
      {compare max. child with k. If k is max, then done.}
      if k >= tree [j ] . key then done := true
      else begin
             tree [j div 2] := tree [j ]; {move jth record up the tree}
             j := 2*j;
          end;
   end;
   tree [j div 2] := r;
end; {of adjust}
```

Program 7.13: Adjusting a max heap

```
procedure HeapSort(var r : alist ; n : integer);
{The list r = (r [1], · · · , r [n ]) is sorted into nondecreasing order of the field key.}
var i : integer; t : records;
begin
   for i := (n div 2) downto 1 do {convert r into a heap}
      adjust (r,i,n);
   for i := (n − 1) downto 1 do {sort r}
   begin
      t := r [i + 1]; r [i + 1] := r [1]; r [1] := t; {interchange r₁ and rᵢ₊₁}
      adjust (r, 1,i); {recreate heap}
   end;
end; {of HeapSort}
```

Program 7.14: Heap sort

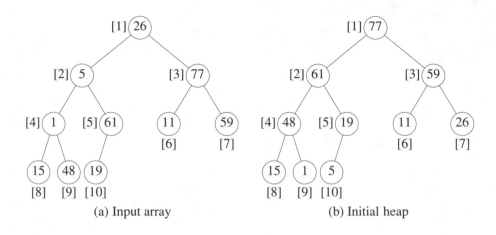

(a) Input array   (b) Initial heap

Figure 7.9: Array interpreted as a binary tree

In the next **for** loop, $n - 1$ applications of *adjust* are made with maximum depth $k = \lceil \log_2 (n + 1) \rceil$. Hence, the computing time for this loop is $O(n \log n)$. Consequently, the total computing time is $O(n \log n)$. Note that apart from some simple variables, the only additional space needed is space for one record to carry out the interchange in the second **for** loop. $\square$

EXERCISES

1. Write the status of the list $F = (12, 2, 16, 30, 8, 28, 4, 10, 20, 6, 18)$ at the end of each phase of *HeapSort* (Program 7.14).

2. Heap sort is unstable. Give an example of an input list in which the order of records with equal keys is not preserved.

7.7   SORTING ON SEVERAL KEYS

We now look at the problem of sorting records on several keys, $K^1, K^2, \cdots, K^r$ (K^1 is the most significant key and K^r the least). A list of records $R_1, \cdots, R_n$ is said to be sorted with respect to the keys $K^1, K^2, \cdots, K^r$ iff for every pair of records i and j, $i < j$ and $(K_i^1, \cdots, K_i^r) \le (K_j^1, \cdots, K_j^r)$. The r-tuple $(x_1, \cdots, x_r)$ is less than or equal to the r-tuple $(y_1, \cdots, y_r)$ iff either $x_i = y_i$, $1 \le i \le j$, and $x_{j+1} < y_{j+1}$ for some $j < r$, or $x_i = y_i$, $1 \le i \le r$.

For example, the problem of sorting a deck of cards may be regarded as a sort on two keys, the suit and face values, with the following ordering relations:

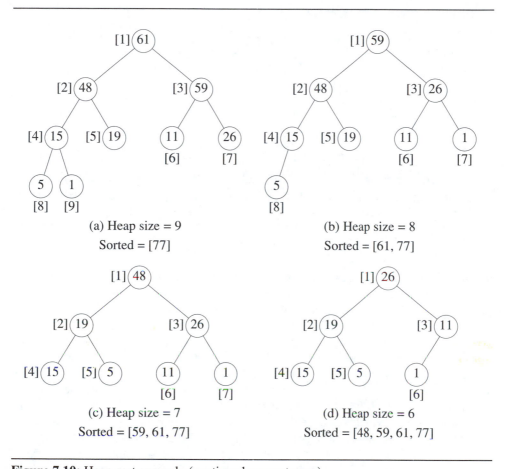

(a) Heap size = 9
Sorted = [77]

(b) Heap size = 8
Sorted = [61, 77]

(c) Heap size = 7
Sorted = [59, 61, 77]

(d) Heap size = 6
Sorted = [48, 59, 61, 77]

Figure 7.10: Heap sort example (continued on next page)

K^1 [Suits]:   ♣ < ♦ < ♥ < ♠

K^2 [Face values]:   2 < 3 < 4 ⋯ < 10 < J < Q < K < A

A sorted deck of cards therefore has the following ordering:

$$2♣, \ldots, A♣, \ldots, 2♠, \ldots, A♠$$

There are two popular ways to sort on multiple keys. In the first, we begin by sorting on the most significant key K^1, obtaining several ''piles'' of records, each having the same value for K^1. Then each of these piles is independently sorted on the key K^2 into ''subpiles'' such that all the records in the same subpile have the same values for K^1 and K^2. The subpiles are then sorted on K^3, and so on, and the piles are combined. Using

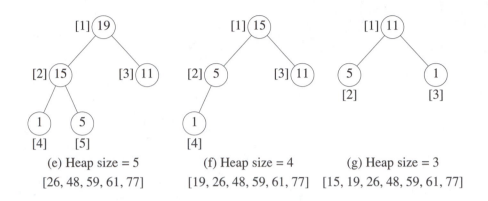

(e) Heap size = 5
[26, 48, 59, 61, 77]

(f) Heap size = 4
[19, 26, 48, 59, 61, 77]

(g) Heap size = 3
[15, 19, 26, 48, 59, 61, 77]

Figure 7.10: Heap sort example

this method on our card deck example, we would first sort the 52 cards into four piles, one for each of the suit values, then sort each pile on the face value. Then we would place the piles on top of each other to obtain the desired ordering.

A sort proceeding in this fashion is referred to as a most-significant-digit-first (MSD) sort. The second way, quite naturally, is to sort on the least significant digit first (LSD). An LSD sort would mean sorting the cards first into 13 piles corresponding to their face values (key K^2). Then, we would place the 3's on top of the 2's, $\cdots$, the kings on top of the queens, the aces on top of the kings; we would turn the deck upside down and sort on the suit (K^1) using a stable sorting method to obtain four piles, each orderd on K^2; and we would combine the piles to obtain the required ordering on the cards.

Comparing the two procedures outlined here (MSD and LSD), we see that LSD is simpler, as the piles and subpiles obtained do not have to be sorted independently (provided the sorting scheme used for sorting on the keys K^i, $1 \le i < r$, is stable). This in turn implies less overhead.

The terms LSD and MSD specify only the order in which the keys are to be sorted. They do not specify how each key is to be sorted. When sorting a card deck manually, we generally use an MSD sort. The sorting on suit is done by a *bin sort* (i.e., four "bins" are set up, one for each suit value and the cards are placed into their corresponding bins). Next, the cards in each bin are sorted using an algorithm similar to insertion sort. However, there is another way to do this. First use a bin sort on the face value. To do this we need 13 bins, one for each distinct face value. Then collect all the cards together as described above and perform a bin sort on the suits using four bins. Note that a bin sort requires only O(n) time if the spread in key values is O(n).

LSD or MSD sorting can be used to sort even when the records have only one key. For this, we interpret the key as being composed of several subkeys. For example, if the keys are numeric, then each decimal digit may be regarded as a subkey. So, if the keys are in the range $0 \leq K \leq 999$, we can use either the LSD or MSD sorts for three keys (K^1, K^2, K^3), where K^1 is the digit in the hundredths place, K^2 the digit in the tens place, and K^3 the digit in the units place. Since $0 \leq K^i \leq 9$ for each key K^i, the sort on each key can be carried out using a bin sort with 10 bins.

In a *radix sort*, we decompose the sort key using some radix r. When r is 10, we get the decimal decomposition described above. When $r = 2$, we get binary decomposition of the keys. In a radix-r sort, the number of bins required is r.

Assume that the records to be sorted are $R_1, \cdots, R_n$. The record keys are decomposed using a radix of r. This results in each key having d digits in the range 0 through $r - 1$. Thus, we shall need r bins. The records are assumed to have a *link* field. The records in each bin will be linked together into a chain with $f[i]$, $0 \leq i \leq r$, a pointer to the first record in bin i and $e[i]$, a pointer to the last record in bin i. These chains will operate as queues. Procedure *RadixSort* (Program 7.15) formally presents the LSD radix-r method. This procedure assumes that *rminus*1 is defined as a constant with value $r - 1$. Also, it is assumed that the key field of each record is an array $key[1 .. d]$ with $0 \leq key[i] < r$.

Analysis of *RadixSort*: *RadixSort* makes d passes over the data, each pass taking $O(n + r)$ time. Hence, the total computing time is $O(d(n + r))$. In the sorting of numeric data, the value of d will depend on the choice of the radix r and also on the largest key. Different choices of r will yield different computing times. □

Example 7.8: Suppose we are to sort 10 numbers in the range $[0, 999]$. Each decimal digit in the key will be regarded as a subkey. So, the value of d is 3, and that of r is 10. The input list is linked and has the form given in Figure 7.11(a). The nodes are labeled $R_1, \cdots, R_{10}$. Figure 7.11 shows the queues formed when sorting on each of the digits, as well as the lists after the queues have been collected from the 10 bins. □

EXERCISES

1. Write the status of the list $F = (12, 2, 16, 30, 8, 28, 4, 10, 20, 6, 18)$ at the end of each phase of *RadixSort* (Program 7.15). Use $r = 10$.

2. Under what conditions would an MSD radix sort be more efficient than an LSD radix sort?

3. Does *RadixSort* result in a stable sort when used to sort numbers as in Example 7.8?

4. Write a sort procedure to sort records $R_1, \cdots, R_n$ lexically on keys $(K^1, \cdots, K^r)$ for the case when the range of each key is much larger than n. In this case, the bin-sort scheme used in *RadixSort* to sort within each key becomes inefficient (why?). What scheme would you use to sort within a key if we desired a procedure with (a) good worst-case behavior, (b) good average behavior, (c) small n, say <15?

---

procedure *RadixSort*(**var** *r* : *alist*; *d,n* : **integer**);
{Records *r* = (*r*[1], $\cdots$, *r*[*n*]) are sorted on the keys *key*[1], $\cdots$, *key*[*d*]. The range
of each key is $0 \le key[i] \le rminus1$. *rminus1* is a constant. Sorting within a key is done
using a bin sort.}
var *e*, *f* :**array** [0 .. *rminus1*] **of integer**; {queue pointers}
   i, j, p, t : **integer**;
   k : 0 .. *rminus* 1;
begin
  for *i* := 1 **to** *n* **do** *r*[*i*] . *link* := *i* +1; {link into a chain starting at *p*}
  r[*n*] . *link* := 0; *p* := 1;
  for *i* := *d* **downto** 1 **do** {sort on *key*[*i*]}
  begin
    for *j* := 0 **to** *rminus*1 **do** *f*[*j*] := 0; {initialize bins to be empty queues}
    while *p* < > 0 **do** {put records into queues}
    begin
      k := *r*[*p*] . *key*[*i*];
      if *f*[*k*] = 0 **then** *f*[*k*] := *p*
            else *r*[*e*[*k*]] . *link* := *p*;
      e[*k*] := *p*;
      p := *r*[*p*] . *link*; {get next record}
    end; {of **while**}
    j := 0;
    while *f*[*j*] = 0 **do** *j* := *j* + 1; {find first nonempty queue}
    p := *f*[*j*]; *t* := *e*[*j*];
    for *k* := *j* +1 **to** *rminus*1 **do** {concatenate remaining queues}
      if *f*[*k*]< >0 **then begin**
               r[*t*] . *link* := *f*[*k*];
               t := *e*[*k*];
           end; {of **if** and **for**}
    r[*t*] . *link* := 0;
  end ; {of **for**}
end; {of *RadixSort*}

Program 7.15: LSD radix sort

5. If we have *n* records with integer keys in the range [0, n^2), then they may be sorted in O(*n* log *n*) time using heap or merge sort. Radix sort on a single key (i.e.,
d = 1 and *r* = n^2) takes O(n^2) time. Show how to interpret the keys as two subkeys so that radix sort will take only O(*n*) time to sort *n* records. (Hint: Each key,
K_i, may be written as $K_i = K_i^1 n + K_i^2$ with K_i^1 and K_i^2 integers in the range [0, *n*).)

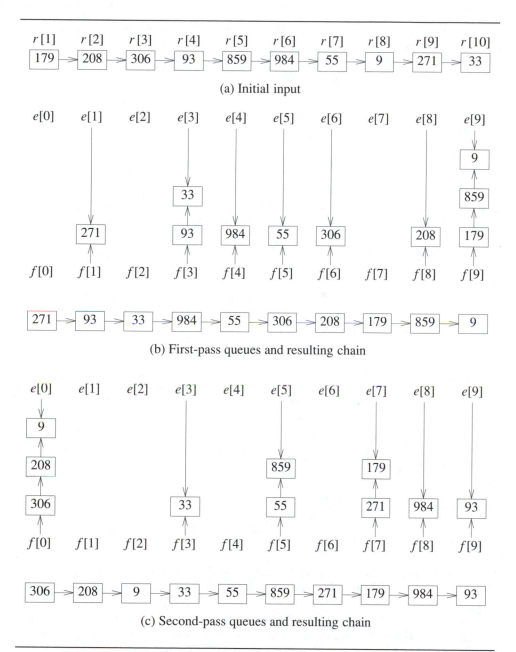

Figure 7.11: Radix sort example (continued on next page)

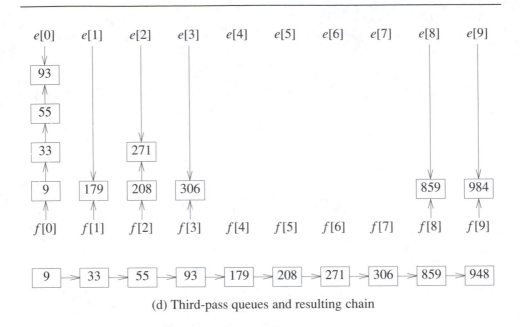

(d) Third-pass queues and resulting chain

Figure 7.11: Radix sort example

6. Generalize the method of the previous exercise to the case of integer keys in the range $(0, n^p)$ obtaining an $O(pn)$ sorting method.

7. Experiment with *RadixSort* to see how it performs relative to the comparison-based sort methods discussed in earlier sections.

7.8 LIST AND TABLE SORTS

Apart from radix sort and recursive merge sort, all the sorting methods we have looked at require excessive data movement. That is, as the result of a comparison, records may be physically moved. This tends to slow down the sorting process when records are large. When sorting lists with large records, it is necessary to modify the sorting methods so as to minimize data movement. Methods such as insertion sort and merge sort can be easily modified to work with a linked list rather than a sequential list. In this case each record will require an additional link field. Instead of physically moving the record, we change its link field to reflect the change in the position of the record in the list. At the end of the sorting process, the records are linked together in the required order. In many applications (e.g., when we just want to sort lists and then output them record by record on some external media in the sorted order), this is sufficient. However, in some applications it is necessary to physically rearrange the records *in place* so that they are in the required order. Even in such cases, considerable savings can be achieved by first performing a linked-list sort and then physically rearranging the records according to the order specified in the list. This rearranging can be accomplished in linear time using some additional space.

If the list, F, has been sorted so that at the end of the sort, p is a pointer to the first record in a linked list of records, then each record in this list will have a key that is greater than or equal to the key of the previous record (if there is a previous record). To physically rearrange these records into the order specified by the list, we begin by interchanging records R_1 and R_p. Now, the record in the position R_1 has the smallest key. If $p \neq 1$, then there is some record in the list whose link field is 1. If we could change this link field to indicate the new position of the record previously as position 1, then we would be left with records R_2, $\cdots$, R_n linked together in nondecreasing order. Repeating the above process will, after $n - 1$ iterations, result in the desired rearrangement. The snag, however, is that in a singly linked list we do not know the predecessor of a node. To overcome this difficulty, our first rearrangement procedure, *list*1 (Program 7.16), begins by converting the singly linked list p into a doubly linked list and then proceeds to move records into their correct places.

```
procedure list1(var r : alist; n, p : integer);
{Rearrange the sorted chain p so that the records r [1],  · · · , r [n ] are in sorted order.
Each record has an additional link field linkb.}
var i, u, s : integer;
    a : records;
begin
  u := 0; s := p;
  while s < > 0 do {convert p into a doubly linked list using linkb}
  begin
    r [s] . linkb := u; u := s; s := r [s] . link;
  end;
  for i := 1 to n − 1 do {move r_p to position i while}
  begin                        {maintaining the list}
    if p < > i then begin
                    if r [i] . link < > 0 then r [r [i] . link ] . linkb := p;
                    r [r [i] . linkb ] . link := p;
                    a := r [p ]; r [p ] := r [i]; r [i] := a;
                end;
    p := r [i] . link;
  end;
end; {of list1}
```

Program 7.16: Rearranging records using a doubly linked list

Example 7.9: After a list sort on the input list (26, 5, 77, 1, 61, 11, 59, 15, 48, 19) has been made, the list is linked as in Figure 7.12(a) (only the key and link fields of each record are shown).

i	R_1	R_2	R_3	R_4	R_5	R_6	R_7	R_8	R_9	R_{10}
key	26	5	77	1	61	11	59	15	48	19
link	9	6	0	2	3	8	5	10	7	1

(a) Linked list following a list sort, $p = 4$

i	R_1	R_2	R_3	R_4	R_5	R_6	R_7	R_8	R_9	R_{10}
key	26	5	77	1	61	11	59	15	48	19
link	9	6	0	2	3	8	5	10	7	1
linkb	10	4	5	0	7	2	9	6	1	8

(b) Corresponding doubly linked list, $p = 4$

Figure 7.12: Sorted linked lists

Following the links starting at R_p, we obtain the logical sequence of records $R_4, R_2, R_6,$ $R_8, R_{10}, R_1, R_9, R_7, R_5,$ and R_3. This sequence corresponds to the key sequence 1, 5, 11, 15, 19, 26, 48, 59, 61, 33. Filling in the backward links, we get the doubly linked list of Figure 7.12(b). Figure 7.13 shows the list following the first four iterations of the **for** loop of *list*1. The changes made in each iteration are shown in boldface. □

Analysis of *list1*: If there are n records in the list, then the time required to convert the chain p into a doubly linked list is O(n). The **for** loop is iterated $n - 1$ times. In each iteration, at most two records are interchanged. This requires three record moves. If each record is m words long, then the cost per interchange is $3m$. The total time is therefore O(nm).

The worst case of $3(n - 1)$ record moves is achievable. For example, consider the input key sequence $R_1, R_2, \cdots, R_n$, with $R_2 < R_3 < \cdots < R_n$ and $R_1 > R_n$. □

Although several modifications to *list*1 are possible, one of particular interest was given by M. D. MacLaren. This modification results in a rearrangement procedure, *list*2, in which no additional link fields are necessary. In this procedure (Program 7.17), after the record R_p is exchanged with R_i, the link field of the new R_i is set to p to indicate that the original record was moved. This, together with the observation that p must always be $\geq i$, permits a correct reordering of the records.

i	$\mathbf{R_1}$	R_2	R_3	$\mathbf{R_4}$	R_5	R_6	R_7	R_8	R_9	R_{10}
key	**1**	5	77	**26**	61	11	59	15	48	19
link	**2**	6	0	**9**	3	8	5	10	7	**4**
linkb	**0**	4	5	**10**	7	2	9	6	4	8

(a) Configuration after first iteration of the **for** loop of *list*1, $p = 2$

i	R_1	R_2	R_3	R_4	R_5	R_6	R_7	R_9	R_9	R_{10}
key	1	5	77	26	61	11	59	15	48	19
link	2	6	0	9	3	8	5	10	7	4
linkb	0	4	5	10	7	2	9	6	4	8

(b) Configuration after second iteration, $p = 6$

i	R_1	R_2	$\mathbf{R_3}$	R_4	R_5	$\mathbf{R_6}$	R_7	R_8	R_9	R_{10}
key	1	5	**11**	26	61	**77**	59	15	48	19
link	2	6	**8**	9	6	**0**	5	10	7	4
linkb	0	4	**2**	10	7	**5**	9	6	4	8

(c) Configuration after third iteration, $p = 8$

i	R_1	R_2	R_3	$\mathbf{R_4}$	R_5	R_6	R_7	$\mathbf{R_8}$	R_9	R_{10}
key	1	5	11	**15**	61	77	59	**26**	48	19
link	2	6	8	**10**	6	0	5	**9**	7	8
linkb	0	4	2	**6**	7	5	9	**10**	8	8

(d) Configuration after fourth iteration, $p = 10$

Figure 7.13: Example for *list*1 (Program 7.16)

Example 7.10: The data is the same as in Example 7.9. After the list sort we have the configuration of Figure 7.12(a). The configuration after each of the first five iterations of the **for** loop of *list*2 is shown in Figure 7.14. □

Analysis of *list*2: The sequence of record moves for *list*2 is identical to that for *list*1. Hence, in the worst case $3(n-1)$ record moves for a total cost of $O(nm)$ are made. No node is examined more than once in the **while** loop. So, the total time for the **while** loop is $O(n)$. □

```
procedure list2(var r :alist; n, p : integer);
{Same function as list1 except that a second link field, linkb, is not required.}
var i,q : integer;
    t : records;
begin
  for i := 1 to n − 1 do
  begin
    {Find correct record to place into ith position. The index of this record must
     be ≥ i, as records in positions 1, 2, · · · , i − 1 are already correctly positioned.}
    while p < i do
        p := r [p ] . link;
    q := r [p ] . link;        {rq is next record with largest key}
    if p < > i      {interchange ri and rp, moving rp to its correct spot as}
    then             {rp has ith smallest key.}
    begin            {also set link from old position of rj to new one}
      t := r [i ];
      r [i ] := r [p ]; r [p ] := t; r [i ] . link := p;
    end; {of if}
    p := q;
  end; {of for}
end; {of list2}
```

Program 7.17: Rearranging records using only one link field

Although the asymptotic computing time for both *list*1 and *list*2 is the same, and the same number of record moves is made in either case, we would expect *list*2 to be slightly faster than *list*1 because each time two records are interchanged, *list*1 does more work than *list*2 does. *list*1 is inferior to *list*2 in both space and time considerations.

The list-sort technique is not well suited for quick sort and heap sort. The sequential representation of the heap is essential to heap sort. For these sort methods, as well as for methods suited to list sort, one can maintain an auxiliary table, t, with one entry per record. The entries in this table serve as an indirect reference to the records. Let this table be of type *TableList*, which is defined as

type *TableList* = **array** [1..*MaxSize*] **of integer**

At the start of the sort, $t[i] = i$, $1 \leq i \leq n$. If the sorting procedure requires an interchange of R_i and R_j, then only the table entries (i.e., $t[i]$ and $t[j]$) need to be interchanged. At the end of the sort, the record with the smallest key is $R_{t[1]}$ and that with the largest $R_{t[n]}$. The required permutation on the records is $R_{t[1]}, R_{t[2]}, \cdots, R_{t[n]}$ (see Figure 7.15). This table is adequate even in situations such as binary search, where a sequentially ordered list is needed. In other situations, it may be necessary to physically rearrange the records according to the permutation specified by t.

i	R_1	R_2	R_3	R_4	R_5	R_6	R_7	R_8	R_9	R_{10}
key	1	5	77	26	61	11	59	15	48	19
link	4	6	0	9	3	8	5	10	7	1

(a) Configuration after first iteration of the **for** loop of *list2*, $p = 2$

i	R_1	R_2	R_3	R_4	R_5	R_6	R_7	R_8	R_9	R_{10}
key	1	5	77	26	61	11	59	15	48	19
link	4	6	0	9	3	8	5	10	7	1

(b) Configuration after second iteration, $p = 6$

i	R_1	R_2	R_3	R_4	R_5	R_6	R_7	R_8	R_9	R_{10}
key	1	5	**11**	26	61	**77**	59	15	48	19
link	4	6	**6**	9	3	**0**	5	10	7	1

(c) Configuration after third iteration, $p = 8$

i	R_1	R_2	R_3	R_4	R_5	R_6	R_7	R_8	R_9	R_{10}
key	1	5	11	**15**	61	77	59	**26**	48	19
link	4	6	6	**8**	3	0	5	**9**	7	1

(d) Configuration after fourth iteration, $p = 10$

i	R_1	R_2	R_3	R_4	R_5	R_6	R_7	R_8	R_9	R_{10}
key	1	5	11	15	**19**	77	59	26	48	**61**
link	4	6	6	8	**10**	0	5	9	7	**3**

(e) Configuration after fifth iteration, $p = 1$

Figure 7.14: Example for *list2* (Program 7.17)

The procedure to rearrange records corresponding to the permutation $t[1]$, $t[2]$, $\cdots$, $t[n]$ is a rather interesting application of a theorem from mathematics: Every permutation is made up of disjoint cycles. The cycle for any element i is made up of i, $t[i]$, $t^2[i]$, $\cdots$, $t^k[i]$, where $t^j[i] = t[t^{j-1}[i]]$, $t^0[i] = i$, and $t^k[i] = i$. Thus, the permutation t of Figure 7.15 has two cycles, the first involving R_1 and R_5 and the second involving R_4, R_3, and R_2. Procedure *table* (Program 7.18) utilizes this cyclic decomposition of a permutation. First, the cycle containing R_1 is followed, and all records are

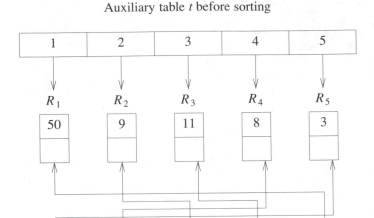

Auxiliary table t before sorting

Table t after sorting

Figure 7.15: Table sort

```
procedure table(var r : alist; n : integer; var t : TableList);
{Rearrange r [1], · · · , r [n] to correspond to the sequence r [t [1]], · · · , r [t [n]], n ≥ 1.}
var i, j, k : integer;
     p : records;
begin
   for i := 1 to n − 1 do
     if t [i] < > i then begin {there is a nontrivial cycle starting at i}
                    p := r [i]; j := i;
                    repeat
                       k := t [j]; r [j] := r [k]; t [j] := j;
                       j := k;
                    until t [j] = i;
                    r [j] := p; {j is position for record p}
                    t [j] := j;
                  end;
end; {of table}
```

Program 7.18: Table sort

moved to their correct positions. The cycle containing R_2 is the next one examined unless this cycle has already been examined. The cycles for $R_3, R_4, \cdots, R_{n-1}$ are followed in this order. The result is a physically sorted list.

When processing a trivial cycle for R_i (i.e., $t[i] = i$), no rearrangement involving record R_i is required, since the condition $t[i] = i$ means that the record with the ith smallest key is R_i. In processing a nontrivial cycle for record R_i (i.e., $t[i] \neq i$), R_i is moved to a temporary position p, then the record at $t[i]$ is moved to i; next the record at $t[t[i]]$ is moved to $t[i]$, and so on until the end of the cycle $t^k[i]$ is reached and the record at p is moved to $t^{k-1}[i]$.

Example 7.11: Suppose we start with the table t of Figure 7.16(a). This figure also shows the record keys. The table configuration is that following a table sort. There are two nontrivial cycles in the permutation specified by t. The first is R_1, R_3, R_8, R_6, R_1. The second is R_4, R_5, R_7, R_4. During the first iteration ($i = 1$) of the **for** loop of *table* (Program 7.18), the cycle $R_1, R_{t[1]}, R_{t^2[1]}, R_{t^3[1]}, R_1$ is followed. Record R_1 is moved to a temporary spot P; $R_{t[1]}$ (i.e., R_3) is moved to the position R_1; $R_{t^2[1]}$ (i.e., R_8) is moved to R_3; R_6 is moved to R_8; and finally P is moved to R_6. Thus, at the end of the first iteration we have the table configuration of Figure 7.16(b).

	R_1	R_2	R_3	R_4	R_5	R_6	R_7	R_8
key	35	14	12	42	26	50	31	18
t	3	2	8	5	7	1	4	6

(a) Initial configuration

key	12	14	18	42	26	35	31	50
t	1	2	3	5	7	6	4	8

(b) Configuration after rearrangement of first cycle

key	12	14	18	26	31	35	42	50
t	1	2	3	4	5	6	7	8

(c) Configuration after rearrangement of second cycle

Figure 7.16: Table sort example

For $i = 2$ or 3, $t[i] = i$, indicating that these records are already in their correct positions. When $i = 4$, the next nontrivial cycle is discovered, and the records on this cycle (R_4, R_5, R_7, R_4) are moved to their correct positions. Following this we have the table configuration of Figure 7.16(c).

For the remaining values of i ($i = 5, 6,$ and 7), $t[i] = i$, and no more nontrivial cycles are found. □

Analysis of *table*: If each record uses m words of storage, then the additional space needed is m words for p plus a few more for variables such as i, j, and k. To obtain an estimate of the computing time, we observe that the **for** loop is executed $n - 1$ times. If for some value of i, $t[i] \neq i$, then there is a nontrivial cycle including $k > 1$ distinct records $R_i, R_{t[i]}, \cdots, R_{t^{k-1}[i]}$. Rearranging these records requires $k + 1$ record moves. Following this, the records involved in this cycle are not moved again at any time in the algorithm, as $t[j] = j$ for all such records R_j. Hence, no record can be in two different nontrivial cycles. Let k_l be the number of records on a nontrivial cycle starting at R_l when $i = l$ in the **for** loop. Let $k_l = 0$ for a trivial cycle. The total number of record moves is

$$\sum_{l=0, k_l \neq 0}^{n-1} (k_l + 1)$$

Since the records on nontrivial cycles must be different, $\sum k_l \leq n$. The total number of record moves is maximum when $\sum k_l = n$ and there are $\lfloor n/2 \rfloor$ cycles. When n is even, each cycle contains two records. Otherwise, one cycle contains three and the others two each. In either case the number of record moves is $\lfloor 3n/2 \rfloor$. One record move costs $O(m)$ time. The total computing time is therefore $O(mn)$. □

Comparing *list2* (Program 7.17) and *table*, we see that in the worst case, *list2* makes $3(n-1)$ record moves, whereas *table* makes only $\lfloor 3n/2 \rfloor$ record moves. For larger values of m it is worthwhile to make one pass over the sorted list of records, creating a table t corresponding to a table sort. This would take $O(n)$ time. Then *table* could be used to rearrange the records in the order specified by t.

EXERCISES

1. Complete Example 7.9.

2. Complete Example 7.10.

3. Write a version of selection sort (see Chapter 1) that works on a linked chain of records.

4. Write a table sort version of quick sort. Now during the sort, records are not physically moved. Instead, $t[i]$ is the index of the record that would have been in position i if records were physically moved around as in *QuickSort* (Program 7.6). Begin with $t[i] = i$, $1 \leq i \leq n$. At the end of the sort, $t[i]$ is the index of the record that should be in the ith position in the sorted list. So now procedure *table* may be used to rearrange the records into the sorted order specified by t. Note that this reduces the amount of data movement taking place when compared to *QuickSort* for the case of large records.

5. Do Exercise 4 for the case of insertion sort.

6. Do Exercise 4 for the case of merge sort.

7. Do Exercise 4 for the case of heap sort.

7.9 SUMMARY OF INTERNAL SORTING

Of the several sorting methods we have studied, no one method is best. Some methods are good for small n, others for large n. Insertion sort is good when the list is already partially ordered. Because of the low overhead of the method, it is also the best sorting method for "small" n. Merge sort has the best worst-case behavior but requires more storage than heap sort. Quick sort has the best average behavior, but its worst-case behavior is $O(n^2)$. The behavior of radix sort depends on the size of the keys and the choice of r.

Figure 7.17 gives the average running times for *InsertionSort* (Program 7.5), *QuickSort* (Program 7.6, using the median-of-three rule), *MergeSort* (Program 7.10), and *HeapSort* (Program 7.14). These were obtained on an IBM-PC. Figure 7.18 is a plot of these times. As can be seen for n up to about 20, *InsertionSort* is the fastest. *QuickSort* is the fastest for larger values of n. In practice, therefore, it would be worthwhile to combine *InsertionSort* and *QuickSort*. *QuickSort* uses *InsertionSort* when the sublist size is below about 20.

EXERCISES

1. [**Count Sort**] The simplest known sorting method arises from the observation that the position of a record in a sorted list depends on the number of records with smaller keys. Associated with each record there is a *count* field used to determine the number of records that must precede this one in the sorted list. Write a procedure to determine the count of each record in an unordered list. Show that if the list has n records, then all the counts can be determined by making at most $n(n-1)/2$ key comparisons.

2. Write a procedure similar to *table* (Program 7.18) to rearrange the records of a list if, with each record, we have a count of the number of records preceding it in the sorted list (see Exercise 1).

3. Obtain Figures 7.17 and 7.18 for the worst-case run time.

4. [**Programming Project**] The objective of this assignment is to come up with a composite sorting procedure that is good on the worst-time criterion. The candidate sort methods are (a) insertion sort, (b) quick sort, (c) merge sort, (d) heap sort.

   To begin with, program these sort methods in Pascal. In each case, assume that n integers are to be sorted. In the case of quick sort, use the median-of-three method. In the case of merge sort, use the iterative method (as a separate exercise, you might wish to compare the run times of the iterative and recursive versions of

n	quick	merge	heap	insert
0	0.041	0.027	0.034	0.032
10	1.064	1.524	1.482	0.775
20	2.343	3.700	3.680	2.253
30	3.700	5.587	6.153	4.430
40	5.085	7.800	8.815	7.275
50	6.542	9.892	11.583	10.892
60	7.987	11.947	14.427	15.013
70	9.587	15.893	17.427	20.000
80	11.167	18.217	20.517	25.450
90	12.633	20.417	23.717	31.767
100	14.275	22.950	26.775	38.325
200	30.775	48.475	60.550	148.300
300	48.171	81.600	96.657	319.657
400	65.914	109.829	134.971	567.629
500	84.400	138.033	174.100	874.600
600	102.900	171.167	214.400	
700	122.400	199.240	255.760	
800	142.160	230.480	297.480	
900	160.400	260.100	340.000	
1000	181.000	289.450	382.250	

Times in hundredths of a second

Figure 7.17: Average times for sort methods

merge sort and determine what the recursion penalty is in your favorite language using your favorite compiler). Check out the correctness of the programs using some test data. Since quite detailed and working procedures are given in the book, this part of the assignment should take little effort. In any case, no points are earned until after this step.

To obtain reasonably accurate run times, you need to know the accuracy of the clock or timer you are using. Determine this by reading the appropriate manual. Let the clock accuracy be δ. Now, run a pilot test to determine ballpark times for your four sorting procedures for $n = 5, 10, 20, 30, 40, 50$, and 100. You will notice times of 0 for many of these values of n. The other times may not be much larger than the clock accuracy.

To time an event that is smaller than or near the clock accuracy, repeat it many times and divide the overall time by the number of repetitions. You should obtain times that are accurate to within 1%.

We need worst-case data for each of the four sort methods. The worst-case data for insertion sort are easy to generate. Just use the sequence $n, n-1, n-2,$

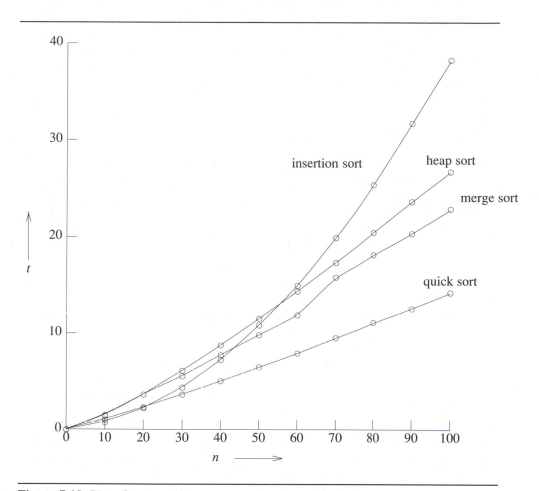

Figure 7.18: Plot of average times

··· , 1. Worst-case data for merge sort can be obtained by working backward. Begin with the last merge your procedure will perform and make this work hardest. Then look at the second-to-last merge, and so on. Use this logic to obtain a program that will generate worst-case data for merge sort for each of the above values of n.

Generating worst-case data for heap sort is the hardest, so, here we shall use a random permutation generator (one is provided in Program 7.19). We shall generate random permutations of the desired size, clock heap sort on each of these, and use the max of these times to approximate to the worst-case time. You will be able to use more random permutations for smaller values of n than for larger. For no value of *n* should you use fewer than 10 permutations. Use the same technique to obtain worst-case times for quick sort.

```
procedure permute(var a : ElementList ; n : integer);
{Random permutation generator.}
var i, j : integer; k : element;
begin
   for i := n downto 2 do
   begin
      j := random (i) + 1;  {j := random integer in the range [0, i −1]}
      k := a [j]; a [j] := a [i ]; a [i ] := k;
   end;
end; {of permute}
```

Program 7.19: Random permutation generator

Having settled on the test data, we are ready to perform our experiment. Obtain the worst-case times. From these times you will get a rough idea when one procedure performs better than the other. Now, narrow the scope of your experiments and determine the exact value of *n* when one sort method outperforms another. For some methods, this value may be 0. For instance, each of the other three methods may be faster than quick sort for all values of *n*.

Plot your findings on a single sheet of graph paper. Do you see the n^2 behavior of insertion sort and quick sort and the $n\log n$ behavior of the other two methods for suitably large *n* (about $n > 20$)? If not, there is something wrong with your test or your clock or with both. For each value of *n* determine the sort procedure that is fastest (simply look at your graph). Write a composite procedure with the best possible performance for all *n*. Clock this procedure and plot the times on the same graph sheet you used earlier.

A word of **CAUTION**: If you are using a multiprocess computer, make all your final runs at about the same time. On these computers, the clocked time will vary significantly with the amount of computer work load. Comparing the run times of an insertion sort run made at 2:00 p.m. with the run times of a merge sort run made at 2:00 a.m. will not be very meaningful.

WHAT TO TURN IN

You are required to submit a report that states the clock accuracy, the number of random permutations tried for heap sort, the worst-case data for merge sort and how you generated it, a table of times for the above values of *n*, the times for the narrowed ranges, the graph, and a table of times for the composite procedure. In addition, your report must be accompanied by a complete listing of the program used by you (this includes the sorting procedures and the main program for timing and test-data generation).

5. Repeat the previous exercise for the case of average run times. Average-case data are usually very difficult to create, so use random permutations. This time, however, do not repeat a permutation many times to overcome clock inaccuracies. Instead, use each permutation once and clock the overall time (for a fixed n).

6. Assume you are given a list of five-letter English words and are faced with the problem of listing these words in sequences such that the words in each sequence are anagrams (i.e., if x and y are in the same sequence, then word x is a permutation of word y). You are required to list out the fewest such sequences. With this restriction, show that no word can appear in more than one sequence. How would you go about solving this problem?

7. Assume you are working in the census department of a small town where the number of records, about 3000, is small enough to fit into the internal memory of a computer. All the people currently living in this town were born in the United States. There is one record for each person in this town. Each record contains (a) the state in which the person was born, (b) county of birth, and (c) name of person. How would you produce a list of all persons living in this town? The list is to be ordered by state. Within each state the persons are to be listed by their counties, the counties being arranged in alphabetical order. Within each county, the names are also listed in alphabetical order. Justify any assumptions you make.

8. [*Bubble Sort*] In a bubble sort several left-to-right passes are made over the array of records to be sorted. In each pass pairs of adjacent records are compared and exchanged if necessary. The sort terminates following a pass in which no records are exchanged.

    (a)   Write a Pascal procedure for bubble sort.

    (b)   What is the worst-case complexity of your procedure?

    (c)   How much time does your procedure take on a sorted array of records?

    (d)   How much time does your procedure take on an array of records that are in the reverse of sorted order?

9. Redo the preceding exercise beginning with an unsorted chain of records and ending with a sorted chain.

7.10 EXTERNAL SORTING

7.10.1 Introduction

In this section, we assume that the lists to be sorted are so large that the whole list cannot be contained in the internal memory of a computer, making an internal sort impossible. We shall assume that the list (or file) to be sorted resides on a disk. Most of the concepts developed for a disk sort also apply when the file resides on a tape. The term *block* refers to the unit of data that is read from or written to a disk at one time. A block generally consists of several records. For a disk, there are three factors contributing to the read/write time:

(1) *Seek time:* time taken to position the read/write heads to the correct cylinder. This will depend on the number of cylinders across which the heads have to move.

(2) *Latency time:* time until the right sector of the track is under the read/write head.

(3) *Transmission time:* time to transmit the block of data to/from the disk.

The most popular method for sorting on external storage devices is merge sort. This method consists of two distinct phases. First, segments of the input list are sorted using a good internal sort method. These sorted segments, known as *runs*, are written onto external storage as they are generated. Second, the runs generated in phase one are merged together following the merge-tree pattern of Figure 7.6, until only one run is left. Because the simple merge procedure *merge* (Program 7.7) requires only the leading records of the two runs being merged to be present in memory at one time, it is possible to merge large runs together. It is more difficult to adapt the other internal sort methods considered in this chapter to external sorting.

Example 7.12: A list containing 4500 records is to be sorted using a computer with an internal memory capable of sorting at most 750 records. The input list is maintained on disk and has a block length of 250 records. We have available another disk that may be used as a scratch pad. The input disk is not to be written on. One way to accomplish the sort using the general procedure outlined above is to

(1) Internally sort three blocks at a time (i.e., 750 records) to obtain six runs R_1 to R_6. A method such as heap sort, merge sort, or quick sort could be used. These six runs are written onto the scratch disk (Figure 7.19).

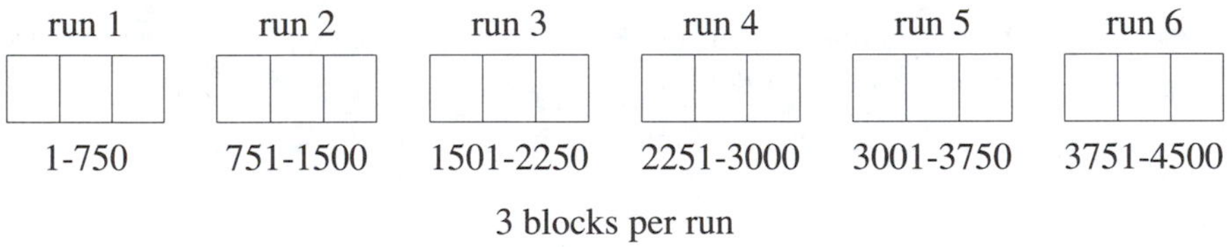

run 1	run 2	run 3	run 4	run 5	run 6
1-750	751-1500	1501-2250	2251-3000	3001-3750	3751-4500

3 blocks per run

Figure 7.19: Blocked runs obtained after internal sorting

(2) Set aside three blocks of internal memory, each capable of holding 250 records. Two of these blocks will be used as input buffers and the third as an output buffer. Merge runs R_1 and R_2. This merge is carried out by first reading one block of each of these runs into input buffers. Blocks of runs are merged from the input buffers into the output buffer. When the output buffer gets full, it is written onto the disk. If an input buffer gets empty, it is refilled with another block from the same run. After runs R_1 and R_2 are merged, R_3 and R_4 and finally R_5 and R_6 are merged. The result of this

pass is three runs, each containing 1500 sorted records or six blocks. Two of these runs are now merged using the input/output buffers set up as above to obtain a run of size 3000. Finally, this run is merged with the remaining run of size 1500 to obtain the desired sorted list (Figure 7.20). □

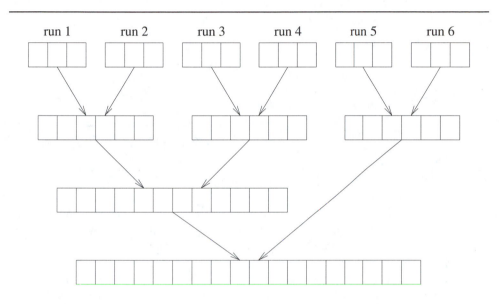

Figure 7.20: Merging the six runs

To analyze the complexity of external sort, we use the following notation:

t_s = maximum seek time

t_l = maximum latency time

t_{rw} = time to read or write one block of 250 records

t_{IO} = time to input or putput one block

$= t_s + t_l + t_{rw}$

t_{IS} = time to internally sort 750 records

nt_m = time to merge n records from input buffers to the output buffer

We shall assume that each time a block is read from or written onto the disk, the maximum seek and latency times are experienced. Although this is not true in general, it will simplify the analysis. The computing times for the various operations in our 4500-record example are given in Figure 7.21.

operation	time
(1) read 18 blocks of input, $18t_{IO}$, internally sort, $6t_{IS}$, write 18 blocks, $18t_{IO}$	$36t_{IO} + 6t_{IS}$
(2) merge runs 1 to 6 in pairs	$36t_{IO} + 4500t_m$
(3) merge two runs of 1500 records each, 12 blocks	$24t_{IO} + 3000t_m$
(4) merge one run of 3000 records with one run of 1500 records	$36t_{IO} + 4500t_m$
total time	$132t_{IO} + 12,000t_m + 6t_{IS}$

Figure 7.21: Computing times for disk sort example

The contribution of seek time can be reduced by writing blocks on the same cylinder or on adjacent cylinders. A close look at the final computing time indicates that it depends chiefly on the number of passes made over the data. In addition to the initial input pass made over the data for the internal sort, the merging of the runs requires 2-2/3 passes over the data (one pass to merge 6 runs of length 750 records, two-thirds of a pass to merge two runs of length 1500, and one pass to merge one run of length 3000 and one of length 1500). Since one full pass covers 18 blocks, the input and output time is $2 \times (2\text{-}2/3 + 1) \times 18\, t_{IO} = 132t_{IO}$. The leading factor of 2 appears because each record that is read is also written out again. The merge time is $2\text{-}2/3 \times 4500t_m = 12,000t_m$. Because of this close relationship between the overall computing time and the number of passes made over the data, future analysis will be concerned mainly with counting the number of passes being made. Another point to note regarding the above sort is that no attempt was made to use the computer's ability to carry out input/output and CPU operation in parallel and thus overlap some of the time. In the ideal situation we would overlap almost all the input/output time with CPU processing so that the real time would be approximately $132\, t_{IO} \approx 12,000\, t_m + 6t_{IS}$.

If we have two disks, we can write on one, read from the other, and merge buffer loads already in memory in parallel. A proper choice of buffer lengths and buffer handling schemes will result in a time of almost $66t_{IO}$. This parallelism is an important consideration when sorting is being carried out in a nonmultiprogramming environment. In this situation, unless input/output and CPU processing is going on in parallel, the CPU is idle during input/output. In a multiprogramming environment, however, the need for the sorting program to carry out input/output and CPU processing in parallel may not be so critical, since the CPU can be busy working on another program (if there are other programs in the system at the time) while the sort program waits for the completion of its input/output. Indeed, in many multiprogramming environments it may not even be possible to achieve parallel input, output, and internal computing because of the structure of the operation system.

The number of merge passes over the runs can be reduced by using a higher-order merge than two-way merge. To provide for parallel input, output, and merging, we need an appropriate buffer-handling scheme. Further improvement in run time can be obtained by generating fewer (or equivalently longer) runs than are generated by the strategy described above. This can be done using a loser tree. The loser-tree strategy to be discussed results in runs that are on the average almost twice as long as those obtained by the above strategy. However, the generated runs are of varying size. As a result, the order in which the runs are merged affects the time required to merge all runs into one. We consider these factors now.

7.10.2   *k*-Way Merging

The two-way merge procedure *merge* (Program 7.7) is almost identical to the merge procedure just described (Figure 7.20). In general, if we start with m runs, the merge tree corresponding to Figure 7.20 will have $\lceil \log_2 m \rceil + 1$ levels, for a total of $\lceil \log_2 m \rceil$ passes over the data list. The number of passes over the data can be reduced by using a higher-order merge (i.e., k-way merge for $k \geq 2$). In this case, we would simultaneously merge k runs together. Figure 7.22 illustrates a four-way merge of 16 runs. The number of passes over the data is now two, versus four passes in the case of a two-way merge. In general, a k-way merge on m runs requires $\lceil \log_k m \rceil$ passes over the data. Thus, the input/output time may be reduced by using a higher-order merge.

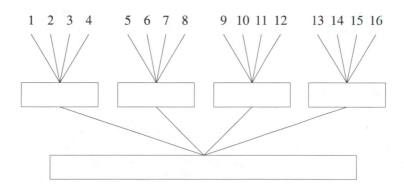

Figure 7.22: A four-way merge on 16 runs

The use of a higher-order merge, however, has some other effects on the sort. To begin with, k runs of size $S_1, S_2, S_3, \cdots, S_k$ can no longer be merged internally in $O(\Sigma_1^k S_i)$ time. In a k-way merge, as in a two-way merge, the next record to be output is the one with the smallest key. The smallest has now to be found from k possibilities and it could be the leading record in any of the k runs. The most direct way to merge k runs is to make $k - 1$ comparisons to determine the next record to output. The computing time for this is $O((k - 1) \Sigma_1^k S_i)$. Since $\log_k m$ passes are being made, the total number of key comparisons is $n(k - 1)\log_k m = n(k - 1)\log_2 m / \log_2 k$, where n is the number of records in the list. Hence, $(k - 1)/\log_2 k$ is the factor by which the number of key comparisons increases. As k increases, the reduction in input/output time will be outweighed by the resulting increase in CPU time needed to perform the k-way merge.

For large k (say, $k \geq 6$) we can achieve a significant reduction in the number of comparisons needed to find the next smallest element by using a loser tree with k leaves (see Chapter 5). In this case, the total time needed per level of the merge tree is $O(n \log_2 k)$. Since the number of levels in this tree is $O(\log_k m)$, the asymptotic internal processing time becomes $O(n \log_2 k \log_k m) = O(n\log_2 m)$. This is independent of k.

In going to a higher-order merge, we save on the amount of input/output being carried out. There is no significant loss in internal processing speed. Even though the internal processing time is relatively insensitive to the order of the merge, the decrease in input/output time is not as much as indicated by the reduction to $\log_k m$ passes. This is so because the number of input buffers needed to carry out a k-way merge increases with k. Although $k + 1$ buffers are sufficient, in the next section we shall see that the use of $2k + 2$ buffers is more desirable. Since the internal memory available is fixed and independent of k, the buffer size must be reduced as k increases. This in turn implies a reduction in the block size on disk. With the reduced block size, each pass over the data results in a greater number of blocks being written or read. This represents a potential increase in input/output time from the increased contribution of seek and latency times involved in reading a block of data. Hence, beyond a certain k value the input/output time will increase despite the decrease in the number of passes being made. The optimal value for k depends on disk parameters and the amount of internal memory available for buffers.

7.10.3 Buffer Handling for Parallel Operation

If k runs are being merged together by a k-way merge, then we clearly need at least k input buffers and one output buffer to carry out the merge. This, however, is not enough if input, output, and internal merging are to be carried out in parallel. For instance, while the output buffer is being written out, internal merging has to be halted, since there is no place to collect the merged records. This can be overcome through the use of two output buffers. While one is being written out, records are merged into the second. If buffer sizes are chosen correctly, then the time to output one buffer will be the same as the CPU time needed to fill the second buffer. With only k input buffers, internal merging will have to be held up whenever one of these input buffers becomes empty and another block from the corresponding run is being read in. This input delay can also be avoided if we have $2k$ input buffers. These $2k$ input buffers have to be used cleverly to avoid reaching a situation in which processing has to be held up because of a lack of input records from any one run. Simply assigning two buffers per run does not solve the problem.

Example 7.13: Assume that a two-way merge is carried out using four input buffers, $in[i]$, $1 \le i \le 4$, and two output buffers, $ou[1]$ and $ou[2]$. Each buffer is capable of holding two records. The first few records of run 1 have key value 1, 3, 5, 7, 8, 9. The first few records of run 2 have key value 2, 4, 6, 15, 20, 25. Buffers $in[1]$ and $in[3]$ are assigned to run 1. The remaining two input buffers are assigned to run 2. We start the merge by reading in one buffer load from each of the two runs. At this time the buffers have the configuration of Figure 7.23(a). Now runs 1 and 2 are merged using records from $in[1]$ and $in[2]$. In parallel with this, the next buffer load from run 1 is input. If we assume that buffer lengths have been chosen such that the times to input, output, and generate an output buffer are all the same, then when $ou[1]$ is full, we have the situation of Figure 7.23(b). Next, we simultaneously output $ou[1]$, input into $in[4]$ from run 2, and merge into $ou[2]$. When $ou[2]$ is full, we have the situation of Figure 7.23(c). Continuing in this way, we reach the configuration of Figure 7.23(e). We now begin to output $ou[2]$, input from run 1 into $in[3]$, and merge into $ou[1]$. During the merge, all records from run 1 get used before $ou[1]$ gets full. Merging must now be delayed until the inputting of another buffer load from run 1 is completed. $\square$

Example 7.13 makes it clear that if $2k$ input buffers are to suffice, then we cannot assign two buffers per run. Instead, the buffer must be floating in the sense that an individual buffer may be assigned to any run depending upon need. In the buffer assignment strategy we shall describe, there will at any time be at least one input buffer containing records from each run. The remaining buffers will be filled on a priority basis (i.e., the run for which the k-way merging algorithm will run out of records first is the one from which the next buffer will be filled). One may easily predict which run's records will be exhausted first by simply comparing the keys of the last record read from each of the k runs. The smallest such key determines this run. We shall assume that in the case of equal keys, the merge process first merges the record from the run with least index. This means that if the key of the last record read from run i is equal to the key of the last record read from run j, and $i < j$, then the records read from i will be exhausted before those from j. So, it is possible to have more than two bufferloads from a given run and only one partially full buffer from another run. All bufferloads from the same run are queued together. Before formally presenting the algorithm for buffer utilization, we make the following assumptions about the parallel processing capabilities of the computer system available:

(1) We have two disk drives and the input/output channel is such that we can simultaneously read from one disk and write onto the other.

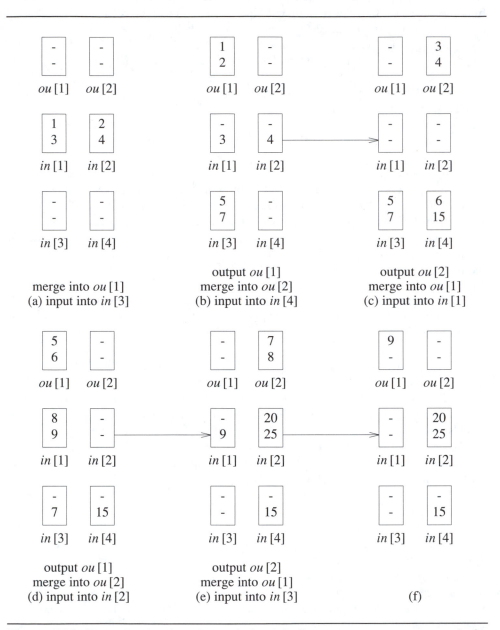

Figure 7.23: Example showing that two fixed buffers per run are not enough for continued parallel operation

(2)   While data transmission is taking place between an input/output device and a block of memory, the CPU cannot make references to that same block of memory. Thus, it is not possible to start filling the front of an output buffer while it is being written out. If this were possible, then by coordinating the transmission and merging rate, only one output buffer would be needed. By the time the first record for the new output block is determined, the first record of the previous output block has been written out.

(3)   To simplify the discussion we assume that input and output buffers are of the same size.

Keeping these assumptions in mind, we provide a high-level description of the algorithm obtained using the strategy outlined earlier and then illustrate how it works through an example. Our algorithm, Program 7.20, merges k-runs, $k \geq 2$, using a k-way merge. $2k$ input buffers and two output buffers are used. Each buffer is a continuous block of memory. Input buffers are queued in k queues, one queue for each run. It is assumed that each input/output buffer is long enough to hold one block of records. Empty buffers are placed on a linked stack. The algorithm also assumes that the end of each run has a sentinel record with a very large key, say $+\infty$. It is assumed that all other records have key value less than that of the sentinel record. If block lengths, and hence buffer lengths, are chosen such that the time to merge one output buffer load equals the time to read a block, then almost all input, output, and computation will be carried out in parallel. It is also assumed that in the case of equal keys, the k-way merge algorithm first outputs the record from the run with the smallest index.

We make the following observations about Program 7.20:

(1)   For large k, determination of the queue that will be exhausted first can be found in $\log_2 k$ comparisons by setting up a loser tree for $last\,[i\,]$, $1 \leq i \leq k$, rather than making $k - 1$ comparisons each time a buffer load is to be read in. The change in computing time will not be significant, since this queue selection represents only a very small fraction of the total time taken by the algorithm.

(2)   For large k, procedure $kwaymerge$ uses a tree of losers (see Chapter 5).

(3)   All input and output except for the input of the initial k blocks and the output of the last block is done concurrently with computing. Since, after k runs have been merged, we would probably begin to merge another set of k runs, the input for the next set can commence during the final merge stages of the present set of runs. That is, when $LastKey\,[NextRun\,] = +\infty$ in Step 6, we begin reading one by one the first blocks from each of the next set of k runs to be merged. So, over the entire sorting of a file the only time that is not overlapped with the internal merging time is the time to input the first k blocks and that to output the last block.

(4)   The algorithm assumes that all blocks are of the same length. Ensuring this may require inserting a few dummy records into the last block of each run following the sentinel record with key $+\infty$.

{Steps in buffering algorithm}

Step 1: Input the first block of each of the k runs, setting up k linked queues, each having one block of data. Put the remaining k input blocks into a linked stack of free input blocks. Set *ou* to 0.

Step 2: Let *LastKey*[i] be the last key input from run i. Let *NextRun* be the run for which *LastKey* is minimum. If *LastKey*[*NextRun*] $\neq +\infty$, then initiate the input of the next block from run *NextRun*.

Step 3: Use a procedure *kwaymerge* to merge records from the k input queues into the output buffer *ou*. Merging continues until either the output buffer gets full or a record with key $+\infty$ is merged into *ou*. If, during this merge, an input buffer becomes empty before the output buffer gets full or before $+\infty$ is merged into *ou*, the *kwaymerge* advances to the next buffer on the same queue and returns the empty buffer to the stack of empty buffers. However, if an input buffer becomes empty at the same time as the output buffer gets full or $+\infty$ is merged into *ou*, the empty buffer is left on the queue, and *kwaymerge* does not advance to the next buffer on the queue. Rather, the merge terminates.

Step 4: Wait for any ongoing disk input/output to complete.

Step 5: If an input buffer has been read, add it to the queue for the appropriate run. Determine the next run to read from by determining *NextRun* such that *LastKey*[*NextRun*] is minimum.

Step 6: If *LastKey*[*NextRun*] $\neq +\infty$, then initiate reading the next block from run *NextRun* into a free input buffer.

Step 7: Initiate the writing of output buffer *ou*. Set *ou* to $1 - ou$.

Step 8: If a record with key $+\infty$ has been not been merged into the output buffer, go back to Step 3. Otherwise, wait for the ongoing write to complete and then terminate.

Program 7.20: k-way merge with floating buffers

Example 7.14: To illustrate the algorithm of Program 7.20, let us trace through it while it performs a three-way merge on the three runs of Figure 7.24. Each run consists of four blocks of two records each; the last key in the fourth block of each of these three runs is $+\infty$. We have six input buffers and two output buffers. Figure 7.25 shows the status of the input buffer queues, the run from which the next block is being read, and the output buffer being output at the beginning of each iteration of the loop of Steps 3 through 8 of the buffering algorithm.

From line 5 of Figure 7.25 it is evident that during the k-way merge, the test for "output buffer full?" should be carried out before the test "input buffer empty?", as the next input buffer for that run may not have been read in yet, so there would be no next

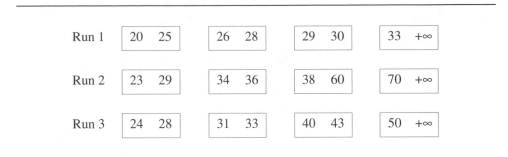

Figure 7.24: Three runs

buffer in that queue. In lines 3 and 4 all six input buffers are in use, and the stack of free buffers is empty. □

We end our discussion of buffer handling by proving that Program 7.20 is correct.

Theorem 7.2: The following are true for Program 7.20:

(1)   In Step 6, there is always a buffer available in which to begin reading the next block.

(2)   During the k-way merge of Step 3, the next block in the queue has been read in by the time it is needed.

Proof: (1) Each time we get to Step 6 of the algorithm, there are at most $k + 1$ buffer loads in memory, one of these being in an output buffer. For each queue there can be at most one buffer that is partially full. If no buffer is available for the next read, then the remaining k buffers must be full. This means that all the k partially full buffers are empty (as otherwise there will be more than $k+1$ buffer loads in memory). From the way the merge is set up, only one buffer can be both unavailable and empty. This may happen only if the output buffer gets full exactly when one input buffer becomes empty. But $k > 1$ contradicts this. So, there is always at least one buffer available when Step 6 is being executed.

(2) Assume this is false. Let run R_i be the one whose queue becomes empty during *kwaymerge*. We may assume that the last key merged was not $+\infty$, since otherwise *kwaymerge* would terminate the merge rather than get another buffer for R_i. This means that there are more blocks of records for run R_i on the input file, and $LastKey[i] \neq +\infty$. Consequently, up to this time whenever a block was output, another was simultaneously read in. Input and output therefore proceeded at the same rate, and the number of available blocks of data was always k. An additional block is being read in, but it does not get queued until Step 5. Since the queue for R_i has become empty first, the selection rule for

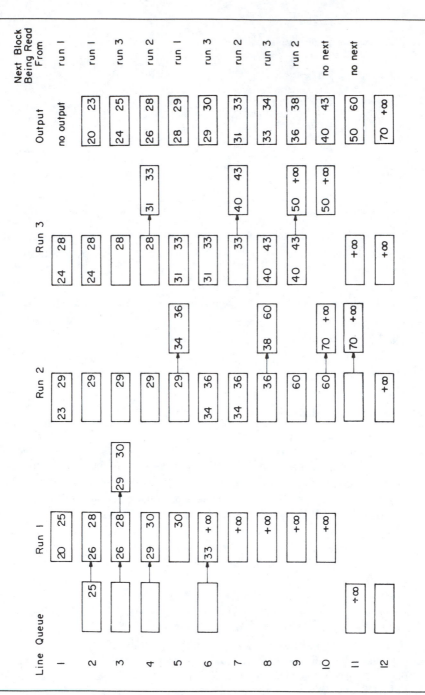

Figure 7.25: Buffering example

choosing the next run to read from ensures that there is at most one block of records for each of the remaining $k - 1$ runs. Furthermore, the output buffer cannot be full at this time, as this condition is tested for before the input-buffer-empty condition. Thus, fewer than k blocks of data are in memory. This contradicts our earlier assertion that there must be exactly k such blocks of data. $\square$

7.10.4   Run Generation

Using conventional internal sorting methods such as those discussed earlier in this chapter, it is possible to generate runs that are only as large as the number of records that can be held in internal memory at one time. Using a tree of losers, it is possible to do better than this. In fact, the algorithm we shall present will, on the average, generate runs that are twice as long as obtainable by conventional methods. This algorithm was devised by Walters, Painter, and Zalk. In addition to being capable of generating longer runs, this algorithm will allow for parallel input, output and internal processing.

We assume that input/output buffers have been set up appropriately for maximum overlapping of input, output, and internal processing. Wherever there is an input/output instruction in the run-generation algorithm, it is assumed that the operation takes place through the input/output buffers. The run generation algorithm uses a tree of losers. We assume that there is enough space to construct such a tree for k records, $r[i]$, $0 \le i < k$. Each node, i, in this tree has one field $l[i]$. $l[i]$, $1 \le i < k$, represents the loser of the tournament played at node i. Each of the k record positions $r[i]$ has a run number field $rn[i]$, $0 \le i < k$. This field enables us to determine whether or not $r[i]$ can be output as part of the run currently being generated. Whenever the tournament winner is output, a new record (if there is one) is input, and the tournament is replayed as discussed in Chapter 5.

Procedure *runs* (Program 7.21) is an implementation of the loser tree strategy just discussed. The variables used in this procedure have the following significance:

$r[i]$, $0 \le i < k$	...	the k records in the tournament tree
$key[i]$, $0 \le i < k$	...	key value of record $r[i]$
$l[i]$, $0 \le i < k$	...	loser of the tournament played at node i
$rn[i]$, $0 \le i < k$	...	the run number to which $r[i]$ belongs
rc	...	run number of current run
q	...	overall tournament winner
rq	...	run number for $r[q]$
$rmax$	...	number of runs that will be generated
$LastKey$	...	key value of last record output

```
1  procedure runs;
2  {Generate runs using a tree of losers.}
3  label 99;
4  var r : array[0 .. k ] of TreeRecord ;
5      key, l, rn : array [0..k ] of integer;
6      rc, q, rq, rmax, LastKey, temp, i, t : integer;
7  begin {runs}
8      for i := 1 to k do {input records into loser tree}
9      begin
10         InputRecord (r [i ]); rn [i ] := 1;
11     end;
12     InitializeLoserTree;
13     q :=  tournament winner;
14     rq := 1; rc := 1; rmax := 1; LastKey := maxint;
15     while true do {output runs}
16     begin
17        if rq < > rc then begin {end of run}
18                            output end of run marker;
19                            if rq > rmax then goto 99
20                               else rc := rq ;
21                      end;
22        WriteRecord (r [q ]); LastKey := key [q ]; {output record r [q ]}
```

Program 7.21: Run generation using a loser tree (continued on next page)

The data type *TreeRecord* is defined as

$$\textbf{type } TreeRecord = \textbf{record}$$
$$key : \textbf{integer}$$
$$\{other\ fields\ declared\ here\}$$
$$\textbf{end};$$

The loop of lines 15 to 44 repeatedly plays the tournament outputting records. The variable *LastKey* is made use of in line 27 to determine whether or not the new record input, $r[q]$, can be output as part of the current run. If $key[q] < LastKey$ then $r[q]$ cannot be output as part of the current run rc, as a record with larger key value has already been output in this run. When the tree is being readjusted (lines 34 to 43), a record with lower run number wins over one with a higher run number. When run numbers are equal, the record with lower key value wins. This ensures that records come out of the tree in nondecreasing order of their run numbers. Within the same run, records come out of the tree in nondecreasing order of their key values. *rmax* is used to terminate the procedure. In line 24, when we run out of input, a record with run number *rmax* + 1 is introduced. When this record is ready for output, the procedure terminates from line 19.

```
23        {input new record into tree}
24        if no more input then rn [q] := rmax + 1;
25        else begin
26              ReadRecord (r [q]);
27              if key [q] < LastKey then
28              begin {new record belongs to next run}
29                  rn [q] := rq + 1; rmax := rq + 1;
30              end
31              else rn [q] := rc;
32           end;
33        {adjust losers}
34        t := (k + q) div 2; {t is parent of q} rq := rn [q];
35        while t < > 0 do
36        begin
37           if (rn [l [t]] < rq) or ((rn [l [t]] = rq) and (key [l [t]] < key [q])) then
38           begin {t is the winner}
39              temp := q; q := l [t]; l [t] := temp;
40              rq := rn [q];
41           end;
42           t := t div 2; {move up tree}
43        end; (of while t < > 0}
44     end; (of while true}
45 99: end; {of runs}
```

Program 7.21: Run generation using a loser tree

Analysis of *runs*: When the input list is already sorted, only one run is generated. On the average, the run size is almost $2k$. The time required to generate all the runs for an n run list is $O(n \log k)$, as it takes $O(\log k)$ time to adjust the loser tree each time a record is output. □

7.10.5 Optimal Merging of Runs

The runs generated by procedure *runs* may not be of the same size. When runs are of different size, the run merging strategy employed so far (i.e., make complete passes over the collection of runs) does not yield minimum run times. For example, suppose we have four runs of length 2, 4, 5, and 15, respectively. Figure 7.26 shows two ways to merge these using a series of two-way merges. The circular nodes represent a two-way merge using as input the data of the children nodes. The square nodes represent the initial runs. We shall refer to the circular nodes as *internal nodes* and the square ones as *external nodes*. Each figure is a *merge tree*.

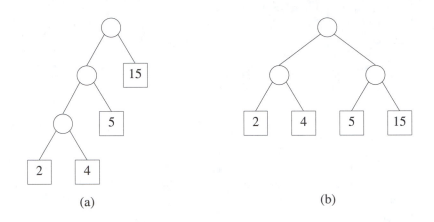

(a)   (b)

Figure 7.26: Possible two-way merges

In the first merge tree, we begin by merging the runs of size 2 and 4 to get one of size 6; next this is merged with the run of size 5 to get a run of size 11; finally this run of size 11 is merged with the run of size 15 to get the desired sorted run of size 26. When merging is done using the first merge tree, some records are involved in only one merge, and others are involved in up to three merges. In the second merge tree, each record is involved in exactly two merges. This corresponds to the strategy in which complete merge passes are repeatedly made over the data.

The number of merges that an individual record is involved in is given by the distance of the corresponding external node from the root. So, the records of the run with 15 records are involved in one merge when the first merge tree of Figure 7.26 is used and in two merges when the second tree is used. Since the time for a merge is linear in the number of records being merged, the total merge time is obtained by summing the products of the run lengths and the distance from the root of the corresponding external nodes. This sum is called the *weighted external path length*. For the two trees of Figure 7.26, the respective weighted external path lengths are

$$2 \cdot 3 + 4 \cdot 3 + 5 \cdot 2 + 15 \cdot 1 = 43$$

and

$$2 \cdot 2 + 4 \cdot 2 + 2 + 5 \cdot 2 + 15 \cdot 2 = 52$$

The cost of a k-way merge of n runs of length q_i, $1 \le i \le n$, is minimized by using a merge tree of degree k that has minimum weighted external path length. We shall consider the case $k = 2$ only. The discussion is easily generalized to the case $k > 2$ (see the exercises).

We briefly describe another application for binary trees with minimum weighted external path length. Suppose we wish to obtain an optimal set of codes for messages

$M_1, \cdots, M_{n+1}$. Each code is a binary string that will be used for transmission of the corresponding message. At the receiving end the code will be decoded using a *decode tree*. A decode tree is a binary tree in which external nodes represent messages. The binary bits in the code word for a message determine the branching needed at each level of the decode tree to reach the correct external node. For example, if we interpret a zero as a left branch and a one as a right branch, then the decode tree of Figure 7.27 corresponds to codes 000, 001, 01, and 1 for messages M_1, M_2, M_3, and M_4, respectively. These codes are called Huffman codes. The cost of decoding a code word is proportional to the number of bits in the code. This number is equal to the distance of the corresponding external node from the root node. If q_i is the relative frequency with which message M_i will be transmitted, then the expected decoding time is

$$\sum_{1 \leq i \leq n+1} q_i d_i$$

where d_i is the distance of the external node for message M_i from the root node. The expected decoding time is minimized by choosing code words resulting in a decode tree with minimal weighted external path length.

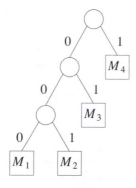

Figure 7.27: A decode tree

A very nice solution to the problem of finding a binary tree with minimum weighted external path length has been given by D. Huffman. The following type declarations are assumed:

$$\textbf{type } TreePointer = \uparrow TreeRecord;$$
$$TreeRecord = \textbf{record}$$
$$LeftChild : TreePointer;$$
$$weight : \textbf{integer};$$
$$RightChild : TreePointer;$$
$$\textbf{end};$$

Procedure *huffman* (Program 7.22) makes use of a list l of extended binary trees. Each node in a tree has three fields: *weight*, *LeftChild*, and *RightChild*. Initially, all trees in l have only one node. For each tree this node is an external node, and its weight is one of the provided q_i's. During the course of the procedure, for any tree in l with root node t and depth greater than one, $t\uparrow.weight$ is the sum of weights of all external nodes in t. Procedure *huffman* uses the procedures *least* and *insert*. *least* determines a tree in l with minimum *weight* and removes it from l; *insert* adds a new tree to the list l.

```
procedure huffman (var l : ListPointer ; n : integer);
{l is a list of n single-node binary trees as described above.}
var t : TreePointer ;
    i : integer;
begin
   for i := 1 to n − 1 do                  {loop n−1 times}
   begin
      new(t);                              {Create a new binary tree}
      t↑.LeftChild := least (l);           {by combining the trees}
      t↑.RightChild := least (l);          {with the two smallest weights}
      t↑.weight := r↑.LeftChild↑.weight + t↑.RightChild↑.weight ;
      insert (l,t);
   end;
end; {of huffman}
```

Program 7.22: Finding a binary tree with minimum weighted external path length

Example 7.15: Suppose we have the weights $q_1 = 2$, $q_2 = 3$, $q_3 = 5$, $q_4 = 7$, $q_5 = 9$, and $q_6 = 13$. Then the sequence of trees we would get is given in Figure 7.28 (the number in a circular node represents the sum of the weights of external nodes in that subtree).

The weighted external path length of this tree is

$$2 \cdot 4 + 3 \cdot 4 + 5 \cdot 3 + 13 \cdot 2 + 7 \cdot 2 + 9 \cdot 2 = 93$$

By comparison, the best complete binary tree has weighted path length 95. □

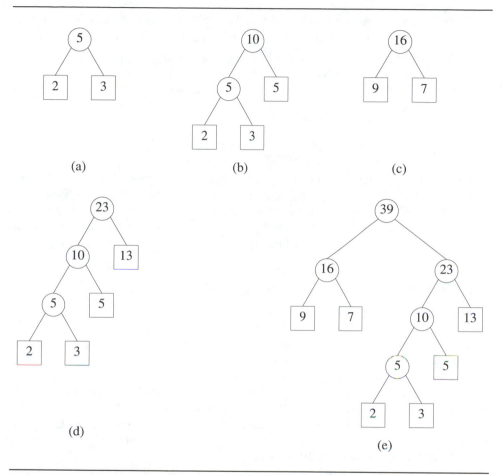

Figure 7.28: Construction of a Huffman tree

Analysis of *huffman:* The main loop is executed $n - 1$ times. If l is maintained as a heap (see Section 5.6), then each call to *least* and *insert* requires only O($\log n$) time. Hence, the asymptotic computing time is O($n \log n$). The correctness proof is left as an exercise. □

EXERCISES

1. (a)   *n* records are to be sorted on a computer with a memory capacity of *S* records ($S \ll n$). Assume that the entire *S*-record capacity may be used for input/output buffers. The input is on disk and consists of *m* runs. Assume that each time a disk access is made, the seek time is t_s and the latency time

is t_l. The transmission time is t_t per record transmitted. What is the total input time for phase two of external sorting if a k-way merge is used with internal memory partitioned into input/output buffers to permit overlap of input, output, and CPU processing as in *buffering* (Program 7.20)?

(b)   Let the CPU time needed to merge all the runs together be t_{CPU} (we may assume it is independent of k and hence constant). Let $t_s = 80\ ms$, $t_l = 20ms$, $n = 200{,}000$, $m = 64$, $t_t = 10^{-3}$ sec/record, and $S = 2000$. Obtain a rough plot of the total input time, t_{input}, versus k. Will there always be a value of k for which $t_{CPU} \approx t_{input}$?

2. (a)   Show that procedure *huffman* (Program 7.22) correctly generates a binary tree of minimal weighted external path length.

(b)   When n runs are to be merged together using an m-way merge, Huffman's method can be generalized to the following rule: "First add $(1 - n) \bmod (m - 1)$ runs of length zero to the set of runs. Then, repeatedly merge the m shortest remaining runs until only one run is left." Show that this rule yields an optimal merge pattern for m-way merging.

7.11   REFERENCES AND SELECTED READINGS

A comprehensive discussion of sorting and searching may be found in *The Art of Computer Programming: Sorting and Searching*, by D. Knuth, vol. 3, Addison-Wesley, Reading, MA, 1973.

Two other useful references on sorting are *Sorting and Sort Systems*, by H. Lorin, Addison-Wesley, Reading, MA, 1975, and *Internal Sorting Methods Illustrated with PL/1 Programs*, by R. Rich, Prentice-Hall, Englewood Cliffs, NJ, 1972.

Two references on quick sort are "Quicksort," by C. A. R. Hoare, *The Computer Journal*, 5, 1962, pp. 10-15, and "The analysis of quicksort programs," by R. Sedgewick, *Acta Informatica*, 7, 1976/77, pp. 327-355.

Figures 7.17 and 7.18 are taken from *Software Development in Pascal*, Third Edition, by S. Sahni, Camelot Publishing Co., MN, 1993.

The O(1)-space, linear-time merge algorithm is from the paper: "Practical in-place merging," by B. Huang and M. Langston, *CACM*, 31:3, 1988, pp. 348-352.

For more on Huffman codes see "An optimum encoding with minimum longest code and total number of digits," by E. Schwartz, *Information and Control*, 7, 1964, pp. 37-44.

CHAPTER **8**

HASHING

8.1 THE SYMBOL TABLE ABSTRACT DATA TYPE

We have all used a *dictionary*, and many of us have a word processor equipped with a limited dictionary, that is, a spelling checker. In this chapter, we consider the dictionary, as an ADT. Examples of dictionaries are found in many applications, including the spelling checker, the thesaurus, the data dictionary found in database management applications, and the symbol tables generated by loaders, assemblers, and compilers.

In computer science, we generally use the term *symbol table* rather than dictionary, when referring to the ADT. Viewed from this perspective, we define a symbol table as a set of name-attribute pairs. The characteristics of the name and attribute vary according to the application. For example, in a thesaurus, the name is a word, and the attribute is a list of synonyms for the word; in a symbol table for a compiler, the name is an identifier, and the attributes might include an initial value and a list of lines that use the identifier.

Generally we want to perform the following operations on a symbol table:

(1) determine if a particular name is in the table

(2) retrieve the attributes of that name

(3) modify the attributes of that name

(4)   insert a new name and its attributes

(5)   delete a name and its attributes

Structure 8.1 provides the complete specification of the symbol table ADT.

---

structure *SymbolTable(SymTab)* is
  objects: A set of name-attribute pairs in which the names are unique.
  functions:
    for all *name* ∈ *Name*, *attr* ∈ *Attribute*, *symtab* ∈ *SymbolTable*, *MaxSize* ∈ integer

Create (*MaxSize*) : *SymTab*	::=	create an empty symbol table with capacity *MaxSize*
IsIn (*symtab*, *name*) : **boolean**	::=	**if** *name* is in *symtab* **then** *IsIn* := **true** **else** *IsIn* := **false**
Find (*symtab*, *name*) : *Attribute*	::=	**if** *name* is in *symtab* **then** *Find* := the corresponding attribute **else** *Find* := null attribute
Insert (*symtab*, *name*, *attr*) : *SymTab*	::=	**if** *name* is in *symtab* **then** replace its existing attribute with *attr* **else** insert the pair (*name*, *attr*) into *symtab*
Delete (*symtab*, *name*) : *SymTab*	::=	**if** *name* is in *symtab* **then** delete (*name*, *attr*) from *symtab*

Structure 8.1: Abstract data type *SymbolTable*

Although Structure 8.1 lists several operations, there are only three basic operations on symbol tables: searching, inserting, and deleting. Therefore, when choosing a symbol table representation, we must make sure that we can implement these operations efficiently. For example, we could use the binary search tree introduced in Chapter 5 to represent a symbol table. If our search tree contained n identifiers, the worst-case complexity for these operations would be $O(n)$. In Chapter 10 we introduce several refinements of the binary search tree data structure that reduce the time per operation to $O(\log n)$. In this chapter we examine a technique for search, insert, and delete operations that has very good expected performance. The technique is referred to as *hashing*. Unlike search tree methods which rely on identifier comparisons to perform a search, hashing relies on a formula called the *hash function*. We divide our discussion of hashing into two parts: *static hashing* and *dynamic hashing*.

8.2   STATIC HASHING

8.2.1   Hash Tables

In *static hashing* the identifiers are stored in a fixed-size table called the *hash table.* The address or location of an identifier, x, is obtained by computing some arithmetic function, h, of x. $h(x)$ gives the address of x in the table. This address will be referred to as the hash or home address of x. The memory available to maintain the symbol table is assumed to be sequential. This memory is referred to as the hash table, ht. The hash table is partitioned into b buckets, $ht[0]$, $\cdots$, $ht[b-1]$. Each bucket is capable of holding s records. Thus, a bucket is said to consist of s slots, each slot being large enough to hold one record. Usually $s = 1$, and each bucket can hold exactly one record. A hash function, $h(x)$, is used to perform an identifier transformation on x. $h(x)$ maps the set of possible identifiers onto the integers 0 through $b-1$. If we limit the identifiers to be at most six characters long, with the first one being a letter and the remaining either letters or decimal digits, then there are $T = \sum_{0 \le i \le 5} 26 \times 36^i > 1.6 \times 10^9$ distinct possible values for x. Any reasonable application, however, uses only a very small fraction of these.

Definition: The *identifier density* of a hash table is the ratio n/T, where n is the number of identifiers in the table and T is the total number of possible identifiers. The *loading density* or *loading factor* of a hash table is $\alpha = n/(sb)$. $\square$

Since the number of identifiers, n, in use is usually several orders of magnitude less than the total number of possible identifiers, T, the number of buckets, b, in the hash table is also much less than T. Therefore, the hash function h must map several different identifiers into the same bucket. Two identifiers, I_1, and I_2, are said to be *synonyms* with respect to h if $h(I_1) = h(I_2)$. Distinct synonyms are entered into the same bucket as long as all the s slots in that bucket have not been used. An *overflow* is said to occur when a new identifier I is mapped or hashed by h into a full bucket. A *collision* occurs when two nonidentical identifiers are hashed into the same bucket. When the bucket size s is 1, collisions and overflows occur simultaneously.

Example 8.1: Consider the hash table ht with $b = 26$ buckets and $s = 2$. Assume that there are $n = 10$ distinct identifiers and that each identifier begins with a letter. The loading factor, α, for this table is $10/52 = 0.19$. The hash function h must map each of the possible identifiers into one of the numbers 0 to 25. If the internal binary representation for the letters A to Z corresponds to the numbers 0 to 25, respectively, then the function h defined by $h(x) =$ the first character of x will hash all identifiers x into the hash table. The identifiers GA, D, A, G, L, A2, A1, A3, A4, and E will be hashed into buckets 6, 3, 0, 6, 11, 0, 0, 0, 0, and 4, respectively, by this function. The identifiers A, A1, A2, A3, and A4 are synonyms. So also are G and GA. Figure 8.1 shows the identifiers GA, D, A, G, and A2 entered into the hash table.

	Slot 1	Slot 2
0	A	A2
1		
2		
3	D	
4		
5		
6	GA	G
⋮	⋮	⋮
25		

Figure 8.1: Hash table with 26 buckets and two slots per bucket

Note that GA and G are in the same bucket and each bucket has two slots. Similarly, the synonyms A and A2 are in the same bucket. The next identifier, A1, hashes into the bucket ht [0]. This bucket is full and a search of the bucket indicates that A1 is not in the bucket. An overflow has now occurred. Where in the table should A1 be entered so that it may be retrieved when needed? □

When no overflows occur, the time required to enter or search for identifiers using hashing depends only on the time required to compute the hash function h and the time to search one bucket. Since the bucket size, s, is usually small (for internal tables s is usually 1) the search for an identifier within a bucket is carried out using a sequential search. The time is independent of n.

The hash function of Example 8.1 is not well suited for the application we have in mind because of the very large number of collisions and resulting overflows that occur. This is so because it is not unusual to find programs in which many of the variables begin with the same letter. Ideally, we would like to choose a function h that is both easy to compute and results in very few collisions. Since the ratio b/T is usually very small, it is impossible to avoid collisions altogether.

In summary, hashing schemes perform an identifier transformation through the use of a hash function h. It is desirable to choose a function h that is easy to compute and also minimizes the number of collisions. Since the size of the identifier space, T, is usually several orders of magnitude larger than the number of buckets, b, and s is small, overflows necessarily occur. Hence, a mechanism to handle overflows is also needed.

8.2.2   Hash Functions

A hash function, h, transforms an identifier, x, into a bucket address in the hash table. As mentioned earlier, the desired properties of such a function are that it be easy to compute and that it minimize the number of collisions. A function such as the one discussed earlier is not a very good choice for a hash function for symbol tables, even though it is easy to compute. The reason for this is that the function depends only on the first character in the identifier. Since many programs use several identifiers with the same first letter, we expect several collisions to occur. In general, then, we would like the function to depend upon all the characters in the identifiers. In addition, we would like the hash function to be such that it does not result in a biased use of the hash table for random inputs; i.e., if x is an identifier chosen at random from the identifier space, then we want the probability that $h(x) = i$ to be $1/b$ for all buckets i. Then a random x has an equal chance of hashing into any of the b buckets. A hash function satisfying this property will be called a *uniform hash function*.

Several kinds of uniform hash functions are in use. We shall describe four of these.

8.2.2.1   Mid-Square

The mid-square function has found much use in symbol table applications. This function, h_m, is computed by squaring the identifier and then using an appropriate number of bits from the middle of the square to obtain the bucket address; the identifier is assumed to fit into one computer word. Since the middle bits of the square usually depend on all the characters in the identifier, different identifiers are expected to result in different hash addresses with high probability, even when some of the characters are the same. Figure 8.2 shows the bit configurations resulting from squaring some sample identifiers. The number of bits to be used to obtain the bucket address depends on the table size. If r bits are used, the range of values is 2^r, so the size of hash tables is chosen to be a power of two when this kind of scheme is used.

8.2.2.2   Division

Another simple choice for a hash function is obtained by using the modulo (**mod**) operator. The identifier x is divided by some number M, and the remainder is used as the hash address for x. The hash function is

$$f_D(x) = x \bmod M$$

Identifier	**Internal Representation**	
x	x	x^2
A	1	1
A1	134	20420
A2	135	20711
A3	136	21204
A4	137	21501
A9	144	23420
B	2	4
C	3	11
G	7	61
DMAX	4150130	21526443617100
DMAX1	415013034	5264473522151420
AMAX	1150130	135423617100
AMAX1	115013034	3454246522151420

Figure 8.2: Internal representations of x and x^2 in octal notation (x is input right-justified, zero-filled, six bits or two octal digits per character)

This function gives bucket addresses in the range 0 through $(M - 1)$, so the hash table is at least of size $b = M$. The choice of M is critical. If M is a power of 2, then $h_D(x)$ depends only on the least significant bits of x. For instance, if each character is represented by six bits, and identifiers are stored right-justified in a 60-bit word with leading bits filled with zeros (Figure 8.3), then with $M = 2^i$, $i \leq 6$, the identifiers A1, B1, C1, X41, DNTXY1, etc., all have the same bucket address. With $M = 2^i$, $i \leq 12$, the identifiers AXY, BXY, WTXY, etc., have the same bucket address.

48 bits

0	0	0	0	0	0	A	1

right-justified zero-filled

48 bits

A	1	0	0	0	0	0	0

left-justified

Figure 8.3: Identifier A1 right- and left-justified and zero-filled (six bits per character)

Since programmers have a tendency to use many variables with the same suffix, the choice of M as a power of two would result in many collisions. This choice of M would have even more disastrous results if the identifier x were stored left-justified and zero-filled. Then, all one-character identifiers would map to the same bucket, 0, for

$M = 2^i, i \le 54$; all two-character identifiers would map to the bucket 0 for $M = 2^i, i \le 48$, and so on. As a result of this observation, we see that when the division function h_D is used as a hash function, the table size should not be a power of two, whereas when the mid-square function h_m is used, the table size is a power of two.

If M is divisible by two, then odd keys are mapped to odd buckets (as the remainder is odd), and even keys are mapped to even buckets. The use of the hash table is thus biased.

Let $x = x_1x_2$ and $y = x_2x_1$ be two identifiers, each consisting of the characters x_1 and x_2. If the internal binary representation of x_1 has value $C(x_1)$, and that for x_2 has value $C(x_2)$, then if each character is represented by six bits, the numeric value of x is $2^6C(x_1) + C(x_2)$, and that for y is $2^6C(x_2) + C(x_1)$. If p is a prime number that divides M, then:

$$(f_D(x) - f_D(y)) \bmod p = (2^6 C(x_1) \bmod p + C(x_2) \bmod p$$
$$- 2^6 C(x_2) \bmod p - C(x_1) \bmod p) \bmod p$$

If $p = 3$, then

$$(f_D(x) - f_D(y)) \bmod p = (64 \bmod 3 \; C(x_1) \bmod 3 + C(x_2) \bmod 3$$
$$- 64 \bmod 3 \; C(x_2) \bmod 3 - C(x_1) \bmod 3) \bmod 3$$
$$= C(x_1) \bmod 3 + C(x_2) \bmod 3 - C(x_2) \bmod 3 - C(x_1) \bmod 3$$
$$= 0 \bmod 3$$

That is, permutations of the same set of characters are hashed at a distance a multiple of three apart. Programs in which many variables are permutations of each other would again result in a biased use of the table and hence result in many collisions. This happens because $64 \bmod 3 = 1$. The same behavior can be expected when 7 divides M, as $64 \bmod 7 = 1$.

These difficulties can be avoided by making M a prime number. Then, the only factors of M are M and 1. Donald Knuth has shown that when M divides $r^k \pm a$, where k and a are small numbers and r is the radix of the character set (in the example above $r = 64$), then $x \bmod M$ tends to be a simple superposition of the characters in x. Thus, a prime number such that M does not divide $r^k \pm a$ for small k and a would be a good choice for M. In Section 8.2.3 we shall see other reasons for choosing M as a prime number. In practice it has been observed that it is sufficient to choose M such that it has no prime divisors less than 20.

8.2.2.3   Folding

In this method the identifier x is partitioned into several parts, all but possibly the last being of the same length. These partitions are then added together to obtain the hash address for x. There are two ways of carrying out this addition. In the first, all but the last partition are shifted so that the least significant bit of each lines up with the corresponding bit of the last partition. The different partitions are now added together to get $h(x)$.

This method is known as *shift folding*. In the second method, *folding at the boundaries*, the identifier is folded at the partition boundaries, and digits falling into the same position are added together to obtain $h(x)$. This is equivalent to reversing every other partition and then adding.

Example 8.2: Suppose that $x = 12320324111220$, and we partition it into parts that are three decimal digits long. The partitions are $P_1 = 123$, $P_2 = 203$, $P_3 = 241$, $P_4 = 112$, and $P_5 = 20$. Using shift folding, we obtain

$$h(x) = \sum_{1=1}^{5} P_i = 123 + 203 + 241 + 112 + 20 = 699$$

When folding at the boundaries is used, we first reverse P_2 and P_4 to obtain 302 and 211, respectively. Next, the five partitions are added to obtain $h(x) = 123 + 302 + 241 + 211 + 20 = 897$. □

8.2.2.4 Digit Analysis

This method is particularly useful in the case of a static file where all the identifiers in the table are known in advance. Each identifier x is interpreted as a number using some radix r. The same radix is used for all the identifiers in the table. Using this radix, the digits of each identifier are examined. Digits having the most skewed distributions are deleted. Enough digits are deleted so that the number of remaining digits is small enough to give an address in the range of the hash table.

In Section 8.2.4, we compare the various methods used to generate a hash address. Of these methods, the one most suitable for general-purpose applications is the division method with a divisor, M, such that M has no prime factors less than 20.

8.2.3 Overflow Handling

8.2.3.1 Open Addressing

There are two ways to handle overflows: *open addressing* and *chaining*. In open addressing, we assume the hash table is an array. For simplicity, we assume that $s = 1$. The data types used are

type *identifier* = **string** [*MaxSize*];
    HashTable = **array**[0 .. *bMinus* 1] **of** *identifer*;

To detect collisions and overflows, the hash table, *ht*, is initialized so that each slot contains the null identifier. When a new identifier is hashed into a full bucket, we need to find another bucket for this identifier. The simplest solution is to find the closest unfilled bucket. This is called *linear probing* or *linear open addressing*.

Example 8.3: Assume we have a 26-bucket table with one slot per bucket and the following identifiers: GA, D, A, G, L, A2, A1, A3, A4, Z, ZA, E. For simplicity we choose the hash function $h(x) =$ first character of x. Initially, all entries in the table are null. Since $h(GA) = 6$, and $ht[6]$ is empty, GA and any other information making up the record are entered into $ht[6]$. D and A get entered into the buckets $ht[3]$ and $ht[0]$, respectively. The next identifier G has $h(G) = 6$. This bucket is already used by GA. The next vacant slot is $ht[7]$, so G is entered there. L enters $ht[11]$. A2 collides with A at $ht[0]$, the bucket overflows, and A2 is entered at the next vacant slot, $ht[1]$. A1, A3, and A4 are entered at $ht[2]$, $ht[4]$, and $ht[5]$, respectively. Z is entered at $ht[25]$, ZA at $ht[8]$ (the hash table is used circularly), and E collides with A3 at $ht[4]$ and is eventually entered at $ht[9]$. Figure 8.4 shows the resulting table. □

0	A
1	A2
2	A1
3	D
4	A3
5	A4
6	GA
7	G
8	ZA
9	E
10	
11	L
12	
13	
24	
25	Z

Figure 8.4: Hash table with linear probing (26 buckets, one slot per bucket)

When linear open addressing is used to handle overflows, a hash table search for identifier x proceeds as follows:

(1)   compute $h(x)$

(2)   examine identifiers at positions $ht[h(x)]$, $ht[h(x) + 1]$, $\cdots$, $ht[h(x) + j]$, in this order, until one of the following happens:

   (a) $ht[h(x) + j] = x$; in this case x is found.

   (b) $ht[h(x) + j]$ is null; x is not in the table.

   (c)   We return to the starting position $h(x)$; the table is full and x is not in the table.

LinearSearch (Program 8.1) is the resulting search procedure.

---

procedure *LinearSearch* (x : *identifier*; ht : *HashTable*; **var** j : **integer**; b : **integer**);
{Search the hash table $ht[0..b-1]$ (each bucket has exactly one slot) for x using linear probing. j is set such that if x is already in the table, then $ht[j] = x$. If x is not in the table and there is a free bucket, then $ht[j] = ''$ and x can be entered here. h is the hash function.}
var i : **integer**; *done* : **boolean**;
begin
 $i := h(x)$; $j := i$; *done* := **false**;
 while ($ht[j] < > x$) **and** ($ht[j] < > ''$) **and** (**not** *done*) **do**
 begin
  $j := (j + 1)$ **mod** b; {treat the table as circular}
  if $j = i$ **then** *done* := **true**; {back to start}
 end;
end; {of *LinearSearch*}

Program 8.1: Linear search

   In Example 8.3 we saw that when linear probing is used to resolve overflows, identifiers tend to cluster together, and moreover, adjacent clusters tend to coalesce, thus increasing the search time. To locate the identifier ZA in the table of Figure 8.4, it is necessary to examine $ht[25]$, $ht[0]$, $\cdots$, $ht[8]$ — a total of 10 comparisons. This is far worse than the worst-case behavior for the tree tables we shall see in Chapter 10. If each of the identifiers in the table of Figure 8.4 is retrieved exactly once, then the number of buckets examined is 1 for A, 2 for A2, 3 for A1, 1 for D, 5 for A3, 6 for A4, 1 for GA, 2 for G, 10 for ZA, 6 for E, 1 for L, and 1 for Z — for a total of 39 buckets examined. The average number examined is 3.25 buckets per identifier.
   An analysis of linear probing shows that the expected average number of identifier comparisons, P, to look up an identifier is approximately $(2 - \alpha)/(2 - 2\alpha)$, where α is the loading density. This is the average over all possible sets of identifiers yielding the given loading density and using a uniform function h. In Example 8.3, $\alpha = 12/26 = .47$ and $P = 1.5$. Even though the average number of probes is small, the worst case can be quite large.

One of the problems with linear open addressing is that it tends to create clusters of identifiers. Moreover, these clusters tend to merge as more identifiers are entered, leading to bigger clusters. Some improvement in the growth of clusters and hence in the average number of probes needed for searching can be obtained by *quadratic probing*. Linear probing was characterized by searching the buckets $(h(x) + i)$ mod b, $0 \leq i \leq b - 1$, where b is the number of buckets in the table. In quadratic probing, a quadratic function of i is used as the increment. In particular, the search is carried out by examining buckets $h(x)$, $(h(x) + i^2)$ mod b, and $(h(x) - i^2)$ mod b for $1 \leq i \leq (b - 1)/2$. When b is a prime number of the form $4j + 3$, for j an integer, the quadratic search described above examines every bucket in the table. (For the proof, refer to the article by Radke cited in the References and Selected Readings section). Figure 8.5 lists some primes of the form $4j + 3$.

Prime	j	Prime	j
3	0	43	10
7	1	59	14
11	2	127	31
19	4	251	62
23	5	503	125
31	7	1019	254

Figure 8.5: Some primes of the form $4j + 3$

An alternative method to retard the growth of clusters is to use a series of hash functions $h_1, h_2, \cdots, h_m$. This method is known as *rehashing*. Buckets $h_i(x)$, $1 \leq i \leq m$ are examined in that order. Yet another alternative, random probing, is explored in the exercises.

8.2.3.2   Chaining

Linear probing and its variations perform poorly because the search for an identifier involves comparison with identifiers that have different hash values. In the hash table of Figure 8.4, for instance, searching for the identifier ZA involves comparisons with the buckets $ht[0]$ to $ht[7]$, even though none of the identifiers in these buckets had a collision with $ht[25]$ and so cannot possibly be ZA. Many of the comparisons can be saved if we maintain lists of identifiers, one list per bucket, each list containing all the synonyms for that bucket. If this is done, a search involves computing the hash address $h(x)$ and examining only those identifiers in the list for $h(x)$. Since the sizes of these lists are not known in advance, the best way to maintain them is as linked chains. Additional space for a link is required in each slot. Each chain has a head node. The head node, however, usually is much smaller than the other nodes, since it has to retain only a link. Since the lists are to be accessed at random, the head nodes should be sequential. We assume that they are numbered 1 to $b - 1$ if the hash function h has range 1 to $b - 1$.

When chaining is used on the data of Example 8.3, the hash chains of Figure 8.6 are obtained. To insert a new identifier, x, into a chain, we must first verify that it is not currently on the chain. Following this, x may be inserted at any position of the chain. In the example of Figure 8.6, new identifiers were inserted at the front of the chains. The number of probes needed to search for any of the identifiers is one for each of A4, D, E, G, L, and ZA; two for each of A3, GA, and Z; three for A1; four for A2; and five for A, for a total of 24. The average is now two, which is considerably less than the average for linear probing.

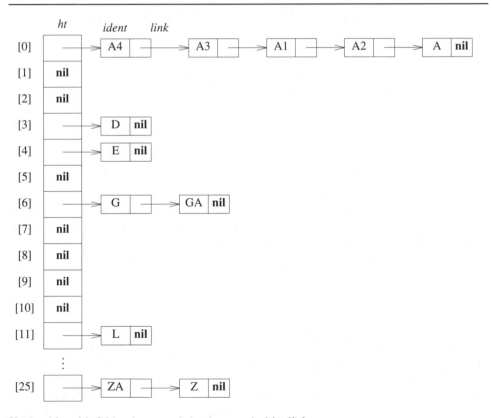

Hash table with 26 buckets; each bucket can hold a link.

Figure 8.6: Hash chains corresponding to Figure 8.4

The search algorithm for hash tables with chaining is given in Program 8.2. The data types are

> **type** *identifier* = **packed array**[1 .. *MaxChar*] **of char**;
> *ListPointer* = ↑*ListNode*;
> *ListNode* = **record**
> *ident* = *identifier*;
> *link* = *ListPointer*;
> **end**;
> *HashTable* = **array**[0 .. *bMinus* 1] **of** *ListPointer*;

---

procedure *ChainSearch* (*x* : *identifier*; **var** *ht* : *HashTable*;
b : **integer**; **var** *j* : *ListPointer*);
{Search the chained hash table *ht* [0 .. *b* − 1] for *x*. On termination, *j* points to the node that contains *x*. If there is no such node, then *j* = **nil**.}
var *found* : **boolean**;
begin
    j := *ht* [*h* (*x*)]; {compute head node address}
    {search the chain starting at *j*}
    found := **false**;
    while (*j* <> **nil**) **and not** *found* **do**
        if *j*↑. *ident* = *x* **then** *found* := **true**
                        else *j* := *j*↑. *link*;
end; {of *ChainSearch*}

Program 8.2: Chain search

The expected number of identifier comparisons can be shown to be ≈ $1 + \alpha/2$, where α is the loading density n/b (b = number of head nodes). For $\alpha = 0.5$ this figure is 1.25, and for $\alpha = 1$ it is about 1.5. This scheme has the additional advantage that only the b head nodes must be sequential and reserved at the beginning. Each head node, however, will be at most one-half to one word long. The other nodes will be much bigger and are allocated only as needed. This could represent an overall reduction in space required for certain loading densities, despite the links. If each record in the table is five words long, $n = 100$, and $\alpha = 0.5$, then the hash table will be of size $200 \times 5 = 1000$ words. Only 500 of these are used, as $\alpha = 0.5$. On the other hand, if chaining is used with one full word per link, then 200 words are needed for the head nodes ($b = 200$). Each head node is one word long. One hundred nodes of six words each are needed for the records. The total space needed is thus 800 words, or 20% less than when no chaining was being used. When α is close to 1, the average number of probes using linear probing or its variations becomes quite large, and the additional space used for chaining can be justified by the reduction in the expected number of probes needed for retrieval. Deletion can be done by removing a node from its chain. The problem of deleting entries when open addressing is used is explored in the exercises.

The results of this section tend to imply that the performance of a hash table depends only on the method used to handle overflows and is independent of the hash function as long as a uniform hash function is used. Although this is true when the identifiers are selected at random from the identifier space, it is not true in practice. In practice, there is a tendency to make a biased use of identifiers. Many identifiers in use have a common suffix or prefix or are simple permutations of other identifiers. Hence, in practice we would expect different hash functions to result in different hash table performance. The table of Figure 8.7 presents the results of an empirical study conducted by Lum, Yuen, and Dodd. The values in each column give the average number of bucket accesses made in searching eight different tables with 33,575, 24,050, 4909, 3072, 2241, 930, 762, and 500 identifiers each. As expected, chaining outperforms linear open addressing as a method for overflow handling. In looking over the figures for the various hash functions, we see that division is generally superior to the other types of hash functions. For a general application it is therefore recommended that the division method be used. The divisor should be a prime number, although choosing a divisor that has no prime factors less than 20 is sufficient. The table also gives the theoretical expected number of bucket accesses based on random keys.

$\alpha = \dfrac{n}{b}$	0.50		0.75		0.90		0.95	
Hash Function	Chain	Open	Chain	Open	Chain	Open	Chain	Open
mid square	1.26	1.73	1.40	9.75	1.45	37.14	1.47	37.53
division	1.19	4.52	1.31	7.20	1.38	22.42	1.41	25.79
shift fold	1.33	21.75	1.48	65.10	1.40	77.01	1.51	118.57
bound fold	1.39	22.97	1.57	48.70	1.55	69.63	1.51	97.56
digit analysis	1.35	4.55	1.49	30.62	1.52	89.20	1.52	125.59
theoretical	1.25	1.50	1.37	2.50	1.45	5.50	1.48	10.50

(Adapted from V. Lum, P. Yuen, and M. Dodd, *CACM*, 14:4, 1971)

Figure 8.7: Average number of bucket accesses per identifier retrieved

8.2.4   Theoretical Evaluation of Overflow Techniques

The experimental evaluation of hashing techniques indicates a very good performance over conventional techniques such as balanced trees. The worst-case performance for hashing can, however, be very bad. In the worst case, an insertion or a search in a hash table with n identifiers may take O(n) time. In this section, we present a probabilistic analysis for the expected performance of the chaining method and state without proof the results of similar analyses for the other overflow handling methods. First, we formalize what we mean by expected performance.

Let $ht[0..b-1]$ be a hash table with b buckets, each bucket having one slot. Let h be a uniform hash function with range $[0, b-1]$. If n identifiers $x_1, x_2, \cdots, x_n$ are entered into the hash table, then there are b^n distinct hash sequences $h(x_1), h(x_2), \cdots, h(x_n)$. Assume that each of these is equally likely to occur. Let S_n denote the expected number of identifier comparisons needed to locate a randomly chosen x_i, $1 \le i \le n$. Then, S_n is the average number of comparisons needed to find the jth key x_j, averaged over $1 \le j \le n$, with each j equally likely, and averaged over all b^n hash sequences, assuming each of these also to be equally likely. Let U_n be the expected number of identifier comparisons when a search is made for an identifier not in the hash table. This hash table contains n identifiers. The quantity U_n may be defined in a manner analogous to that used for S_n.

Theorem 8.1: Let $\alpha = n/b$ be the loading density of a hash table using a uniform hashing function h. Then

(1) for linear open addressing

$$U_n \approx \frac{1}{2}\left[1 + \frac{1}{(1-\alpha)^2}\right]$$

$$S_n \approx \frac{1}{2}\left[1 + \frac{1}{1-\alpha}\right]$$

(2) for rehashing, random probing, and quadratic probing

$$U_n \approx 1/(1-\alpha)$$

$$S_n \approx -\left[\frac{1}{\alpha}\right]\log_e(1-\alpha)$$

(3) for chaining

$$U_n \approx \alpha$$

$$S_n \approx 1 + \alpha/2$$

Proof: Exact derivations of U_n and S_n are fairly involved and can be found in Knuth's book *The Art of Computer Programming: Sorting and Searching* (see the References and Selected Readings section). Here we present a derivation of the approximate formulas for chaining. First, we must make clear our count for U_n and S_n. If the identifier x being sought has $h(x) = i$, and chain i has k nodes on it (not including the head node), then k comparisons are needed if x is not on the chain. If x is j nodes away from the head node, $1 \le j \le k$, then j comparisons are needed.

When the n identifiers are distributed uniformly over the b possible chains, the expected number in each chain is $n/b = \alpha$. Since U_n equals the expected number of identifiers on a chain, we get $U_n = \alpha$.

When the ith identifier, x_i, is being entered into the table, the expected number of identifiers on any chain is $(i - 1)/b$. Hence, the expected number of comparisons needed to search for x_i after all n identifiers have been entered is $1 + (i - 1)/b$ (this assumes that new entries will be made at the end of the chain). Thus,

$$S_n = \frac{1}{n}\sum_{i=1}^{n}\{1 + (i - 1)/b\} = 1 + \frac{n - 1}{2b} \approx 1 + \frac{\alpha}{2} \quad \square$$

EXERCISES

1. Write an algorithm to delete identifier x from a hash table that uses hash function h and linear open addressing to resolve collisions. Show that simply setting the slot previously occupied by x to null does not solve the problem. How must algorithm *LinearSearch* (Program 8.1) be modified so that a correct search is made in the situation when deletions are permitted? Where can a new identifier be inserted?

2. (a) Show that if quadratic searching is carried out in the sequence $(h(x) + q^2)$, $(h(x) + (q - 1)^2)$, $\cdots$, $(h(x) + 1)$, $h(x)$, $(h(x) - 1)$, $\cdots$, $(h(x) - q^2)$ with $q = (b - 1)/2$, then the address difference mod b between successive buckets being examined is

$$b - 2, b - 4, b - 6, \ldots, 5, 3, 1, 1, 3, 5, \ldots, b - 6, b - 4, b - 2$$

   (b) Write an algorithm to search a hash table $ht[0 .. b - 1]$ of size b for the identifier x. Use h as the hash function and the quadratic probe scheme discussed in the text to resolve overflows. If x is not in the table, it is to be entered. Use the results of part (a) to reduce the computations.

3. [*Morris 1968*] In random probing, the search for an identifier, x, in a hash table with b buckets is carried out by examining the buckets in the order $h(x)$, $(h(x) + S(i))$ mod b, $1 \le i \le b - 1$ where $S(i)$ is a pseudo random number. The random number generator must satisfy the property that every number from 1 to $b - 1$ must be generated exactly once as i ranges from 1 to $b - 1$.

   (a) Show that for a table of size 2^r, the following sequence of computations generates numbers with this property:

   Initialize R to 1 each time the search routine is called.
   On successive calls for a random number do the following:
   $R := R * 5$
   $R :=$ low order $r + 2$ bits of R
   $S(i) := R/4$

   (b) Write search and insert algorithms for a hash table using random probing and the mid-square hash function. Use the random number generator of (a).

It can be shown that for this method, the expected value for the average number of comparisons needed to search for x is $-(1/\alpha)\log(1 - \alpha)$ for large tables (α is the loading factor).

4. Write an algorithm to list all the identifiers in a hash table in lexicographic order. Assume the hash function h is $h(x) =$ first character of x, and linear probing is used. How much time does your algorithm take?

5. Let the binary representation of identifier x be $x_1 x_2$. Let $|x|$ denote the number of bits in x and let the first bit of x_1 be 1. Let $|x_1| = \lceil |x|/2 \rceil$ and $|x_2| = \lfloor |x|/2 \rfloor$. Consider the following hash function

$$h(x) = \text{middle } k \text{ bits of } (x_1 \text{ XOR } x_2)$$

where XOR is the exclusive-or operator. Is this a uniform hash function if identifiers are drawn at random from the space of allowable Pascal identifiers? What can you say about the behavior of this hash function in actual symbol table usage?

6. [**T. Gonzalez**] Design a symbol table representation that allows you to search, insert, and delete an identifier x in O(1) time. Assume that $1 \leq x \leq m$ and that $m + n$ units of space are available, where n is the number of insertions to be made. (Hint: Use two arrays, $a[1 .. n]$ and $b[1 .. m]$, where $a[i]$ will be the ith identifier inserted into the table. If x is the ith identifier inserted, then $b[x] = i$.) Write algorithms to search, insert, and delete identifiers. Note that you cannot initialize either a or b to zero as this would take O($n + m$) time. Note that x is an integer.

7. [**T. Gonzalez**] Let $S = \{x_1, x_2, \cdots, x_n\}$ and $T = \{y_1, y_2, \cdots, y_r\}$ be two sets. Assume $1 \leq x_i \leq m$, $1 \leq i \leq n$, and $1 \leq y_i \leq m$, $1 \leq i \leq r$. Using the idea of Exercise 6, write an algorithm to determine if $S \subseteq T$. Your algorithm should work in O($r + n$) time. Since $S \equiv T$ iff $S \subseteq T$ and $T \subseteq S$, one can determine in linear time whether two sets are equivalent. How much space is needed by your algorithm?

8. [**T. Gonzalez**] Using the idea of Exercise 6, write an O($n + m$) time algorithm to carry out the function of algorithm *verify2* (Program 7.3). How much space does your algorithm need?

9. Using the notation of Section 8.2.4, show that when linear open addressing is used

$$S_n = \frac{1}{n} \sum_{i=0}^{n-1} U_i$$

Using this equation and the approximate equality

$$U_n \approx \frac{1}{2} \left[1 + \frac{1}{(1 - \alpha)^2} \right] \quad \text{where } \alpha = \frac{n}{b}$$

show that

$$S_n \approx \frac{1}{2}\left[1 + \frac{1}{(1-\alpha)}\right]$$

10. [*Guttag*] The following set of operations defines a symbol table that handles a language with block structure. Write a specification for this data type in the style of Structure 8.1.

INIT	creates an empty table
ENTERB	indicates a new block has been entered
ADD	places an identifier and its attributes in the table
LEAVEB	deletes all identifiers that are defined in the innermost block
RETRIEVE	returns the attributes of the most recently defined identifier
ISINB	returns true if the identifier is defined in the innermost block, else false

8.3   DYNAMIC HASHING

8.3.1   Motivation for Dynamic Hashing

One of the most important classes of software is the database management system, or DBMS. In a DBMS the user enters a query, and the system translates it and retrieves the resulting data. Fast access time is essential, as a DBMS typically holds large sets of information. Another key characteristic of a DBMS is that the amount of information can vary a great deal with time. Various data structures have been suggested for storing the data in a DBMS. In this section, we examine an extension of hashing that permits the technique to be used by a DBMS.

Traditional hashing schemes as described in the previous section are not ideal. This follows from the fact that one must statically allocate a portion of memory to hold the hash table. This hash table is used to point to the pages used to hold identifiers, or it may actually hold the identifiers themselves. In either case, if the table is allocated to be as large as possible, then space can be wasted. If it is allocated to be too small, then when the data exceed the capacity of the hash table, the entire file must be restructured, a time-consuming process. The purpose of *dynamic hashing* (also referred to as *extendible hashing*) is to retain the fast retrieval time of conventional hashing while extending the technique so that it can accommodate dynamically increasing and decreasing file size without penalty.

We assume that a file F is a collection of records R. Each record has a key field K by which it is identified. Records are stored in pages or buckets whose capacity is p. We will try to develop algorithms that minimize access to pages, since they are typically stored on disk and their retrieval into memory dominates any operation. The measure of space utilization is the ratio of the number of records, n, divided by the total space, mp, where m is the number of pages.

8.3.2   Dynamic Hashing Using Directories

Consider an example in which an identifier consists of two characters, and each character is represented by three bits. Figure 8.8 gives a list of some of these identifiers.

identifiers	binary represenation
A0	100 000
A1	100 001
B0	101 000
B1	101 001
C0	110 000
C1	110 001
C2	110 010
C3	110 011

Figure 8.8: Some identifiers that require three bits per character

Consider placing these identifiers into a table that has four pages. Each page can hold at most two identifiers, and each page is indexed by the two-bit sequence 00, 01, 10, and 11, respectively. We use the two low-order bits of each identifier to determine in which page of the table to place it. The result of placing A0, B0, C2, A1, B1, and C3 is shown in Figure 8.9. Note that we select the bits from least significant to most significant.

Branching at the root is determined by the least significant bit. If this bit is zero, the upper branch is taken; otherwise, the lower branch is taken. Branching at the next level is determined by the second least significant bit, and so on. A0 and B0 are in the first page since their two low-order bits are 0 and 0. The second page contains only C2. To reach this page, we first branch on the least significant bit of C2 (i.e., 0) and then on the next bit (i.e., 1). The third page contains A1 and B1. To reach this page, we first branch on the least significant bit of A1 or B1. This bit is one for both A1 and B1. Next, we branch on the next bit, which is zero for both. The last page contains C3, with a bit pattern of 11. We use the term *trie* to denote a binary tree in which we locate an identifier by following its bit sequence. (We shall describe tries in greater detail in Chapter 10.) Notice that the nodes of this trie always branch in two directions corresponding to 0 or 1. Only the leaf nodes of the trie contain a pointer to a page.

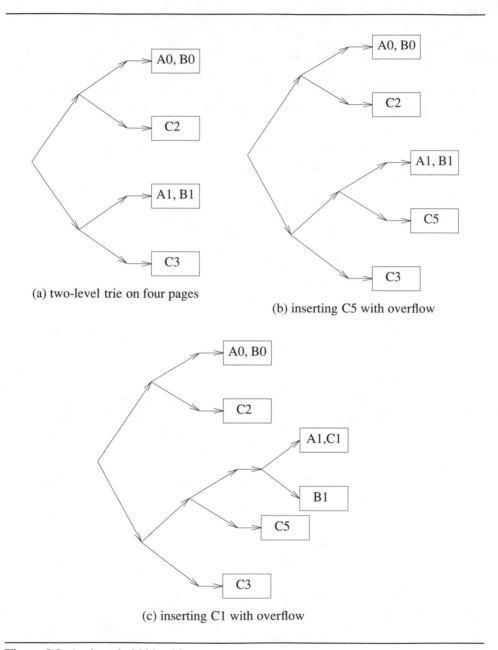

(a) two-level trie on four pages

(b) inserting C5 with overflow

(c) inserting C1 with overflow

Figure 8.9: A trie to hold identifiers

Now suppose we try to insert a new identifier, say C5, into Figure 8.9(a). Since the two low-order bits of C5 are 1 and 0, we must place it in the third page. However, this page is full, and an overflow occurs. A new page is added, and the depth of the trie increases by one level. This is shown in Figure 8.9(b). If we now try to insert the new identifier C1, an overflow of the page containing A1 and B1 occurs. A new page is obtained, and the three identifiers are divided between the two pages according to their four low-order bits.

From this example one can see that two major problems exist. First, the access time for a page depends on the number of bits needed to distinguish the identifiers. Second, if the identifiers have a skewed distribution, the tree is also skewed. Both of these factors increase the retrieval time. Fagin et al. (1979) present a method, which they call *extendible hashing*, for solving these problems. To avoid the skewed distribution of identifiers, a hash function is used. This function takes the key and produces a random set of binary digits. To avoid the long search down the trie, the trie is mapped to a directory.

A *directory* is a table of page pointers. If k bits are needed to distinguish the identifiers, the directory has 2^k entries indexed $0, \cdots, 2^k-1$. To find the page for an identifier, we use the integer with binary representation equal to the last k bits of the identifier. The page pointed at by this directory entry is searched. Figure 8.10 shows the directories corresponding to the three tries in Figure 8.9. The first directory contains four entries indexed from 0 to 3 (the binary representation of each index is shown in Figure 8.10). Each entry contains a pointer to a page. This pointer is shown as an arrow in the figure. The letter above each pointer is a page label. The page labels were obtained by labeling the pages of Figure 8.9(a) top to bottom, beginning with the label a. The page contents are shown immediately after the page pointer. To see the correspondence between the directory and the trie, notice that if the bits in the directory index are used to follow a path in the trie (beginning with the least significant bit), we will reach the page pointed at by the corresponding directory entry.

The second directory contains eight entries indexed from 0 to 7, and the third has 16 entries indexed from 0 to 15. Page a of the second directory (Figure 8.10(b)) has two directory entries (000 and 100) pointing to it. The page contents are shown only once. Page b has two pointers to it, page c has one pointer, page d has one pointer, and page e has two pointers. In Figure 8.10(c) there are six pages with the following number of pointers, respectively: 4, 4, 1, 1, 2, and 4.

Using a directory to represent a trie allows the table of identifiers to grow and shrink dynamically. This, of course, assumes that the operating system can give us more pages or return pages to available storage with little or no difficulty. In addition, accessing any page requires only two steps. In the first step, we use the hash function to find the address of the directory entry, and in the second, we retrieve the page associated with the address.

Unfortunately, if the keys are not uniformly divided among the pages, the directory can grow quite large. However, most of the entries point to the same pages. To prevent this from happening, we cannot use the bit sequence of the keys themselves. Instead we translate the bits into a random sequence using a *uniform hash function* as dis-

00 $\xrightarrow{a}$ A0, B0	000 $\xrightarrow{a}$ A0, B0	0000 $\xrightarrow{a}$ A0, B0
01 $\xrightarrow{c}$ A1, B1	001 $\xrightarrow{c}$ A1, B1	0001 $\xrightarrow{c}$ A1, C1
10 $\xrightarrow{b}$ C2	010 $\xrightarrow{b}$ C2	0010 $\xrightarrow{b}$ C2
11 $\xrightarrow{d}$ C3	011 $\xrightarrow{e}$ C3	0011 $\xrightarrow{f}$ C3
	100 $\xrightarrow{a}$	0100 $\xrightarrow{a}$
	101 $\xrightarrow{d}$ C5	0101 $\xrightarrow{e}$ C5
	110 $\xrightarrow{b}$	0110 $\xrightarrow{b}$
	111 $\xrightarrow{e}$	0111 $\xrightarrow{f}$
		1000 $\xrightarrow{a}$
		1001 $\xrightarrow{d}$ B1
		1010 $\xrightarrow{b}$
		1011 $\xrightarrow{f}$
		1100 $\xrightarrow{a}$
		1101 $\xrightarrow{e}$
		1110 $\xrightarrow{b}$
		1111 $\xrightarrow{f}$

    (a) 2 bits   (b) 3 bits   (c) 4 bits

Figure 8.10: Tries collapsed into directories

cussed in the previous section. In contrast to the previous section, however, we need a *family* of hash functions, because, at any point, we may require a different number of bits to distinguish the new key. One solution is the family

$$hash_i: key \rightarrow \{0 \ldots 2^{i-1}\}, \ 1 \le i \le d$$

where $hash_i$ is simply $hash_{i-1}$ with either a zero or one appended as the new leading bit of the result. Thus, $hash(key, i)$ might be a function that produces a random number of i bits from the identifier *key*.

    Some important twists are associated with this approach. For example, suppose a page identified by i bits overflows. We allocate a new page and rehash the identifiers into those two pages. The identifiers in both pages have their low-order i bits in common. We refer to these pages as *buddies*. When the number of identifiers in two buddy pages is no more than the capacity of a single page, then we coalesce the two pages into one.

Suppose a page that can hold only p records now contains p records, and a new record is to be added. The operating system allocates a new page. All $p + 1$ keys are rehashed, using one more bit and divided between the two pages. If the number of bits used is greater than the depth (the number of bits or $\log_2$ of the directory size) of the directory, the whole directory doubles in size and its depth increases by 1. If all $p + 1$ records are hashed to one of the two pages, the split operation has to be repeated. Fortunately, this is a fairly rare occurrence. When this happens, the depth of the directory can be reduced using a compressed trie as discussed in Chapter 10.

Program 8.3 contains a set of pseudo-Pascal programs that provide many of the details for implementing directory-based dynamic hashing.

```
program DynamicHashing (input, output);
const WordSize = 5; {maximum number of directory bits}
      PageSize = 10; {maximum size of a page}
      MaxDir = 32; {maximum size of a directory}
type NumBits = 1 .. WordSize;
     TwoChars = array[1 .. 2] of char; {holds an identifier}
     GlobalDepth = 1 .. WordSize; { 2^GlobalDepth = number of directory entries}
     paddr = ↑ page;
     directory = array[0 .. MaxDir] of paddr;
     page = record
                 LocalDepth : integer; {number of bits to distinquish identifiers}
                 names : array [1 .. PageSize] of TwoChars; {the actual identifiers}
                 NumIdents : integer; {number of identifiers in this page}
            end;
     brecord = record {a sample record}
                 KeyField : TwoChars;
                 IntegerData : integer;
                 CharData : char;
              end;
var gdepth : GlobalDepth;
    rdirectory : directory; {will contain pointers to pages}

function hash (key : TwoChars ; precision : NumBits) : paddr;
begin
   {key is hashed using a uniform hash function, and the low-order precision bits are re-
   turned as the page address.}
end; {hash}
```

function *buddy* (*index* : *paddr*) : *paddr*;
begin
    {Take an address of a page and return the page's buddy (i.e., the leading bit is complemented).}
end; {*buddy*}

function *size*(*ptr* : *paddr*) : **integer**;
    {Return the number of identifiers in the page.}
end; {*size*}

 function *coalesce* (*ptr*, *buddy* : *paddr*) : *paddr*;
    {Combine page *ptr* and its buddy, *buddy*, into a single page.}
end; {*coalesce*}

function *PageSearch* (*key* : *TwoChars* ; *index* : *paddr*) : **boolean**;
begin
    {Search a page for a key. If found, return **true**; otherwise return **false**.}
end; {*PageSearch*}

function *convert* (*p* : *paddr*) : **integer**;
begin
    {Convert a pointer to a page to an equivalent integer.}
end; {*convert*}

procedure *enter* (*r* : *brecord* ; *p* : *paddr*);
begin
    {Insert a new record into the page pointed at by *p*.}
end; {*enter*}

procedure *PageDelete* (*key* : *twochar* ; *p* : *pointer*);
begin
    {Remove the record with key *key* from the page pointed at by *p*.}
end; {*PageDelete*}

procedure *find* (*key* : *TwoChars* ; **var** *p* : *paddr* ; *found* : **boolean**);
{Takes a key and searches for a record with this identifier in the file. If found, sets *found* to true and returns the address of the page in *p*. If not found, sets *found* to false.}
var *index*, *ptr* : *paddr* ; *IntIndex* : **integer**;
begin
    index := *hash* (*key*, *gdepth*);
    IntIndex := *convert* (*index*); {change an address to an integer}
    ptr := *rdirectory* [*IntIndex*]; {retrieve a pointer to a page}
    found := *PageSearch* (*key*, *ptr*);
end; {*find*}

procedure *insert* (*r* : *brecord*, *key* : *TwoChars*);
{Insert a new record into the file pointed at by the directory.}
var *found* : **boolean**; *p* : *paddr* ;
label 99;
begin
  find (*key*, *p*, *found*) {check if key is present}
  if *found* **then goto** 99; {key already in}
  else if *p* ↑. *NumIdents* < > *PageSize* {page not full}
    then begin
        enter (*r*, *p*); *p* ↑. *NumIdents* := *p* ↑. *NumIdents* + 1; **goto** 99;
      end
    else begin
        Split the page into two, insert the new key, and
        update *GlobalDepth* if necessary;
        if this causes *GlobalDepth* to exceed *WordSize*,
        then print an error and terminate;
      end;
99:**end**; {*insert*}

procedure *delete* (*key* : *TwoChars*);
{Find and delete the record with key *key*.}
var *found* : **boolean**; *p* : *paddr*;
label 99;
begin
  find (*key*, *p*, *found*);
  if not *found* **then goto** 99;
  PageDelete (*key*, *p*);
  if *size* (*p*) + *size* (*buddy* (*p*)) <= *PageSize* **then** *coalesce* (*p*, *buddy* (*p*));
99:**end**; {*delete*}
begin
{main program}
end; {*DynamicHashing*}

Program 8.3: Extendible hashing

8.3.3   Analysis of Directory-based Dynamic Hashing

The most important feature of the directory version of extendible hashing is the guarantee that retrieving any page requires only two disk accesses. Thus, its performance is very good. However, we pay for this performance in space. Recall that adding identifiers that are not uniformly distributed can double the directory size. Since many of the pointers could point to the same page, we have a lot of wasted storage.

A second criterion for judging hashing schemes is the space utilization. This is defined as the ratio of the number of records stored in the table divided by the total amount of space allocated. Several researchers (Fagin, Larson, and Mendelson) have analyzed this measure for different variations of dynamic hashing. They have all reached similar conclusions, namely, that without any special strategies for handling overflows, the space utilization is approximately 69%. Each of their derivations is complex and relies on assumptions about the distribution of the identifiers. Here we will follow the derivation given by Mendelson.

Let $L(k)$ stand for the expected number of leaf nodes needed to hold k records. When all the records fit in a single page, $L(k) = 1$. The interesting case is when k exceeds the page size. In this case, the number of records in the two subtrees of the root have a symmetric binomial distribution. From this it follows that there will be j keys in the left subtree and $k - j$ in the right, each with a given probability, which is

$$\binom{k}{j} (1/2)^k$$

This implies that the number of leaf pages in the left subtree is $L(j)$ and the number in the right subtree is $L(k - j)$. Thus, one can express $L(k)$ by the following formula:

$$L(k) = \frac{1}{2^k} \sum_{j=0}^{k} \binom{k}{j} \{L(j) + L(k-j)\} = 2^{1-k} \sum_{j=0}^{k} \binom{k}{j} L(j)$$

Mendelson goes on to show that

$$L(k) \approx \frac{k}{p \ln 2}$$

It follows that the storage utilization is the number of records k divided by the product of the page size p and the number of leaf nodes $L(k)$, or that

$$utilization = \frac{k}{pL(k)} \approx \ln 2 \approx 0.69$$

To see that Mendelson's estimate is reasonable, suppose there is no overflow strategy other than doubling the directory size. We have a full page with p records and attempt to insert a $p+1$'st record, which causes an overflow. With a uniform hash function we now have two pages, each containing about $p/2$ identifiers, or a space utilization of 50%. After the process of inserting and deleting continued for a while, we expect that a recently split page would be at least half full. Thus, space utilization should be at least 50% but certainly less than 100%.

When a page overflows, it may double the directory size. To avoid this, we introduce the concept of overflow pages. Instead of increasing the directory, an overflow causes the allocation of a new page. The pointer to this page is stored in the main page. Rather than storing new identifiers in the main page, we place them in the overflow page. As we shall see, this increases storage utilization, but at the expense of increased retrieval time.

Assume that an overflow page is the same size as a regular page and that both pages are full with p records, making a total of $2p$ records. Suppose an overflow now occurs. We obtain a new page and distribute the keys among the three pages. The utilization is $2p/3p$, or 66%. On the other hand, suppose that the overflow page has a capacity of $p/2$ rather than p. If we redistribute the keys as before, then a total of $3p/2$ records is divided over a capacity of $2p$. This produces a utilization of 3/4, or 75%. Thus, we see that although overflow pages increase utilization, they also increase retrieval time.

Determining the ideal size for the overflow page has been investigated by Larson and others. Larson concludes that if a space utilization below 80% is sufficient, then the size of the overflow pages can vary widely, say from p to $p/2$. However, higher space utilizations require an increasingly narrow range of overflow page sizes, because utilization begins to oscillate, and access time increases significantly. To cope with this problem, we could monitor the space utilization of the file so that when it achieves some predetermined amount, say the 80 percent ratio, the algorithm resumes splitting.

We can also analyze the size of the directory in terms of the number of records, n, that are stored in the file. Fagin estimates this as

$$2 \left\lceil \log \frac{n}{p \ln 2} \right\rceil$$

Figure 8.11 contains a table given by Flajolet that shows the expected directory size for various numbers of records, n, and page size, p. For example, we would need a directory of size 62,500 to store one million records using a page size of 50. This is substantial and indicates that the directory may have to be stored using auxiliary storage.

			p			
n	5	10	20	50	100	200
10^3	1.5K	0.3K	0.1K	0.0K	0.0K	0.0K
10^4	25.6K	4.8K	1.7K	0.5K	0.2K	0.00K
10^5	424.1K	68.2K	16.8K	4.1K	2.0K	1.0K
10^6	6.9M	1.02M	0.26M	62.5K	16.8K	8.1K
10^7	111.11M	11.64M	2.25M	0.52M	0.26M	0.13M

Figure 8.11: Directory size given n records and p page size

In the event that the hash function does not evenly distribute the identifiers across the pages, more sophisticated techniques are required. Lomet suggests that, in the directory scheme, we do not view pages as of a fixed size but allow them to grow. Thus, any given page may be composed of several subpages. As more identifiers map to this page, its storage is expanded. This leads to different strategies for maintaining the identifiers within the page. The simplest strategy is to keep the identifiers in the order they were entered into the table. However, sequential searching is time-consuming, especially as the identifier list gets long. An alternate strategy is to treat each subpage as a dynamically hashed directoryless structure. We describe its maintenance in Section 8.3.3.

Simulation

One important way to measure the performance of any new data structure is to carry out a series of experiments. Each experiment makes use of the algorithms that implement the data structure. Various distributions of identifiers are given to the algorithms with the resultant behavior tabulated. In the case of dynamic hashing, three factors are especially important to monitor. These are (1) access time, (2) insertion time, and (3) total space. The dependent parameters are (1) the number of records, (2) the page size, (3) the directory size, (4) the size of main memory for holding the directory and identifiers, and (5) the time to process page faults.

Fagin et al. have done such a series of experiments. They found that in all cases, extendible hashing performed at least as well or better than B-trees, a popular competitor. In the case of access time and insertion time, extendible hashing was clearly superior. For space utilization the two methods were about equal.

8.3.4 Directoryless Dynamic Hashing

The previous section assumed the existence of a directory that points to pages. One criticism of this approach is that it always requires at least one level of indirection. If we assume that we have a continuous address space large enough to hold all the records, we can eliminate the directory. In effect, this leaves it to the operating system to break the address space into pages and to manage moving them into and out of memory. This scheme is referred to as *directoryless hashing* or *linear hashing*.

Consider the trie of Figure 8.9(a), which has two levels and indexes four pages. In the new method, the two-bit addresses are the actual addresses of these pages (actually they are an offset of some base address). Thus, the hash function delivers the actual address of a page containing the key. Moreover, every value produced by the hash function must point to an actual page. In contrast to the directory scheme, in which a single page might be pointed at by several directory entries, in the directoryless scheme there must exist a unique page for every possible address. Figure 8.12 shows a simple trie and its mapping to contiguous memory without a directory.

What happens when a page overflows? We could double the size of the address space, but this is wasteful. Instead, whenever an overflow occurs, we add a new page to the end of the file and divide the identifiers in one of the pages between its original page and the new page. This complicates the handling of the family of hash functions somewhat. However, if we had simply added one bit to the result of the hash function, the table size would have to be doubled. By adding only one page, the hash function must distinguish between pages addressed by r bits and those addressed by $r+1$ bits. We will show how this is done in a moment.

Figure 8.13 provides an example of directoryless hashing after two insertions. Initially, there are four pages, each addressed by two bits (Figure 8.13(a)). Two of the pages are full, and two have one identifier each. When C5 is inserted, it hashes to the

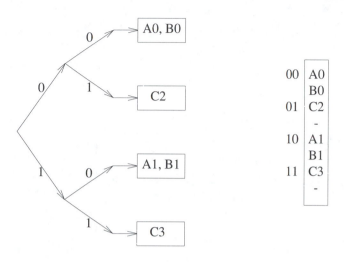

Figure 8.12: A trie mapped to directoryless, continuous storage

page whose address is 10 (Figure 8.13(b)). Since that page is full, an overflow node is allocated to hold C5. At the same time, we add a new page at the end of the storage, rehash the identifiers in the first page, and split them between the first and new page. Unfortunately, none of the new identifiers go into the new page. The first page and the new page are now addressed by three bits, not two as shown in Figure 8.13(b). In the next step, we insert the identifier C1. Since it hashes to the same page as C5, we use another overflow node to store it. We add another new page to the end of the file and rehash the identifiers in the second page. Once again none go into the new page. (Note that this is largely a result of not using a uniform hash function.) Now the first two pages and the two new pages are all addressed using three bits. Eventually the number of pages will double, thereby completing one phase. A new phase then begins.

Consider Figure 8.14, which shows the state of file expansion during the rth phase at some time q. At the beginning of the rth phase, there are 2^r pages, all addressed by r bits. In the figure, q new pages have been added. To the left of the q line are the pages that have already been split. To the right of the q line are the pages remaining to be split up to the line labeled r. To the right of the r line are the pages that have been added during this phase of the process. Each page in this section of the file is addressed by $r + 1$ bits. Note that the q line is an indicator of which page gets split next. The modified hash function is given in Program 8.4. All pages less than q require $r + 1$ bits. The function $hash(key,r)$ is in the range $[0, 2^{r-1}]$, so if the result is less than q, we rehash using $r + 1$ bits. This gives us either the page to the left of q or the one above $2^r - 1$. The directoryless method always requires overflows.

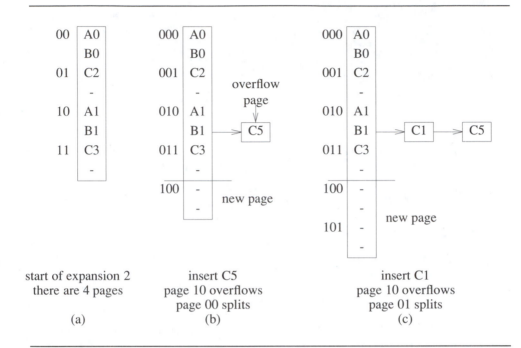

Figure 8.13: An example with two insertions

One sees that for many retrievals the time will be one access, namely, for those identifiers that are in the page directly addressed by the hash function. However, for others, substantially more than two accesses might be required as one moves along the overflow chain. When a new page is added and the identifiers split across the two pages, all identifiers including the overflows are rehashed.

Another fact about this method is that space utilization is not good. As can be seen from Figure 8.13, some extra pages are empty, and yet overflow pages are being used. Litwin has shown that space utilization is approximately 60%. He offers an alternate strategy pursued in the exercises. The term *controlled splitting* refers to splitting the "next page" only when storage utilization exceeds a predefined amount. Litwin suggests that until 80% utilization is reached, other pages continue to overflow.

A natural way to handle overflows is to use one of the traditional hashing schemes discussed earlier, such as open addressing. Recall that open addressing searches the file linearly from the home bucket, looking either for the identifier or for an open spot.

From the example, one sees that the longest overflow chains will occur for those pages that are near the end of the expansion phase, as they are the last to be split. By contrast, those pages that are split early are generally not full.

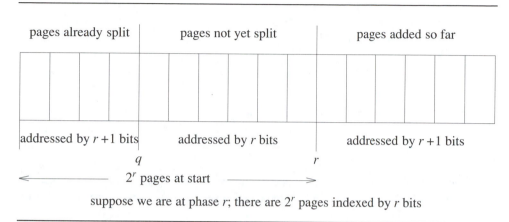

addressed by $r+1$ bits addressed by r bits addressed by $r+1$ bits

suppose we are at phase r; there are 2^r pages indexed by r bits

Figure 8.14: The rth phase of expansion of directoryless method

if *hash*(*key*,*r*) < *q* **then** *page* := *hash*(*key*,*r*+1)
else *page* := *hash*(*key*,*r*);
If neccessary, then follow overflow pointers.

Program 8.4: Modified hash function

EXERCISES

1. The text points out that nonuniform distributions of keys cause a skewed directory and a waste of directory space. One way to avoid this problem in the directory scheme is to store the directory not as a table but as a forest of tries. A new key is hashed to one of the tries, and then its nodes are traversed to a leaf node that points to a page containing the desired record. Splitting is still required. The tries grow and contract with respect to the file. Write out the algorithms for maintaining a trie as a directory.

2. In extendible hashing, given a directory of size *d*, suppose two pointers point to the same page. All identifiers will share a number of low-order bits in common. How many? If four pointers point to the same page, how many bits do the identifiers have in common?

3. Another way of handling overflows in directory-based dynamic hashing is to permit a page to be divided into as many multiple pages as necessary to hold all identifiers that hash to that page. Then you assign a limit on the size of the directory you are willing to accept, and once that size has been reached, a page just

continues to grow. Modify the algorithms in Program 8.3 to implement this strategy.

4. Prove that in directory-based dynamic hashing, a page can be pointed at by a number of pointers that is a power of two.

5. We have not talked much about how to organize the identifiers within a page for fast retrieval. Consider an unordered list, an ordered list, and hashing and compare their merits.

6. Procedure *insert* (Program 8.3) is a complete Pascal program except for a few lines of pseudocode. Replace the pseudocode by actual Pascal code that places all identifiers in page *p* into the *temp* area and then rehashes those identifiers back into either page *p* or *q*.

7. Program 8.3 contains a reference to a procedure *coalesce* that combines the identifiers in two pages into a single page. Using the types and procedures already defined, write a Pascal version of this procedure.

8. Take the formula given by Mendelson for the number of leaf pages required to store *k* records in a directory-based dynamic hashing scheme and formally derive the approximation that $L(k)$ is about equal to $k/(pln\,2)$, where *p* is the page size.

9. Larson has suggested using open addressing in a directoryless dynamic hashing method to handle overflows. The problem is that pages that have yet to be split will have the most overflows, but these pages are stored contiguously. Instead, he suggests that pages be split alternately, so that next to an unsplit page is a split page. Show how the hashing function must be rewritten to handle this scheme.

8.4   REFERENCES AND SELECTED READINGS

Several interesting and enlightening works on hash tables exist. Some of these are "Scatter storage techniques," by R. Morris, *CACM*, 11:1, 1968, pp. 38-44; "Key to address transform techniques: A fundamental performance study on large existing formatted files," by V. Lum, P. Yuen, and M. Dodd, *CACM*, 14:4, 1971, pp. 228-239; "The quadratic quotient method: A hash code eliminating secondary clustering," by J. Bell, *CACM*, 13:2, 1970, pp. 107-109; "Full table quadratic searching for scatter storage," by A. Day, *CACM*, 13:8, 1970, pp. 481-482; "Identifier search mechanisms: A survey and generalized model," by D. Severence, *ACM Computing Surveys*, 6:3, 1974, pp. 175-194; "Hash table methods," by W. Mauer and T. Lewis, *ACM Computing Surveys*, 7:1, 1975, pp. 5-20; *The Art of Computer Programming: Sorting and Searching*, vol. 3, by D. Knuth, Addison-Wesley, Reading, MA, 1973; "Reducing the retrieval time of scatter storage techniques," by R. Brent, *CACM*, 16:2, 1973, pp. 105-109; "General performance analysis of key-to-address transformation methods using an abstract file concept," by V. Lum, *CACM*, 16:10, 1973, pp. 603-612; and "The use of quadratic residue research," by C. Radke, *CACM*, 13:2, 1970, pp. 103-105.

In the literature, Larson was the first to introduce a method he called dynamic hashing. Litwin followed. Fagin et al. called their method extendible hashing. Fagin uses a directory scheme that doubles in size on expansion. Larson used a linked tree structure as the representation of the directory with pointers to pages in the leaves. The references are "Dynamic hashing," by P. Larson, *BIT*, 18, 1978, pp. 184-201; "Virtual hashing: A dynamically changing hashing," by W. Litwin, *Proc. Int. Conf. on Very Large Databases*, Berlin, 1978, pp. 517-523; and "Extendible hashing - A fast access method for dynamic files," by R. Fagin, J. Nievergelt, N. Pippenger, and H. Strong, *ACM Trans. on Database Systems*, 4:3, 1979, pp. 315-344.

An excellent overview of dynamic hashing techniques and variations can be found in: "Dynamic hashing schemes," by R. Enbody and H. Du, *ACM Computing Surveys*, 20:2, 1988, pp. 85-113.

Some other papers on dynamic hashing are: "On the performance evaluation of extendible hashing and trie searching," by P. Flajolet, *Acta Informatica*, 20, 1983, pp. 345-369; "Bounded index exponential hashing," by D. Lomet, *ACM Trans. on Database Systems*, 8:1, 1983, pp. 136-165; "Analysis of extendible hashing," by H. Mendelson, *IEEE Trans. on Software Engineering*, se-8, 6, 1982, pp. 611-619; and "Dynamic hashing schemes," by K. Ramamohanarao and J. Lloyd, *The Computer Journal*, 25:4, 1982, pp. 478-485.

Scholl introduces two methods to improve storage utilization by deferring the splitting of pages and handling overflows internally. This gives a tradeoff between storage utilization and access time. See "New file organizations based on dynamic hashing," by M. Scholl, *ACM Trans. Database Systems*, 6:1, 1981, pp. 194-211.

CHAPTER 9

HEAP STRUCTURES

9.1 MIN-MAX HEAPS

9.1.1 Definitions

A *double-ended priority queue* is a data structure that supports the following operations:

(1) inserting an element with an arbitrary key

(2) deleting an element with the largest key

(3) deleting an element with the smallest key

When only insertion and one of the two deletion operations are to be supported, a min heap or a max heap may be used (see Chapter 5). A min-max heap supports all of the above operations.

Definition: A *min-max heap* is a complete binary tree such that if it is not empty, each element has a field called *key*. Alternating levels of this tree are min levels and max levels, respectively. The root is on a min level. Let x be any node in a min-max heap. If x is on a min (max) level then the element in x has the minimum (maximum) key from among all elements in the subtree with root x. A node on a min (max) level is called a *min* (*max*) node. □

An example of a min-max heap with 12 elements is shown in Figure 9.1. The value in each node is the key of the element in that node.

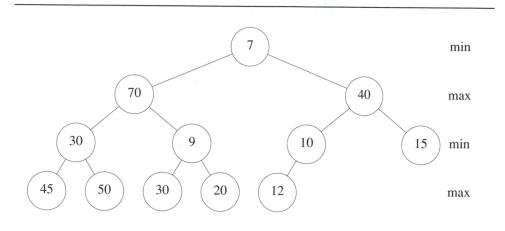

Figure 9.1: A 12-element min-max heap

9.1.2   Insertion into a Min-Max Heap

Suppose we wish to insert the element with key 5 into this min-max heap. Following the insertion, we will have a 13-element min-max heap with the shape shown in Figure 9.2.

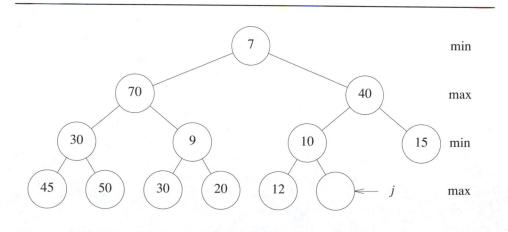

Figure 9.2: Min-max heap of Figure 9.1 with new node j

As in the case of heaps, the insertion algorithm for min-max heaps follows the path from the new node j to the root. Comparing the new key 5 with the key 10 that is in the parent of j, we see that since the node with key 10 is on a min level, and $5 < 10$, 5 is guaranteed to be smaller than all keys in nodes that are both on max levels and on the path from j to the root. Hence, the min-max heap property is to be verified only with respect to min nodes on the path from j to the root. First, the element with key 10 is moved to node j. Then the element with key 7 is moved to the former position of 10. Finally, the new element with key 5 is inserted into the root. The min-max heap following the insertion is shown in Figure 9.3(a).

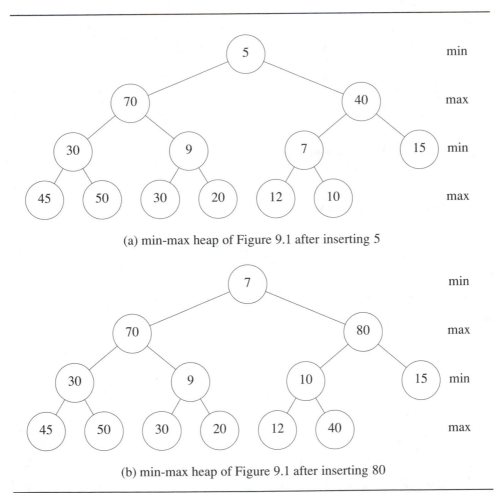

(a) min-max heap of Figure 9.1 after inserting 5

(b) min-max heap of Figure 9.1 after inserting 80

Figure 9.3: Insertion into a min-max heap

Next, suppose we wish to insert an element with key 80 into the min-max heap of Figure 9.1. The resulting min-max heap has 13 elements and has the shape shown in

Figure 9.2. Since $80 > 10$, and 10 is on a min level, we are assured that 80 is larger than all keys in nodes that are both on min levels and on the path from j to the root. Hence, the min-max heap property is to be verified only with respect to max nodes on the path from j to the root. There is only one such node in the min-max heap of Figure 9.1. This node has key 40. The element with key 40 is moved to j, and the new element is inserted into the node formerly occupied by this element. The resulting min-max heap is shown in Figure 9.3(b).

The preceding insertion examples lead to procedure *MinMaxInsert* (Program 9.1).

```
procedure MinMaxInsert (var h : MinMaxHeap ; var n : integer ; x : element);
{Insert x into the min-max heap h, which presently has n elements.}
var p : integer;
begin
   if n = MaxElements then MinMaxFull
   else begin
        n := n +1; p := n div 2; {p is the parent of the new node}
        if p = 0 then h [1] := x {insertion into an initially empty heap}
        else case level (p) of
             min: if x.key < h [p ].key
                    then begin {follow min levels}
                         h [n ] := h [p ];
                         VerifyMin (h, p, x);
                       end
                  else VerifyMax (h, n, x); {follow max levels}
             max: if x.key > h [p ].key
                    then begin {follow max levels}
                         h [n ] := h [p ];
                         VerifyMax (h, p, x);
                       end
                  else VerifyMin (h, n, x); {follow min levels}
        end; {of case and if p = 0}
   end; {of if n = MaxElements}
end; {of MinMaxInsert}
```

Program 9.1: Insertion into a min-max heap

The data type *MinMaxHeap* is defined as

type *MinMaxHeap* = **array** [1.. *MaxElements*] of *element*;

and *element* has at least the field *key*. A min-max heap is stored in a one-dimensional array using the standard array representation of a complete binary tree (see Section 5.2.3.1). Procedure *MinMaxInsert* makes use of the two procedures *VerifyMax* and *Veri-*

fyMin and the function *level*. The function *level* determines whether a node is on a min or a max level of a min-max heap. The procedure *VerifyMax* (Program 9.2) begins at a max node *i* and follows along the path of max nodes from *i* to the root of the min-max heap *h*. It searches for the correct node to insert the element *x*. This node has the property that all max nodes above it and on the path to the root have key values at least as large as *x.key*. Further, all max nodes below it and on the path from *i* have key values smaller than *x.key*. During the search, max nodes with keys smaller than *x.key* are moved down one max level.

---

procedure *VerifyMax* (**var** *h* : *MinMaxHeap* ; *i* : **integer** ; *x* : *element*);
{Follow max nodes from the max node *i* to the root and insert *x* at proper place.}
var *gp* : **integer**;
begin
    gp := *i* **div** 4; {grandparent of *i*}
    while *gp* <> 0 **do**
      if *x.key* > *h* [*gp*].*key* **then begin** {move *h* [*gp*] to *h* [*p*]}
                          h [*i*] := *h* [*gp*];
                          i := *gp*; *gp* := *gp* **div** 4;
              end
           else *gp* := 0; {*x* is to be inserted into node *i*}
    h [*i*] := *x*;
end; {of *VerifyMax*}

Program 9.2: Searching for the correct max node for insertion

The procedure *VerifyMin* is quite similar to *VerifyMax* except that it begins at a min node *i* and follows along the path of min nodes from *i* to the root. *x* is inserted into one of the encountered min nodes to preserve the min-max heap property. The formal development of *VerifyMin* and *level* is left as an exercise.

Analysis of *MinMaxInsert*: The correctness of *MinMaxInsert* is easily established. Further, since a min-max heap with *n* elements has O(log *n*) levels, the complexity of procedure *MinMaxInsert* is O(log *n*). □

9.1.3 Deletion of the Min Element

If we wish to delete the element with the smallest key, then this element is in the root. In the case of the min-max heap of Figure 9.1, we are to delete the element with key 7. Following the deletion, we will be left with a min-max heap that has 11 elements. Its shape is that shown in Figure 9.4. The node with key 12 is deleted from the heap, and the element with key 12 is reinserted into the heap. As in the case of deletion from a min or max heap, the reinsertion is done by examining the nodes of Figure 9.4 from the root down toward the leaves.

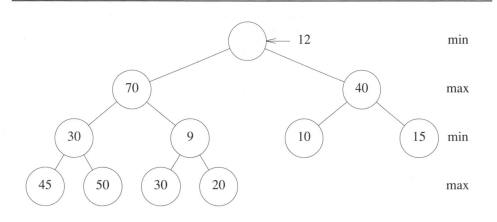

Figure 9.4: Shape of Figure 9.1 following deletion of the min item

In a general situation, we are to reinsert an element x into a min-max heap, h, whose root is empty. We consider the two cases:

(1) *The root has no children.* In this case x is to be inserted into the root.

(2) *The root has at least one child.* Now the smallest key in the min-max heap is in one of the children or grandchildren of the root. We determine which of these nodes has the smallest key. Let this be node k. The following possibilities need to be considered:

    (a) $x.key \leq h[k].key$. x may be inserted into the root, as there is no element in h with key smaller than $x.key$.

    (b) $x.key > h[k].key$ and k is a child of the root. Since k is a max node, it has no descendants with key larger than $h[k].key$. Hence, node k has no descendants with key larger than $x.key$. So, the element $h[k]$ may be moved to the root, and x can be inserted into node k.

    (c) $x.key > h[k].key$, and k is a grandchild of the root. In this case, too, $h[k]$ may be moved to the root. Let p be the parent of k. If $x.key > h[p].key$, then $h[p]$ and x are to be interchanged. This ensures that the max node p contains the largest key in the subheap with root p. At this point we are faced with the problem of inserting x into the subheap with root k. The root of this sub-min-max heap is presently empty. This is quite similar to our initial situation, in which we were to insert x into the min-max heap h with root 1, and node 1 was initially empty.

In our example, $x.key = 12$, and the smallest key in the children and grandchildren of the root node is 9. Let k denote the node that contains this key, and let p be its parent. Since $9 < 12$ and k is a grandchild of the root, we are in case 2(c). The element with key 9 (i.e., $h[k]$) is moved to the root. Since $x.key = 12 < 70 = h[p].key$, we do not interchange x and $h[p]$. The present configuration is shown in Figure 9.5. We must now reinsert x into the sub-min-max heap with root k. The smallest key from among the children and grandchildren of node k is 20. Since $12 < 20$, we are in case 2(a), and the element x is inserted into $h[k]$.

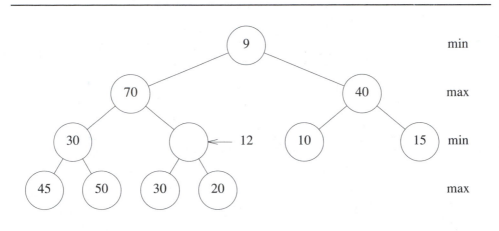

Figure 9.5: Figure 9.4 following the move of the element with key 9

The preceding discussion results in the procedure *DeleteMin* (Program 9.3). This procedure uses a function, *MinChildGrandChild* (i), that determines the child or grandchild of the node i that has the smallest key. If both a child and a grandchild of i have the smallest key, it is preferable that *MinChildGrandChild* return the address of the child, as this prevents further iterations of the **while** loop of *DeleteMin*. Notice that even though *DeleteMin* does not explicitly check for the case when $n = 1$ initially, this is handled correctly, and an empty min-max heap results from the deletion.

Analysis of *DeleteMin*: In each iteration of the **while** loop of *DeleteMin*, a constant amount of work is done. Also, in each iteration (except possibly the last), i moves down two levels. Since a min-max heap is a complete binary tree, h has O(log n) levels. Hence, the complexity of *DeleteMin* is O(log n). $\square$

---

procedure *DeleteMin* (**var** *h* : *MinMaxHeap* ; **var** *y* : *element* ; **var** *n* : **integer**);
{Delete an element with minimum key in the min-max heap *h*. *n* is the number of elements in *h*. The deleted element is returned in *y*.}
var *i*, *j*, *k*, *p* : **integer**;
    x, *t* : *element*;
    NotDone : **boolean**;
begin
  if *n* = 0 **then** *EmptyMinMaxHeap*
  else begin
      {Save root and last elements and update heap size}
      y := *h* [1]; *x* := *h* [*n*]; *n* := *n*−1;

      {Initialize for reinsertion of *x*}
      NotDone := **true**; *i* := 1; {empty node} *j* := *n* **div** 2; {last node with a child}

      {Find place to insert *x*}
      while (*i* <= *j*) **and** *NotDone* **do**
      begin {*i* has a child, case (2)}
        k := *MinChildGrandChild* (*i*);
        if *x*.*key* <= *h* [*k*].*key*
        then *NotDone* := **false** {case 2(a), *x* is to be inserted into *h* [*i*]}
        else begin {case 2(b) or (c)}
            h [*i*] := *h* [*k*];
            if *k* <= 2∗*i*+1
            then *NotDone* := **false** {*k* is a child of *i*, case 2(b)}
            else begin {*k* is a grandchild of *i*, case 2(c)}
                p := *k* **div** 2; {parent of *k*}
                if *x*.*key* > *h* [*p*].*key*
                then begin *t* := *h* [*p*]; *h* [*p*] := *x* ; *x* := *t*; **end**;
              end; {of **if** *k* <= 2∗*i* +1}
            i := *k*;
          end; {of **if** *x*.*key* <= *h* [*k*].*key*}
      end; {of **while**}
      h [*i*] := *x*; {insert *x*}
    end; {of **if** *n* = 0}
end; {of *DeleteMin*}

Program 9.3: Deleting the element with minimum key

EXERCISES

1. Write the procedure *VerifyMin* defined in connection with insertion into a min-max heap.

2. Write the function *level* (i), which determines whether node i of a min-max heap is on a min or a max level.

3. Write the function *MinChildGrandChild* (i), which returns the child or grandchild of node i of a min-max heap that has the smallest key. You may assume that i has at least one child.

4. Write a procedure *DeleteMax* to delete the element with maximum key in a min-max heap. Your algorithm should run in O(log n) time for a min-max heap with n elements.

5. Write a procedure to initialize a min-max heap with n elements. Do this using a series of adjust steps as used in the initialization of a max heap (see Chapter 5). Show that your procedure takes O(n) time rather than the O(n log n) time that would be taken if initialization were done by performing n insertions into an initially empty heap.

9.2   DEAPS

9.2.1   Definition

A deap is a double-ended heap that supports the double-ended priority-queue operations of insert, delete-min, and delete-max. As in the case of the min-max heap, these operations take logarithmic time on a deap. However, the deap is faster by a constant factor, and the algorithms are simpler.

Definition: A *deap* is a complete binary tree that is either empty or satisfies the following properties:

(1)   The root contains no element.

(2)   The left subtree is a min heap.

(3)   The right subtree is a max heap.

(4)   If the right subtree is not empty, then let i be any node in the left subtree. Let j be the corresponding node in the right subtree. If such a j does not exist, then let j be the node in the right subtree that corresponds to the parent of i. The key in node i is less than or equal to that in j. $\square$

An example 11-element deap is shown in Figure 9.6. The root of the min heap contains 5, and the root of the max heap contains 45. The min heap node with 10 corresponds to the max heap node with 25, whereas the min heap node with 15 corresponds to the max heap node with 20. For the node containing 9, the node j defined in property (4) of the deap definition is the max heap node that contains 40.

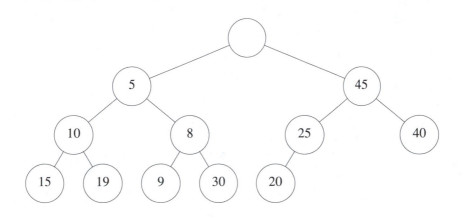

Figure 9.6: An 11-element deap

From the definition of a deap, it is evident that in an n-element deap, $n > 1$, the min element is in the root of the min heap, and the max element is in the root of the max heap. If $n = 1$, then the min and max elements are the same and are in the root of the min heap. Since a deap is a complete binary tree, it may be stored as an implicit data structure in a one-dimensional array in much the same way as min, max, and min-max heaps are stored. In the case of a deap, position 1 of the array is not utilized (we may simply begin the array indexing at 2 rather than at 1). Let n denote the last occupied position in this array. Then the number of elements in the deap is $n - 1$. If i is a node in the min heap, then its corresponding node in the max heap is $i + 2^{\lfloor \log_2 i \rfloor - 1}$. Hence, the j defined in property (4) of the definition is given by

$$j := i + 2^{\lfloor \log_2 i \rfloor - 1};$$
$$\textbf{if } j > n \textbf{ then } j := j \textbf{ div } 2;$$

Notice that if property (4) of the deap definition is satisfied by all leaf nodes of the min heap, then it is also satisfied by all remaining nodes of the min heap.

9.2.2   Insertion into a Deap

Suppose we wish to insert an element with key 4 into the deap of Figure 9.6. Following this insertion, the deap will have 12 elements in it and will thus have the shape shown in Figure 9.7. j points to the new node in the deap.

The insertion process begins by comparing the key 4 to the key in j's corresponding node, i, in the min heap. This node contains 19. To satisfy property (4), we move the

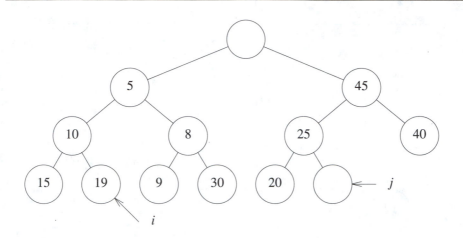

Figure 9.7: Shape of a 12-element deap

19 to node j. Now, if we use the min heap insertion algorithm (see Chapter 5) to insert 4 into position i, we get the deap of Figure 9.8.

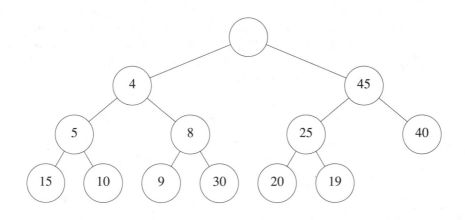

Figure 9.8: Deap of Figure 9.6 following the insertion of 4

If instead of inserting a 4, we were to insert a 30 into the deap of Figure 9.6, then the resulting deap would have the same shape as in Figure 9.7. Comparing 30 with the key 19 in the corresponding node i, we see that property (4) may be satisfied by using the max heap insertion algorithm to insert 30 into position j. This results in the deap of Figure 9.9.

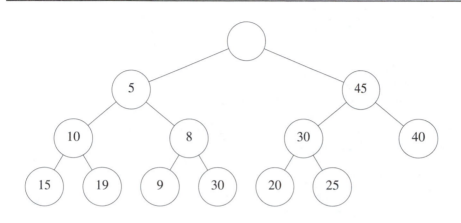

Figure 9.9: Deap of Figure 9.6 following the insertion of 30

The case in which the new node, j, is a node of the min heap is symmetric to the case just discussed. The procedure to insert into a deap is given in Program 9.4. The data type *deap* is defined to be an array [2 .. *MaxElements*] of *element*. n is the position of the last element in the deap. $n = 1$ denotes an empty deap.

The procedures and functions used by *DeapInsert* are specified as follows:

(1)   *DeapFull*. This signals an error. The insertion cannot proceed, as there is no space in the deap to accommodate the additional element.

(2)   *MaxHeap*. This is a boolean function that returns the value **true** iff n is a position in the max heap of the deap.

(3)   *MinPartner*. This function computes the min heap node that corresponds to the max heap position n. This is given by $n - 2^{\lfloor \log_2 n \rfloor - 1}$.

(4)   *MaxPartner*. This function computes the max heap node that corresponds to the parent of the min heap position n. This is given by $(n + 2^{\lfloor \log_2 n \rfloor - 1})$ **div** 2.

(5)   The procedures *MinInsert* and *MaxInsert* insert an element into a specified position of a min and max heap, respectively, by following the path from this position toward the root of the respective heap. Elements are moved down as necessary until the correct place to insert the new element is found. This process differs from that used in Chapter 5 to insert into a min or max heap only in that the root is now at position 2 or 3 rather than at 1.

---

procedure *DeapInsert* (**var** *d* : *deap* ; **var** *n* : **integer** ; *x* : *element*);
{Insert *x* into the deap *d* of size *n* −1.}
var *i* : integer;
begin
  if *n* =*MaxElements* **then** *DeapFull*
  else begin
       n := *n* +1;
       if *n* = 2 **then** *d* [2] := *x* {insertion into an initially empty deap}
       else case *MaxHeap* (*n*) **of**
           true : **begin** {*n* is a position in the max heap}
               i := *MinPartner* (*n*);
               if *x.key* < *d* [*i*].*key*
               then begin
                   d [*n*] := *d* [*i*];
                   MinInsert (*d*, *i*, *x*);
                 end
               else *MaxInsert* (*d*, *n*, *x*);
           false : **begin** {*n* is a position in the min heap}
               i := *MaxPartner* (*n*);
               if *x.key* > *d* [*i*].*key*
               then begin
                   d [*n*] := *d* [*i*];
                   MaxInsert (*d*, *i*, *x*);
                 end
               else *MinInsert* (*d*, *n*, *x*);
         end; {of **case** and **if** *n* = 2}
      end; {of **if** *n* = *MaxElements*}
end; {of *DeapInsert*}

Program 9.4: Inserting into a deap

Analysis of *DeapInsert*: The correctness of procedure *DeapInsert* is easily established. Its complexity is O(log *n*), as the time taken is linear in the height of the deap, which is O(log *n*). □

9.2.3 Deletion of the Min Element

A high-level description of the deletion process is given in Program 9.5. The strategy is first to transform the deletion of the element from the root of the min heap to the deletion of an element from a leaf position in the min heap. This is done by following a root-to-leaf path in the min heap, ensuring that the min heap properties are satisfied on the preceding levels of the heap. This process has the effect of shifting the empty position initially at the min heap root to a leaf node p. This leaf node is then filled by the element, t, initially in the last position of the deap. The insertion of t into position p of the min heap is done as in *DeapInsert* (Program 9.4) except that the specification of *MaxPartner* (i) is changed to

$$j := i + 2^{\lfloor \log_2 i \rfloor - 1};$$
$$\text{if } j > n \text{ then } j := j \text{ div } 2;$$

and the insertion does not increase the size of the deap.

---

procedure *DeapDeleteMin* (**var** d : *deap* ; **var** n : **integer** ; **var** x : *element*);
{Delete the min element from the deap d. The deleted element is returned in x.}
var i : **integer**;
    t : *element*;
begin
  if $n < 2$ **then** *DeapEmpty*
  else begin
      $x := d[2]$;
      $t := d[n]; n := n-1$;
      $i := 2$;
      while i has a child **do**
      begin
        Let j be the child with smaller key;
        $d[i] := d[j]$;
        $i := j$;
      end;
      Do a deap insertion of t at position i;
    end; {of **if** $n < 2$}
end; {of *DeapDeleteMin*}

Program 9.5: Deleting the min element

Suppose we wish to remove the minimum element from the deap of Figure 9.6. We first place the last element (i.e., the one with key 20) into a temporary element t. Next, the vacancy created in position 2 by the deletion of the min element is filled by moving from position 2 to a leaf. Each move is preceded by a step that moves the smaller of the elements in the children of the current node up. Then, we move to the position previously occupied by the moved element. First, the 8 is moved up to position 2. Then the 9 is moved to position 5, which was formerly occupied by the 8. Now we have an empty leaf (position 10). To do a deap insertion here, we compare 20 with the key 40 in its max partner. Since $20 < 40$, no exchange is needed, and we proceed to insert the 20 into the min heap beginning at the empty leaf 10. This results in the deap of Figure 9.10.

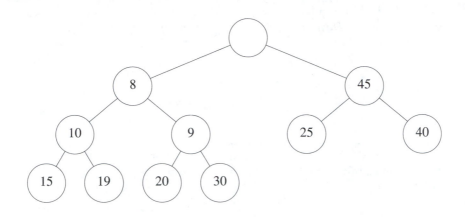

Figure 9.10: Deap of Figure 9.6 following deletion of the min element

Analysis of *DeapDeleteMin:* One may verify that *DeapDeleteMin* works correctly regardless of whether the last position in the deap is in the min or max heap. The complexity is O(log n), as the height of a deap is O(log n). □

EXERCISES

1. Complete procedure *DeapInsert* (Program 9.4) by writing all the procedures and functions it uses. Test the insertion procedure by running it on a computer. Generate your own test data.

2. Refine procedure *DeapDeleteMin* (Program 9.5) into a Pascal procedure. Test the correctness of your procedure running the procedure on a computer using test data of your choice.

3. Write a procedure to initialize a deap with n elements. Your procedure must run in O(n) time. Show that your procedure actually has this running time. (Hint: Proceed as in the initialization of a min heap or max heap.)

4. Write the procedures to perform all double-ended priority-queue operations, both for a min-max heap and for a deap.

   (a) Use suitable test data to test the correctness of your procedures.

   (b) Create a random list of n elements and a random sequence of insert, delete-min, and delete-max operations of length m. This latter sequence is created such that the probability of an insert is approximately 0.5, whereas that of each type of delete is approximately 0.25. Initialize a min-max heap and a deap to contain the n elements in the first random list. Now, measure the time to perform the m operations using the min-max heap as well as the deap. Divide this time by m to get the average time per operation. Do this for $n = 100, 500, 1000, 2000, \cdots, 5000$. Let m be 5000. Tabulate your computing times.

(c) Based on your experiments, what can you say about the relative merits of the two double-ended priority-queue schemes?

5. Use a two-array representation for a deap. One of these arrays, say A, represents the min heap, and the other, say B, represents the max heap. Let n_A be the number of elements in A and n_B the number of elements in B. The number of elements, n, in the deap is $n_A + n_B$.

(a) Obtain an upper and lower bound for n_A as a function of n_B (i.e., determine $g(n_B)$ and $h(n_B)$ such that $g(n_B) \leq n_A \leq h(n_B)$).

(b) Which node of max heap B corresponds to min heap node $A[i]$, $1 \leq i \leq n_A$?

(c) Write deap-insert, delete-min, and delete-max procedures using this two-array representation.

(d) Use suitable test data to test the correctness of your procedures.

(e) Compare the performance of the two-array representation and that of the single array representation. For this comparison, design an experiment similar to that described in part (b) of the previous exercise.

6. Obtain an exact count of the worst-case number of key comparisons that can be made during each of the double-ended priority-queue operations when a min-max heap is used. Do this also for the case when a deap is used. What can you say about the expected worst-case performance of these two methods? Can you think of a way to reduce the worst-case number of comparisons using a binary search (without affecting the number of element moves)?

9.3 LEFTIST TREES

In the preceding section we extended the definition of a priority queue by requiring that both delete-max and delete-min operations be permissible. In this section, we consider a different extension. Suppose that in addition to the normal priority-queue operations, we are also required to support the operation of *combine*. This requires us to combine two priority queues into a single priority queue. One application for this is when the server for one priority queue shuts down. At this time, it is necessary to combine its priority queue with that of a functioning server.

Let n be the total number of elements in the two priority queues that are to be combined. If heaps are used to represent priority queues, then the combine operation takes $O(n)$ time. Using a leftist tree, the combine operation as well as the normal priority-queue operations take logarithmic time.

Leftist trees are defined using the concept of an extended binary tree. An *extended binary tree* is a binary tree in which all empty binary subtrees have been replaced by a square node. Figure 9.11 shows two examples of binary trees. Their corresponding extended binary trees are shown in Figure 9.12. The square nodes in an extended binary tree are called *external nodes*. The original (circular) nodes of the binary tree are called *internal nodes*.

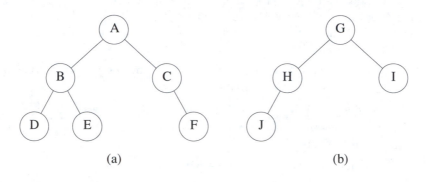

(a)   (b)

Figure 9.11: Two binary trees

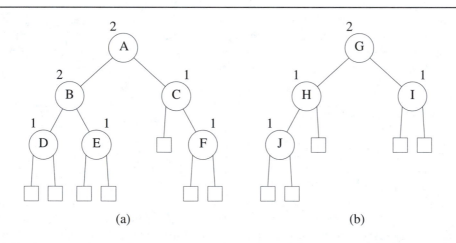

(a)   (b)

Figure 9.12: Extended binary trees corresponding to Figure 9.11

Let x be a node in an extended binary tree. Let *LeftChild*(x) and *RightChild*(x), respectively, denote the left and right children of the internal node x. Define *shortest*(x) to be the length of a shortest path from x to an external node. It is easy to see that *shortest*(x) satisfies the following recurrence:

$$shortest\,(x) = \begin{cases} 0 & \text{if } x \text{ is an external node} \\ 1 + \min\,\{shortest\,(LeftChild\,(x)),\ shortest\,(RightChild\,(x))\} & \text{otherwise} \end{cases}$$

The number outside each internal node x of Figure 9.12 is the value of $shortest\,(x)$.

Definition: A *leftist tree* is a binary tree such that if it is not empty, then

$$shortest\,(LeftChild\,(x)) \geq shortest\,(RightChild\,(x))$$

for every internal node x. $\square$

The binary tree of Figure 9.11(a), which corresponds to the extended binary tree of Figure 9.12(a), is not a leftist tree, as $shortest\,(LeftChild\,(C)) = 0$, whereas $shortest\,(RightChild(C)) = 1$. The binary tree of Figure 9.11(b) is a leftist tree.

Lemma 9.1: Let x be the root of a leftist tree that has n (internal) nodes.

(a) $n \geq 2^{shortest(x)} - 1$

(b)   The rightmost root to external node path is the shortest root to external node path. Its length is $shortest\,(x)$.

Proof: (a) From the definition of $shortest\,(x)$ it follows that there are no external nodes on the first $shortest\,(x)$ levels of the leftist tree. Hence, the leftist tree has at least

$$\sum_{i=1}^{shortest(x)} 2^{i-1} = 2^{shortest(x)} - 1$$

internal nodes. (b) This follows directly from the definition of a leftist tree. $\square$

Leftist trees are represented using nodes that have the following fields: *LeftChild*, *RightChild*, *shortest*, and *data*. We assume that *data* is a record type with at least the field *key*. We note that the concept of an external node is introduced merely to arrive at clean definitions. The external nodes are never physically present in the representation of a leftist tree. Rather the appropriate child field (*LeftChild* or *RightChild*) of the parent of an external node is set to **nil**.

Definition: A *min leftist tree* (*max leftist tree*) is a leftist tree in which the key value in each node is no larger (smaller) than the key values in its children (if any). In other words, a min (max) leftist tree is a leftist tree that is also a min (max) tree. $\square$

Two min leftist trees are shown in Figure 9.13. The number inside a node x is the key of the element in x, and the number outside x is $shortest\,(x)$. The operations insert, delete-min (delete-max), and combine can be performed in logarithmic time using a min (max) leftist tree. We shall continue our discussion using min leftist trees.

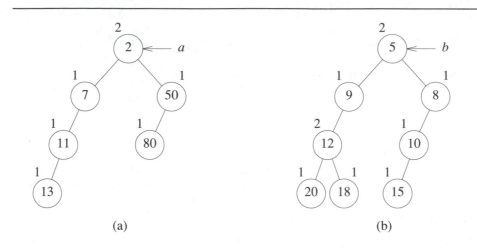

(a)   (b)

Figure 9.13: Examples of min leftist trees

The insert and delete-min operations can both be performed by using the combine operation. To insert an element x into a min leftist tree a, we first create a min leftist tree b that contains the single element x. Then we combine the min leftist trees a and b. To delete the min element from a nonempty min leftist tree a, we combine the min leftist trees $a\uparrow.LeftChild$ and $a\uparrow.RightChild$ and delete the node a.

The combine operation itself is quite simple. Suppose that the min leftist trees a and b are to be combined. First, a new binary tree containing all elements in a and b is obtained by following the rightmost paths in a and/or b. This binary tree has the property that the key in each node is no larger than the keys in its children (if any). Next, the left and right subtrees of nodes are interchanged as necessary to convert this binary tree into a leftist tree.

As an example, consider combining the min leftist trees a and b of Figure 9.13. To obtain a binary tree that contains all the elements in a and b and that satisfies the required relationship between parent and child keys, we first compare the root keys 2 and 5. Since $2 < 5$, the new binary tree should have 2 in its root. We shall leave the left subtree of a unchanged and combine the right subtree of a with the entire binary tree b. The resulting binary tree will become the new right subtree of a. When combining the right subtree of a and the binary tree b, we notice that $5 < 50$. So, 5 should be in the root of the combined tree. Now, we proceed to combine the subtrees with root 8 and 50. Since $8 < 50$ and 8 has no right subtree, we can make the subtree with root 50 the right subtree of 8. This gives us the binary tree of Figure 9.14(a). Hence, the result of combining the right subtree of a and the tree b is the tree of Figure 9.14(b). When this is made the right subtree of a, we get the binary tree of Figure 9.14(c). To convert this into a leftist tree, we begin at the last modified root (i.e., 8) and trace back to the overall root, ensuring that *shortest* (*LeftChild* ( )) ≥ *shortest* (*RightChild* ( )). This inequality holds at 8 but not at 5 and 2. Simply interchanging the left and right subtrees at these nodes causes the inequality to hold. The result is the leftist tree of Figure 9.14(d).

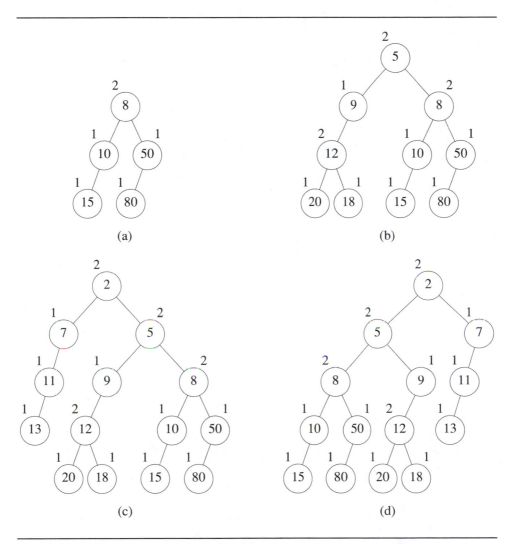

Figure 9.14: Combining the min leftist trees of Figure 9.13

The procedure to combine two leftist trees is given in Program 9.6. This procedure makes use of the recursive procedure *MinUnion* which combines two nonempty leftist trees. Procedure *MinUnion* intertwines the following two steps:

---

procedure *MinCombine* (**var** *a*, *b* : *LeftistTree*);
{Combine the two min leftist trees *a* and *b*. The resulting min leftist
tree is returned in *a* and *b* is set to **nil**.}
begin
   if *a* = **nil then** *a* := *b*
        else if *b* < > **nil then** *MinUnion* (*a*, *b*);
   b := **nil**;
end; {of *MinCombine*}

procedure *MinUnion* (**var** *a*, *b* : *LeftistTree*);
{Recursive procedure to combine two nonempty min leftist trees.}
var *t* : *LeftistTree*;
begin
   {Set *a* to be min leftist tree with smaller root}
   if *a*↑.*data* .*key* > *b*↑.*data* .*key*
   then begin *t* := *a*; *a* := *b*; *b* := *t*; **end**;

   {Create binary tree such that the smallest key in each subtree is in the root}
   if *a*↑.*RightChild* = **nil**
   then *a*↑.*RightChild* := *b*
   else *MinUnion* (*a*↑.*RightChild*, *b*);

   {Leftist tree property}
   if *a*↑.*LeftChild* = **nil**
   then begin {interchange subtrees}
        a↑.*LeftChild* := *a*↑.*RightChild*; *a*↑.*RightChild* := **nil**;
     end
   else if *a*↑.*LeftChild*↑.*shortest* < *a*↑.*RightChild*↑.*shortest*
   then begin {interchange *a*'s subtrees}
      t := *a*↑.*LeftChild*; *a*↑.*LeftChild* := *a*↑.*RightChild*; *a*↑.*RightChild* := *t*;
     end;

   {Set *shortest* field of *a*}
   if *a*↑.*RightChild* = **nil**
   then *a*↑.*shortest* := 1
   else *a*↑.*shortest* := *a*↑.*RightChild*↑.*shortest* + 1;
end; {of *MinUnion*}

Program 9.6: Combining two min leftist trees

(1)   create a binary tree that contains all the elements, the root of each subtree has the smallest key in that subtree

(2)   ensure that each node has a left subtree whose *shortest* value is greater than or equal to that of its right subtree

Analysis of *MinCombine*: Since *MinUnion* moves down the rightmost paths in the two leftist trees being combined, and since the lengths of these paths are at most logarithmic in the number of elements in each tree, the combining of two leftist trees with a total of n elements is done in time O(log n). □

EXERCISES

1.   Let t be an arbitrary binary tree represented using the node structure for a leftist tree.

   (a)   Write a procedure to initialize the *shortest* field of each node in t.

   (b)   Write a procedure to convert t into a leftist tree.

   (c)   What is the complexity of each of these two procedures?

2.   Compare the performance of leftist trees and min heaps under the assumption that the only operations to be performed are insert and delete-min. For this, do the following:

   (a)   Create a random list of n elements and a random sequence of insert and delete-min operations of length m. The latter sequence is created such that the probability of an insert or delete-min operation is approximately 0.5. Initialize a min leftist tree and a min heap to contain the n elements in the first random list. Now, measure the time to perform the m operations using the min leftist tree as well as the min heap. Divide this time by m to get the average time per operation. Do this for $n = 100, 500, 1000, 2000, \cdots,$ 5000. Let m be 5000. Tabulate your computing times.

   (b)   Based on your experiments, make some statements about the relative merits of the two priority-queue schemes.

3.   Write a procedure to initialize a min leftist tree with n elements. Assume that the node structure is the same as that used in the text. Your procedure must run in $\Theta(n)$ time. Show that this is the case. Can you think of a way to do this initialization in $\Theta(n)$ time such that the resulting min leftist tree is also a complete binary tree?

4.   Write a procedure to delete the element in node x of the min leftist tree a. Assume that each node has the fields *LeftChild*, *RightChild*, *parent*, *shortest*, and *data*. The *parent* field of a node points to its parent in the leftist tree. What is the complexity of your algorithm?

5.   [*Lazy deletion*] Another way to handle the deletion of arbitrary elements from a min leftist heap is to use a Boolean field, *deleted*, in place of the *parent* field of the previous exercise. When an element is deleted, its *deleted* field is set to **true**. However, the node is not physically deleted. When a delete-min operation is performed, we first search for the minimum element not deleted by performing a limited preorder search. This preorder search traverses only the upper part of the tree as needed to identify the min element. All deleted elements encountered are physically deleted, and their subtrees are combined to obtain the new min leftist tree.

   (a)   Write a procedure to delete the element in node x of the min leftist tree a.

   (b)   Write another procedure to delete the min element from a min leftist tree from which several elements have been deleted using the former procedure.

   (c)   What is the complexity of the latter procedure as a function of the number of deleted elements encountered and the number of elements in the entire tree?

6.   [*Skewed heaps*] A *skewed heap* is a min tree that supports the min leftist tree operations: insert, delete-min, and combine in amortized time (the Section 9.4 for a definition of amortized time) $O(\log n)$ per operation. As in the case of min leftist trees, insertions and deletions are performed using the combine operation, which is carried out by following the rightmost paths in the two heaps being combined. However, unlike min leftist trees, the left and right subtrees of all nodes (except the last) on the rightmost path in the resulting heap are interchanged.

   (a)   Write insert, delete-min, and combine procedures for skewed heaps.

   (b)   Compare the running times of these with those for the same operations on a min leftist tree. Use random sequences of insert, delete-min, and combine operations.

9.4   BINOMIAL HEAPS

9.4.1   Cost Amortization

A *binomial heap* is a data structure that supports the same functions (i.e., insert, delete-min (or delete-max), and combine) as those supported by leftist trees. Unlike leftist trees, where an individual operation can be performed in $O(\log n)$ time, it is possible that certain individual operations performed on a binomial heap may take $O(n)$ time. However, if we amortize part of the cost of expensive operations over the inexpensive ones, then the amortized complexity of an individual operation is either $O(1)$ or $O(\log n)$ depending on the type of operation.

Let us examine more closely the concept of cost amortization (we shall use the terms *cost* and *complexity* interchangeably). Suppose that a sequence I1, I2, D1, I3, I4, I5, I6, D2, I7 of insert and delete-min operations is performed. Assume that the *actual cost* of each of the seven inserts is one. By this, we mean that each insert takes one unit of time. Further, suppose that the delete-min operations D1 and D2 have an actual cost of eight and ten, respectively. So, the total cost of the sequence of operations is 25.

In an amortization scheme we charge some of the actual cost of an operation to other operations. This reduces the charged cost of some operations and increases that of others. The *amortized cost* of an operation is the total cost charged to it. The cost transferring (amortization) scheme is required to be such that the sum of the amortized costs of the operations is greater than or equal to the sum of their actual costs. If we charge one unit of the cost of a delete-min operation to each of the inserts since the last delete-min operation (if any), then two units of the cost of D1 get transferred to I1 and I2 (the charged cost of each increases by one), and four units of the cost of D2 get transferred to I3 to I6. The amortized cost of each of I1 to I6 becomes two, that of I7 is equal to its actual cost (i.e., one), and that of each of D1 and D2 becomes 6. The sum of the amortized costs is 25, which is the same as the sum of the actual costs.

Now suppose we can prove that no matter what sequence of insert and delete-min operations is performed, we can charge costs in such a way that the amortized cost of each insertion is no more than two and that of each deletion is no more than six. This will enable us to make the claim that the actual cost of any insert / delete-min sequence is no more than $2 * i + 6 * d$ where i and d are, respectively, the number of insert and delete-min operations in the sequence. Suppose that the actual cost of a deletion is no more than ten, and that of an insertion is one. Using actual costs, we can conclude that the sequence cost is no more than $i + 10 * d$. Combining these two bounds, we obtain $\min\{2 * i + 6 * d, i + 10 * d\}$ as a bound on the sequence cost. Hence, using the notion of cost amortization, we can obtain tighter bounds on the complexity of a sequence of operations. We shall use the notion of cost amortization to show that although individual delete operations on a binomial heap may be expensive, the cost of any sequence of binomial heap operations is actually quite small.

9.4.2 Definition of Binomial Heaps

As in the case of heaps and leftist trees, there are two varieties of binomial heaps, min and max. A *min binomial heap* is a collection of min trees; a *max binomial heap* is a collection of max trees. We shall explicitly consider min binomial heaps only. These will be referred to as *B-heaps*. Figure 9.15 shows an example of a B-heap that is made up of three min trees.

Using B-heaps, we can perform an insert and a combine in O(1) actual and amortized time and a delete-min in O(log n) amortized time. B-heaps are represented using nodes that have the following fields: *degree*, *child*, *link*, and *data*. The *degree* of a node is the number of children it has; the *child* field is used to point to any one of its children (if any); the *link* field is used to maintain singly linked circular lists of siblings. All the children of a node form a singly linked circular list, and the node points to one of these children. Additionally, the roots of the min trees that comprise a B-heap are linked to form a singly linked circular list. The B-heap is then pointed at by a single pointer to the min tree root with smallest key.

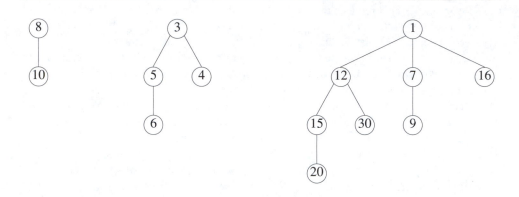

Figure 9.15: A B-heap with three min trees

Figure 9.16 shows the representation for the example of Figure 9.15. To enhance the readability of this figure, we have used bidirectional arrows to join together nodes that are in the same circular list. When such a list contains only one node, no such arrows are drawn. Each of the key sets {10}, {6}, {5,4}, {20}, {15, 30}, {9}, {12, 7, 16}, and {8, 3, 1} denotes the keys in one of the circular lists of Figure 9.16. *a* is the pointer to the B-heap. Note that an empty B-heap has a **nil** pointer.

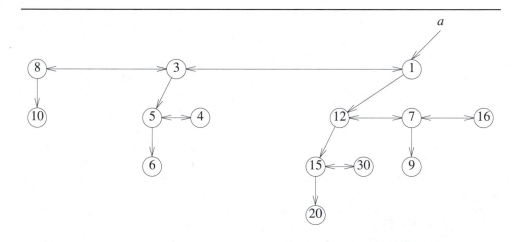

Figure 9.16: B-heap of Figure 9.15 showing child pointers and sibling lists

9.4.3 Insertion into a Binomial Heap

An element x may be inserted into a B-heap a by first putting x into a new node and then inserting this node into the circular list pointed at by a. The pointer a is reset to this new node only if a is **nil** or the key of x is smaller than the key in the node pointed at by a. It is evident that these insertion steps can be performed in $O(1)$ time.

9.4.4 Combining Two Binomial Heaps

To combine two nonempty B-heaps a and b, we combine the top circular lists of a and b into a single circular list. The new B-heap pointer is either a or b, depending on which has the smaller key. This can be determined with a single comparison. Since two circular lists can be combined into a single one in $O(1)$ time, a combine takes only $O(1)$ time.

9.4.5 Deletion of Min Element

Let a be the pointer of the B-heap from which the min element is to be deleted. If a is **nil**, then the B-heap is empty, and a deletion cannot be performed. Assume that a is not **nil**. a points to the node that contains the min element. This node is deleted from its circular list. The new B-heap consists of the remaining min trees and the sub-min trees of the deleted root. Figure 9.17 shows the situation for the example of Figure 9.15.

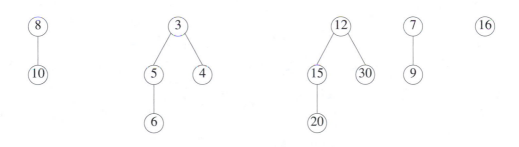

Figure 9.17: The B-heap of Figure 9.15 following the deletion of the min element

Before forming the circular list of min tree roots, we repeatedly join together pairs of min trees that have the same degree (the degree of a nonempty min tree is the degree of its root). *This min tree joining is done by making the min tree whose root has a larger key a subtree of the other (ties are broken arbitrarily).* When two min trees are joined, the degree of the resulting min tree is one larger than the original degree of each min tree, and the number of min trees decreases by one. For our example, we may first join either the min trees with roots 8 and 7 or those with roots 3 and 12. If the first pair is joined, the min tree with root 8 is made a subtree of the min tree with root 7. We now have the min tree collection of Figure 9.18. There are three min trees of degree two in this collection. If the pair with roots 7 and 3 is picked for joining, the resulting min tree collection is that of Figure 9.19. Since the min trees in this collection have different degrees, the min tree joining process terminates.

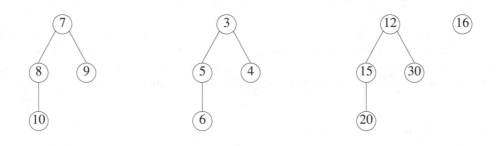

Figure 9.18: The B-heap of Figure 9.17 following the joining of the two degree-one min trees

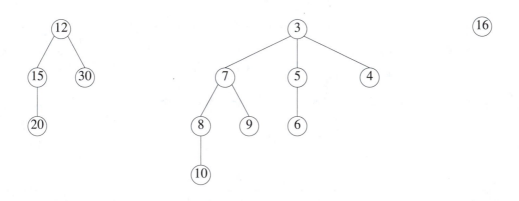

Figure 9.19: The B-heap of Figure 9.18 following the joining of two degree-two min trees

The min tree joining step is followed by a step in which the min tree roots are linked together to form a circular list and the B-heap pointer is reset to point to the min tree root with smallest key. The steps involved in a delete-min operation are summarized in Program 9.7.

{Delete the min element from a B-heap a. This element is returned in x.}

Step 1: [Handle empty B-heap] **if** a = **nil then** *DeletionError* **else** perform Steps 2 to 4;

Step 2: [Deletion from nonempty B-heap] $x := a\uparrow.data$; $y := a\uparrow.child$; delete a from its circular list; following this deletion, a points to any remaining node in the resulting list; if there is no such node, then a = **nil**;

Step 3: [Min-tree joining] Consider the min trees in the lists a and y; join together pairs of min trees of the same degree until all remaining min trees have different degrees;

Step 4: [Form min tree root list] Link the roots of the remaining min trees (if any) together to form a circular list; set a to point to the root (if any) with minimum key;

Program 9.7: Steps in a delete-min operation

Step 1 takes $O(1)$ time. Step 2 can be done in $O(1)$ time by copying over the data from the next node (if any) in the circular list and physically deleting that node instead. However, since Step 3 requires us to visit all nodes in the circular list of roots, it is not necessary to delete a and leave behind a circular list. In Step 3, we can simply examine all nodes other than a in the root-level circular list.

Step 3 may be implemented by using an array, *tree*, that is indexed from 0 to the maximum possible degree, *MaxDegree*, of a min tree. Initially all entries in this array are **nil**. Let s be the number of min trees in a and y. The lists a and y created in Step 2 are scanned. For each min tree p in the lists a and y created in Step 2, the code of Program 9.8 is executed. The procedure *JoinMinTrees* makes the input tree with larger root a subtree of the other tree. The resulting tree is returned in the first parameter. In the end, the array *tree* contains pointers to the min trees that are to be linked together in Step 4. Since each time a pair of min trees is joined the total number of min trees decreases by one, the number of joins is at most $s - 1$. Hence, the complexity of Step 3 is $O(MaxDegree + s)$.

Step 4 is accomplished by scanning *tree* $[0 .. MaxDegree]$ and linking together the min trees found. During this scan, the min tree with minimum key may also be determined. The complexity of Step 4 is $O(MaxDegree)$.

9.4.6 Analysis

Definition: The *binomial tree, B_k, of degree k* is a tree such that if $k = 0$, then the tree has exactly one node, and if $k > 0$, then the tree consists of a root whose degree is k and whose subtrees are $B_0, B_1, \cdots, B_{k-1}$. $\square$

```
d := p ↑. degree;
while tree [d] < > nil do
begin
    JoinMinTrees (p, tree [d]);
    tree [d] := nil;
    d := d + 1;
end;
tree [d] := p;
```

Program 9.8: Code to handle min tree p encountered during a scan of lists a and y

The min trees of Figure 9.15 are B_1, B_2, and B_3, respectively. One may verify that B_k has exactly 2^k nodes. Further, if we start with a collection of empty B-heaps and perform inserts, combines, and delete-mins only, then the min trees in each B-heap are binomial trees. These observations enable us to prove that when only inserts, combines, and delete-mins are performed, we can amortize costs such that the amortized cost of each insert and combine is O(1), and that of each delete-min is O(log n).

Lemma 9.2: Let a be a B-heap with n elements that results from a sequence of insert, combine, and delete-min operations performed on a collection of initially empty B-heaps. Each min tree in a has degree $\leq \log_2 n$. Consequently, $MaxDegree \leq \lfloor \log_2 n \rfloor$, and the actual cost of a delete-min operation is O(log $n + s$).

Proof: Since each of the min trees in a is a binomial tree with at most n nodes, none can have degree greater than $\lfloor \log_2 n \rfloor$. □

Theorem 9.1: If a sequence of n insert, combine, and delete-min operations is performed on initially empty B-heaps, then we can amortize costs such that the amortized time complexity of each insert and combine is O(1), and that of each delete-min operation is O(log n).

Proof: For each B-heap, define the quantities *#insert* and *LastSize* in the following way: When an initially empty B-heap is created or when a delete-min operation is performed on a B-heap, its *#insert* value is set to zero. Each time an insert is done on a B-heap, its *#insert* value is increased by one. When two B-heaps are combined, the *#insert* value of the resulting B-heap is the sum of the *#insert* values of the B-heaps combined. Hence, *#insert* counts the number of inserts performed on a B-heap or its constituent B-heaps since the last delete-min operation performed in each. When an initially empty B-heap is created, its *LastSize* value is zero. When a delete-min operation is performed on a B-heap, its *LastSize* is set to the number of min trees it contains following this delete. When two B-heaps are combined, the *LastSize* value for the resulting B-heap is the sum of the *LastSize* values in the two B-heaps that were combined. One may verify that the number of min trees in a B-heap is always equal to *#insert* + *LastSize*.

Consider any individual delete-min operation in the operation sequence. Assume this is from the B-heap *a*. Observe that the total number of elements in all the B-heaps is at most *n*, as only inserts add elements, and at most *n* inserts can be present in a sequence of *n* operations. Let $u = a \uparrow . degree \leq \log_2 n$.

From Lemma 9.2, the actual cost of this delete-min operation is O(log *n* + *s*). The log *n* term is due to *MaxDegree* and represents the time needed to initialize the array *tree* and to complete Step 4. The *s* term represents the time to scan the lists *a* and *y* and to perform the *s* − 1 (at most) min tree joins. We see that *s* = *#insert* + *LastSize* + *u* − 1. If we charge *#insert* units of cost to the insert operations that contribute to the count *#insert* and *LastSize* units to the delete-mins that contribute to the count *LastSize* (each such delete-min operation is charged a number of cost units equal to the number of min trees it left behind), then only *u* − 1 of the *s* cost units remain. Since $u \leq \log_2 n$, and since the number of min trees in a B-heap immediately following a delete-min operation is $\leq \log_2 n$, the amortized cost of a delete-min operation becomes O($\log_2 n$).

Since this charging scheme adds at most one unit to the cost of any insert, the amortized cost of an insert becomes O(1). The amortization scheme used does not charge anything extra to a combine. So, the actual and amortized costs of a combine are also O(1). □

From the preceding theorem and the definition of cost amortization, it follows that the actual cost of any sequence of *i* inserts, *c* combines, and *dm* delete-min operations is O(*i* + *c* + *dm* log *i*).

EXERCISES

1. Let *S* be an initially empty stack. We wish to perform two operations on *S*: *add* (*x*) and *DeleteUntil* (*x*). These are defined as follows:

    (a) *add* (*x*): Add the element *x* to the top of the stack *S*. This operation takes O(1) time per invocation.

    (b) *DeleteUntil* (*x*): Delete elements from the top of the stack up to and including the first *x* encountered. If *p* elements are deleted, the time taken is O(*p*).

    Consider any sequence of *n* stack operations (*add*s and *DeleteUntil*s). Show how to amortize the cost of the *add* and *DeleteUntil* operations so that the amortized cost of each is O(1). From this, conclude that the time needed to perform any such sequence of operations is O(*n*).

2. Let *x* [1 .. *n*] be an unsorted array of *n* elements. The procedure *search* (*x*,*n*,*i*,*y*) searches *x* [*i* .. *n*] for *y* by examining *x* [*i*], [*i* +1], and so on, in that order, for the least *j* such that *x* [*j*] = *y*. If no such *j* is found, *j* is set to *n* + 1. On termination, procedure *search* sets *i* to *j*. Assume that the time required to examine a single element of *x* is O(1).

(a)   What is the worst-case complexity of *search*?

(b)   Suppose that a sequence of m searches is performed beginning with $i = 1$. Use a cost amortization scheme that assigns costs both to elements and to search operations. Show that it is always possible to amortize costs so that the amortized cost of each element is $O(1)$ and that of each search is also $O(1)$. From this, conclude that the cost of the sequence of m searches is $O(m + n)$.

3.   Prove that the binomial tree B_k has 2^k nodes, $k \geq 0$.

4.   Compare the performance of leftist trees and B-heaps under the assumption that the only permissible operations are insert and delete-min. For this, do the following:

(a)   Create a random list of n elements and a random sequence of insert and delete-min operations of length m. The number of delete-mins and inserts should be approximately equal. Initialize a min leftist tree and a B-heap to contain the n elements in the first random list. Now, measure the time to perform the m operations using the min leftist tree as well as the B-heap. Divide this time by m to get the average time per operation. Do this for $n = 100, 500, 1000, 2000, \cdots, 5000$. Let m be 5000. Tabulate your computing times.

(b)   Based on your experiments, make some statements about the relative merits of the two data structures.

9.5   FIBONACCI HEAPS

9.5.1   Definition

A *Fibonacci heap* is a data structure that supports the three binomial heap operations: insert, delete-min (or delete-max), and combine, as well as the following additional operations:

(1)   *decrease key*: Decrease the key of a specified node by a given positive amount.

(2)   *delete*: Delete the element in a specified node.

The first of these can be done in $O(1)$ amortized time and the second in $O(\log n)$ amortized time. The binomial heap operations can be performed in the same asymptotic times using a Fibonacci heap as they can be using a binomial heap.

There are two varieties of Fibonacci heaps: min and max. A *min Fibonacci heap* is a collection of min trees; a *max Fibonacci heap* is a collection of max trees. We shall explicitly consider min Fibonacci heaps only. These will be referred to as *F-heaps*. B-heaps are a special case of F-heaps. Thus, all the examples of B-heaps in the preceding section are also examples of F-heaps. As a consequence, in this section, we shall refer to these examples as F-heaps. To represent an F-heap, the B-heap representation is augmented by adding two fields, *parent* and *ChildCut*, to each node. The *parent* field is used to point to the node's parent (if any). The significance of the *ChildCut* field will be described later. In addition, the singly linked circular lists are replaced by doubly linked circular lists. This requires us to replace the field *link* by the fields *LeftLink* and *Right-Link*.

The basic operations insert, delete-min, and combine are performed exactly as for the case of B-heaps. We examine the remaining two operations: (1) delete an arbitrary node b from the F-heap a, and (2) decrease the key in the arbitrary node b by a positive amount.

9.5.2   Deletion from an F-Heap

To delete an arbitrary node b from the F-heap a, we do the following:

(1)   If $a = b$, then do a delete-min; otherwise do Steps 2, 3, and 4 below.

(2)   Delete b from its doubly linked list.

(3)   Combine the doubly linked list of b's children with the doubly linked list of a's min tree roots into a single doubly linked list. Trees of equal degree are not joined as in a delete-min operation.

(4)   Dispose of node b.

For example, if we delete the node containing 12 from the F-heap of Figure 9.15, we get the F-heap of Figure 9.20. The actual cost of an arbitrary delete is O(1) unless the min element is being deleted. In this case the deletion time is the time for a delete-min operation.

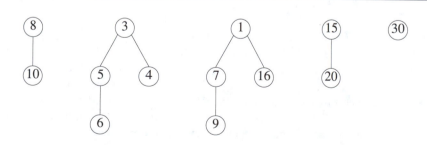

Figure 9.20: F-heap of Figure 9.15 following the deletion of 12

9.5.3   Decrease Key

To decrease the key in node b we do the following:

(1)   Reduce the key in b.

(2)   If b is not a min tree root and its key is smaller than that in its parent, then delete b from its doubly linked list and insert it into the doubly linked list of min tree roots.

(3)   Change a to point to b if the key in b is smaller than that in a.

Suppose we decrease the key 15 in the F-heap of Figure 9.15 by 4. The resulting F-heap is shown in Figure 9.21. The cost of performing a decrease-key operation is O(1).

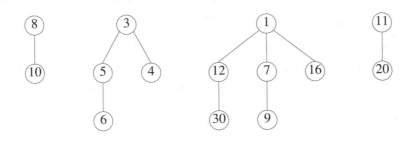

Figure 9.21: F-heap of Figure 9.15 following the reduction of 15 by 4

9.5.4   Cascading Cut

With the addition of the delete and decrease-key operations, the min trees in an F-heap need not be binomial trees. In fact, it is possible to have degree-k min trees with as few as $k+1$ nodes. As a result, the analysis of Theorem 9.1 is no longer valid. The analysis of Theorem 9.1 requires that each min tree of degree k have an exponential (in k) number of nodes. When decrease-key and delete operations are performed as described above, this is no longer true. To ensure that each min tree of degree k has at least c^k nodes for some c, $c > 1$, each delete and decrease-key operation must be followed by a *cascading-cut* step. For this, we add the Boolean field *ChildCut* to each node. The value of this field is useful only for nodes that are not the root of a min tree. In this case, the *ChildCut* field of node x has the value **true** iff one of the children of x was cut off (i.e., removed) after the most recent time x was made the child of its current parent. This means that each time two min trees are joined in a delete-min operation, the *ChildCut* field of the root with larger key should be set to **false**. Further, whenever a delete or decrease-key operation deletes a node q that is not a min tree root from its doubly linked list (Step 2 of delete and decrease key), then the cascading-cut step is invoked. During this step, we examine the nodes on the path from the parent p of the deleted node q up to the nearest ancestor of the deleted node with *ChildCut* = **false**. If there is no such ancestor, then the path goes from p to the root of the min tree containing p. All nonroot nodes on this path with *ChildCut* field **true** are deleted from their respective doubly linked lists and added to the doubly linked list of min tree root nodes of the F-heap. If the path has a node with *ChildCut* field **false**, this field is changed to **true**.

Figure 9.22 gives an example of a cascading cut. Figure 9.22(a) is the min tree containing 14 before a decrease-key operation that reduces this key by 4. The *ChildCut* fields are shown only for the nodes on the path from the parent of 14 to its nearest ancestor with *ChildCut* = **false**. A **true** value is indicated by "T." During the decrease-key operation, the min tree with root 14 is deleted from the min tree of Figure 9.22(a) and becomes a min tree of the F-heap. Its root now has key 10. This is the first min tree of Figure 9.22(b). During the cascading cut, the min trees with roots 12, 10, 8, and 6 are cut off from the min tree with root 2. Thus, the single min tree of Figure 9.22(a) becomes six min trees of the resulting F-heap. The *ChildCut* value of 4 becomes **true**. All other *ChildCut* values are unchanged.

9.5.5 Analysis

Lemma 9.3: Let a be an F-heap with n elements that results from a sequence of insert, combine, delete-min, delete, and decrease-key operations performed on initially empty F-heaps.

(a)   Let b be any node in any of the min trees of a. The degree of b is at most $\log_\phi m$, where $\phi = (1+\sqrt5)/2$, and m is the number of elements in the subtree with root b.

(b)   *MaxDegree* $\leq \lfloor \log_\phi n \rfloor$, and the actual cost of a delete-min operation is $O(\log n + s)$.

Proof: We shall prove (a) by induction on the degree of b. Let N_i be the minimum number of elements in the subtree with root b when b has degree i. We see that $N_0 = 1$ and $N_1 = 2$. So, the inequality of (a) holds for degrees 0 and 1. For $i > 1$, let $c_1, \cdots, c_i$ be the i children of b. Assume that c_j was made a child of b before c_{j+1}, $j < i$. Hence, when c_k, $k \leq i$, was made a child of b, the degree of b was at least $k - 1$. The only F-heap operation that makes one node a child of another is delete-min. Here, during a join min tree step, one min tree is made a subtree of another min tree of equal degree. Hence, at the time of joining, the degree of c_k must have been equal to that of b. Subsequent to joining, its degree can decrease as a result of a delete or decrease-key operation. However, following such a join, the degree of c_k can decrease by at most one, as an attempt to cut off a second child of c_k results in a cascading cut at c_k. Such a cut causes c_k to be-

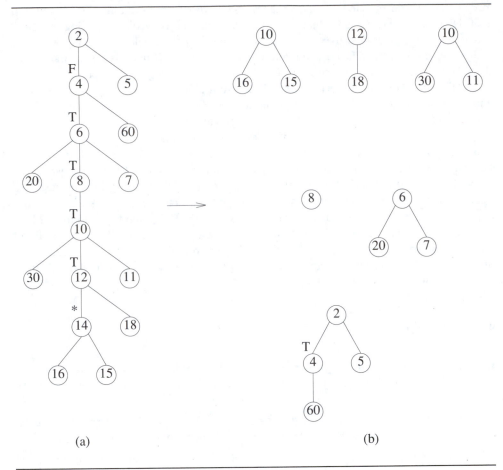

Figure 9.22: A cascading cut following a decrease of key 14 by 4

come the root of a min tree of the F-heap. Hence, the degree, d_k, of c_k is at least $\max\{0, k-2\}$. So, the number of elements in c_k is at least N_{d_k}. This implies that

$$N_i = N_0 + \sum_{k=0}^{i-2} N_k + 1 = \sum_{k=0}^{i-2} N_k + 2$$

One may show (see the exercises) that the Fibonacci numbers satisfy the equality

$$F_h = \sum_{k=0}^{h-2} F_k + 1, h > 1, F_0 = 0, \text{ and } F_1 = 1$$

From this we may obtain the equality $N_i = F_{i+2}$, $i \geq 0$. Further, since $F_{i+2} \geq \phi^i$, $N_i \geq \phi^i$. Hence, $i \leq \log_\phi m$. (b) is a direct consequence of (a). □

Theorem 9.2: If a sequence of n insert, combine, delete-min, delete, and decrease-key operations is performed on an initially empty F-heap, then we can amortize costs such that the amortized time complexity of each insert, combine, and decrease-key operation is O(1) and that of each delete-min and delete operation is O(log n). The total time complexity of the entire sequence is the sum of the amortized complexities of the individual operations in the sequence.

Proof: The proof is similar to that of Theorem 9.1. The definition of #*insert* is unchanged. However, that of *LastSize* is augmented by requiring that following each delete and decrease-key operation, *LastSize* be changed by the net change in the number of min trees in the F-heap (in the example of Figure 9.22 *LastSize* is increased by 5). With this modification, we see that at the time of a delete-min operation $s = $ #*insert* + *LastSize* + $u - 1$. #*insert* units of cost may be charged, one each, to the #*insert* insert operations that contribute to this count, and *LastSize* units may be charged to the delete-min, delete, and decrease-key operations that contribute to this count. This results in an additional charge of at most $\log_\phi n$ to each contributing delete-min and delete operation and of one to each contributing decrease-key operation. As a result, the amortized cost of a delete-min operation is O(log n).

Since the total number of cascading cuts is limited by the total number of deletes and decrease-key operations (as these are the only operations that can set *ChildCut* to **true**), the cost of these cuts may be amortized over the delete and decrease-key operations by adding one to their amortized costs. The amortized cost of deleting an element other than the min element becomes O(log n), as its actual cost is O(1) (excluding the cost of the cascading-cut sequence that may be performed); at most one unit is charged to it from the amortization of all the cascading cuts; and at most $\log_\phi n$ units are charged to it from a delete-min operation.

The amortized cost of a decrease-key operation is O(1), as its actual cost is O(1) (excluding the cost of the ensuing cascading cut); at most one unit is charged to it from the amortization of all cascading cuts; and at most one unit is charged from a delete-min operation.

The amortized cost of an insert is O(1), as its actual cost is one, and at most one cost unit is charged to it from a delete-min operation. Since the amortization scheme transfers no charge to a combine operation, its actual and amortized costs are the same. This cost is O(1). □

From the preceding theorem, it follows that the complexity of any sequence of F-heap operations is O($i + c + dk + (dm + d)$ log i) where i, c, dk, dm, and d are, respectively, the number of insert, combine, decrease-key, delete-min, and delete operations in the sequence.

9.5.6 Application to the Shortest-Paths Problem

We conclude this section on F-heaps by considering their application to the single-source/all-destinations algorithm of Chapter 6. Let S be the set of vertices to which a shortest path has been found and let $dist(i)$ be the length of a shortest path from the source vertex to vertex i, $i \in S$, that goes through only vertices in S. On each iteration of the shortest-path algorithm, we need to determine an i, $i \in S$, such that $dist(i)$ is minimum and add this i to S. This corresponds to a delete-min operation on S. Further, the $dist$ values of the remaining vertices in S may decrease. This corresponds to a decrease-key operation on each of the affected vertices. The total number of decrease-key operations is bounded by the number of edges in the graph, and the number of delete-min operations is $n - 2$. S begins with $n - 1$ vertices. If we implement S as an F-heap using $dist$ as the key, then $n - 1$ inserts are needed to initialize the F-heap. Additionally, $n - 2$ delete-min operations and at most e decrease-key operations are needed. The total time for all these operations is the sum of the amortized costs for each. This is $O(n \log n + e)$. The remainder of the algorithm takes $O(n)$ time. Hence if an F-heap is used to represent S, the complexity of the shortest-path algorithm becomes $O(n \log n + e)$. This is an asymptotic improvement over the implementation discussed in Chapter 6 if the graph does not have $\Omega(n^2)$ edges. If this single-source algorithm is used n times, once with each of the n vertices in the graph as the source, then we can find a shortest path between every pair of vertices in $O(n^2 \log n + ne)$ time. Once again, this represents an asymptotic improvement over the $O(n^3)$ dynamic programming algorithm of Chapter 6 for graphs that do not have $\Omega(n^2)$ edges. It is interesting to note that $O(n \log n + e)$ is the best possible implementation of the single-source algorithm of Chapter 6, as the algorithm must examine each edge and may be used to sort n numbers (which takes $O(n \log n)$ time).

EXERCISES

1. Prove that if we start with empty F-heaps and perform only the operations insert, combine, and delete-min, then all min trees in the F-heaps are binomial trees.

2. Can all the functions on an F-heap be performed in the same amount of time using singly linked circular lists rather than doubly linked circular lists? (Note that we can delete from an arbitrary node x of a singly linked circular list by copying over the data in the next node and then deleting the next node rather than the node x.)

3. Show that if we start with empty F-heaps and do not perform cascading cuts, then it is possible for a sequence of F-heap operations to result in degree-k min trees that have only $k + 1$ nodes, $k \geq 1$.

4. Suppose we change the rule for a cascading cut so that such a cut is performed only when a node loses a third child rather than when it loses a second child. For this, the *ChildCut* field is changed so that it can have the values 0, 1, and 2. When a node acquires a new parent, its *ChildCut* field is set to 1. Each time a node has a child cut off (during a delete or decrease-key operation), its *ChildCut* field is in-

creased by one (unless this field is already two). If the *ChildCut* field is already two, a cascading cut is performed.

(a) Obtain a recurrence equation for N_i, the minimum number of nodes in a min tree with degree i. Assume that we start with an empty F-heap and that all operations (except cascading cut) are performed as described in the text. Cascading cuts are performed as described above.

(b) Solve the recurrence of part (a) to obtain a lower bound on N_i.

(c) Does the modified rule for cascading cuts ensure that the minimum number of nodes in any min tree of degree i is exponential in i?

(d) For the new cascading-cut rule, can you establish the same amortized complexities as for the original rule? Prove the correctness of your answer.

(e) Answer parts (c) and (d) under the assumption that cascading cuts are performed only after k children of a node have been cut off. Here, k is a fixed constant ($k = 2$ for the rule used in the text, and $k = 3$ for the rule used earlier in this exercise).

(f) How do you expect the performance of F-heaps to change as larger values of k (see part (e)) are used?

5. Write Pascal procedures to do the following:

(a) Create an empty F-heap.

(b) Insert element x into an F-heap.

(c) Perform a delete-min operation on an F-heap. The deleted element is to be returned in z.

(d) Delete the element in node b of an F-heap a. The deleted element is to be returned in z.

(e) Decrease the key in the node b of an F-heap a by some positive amount c.

Note that all operations must leave behind properly structured F-heaps. Your procedures for (d) and (e) must perform cascading cuts. Test the correctness of your procedures by running them on a computer using suitable test data.

6. For the Fibonacci numbers F_k and the numbers N_i of Lemma 9.3, prove the following:

(a) $F_h = \sum\limits_{k=0}^{h-2} F_k + 1, h > 1.$

(b) Use (a) to show that $N_i = F_{i+2}, i \geq 0.$

(c) Use the equality

$$F_k = \frac{1}{\sqrt{5}}(\frac{1+\sqrt{5}}{2})^k - \frac{1}{\sqrt{5}}(\frac{1-\sqrt{5}}{2})^k, k \geq 0$$

to show that $F_{k+2} \geq \phi^k, k \geq 0$, where $\phi = (1+\sqrt{5})/2$.

7. Implement the single-source shortest-path algorithm of Chapter 6 using the data structures recommended there as well as F-heaps. However, use adjacency lists rather than an adjacency matrix. Generate 10 connected undirected graphs with different edge densities (say 10%, 20%, $\cdots$, 100% of maximum) for each of the cases $n = 100, 200, \cdots, 500$. Assign random costs to the edges (use a uniform random number generator in the range [1, 1000]). Measure the run times of the two implementations of the shortest-path algorithms. Plot the average times for each n.

9.6 REFERENCES AND SELECTED READINGS

Min-max heaps were developed in "Min-max heaps and generalized priority queues," by M. Atkinson, J. Sack, N. Santoro, and T. Strothotte, *Communications of the ACM*, 29:10, 1986, pp. 996-1000. This paper also contains extensions of min-max heaps.

The deap data structure was invented by Svante Carlsson. The reference is "The deap: A double-ended heap to implement double-ended priority queues," *Information Processing Letters*, 26, 1987, pp. 33-36.

Leftist trees were invented by C. Crane. See, *Linear Lists and Priority Queues as Balanced Binary Trees*, Technical report CS-72-259, Computer Science Dept., Stanford University, Palo Alto, CA, 1972.

Further discussion of leftist trees may be found in *Data Structures and Network Algorithms*, by R. Tarjan, SIAM, Philadelphia, PA, 1983.

The exercise on lazy deletion is from "Finding minimum spanning trees," by D. Cheriton and R. Tarjan, *SIAM Journal on Computing*, 5, 1976, pp. 724-742.

B-heaps and F-heaps were invented by M. Fredman and R. Tarjan. Their work is reported in the paper "Fibonacci heaps and their uses in improved network optimization algorithms," *JACM*, 34:3, 1987, pp. 596-615. This paper also describes several variants of the basic F-heap as discussed here, as well as the application of F-heaps to the assignment problem and to the problem of finding a minimum-cost spanning tree. Their result is that using F-heaps, minimum-cost spanning trees can be found in $O(e\beta(e,n))$ time, where $\beta(e,n) \le \log^* n$ when $e \ge n$. $\log^* n = \min\{i \mid \log^{(i)} n \le 1\}$, $\log^{(0)} n = n$, and $\log^{(i)} n = \log(\log^{(i-1)} n)$. The complexity of finding minimum-cost spanning trees has been further reduced to $O(e\log\beta(e,n))$. The reference for this is "Efficient algorithms for finding minimum spanning trees in undirected and directed graphs," by H. Gabow, Z. Galil, T. Spencer, and R. Tarjan, *Combinatorica*, 6:2, 1986, pp. 109-122.

CHAPTER 10

SEARCH STRUCTURES

10.1 OPTIMAL BINARY SEARCH TREES

Binary search trees were introduced in Chapter 5. In this section, we consider the construction of binary search trees for a static set of identifiers. That is, we make no additions to or deletions from the set. Only searches are performed.

A sorted file can be searched using a binary search. For this search, we can construct a binary search tree with the property that searching this tree using the function *search* (Program 5.17) is equivalent to performing a binary search on the sorted file. For instance, a binary search on the file (**do, if, while**) corresponds to using algorithm *search* on the binary search tree of Figure 10.1. Although this tree is a full binary tree, it may not be the optimal binary search tree to use when the probabilities with which different identifiers are sought are different.

To find an optimal binary search tree for a given static file, we must first decide on a cost measure for search trees. When searching for an identifier at level k, function *search* makes k iterations of the **while** loop. Since this **while** loop determines the cost of the search, it is reasonable to use the level number of a node as its cost.

Consider the two search trees of Figure 10.2. The second of these requires at most three comparisons to decide whether the identifier being sought is in the tree. The first binary tree may require four comparisons, since any identifier that alphabetically follows **for** but precedes **if** will test four nodes. Thus, as far as worst-case search time is concerned, the second binary tree is more desirable than the first. To search for an identifier

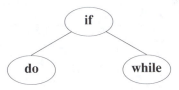

Figure 10.1: Binary search tree corresponding to a binary search on the file (**do, if, while**)

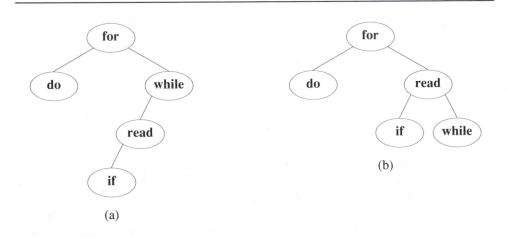

Figure 10.2: Two binary search trees

in the first tree takes one comparison for the **for**, two for each of **do** and **while**, three for **read**, and four for **if**. Assuming that each identifier is sought with equal probability, the average number of comparisons for a successful search is 2.4. For the second binary search tree this amount is 2.2. Thus, the second tree has a better average behavior, too.

In evaluating binary search trees, it is useful to add a special "square" node at every null link. Doing this to the trees of Figure 10.2 yields the trees of Figure 10.3. Remember that every binary tree with n nodes has $n + 1$ null links and therefore will have $n + 1$ square nodes. We shall call these nodes *external* nodes because they are not part of the original tree. The remaining nodes will be called *internal* nodes. Each time a binary search tree is examined for an identifier that is not in the tree, the search terminates at an external node. Since all such searches are unsuccessful searches, external

nodes will also be referred to as *failure nodes*. A binary tree with external nodes added
is an *extended binary tree*. The concept of an extended binary tree as just defined is the
same as that defined in connection with leftist trees in Chapter 9. Figure 10.3 shows the
extended binary trees corresponding to the search trees of Figure 10.2.

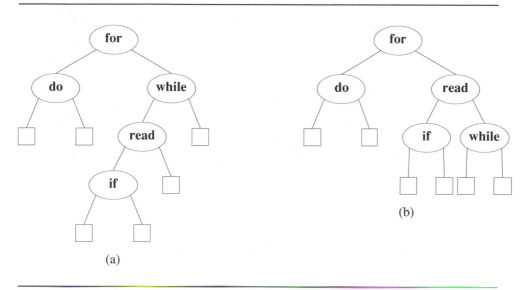

(a)

(b)

Figure 10.3: Extended binary trees corresponding to search trees of Figure 10.2

We define the *external path length* of a binary tree to be the sum over all external
nodes of the lengths of the paths from the root to those nodes. Analogously, the *internal
path length* is the sum over all internal nodes of the lengths of the paths from the root to
those nodes. The internal path length, I, for the tree of Figure 10.3(a) is

$$I = 0 + 1 + 1 + 2 + 3 = 7$$

Its external path length, E, is

$$E = 2 + 2 + 4 + 4 + 3 + 2 = 17$$

Exercise 1 of this section shows that the internal and external path lengths of a
binary tree with n internal nodes are related by the formula $E = I + 2n$. Hence, binary
trees with the maximum E also have maximum I. Over all binary trees with n internal
nodes, what are the maximum and minimum possible values for I? The worst case,
clearly, is when the tree is skewed (i.e., when the tree has a depth of n). In this case,

$$I = \sum_{i=0}^{n-1} i = n(n-1)/2$$

To obtain trees with minimal I, we must have as many internal nodes as close to the root as possible. We can have at most 2 nodes at distance 1, 4 at distance 2, and in general, the smallest value for I is

$$0 + 2 * 1 + 4 * 2 + 8 * 3 + \cdots +$$

One tree with minimal internal path length is the complete binary tree defined in Section 5.2. If we number the nodes in a complete binary tree as in Section 5.3, then we see that the distance of node i from the root is $\lfloor \log_2 i \rfloor$. Hence, the smallest value for I is

$$\sum_{1 \leq i \leq n} \lfloor \log_2 i \rfloor = O(n \log_2 n)$$

Let us now return to our original problem of representing a symbol table as a binary search tree. If the binary search tree contains the identifiers $a_1, a_2, \cdots, a_n$ with $a_1 < a_2 < \cdots < a_n$, and the probability of searching for each a_i is p_i, then the total cost of any binary search tree is

$$\sum_{1 \leq i \leq n} p_i \cdot \text{level}(a_i)$$

when only successful searches are made. Since unsuccessful searches (i.e., searches for identifiers not in the table) will also be made, we should include the cost of these searches in our cost measure, too. Unsuccessful searches terminate with *search* := **nil** in algorithm *search* (Program 5.17). Every node with a null subtree defines a point at which such a termination can take place. Let us replace every null subtree by a failure node. The identifiers not in the binary search tree may be partitioned into $n + 1$ classes $E_i, 0 \leq i \leq n$. E_0 contains all identifiers X such that $X < a_1$. E_i contains all identifiers X such that $a_i < X < a_{i+1}, 1 \leq i < n$, and E_n contains all identifiers $X, X > a_n$. It is easy to see that for all identifiers in a particular class E_i, the search terminates at the same failure node, and it terminates at different failure nodes for identifiers in different classes. The failure nodes may be numbered 0 to n, with i being the failure node for class $E_i, 0 \leq i \leq n$. If q_i is the probability that the identifier being sought is in E_i, then the cost of the failure nodes is

$$\sum_{0 \leq i \leq n} q_i \cdot (\text{level(failure node } i) - 1)$$

Therefore, the total cost of a binary search tree is

$$\sum_{1 \leq i \leq n} p_i \cdot \text{level}(a_i) + \sum_{0 \leq i \leq n} q_i \cdot (\text{level (failure node } i) - 1) \qquad (10.1)$$

An *optimal binary search tree* for the identifier set $a_1, \cdots, a_n$ is one that minimizes Eq. (10.1) over all possible binary search trees for this identifier set. Note that since all searches must terminate either successfully or unsuccessfully, we have

$$\sum_{1 \le i \le n} p_i + \sum_{0 \le i \le n} q_i = 1$$

Example 10.1: Figure 10.4 shows the possible binary search trees for the identifier set $(a_1, a_2, a_3) = ($**do, if, while**$)$.

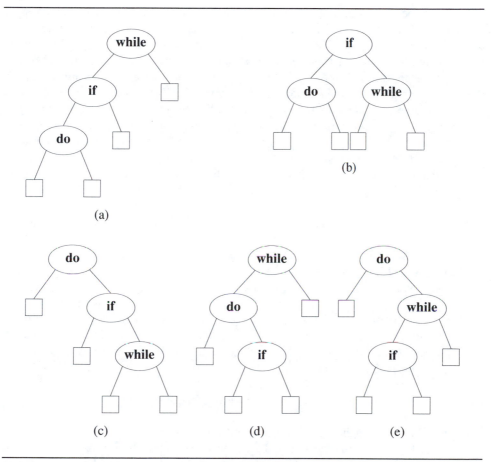

(a)

(b)

(c)

(d)

(e)

Figure 10.4: Binary search trees with three identifiers

With equal probabilities, $p_i = q_j = 1/7$ for all i and j, we have

cost (tree a) = 15/7; cost (tree b) = 13/7
cost (tree c) = 15/7; cost (tree d) = 15/7
cost (tree e) = 15/7

As expected, tree b is optimal. With $p_1 = 0.5$, $p_2 = 0.1$, $p_3 = 0.05$, $q_0 = 0.15$, $q_1 = 0.1$, $q_2 = 0.05$, and $q_3 = 0.05$ we have

$$\text{cost (tree } a) = 2.65; \text{ cost (tree } b) = 1.9$$
$$\text{cost (tree } c) = 1.5; \text{ cost (tree } d) = 2.05$$
$$\text{cost (tree } e) = 1.6$$

Tree c is optimal with this assignment of p's and q's. $\square$

How does one determine the optimal binary search tree? We could proceed as in Example 10.1 and explicitly generate all possible binary search trees, then compute the cost of each tree, and determine the tree with minimum cost. Since the cost of an n-node binary search tree can be determined in $O(n)$ time, the complexity of the optimal binary search tree algorithm is $O(n\,N(n))$, where $N(n)$ is the number of distinct binary search trees with n identifiers. From Section 5.11 we know that $N(n) = O(4^n/n^{3/2})$. Hence, this brute-force algorithm is impractical for large n. We can find a fairly efficient algorithm by making some observations about the properties of optimal binary search trees.

Let $a_1 < a_2 < \cdots < a_n$ be the n identifiers to be represented in a binary search tree. Let T_{ij} denote an optimal binary search tree for $a_{i+1}, \cdots, a_j, i < j$. By convention T_{ii} is an empty tree for $0 \le i \le n$, and T_{ij} is not defined for $i > j$. Let c_{ij} be the cost of the search tree T_{ij}. By definition c_{ii} will be 0. Let r_{ij} be the root of T_{ij}, and let

$$w_{ij} = q_i + \sum_{k=i+1}^{j} (q_k + p_k)$$

be the weight of T_{ij}. By definition $r_{ii} = 0$, and $w_{ii} = q_i$, $0 \le i \le n$. Therefore, T_{0n} is an optimal binary search tree for $a_1, \cdots, a_n$. Its cost is c_{0n}, its weight is w_{0n}, and its root is r_{0n}.

If T_{ij} is an optimal binary search tree for $a_{i+1}, \cdots, a_j$, and $r_{ij} = k$, then k satisfies the inequality $i < k \le j$. T_{ij} has two subtrees L and R. L is the left subtree and contains the identifiers $a_{i+1}, \cdots, a_{k-1}$, and R is the right subtree and contains the identifiers $a_{k+1}, \cdots, a_j$ (Figure 10.5). The cost c_{ij} of T_{ij} is

$$c_{ij} = p_k + \text{cost}(L) + \text{cost}(R) + \text{weight}(L) + \text{weight}(R) \qquad (10.2)$$

where $\text{weight}(L) = \text{weight}(T_{i,k-1}) = w_{i,k-1}$, and $\text{weight}(R) = \text{weight}(T_{kj}) = w_{kj}$.

From Eq. (10.2) it is clear that if c_{ij} is to be minimal, then $\text{cost}(L) = c_{i,k-1}$ and $\text{cost}(R) = c_{kj}$, as otherwise we could replace either L or R by a subtree with a lower cost, thus getting a binary search tree for $a_{i+1}, \cdots, a_j$ with a lower cost than c_{ij}. This violates the assumption that T_{ij} is optimal. Hence, Eq. (10.2) becomes

$$c_{ij} = p_k + c_{i,k-1} + c_{kj} + w_{i,k-1} + w_{kj}$$

$$= w_{ij} + c_{i,k-1} + c_{kj} \qquad (10.3)$$

Figure 10.5: An optimal binary search tree T_{ij}

Since T_{ij} is optimal, it follows from Eq. (10.3) that $r_{ij} = k$ is such that

$$w_{ij} + c_{i,k-1} + c_{kj} = \min_{i<l\leq j}\{w_{ij} + c_{i,l-1} + c_{lj}\}$$

or

$$c_{i,k-1} + c_{kj} = \min_{i<l\leq j}\{c_{i,l-1} + c_{lj}\} \tag{10.4}$$

Equation (10.4) gives us a means of obtaining T_{0n} and c_{0n}, starting from the knowledge that $T_{ii} = \phi$ and $c_{ii} = 0$.

Example 10.2: Let $n = 4$ and $(a_1, a_2, a_3, a_4) = (\textbf{do}, \textbf{if}, \textbf{read}, \textbf{while})$. Let $(p_1, p_2, p_3, p_4) = (3, 3, 1, 1)$ and $(q_0, q_1, q_2, q_3, q_4) = (2, 3, 1, 1, 1)$. The p's and q's have been multiplied by 16 for convenience. Initially, $w_{ii} = q_i$, $c_{ii} = 0$, and $r_{ii} = 0$, $0 \leq i \leq 4$. Using Eqs. (10.3) and (10.4), we get

$$
\begin{aligned}
w_{01} &= p_1 + w_{00} + w_{11} = p_1 + q_1 + w_{00} = 8 \\
c_{01} &= w_{01} + \min\{c_{00} + c_{11}\} = 8 \\
r_{01} &= 1 \\
w_{12} &= p_2 + w_{11} + w_{22} = p_2 + q_2 + w_{11} = 7 \\
c_{12} &= w_{12} + \min\{c_{11} + c_{22}\} = 7 \\
r_{12} &= 2 \\
w_{23} &= p_3 + w_{22} + w_{33} = p_3 + q_3 + w_{22} = 3 \\
c_{23} &= w_{23} + \min\{c_{22} + c_{33}\} = 3
\end{aligned}
$$

$$r_{23} = 3$$

$$w_{34} = p_4 + w_{33} + w_{44} = p_4 + q_4 + w_{33} = 3$$

$$c_{34} = w_{34} + \min\{c_{33} + c_{44}\} = 3$$

$$r_{34} = 4$$

Knowing $w_{i,i+1}$ and $c_{i,i+1}$, $0 \le i < 4$, we can use Eqs. (10.3) and (10.4) again to compute $w_{i,i+2}$, $c_{i,i+2}$, $r_{i,i+2}$, $0 \le i < 3$. This process may be repeated until w_{04}, c_{04}, and r_{04} are obtained. The table of Figure 10.6 shows the results of this computation. From the table, we see that $c_{04} = 32$ is the minimal cost of a binary search tree for a_1 to a_4. The root of tree T_{04} is a_2. Hence, the left subtree is T_{01} and the right subtree T_{24}. T_{01} has root a_1 and subtrees T_{00} and T_{11}. T_{24} has root a_3; its left subtree is therefore T_{22} and right subtree T_{34}. Thus, with the data in the table it is possible to reconstruct T_{04}. Figure 10.7 shows T_{04}. □

	0	1	2	3	4
0	$w_{00} = 2$ $c_{00} = 0$ $r_{00} = 0$	$w_{11} = 3$ $c_{11} = 0$ $r_{11} = 0$	$w_{22} = 1$ $c_{22} = 0$ $r_{22} = 0$	$w_{33} = 1$ $c_{33} = 0$ $r_{33} = 0$	$w_{44} = 1$ $c_{44} = 0$ $r_{44} = 0$
1	$w_{01} = 8$ $c_{01} = 8$ $r_{01} = 1$	$w_{12} = 7$ $c_{12} = 7$ $r_{12} = 2$	$w_{23} = 3$ $c_{23} = 3$ $r_{23} = 3$	$w_{34} = 3$ $c_{34} = 3$ $r_{34} = 4$	
2	$w_{02} = 12$ $c_{02} = 19$ $r_{02} = 1$	$w_{13} = 9$ $c_{13} = 12$ $r_{13} = 2$	$w_{24} = 5$ $c_{24} = 8$ $r_{24} = 3$		
3	$w_{03} = 14$ $c_{03} = 25$ $r_{03} = 2$	$w_{14} = 11$ $c_{14} = 19$ $r_{14} = 2$			
4	$w_{04} = 16$ $c_{04} = 32$ $r_{04} = 2$				

Figure 10.6: Computation of c_{04} and r_{04}. The computation is carried out by row from row 0 to row 4

Example 10.2 illustrates how Eq. (10.4) may be used to determine the c's and r's, as well as how to reconstruct T_{0n} knowing the r's. Let us examine the complexity of this procedure to evaluate the c's and r's. The evaluation procedure described in Example

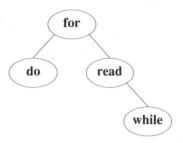

Figure 10.7: Optimal binary search tree for Example 10.2

10.2 requires us to compute c_{ij} for $(j - i) = 1, 2, \cdots, n$ in that order. When $j - i = m$, there are $n - m + 1$ c_{ij}'s to compute. The computation of each of these c_{ij}'s requires us to find the minimum of m quantities (see Eq. (10.4)). Hence, each such c_{ij} can be computed in time O(m). The total time for all c_{ij}'s with $j - i = m$ is therefore O($nm - m^2$). The total time to evaluate all the c_{ij}'s and r_{ij}'s is

$$\sum_{1 \leq m \leq n} (nm - m^2) = O(n^3)$$

Actually we can do better than this using a result from D. E. Knuth that states that the optimal l in Eq. (10.4) may be found by limiting the search to the range $r_{i,j-1} \leq l \leq r_{i+1,j}$. In this case, the computing time becomes O(n^2) (see Exercise 3). Algorithm *obst* (Program 10.1) uses this result to obtain in O(n^2) time the values of w_{ij}, r_{ij}, and c_{ij}, $0 \leq i \leq j \leq n$. The actual tree T_{0n} may be constructed from the values of r_{ij} in O(n) time. The algorithm for this is left as an exercise. The data types used by *obst* are

> **type** *identifier* = **packed array [1 ..** *MaxChar*] **of char;**
> *IdentArray* = **array**{1 .. *n*] **of** *identifier*;
> *parray* = **array**[1 .. *n*] **of integer;**
> *qarray* = **array**[0 .. *n*] **of integer;**
> *carray* = **array**[0 .. *n*, 0 .. *n*] **of integer;**

EXERCISES

1. (a) Prove by induction that if T is a binary tree with n internal nodes, I its internal path length, and E its external path length, then $E = I + 2n$, $n \geq 0$.

   (b) Using the result of (a), show that the average number of comparisons s in a successful search is related to the average number of comparisons, u, in an unsuccessful search by the formula

---

procedure *obst* (p : *parray*; q : *qarray*; a : *IdentArray*; **var** c,r,w : *carray*);
{Given n distinct identifiers $a_1 < a_2 < \cdots < a_n$, and probabilities p_j, $1 \le j \le n$, and q_i, $0 \le i \le n$ this algorithm computes the cost c_{ij} of optimal binary search trees t_{ij} for identifiers $a_{i+1}, \cdots, a_j$. It also computes r_{ij}, the root of t_{ij}. w_{ij} is the weight of t_{ij}.}
var i, j, k, l, m : **integer**;
begin
  for $i := 0$ **to** $n - 1$ **do**
  begin
    $w[i,i] := q[i]$; $r[i,i] = 0$; $c[i,i] := 0$; {initialize}
    $w[i, i+1] := q[i] + q[i+1] + p[i+1]$; {optimal trees with one node}
    $r[i, i+1] := i + 1$;
    $c[i, i+1] := w[i, i+1]$;
  end;
  $w[n,n] := q[n]$; $r[n,n] := 0$; $c[n,n] := 0$;
  for $m := 2$ **to** n **do** {find optimal trees with m nodes}
    for $i := 0$ **to** $n - m$ **do**
    begin
      $j := i + m$;
      $w[i,j] := w[i, j-1] + p[j] + q[j]$;
      $k := KnuthMin(c, r, i, j)$;
      {*KnuthMin* returns a value k in the range $[r[i, j-1], r[i+1, j]]$
      minimizing $c[i, k-1] + c[k,j]$}
      $c[i,j] := w[i,j] + c[i, k-1] + c[k,j]$; {Eq. (10.3)}
      $r[i,j] := k$;
    end;
end; {of *obst*}

Program 10.1: Finding an optimal binary search tree

$$s = (1 + 1/n)u - 1, \; n \ge 1.$$

2. Using algorithm *obst* (Program 10.1), compute w_{ij}, r_{ij}, and c_{ij}, $0 \le i < j \le 4$, for the identifier set $(a_1, a_2, a_3, a_4) = ($**end, goto, print, read**$)$, with $p_1 = 1/20$, $p_2 = 1/5$, $p_3 = 1/10$, $p_4 = 1/20$, $q_0 = 1/5$, $q_1 = 1/10$, $q_2 = 1/5$, $q_3 = 1/20$, and $q_4 = 1/20$. Using the r_{ij}'s, construct the optimal binary search tree.

3. (a) Complete procedure *obst* by providing the code for function *KnuthMin*.

    (b) Show that the computing time of algorithm *obst* is $O(n^2)$.

    (c) Write an algorithm to construct the optimal binary search tree T_{on} given the roots r_{ij}, $0 \le i < j \le n$. Show that this can be done in time $O(n)$.

4. Since, often, only the approximate values of the p's and q's are known, it is perhaps just as meaningful to find a binary search tree that is nearly optimal (i.e., its cost, Eq. (10.1), is almost minimal for the given p's and q's). This exercise explores an $O(n \log n)$ algorithm that results in nearly optimal binary search trees. The search tree heuristic we shall study is

Choose the root a_k such that $|w_{0,k-1} - w_{k,n}|$ is as small as possible. Repeat this procedure to find the left and right subtrees of a_k.

(a) Using this heuristic obtain the resulting binary search tree for the data of Exercise 2. What is its cost?

(b) Write a Pascal algorithm implementing the above heuristic. The time complexity of your algorithm should be $O(n \log n)$.

An analysis of the performance of this heuristic may be found in the paper by Melhorn (see the References and Selected Readings section).

10.2 AVL TREES

Dynamic tables may also be maintained as binary search trees. In Chapter 5, we saw how insertions and deletions can be performed on binary search trees. Figure 10.8 shows the binary search tree obtained by entering the months JANUARY to DECEMBER in that order into an initially empty binary search tree. Procedure *insert* (Program 5.19) is used.

The maximum number of comparisons needed to search for any identifier in the tree of Figure 10.8 is six for NOVEMBER. The average number of comparisons is (1 for JANUARY + 2 each for FEBRUARY and MARCH + 3 each for APRIL, JUNE and MAY + $\cdots$ + 6 for NOVEMBER)/12 = 42/12 = 3.5. If the months are entered in the order JULY, FEBRUARY, MAY, AUGUST, DECEMBER, MARCH, OCTOBER, APRIL, JANUARY, JUNE, SEPTEMBER, NOVEMBER, then the tree of Figure 10.9 is obtained.

The tree of Figure 10.9 is well balanced and does not have any paths to a node with a null link that are much longer than others. This is not true of the tree of Figure 10.8, which has six nodes on the path from the root to NOVEMBER and only two nodes on the path to APRIL. Moreover, during the construction of the tree of Figure 10.9, all intermediate trees obtained are also well balanced. The maximum number of identifier comparisons needed to find any identifier is now 4, and the average is $37/12 \approx 3.1$. If instead the months are entered in lexicographic order, the tree degenerates to a chain as in Figure 10.10. The maximum search time is now 12 identifier comparisons, and the average is 6.5. Thus, in the worst case, binary search trees correspond to sequential searching in an ordered file. When the identifiers are entered in a random order, the tree tends to be balanced as in Figure 10.9. If all permutations are equally probable, then the average search and insertion time is $O(\log n)$ for an n-node binary search tree.

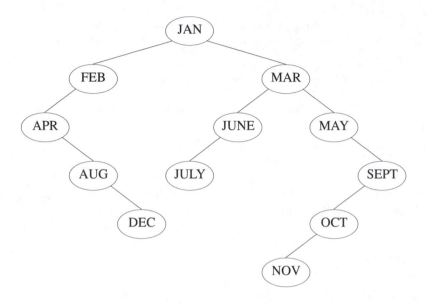

Figure 10.8: Binary search tree obtained for the months of the year

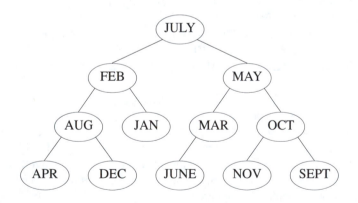

Figure 10.9: A balanced tree for the months of the year

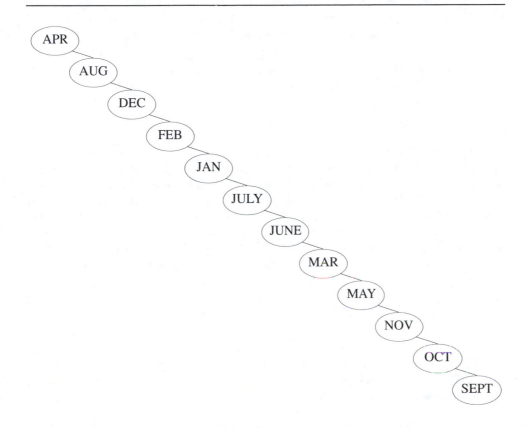

Figure 10.10: Degenerate binary search tree

From our earlier study of binary trees, we know that both the average and maximum search time will be minimized if the binary search tree is maintained as a complete binary tree at all times. However, since we are dealing with a dynamic situation, it is difficult to achieve this ideal without making the time required to insert an identifier very high. This is so because in some cases it would be necessary to restructure the whole tree to accommodate the new entry and at the same time have a complete binary search tree. It is, however, possible to keep the trees balanced to ensure both an average and worst-case retrieval time of O(log n) for a tree with n nodes. In this section, we study one method of growing balanced binary trees. These balanced trees will have satisfactory search and insertion time properties. Other ways to maintain balanced search trees are studied in later sections.

In 1962, Adelson-Velskii and Landis introduced a binary tree structure that is balanced with respect to the heights of subtrees. As a result of the balanced nature of this type of tree, dynamic retrievals can be performed in O(log n) time if the tree has n nodes in it. At the same time, a new identifier can be entered or deleted from such a tree in time O(log n). The resulting tree remains height-balanced. This tree structure is called an AVL tree. As with binary trees, it is natural to define AVL trees recursively.

Definition: An empty tree is height-balanced. If T is a nonempty binary tree with T_L and T_R as its left and right subtrees respectively, then T is *height-balanced* iff (1) T_L and T_R are height-balanced and (2) $| h_L - h_R | \leq 1$ where h_L and h_R are the heights of T_L and T_R, respectively. □

The definition of a height-balanced binary tree requires that every subtree also be height-balanced. The binary tree of Figure 10.8 is not height-balanced, since the height of the left subtree of the tree with root APRIL is 0 and that of the right subtree is 2. The tree of Figure 10.9 is height-balanced while that of Figure 10.10 is not. To illustrate the processes involved in maintaining a height-balanced binary search tree, let us try to construct such a tree for the months of the year. This time let us assume that the insertions are made in the following order: MARCH, MAY, NOVEMBER, AUGUST, APRIL, JANUARY, DECEMBER, JULY, FEBRUARY, JUNE, OCTOBER, SEPTEMBER. Figure 10.11 shows the tree as it grows and the restructuring involved in keeping the tree balanced. The numbers above each node represent the difference in heights between the left and right subtrees of that node. This number is referred to as the balance factor of the node.

Definition: The *balance factor*, $BF(T)$, of a node T in a binary tree is defined to be $h_L - h_R$, where h_L and h_R, respectively, are the heights of the left and right subtrees of T. For any node T in an AVL tree, $BF(T) = -1, 0,$ or 1. □

Inserting MARCH and MAY results in the binary search trees (a) and (b) of Figure 10.11. When NOVEMBER is inserted into the tree, the height of the right subtree of MARCH becomes 2, whereas that of the left subtree is 0. The tree has become unbalanced. To rebalance the tree, a rotation is performed. MARCH is made the left child of MAY, and MAY becomes the root (Figure 10.11(c)). The introduction of AUGUST leaves the tree balanced (Figure 10.11(d)).

The next insertion, APRIL, causes the tree to become unbalanced again. To rebalance the tree, another rotation is performed. This time, it is a clockwise rotation. MARCH is made the right child of AUGUST, and AUGUST becomes the root of the subtree (Figure 10.11(e)). Note that both of the previous rotations were carried out with respect to the closest parent of the new node that had a balance factor of ±2. The insertion of JANUARY results in an unbalanced tree. This time, however, the rotation involved is somewhat more complex than in the earlier situations. The common point, however, is that the rotation is still carried out with respect to the nearest parent of JANUARY with a balance factor ±2. MARCH becomes the new root. AUGUST, together with its left subtree, becomes the left subtree of MARCH. The left subtree of

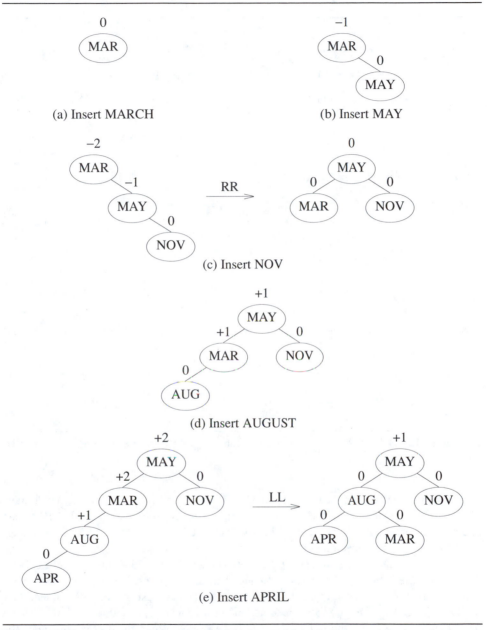

Figure 10.11: Balanced trees obtained for the months of the year (continued on next page)

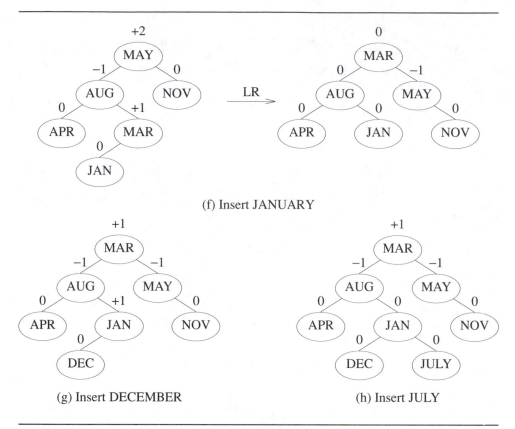

(f) Insert JANUARY

(g) Insert DECEMBER   (h) Insert JULY

Figure 10.11: Balanced trees obtained for the months of the year (continued on next page)

MARCH becomes the right subtree of AUGUST. MAY and its right subtree, which have identifiers greater than MARCH, become the right subtree of MARCH. (If MARCH had had a nonempty right subtree, this could have become the left subtree of MAY, since all identifiers would have been less than MAY.)

Inserting DECEMBER and JULY necessitates no rebalancing. When FEBRUARY is inserted, the tree becomes unbalanced again. The rebalancing process is very similar to that used when JANUARY was inserted. The nearest parent with balance factor ±2 is AUGUST. DECEMBER becomes the new root of that subtree. AUGUST, with its left subtree, becomes the left subtree. JANUARY, with its right subtree, becomes the right subtree of DECEMBER; FEBRUARY becomes the left subtree of JANUARY. (If DECEMBER had had a left subtree, it would have become the right subtree of AUGUST.) The insertion of JUNE requires the same rebalancing as in Figure 10.11(f). The

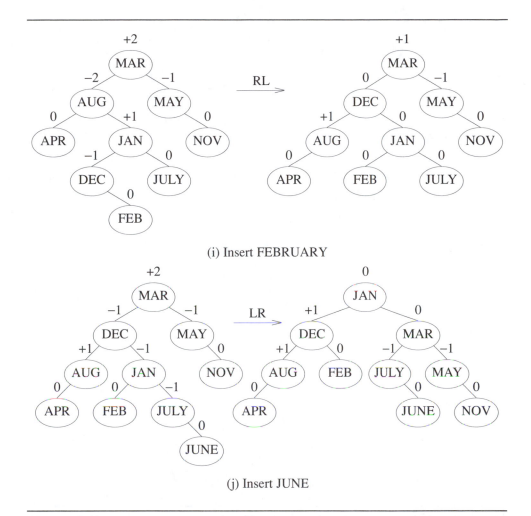

(i) Insert FEBRUARY

(j) Insert JUNE

Figure 10.11: Balanced trees obtained for the months of the year (continued on next page)

rebalancing following the insertion of OCTOBER is identical to that following the insertion of NOVEMBER. Inserting SEPTEMBER leaves the tree balanced.

In the preceding example we saw that the addition of a node to a balanced binary search tree could unbalance it. The rebalancing was carried out using four different kinds of rotations: LL, RR, LR, and RL (Figure 10.11 (e), (c), (f), and (i), respectively). LL and RR are symmetric, as are LR and RL. These rotations are characterized by the nearest ancestor, A, of the inserted node, Y, whose balance factor becomes ± 2. The following characterization of rotation types is obtained:

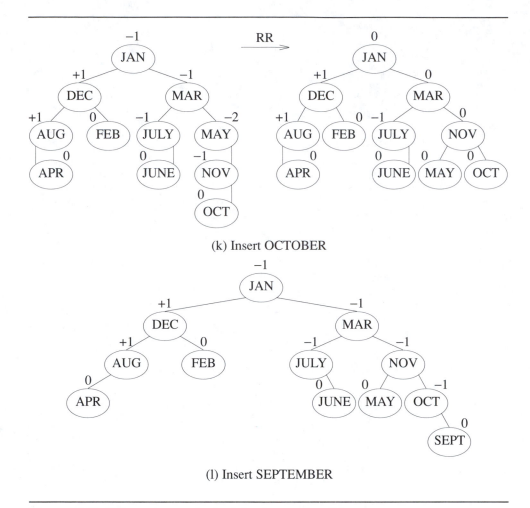

Figure 10.11: Balanced trees obtained for the months of the year

LL: new node Y is inserted in the left subtree of the left subtree of A

LR: Y is inserted in the right subtree of the left subtree of A

RR: Y is inserted in the right subtree of the right subtree of A

RL: Y is inserted in the left subtree of the right subtree of A

Figure 10.12 shows the LL, LR, and RR rotations in terms of abstract binary trees. The RL rotations are similar to the LR rotations. The root node in each of the trees of the figures represents the nearest ancestor whose balance factor has become ±2 as a

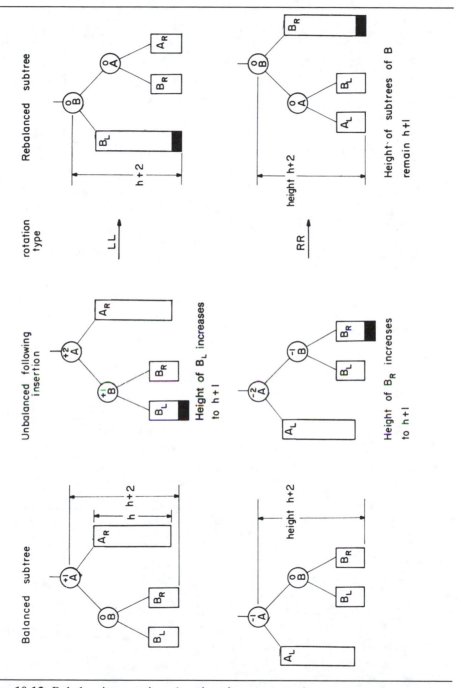

Figure 10.12: Rebalancing rotations (continued on next page)

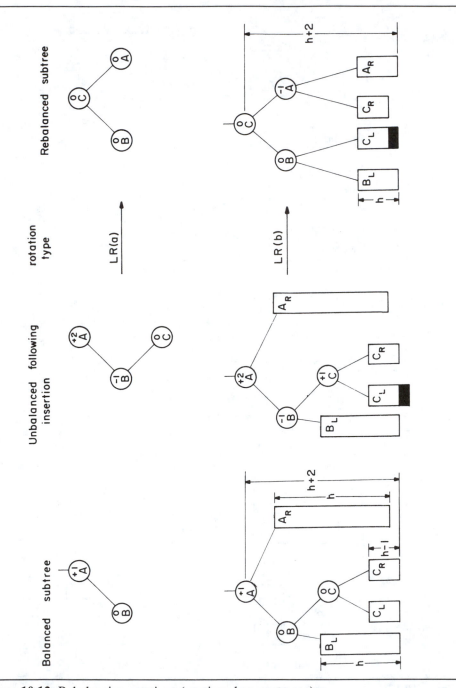

Figure 10.12: Rebalancing rotations (continued on next page)

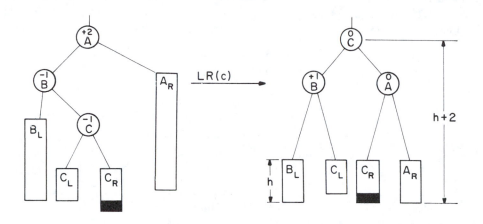

Figure 10.12: Rebalancing rotations

result of the insertion. A moment's reflection will show that if a height-balanced binary tree becomes unbalanced as a result of an insertion, then these are the only four cases possible for rebalancing. In the example of Figure 10.11 and in the rotations of Figure 10.12, notice that the height of the subtree involved in the rotation is the same after rebalancing as it was before the insertion. This means that once the rebalancing has been carried out on the subtree in question, examining the remaining tree is unneccessary. The only nodes whose balance factors can change are those in the subtree that is rotated.

To carry out the rotations of Figure 10.12, it is necessary to locate the node A around which the rotation is to be performed. As remarked earlier, this is the nearest ancestor of the newly inserted node whose balance factor becomes ± 2. For a node's balance factor to become ± 2, its balance factor must have been ± 1 before the insertion. Therefore, before the insertion, the balance factors of all nodes on the path from A to the new insertion point must have been 0. With this information, the node A is readily determined to be the nearest ancestor of the new node having a balance factor ± 1 before insertion. To complete the rotations, the address of F, the parent of A, is also needed. The changes in the balance factors of the relevant nodes are shown in Figure 10.12. Knowing F and A, these changes can be carried out easily.

What happens when the insertion of a node does not result in an unbalanced tree (see Figure 10.11 (a), (b), (d), (g), (h), and (l))? Although no restructuring of the tree is needed, the balance factors of several nodes change. Let A be the nearest ancestor of the new node with balance factor ± 1 before insertion. If, as a result of the insertion, the tree did not get unbalanced, even though some path length increased by 1, it must be that the new balance factor of A is 0. If there is no ancestor A with a balance factor ± 1 (as in Figure 10.11 (a), (b), (d), (g), and (l)), let A be the root. The balance factors of nodes from A to the parent of the new node will change to ± 1 (see Figure 10.11 (h); $A =$ JANUARY). Note that in both cases, the procedure to determine A is the same as when rebalancing is needed. The remaining details of the insertion-rebalancing process are spelled out in algorithm *AvlInsert* (Program 10.2). The type definitions in use are

type *identifier* = **packed array** [1..*MaxChar*] **of char**;
    TreePointer = ↑*TreeRecord*;
    TreeRecord = **record**
                LeftChild : *TreePointer*;
                ident : *identifier*;
                RightChild : *TreePointer*;
                bf : $-1..1$;
        end;

```
procedure AvlInsert (x : identifier; var t : TreePointer);
{The identifier x is inserted into the AVL tree with root t.}
var a, b, c, f, p, q, y, clchild, crchild : TreePointer;
    found, unbalanced : boolean;
    d : integer;
begin
  if t = nil then begin {special case: empty tree}
          new(y); y↑.ident := x; t := y; t↑.bf := 0;
          t↑.LeftChild := nil; t↑.RightChild := nil;
        end
  else begin
    {phase 1: Locate insertion point for x. a keeps track of the most recent node with
      balance factor ±1, and f is the parent of a. q follows p through the tree.}
    f := nil; a := t; p := t; q :=nil; found := false;
    while (p < > nil) and (not found) do
    begin {search t for insertion point for x}
      if p↑.bf < > 0 then begin
              a := p; f := q;
            end;
      if x < p↑.ident then begin {take left branch}
              q := p; p := p↑.LeftChild;
            end
          else if x > p↑.ident then begin {take right branch}
                    q := p; p := p↑.RightChild;
                  end
              else begin {x is in t}
                    y := p; found :=true;
                  end;
    end; {of while}
```

if not *found* **then**
begin
    {phase 2: Insert and rebalance. x is not in t and may be inserted as the appropriate child of q.}
    new(y); $y \uparrow. ident := x$; $y \uparrow. LeftChild :=$ **nil**;
    $y \uparrow. RightChild :=$ **nil**; $y \uparrow. bf := 0$;
    if $x < q \uparrow. ident$ **then** $q \uparrow. LeftChild := y$ {insert as left child}
                        else $q \uparrow. RightChild := y$; {insert as right child}
    {Adjust balance factors of nodes on path from a to q. Note that by the definition of a, all nodes on this path must have balance factors of 0 and so will change to ± 1. $d = +1$ implies that x is inserted in the left subtree of a. $d = -1$ implies that x is inserted in the right subtree of a.}
    if $x > a \uparrow. ident$ **then begin**
                        $p := a \uparrow. RightChild$; $b := p$; $d := -1$;
               end
               else begin
                        $p := a \uparrow. LeftChild$; $b := p$; $d := +1$;
               end;
  while $p < > y$ **do**
    if $x > p \uparrow. ident$ **then begin** {height of right increases by 1}
                    $p \uparrow. bf := -1$; $p := p \uparrow. RightChild$;
               end
               else begin {height of left increases by 1}
                   $p \uparrow. bf := +1$; $p := p \uparrow. LeftChild$;
               end;
  {Is tree unbalanced?}
  unbalanced := **true**;
  if $(a \uparrow. bf = 0)$ **or** $(a \uparrow. bf + d = 0)$
  then begin {tree still balanced}
    $a \uparrow. bf := a \uparrow. bf + d$; *unbalanced* := **false**;
    end;
  if *unbalanced* **then** {tree unbalanced, determine rotation type}
  begin
    if $d = +1$ **then** {left imbalance}
    begin
      if $b \uparrow. bf = +1$ **then** {rotation type LL}
      begin
        $a \uparrow. LeftChild := b \uparrow. RightChild$;
        $b \uparrow. RightChild := a$; $a \uparrow. bf := 0$; $b \uparrow. bf := 0$;
      end
      else begin {LR}
        $c := b \uparrow. RightChild$;
        $b \uparrow. RightChild = c \uparrow. LeftChild$;
        $a \uparrow. LeftChild := c \uparrow. RightChild$;

```
            c↑.LeftChild := b;
            c↑.RightChild := a;
            case c↑.bf of
                +1 : begin {LR(b)}
                          a↑.bf := -1; b↑.bf := 0;
                      end
                -1 : begin {LR(c)}
                          b↑.bf := 1; a↑.bf := 0;
                      end;
                 0 : begin {LR(a)}
                          b↑.bf := 0; a↑.bf := 0;
                      end;
                end; {of case}
            c↑.bf := 0; b := c; {b is a new root}
          end; {of LR}
      end {of then left imbalance}
      else {right imbalance (this is symmetric to left imbalance)}
      begin
      end;
      {Subtree with root b has been rebalanced and is the new subtree.}
      if f = nil then t := b
      else if a = f↑.LeftChild then f↑.LeftChild := b
          else if a = f↑.RightChild then f↑.RightChild := b;
    end; {of if unbalanced}
  end; {of if not found}
end; {of if t = nil}
end; {of AvlInsert}
```

Program 10.2: Insertion into an AVL tree

To really understand the insertion algorithm, you should try it out on the example of Figure 10.11. An analysis of the algorithm reveals that if h is the height of the tree before insertion, then the time to insert a new identifier is $O(h)$. This is the same as for unbalanced binary search trees, although the overhead is significantly greater now. In the case of binary search trees, however, if there were n nodes in the tree, then h could, in the worst case, be n (Figure 10.10), and the worst case insertion time would be $O(n)$. In the case of AVL trees, however, h can be at most $O(\log n)$, so the worst-case insertion time is $O(\log n)$. To see this, let N_h be the minimum number of nodes in a height-balanced tree of height h. In the worst case, the height of one of the subtrees will be $h - 1$ and that of the other $h - 2$. Both of these subtrees are also height balanced. Hence, $N_h = N_{h-1} + N_{h-2} + 1$, and $N_0 = 0$, $N_1 = 1$ and $N_2 = 2$. Note the similarity between this recursive definition for N_h and that for the Fibonacci numbers $F_n = F_{n-1} + F_{n-2}$, $F_0 = 0$, and $F_1 = 1$. In fact, we can show that $N_h = F_{h+2} - 1$ for $h \geq 0$ (see Exercise 2). From Fibonacci number theory it is known that $F_h \approx \phi^h / \sqrt{5}$, where

$\phi = (1 + \sqrt{5})/2$. Hence, $N_h \approx \phi^{h+2} / \sqrt{5} - 1$. This means that if there are n nodes in the tree, then its height, h, is at most $\log_\phi (\sqrt{5}(n + 1)) - 2$. The worst-case insertion time for a height-balanced tree with n nodes is, therefore, $O(\log n)$.

The exercises show that it is possible to find and delete a node with identifier X and to find and delete the kth node from a height-balanced tree in $O(\log n)$ time. Results of an empirical study of deletion in height-balanced trees may be found in the paper by Karlton et al. (see the References and Selected Readings section). Their study indicates that a random insertion requires no rebalancing, a rebalancing rotation of type LL or RR, and a rebalancing rotation of type LR and RL, with probabilities 0.5349, 0.2327, and 0.2324, respectively. Figure 10.13 compares the worst-case times of certain operations on sorted sequential lists, sorted linked lists, and AVL trees.

Operation	Sequential list	Linked list	AVL tree
Search for x	$O(\log n)$	$O(n)$	$O(\log n)$
Search for kth item	$O(1)$	$O(k)$	$O(\log n)$
Delete x	$O(n)$	$O(1)^1$	$O(\log n)$
Delete kth item	$O(n - k)$	$O(k)$	$O(\log n)$
Insert x	$O(n)$	$O(1)^2$	$O(\log n)$
Output in order	$O(n)$	$O(n)$	$O(n)$

1. Doubly linked list and position of x known
2. Position for insertion known

Figure 10.13: Comparison of various structures

EXERCISES

1. (a) Convince yourself that Figure 10.12 takes care of all the possible situations that may arise when a height-balanced binary tree becomes unbalanced as a result of an insertion. Alternately, come up with an example that is not covered by any of the cases in this figure.

   (b) Complete Figure 10.12 by drawing the tree configurations for the rotations RL (a), (b), and (c).

2. Prove by induction that the minimum number of nodes in an AVL tree of height h is $N_h = F_{h+2} - 1$, $h \geq 0$.

3. Complete algorithm *AvlInsert* (Program 10.2) by filling in the steps needed to rebalance the tree if the imbalance is of type RL.

4. Obtain the height-balanced trees corresponding to those of Figure 10.11 using algorithm *AvlInsert*, starting with an empty tree, on the following sequence of insertions: DECEMBER, JANUARY, APRIL, MARCH, JULY, AUGUST, OCTOBER, FEBRUARY, NOVEMBER, MAY, JUNE. Label the rotations according to type.

5. Assume that each node in an AVL tree t has the field *lsize*. For any node, a, $a\uparrow.lsize$ is the number of nodes in its left subtree plus one. Write an algorithm *avlfind* (t,k) to locate the kth smallest identifier in the subtree t. Show that this can be done in $O(\log n)$ time if there are n nodes in t.

6. Rewrite algorithm *AvlInsert* with the added assumption that each node has an *lsize* field as in Exercise 5. Show that the insertion time remains $O(\log n)$.

7. Write an algorithm to list the nodes of an AVL tree T in ascending order of *ident* fields. Show that this can be done in $O(n)$ time if T has n nodes.

8. Write an algorithm to delete the node with identifier x from an AVL tree t. The resulting tree should be restructured if necessary. Show that the time required for this is $O(\log n)$ when there are n nodes in t. [Hint: If x is not in a leaf, then replace x by the largest value in its left subtree or the smallest value in its right subtree. Continue until the deletion propagates to a leaf. Deletion from a leaf can be handled using the reverse of the transformations used for insertion.]

9. Do Exercise 8 for the case when each node has an *lsize* field and the kth smallest identifier is to be deleted.

10. Write an algorithm to merge the nodes of the two AVL trees T_1 and T_2 to obtain a new AVL tree. What is the computing time of your algorithm?

11. Write an algorithm to split an AVL tree, T, into two AVL trees, T_1 and T_2, such that all identifiers in T_1 are $\le x$, and all those in T_2 are $> x$.

12. Complete Figure 10.13 by adding a column for hashing.

13. For a fixed k, $k \ge 1$, we define a height-balanced tree $HB(k)$ as below:

   Definition: An empty binary tree is an $HB(k)$ tree. If T is a nonempty binary tree with T_L and T_R as its left and right subtrees, then T is $HB(k)$ iff (a) T_L and T_R are $HB(k)$ and (b) $|h_L - h_R| \le k$, where h_L and h_R are the heights of T_L and T_R, respectively. $\square$

   (a) Obtain the rebalancing transformations for $HB(2)$.

   (b) Write an insertion algorithm for $HB(2)$ trees.

10.3   2-3 TREES

10.3.1   Definition and Properties

By considering search trees of degree greater than 2, we can arrive at tree structures for which the insertion and deletion algorithms are simpler than those for AVL trees. Yet these algorithms have O(log n) complexity. In this section, we shall look at a special case of B-trees. General B-trees are studied in a later section. The special case we shall consider here is called a 2-3 tree. This name reflects the fact that each internal node in a 2-3 tree has degree two or three. A degree-two node is called a 2-*node*; a degree-three node is called a 3-*node*.

Definition: A *2-3 tree* is a search tree that either is empty or satisfies the following properties:

(1)   Each internal node is a 2-node or a 3-node. A 2-node has one element; a 3-node has two elements.

(2)   Let *LeftChild* and *MiddleChild* denote the children of a 2-node. Let *dataL* be the element in this node, and let *dataL.key* be its key. All elements in the 2-3 subtree with root *LeftChild* have key less than *dataL.key*, whereas all elements in the 2-3 subtree with root *MiddleChild* have key greater than *dataL.key*.

(3)   Let *LeftChild*, *MiddleChild*, and *RightChild* denote the children of a 3-node. Let *dataL* and *dataR* be the two elements in this node. Then, *dataL.key* < *dataR.key*; all keys in the 2-3 subtree with root *LeftChild* are less than *dataL.key*; all keys in the 2-3 subtree with root *MiddleChild* are less than *dataR.key* and greater than *dataL.key*; and all keys in the 2-3 subtree with root *RightChild* are greater than *dataR.key*.

(4)   All external nodes are at the same level. □

An example of a 2-3 tree is given in Figure 10.14. As in the case of leftist trees, external nodes are introduced only to make it easier to define and talk about 2-3 trees. External nodes are not physically represented inside a computer. Rather, the corresponding child field of the parent of each external node is set to **nil**.

The number of elements in a 2-3 tree with height h (i.e., the external nodes are at level $h+1$) is between $2^h - 1$ and $3^h - 1$. To see this, note that the first bound applies when each internal node is a 2-node, and the second bound applies when each internal node is a 3-node. These two cases represent the two extremes. A 2-3 tree with some 2-nodes and some 3-nodes will have a number of elements somewhere between these two bounds. Hence, the height of a 2-3 tree with n elements is between $\lceil \log_3(n+1) \rceil$ and $\lceil \log_2(n+1) \rceil$.

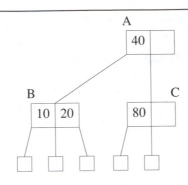

Figure 10.14: Example of a 2-3 tree

A 2-3 tree may be represented using nodes of the type *TwoThree*, defined as

type *TwoThreePtr* = ↑ *TwoThree*;
    TwoThree = **record**
        dataL : *element*;
        dataR : *element*;
        LeftChild : *TwoThreePtr*;
        MiddleChild : *TwoThreePtr*;
        RightChild : *TwoThreePtr*;
    end;

We shall assume that no element has key **maxint** and adopt the convention that a 2-node has *dataR.key* = **maxint**. Its single element is kept in *dataL*, and *LeftChild* and *MiddleChild* point to its two children. Its *RightChild* field may be assigned any arbitrary value.

10.3.2 Searching a 2-3 Tree

The search algorithm for binary search trees is easily extended to obtain the search procedure *search* 23 (Program 10.3), which searches a 2-3 tree *t* for a node that contains an element with key *x*. The element keys are assumed to be of type integer. The search procedure uses a function *compare* that compares a key *x* with the keys in a given node *p*. It returns the value 1, 2, 3, or 4, respectively, depending upon whether *x* is less than the first key, between the first and second keys, greater than the second key, or equal to one of the keys in node *p*. The number of iterations of the **while** loop is bounded by the height of the 2-3 tree *t*. Hence, if *t* has *n* nodes, the complexity of *search* 23 is O(log *n*).

---

procedure *search* 23(*t* : *TwoThreePtr* ; *x* : **integer**; **var** *p* : *TwoThreePtr*);
{Search the 2-3 tree *t* for an element with key *x*. If this key is not in the tree, then return **nil** in *p*. Otherwise, return a pointer to the node that contains this key.}
var *NotDone* : **boolean**;
begin
  NotDone := **true**; *p* := *t*;
  while (*p* < > **nil**) **and** *NotDone* **do**
  case *compare* (*x*, *p*) **of**
    1: {*x* < *p*↑.*dataL*.*key*}
      p := *p*↑.*LeftChild*;
    2: {*p*↑.*dataL*.*key* < *x* < *p*↑.*dataR*.*key*}
      p := *p*↑.*MiddleChild*;
    3: {*x* > *p*↑.*dataR*.*key*}
      p := *p*↑.*RightChild*;
    4: {*x* is one of the keys in *p*}
      NotDone := **false**;
  end; {of **case** and **while**}
end; {of *search* 23}

Program 10.3: Searching a 2-3 tree

10.3.3   Insertion into a 2-3 Tree

Insertion into a 2-3 tree is fairly simple. Consider inserting an element with key 70 into the 2-3 tree of Figure 10.14. First we search for this key. If the key is already in the tree, then the insertion fails, as all keys in a 2-3 tree are distinct. Since 70 is not in our example 2-3 tree, it may be inserted. For this, we need to know the leaf node encountered during the search for 70. Note that whenever we search for a key that is not in the 2-3 tree, the search encounters a unique leaf node. The leaf node encountered during the search for 70 is the node C, with key 80. Since this node has only one element, the new element may be inserted here. The resulting 2-3 tree is shown in Figure 10.15(a).

Next, consider inserting an element *x* with key 30. This time the search encounters the leaf node B. Since B is a 3-node, it is necessary to create a new node, D. D will contain the element that has the larger key of the two elements currently in B and *x*. The element with the smallest key will be in B, and the element with the median key, together with a pointer to D, will be inserted into the parent A of B. The resulting 2-3 tree is shown in Figure 10.15(b).

As a final example, consider the insertion of an element *x* with key 60 into the 2-3 tree of Figure 10.15(b). The leaf node encountered during the search for 60 is node C. Since C is a 3-node, a new node, E, is created. Node E contains the element with the largest key (80). Node C contains the element with the smallest key (60). The element

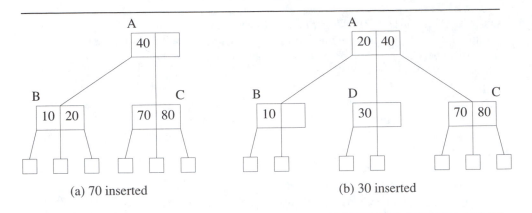

(a) 70 inserted   (b) 30 inserted

Figure 10.15: Insertion into the 2-3 tree of Figure 10.14

with the median key (70), together with a pointer to the new node, E, is to be inserted into the parent A of C. Again, since A is a 3-node, a new node, F, containing the element with the largest key among {20, 40, 70} is created. As before, A contains the element with the smallest key. B and D remain the left and middle children of A, respectively, and C and E become these children of F. If A had a parent, then the element with the median key 40 and a pointer to the new node, F, would be inserted into this parent node. Since A does not have a parent, we create a new root, G, for the 2-3 tree. Node G contains the element with key 40, together with a left-child pointer to A and a middle-child pointer to F. The new 2-3 tree is as shown in Figure 10.16.

Each time an attempt is made to add an element into a 3-node p, a new node q is created. This is referred to as a node *split*. We say that node p is split into p, q, and the median element. Putting the ideas in the preceding discussion together, we get the insertion procedure of Program 10.4.

This procedure makes use of several procedures whose development is left as an exercise. We specify the task performed by each below:

(1)   *NewRoot*: This is invoked when the root of t is to change. The inputs to this procedure are the left child of the new root, its single element, and its middle child. A pointer to the new root is returned in the first of these parameters.

(2)   *FindNode*: This is a modified version of *search* 23 (Program 10.3). It searches a nonempty 2-3 tree t for the presence of an element with key $y.key$. If this key is present in t, then p is set to **nil**. Otherwise, p is set to point to the leaf node encountered in the search. Additionally, *FindNode* creates a global data structure that enables us to return from p to the root t. This data structure could be a list of the nodes on the path from t to p. Such a list is needed, as following a node split, it is necessary to access the parent of the node that was split.

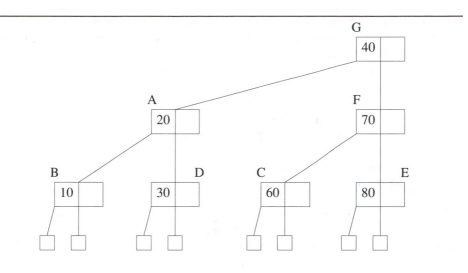

Figure 10.16: Insertion of 60 into the 2-3 tree of Figure 10.15(b)

(3) *InsertionError*: When an attempt to insert an element whose key corresponds to that of an element already in the 2-3 tree is made, an insertion error occurs. This procedure signals an error and causes the program to terminate.

(4) *PutIn*: This procedure is used to insert an element *y* into a node *p* that has exactly one element in it. The subtree *a* is to be placed immediately to the right of *y*. So, if *y* becomes *dataL*, then *a* becomes *MiddleChild*, and the previous values of *dataL* and *MiddleChild* move to *dataR* and *RightChild*, respectively. If *y* becomes *dataR*, then *a* becomes *RightChild*.

(5) *split*: This takes a node *p* that has two elements in it and creates a new node. The new node will contain the record with the largest key from among the elements initially in *p* and the element *y*. The element with the smallest key will be the only element left in *p*. The three original children pointers of *p* and the pointer *a* will occupy the four children fields that need to be defined in *p*, and the new node. On return, *y* is the element with the median key, and *a* points to the newly formed node.

In *insert* 23, *y* denotes the element to be inserted into node *p*, and *a* denotes the node that was newly created at the last iteration of the **while** loop. As for the complexity analysis, we see that the total time taken is proportional to the height of the 2-3 tree *t*. Hence, insertion into a 2-3 tree with *n* elements takes O(log *n*) time.

---

procedure *insert* 23(**var** *t* : *TwoThreePtr* ; *y* : *element*);
{Insert the element *y* into the 2-3 tree *t* provided that *t* does not already contain an element with the same key.}
var *a*, *p* : *TwoThreePtr* ;
   NotDone : **boolean;**
begin
  if *t* = **nil then** *NewRoot* (*t*, *y*, **nil**)
  else begin {insertion into a nonempty 2-3 tree}
       p := *FindNode* (*t*, *y*.*key*);
       if *p* = **nil then** *InsertionError* {key already in *t*}
       else begin {*y*.*key* not in *t*}
           a := **nil**; *NotDone* := **true**;
           while *NotDone* **do**
              if $p \uparrow$. *dataR* .*key* = **maxint**
              then begin {*p* is a 2-node}
                  PutIn (*p*, *y*, *a*);
                  NotDone := **false**;
              end
              else begin {*p* is a 3-node}
                split (*p*, *y*, *a*);
                if *p* = *t* **then begin** {root has been split}
                      NewRoot (*t*, *y*, *a*);
                      NotDone := **false**;
                  end
                else *p* := parent of *p*;
              end; {of *p* is a 3-node}
          end; {of *y*.*key* not in *t*}
      end; {of insertion into a nonempty 2-3 tree}
end; {of *insert* 23}

Program 10.4: Insertion into a 2-3 tree

10.3.4   Deletion from a 2-3 Tree

Deletion from a 2-3 tree is conceptually no harder than insertion. If we are deleting an element that is not in a leaf node, then we transform this into a deletion from a leaf node by replacing the deleted element with a suitable element that is in a leaf. For example, if we are to delete the element with key 50 that is in the root of Figure 10.17(a), then this element may be replaced by either the element with key 20 or the element with key 60. Both are in leaf nodes. In a general situation, we may use either the element with the largest key in the subtree on the left or the element with the smallest key in the subtree on the right of the element being deleted.

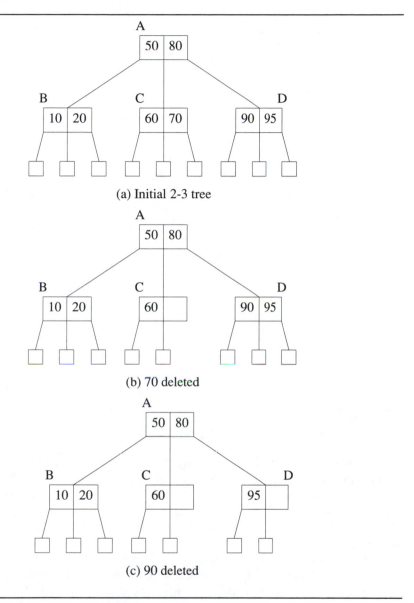

(a) Initial 2-3 tree

(b) 70 deleted

(c) 90 deleted

Figure 10.17: Deletion from a 2-3 tree (continued on next page)

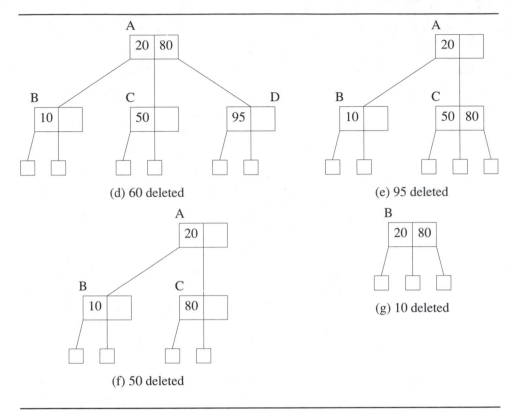

(d) 60 deleted

(e) 95 deleted

(f) 50 deleted

(g) 10 deleted

Figure 10.17: Deletion from a 2-3 tree

Henceforth, we shall consider only the case of deletion from a leaf node. Let us begin with the tree of Figure 10.17(a). To delete the element with key 70, we must merely set *dataR.key* = **maxint** in node C. The result is shown in Figure 10.17(b). To delete the element with key 90 from the 2-3 tree of Figure 10.17(b), we need to shift *dataR* to *dataL* and set *data 2.key* = **maxint** in node D. This results in the 2-3 tree of Figure 10.17(c).

Next consider the deletion of the element with key 60. This leaves node C empty. Since the left sibling, B, of C is a 3-node, we can move the element with key 20 into the *dataL* position of the parent node A and move the element with key 50 from the parent to node C. After setting *dataR.key* = **maxint** in B, the 2-3 tree takes the form shown in Figure 10.17(d). This data movement operation is called a *rotation*. When the element with key 95 is deleted, node D becomes empty. The rotation performed when the 60 was deleted is not possible now, as the left sibling, C, is a 2-node. This time we move the 80 into the left sibling, C, and delete node D. We shall refer to this operation as a *combine*. In a combine, one node is deleted, whereas in a rotation, no nodes are deleted. The deletion of 95 results in the 2-3 tree of Figure 10.17(e). Deleting the element with key 50 from this tree results in the 2-3 tree of Figure 10.17(f). Now consider deleting the element with key 10 from this tree. Node B becomes empty. At this time, we examine B's right sibling, C, to see if it is a 2-node or a 3-node. If it is a 3-node, we can perform a rotation similar to that done during the deletion of 60. If it is a 2-node, then a combine is performed. Since C is a 2-node, we proceed in a manner similar to the deletion of 95. This time the elements with keys 20 and 80 are moved into B, and node C is deleted. This, however, causes the parent node A to have no elements. If the parent had not been a root, we would examine its left or right sibling, as we did when nodes C (deletion of 60) and D (deletion of 95) became empty. Since A is the root, it is simply deleted, and B becomes the new root (Figure 10.17(g)).

The steps involved in deletion from a leaf node p of a 2-3 tree t are summarized in Program 10.5.

Step 1: Modify node p as necessary to reflect its status after the desired element has been deleted.

Step 2: **while** p has zero elements and p is not the root **do**
  begin
    let r be the parent of p, and let q be the left or right sibling of p (as appropriate);
    if q is a 3-node
    then perform a rotation
    else perform a combine;
    $p := r$;
  end;

Step 3: If p has zero elements, then p must be the root. The left child of p becomes the new root, and node p is deleted.

Program 10.5: Steps in deletion from a leaf of a 2-3 tree

For a rotation, there are three cases, depending on whether p is the left, middle, or right child of its parent, r. If p is the left child of r, then let q be the right sibling of p. Otherwise, let q be the left sibling of p. Note that regardless of whether r is a 2-node or a 3-node, q is well defined. The three rotation cases are shown pictorially in Figure 10.18. A ''?'' denotes a situation in which the content of the field is irrelevant. a, b, c, and d denote the children (i.e., roots of subtrees) of nodes.

Figure 10.19 shows the two cases for a combine when p is the left child of r. We leave it as an exercise to obtain the figures for the cases when p is a middle child and when p is a right child.

The refinement of Step 1 of Program 10.5 into Pascal code is shown in Program 10.6. The codes for rotation and combine for the case when p is the left child of r are given in Programs 10.7 and 10.8, respectively. We leave the development of the complete deletion procedure as an exercise.

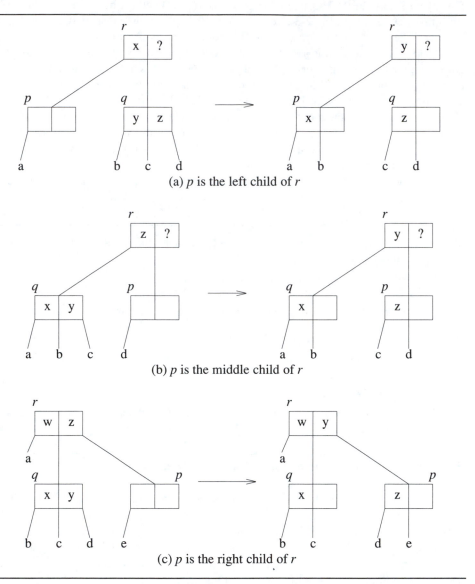

(a) *p* is the left child of *r*

(b) *p* is the middle child of *r*

(c) *p* is the right child of *r*

Figure 10.18: The three cases for rotation in a 2-3 tree

Analysis of 2-3 tree deletion: It should be evident that an individual rotation or combine takes O(1) time. If a rotation is performed, deletion is completed. If a combine is performed, *p* moves up one level in the 2-3 tree. Hence, the number of combines that can be performed during a deletion cannot exceed the height of the 2-3 tree. Consequently, deletion from a 2-3 tree with *n* elements takes O(log *n*) time. □

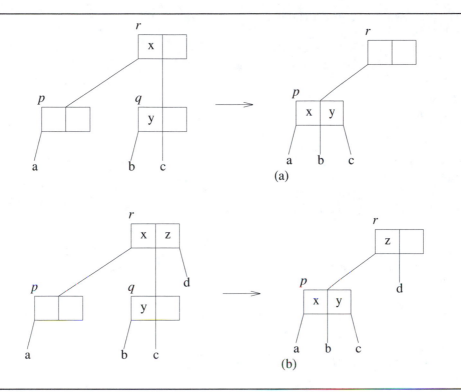

Figure 10.19: Combining in a 2-3 tree when p is the left child of r

```
{Key x is to be deleted from the leaf node p.}
with p do
   if x = dataL.key {delete first element}
   then if p↑.dataR.key <> maxint
        then begin {p is a 3-node}
                dataL := dataR; dataR.key := maxint;
             end
        else dataL.key := maxint {p is a 2-node}
   else dataR.key := maxint; {delete second element}
```

Program 10.6: Refinement of Step 1 of Program 10.5

```
{Rotation when p is the left child of r.  q is the middle child of r.}
p↑.dataL := r↑.dataL;
p↑.MiddleChild := q↑.LeftChild;
r↑.dataL := q↑.dataL;
with q do
begin
   dataL := dataR;
   LeftChild := MiddleChild;
   MiddleChild := RightChild;
   dataR.key := maxint;
end;
```

Program 10.7: Pascal code for a rotation when p is the left child of r

---

```
{Combine when p is the left child of r.  q is the right sibling of p.}
with p do
begin
   dataL := r↑.dataL;
   dataR := q↑.dataL;
   MiddleChild := q↑.LeftChild;
   RightChild := q↑.MiddleChild;
end;
with r do
   if dataR.key = maxint {r was a 2-node}
   then dataL.key = maxint
   else begin
         dataL := dataR;
         dataR.key := maxint;
         MiddleChild := RightChild;
      end;
```

Program 10.8: Code to perform a combine when p is the left child of r

EXERCISES

1. Write the function *compare* used in Program 10.3.

2. (a) Develop the procedures *FindNode*, *NewRoot*, *PutIn*, and *split* used by procedure *insert*23 (Program 10.4). Put these together and test the correctness of procedure *insert*23.

   (b) Use random insertions and measure the height of the resulting 2-3 trees with $n = 100$, 1000, and 10,000 elements.

3. Complete Figure 10.19 by providing the figures for the case in which p is a middle child and p is a right child.

4. Develop a complete Pascal procedure to delete the element with key x from the 2-3 tree t. Test this procedure using at least five different 2-3 trees of your choice. For each of these perform at least six successive deletions.

5. Write a procedure to perform the *ThreeWayJoin* operation defined in Section 5.7.5 for binary search trees. This time, assume that A and B are 2-3 trees and that the result of the join is also a 2-3 tree. You may assume that the heights of the two input 2-3 trees are known. You should be able to perform the join in $O(\mid height(A) - height(B) \mid)$ time. (Hint: If $height(A) > height(B)$, follow the rightmost path from A to a node Y such that $height(Y) = height(B) + 1$; now attempt to insert x, together with a pointer to B, into node Y.)

6. Do the previous exercise for the case of a *TwoWayJoin* (see Section 5.7.5).

7. Write a procedure to perform the *Split* operation defined in Section 5.7.5 for binary search trees. This time, assume that A is a 2-3 tree and that the resulting trees B and C are also 2-3 trees. Can you do this operation in $O(height(A))$ time?

8. Any algorithm that merges two sorted lists of size n and m, respectively, must make at least $n + m - 1$ comparisons in the worst case. What implications does this result have on the time complexity of a comparison-based algorithm that combines two 2-3 trees that have n and m elements, respectively?

9. In Chapter 7, we showed that every comparison-based algorithm to sort n elements must make $O(n \log n)$ comparisons in the worst case. What implications does this result have on the complexity of initializing a 2-3 tree with n elements?

10. Consider a variation of a 2-3 tree in which elements are kept only in leaf nodes. Each leaf has exactly one element. The remaining nodes are 2-nodes or 3-nodes. Each such node keeps only the values *largeA* = largest key in any leaf in its left subtree and *largeB* = largest key in any leaf in its middle subtree. As before, all external nodes are at the same level.

    (a) Define two node structures such that one is suitable to represent a leaf node and the other to represent a nonleaf node.

    (b) Write a procedure to search a 2-3 tree represented in this way.

    (c) Write a procedure to insert an element x into this tree.

    (d) Write a deletion procedure for such a 2-3 tree.

    (e) Show that each of the above operations can be performed in $O(\log n)$ time, where n is the number of elements (i.e., leaf nodes) in the tree.

11. Let T and U be two 2-3 trees in which keys are kept in the leaves only (see preceding exercise). Let V be a similar tree thet contains all key values in T and U. Write an algorithm to construct V from T and U. What is the complexity of your algorithm?

12.   Write insertion and deletion algorithms for 2-3 trees assuming that an additional field, f, is associated with each key value. $f = 1$ iff the corresponding key value has not been deleted. Deletions should be accomplished by setting the corresponding $f = 0$, and insertions should make use of deleted space whenever possible without restructuring the tree.

13.   Write algorithms to search and delete keys from a 2-3 tree by position; that is, *search* (k) finds the kth smallest key, and *delete* (k) deletes the kth smallest key in the tree. (Hint: To do this efficiently, additional information must be kept in each node. With each pair (K_i, A_i) keep $N_i = \Sigma_{j=0}^{i-1}$ (number of key values in the subtree $A_j + 1$).) What are the worst-case computing times of your algorithms?

14.   Modify the 2-3 insertion (Program 10.4) algorithm so that we first check to see if either the nearest left sibling or the nearest right sibling of p has fewer than two keys. If so, no node is split. Instead, a rotation is performed, moving either the smallest or largest key in p to its parent. The corresponding key in the parent, together with a subtree, is moved to the sibling of p, which has space for another key value.

10.4   2-3-4 TREES

10.4.1   Definition and Properties

A 2-3-4 tree is an extension of a 2-3 tree to the case in which 4-nodes (i.e., nodes with four children) are also permitted.

Definition: A *2-3-4 tree* is a search tree that either is empty or satisfies the following properties:

(1)   Each internal node is a 2-, 3-, or 4-node. A 2-node has one element, a 3-node has two elements, and a 4-node has three elements.

(2)   Let *LeftChild* and *LeftMidChild* denote the children of a 2-node. Let *dataL* be the element in this node, and let *dataL.key* be its key. All elements in the 2-3-4 subtree with root *LeftChild* have key less than *dataL.key*, and all elements in the 2-3-4 subtree with root *LeftMidChild* have key greater than *dataL.key*.

(3)   Let *LeftChild*, *LeftMidChild*, and *RightMidChild* denote the children of a 3-node. Let *dataL* and *dataM* be the two elements in this node. Then, *dataL.key* < *dataM.key*; all keys in the 2-3-4 subtree with root *LeftChild* are less than *dataL.key*; all keys in the 2-3-4 subtree with root *LeftMidChild* are less than *dataM.key* and greater than *dataL.key*; and all keys in the 2-3-4 subtree with root *RightMidChild* are greater than *dataM.key*.

(4)   Let *LeftChild*, *LeftMidChild*, *RightMidChild* and *RightChild* denote the children of a 4-node. Let *dataL*, *dataM*, and *dataR* be the three elements in this node. Then,

dataL.key < *dataM.key* < *dataR.key*; all keys in the 2-3-4 subtree with root *LeftChild* are less than *dataL.key*; all keys in the 2-3-4 subtree with root *LeftMidChild* are less than *dataM.key* and greater than *dataL.key*; all keys in the 2-3-4 subtree with root *RightMidChild* are greater than *dataM.key* but less than *dataR.key*; and all keys in the 2-3-4 subtree with root *RightChild* are greater than *dataR.key*.

(5) All external nodes are at the same level. □

A 2-3-4 tree may be represented using nodes of the type *TwoThreeFour*, defined as

> **type** *TwoThreeFourPtr* = ↑ *TwoThreeFour*;
>   *TwoThreeFour* = **record**
>   *dataL* : *element*;
>   *dataM* : *element*;
>   *dataR* : *element*;
>   *LeftChild* : *TwoThreeFourPtr*;
>   *LeftMidChild* : *TwoThreeFourPtr*;
>   *RightMidChild* : *TwoThreeFourPtr*;
>   *RightChild* : *TwoThreeFourPtr*;
>   **end**;

As in the case of 2-3 trees, we shall assume that no element has key **maxint**. We shall adopt the convention that a 2-node will have *dataM.key* = **maxint**. The single element is kept in *dataL*, and *LeftChild* and *LeftMidChild* point to its two children. A 3-node has *dataR.key* = **maxint** and the *LeftChild*, *LeftMidChild*, and *RightMidChild* fields point to its three subtrees. An example of a 2-3-4 tree using these conventions and nodes of type *TwoThreeFour* is shown in Figure 10.20.

If a 2-3-4 tree of height h has only 2-nodes, then it contains $2^h - 1$ elements. If it contains only 4-nodes, then the number of elements is $4^h - 1$. A 2-3-4 tree of height h with a mixture of 2-, 3-, and 4-nodes, has between $2^h - 1$ and $4^h - 1$ elements. In other words, the height of a 2-3-4 tree with n elements is between $\lceil \log_4(n+1) \rceil$ and $\lceil \log_2(n+1) \rceil$.

2-3-4 trees have an advantage over 2-3 trees in that insertion and deletion can be performed by a single root-to-leaf pass rather than by a root-to-leaf pass followed by a leaf-to-root pass. As a result, the corresponding algorithms are simpler. More interestingly, a 2-3-4 tree can be represented efficiently as a binary tree (called a red-black tree). This results in a more efficient utilization of space than does the use of nodes of type *TwoThree* in the case of 2-3 trees and of type *TwoThreeFour* in the case of 2-3-4 trees. Note that modifying the definitions of the types *TwoThree* and *TwoThreeFour* to use variant records that have only as many fields as necessary for the variant in use does not improve the efficiency of space utilization, as enough space to accommodate the largest variant is allocated whenever a variable of variant type is created. Using different record types for 2-nodes, 3-nodes, and 4-nodes improves space utilization but introduces addi-

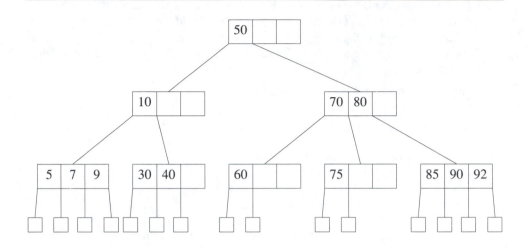

Figure 10.20: Example of a 2-3-4 tree

tional complexity in terms of memory management and the requirement for pointer fields that can point to three different types of nodes.

We shall examine the representation of 2-3-4 trees as binary trees in the next section. In this section, we shall see how insertions and deletions can be performed by making a single top-down, root-to-leaf pass over the 2-3-4 tree.

10.4.2 Top-down Insertion

If the leaf node into which the element is to be inserted is a 4-node, then this node splits and a backward (leaf-to-root) pass is initiated. This backward pass terminates when either a 2- or 3-node is encountered, or when the root is split. To avoid the backward pass, we split 4-nodes on the way down the tree. As a result, the leaf node into which the insertion is to be made is guaranteed to be a 2- or 3-node. The element to be inserted may be added to this node without any further node-splitting.

There are three different situations to consider for a 4-node:

(1)   It is the root of the 2-3-4 tree.

(2)   Its parent is a 2-node.

(3)   Its parent is a 3-node.

The splitting transformations for cases (1) and (2) are shown in Figures 10.21 and 10.22, respectively. For case (3), Figure 10.23 shows the transformation when the 4-

node is the left child of the 3-node, and Figure 10.24 shows it for the case when the 4-node is the left middle child. The remaining case, when the 4-node is the right middle child of the 3-node, is symmetric to the case when it is the left child and is left as an exercise. It is easy to see that if the transformations of Figures 10.21, 10.22, and 10.23 are used to split 4-nodes on the way down the 2-3-4 tree, then whenever a nonroot 4-node is encountered, its parent cannot be a 4-node. Notice that the transformation for a root 4-node increases the height of the 2-3-4 tree by one, whereas the remaining transformations do not affect its height.

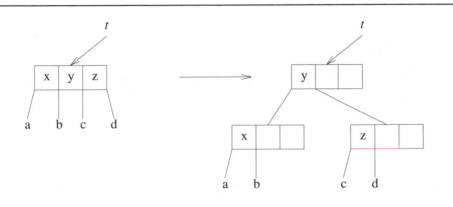

Figure 10.21: Transformation when the 4-node is the root

The procedure to insert element y into the 2-3-4 tree t represented with nodes of type *TwoThreeFour* takes the form given in Program 10.9. The procedures and functions used by this program are specified below:

(1) *NewRoot*: This creates a single-node 2-3-4 tree t with only the element y in it.

(2) *FourNode*: This is a Boolean-valued function that returns the value **true** iff the given node is a 4-node.

(3) *SplitRoot*: This uses the transformation of Figure 10.21 to split a root that is a 4-node.

(4) *NodeType*: This function returns the value TwoNode if the given node is a 2-node and the value ThreeNode otherwise.

(5) *SplitChildOf2*: This uses the transformations of Figure 10.22 to split a 4-node that is a child of a 2-node.

(6) *SplitChildOf3*: This uses the transformations of Figures 10.23 and 10.24 to split a 4-node that is a child of a 3-node.

(7) *compare*: This compares the key of the given element y with the keys in the given

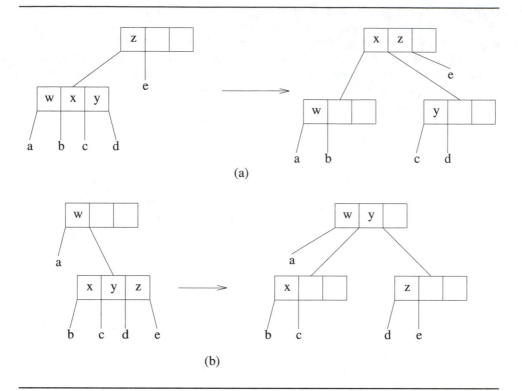

Figure 10.22: Transformation when the 4-node is the child of a 2-node

node p. The possible outputs from this function and the corresponding conditions are

(a)   equal: $y.key$ equals the key of one of the elements in p

(b)   leaf: p is a leaf node

(c)   lChild: $y.key < p\uparrow.dataL.key$

(d)   lmChild: $p\uparrow.dataL.key < y.key < p\uparrow.dataM.key$

(e)   rmChild: $p\uparrow.dataM.key < y.key < p\uparrow.dataR.key$

(f)   rChild: $y.key > p\uparrow.dataR.key$

If y and p satisfy more than one of these conditions, then the first is used.

(8)   *InsertionError*: This handles the case when the element y to be inserted has a key equal to that of an element already in the 2-3-4 tree.

(9)   *PutIn*: This adds the element to be inserted to the given leaf node. This leaf node is either a 2-node or a 3-node.

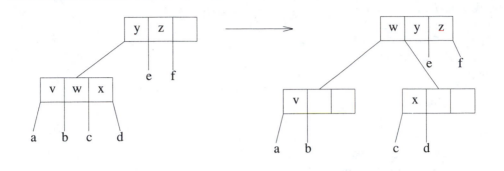

Figure 10.23: Transformation when the 4-node is the left child of a 3-node

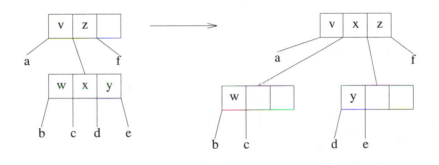

Figure 10.24: Transformation when the 4-node is the left middle child of a 3-node

The complexity of *insert* 234 is readily seen to be O(log *n*), where *n* is the number of elements in *t*.

10.4.3   Top-down Deletion

As in the case of 2-3 trees, the deletion of an arbitrary element from a 2-3-4 tree may be reduced to that of a deletion of an element that is in a leaf node. If the element to be deleted is in a leaf that is a 3-node or a 4-node, then its deletion leaves behind a 2-node or a 3-node. In this case, no restructuring work is required. Hence, to avoid a backward (leaf-to-root) restructuring path (as performed in the case of 2-3 trees), it is necessary to

```
procedure insert 234(var t : TwoThreeFourPtr ; y : element );
{Insert element y into the 2-3-4 tree t.}
var p, q : TwoThreeFourPtr;
    NotDone : boolean;
begin
   if t = nil then NewRoot (t, y)  {insertion into an empty 2-3-4 tree}
   else begin
           if FourNode (t) then SplitRoot (t);
           p := t; q := nil;  {q is parent of p}
           NotDone := true;
           while NotDone do
           begin
             if FourNode (p)
             then begin
                     if NodeType (q) =  TwoNode then SplitChildOf2(p, q)
                                               else SplitChildOf3(p, q);
                     p := q; {back up to parent for next comparison}
                   end; {of FourNode (p)}
             q := p;
             case compare (y, p) of
                equal : InsertionError; {key is duplicated}
                leaf : begin PutIn (y, p); NotDone := false; end;
                lChild : p := p ↑.LeftChild;
                lmChild : p := p ↑.LeftMidChild;
                rmChild : p := p ↑.RightMidChild;
                rChild : p := p ↑.RightChild;
             end; {of case}
           end; {of while}
        end; {of else begin}
end; {of insert 234}
```

Program 10.9: Insertion into a 2-3-4 tree

ensure that at the time of deletion, the element to be deleted is in a 3-node or a 4-node. This is accomplished by restructuring the 2-3-4 tree during the downward (root-to-leaf) pass.

The restructuring strategy requires that whenever the search moves to a node on the next level, this node must be a 3-node or a 4-node. Suppose the search is presently at node p and will move next to node q. Note that q is a child of p and is determined by the relationship between the key of the element to be deleted and the keys of the elements in p. The following cases are to be considered:

(1)   *p* is a leaf. In this case, the element to be deleted is either in *p* or not in the tree. If the element to be deleted is not in *p*, then the deletion is unsuccessful. Assume that this is not the case. By the nature of the restructuring process, *p* can be a 2-node only if it is also the root. The deletion results in an empty tree.

(2)   *q* is not a 2-node. In this case, the search moves to *q*, and no restructuring is needed.

(3)   *q* is a 2-node, and its nearest sibling, *r*, is also a 2-node (if *q* is the left child of *p*, then its nearest sibling is the left middle child of *p*; otherwise, the nearest sibling is its left sibling). Now, if *p* is a 2-node, it must be the root, and we perform the transformation of Figure 10.21 in reverse. That is, *p*, *q*, and *r* are combined to form a 4-node, and the height of the tree decreases by 1. If *p* is a 3-node or a 4-node, then we perform, in reverse, the 4-node splitting transformation for the corresponding case (Figures 10.22 through 10.24).

(4)   *q* is a 2-node, and its nearest sibling, *r*, is a 3-node. In this case, we perform the transformation of Figure 10.25. This figure shows only the transformations for the case when *q* is the left child of a 3-node *p*. The cases when *q* is the left middle child, right middle child, or right child, and when *p* is a 2-node (in this case *p* is the root) or a 4-node are similar.

(5)   *q* is a 2-node and its nearest sibling, *r*, is a 4-node. This is similar to the case when *r* is a 3-node.

These transformations guarantee that a backward restructuring pass is not needed following the deletion from a leaf node. We leave the development of the deletion procedure as an exercise.

EXERCISES

1.   Complete Figure 10.23 by drawing the splitting transformations for the case when the 4-node is the right middle child of a 3-node.

2.   Complete procedure *insert*234 (Program 10.9) by writing the code for all the procedures and functions used. Test your procedure using randomly generated keys.

3.   Use the deletion transformations described in the text to obtain a procedure to delete an element *y* from a 2-3-4 tree represented using nodes of type *TwoThreeFour*. The deletion should be performed in a top-down manner. To handle deletion from an interior node, you may need to make two top-down passes. Show that the complexity of your algorithm is O(log *n*), where *n* is the number of elements initially in the tree.

4.   Write a procedure to perform the *ThreeWayJoin* operation defined in Section 5.7.5 for binary search trees. This time, assume that *A* and *B* are 2-3-4 trees and that the result of the join is also a 2-3-4 tree. You may assume that the heights of the two input 2-3-4 trees are known. You should be able to perform the join in O($|$ *height* (*A*) $-$ *height* (*B*) $|$) time. (Hint: If *height* (*A*) > *height* (*B*), follow the

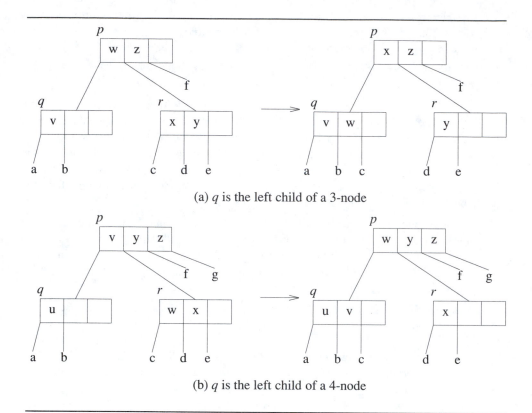

(a) q is the left child of a 3-node

(b) q is the left child of a 4-node

Figure 10.25: Deletion transformation when the nearest sibling is a 3-node

rightmost path from A to a node Y such that *height* $(Y) =$ *height* $(B) + 1$; now attempt to insert x, together with a pointer to B, into node Y.)

5. Do the previous exercise for the case of a *TwoWayJoin* (see Section 5.7.5).

6. Write a procedure to perform the *Split* operation (see Section 5.7.5) for binary search trees. This time, assume that A is a 2-3-4 tree and that the resulting trees, B and C, are also 2-3-4 trees. Can you do this operation in $O(height (A))$ time?

10.5 RED-BLACK TREES

10.5.1 Definition and Properties

A *red-black tree* is a binary tree representation of a 2-3-4 tree. The child pointers of a node in a red-black tree are of two types: red and black. If the child pointer was present in the original 2-3-4 tree, it is a black pointer. Otherwise, it is a red pointer. The node structure, *RedBlack*, is defined as

> **type** *color* = (red, black);
> *RedBlackPtr* = ↑*RedBlack*;
> *RedBlack* = **record**
> > *data* : *element*;
> > *LeftChild* : *RedBlackPtr*;
> > *RightChild* : *RedBlackPtr*;
> > *LeftColor* : *color*;
> > *RightColor* : *color*;
> **end**;

An alternate node structure in which each node has a single color field may be used instead. The value of this field is the color of the pointer from the node's parent. Thus, a red node has a red pointer from its parent, and a black node has a black pointer from its parent. The root node, is by definition, a black node. We examine this structure in the exercises. The former structure is better suited for top-down insertion and deletion; the latter is better suited for algorithms that make a bottom-to-top restructuring pass. When drawing a red-black tree, we shall use a solid line to represent a black pointer and a broken one to represent a red pointer. A 2-3-4 tree represented using nodes of type *TwoThreeFour* is transformed into its red-black representation as follows:

(1) A 2-node p is represented by a *RedBlack* node q with both its color fields black, and *data* = *dataL*; q↑.*LeftChild* = p↑.*LeftChild*, and q↑.*RightChild* = p↑.*LeftMidChild*.

(2) A 3-node p is represented by two *RedBlack* nodes connected by a red pointer. There are two ways in which this may be done (see Figure 10.26; color fields are not shown).

(3) A 4-node is represented by three *RedBlack* nodes, one of which is connected to the remaining two by red pointers (see Figure 10.27; color fields are not shown).

The red-black tree representation of the 2-3-4 tree of Figure 10.20 is given in Figure 10.28. External nodes and color fields are not shown. One may verify that a red-black tree satisfies the following properties:

(P1) It is a binary search tree.

(P2) Every root-to-external-node path has the same number of black links (this follows

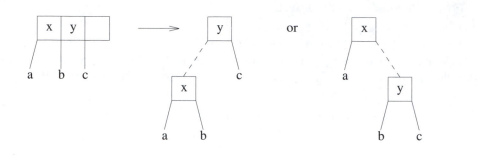

Figure 10.26: Transforming a 3-node into two *RedBlack* nodes

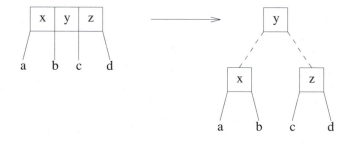

Figure 10.27: Transforming a 4-node into three *RedBlack* nodes

from the fact that all external nodes of the original 2-3-4 tree are on the same level, and black pointers represent original pointers).

(P3) No root-to-external-node path has two or more consecutive red pointers (this follows from the nature of the transformations of Figures 10.26 and 10.27).

An alternate definition of red-black trees is possible. In this definition, we associate a rank with each node x in the tree. This value is not explicitly stored in each node. Rather, if the rank of the root (also called the rank of the tree) is known, then the rank of every other node can be computed by traversing the binary tree and using the color information of the nodes/pointers. A binary tree is a red-black tree iff it satisifies the following properties:

(Q1) It is a binary search tree.

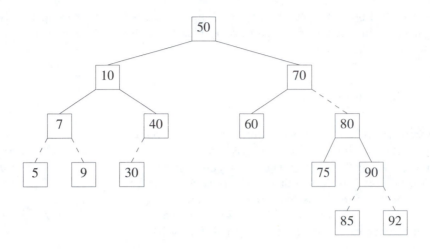

Figure 10.28: Red-black representation of the 2-3-4 tree of Figure 10.20

(Q2) The rank of each external node is 0.

(Q3) Every internal node that is the parent of an external node has rank 1.

(Q4) For every node x that has a parent $p(x)$, $rank(x) \leq rank(p(x)) \leq rank(x) + 1$.

(Q5) For every node x that has a grandparent $gp(x)$, $rank(x) < rank(gp(x))$.

Intuitively, we see that each node x of a 2-3-4 tree T is represented by a collection of nodes in its corresponding red-black tree. All nodes in this collection have a rank equal to $height(T) - level(x) + 1$. So, each time there is a rank change in a path from the root of the red-black tree, there is a level change in the corresponding 2-3-4 tree. Black pointers go from a node of a certain rank to one whose rank is one less; red pointers connect two nodes of the same rank. Lemma 10.1 is an immediate consequence of the properties of a 2-3-4 tree.

Lemma 10.1: Every red-black tree RB with n (internal) nodes satisifies the following:

(1) $height(RB) \leq 2\lceil \log_2(n+1) \rceil$

(2) $height(RB) \leq 2rank(RB)$

(3) $rank(RB) \leq \lceil \log_2(n+1) \rceil$ □

10.5.2   Searching a Red-Black Tree

Since every red-black tree is a binary search tree, it can be searched using exactly the same algorithm as used to search an ordinary binary search tree. The pointer colors are not used during this search.

10.5.3   Top-down Insertion

An insertion can be carried out in one of two ways: top-down or bottom-up. In a top-down insertion, a single root-to-leaf pass is made over the red-black tree. A bottom-up insertion makes both a root-to-leaf and a leaf-to-root pass. To make a top-down insertion, we use the 4-node splitting transformations described in Figures 10.21 through 10.24. In terms of red-black trees, these transformations take the form given in Figures 10.29 through 10.32. The case when a 4-node is the right middle child of a 3-node is symmetric to the case when it is the left child (Figure 10.31).

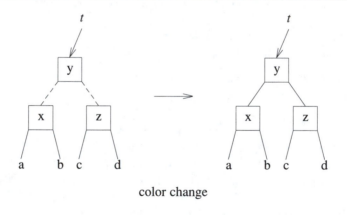

color change

Figure 10.29: Transformation for a root 4-node

We can detect a 4-node simply by looking for nodes q for which both color fields are red. Such nodes, together with their two children, form a 4-node. When such a q is detected, the transformations of Figures 10.29 through 10.32 are accomplished as follows:

(1)   Change both of the colors of q to black.

(2)   If q is the left (right) child of its parent, then change the left (right) color of its parent to red.

(3)   If we now have two consecutive red pointers, then one is from the grandparent, gp,

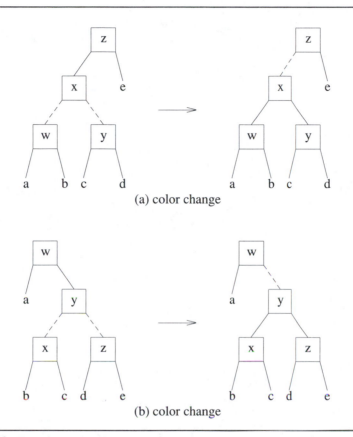

(a) color change

(b) color change

Figure 10.30: Transformation for a 4-node that is the child of a 2-node

of q to the parent, p, of q and the other from p to q. Let the direction of the first of these be X and that of the second be Y. We shall use L (R) to denote a left (right) direction. XY = LL, LR, and RL in Figures 10.31(a), 10.32(a), and 10.32(b), respectively. For the case symmetric to Figure 10.31(a) that arises when the 4-node is a right middle child of a 3-node, XY = RR. A rotation similar to that performed in AVL trees is needed. We describe the rotation for the case XY = LL. Now, node p takes the place previously occupied by gp; the right child of p becomes the left child of gp, and gp becomes the right child of p.

Note that when the 4-node to be split is a root or the child of a 2-node or that of a ''nicely'' oriented 3-node (as in Figure 10.31(b)), color changes suffice. Pointers need to be changed only when the 4-node is the child of a 3-node that is not ''nicely'' oriented (as in Figures 10.31(a) and 10.32). We leave the development of the formal insertion procedure as an exercise.

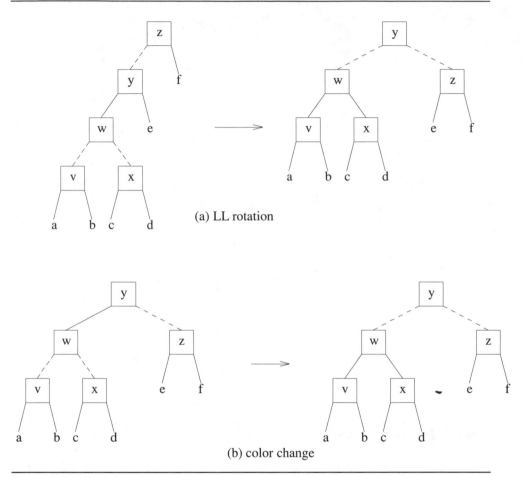

(a) LL rotation

(b) color change

Figure 10.31: Transformation for a 4-node that is the left child of a 3-node

10.5.4   Bottom-up Insertion

In a bottom-up insertion, we search the red-black tree for the key to be inserted. This search is unsuccessful. No transformations are made during this downward pass. The element to be inserted is added as the appropriate child of the node last encountered. A red pointer is used to join the new node to its parent. Following this, all root-to-external-node paths have the same number of black pointers. However, it is possible for one such path to have two consecutive red pointers. This violates the red-black property P3 that no root-to-external-node path has two consecutive red pointers. Let these two pointers be $<p, q>$ and $<q, r>$. The first is from node p to node q, and the second is from node q to node r. Let s be the sibling (if any) of node q. $s =$ **nil**, if q has no sibling.

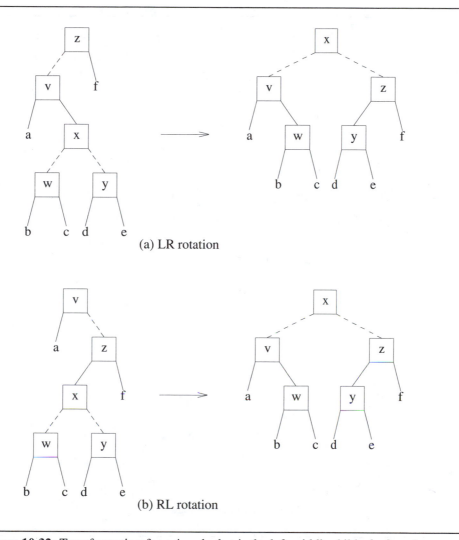

(a) LR rotation

(b) RL rotation

Figure 10.32: Transformation for a 4-node that is the left middle child of a 3-node

The violation is classified as an XYZ violation, where X = L if <p, q> is a left pointer, and X = R otherwise; Y = L if <q, r> is a left pointer, and Y = R otherwise; and Z = r if s ≠ **nil** and <p, s> is a red pointer, and Z = b otherwise.

The color change transformations of Figure 10.33 handle the violation cases LLr and LRr. Similar transformations handle the cases RRr and RLr. In these figures, the subtrees a, b, c, d, and e may be empty and the pointer from the parent of y nonexistent (if y is the root). These color changes potentially propagate the violation up the tree and may need to be reapplied several times. Note that the color change does not affect the

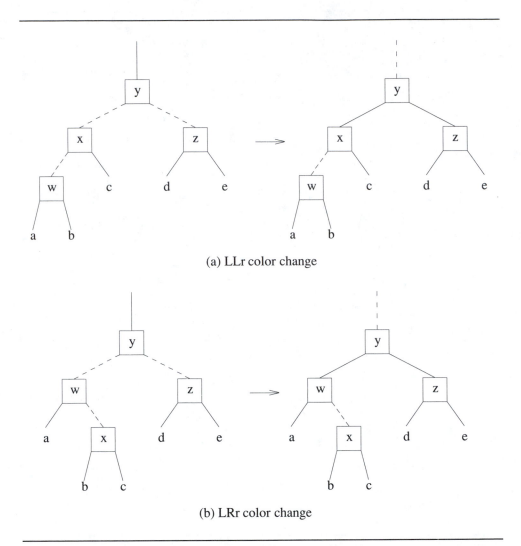

(a) LLr color change

(b) LRr color change

Figure 10.33: LLr and LRr color changes for bottom-up insertion

number of black pointers on a root-to-external-node path. Figure 10.34 shows the rotations needed for the cases LLb and LRb. The cases RRb and RLb are symmetric to LLb and LRb, respectively. The rotations of this figure do not propagate the violation. Hence, at most one rotation can be performed. Once again, we observe that these rotations do not affect the number of black pointers on any root-to-external-node path.

In comparing the top-down and the bottom-up insertion methods, we note that in the top-down method, $O(\log n)$ rotations can be performed, whereas only one rotation is

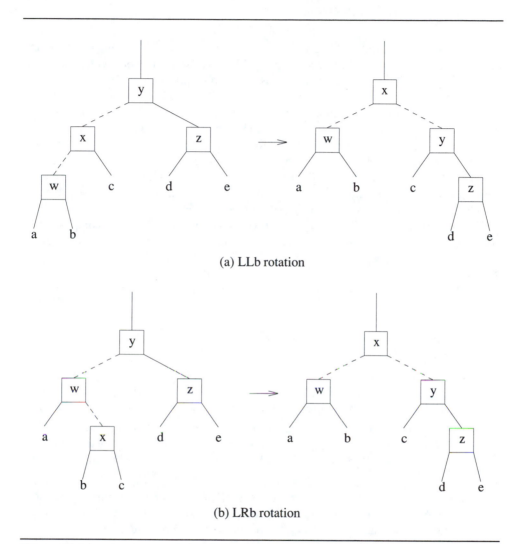

(a) LLb rotation

(b) LRb rotation

Figure 10.34: LLb and LRb rotations for bottom-up insertion

possible in the bottom-up method. Both methods may perform O(log *n*) color changes. However, the top-down method can be used in pipeline mode to perform several insertions in sequence. The bottom-up method cannot be used in this way.

10.5.5 Deletion from a Red-Black Tree

For top-down deletion from a leaf, we note that if the leaf from which the deletion is to occur is the root, then the result is an empty red-black tree. If the leaf is connected to its parent by a red pointer, then it is part of a 3-node or a 4-node, and the leaf may be deleted from the tree. If the pointer from the parent to the leaf is a black pointer, then the leaf is a 2-node. Deletion from a 2-node requires a backward restructuring pass. To avoid this, we ensure that the deletion leaf has a red pointer from its parent. This is accomplished by using the insertion transformations in the reverse direction, together with red-black transformations corresponding to the 2-3-4 deletion transformations (3) and (4) (q is a 2-node whose nearest sibling is a 3- or 4-node), and a 3-node transformation that switches from one 3-node representation to the other as necessary to ensure that the search for the element to be deleted moves down a red pointer.

Since most of the insertion and deletion transformations can be accomplished by color changes and require no pointer changes or data shifts, these operations take less time using red-black trees than when a 2-3-4 tree is represented using nodes of type *TwoThreeFour*.

The development of the bottom-up deletion transformations is left as an exercise.

10.5.6 Joining and Splitting Red-Black Trees

In Section 5.7.5, we defined the following operations on binary search trees: *ThreeWay-Join*, *TwoWayJoin*, and *Split*. Each of these can be performed in logarithmic time on red-black trees. The operation *ThreeWayJoin* (A,x,B,C) can be performed as follows:

Case 1: If A and B have the same rank (see properties Q1 to Q5), then let C be constructed by creating a new root with *data* field x; color fields black; *LeftChild* field A; and *RightChild* field B. The rank of C is one more than the ranks of A and B.

Case 2: If $rank(A) > rank(B)$, then follow *RightChild* pointers from A to the first node Y that has rank equal to $rank(B)$. Properties Q1 to Q5 guarantee the existence of such a node. Let $p(Y)$ be the parent of Y. From the definition of Y, it follows that $rank(p(Y)) = rank(Y) + 1$. Hence, the pointer from $p(Y)$ to Y is a black pointer. Create a new node, Z, with *data* field x; color fields black; *LeftChild* Y (i.e., node Y and its subtrees become the left subtree of Z); and *RightChild* B. Z is made the right child of $p(Y)$, and the link from $p(Y)$ to Z has color red. Note that this transformation does not change the number of black pointers on any root-to-external-node path. However, it may cause the path from the root to Z to contain two consecutive red pointers. If this happens, then the transformations used to handle this in a bottom-up insertion are performed. These transformations may increase the rank of the tree by one.

Case 3: The case $rank(A) < rank(B)$ is similar to Case 2.

Analysis of join: The correctness of the procedure just described is easily established. Case 1 takes O(1) time; each of the remaining two cases takes O($| rank(A) - rank(B) |$) time under the assumption that the rank of each red-black tree is known prior to computing the join. Hence, a three-way join can be done in O(log n) time, where n is the number of nodes in the two trees being joined. A two-way join can be performed in a similar manner. Note that there is no need to add parent fields to the nodes to perform a join, as the needed parents can be saved on a stack as we move from the root to the node Y. □

We now turn our attention to the split operation. Assume for simplicity that the splitting key, i, is actually present in the red-black tree A. Under this assumption, the split operation can be performed as in Program 10.10.

Step 1: Search A for the node P that contains the record x with key i. Initialize B and C to be the left and right subtrees of P, respectively.

Step 2:
```
Q := parent (P);
while Q <> nil do
begin
    if P = Q↑.LeftChild
    then ThreeWayJoin (C, Q↑.data, Q↑.RightChild, C)
    else ThreeWayJoin (Q↑.LeftChild, Q↑.data, B, B);
    P := Q;
    Q := parent (Q);
end;
```

Program 10.10: Splitting a red-black tree

We first locate the splitting record, x, in the red-black tree. Let P be the node that contains this record. The left subtree of P contains records with key less than i. B is initialized to be this subtree. All records in the right subtree of P have a key larger than i, and C is initialized to be this subtree. In Step 2, we trace the path from P to the root of the red-black tree A. During this traceback, two kinds of subtrees are encountered. One of these contains records with keys that are larger than i as well as all keys in C. This happens when the traceback moves from a left child of a node to its parent. The other kind of subtree contains records with keys that are smaller than i, as well as smaller than all keys in B. This happens when we move from a right child to its parent. In the former case a three-way join with C is performed, and in the latter a three-way join with B is performed. One may verify that the two-step procedure outlined here does indeed implement the split operation for the case when i is the key of a record in the tree A. It is easily extended to handle the case when the tree A contains no record with key i.

Analysis of split: Call a node red if the pointer to it from its parent is red. The root and all nodes that have a black pointer from their parent are black. Let $r(X)$ be the rank of node X in the unsplit tree. First, we shall show that during a split, if P is a black node in the unsplit tree, and $Q \neq$ **nil**, then

$$r(Q) \geq \max\{r(B), r(C)\}$$

where P, Q, B, and C are as defined at the start of an iteration of the **while** loop in Step 2.

From the definition of rank, the inequality holds at the start of the first iteration of the **while** loop regardless of the color of P. If P is red initially, then its parent, Q, exists and is black. Let q' be the parent of Q. If $q' =$ **nil**, then there is no Q at which the inequality is violated. So, assume $q' \neq$ **nil**. From the definition of rank and the fact that Q is black, it follows that $r(q') = r(Q) + 1$. Let B' and C' be the trees B and C following the three-way join of Step 2. Since $r(B') \leq r(B) + 1$ and $r(C') \leq r(C) + 1$, $r(q') = r(Q) + 1 \geq \max\{r(B), r(C)\} + 1 \geq \max\{r(B'), r(C')\}$. So, the inequality holds the first time Q points to a node with a black child P (i.e., at the start of the second iteration of the **while** loop, when $Q = q'$).

Having established the induction base, we can proceed to show that the inequality holds at all subsequent iterations when Q points to a node with a black child P. Suppose Q is currently pointing to a node q with a black child $P = p$. Assume that the inequality holds. We shall show that it will hold again the next time Q is at a node with a black P. For there to be such a next time, the parent q' of q must exist. If q is black, the proof is similar to that provided for a black Q and a red P in the induction base.

If q is red, then q' is black. Further, for there to be a next time when Q is at a node with a black P, q must have a grandparent q'', as when Q moves to q' and P to q, $Q = q'$ has a red child $P = q$. Let B' and C' represent the B and C trees following the iteration that begins with $P = p$ and $Q = q$. Similarly, let B'' and C'' represent these trees following the iteration that begins with $P = q$ and $Q = q'$.

Suppose that C is joined with q and its right subtree R to create C'. If $r(C) = r(R)$, then $r(C') = r(C) + 1$, and C' has two black children (recall that when the rank increases by one, the root has two black children). If $C'' = C'$, then $B = B'$ is combined with q' and its left subtree L' to form B''. Since $r(L') \leq r(q')$, $r(B'') \leq \max\{r(B), r(L')\} + 1$, and $r(q'') = r(q') + 1 = r(q) + 1$, $r(B'') \leq r(q'')$. Also, $r(C'') = r(C') = r(C) + 1 \leq r(q) + 1 \leq r(q'')$. So, the inequality holds when $Q = q''$. If $C'' \neq C'$, then C' is combined with q' and its right subtree R' to form C''. If $r(R') \geq r(C')$, then $r(C'') \leq r(R') + 1 \leq r(q') + 1 = r(q'')$. If $r(R') < r(C')$, then $r(C'') = r(C')$, as C' has two black children, and the join of C', q', and R' does not increase the rank. Once again, $r(C'') \leq r(q'')$, and the inequality holds when $Q = q''$.

If $r(C) > r(R)$ and $r(C') = r(C)$, then $r(q'') = r(q) + 1 \geq \max\{r(B), r(C)\} + 1 \geq \max\{r(B''), r(C'')\}$. If $r(C') = r(C) + 1$, then C' has two black children, and $r(C'') \leq r(q) + 1 = r(q'')$. Also, $r(B'') \leq r(q'')$. So, the inequality holds when $Q = q''$. The case $r(C) < r(R)$ is similar.

The case when B is joined with q and its left subtree L is symmetric.

Using the rank inequality just established, we can show that whenever Q points to a node with a black child, the total work done in Step 2 of the splitting algorithm from initiation to the time Q reaches this node is $O(r(B) + r(C) + r(Q))$. Here, B and C are, respectively, the current red-black trees with values smaller and larger than the splitting value. Since $r(Q) \geq \max\{r(B), r(C)\}$, the total work done in Step 2 is $O(r(Q))$. From this, it follows that the time required to perform a split is $O(\log n)$, where n is the number of nodes in the tree to be split. $\square$

EXERCISES

1. (a) Show that every binary tree obtained by transforming a 2-3-4 tree as described in the text satisfies properties Q1 to Q5.

    (b) Show that every binary tree that satisfies properties Q1 to Q5 represents a 2-3-4 tree and can be obtained from this 2-3-4 tree using the transformations of the text.

2. Write a procedure to convert a 2-3-4 tree into its red-black representation. What is the time complexity of your procedure?

3. Write a procedure to convert a red-black tree into its 2-3-4 representation. What is the time complexity of your procedure?

4. Let T be a red-black tree with rank r. Write a procedure to compute the rank of each node in the tree. The time complexity of your procedure should be linear in the number of nodes in the tree. Show that this is the case.

5. Compare the worst-case height of a red-black tree with n nodes and that of an AVL tree with the same number of nodes.

6. Rewrite procedure *insert* 234 (Program 10.9) so that it inserts an element into a 2-3-4 tree represented as a red-black tree.

7. Obtain the symmetric transformations for Figures 10.33 and 10.34.

8. Obtain a procedure to delete an element y from a 2-3-4 tree represented as a red-black tree. Use the top-down method. Test the correctness of this procedure by running it on a computer. Generate your own test data.

9. Do the Exercise 8 using the bottom-up method.

10. The number of color fields in a node of a red-black tree may be reduced to one. In this case the color of a node represents the color of the pointer (if any) from the node's parent to that node. Write the corresponding insert and delete procedures using the top-down approach. How would this change in the node structure affect the efficiency of the insert and delete procedures?

11. Do the Exercise 10 using the bottom-up approach.

12. (a) Use the strategy described in the text to obtain a Pascal procedure to compute a three-way join. Assume the existence of a procedure *rebalance* (X) that performs the necessary transformations if the tree pointer to node X is the second of two consecutive red pointers. The complexity of this procedure may be assumed to be $O(level(X))$.

(b)   Prove the correctness of your procedure.

(c)   What is the time complexity of your procedure?

13.   Obtain a procedure to perform a two-way join on red-black trees. You may assume the existence of procedures to search, insert, delete, and perform a three-way join. What is the time complexity of your two-way join procedure?

14.   Use the strategy suggested in the text to obtain a Pascal procedure to perform the split operation in a red-black tree T. The complexity of your algorithm must be $O(height\ (T))$. Your procedure must work when the splitting key i is present in T and when it is not present in T.

15.   Complete the complexity proof for the split operation by showing that whenever Q has a black child, the total work done in Step 2 of the splitting algorithm from initiation to the time that Q reaches the current node is $O(r\ (Q))$.

16.   Program the search, insert, and delete operations for AVL trees, 2-3 trees, 2-3-4 trees, and red-black trees.

(a)   Test the correctness of your procedures.

(b)   Generate a random sequence of n inserts of distinct values. Use this sequence to initialize each of the data structures. Next, generate a random sequence of searches, inserts, and deletes. In this sequence, the probability of a search should be 0.5, that of an insert 0.25, and that of a delete 0.25. The sequence length is m. Measure the time needed to perform the m operations in the sequence using each of the above data structures.

(c)   Do part (b) for $n = 100$, 1000, 10,000, and 100,000 and $m = n$, $2n$, and $4n$.

(d)   What can you say about the relative performance of these data structures?

10.6   B-TREES

10.6.1   Definition of m-Way Search Trees

The balanced search trees that we have studied so far (AVL trees, 2-3 trees, 2-3-4 trees, and red-black trees) allow us to search, insert, and delete entries from a table in $O(\log n)$ time, where n is the number of entries in the table. These structures are well suited to applications in which the table is small enough to be accommodated in internal memory. However, when the table is too large for this, these structures do not have good performance. This is because we must now retrieve the nodes of the search tree structure from a disk (for example). These nodes are retrieved one at a time as needed. So, for example, when searching a 2-3 tree for an element with key x, we would retrieve only those nodes that are on the search path from the root to the node that contains the desired element. As a result, the number of disk accesses for a search is $O(h)$, where h is the height of the 2-3 tree. When $n = 1000$, h can be as high as 10. So, searching a 2-3 tree that is stored on a disk and that has 1000 elements could require up to 10 disk accesses. Since the time required for a disk access is significantly more than that for an internal memory access, we seek structures that would reduce the number of disk accesses.

We shall use the term *index* to refer to a symbol table that resides on a disk. The symbol table may be assumed to be too large to be accommodated in the internal memory of the target computer. To obtain better performance, we shall use search trees whose degree is quite large.

Definiton: An *m-way search tree*, either is empty or satisfies the following properties:

(1)   The root has at most *m* subtrees and has the following structure:

$$n, A_0, (K_1, A_1), (K_2, A_2), \cdots, (K_n, A_n)$$

where the A_i, $0 \leq i \leq n < m$, are pointers to subtrees, and the K_i, $1 \leq i \leq n < m$, are key values.

(2) $K_i < K_{i+1}$, $1 \leq i < n$.

(3)   All key values in the subtree A_i are less than K_{i+1} and greater than K_i, $0 < i < n$.

(4)   All key values in the subtree A_n are greater than K_n, and those in A_0 are less than K_1.

(5)   The subtrees A_i, $0 \leq i \leq n$, are also *m*-way search trees. □

We may verify that AVL trees are two-way search trees, 2-3 trees are three-way search trees, and 2-3-4 trees are four-way search trees. Of course, there are two-way search trees that are not AVL trees, three-way search trees that are not 2-3 trees, and four-way search trees that are not 2-3-4 trees. A three-way search tree that is not a 2-3 tree is shown in Figure 10.35.

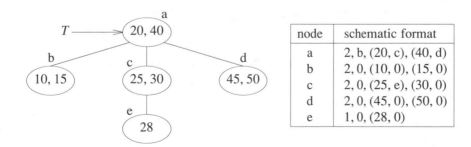

node	schematic format
a	2, b, (20, c), (40, d)
b	2, 0, (10, 0), (15, 0)
c	2, 0, (25, e), (30, 0)
d	2, 0, (45, 0), (50, 0)
e	1, 0, (28, 0)

Figure 10.35: Example of a three-way search tree that is not a 2-3 tree

10.6.2 Searching an m-Way Search Tree

Suppose we wish to search the m-way search tree T for the key value x. Assume that T resides on a disk. We begin by retrieving the root node from the disk. Assume that this node has the structure given in the definition of an m-way search tree. For convenience, assume that $K_0 = -\infty$ and $K_{n+1} = +\infty$. By searching the keys of the root, we determine i such that $K_i \le x < K_{i+1}$. If $x = K_i$, then the search is complete. If $x \ne K_i$, then from the definition of an m-way search tree, it follows that if x is in the tree, it must be in subtree A_i. So, we retrieve the root of this subtree from the disk and proceed to search it. This process continues until either we find x or we have determined that x is not in the tree (the search leads us to an empty subtree). When the number of keys in the node being searched is small, a sequential search (as in the case of 2-3 and 2-3-4 trees) is used. When this number is large, a binary search may be used. A high-level description of the algorithm to search an m-way search tree is given in Program 10.11.

---

procedure *msearch* $(t : mtree ; x : \textbf{integer}; \textbf{var } p : mtree ; \textbf{var } i,j : \textbf{integer})$;
{Search the m-way search tree t residing on disk for the key value x. Individual node format is $n, A_0, (K_1,A_1), \cdots, (K_n,A_n), n < m$. A triple (p,i,j) is returned. $j = 1$ implies that x is found at node location p with key K_i. Otherwise, $j = 0$, and p is the location of the node into which x can be inserted.}
label 99;
begin
$\quad p := t; K_0 := -\textbf{maxint}; q := \textbf{nil}; j := 1;$ {q is the parent of p}
$\quad$ **while** $p < > 0$ **do**
$\quad$ **begin**
$\quad\quad$ input node located at p from disk;
$\quad\quad$ let this node define $n, A_0, (K_1, A_1), \cdots, (K_n, A_n)$;
$\quad\quad K_{n+1} := \textbf{maxint}$;
$\quad\quad$ let i be such that $K_i <= x < K_{i+1}$;
$\quad\quad$ **if** $x = K_i$ **then** {x has been found; return $(p, i, 1)$} **goto** 99;
$\quad\quad q := p; p := A_i;$
$\quad$ **end**;
$\quad$ {x is not in t; return location of node into which insertion can take place}
$\quad p := q; j := 0;$ {**return** $(q, i, 0)$}
99: **end**; {of *msearch*}

Program 10.11: Searching an m-way search tree

In a tree of degree m and height h, the maximum number of nodes is

$$\sum_{0 \le i \le h-1} m^i = (m^h - 1)/(m - 1)$$

Since each node has at most $m - 1$ keys, the maximum number of keys in an m-way tree index of height h is $m^h - 1$. For a binary tree with $h = 3$ this figure is 7. For a 200-way tree with $h = 3$ we have $m^h - 1 = 8 * 10^6 - 1$.

Clearly, the potentials of high-order search trees are much greater than those of low-order search trees. To achieve a performance close to that of the best m-way search trees for a given number of keys n, the search tree must be balanced. The particular variety of balanced m-way search trees we shall consider here is known as a B-tree. In defining a B-tree, it is convenient to reintroduce the concept of failure nodes. Recall that a failure node represents a node that can be reached during a search only if the value x being sought is not in the tree.

10.6.3   Definition and Properties of a B-Tree

Definition: A *B-tree of order m* is an m-way search tree that either is empty or satisfies the following properties:

(1)   The root node has at least two children.

(2)   All nodes other than the root node and failure nodes have at least $\lceil m/2 \rceil$ children.

(3)   All failure nodes are at the same level. $\square$

Observe that a 2-3 tree is a B-tree of order 3, and a 2-3-4 tree is a B-tree of order 4. Also, notice that all B-trees of order 2 are full binary trees. Hence, B-trees of order 2 exist only when the number of key values is $2^k - 1$ for some k. However, for any $n \geq 0$ and any $m > 2$, there is a B-tree of order m that contains n keys.

10.6.3.1   Number of Key Values in a B-Tree

A B-tree of order m in which all failure nodes are at level $l+1$ has at most $m^l - 1$ keys. What is the minumum number, N, of keys in such a B-tree? From the definition of a B-tree we know that if $l > 1$, the root node has at least two children. Hence, there are at least two nodes at level 2. Each of these nodes must have at least $\lceil m/2 \rceil$ children. Thus, there are at least $2\lceil m/2 \rceil$ nodes at level 3. At level 4 there must be at least $2\lceil m/2 \rceil^2$ nodes, and continuing this argument, we see that there are at least $2\lceil m/2 \rceil^{l-2}$ nodes at level l when $l > 1$. All of these nodes are nonfailure nodes. If the key values in the tree are $K_1, K_2, \cdots, K_N$ and $K_i < K_{i+1}, 1 \leq i < N$, then the number of failure nodes is $N + 1$. This is so because failures occur for $K_i < x < K_{i+1}, 0 \leq i \leq N$, where $K_0 = -\infty$ and $K_{N+1} = +\infty$. This results in $N + 1$ different nodes that one could reach while searching for a key value x that is not in the B-tree. Therefore, we have

$$N + 1 = \text{number of failure nodes}$$
$$= \text{number of nodes at level } l + 1$$
$$\geq 2\lceil m/2 \rceil^{l-1}$$

so $N \geq 2\lceil m/2 \rceil^{l-1} - 1$, $l \geq 1$.

This in turn implies that if there are N key values in a B-tree of order m, then all nonfailure nodes are at levels less than or equal to l, $l \leq \log_{\lceil m/2 \rceil}\{(N + 1)/2\} + 1$. The maximum number of accesses that have to be made for a search is l. Using a B-tree of order $m = 200$, an index with $N \leq 2 \times 10^6 - 2$ will have $l \leq \log_{100}\{(N + 1)/2\} + 1$. Since l is an integer, we obtain $l \leq 3$. For $n \leq 2 \times 10^8 - 2$ we get $l \leq 4$. Thus, the use of a high-order B-tree results in a tree index that can be searched making a very small number of disk accesses, even when the number of entries is very large.

10.6.3.2 Choice of m

B-trees of high order are desirable, since they result in a reduction in the number of disk accesses needed to search an index. If the index has N entries, then a B-tree of order $m = N + 1$ has only one level. This choice of m clearly is not reasonable, since by assumption the index is too large to fit in internal memory. Consequently, the single node representing the index cannot be read into memory and processed. In arriving at a reasonable choice for m, we must keep in mind that we are really interested in minimizing the total amount of time needed to search the B-tree for a value x. This time has two components: (1) the time for reading in the node from the disk and (2) the time needed to search this node for x. Let us assume that each node of a B-tree of order m is of a fixed size and is large enough to accommodate n, A_0, and $m-1$ triples (K_i, A_i, B_i), $1 \leq j < m$. Notice that although in the definition of an m-way search tree we had pairs (K_i, A_i), in practice, these will be triples (K_i, A_i, B_i), where B_i gives the address, on disk, of the record with key K_i (as before, A_i points to a subtree of the B-tree). If the K_i are at most α characters long and the A_i and B_i each β characters long, then the size of a node is approximately $m(\alpha + 2\beta)$ characters. The time required to read in a node is therefore

$$t_s + t_l + m(\alpha + 2\beta)\, t_c = a + bm$$

where

$$a = t_s + t_l = \text{seek time} + \text{latency time}$$
$$b = (\alpha + 2\beta)t_c, \text{ and } t_c = \text{transmission time per character}$$

If binary search is used to search each node of the B-tree, then the internal processing time per node is $c \log_2 m + d$ for some constants c and d. The total processing time per node is thus

$$\tau = a + bm + c \log_2 m + d$$

For an index with N entries, the number of levels, l, is bounded by

$$l \leq \log_{\lceil m/2 \rceil} \{(N+1)/2\} + 1 \leq f \frac{\log_2 \{(N+1)/2\}}{\log_2 m} \quad \text{for some constant } f$$

The maximum search time is therefore

$$g \left\{ \frac{a+d}{\log_2 m} + \frac{bm}{\log_2 m} + c \right\} \text{ seconds}$$

where $g = f * \log_2 \{(N + 1)/2\}$.

We therefore desire a value of m that minimizes the maximum search time. If the disk drive available has $t_s = 1/100$ sec and $t_l = 1/40$ sec, then $a = 0.035$ sec. Since d is typically a few microseconds, we may ignore it in comparison with a. Hence, $a + d \approx a = 0.035$ sec. If each key value is at most six characters long, and each A_i and B_i is three characters long, $\alpha = 6$ and $\beta = 3$. If the transmission rate t_c is 5×10^{-6} sec/charac (corresponding to a track capacity of 5000 characters), then $b = (\alpha + 2\beta)t_c = 6 \times 10^{-5}$ sec. The formula for the maximum search time now becomes

$$g \left\{ \frac{35}{\log_2 m} + \frac{0.06m}{\log_2 m} + 1000c \right\} \text{ milliseconds}$$

This function is tabulated in Figure 10.36 and plotted in Figure 10.37. It is evident that there is a wide range of values of m for which nearly optimal performance is achieved. This corresponds to the almost flat region $m \in [50,400]$. If the lowest value of m in this region results in a node size greater than the allowable capacity of an input buffer, the value of m will be determined by the buffer size.

10.6.4   Insertion into a B-Tree

The algorithm to insert a new key into a B-tree is a generalization of the two-pass insertion algorithm for 2-3 trees. Although for $m > 3$ we could also generalize the top-down insertion algorithm described for 2-3-4 trees, this is not desirable, as this algorithm splits many nodes, and each time we change a node, it has to be written to disk. This increases the number of disk accesses.

The insertion algorithm for B-trees of order m first performs a search to determine the leaf node, p, into which the new key is to be inserted. If the insertion of the new key into p results in p having m keys, the node p is split. Otherwise, the new p is written to the disk, and the insertion is complete. To split the node, assume that following the insertion of the new key, p, has the format

$$m, A_0, (K_1, A_1), \cdots, (K_m, A_m), \quad \text{and} \quad K_i < K_{i+1}, 1 \leq i < m$$

m	Search time (sec)
2	35.12
4	17.62
8	11.83
16	8.99
32	7.38
64	6.47
128	6.10
256	6.30
512	7.30
1024	9.64
2048	14.35
4096	23.40
8192	40.50

Figure 10.36: Values of $(35 + .06m)/\log_2 m$

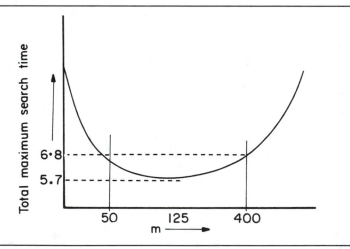

Figure 10.37: Plot of $(35+.06m)/\log_2 m$

The node is split into two nodes, p and q, with the following formats:

$$\text{node } p: \lceil m/2 \rceil - 1, A_0, (K_1 A_1), \cdots, (K_{\lceil m/2 \rceil - 1}, A_{\lceil m/2 \rceil - 1}) \qquad (10.5)$$

$$\text{node } q: m - \lceil m/2 \rceil, A_{\lceil m/2 \rceil}, (K_{\lceil m/2 \rceil + 1}, A_{\lceil m/2 \rceil + 1}), \cdots, (K_m, A_m)$$

The remaining key, $K_{\lceil m/2 \rceil}$, and a pointer to the new node, q, form a tuple $(K_{\lceil m/2 \rceil}, q)$. This is to be inserted into the parent of p. Before attempting this, the nodes p and q are written to disk.

As in the case of 2-3 trees, inserting into the parent may require us to split the parent, and this splitting process can propagate all the way up to the root. When the root splits, a new root with a single key is created, and the height of the B-tree increases by one. A high-level description of the insertion algorithm is given in Program 10.12.

```
procedure BtreeInsert(var t : mtree ; x : integer);
{Key value x is inserted into the B-tree, t, of order m. t resides on a disk.}
label 99;
var A, p, q, t : mtree; i, j, K : integer;
begin
    A := nil; K := x; {(K,A) is tuple to be inserted}
    msearch (t, x, p, i, j); {p is location of node for insertion}
    if j <> 0 then goto 99; {x is already in t}
    while p <> 0 do
    begin
        insert (K,A) into appropriate position in node at location p;
        let the resulting node have the form: n, A_0, (K_1, A_1), ···, (K_n, A_n);
        if n <= m - 1 then begin {resulting node is not too big}
            output node located at p onto disk; goto 99; end;
        {node located at p has to be split}
        let node p and node q be defined as in Eq. (10.5);
        output nodes p and q onto the disk;
        K := K_⌈m/2⌉; A := q; p := parent [p ];
    end;
    {a new root is to be created}
    Create a new node r with format 1, t, (K, A);
    t := r; output t onto disk;
99: end; {of BtreeInsert]
```

Program 10.12: Insertion into a B-tree

Analysis of BtreeInsert: If h is the height of the B-tree, then h disk accesses are made during the top-down search. In the worst case, all h of the accessed nodes may split during the bottom-up splitting pass. When a node other than the root splits, we need to write out two nodes. When the root splits, three nodes are written out. If we assume that the h nodes read in during the top-down pass can be saved in memory so that they are not to be retrieved from disk during the bottom-up pass, then the number of disk accesses for an insertion is at most h (downward pass) + $2(h - 1)$ (nonroot splits) + 3 (root split) = $3h + 1$.

The average number of disk accesses is, however, approximately $h + 1$ for large m. To see this, suppose we start with an empty B-tree and insert N values into it. The total number of nodes split is at most $p - 2$, where p is the number of nonfailure nodes in the final B-tree with N entries. This upper bound of $p - 2$ follows from the observation that each time a node splits, at least one additional node is created. When the root splits, two additional nodes are created. The first node created results from no splitting, and if a B-tree has more than one node, then the root must have split at least once. Figure 10.38 shows that $p - 2$ is the best possible upper bound on the number of nodes split in the creation of a p-node B-tree when $p > 2$ (note that there is no B-tree with $p = 2$). A B-tree of order m with p nodes has at least $1 + (\lceil m/2 \rceil - 1)(p - 1)$ keys, as the root has at least one key and remaining nodes have at least $\lceil m/2 \rceil - 1$ keys each. The average number of splits, s_{avg}, may now be determined as follows:

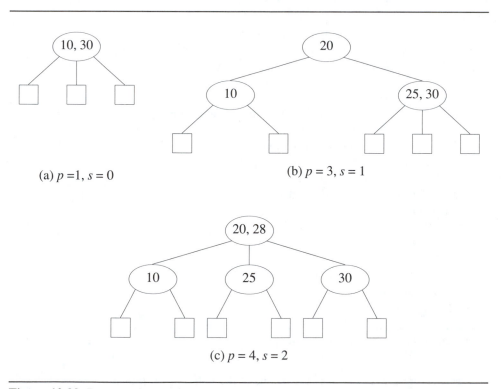

(a) $p = 1, s = 0$

(b) $p = 3, s = 1$

(c) $p = 4, s = 2$

Figure 10.38: B-trees of order 3

$$s_{avg} = \text{(total number of splits)}/N$$
$$\leq (p-2)/\{1 + (\lceil m/2 \rceil - 1)(p-1)\}$$
$$< 1/(\lceil m/2 \rceil - 1)$$

For $m = 200$ this means that the average number of node splits is less than $1/99$ per key inserted. The number of disk accesses in an insertion is $h + 2s - 1$, where s is the number of nodes that are split during the insertion. So, the average number of disk accesses is $h + 2s_{avg} + 1 < h + 101/99 \approx h + 1$. $\square$

10.6.5   Deletion from a B-Tree

The deletion algorithm for B-trees is also a generalization of the deletion algorithm for 2-3 trees. First, we search for the key x that is to be deleted. If x is found in a node, z, that is not a leaf, then the position occupied by x in z is filled by a key from a leaf node of the B-tree. Suppose that x is the ith key in z (i.e., $x = K_i$). Then x may be replaced by either the smallest key in the subtree A_i or the largest in the subtree A_{i-1}. Both of these keys are in leaf nodes. In this way the deletion of x from a nonleaf node is transformed into a deletion from a leaf.

There are four possible cases when deleting from a leaf node p. In the first, p is also the root. If the root is left with at least one key, the changed root is written to disk and we are done. Otherwise, the B-tree is empty following the deletion. In the remaining cases, p is not the root. In the second case, following the deletion, p has at least $\lceil m/2 \rceil - 1$ keys. The modified leaf is written to disk, and we are done.

In the third case, p has $\lceil m/2 \rceil - 2$ keys, and its nearest sibling, q, has at least $\lceil m/2 \rceil$ keys. To determine this, we examine only one of the two (at most) nearest siblings that p may have. p is deficient, as it has one less than the minimum number of keys required. q has more keys than the minimum required. As in the case of a 2-3 tree, a rotation is performed. In this rotation, the number of keys in q decreases by one, and the number in p increases by one. As a result, neither p nor q is deficient following the rotation. The rotation leaves behind a valid B-tree. Let r be the parent of p and q. If q is the nearest right sibling of p, then let i be such that K_i is the ith key in r, all keys in p are less than K_i, and all those in q are greater than K_i. For the rotation, K_i is replaced by the first (i.e., smallest) key in q, K_i becomes the rightmost key in p, and the leftmost subtree of q becomes the rightmost subtree of p. The changed nodes p, q, and r are written to disk, and the deletion is complete. The case when q is the nearest left sibling of p is similar.

In the fourth case for deletion, p has $\lceil m/2 \rceil - 2$ keys, and q has $\lceil m/2 \rceil - 1$ keys. So, p is deficient, and q has the minimum number of keys permissible for a nonroot node. Now, nodes p and q and the key K_i are combined to form a single node. The combined node has $(\lceil m/2 \rceil - 2) + (\lceil m/2 \rceil - 1) + 1 = 2\lceil m/2 \rceil - 2 \leq m - 1$ keys, which will, at most, fill the node. The combined node is written to disk. The combining operation reduces the number of keys in the parent node, r, by one. If the parent does not become deficient (i.e., it has at least one key if it is the root and at least $\lceil m/2 \rceil - 1$ keys if it is not the root), the changed parent is written to disk, and we are done. Otherwise, if the deficient parent is the root, it is discarded, as it has no keys. If the deficient parent is not the root, it has exactly $\lceil m/2 \rceil - 2$ keys. To remove this deficiency, we first attempt a rotation with one of r's nearest siblings. If this is not possible, a combine is done. This process of combining can continue up the B-tree only until the children of the root are combined.

The details are provided in algorithm *BtreeDelete* (Program 10.13). To reduce the worst-case performance of the algorithm, only the nearest left or nearest right sibling of a node is examined.

```
1  procedure BtreeDelete (var t : mtree; x : integer);
     {Delete x from B-tree t of order m. t resides on a disk.}
2  label 99;
3  var i,j : integer; t,p,q,y,z : mtree;
4  begin
5     msearch (t, x, p, i, j);
6     if j <> 1 then goto 99; {x is not in t}
7     let p be of the form n, A_0, (K_1,A_1), ···, (K_n,A_n) and K_i = x;
8     if A_0 <> 0 then {deletion from a nonleaf; find key to move up}
9     begin
10        q := A_i; {move to right subtree}
11        whle q is not a leaf node do
12        begin
13           let q be of the form  n_q, A_0^q, (K_1^q, A_1^q), ···, (K_n^q, A_n^q);
14           q := A_0^q;
15        end;
16        let q be of the form n_q, A_0^q, (K_1^q, A_1^q), ···, (K_n^q, A_n^q);
17        replace K_i in node p by K_1^q and write the altered node p onto disk;
18        p := q; i := 1;
19        let n, A_0, (K_1,A_1), ···, (K_n,A_n) be as defined by the new node p;
20     end {of if A_0 <> 0}
21     {delete K_i from node p, a leaf}
22     delete (K_i, A_i) from p = [n, A_0, (K_1,A_1), ···, (K_n,A_n)]; replace n by n − 1;
23     while (n < ⌈m/2⌉ − 1) and p <> t do
24        if p has a nearest right sibling y then
25        begin
26           let y : n_y, A_0^y, (K_1^y, A_1^y), ···, (K_n^y, A_n^y);
27           let z : n_z, A_0^z, (K_1^z, A_1^z), ···, (K_n^z, A_n^z) be the parent of p and y;
28           let A_j^z = y and A_{j-1}^z = p;
```

Program 10.13: Deletion from a B-tree (continued on next page)

```
29          if n_y > = ⌈m/2⌉ then {redistribute key values}
30             begin
31                (K_{n+1}, A_{n+1}) := (K_j^z, A_0^y); n := n + 1; {update node p}
32                K_j^z := K_1^y; {update node z}
33                (n_y, A_0^y, (K_1^y, A_1^y), ···) := (n_y−1, A_1^y, (K_2^y, A_2^y, ···); {update node y}
34                output nodes p, y, z onto disk;
35                goto 99;
36             end; {of if n_y > = ⌈m/2⌉}
37          {combine nodes p, K_j^z, and y}
38          r := 2* ⌈m/2⌉ − 2;
39          output r, A_0, (K_1, A_1), ···, (K_n, A_n), (K_j^z, A_0^y), (K_1^y, A_1^y), ···, (K_n^y, A_n^y)
40             onto disk at location p;
41          {update}
42          (n, A_0 ···) := (n_z−1, A_0^z, ···, (K_{j−1}^z, A_{j−1}^z), (K_{j+1}^z, A_{j+1}^z) ···)
43          p := z;
44       end {of if p has a nearest right sibling}
45       else begin {node p must have a left sibling}
46                {this is symmetric to lines 25 to 44 and is left as an exercise}
47             end; {of if and while}
48    if n <> 0 then output p: (n, A_0, ···, (K_n,A_n))
49             else t := A_0; {change root}
50 99: end; {of BtreeDelete}
```

Program 10.13: Deletion from a B-tree

Analysis of *BtreeDelete*: Once again, we assume that disk nodes accessed during the downward search pass may be saved in a stack, so they do not need to be reaccessed from the disk during the upward restructuring pass. For a B-tree of height h, h disk accesses are made to find the node from which the key is to be deleted and to transform the deletion to a deletion from a leaf. In the worst case, a combine takes place at each of the last $h − 2$ nodes on the root-to-leaf path, and a rotation takes place at the second node on this path. The $h − 2$ combines require this many disk accesses to retrieve a nearest sibling for each node and another $h − 2$ accesses to write out the combined nodes. The rotation requires one access to read a nearest sibling and three to write out the three nodes that are changed. The total number of disk accesses is $3h$.

The deletion time can be reduced at the expense of disk space and a slight increase in node size by including a delete bit, F_i, for each key value, K_i, in a node. Then we can set $F_i = 1$ if K_i has not been deleted and $F_i = 0$ if it has. No physical deletion takes place. In this case a delete requires a maximum of $h + 1$ accesses (h to locate the node containing x and 1 to write out this node with the appropriate delete bit set to 0). With this strategy, the number of nodes in the tree never decreases. However, the space used by deleted entries can be reused during further insertions (see exercises). As a result, this strategy has little effect on search and insert times (the number of levels increases very slowly when m is large). The time taken to insert an item may even decrease slightly because of the ability to reuse deleted entry space. Such reuses would not require us to split any nodes. □

Some variations of B-trees are examined in the exercises.

10.6.6   Variable-Size Key Values

With a node format of the form n, A_0, (K_1,A_1), $\cdots$, (K_n,A_n), the first problem created by the use of variable-size key values, K_i, is that a binary search can no longer be carried out, since, given the location of the first tuple (K_1,A_1), and n, we cannot easily determine K_n or even the location of $K_{(1+n)/2}$. When the range of key value size is small, it is best to allocate enough space for the largest key value. When the range in sizes is large, storage may be wasted, and another node format may be better (i.e., the format n, A_0, α_1, α_2, $\cdots$, α_n, (K_1,A_1), $\cdots$, (K_n,A_n), where α_i is the address of K_i in internal memory, i.e., K_i = memory (α_i)). In this case, a binary search of the node can still be made. The use of variable-size nodes is not recommended, since this would require a more complex storage management system. More importantly, the use of variable-size nodes would result in degraded performance during insertion, as insertion into a node requires requesting a larger node to accommodate the new value being inserted. Consequently, nodes of a fixed size should be used. The size should allow for at least $m - 1$ key values of the largest size. During insertions, however, we can relax the requirement that each node have $\leq m - 1$ key values. Instead, a node will be allowed to hold as many values as can fit into it and will contain at least $\lceil m/2 \rceil - 1$ values. The resulting performance will be at least as good as that of a B-tree of order m. Another possibility is to use some kind of key sampling scheme to reduce the key value size so as not to exceed some predetermined size d. Some possibilities are truncating prefixes and suffixes, removing vowels, etc. Whatever scheme is used, some provision will have to be made for handling synonyms (i.e., distinct key values that have the same sampled value).

EXERCISES

1. Show that all B-trees of order 2 are full binary trees.

2. (a) Insert the keys 62, 5, 85, and 75 one at a time into the order-5 B-tree of Figure 10.39. Show the new tree after each key is added. Do the insertion using the insertion process described in the text.

    (b) Assuming that the tree is kept on a disk and one node may be retrieved at a time, how many disk accesses are needed to make each insertion? State any assumptions you make.

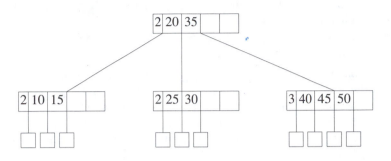

Figure 10.39: B-tree of order 5

(c) Delete the keys 45, 40, 10, and 25 from the order-5 B-tree of Figure 10.39. Show the tree following each deletion. The deletions are to be performed using the deletion process described in the text.

(d) How many disk accesses are made for each of the deletions?

3. Complete line 46 of algorithm *BtreeDelete* (Program 10.13).

4. Write insertion and deletion algorithms for B-trees assuming that with each key value is associated an additional field, f, such that $f = 1$ iff the corresponding key value has not been deleted. Deletions should be accomplished by setting the corresponding $f = 0$, and insertions should make use of deleted space whenever possible without restructuring the tree.

5. Write algorithms to search and delete keys from a B-tree by position; that is, *search* (k) finds the kth smallest key, and *delete* (k) deletes the kth smallest key in the tree. (Hint: To do this efficiently, additional information must be kept in each node. With each pair (K_i, A_i) keep $N_i = \Sigma_{j=0}^{i-1}$ (number of key values in the subtree $A_j + 1$).) What are the worst-case computing times of your algorithms?

6. The text assumed a node structure that was sequential. However, we need to perform the following functions on a B-tree node: search, insert, delete, join, and split.

(a) Explain why each of the these functions is important during a search, insert, and delete operation in the B-tree.

(b) Explain how a red-black tree could be used to represent each node. You will need to use integer pointers and regard each red-black tree as embedded in an array.

(c) What kind of performance gain/loss do you expect using red-black trees for each node instead of a sequential organization? Try to quantify your answer.

7. Modify algorithm *BtreeInsert* (Program 10.12) so that when node *P* has *m* keys, we first check to see if either the nearest left sibling or the nearest right sibling of *P* has fewer than $m - 1$ key values. If so, *P* is not split. Instead, a rotation is performed moving either the smallest or largest key in *P* to its parent. The corresponding key in the parent, together with a subtree, is moved to the sibling of *P* that has space for another key value.

8. [***Bayer and McCreight***] The idea of the preceding exercise can be extended to obtain improved B-tree performance. If the nearest sibling, *Q*, of *P* already has $m - 1$ key values, then we can split both *P* and *Q* to obtain three nodes *P*, *Q*, and *R* with each node containing $\lfloor (2m - 2)/3 \rfloor$, $\lfloor (2m - 1)/3 \rfloor$, and $\lfloor 2m/3 \rfloor$ key values. Figure 10.40 describes the splitting procedure when *Q* is *P*'s nearest right sibling.

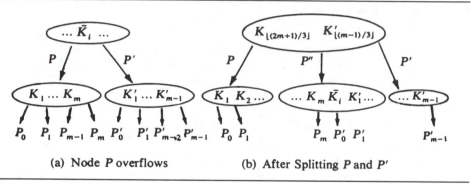

(a) **Node *P* overflows**   (b) **After Splitting *P* and *P'***

Figure 10.40: Splitting *P* and its nearest right sibling, *P´*

Rewrite algorithm *BtreeInsert* so that node splittings occur only as described here.

9. A *B*-tree*, *t*, of order *m* is a search tree that either is empty or satisfies the following properties:

    (a)   The root node has at least two and at most $2\lfloor (2m - 2)/3 \rfloor + 1$ children.

    (b)   The remaining nonfailure nodes have at most *m* and at least $\lceil (2m - 1)/3 \rceil$ children each.

    (c)   All failure nodes are on the same level.

    For a B*-tree of order *m* that contains *N* key values, show that if $x = \lceil (2m - 1)/3 \rceil$, then

    (a)   the height, *h*, of the B*-tree satisfies $h \le 1 + \log_x\{(N + 1)/2\}$

    (b)   the number of nodes *p* in the B*-tree satisifies $p \le 1 + (N - 1)/(x - 1)$

    What is the average number of splits per insert if a B*-tree is built up starting from an empty B*-tree?

10. Using the splitting technique of Exercise 8, write an algorithm to insert a new key value, x, into a B*-tree, t, of order m. How many disk accesses are made in the worst case and on the average? Assume that t was initially of depth l and that t is maintained on a disk. Each access retrieves or writes one node.

11. Write an algorithm to delete the identifier x from the B*-tree, t, of order m. What is the maximum number of accesses needed to delete x from a B*-tree of depth l? Make the same assumptions as in Exercise 10.

12. The basic idea of a B-tree may be modified to obtain a B'-tree. A B'-tree of order m is similar to a B-tree of order m except that in a B'-tree all identifiers are placed in leaf nodes. If P is a nonleaf node in a B'-tree and is of degree j, then the node format for P is $j, L(1), L(2), \cdots, L(j-1)$, where $L(i), 1 \le i < j$, is the value of the largest key in the ith subtree of P. Figure 10.41 shows a B'-tree of order 5. Notice that in a B'-tree, the key values in the leaf nodes increase from left to right. Only the leaf nodes contain such information as the address of records having that key value. If there are n key values in the tree, then there are n leaf nodes. Write an algorithm to search for x in a B'-tree t of order m. How many disk accesses are needed?

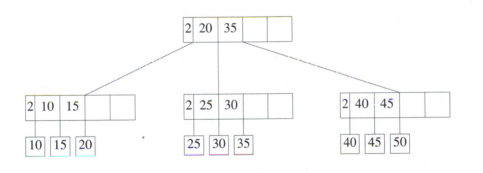

Figure 10.41: Example of a B'-tree

13. For a B'-tree of order m write an algorithm to insert x. How many disk accesses are needed?

14. Write an algorithm to delete x from a B'-tree, t, of order m. Since all key values are in leaf nodes, this deletion always corresponds to a deletion from a leaf. What is the number of disk accesses?

15. Let T and U be two B'-trees of order m. Let V be a B'-tree of order m containing all key values in T and U. Write an algorithm to construct V from T and U. How many disk accesses are made?

16. Obtain search, insert, and delete algorithms for B'-trees of order m. If the tree resides on disk, how many disk accesses are needed in the worst case for each of the three operations? Assume the tree has n leaf nodes.

17. [***Programming Project***] Evaluate the relative performance of B-trees, B*-trees, and B'-trees for search, insert, and delete operations.

10.7   SPLAY TREES

We have studied balanced search trees that allow one to perform operations such as search, insert, delete, join, and split in O(log n) worst-case time per operation. In the case of priority queues, we saw that if we are interested in amortized complexity rather than worst-case complexity, simpler structures can be used. This is also true for search trees. Using a splay tree, we can perform the operations in O(log n) amortized time per operation.

A *splay tree* is a binary search tree in which each search, insert, delete, and join operation is performed in the same way as in an ordinary binary search tree (see Chapter 5) except that each of these operations is followed by a *splay*. A splay consists of a sequence of rotations. In a split, however, we first perform a splay. This makes the split very easy to perform. For simplicity, we assume that each of the operations is always successful. A failure can be modeled as a different successful operation. For example, an unsuccesful search may be modeled as a search for the element in the last node encountered in the unsuccessful search, and an unsuccessful insert may be modeled as a successful search. With this assumption, the start node for a splay is obtained as follows:

(1) *search*: The splay starts at the node containing the element being sought.

(2) *insert*: The start node for the splay is the newly inserted node.

(3) *delete*: The parent of the physically deleted node is used as the start node for the splay. If this node is the root, then no splay is done.

(4) *ThreeWayJoin*: No splay is done.

(5) *split*: Suppose that we are splitting with respect to the key i and that key i is actually present in the tree. We first perform a splay at the node that contains i and then split the tree. As we shall see, splitting following a splay is very simple.

Splay rotations are performed along the path from the start node to the root of the binary search tree. These rotations are similar to those performed for AVL trees and red-black trees. Let q be the node at which the splay is being performed. Initially, q is the node at which the splay starts. The following steps define a splay:

(1) If q either is **nil** or the root, then the splay terminates.

(2) If q has a parent, p, but no grandparent, then the rotation of Figure 10.42 is performed, and the splay terminates.

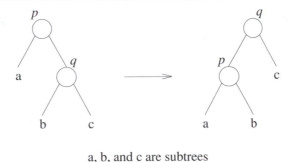

a, b, and c are subtrees

Figure 10.42: Rotation when q is a right child and has no grandparent

(3)   If q has a parent, p, and a grandparent, gp, then the rotation is classified as LL (p is the left child of gp, and q is the left child of p), LR (p is the left child of gp, and q is the right child of p), RR, or RL. The RR and RL rotations are shown in Figure 10.43. LL and LR rotations are symmetric to these. The splay is repeated at the new location of q.

Notice that all rotations move q up the tree and that following a splay, q becomes the new root of the search tree. As a result, splitting the tree with respect to a key, i, is done simply by performing a splay at i and then splitting at the root. Figure 10.44 shows a binary search tree before, during, and after a splay at node *.

In the case of Fibonnaci heaps, we obtained the amortized complexity of an operation by using an explicit cross-charging scheme. The analysis for splay trees will use a *potential* technique. Let P_0 be the initial potential of the search tree, and let P_i be its potential following the ith operation in a sequence of n operations. The amortized time for the ith operation is defined to be

$$\text{(actual time for the } i\text{th operation)} + P_i - P_{i-1}$$

That is, the amortized time is the actual time plus the change in the potential. Rearranging terms, we see that the actual time for the ith operation is

$$\text{(amortized time for the } i\text{th operation)} + P_{i-1} - P_i$$

Hence, the actual time needed to perform the n operations in the sequence is

$$\sum_i \text{(amortized time for the } i\text{th operation)} + P_0 - P_n$$

Since each operation other than a join involves a splay whose actual complexity is of the same order as that of the whole operation, and since each join takes $O(1)$ time, it is sufficient to consider only the time spent performing splays.

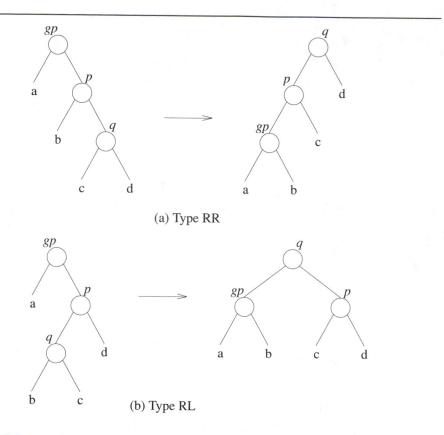

(a) Type RR

(b) Type RL

Figure 10.43: RR and RL rotations

Each splay consists of several rotations. We shall assign to each rotation a fixed cost of one unit. The choice of a potential function is rather arbitrary. The objective is to use one that results in as small a bound on the time complexity as is possible. We now define the potential function we shall use. Let the size, $s(i)$, of the subtree with root i be the total number of nodes in it. The rank, $r(i)$, of node i is equal to $\lfloor \log_2 s(i) \rfloor$. The potential of the tree is $\sum_i r(i)$. The potential of an empty tree is defined to be zero.

Suppose that in the tree of Figure 10.44(a), the subtrees a, b, $\cdots$, j are all empty. Then $(s(1), \cdots, s(9)) = (9, 6, 3, 2, 1, 4, 5, 7, 8)$; $r(3) = r(4) = 1$; $r(5) = 0$; and $r(9) = 3$. In Lemma 10.2 we use r and r', respectively, to denote the rank of a node before and after a rotation.

Lemma 10.2: Consider a binary search tree that has n elements/nodes. The amortized cost of a splay operation that begins at node q is at most $3(\lfloor \log_2 n \rfloor - r(q)) + 1$.

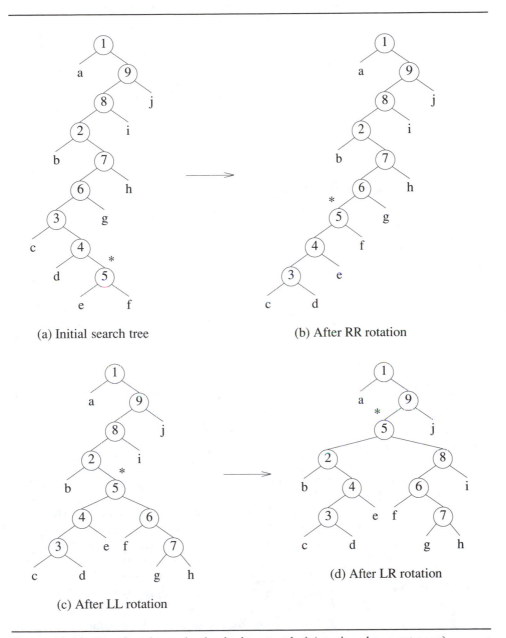

(a) Initial search tree

(b) After RR rotation

(c) After LL rotation

(d) After LR rotation

Figure 10.44: Rotations in a splay beginning at node * (continued on next page)

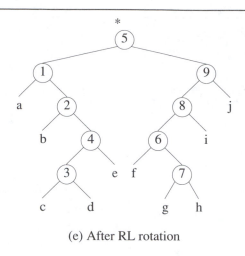

(e) After RL rotation

Figure 10.44: Rotations in a splay beginning at node *

Proof: Consider the three steps in the definition of a splay:

(1) In this case, q either is **nil** or the root. This step does not alter the potential of the tree, so its amortized and actual costs are the same. This cost is 1.

(2) In this step, the rotation of Figure 10.42 (or the symmetric rotation for the case when q is the left child of p) is performed. Since only the ranks of p and q are affected, the potential change, ΔP, is $r'(p) + r'(q) - r(p) - r(q)$. Further, since $r'(p) \le r(p)$, $\Delta P \le r'(q) - r(q)$. The amortized cost of this step (actual cost plus potential change) is, therefore, no more than $r'(q) - r(q) + 1$.

(3) In this step only the ranks of q, p, and gp change. So, $\Delta P = r'(q) + r'(p) + r'(gp) - r(q) - r(p) - r(gp)$. Since, $r(gp) = r'(q)$, $\Delta P = r'p + r'(gp) - r(q) - r(p)$.

Consider an RR rotation. From Figure 10.43(a), we see that $r'(p) \le r'(q)$, $r'(gp) \le r'(q)$, and $r(q) \le r(p)$. So, $\Delta P \le 2(r'(q) - r(q))$. If $r'(q) > r(q)$, $\Delta P \le 3(r'(q) - r(q)) - 1$. If $r'(q) = r(q)$, then $r'(q) = r(q) = r(p) = r(gp)$. Also, $s'(q) > s(q) + s'(gp)$. Consequently, $r'(gp) < r'(q)$. To see this, note that if $r'(gp) = r'(q)$, then $s'(q) > 2^{r'(q)} + 2^{r'(gp)} = 2^{r'(q)+1}$, which violates the definition of rank. Hence, $\Delta P \le 2(r'(q) - r(q)) - 1 = 3(r'(q) - r(q)) - 1$. So, the amortized cost of an RR rotation is at most $1 + 3(r'(q) - r(q)) - 1 = 3(r'(q) - r(q))$.

This bound may be obtained for LL, LR, and RL rotations in a similar way.

The lemma now follows by observing that Steps 1 and 2 are mutually exclusive and can occur at most once. Step 3 occurs zero or more times. Summing up over the amortized cost of a single occurrence of Steps 1 or 2 and all occurrences of Step 3, we obtain the bound of the lemma. □

Theorem 10.1: The total time needed for a sequence of n search, insert, delete, join, and split operations performed on a collection of initially empty splay trees is $O(n \log i)$, where $i, i > 0$, is the number of inserts in the sequence.

Proof: Since none of the splay trees has more than i nodes, no node has rank more than $\lfloor \log_2 i \rfloor$. A search (excluding the splay) does not change the rank of any node and hence does not affect the potential of the splay tree involved. An insert (excluding the splay) increases, by one, the size of every node on the path from the root to the newly inserted node. This causes the ranks of the nodes with size $2^k - 1$ to change. There are at most $\lfloor \log_2 i \rfloor + 1$ such nodes on any insert path. So, each insert (excluding the splay) increases the potential by at most this much. Each join increases the total potential of all the splay trees by at most $\lfloor \log_2 i \rfloor$. Deletions do not increase the potential of the involved splay tree except for any increase that results from the splay step. The split operation (excluding the splay step) reduces the overall potential by an amount equal to the rank of the tree just before the split (but after the splay that precedes it). So, the potential increase, PI, attributable to the n operations (exclusive of that attributable to the splay steps of the operations) is $O(n \log i)$.

From our definition of the amortized cost of a splay operation, it follows that the time for the sequence of operations is the sum of the amortized costs of the splays, the potential change $P_0 - P_n$, and PI. From Lemma 10.2, it follows that the sum of the amortized costs is $O(n \log i)$. The initial potential, P_0, is 0, and the final potential, P_n, is ≥ 0. So, the total time is $O(n \log i)$. $\square$

EXERCISES

1. Obtain figures corresponding to Figures 10.42 and 10.43 for the symmetric splay rotations.

2. What is the maximum height of a splay tree that is created as the result of n insertions made into an initially empty splay tree? Give an example of a sequence of inserts that results in a splay tree of this height.

3. Complete the proof of Lemma 10.2 by providing the proof for the case of an RL rotation. Note that the proofs for LL and LR rotations are similar to those for RR and RL rotations, respectively, as the rotations are symmetric.

4. Explain how a two-way join should be performed in a splay tree so that the amortized cost of each splay tree operation remains $O(\log n)$.

5. Explain how a split with respect to key i is to be performed when key i is not present in the splay tree. The amortized cost of each splay tree operation should be $O(\log n)$.

6. [*Sleator and Tarjan*] Suppose we modify the definition of $s(i)$ used in connection with the complexity analysis of splay trees. Let each node i have a positive weight $p(i)$. Let $s(i)$ be the sum of the weights of all nodes in the subtree with root i. The rank of this subtree is $\log_2 s(i)$.

(a) Let t be a splay tree. Show that the amortized cost of a splay that begins at node q is at most $3(r(t) - r(q)) + 1$, where r is the rank just before the splay.

(b) Let S be a sequence of n inserts and m searches. Assume that each of the n inserts adds a new element to the splay tree and that all searches are successful. Let $p(i)$, $p(i) > 0$, be the number of times element i is sought. The $p(i)$'s satisfy the following equality:

$$\sum_{i=1}^{n} p(i) = m$$

Show that the total time spent on the m searches is

$$O(m + \sum_{i=1}^{n} p(i) \log(m/p(i)))$$

Note that since $\Omega(m + \sum_{i=1}^{n} p(i) \log(m/p(i)))$ is an information theoretic bound on the search time in a static search tree (the optimal binary search tree of Section 10.1 is an example of such a tree), splay trees are optimal to within a constant factor for the representation of a static set of elements.

10.8 DIGITAL SEARCH TREES

10.8.1 Definition

A *digital search tree* is a binary tree in which each node contains one element. The element-to-node assignment is determined by the binary representation of the element keys. Suppose that we number the bits in the binary representation of a key from left to right beginning at one. Then bit one of 1000 is 1, and bits two, three, and four are 0. All keys in the left subtree of a node at level i have bit i equal to zero whereas those in the right subtree of nodes at this level have bit $i = 1$. Figure 10.45(a) shows a digital search tree. This tree contains the keys 1000, 0010, 1001, 0001, 1100, and 0000.

Suppose we are to search for the key $k = 0011$ in the tree of Figure 10.45(a). k is first compared with the key in the root. Since k is different from the key in the root, and since bit one of k is 0, we move to the left child, b, of the root. Now, since k is different from the key in node b, and bit two of k is 0, we move to the left child, d, of b. Since k is different from the key in node d and since bit three of k is one, we move to the right child of d. Node d has no right child to move to. From this we conclude that $k = 0011$ is not in the search tree. If we wish to insert k into the tree, then it is to be added as the right child of d. When this is done, we get the digital search tree of Figure 10.45(b).

The digital search tree procedures to search and insert are quite similar to the corresponding procedures for binary search trees. The essential difference is that the subtree to move to is determined by a bit in the search key rather than by the result of the comparison of the search key and the key in the current node. The deletion of an item in

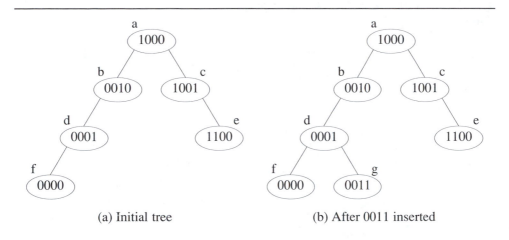

(a) Initial tree (b) After 0011 inserted

Figure 10.45: Digital search trees

a leaf is done by removing the leaf node. To delete from any other node, the deleted item must be replaced by a value from any leaf in its subtree and that leaf removed.

Each of these operations can be performed in $O(h)$ time, where h is the height of the digital search tree. If each key in a digital search tree has *KeySize* bits, then the height of the digital search tree is at most *KeySize* + 1.

10.8.2 Binary Tries

When we are dealing with very long keys, the cost of a key comparison is high. We can reduce the number of key comparisons to one by using a related structure called *Patricia* (*P*ractical *a*lgorithm *t*o *r*etrieve *i*nformation *c*oded *i*n *a*lphanumeric). We shall develop this structure in three steps. First, we introduce a structure called a binary trie. Then we transform binary tries into compressed binary tries. Finally, from compressed binary tries we obtain Patricia. Since binary tries and compressed binary tries are introduced only as a means of arriving at Patricia, we do not dwell much on how to manipulate these structures. A more general version of binary tries (called a trie) is considered later.

A *binary trie* is a binary tree that has two kinds of nodes: *branch nodes* and *element nodes*. A branch node has the two fields *LeftChild* and *RightChild*. It has no *data* field. An element node has the single field *data*. Branch nodes are used to build a binary tree search structure similar to that of a digital search tree. This search structure leads to element nodes.

Figure 10.46 shows a six-element binary trie. To search for an element with key k, we use a branching pattern determined by the bits of k. The ith bit of k is used at level i.

If it is zero, the search moves to the left subtree. Otherwise, it moves to the right subtree. To search for 0010 we first follow the left child, then again the left child, and finally the right child.

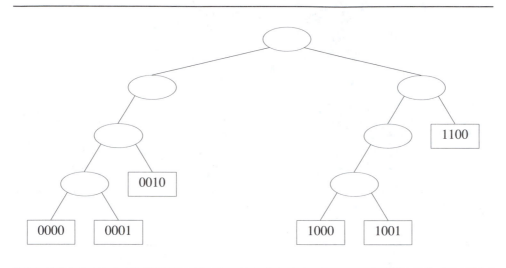

Figure 10.46: Example of a binary trie

Observe that a successful search in a binary trie always ends at an element node. Once this element node is reached, the key in this node is compared with the key we are searching for. This is the only key comparison that takes place. An unsuccessful search may terminate either at an element node or at a **nil** pointer.

The binary trie of Figure 10.46 contains branch nodes whose degree is one. By adding another field, *BitNumber*, to each branch node, we can eliminate all degree-one branch nodes from the trie. The *BitNumber* field of a branch node gives the bit number of the key that is to be used at this node. Figure 10.47 gives the binary trie that results from the elimination of degree-one branch nodes from the binary trie of Figure 10.46. The number outside a node is its *BitNumber*. A binary trie that has been modified in this way to contain no branch nodes of degree one is called a *compressed binary trie*.

10.8.3   Patricia

Compressed binary tries may be represented using nodes of a single type. The new nodes, called *augmented branch nodes*, are the original branch nodes augmented by the field *data*. The resulting structure is called *Patricia* and is obtained from a compressed binary trie in the following way:

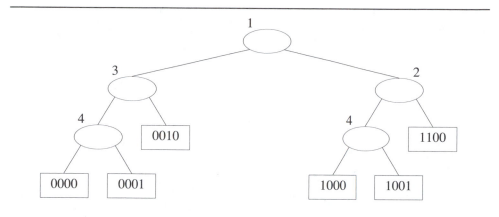

Figure 10.47: Binary trie of Figure 10.46 with degree-one nodes eliminated

(1)   Replace each branch node by an augmented branch node.

(2)   Eliminate the element nodes.

(3)   Store the data previously in the element nodes in the data fields of the augmented branch nodes. Since every nonempty compressed binary trie has one less branch node than it has element nodes, it is necessary to add one augmented branch node. This node is called the *head node*. The remaining structure is the left subtree of the head node. The head node has *BitNumber* equal to zero. Its right-child field is not used. The assignment of data to augmented branch nodes is done in such a way that the *BitNumber* in the augmented branch node is less than or equal to that in the parent of the element node that contained this data.

(4)   Replace the original pointers to element nodes by pointers to the respective augmented branch nodes.

When these transformations are performed on the compressed trie of Figure 10.47, we get the structure of Figure 10.48. Let *t* be an instance of Patricia. *t* is **nil** iff the instance is empty. An instance, *t*, with one element is represented by a head node whose left-child field points to itself (Figure 10.49(a)).

We can distinguish between pointers that pointed originally to branch nodes and those that pointed to element nodes by noting that, in Patricia, the former pointers are directed to nodes with a greater *BitNumber* value, whereas pointers of the latter type are directed to nodes whose *BitNumber* value either is equal to or less than that in the node where the pointer originates.

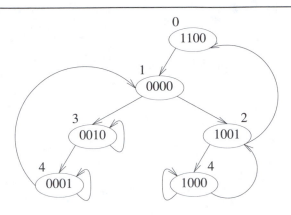

Figure 10.48: An example of Patricia

10.8.3.1 Search

To search for an element with key k, we begin at the head node and follow a path determined by the bits in k. When an element pointer is followed, the key in the node reached is compared with k. This is the only key comparison made. No comparisons are made on the way down. Suppose we wish to search for $k = 0000$ in the Patricia instance of Figure 10.48. We begin at the head node and follow the left-child pointer to the node with 0000. The bit-number field of this node is 1. Since bit one of k is 0, we follow the left child pointer to the node with 0010. Now bit three of k is used. Since this is 0, the search moves to the node with 0001. The bit-number field of this node is 4. The fourth bit of k is zero, so we follow the left-child pointer. This brings us to a node with bit-number field less than that of the node we moved from. Hence, an element pointer was used. Comparing the key in this node with k, we find a match, and the search is successful.

Next, suppose that we are to search for $k = 1011$. We begin at the head node. The search moves successively to the nodes with 0000, 1001, 1000, and 1001. k is compared with 1001. Since k is not equal to 1001, we conclude that there is no element with this key. The procedure to search an instance t of Patricia is given in Program 10.14. This procedure returns, in y, a pointer to the last node encountered in the search. If the key in this node is k, the search is successful. Otherwise, t contains no element with key k. The function $bit(i, j)$ returns the jth bit (the leftmost bit is bit one) of i.

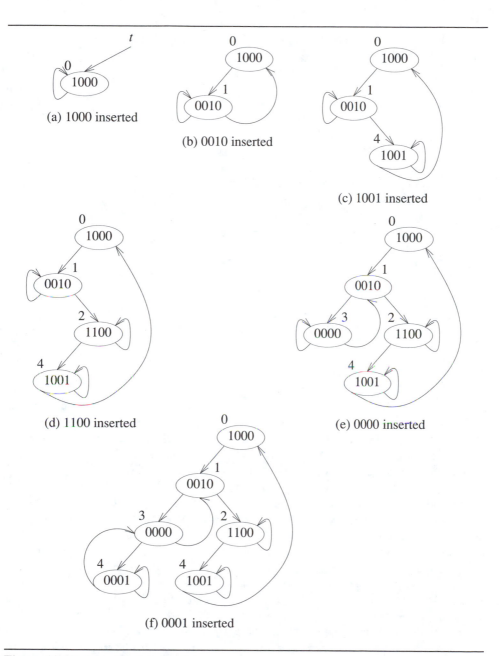

Figure 10.49: Insertion into Patricia

```
procedure PatriciaSearch (t : Patricia ; k : KeyType ; var y : Patricia );
{Search t for the key k.  y is set to point to the last node encountered.}
var p : Patricia;
begin
   if t = nil
   then y := nil {t is empty}
   else begin
           y := t ↑. LeftChild; {move to left child of head node}
           p := t; {p is the parent of y}
           while y ↑. BitNumber > p ↑. BitNumber do
           begin {follow a branch pointer}
               p := y;
               if bit (k, y ↑. BitNumber) = 0 then y := y ↑. LeftChild
                                              else y := y ↑. RightChild;
           end;
       end;
end; {of PatriciaSearch}
```

Program 10.14: Searching Patricia

10.8.3.2   Insertion

Let us now examine how we can insert new elements. Suppose we begin with an empty instance and wish to insert an element with key 1000. The result is an instance that has only a head node (Figure 10.49(a)). Next, consider inserting an element with key $k = 0010$. First, we search for this key using procedure *PatriciaSearch* (Program 10.14). The search terminates at the head node. Since 0010 is not equal to the key $q = 1000$ in this node, we know that 0010 is not currently in the Patricia instance, so the element may be inserted. For this, the keys k and q are compared to determine the first (i.e., leftmost) bit at which they differ. This is bit one. A new node containing the element with key k is added as the left-child of the head node. Since bit one of k is zero, the left child field of this new node points to itself, and its right-child field points to the head node. The bit-number field is set to 1. The resulting Patricia instance is shown in Figure 10.49(b).

Suppose that the next element to be inserted has $k = 1001$. The search for this key ends at the node with $q = 1000$. The first bit at which k and q differ is bit $j = 4$. Now we search the instance of Figure 10.49(b) using only the first $j - 1 = 3$ bits of k. The last move is from the node with 0010 to that with 1000. Since this is a right-child move, a new node containing the element with key k is to be inserted as the right child of 0010. The bit-number field of this node is set to $j = 4$. As bit four of k is 1, the right-child field of the new node points to itself and its left-child field points to the node with q. Figure 10.49(c) shows the resulting structure.

To insert $k = 1100$ into Figure 10.49(c), we first search for this key. Once again, $q = 1000$. The first bit at which k and q differ is $j = 2$. The search using only the first $j - 1$ bits ends at the node with 1001. The last move is a right child move from 0010. A new node containing the element with key k and bit-number field $j = 2$ is added as the right child of 0010. Since bit j of k is one, the right-child field of the new node points to itself. Its left-child field points to the node with 1001 (this was previously the right child of 0010). The new Patricia instance is shown in Figure 10.49(d). Figure 10.49(e) shows the result of inserting an element with key 0000, and Figure 10.49(f) shows the Patricia instance following the insertion of 0001.

The preceding discussion leads to the insertion procedure *PatriciaInsert* (Program 10.15). Its complexity is $O(h)$, where h is the height of t. h can be as large as $\min\{KeySize + 1, n\}$, where $KeySize$ is the number of bits in a key and n is the number of elements. When the keys are uniformly distributed, the height is $O(\log n)$. We leave the development of the deletion procedure as an exercise.

EXERCISES

1. Write the digital search tree procedures for the search, insert, and delete operations. Assume that each key has $KeySize$ bits and that the function $bit(k, i)$ returns the ith (from the left) bit of the key k. Show that each of your procedures has complexity $O(h)$, where h is the height of the digital search tree.

2. Write the binary trie procedures for the search, insert, and delete operations. Assume that each key has $KeySize$ bits and that the function $bit(k, i)$ returns the ith (from the left) bit of the key k. Show that each of your procedures has complexity $O(h)$, where h is the height of the binary trie.

3. Write the compressed binary trie procedures for the search, insert, and delete operations. Assume that each key has $KeySize$ bits and that the function $bit(k, i)$ returns the ith (from the left) bit of the key k. Show that each of your procedures has complexity $O(h)$, where h is the height of the compressed binary trie.

4. Write a procedure to delete the element with key k from the Patricia instance t. The complexity of your procedure should be $O(h)$, where h is the height of t. Show that this is the case.

10.9 TRIES

10.9.1 Definition

A trie is an index structure that is particulary useful when key values are of varying size. This data structure is a generalization of the binary trie that was developed in the preceding section.

A *trie* is a tree of degree $m \geq 2$ in which the branching at any level is determined not by the entire key value, but by only a portion of it. As an example, consider the trie

---

```
procedure PatriciaInsert (var t : Patricia; x : element );
{Insert x into the Patricia instance t.}
var p, s, y, z : Patricia; j : integer; k : KeyType ;
begin
   if t = nil
   then begin {t is empty}
           new (t); t ↑. BitNumber := 0; t ↑. data := x; t ↑.LeftChild := t;
       end
   else begin
           k := x.key ;
           PatriciaSearch (t, k, y);
           if k = y ↑. data. key then InsertionError
           else begin
               {find first bit where k and y ↑. data.key differ}
               j := 1; while bit (k, j) = bit (y ↑. data. key, j) do j := j + 1;

               {Search t using first j − 1 bits of k}
               s := t ↑. LeftChild; p := t;
               while (s ↑. BitNumber > p ↑. BitNumber ) and (s ↑. BitNumber < j) do
               begin
                 p := s ;
                 if bit (k, s ↑. BitNumber ) = 0 then s := s ↑. LeftChild
                                                 else s := s ↑. RightChild;
               end;

               {Insert x as a child of p}
               new (z);
               with z do
               begin
                 data := x ; BitNumber := j;
                 if bit (k, j) = 0 then begin LeftChild := z; RightChild := s; end
                                   else begin LeftChild := s; RightChild := z; end;
               end;
               if s = p ↑. LeftChild then p ↑. LeftChild := z
                                     else p ↑. RightChild := z;
           end;
       end;
end; {of PatriciaInsert}
```

Program 10.15: Insertion into Patricia

of Figure 10.50. The trie contains two types of nodes: *element node*, and *branch node*. An element node has only a data field; a branch node contains pointers to subtrees. Since we assume that each character is one of the 26 letters of the alphabet, a branch node has 27 pointer fields. The extra pointer field is used for the blank character (denoted þ). This character is used to terminate all keys, as a trie requires that no key be a prefix of another (see Figure 10.51).

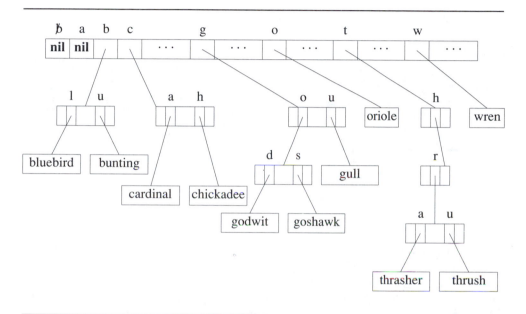

Figure 10.50: Trie created using characters of key value from left to right, one at a time

At the first level all key values are partitioned into disjoint classes depending on their first character. Thus, $t\uparrow.link[i]$ points to a subtrie containing all key values beginning with the ith letter (t is the root of the trie). On the jth level the branching is determined by the jth character. When a subtrie contains only one key value, it is replaced by a node of type element. This node contains the key value, together with other relevant information, such as the address of the record with this key value.

10.9.2 Searching a Trie

Searching a trie for a key value x requires breaking up x into its constituent characters and following the branches determined by these characters. The function *SearchTrie* (Program 10.16) assumes that $p = $ **nil** is not a branch node and that $p\uparrow.key$ is the key value represented in p if p is an element node.

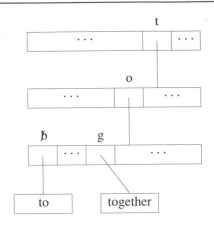

Figure 10.51: Trie showing need for a terminal character (in this case a blank)

function *SearchTrie*(**var** *t,p* : *TriePointer* ; *x* : *key*) : *TriePointer*;
{Search a trie *t* for key value *x*. It is assumed that branching on the *i*th level is determined by the *i*th character of the key value.}
var *c* : **char**; *i,k* : **integer**;
begin
{Assume we can always concatenate at least one trailing blank to *x*.}
k := *x* ; *concatenate* (*k*,' ');
i := 1; *p* := *t*;
while *p* is a branch node **do**
  begin
      c := *i*th character of *k*;
      p := *p* ↑. *link* [*c*];
      i := *i* + 1;
  end;
if *p* = **nil or** *p* ↑. *key* < > *x* **then** *trie* := **nil**
                                         else *trie* := *p*
end; {of *SearchTrie*}

Program 10.16: Searching a trie

Analysis of *SearchTrie*: The search algorithm for tries is very straightforward, and one may readily verify that the worst-case search time is $O(l)$, where l is the number of levels in the trie (including both branch and element nodes).

In the case of an index, all trie nodes will reside on disk, so at most l disk accesses will be made during search. When the nodes reside on disk, the Pascal pointer type cannot be used, as Pascal does not allow input/output of pointers. The link field will now be implemented as an integer. ☐

10.9.3   Sampling Strategies

Given a set of key values to be represented in an index, the number of levels in the trie will depend on the strategy or key sampling technique used to determine the branching at each level. This can be defined by a sampling function, *sample* (x,i), which appropriately samples x for branching at the ith level. In the trie of Figure 10.50 and in the search algorithm *SearchTrie* (Program 10.16) this function is *sample* $(x,i) = i$th character of x. Some other choices for this function are

(1)   *sample* $(x,i) = x_{n-i+1}$

(2)   *sample* $(x,i) = x_{r(x,i)}$ for $r(x,i)$ a randomization function

(3)   *sample* $(x,i) = \begin{cases} x_{i/2} \text{ if } i \text{ is even} \\ x_{n-(i-1)/2} \text{ if } i \text{ is odd} \end{cases}$

where $x = x_1 x_2 \cdots x_n$.

For each of these functions, one may easily construct key value sets for which the particular function is best (i.e., it results in a trie with the fewest number of levels). The trie of Figure 10.50 has five levels. Using function (1) on the same key values yields the trie of Figure 10.52, which has only three levels. An optimal sampling function for this data set will yield a trie that has only two levels (Figure 10.53). Choosing the optimal sampling function for any particular set of values is very difficult. In a dynamic situation, with insertion and deletion, we wish to optimize average performance. In the absence of any further information on key values, probably the best choice would be function (2).

Although all our examples of sampling have involved single-character sampling we need not restrict ourselves to this. The key value may be interpreted as consisting of digits using any radix we desire. Using a radix of 27^2 would result in two-character sampling. Other radixes would give different samplings.

The maximum number of levels in a trie can be kept low by adopting a different strategy for element nodes. These nodes can be designed to hold more than one key value. If the maximum number of levels allowed is l, then all key values that are synonyms up to level $l - 1$ are entered into the same element node. If the sampling function is chosen correctly, there will be only a few synonyms in each element node. The element node will therefore be small and can be processed in internal memory. Figure

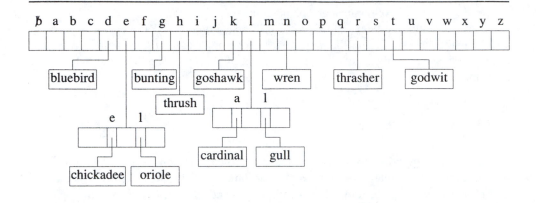

Figure 10.52: Trie constructed for data of Figure 10.50 sampling one character at a time, from right to left

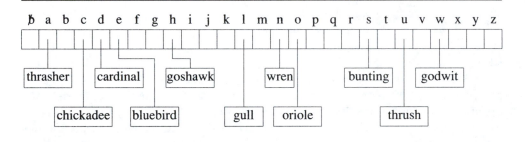

Figure 10.53: An optimal trie for the data of Figure 10.50 sampling on the first level done by using the fourth character of the key values

10.54 shows the use of this strategy on the trie of Figure 10.50 with $l = 3$. In further discussion we shall, for simplicity, assume that the sampling function in use is *sample* (x, i) = ith character of x and that no restriction is placed on the number of levels in the trie.

10.9.4 Insertion into a Trie

Insertion into a trie is straightforward. We shall illustrate the procedure by two examples and leave the formal writing of the algorithm as an exercise. Let us consider the trie of Figure 10.50 and insert into it the keys bobwhite and bluejay. First, we have $x =$

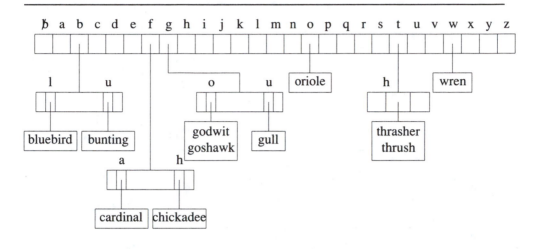

Figure 10.54: Trie obtained for data of Figure 10.50 when number of levels is limited to 3; keys have been sampled from left to right, one character at a time

bobwhite and we attempt to search for bobwhite. This leads us to node σ, where we discover that $\sigma.link[\text{'o'}] = \textbf{nil}$. Hence, x is not in the trie and may be inserted here (see Figure 10.55). Next, $x = $ bluejay, and a search of the trie leads us to the element node that contains bluebird. The keys bluebird and bluejay are sampled until the sampling results in two different values. This happens at the fifth letter. Figure 10.55 shows the trie after both insertions.

10.9.5 Deletion from a Trie

Once again, we shall not present the deletion algorithm formally but will look at two examples to illustrate some of the ideas involved in deleting entries from a trie. From the trie of Figure 10.55, let us first delete bobwhite. To do this we set $\sigma.link[\text{'o'}]$ equal to **nil**. No other changes need to be made. Next, let us delete bluejay. This deletion leaves us with only one key value in the subtrie, δ_3. This means that the node δ_3 may be deleted, and ρ can be moved up one level. The same can be done for nodes δ_1 and δ_2. Finally, the node σ is reached. The subtrie with root σ has more than one key value. Therefore, ρ cannot be moved up any more levels, and we set $\sigma.link[\text{'l'}]$ equal to ρ. To facilitate deletions from tries, it is useful to add a *count* field in each branch node. This field contains the number of children the node has.

As in the case of binary tries, we can define compressed tries in which each branch node has at least two children. In this case, each branch node is augmeneted to have an

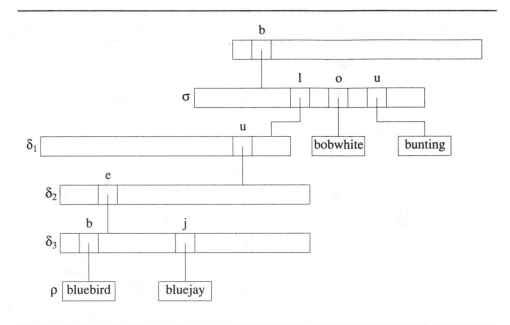

Figure 10.55: Section of trie of Figure 10.50 showing changes resulting from inserting bobwhite and bluejay

additional field, *skip*, that indicates the number of levels of branching that have been eliminated (alternately, we can have a field, *sample*, that indicates the sampling level to use).

10.9.6   Node Structure

So far, we have assumed that each branch node has a number of pointer fields equal to the number of distinct values for *sample*(*x*,*i*). This permits an access time of O(1) for any pointer in the node. However, many of the pointer fields in a branch node can be expected to be **nil**. We can improve the space requirements of tries at the expense of increased pointer access time. One possibility is to set up each node as a hash table of pointers. In this case, Pascal pointers cannot be used. Rather, we must simulate pointers using integers. The use of hash tables results in an expected access time of O(1) per (simulated) pointer. Another possibility is to represent each branch node as a linked list (chain) in which each node represents one of the non-**nil** pointers of the branch node. The access time for a pointer is now linear in the number of nodes on the chain.

EXERCISES

1. (a) Draw the trie obtained for the following data:

   AMIOT, AVENGER, AVRO, HEINKEL, HELLDIVER, MACCHI, MARAUDER, MUSTANG, SPITFIRE, SYKHOI

   Sample the keys from left to right one character at a time.

   (b) Using single-character sampling, obtain a trie with the fewest number of levels.

2. Explain how a trie could be used to implement a spelling checker.

3. Explain how a trie could be used to implement an auto-command completion program. Such a program would maintain a library of valid commands. It would then accept a user command character by character from a keyboard. When a sufficient number of characters had been input to uniquely identify the command, it would display the complete command on the computer monitor.

4. Write an algorithm to insert a key value x into a trie in which the keys are sampled from left to right, one character at a time.

5. Do Exercise 4 with the added assumption that the trie is to have no more than six levels. Synonyms are to be packed into the same element node.

6. Write an algorithm to delete x from a trie t under the assumptions of Exercise 4. Assume that each branch node has a *count* field equal to the number of element nodes in the subtrie for which it is the root.

7. Do Exercise 6 for the trie of Exercise 5.

8. In the trie of Figure 10.55 the nodes δ_1 and δ_2 each have only one child. Branch nodes with only one child may be eliminated from tries by maintaining a *skip* field with each node. The value of this field equals the number of characters to be skipped before obtaining the next character to be sampled. Thus, we can have *skip* $[\delta_3] = 2$ and delete the nodes δ_1 and δ_2. Write algorithms to search, insert, and delete from tries in which each branch node has a *skip* field.

9. Assume that the branch nodes of a compressed trie are represented using a hash table (one for each node). Each such hash table is augmented with a count and skip value as described above. Describe how this change to the node structure affects the time and space complexity of the trie data structure.

10. Do the previous exercise for the case when each branch node is represented by a chain in which each node has two fields: *pointer* and *link*, where *pointer* points to a subtrie and *link* points to the next node in the chain. The number of nodes in the chain for any branch node equals the number of non-**nil** pointers in that node. Each chain is augmented by a skip value. Draw the chain representation of the compressed version of the trie of Figure 10.50.

10.10   DIFFERENTIAL FILES

10.10.1   The Concept

Consider an application where we are maintaining an indexed file. For simplicity, assume that there is only one index and hence just a single key. Further assume that this is a dense index (i.e., one that has an entry for each record in the file) and that updates to the file (inserts, deletes, and changes to an existing record) are permitted. It is necessary to keep a backup copy of the index and file so that we can recover from accidental loss or failure of the working copy. This loss or failure may occur for a variety of reasons, which include corruption of the working copy due to a malfunction of the hardware or software. We shall refer to the working copies of the index and file as the *master index* and *master file*, respectively.

Since updates to the file and index are permitted, the backup copies of these generally differ from the working copies at the time of failure. So, it is possible to recover from the failure only if, in addition to the backup copies, we have a log of all updates made since the backup copies were created. We shall call this log the *transaction log*. To recover from the failure, it is necessary to process the backup copies and the transaction log to reproduce an index and file that correspond to the working copies at the time of failure. The time needed to recover is therefore a function of the sizes of the backup index and file and the size of the transaction log. The recovery time can be reduced by making more frequent backups. This results in a smaller transaction log. Making sufficiently frequent backups of the master index and file is not practical when these are very large and when the update rate is very high.

When only the file (but not the index) is very large, a reduction in the recovery time may be obtained by keeping updated records in a separate file called the *differential file*. The master file is unchanged. The master index is, however, changed to reflect the position of the most current version of the record with a given key. We assume that the addresses for differential-file records and master-file records are different. As a result, by examining the address obtained from a search of the master index, we can tell whether the most current version of the record we are seeking is in the master file or in the differential file. The steps to follow when accessing a record with a given key are given in Program 10.17(b). Program 10.17(a) gives the steps when a differential file is not used.

Notice that when a differential file is used, the backup file is an exact replica of the master file. Hence, it is necessary to backup only the master index and differential file frequently. Since these are relatively small, it is feasible to do this. To recover from a failure of the master index or differential file, the transactions in the transaction log need to be processed using the backup copies of the master file, index, and differential file. The transaction log can be expected to be relatively small, as backups are done more frequently. To recover from a failure of the master file, we need merely make a new copy of its backup. When the differential file becomes too large, it is necessary to create a new version of the master file by merging the old master file and the differential file.

Step 1:   Search master index for record address.

Step 2:   Access record from this master file address.

Step 3:   If this is an update, then update master index, master file, and transaction log.

(a) No differential file

Step 1:   Search master index for record address.

Step 2:   Access record from either the master file or the differential file, depending on the address obtained in Step 1.

Step 3:   If this is an update, then update master index, differential file, and transaction log.

(b) Differential file in use

Step 1:   Search differential index for record address. If the search is unsuccessful, then search the master index.

Step 2:   Access record from either the master file or the differential file, depending on the address obtained in Step 1.

Step 3:   If this is an update, then update differential index, differential file, and transaction log.

(c) Differential index and file in use

Step 1:   Query the Bloom filter. If the answer is "maybe," then search differential index for record address. If the answer is "no" or if the differential index search is unsuccessful, then search the master index.

Step 2:   Access record from either the master file or the differential file, depending on the address obtained in Step 1.

Step 3:   If this is an update, then update Bloom filter, differential index, differential file, and transaction log.

(d) Differential index and file and Bloom filter in use

Program 10.17: Access steps

This also results in a new index and an empty differential file. It is interesting to note that using a differential file as suggested does not affect the number of disk accesses needed to perform a file operation (see Program 10.17).

Suppose that both the index and the file are very large. In this case the differential-file scheme discussed above does not work as well, as it is not feasible to backup the master index as frequently as is necessary to keep the transaction log sufficiently small. We can get around this difficulty by using a differential file and a differential index. The master index and master file remain unchanged as updates are performed. The differential file contains all newly inserted records and the current versions of all changed records. The differential index is an index to the differential file. This also has null address entries for deleted records. The steps needed to perform a file operation when both a differential index and file are used are given in Program 10.17(c). Comparing with Program 10.17(a), we see that additional disk accesses are frequently needed, as we will often first query the differential index and then the master index. Observe that the differential file is much smaller than the master file, so most requests are satisfied from the master file.

When a differential index and file are used, we must backup both of these with high frequency. This is possible, as both are relatively small. To recover from a loss of the differential index or file, we need to process the transactions in the transaction log using the available backup copies. To recover from a loss of the master index or master file, a copy of the appropriate backup needs to be made. When the differential index and/or file becomes too large, the master index and/or file is reorganized so that the differential index and/or file becomes empty.

10.10.2 Bloom Filters

The performance degradation that results from the use of a differential index can be considerably reduced by the use of a *Bloom filter*. This is a device that resides in internal memory and accepts queries of the following type: Is key k in the differential index? If queries of this type can be answered accurately, then there will never be a need to search both the differential and master indexes for a record address. Clearly, the only way to answer queries of this type accurately is to have a list of all keys in the differential index. This is not possible for differential indexes of reasonable size.

A Bloom filter does not answer queries of the above type accurately. Instead of returning one of "yes" and "no" as its answer, it returns one of "maybe" and "no". When the answer is "no," then we are assured that the key k is not in the differential index. In this case, only the master index is to be searched, and the number of disk accesses is the same as when a differential index is not used. If the answer is "maybe," then the differential index is searched. The master index needs to be searched only if k is not found in the differential index. Program 10.17(d) gives the steps to follow when a Bloom filter is used in conjunction with a differential index.

A *filter error* occurs whenever the answer to the Bloom filter query is "maybe" and the key is not in the differential index. Both the differential and master indexes are searched only when a filter error occurs. To obtain a performance close to that when a differential index is not in use, we must ensure that the probability of a filter error is close to zero.

Let us take a look at a Bloom filter. Typically, it consists of m bits of memory and h uniform and independent hash functions $f_1, \cdots, f_h$. Initially all m filter bits are zero, and the differential index and file are empty. When key k is added to the differential index, bits $f_1(k), \cdots, f_h(k)$ of the filter are set to 1. When a query of the type ''Is key k in the differential index?'' is made, bits $f_1(k), \cdots, f_h(k)$ are examined. The query answer is ''maybe'' if all these bits are 1. Otherwise, the answer is ''no.'' One may verify that whenever the answer is ''no,'' the key cannot be in the differential index and that when the answer is ''maybe,'' the key may or may not be in the differential index.

We can compute the probability of a filter error in the following way. Assume that initially there are n records and that u updates are made. Assume that none of these is an insert or a delete. Hence, the number of records remains unchanged. Further, assume that the record keys are uniformly distributed over the key (or identifier) space and that the probability that an update request is for record i is $1/n$, $1 \le i \le n$. From these assumptions, it follows that the probability that a particular update does not modify record i is $1 - 1/n$. So, the probability that none of the u updates modifies record i is $(1 - 1/n)^u$. Hence, the expected number of unmodified records is $n(1 - 1/n)^u$, and the probability that the $(u + 1)$'st update is for an unmodified record is $(1 - 1/n)^u$.

Next, consider bit i of the Bloom filter and the hash function f_j, $1 \le j \le h$. Let k be the key corresponding to one of the u updates. Since f_j is a uniform hash function, the probability that $f_j(k) \ne i$ is $1 - 1/m$. As the h hash functions are independent, the probability that $f_j(k) \ne i$ for all h hash functions is $(1 - 1/m)^h$. If this is the only update, the probability that bit i of the filter is zero is $(1 - 1/m)^h$. From the assumption on update requests, it follows that the probability that bit i is zero following the u updates is $(1 - 1/m)^{uh}$. From this, we conclude that if after u updates we make a query for an unmodified record, the probability of a filter error is $(1 - (1 - 1/m)^{uh})^h$. The probability, $P(u)$, that an arbitrary query made after u updates results in a filter error is this quantity times the probability that the query is for an unmodified record. Hence,

$$P(u) = (1 - 1/n)^u (1 - (1 - 1/m)^{uh})^h$$

Using the approximation

$$(1 - 1/x)^q \sim e^{-q/x}$$

for large x, we obtain

$$P(u) \sim e^{-u/n}(1 - e^{-uh/m})^h$$

when n and m are large.

Suppose we wish to design a Bloom filter that minimizes the probability of a filter error. This probability is highest just before the master index is reorganized and the differential index becomes empty. Let u denote the number of updates done up to this time. In most applications, m is determined by the amount of memory available, and n is fixed. So, the only variable in design is h. Differentiating $P(u)$ with respect to h and setting the result to zero yields

$$h = (\log_e 2)m/u \sim 0.693m/u$$

We may verify that this h yields a minimum for $P(u)$. Actually, since h has to be an integer, the number of hash functions to use either is $\lceil 0.693m/u \rceil$ or $\lfloor 0.693m/u \rfloor$, depending on which one results in a smaller $P(u)$.

EXERCISES

1. By differentiating $P(u)$ with respect to h, show that $P(u)$ is minimized when $h = (\log_e 2)m/u$.

2. Suppose that you are to design a Bloom filter with minimum $P(u)$ and that $n = 100,000$, $m = 5000$, and $u = 1000$.

    (a) Using any of the results obtained in the text, compute the number, h, of hash functions to use. Show your computations.

    (b) What is the probability, $P(u)$, of a filter error when h has this value?

10.11   REFERENCES AND SELECTED READINGS

The $O(n^2)$ optimum binary search tree algorithm is from ''Optimum binary search trees,'' by D. Knuth, *Acta Informatica*, 1:1, 1971, pp. 14-25.

For a discussion of heuristics that obtain in $O(n \log n)$ time nearly optimal binary search trees, see ''Nearly optimal binary search trees,'' by K. Melhorn, *Acta Informatica*, 5, 1975, pp. 287-295; and ''Binary search trees and file organization,'' by J. Nievergelt, *ACM Computing Surveys*, 6:3, 1974, pp. 195-207.

The original paper on AVL trees by G. M. Adelson-Velskii and E. M. Landis appears in *Dokl. Acad. Nauk.,* SSR (Soviet Math), 3, 1962, pp. 1259-1263. Additional algorithms to manipulate AVL trees may be found in ''Linear lists and priority queues as balanced binary trees,'' by C. Crane, Technical Report STAN-CS-72-259, Computer Science Dept., Stanford University, Palo Alto, CA, 1972; and *The Art of Computer Programming: Sorting and Searching* by D. Knuth, Addison-Wesley, Reading, MA, 1973 (Section 6.2.3).

Results of an empirical study of height-balanced trees appear in ''Performance of height-balanced trees,'' by P. L. Karlton, S. H. Fuller, R. E. Scroggs, and E. B. Koehler, *CACM*, 19:1, 1976, pp. 23-28.

2-3 trees and 2-3-4 trees are a special case of B-trees. A good reference is *The Art of Computer Programming: Sorting and Searching*, by D. Knuth, Addison-Wesley, Reading, MA, 1973. The variations of 2-3 trees referred to in the exercises are from *The Design and Analysis of Computer Algorithms*, by A. Aho, J. Hopcroft, and J. Ullman, Addison-Wesley, Reading, MA, 1974; and *Data Structures and Algorithms*, by A. Aho, J. Hopcroft, and J. Ullman, Addison-Wesley, Reading, MA, 1983.

Red-black trees were invented by R. Bayer. The reference is ''Symmetric binary B-trees: Data structure and maintenance,'' *Acta Informatica*, 1:4, 1972, pp. 290-306.

Our treatment of red-black trees is taken from Guibas and Sedgewick. The top-down single-pass insertion and deletion algorithms for 2-3-4 trees are also from them. The reference is ''A dichromatic framework for balanced trees,'' by L. Guibas and R. Sedgewick, *Proceedings of the 19th IEEE Symposium on Foundations of Computer Science*, 1978, pp. 8-21.

Bottom-up insertion and deletion algorithms for red-black trees were proposed by R. Tarjan in the paper "Updating a balanced search tree in O(1) rotations," *Information Processing Letters*, 16:5, 1983, pp. 253-257.

The paper "Planar point location using persistent search trees," by N. Sarnak and R. Tarjan, *CACM*, 27:7, 1986, pp. 669-679, develops a persistent variety of red-black trees. A persistent data structure is one in which all previous versions plus the current version of the data structure can be accessed efficiently. This paper also applies persistent red-black trees to the planar point location problem.

Splay trees were invented by D. Sleator and R. Tarjan. Their paper "Self-adjusting binary search trees," *JACM*, 32:3, 1985, pp. 652-686, provides several other analyses of splay trees, as well as variants of the basic splaying technique discussed in the text. Our analysis is modeled after that in *Data Structures and Network Algorithms*, by R. Tarjan, SIAM Publications, Philadelphia, PA, 1983.

Several other data structures provide good amortized performance for priority-queue and search-tree operations. The exercises examine some of these. The references for these additional structures are "Self-adjusting heaps," by D. Sleator and R. Tarjan, *SIAM Journal on Computing*, 15:1, 1986, pp. 52-69; and "Biased search trees," by S. Bent, D. Sleator, and R. Tarjan, *SIAM Journal on Computing*, 14:3, 1985, pp. 545-568.

Digital search trees were first proposed by E. Coffman and J. Eve in *CACM*, 13, 1970, pp. 427-432.

The structure Patricia was developed by D. Morrison. Digital search trees, tries, and Patricia are analyzed in the book *The Art of Computer Programming: Sorting and Searching* by D. Knuth, Addison-Wesley, Reading, MA, 1973.

The linear time suffix tree construction algorithm is from E. McCreight. It is described in "A space-economical suffix tree construction algorithm," by E. McCreight, *JACM*, 23:2, 1978, pp. 262-272.

Our development of differential files parallels that of Severence and Lohman in the paper "Differential files: Their application to the maintenance of large databases," by D. Severence and G. Lohman, *ACM Transactions on Database Systems*, 1:3, 1976, pp. 256-267. This paper also provides several advantages of using differential files. The assumptions of uniformity made in the filter error analysis are unrealistic, as, in practice, future accesses are more likely to be for records previously accessed. Several authors have attempted to take this into account. Two references are "A practical guide to the design of differential file architectures," by H. Aghili and D. Severance, *ACM Transactions on Database Systems*, 7:2, 1982, pp. 540-565; and "A regression approach to performance analysis for the differential file architecture," by T. Hill and A. Srinivasan, *Proceedings of the Third IEEE International Conference on Data Engineering*, 1987, pp. 157-164.

INDEX